More Praise

"Dr. Jess Shatkin has synthesized an immense body of knowledge into a text that is clearly a must-read for anybody dealing with the mental health of children and adolescents. It is the most current and definitive work on this subject. The writing is straightforward, accurate, and very accessible. I am certain that this book will directly improve the lives of millions of children suffering from mental illness."

—David T. Feinberg, MD, MBA,
President & CEO Geisinger Health System

"The book that I wish I had written. Fact-based and supported by references, this comprehensive, practical, and user-friendly text is a must-read for all child mental health practitioners (whether in practice or in training), parents of children and adolescents, and the general public as well. Dr. Shatkin's knowledge, wealth of clinical and teaching experience, and sensitivity to children, families, and the developmental process make this book different. A truly unique and original contribution."

—Thomas F. Anders, MD, Distinguished Professor (Emeritus),
University of California, Davis, Department of Psychiatry
and Behavioral Sciences and M.I.N.D. Institute,
and Past President, American Academy
of Child and Adolescent Psychiatry

"This is an extremely thorough and comprehensive overview of psychiatric disorders affecting children and adolescents, including diagnostic criteria and available treatments. The book is written as a broad spectrum guide for the wide variety of health care workers who treat children, such as pediatricians, family practitioners, general psychiatrists, psychologists, social workers and others, as well as psychiatric residents and psychology interns. I enthusiastically recommend it as an outstanding reference for anyone who has struggled to understand the many issues underlying childhood psychopathology, including school counselors, teachers, and parents."

—Carol A. Bernstein, MD, Associate Professor
of Psychiatry, Vice Chair for Education,
Department of Psychiatry, New York University
School of Medicine and Past President,
American Psychiatric Association

Child & Adolescent Mental Health

A Norton Professional Book

Child & Adolescent Mental Health

A Practical, All-in-One Guide

Jess P. Shatkin, MD, MPH

Foreword by Harvey Karp, MD, FAAP

W. W. Norton & Company

New York • London

Copyright © 2015. 2009 by Jess P. Shatkin, MD

Previous edition published as TREATING CHILD AND ADOLESCENT MENTAL
ILLNESS: A Practical, All-in-One Guide

For information about permission to reproduce selections from this book, write to
Permissions, W. W. Norton & Company, Inc., 500 Fifth Avenue, New York, NY 10110

For information about special discounts for bulk purchases, please contact
W. W. Norton Special Sales at specialsales@wwnorton.com or 800-233-4830

Manufacturing by Maple Press
Production manager: Christine Critelli

Library of Congress Cataloging-in-Publication Data

Shatkin, Jess P., author.
  [Treating child and adolescent mental illness]
  Child & adolescent mental health : a practical, all-in-one guide / Jess P. Shatkin ;
foreword by Harvey Karp.
    p. ; cm.
  Child and adolescent mental health
  Previous edition published as TREATING CHILD AND ADOLESCENT MENTAL
ILLNESS, A Practical, All-in-One Guide
  «A Norton Professional Book.»
  Includes bibliographical references and index.
  ISBN 978-0-393-71060-1 (pbk.)
  I. Title. II. Title: Child and adolescent mental health.
  [DNLM: 1. Mental Disorders—diagnosis. 2. Mental Disorders—therapy. 3.
Adolescent. 4. Child. WS 350]
  RC454
  616.89--dc23   2014038705

ISBN: 978-0-393-71060-1 (pbk.)

W. W. Norton & Company, Inc., 500 Fifth Avenue, New York, N.Y. 10110
www.wwnorton.com
W. W. Norton & Company Ltd., Castle House, 75/76 Wells Street, London W1T 3QT

1 2 3 4 5 6 7 8 9 0

For my mother, Joyce, who showed me the wonder of childhood; and for my father, Eugene, whose dinner table stories about his patients kept me on the edge of my seat.

Contents

Acknowledgments

Upon completion of my residency in general psychiatry and my fellowship in child and adolescent psychiatry at the UCLA Neuropsychiatric Institute, I found myself in central Arkansas providing care to both children and adults as a National Health Service Corps scholar. I had sought out this opportunity while still a medical student, signing on to work as a physician in a federally designated Health Professional Shortage Area in exchange for educational loan support—a decision driven by both idealistic and financial considerations. Once away from the safe confines of the university and the big city, I immediately had two realizations. First, although I was equipped to provide a wide range of patient care, I was still really a novice in the field of child, adolescent, and family mental health. Second, most of the mental health care for youth in our country is provided by individuals who are not specifically trained to do this work.

As I began seeing children and families at the Western Arkansas Counseling and Guidance Center in Fort Smith, I felt the need to codify my knowledge. I reviewed my notes from residency. I reached for other sources as well and read avidly. I started teaching family practice residents in Fort Smith at the local community hospital. I met with a group of therapists at my clinic each week and learned a great deal from them as we reviewed our cases together. I also met regularly with primary care practitioners in and around Fort Smith and found that they felt poorly equipped to treat child and adolescent mental illness, even though they were often called upon to do so.

After completing my service in Arkansas, I moved to Pittsburgh and took my first academic position as an assistant professor at the Western Psychiatric Institute and Clinic at the University of Pittsburgh. Now two years into my career, I felt more knowledgeable, and for the next three years I continued to expand both my clinical experience and my teaching. The book you have before you began in Pittsburgh with the lectures and seminars that I gave to the general psychiatry residents, developmental-behavioral pediatric fellows, child and adolescent psychiatry fellows, and psychotherapists whom I supervised and taught in my role as medical director of the Center for Children and Families. In 2005, I moved to New York University, where I took a newly created position as director of education and training. I have continued to see patients and teach about child and adolescent mental health to trainees, medical students, psychotherapists, and undergraduate and graduate students.

The first I need to thank are my former teachers from UCLA. Although they are far too numerous to name them all, Mark DeAntonio, David Feinberg, Fred Frankel, James McCracken, Caroly Pataki, James Spar, and Michael Strober deserve special mention for training me and even now continuing to share their wise counsel and friendship with me. At the University of Pittsburgh, I worked alongside Boris Birmaher, David Brent, David Kupfer, Martin Lubetsky, Ken Nash, Harold Pincus, and Neal Ryan, each of whom generously mentored me. At the New York University Child Study Center and Bellevue Hospital Center, where I currently work, there are too many to thank, but I am particularly indebted to Lori Evans and Matthew Cruger for educating me on the finer points of behavioral therapies and neuropsychological testing. Surely, few child and adolescent psychiatrists are so fortunate as to count among their friends and colleagues such a star-studded cast of characters.

I must also thank the many therapists, primary care practitioners, general psychiatry residents, pediatric residents, family medicine residents, child and adolescent psychiatry fellows, and undergraduate and graduate students who have participated in my seminars on psychopathology and evidence-based treatment over the past decade. They have taught me, challenged me, and helped me to sharpen my teaching, contributing immeasurably to this book, although I alone bear the fault of any shortcomings. I would also like to thank the children, adolescents, parents, and teachers who have shared their stories with me and allowed me a privileged glimpse into their lives.

There are a number of individuals who have directly supported this project. Harold S. Koplewicz, founder and director of the NYU Child Study Center, who brought me to NYU and whose mentorship and encouragement are enormously appreciated, was instrumental in starting me on this book. Completing all the research and references was a monumental task, and the assistance provided by Zoe Scott, Nadia Addasi, and Elana Bloomfield was simply outstanding. Regis Scott demonstrated remarkable patience as she designed (and countless times redesigned!) the graphics for this book. Kalma Mitchell deserves special mention for her expert transcription of the first draft and her undying support for my efforts. At W. W. Norton, I would like to thank my editor, Andrea Costella, who believed in this project and was kind, patient, encouraging, and at her desk every single time I called, and Kristen Holt-Browning, who thoughtfully guided me through every step of the editing process.

Four individuals who represent the target audience of this text have given generously of their time by reading each chapter and providing me with comments, critique, and areas for further consideration: my best friend, Charles J. Mayer, MD, MPH, a family practitioner in Seattle, Washington, with whom I took an oath in fifth grade that we both would one day become physicians; my best friend-in-law, Mira Renchner-Kelly, LCSW, a psychotherapist in Mt. Kisco, New York; my colleague and friend, Rahil Jummani, MD, a child and adolescent psychiatrist at NYU; and my father, Eugene P. Shatkin, MD, a pediatrician and child and adolescent psychiatrist in Novato, California. My goal in writing this book has been to translate the core knowledge of this wonderful and vibrant field, and the essential material that a high-functioning clinician must understand (as I have learned it myself), into a digestible and useful format. These four individuals have helped me considerably with that task.

Finally, and most importantly, I wish to thank my wife, Alice Jankell, our daughter Parker Tillie, and our son Julian, who constantly distracted me with games, theater, swimming, piano practice, wrestling, reading, movies, baseball, gymnastics, chess, tall tales, and all manner of shenanigans, and without whom I would have completed this book far sooner. May it always be so.

ACKNOWLEDGMENTS FOR THE SECOND EDITION

As with the first edition of this book, many thanks are due to colleagues, residents, students, and, most importantly, the patients who continue to teach me each day. I also want to thank Gabrielle Lasher, whose thorough literature review was essential in helping me to update this edition. Nicole Aujero also deserves heartfelt thanks for her assistance with references and publisher approvals, not to mention her extraordinary kindness. Andrea Costella, my editor at W. W. Norton, continues to believe in this book, and I am grateful for her support and passion for the material. I also wish to thank the entire Department of Child and Adolescent Psychiatry at New York University School of Medicine, my home for the past nine years, where I have been encouraged to flourish as a clinician, educator, administrator, researcher, and learner. I thank Harvey Karp, whose foreword beautifully lays out my best intentions for this book (*and would make any mother proud!*), and owe him a large debt of gratitude. Finally, I wish to once again thank my wife, Alice Jankell, and our now teenage children, Parker Tillie and Julian. It only becomes more clear to me with each passing year how much you influence my every thought and how lost I would be without you.

Preface

Emerging evidence continues to point to an increase in the prevalence of mental health problems among children, adolescents, and young adults. The surgeon general reports that 20% of children and adolescents within the United States—15 million youth—have a diagnosable psychiatric or developmental disorder (U.S. Department of Health and Human Services, 1999). Whether this increase is due to better diagnosis, an actual increase in prevalence, or both is unknown, but half of all lifetime cases of mental illness are now recognized to begin by age 14 and three quarters by age 24 (R. C. Kessler, Berglund, et al., 2005). Despite effective treatments, however, there are typically long delays, sometimes decades, between when individuals first experience clinically significant symptoms and when they first seek and receive treatment. In fact, the median amount of time between when children first experience a psychiatric disturbance and when they first receive treatment is nine years (R. C. Kessler, Berglund, et al., 2005).

Diagnosable anxiety disorders affect approximately 32% of adolescents aged 13 to 18 years; disruptive behavior disorders impact 19%, mood disorders impair over 14%, and substance use disorders affect over 11% (Fleming & Offord, 1990; Kashani, Sherman, Parker, & Reid, 1990; R. C. Kessler & Walters, 1998; Merikangas, He, Burstein, et al., 2010; D. Shaffer et al., 1996). Other mental illnesses, such as attention-deficit/hyperactivity disorder (ADHD, with a prevalence of 3% to 11%), affect smaller numbers but are ubiquitous among children, adolescents, and young adults, causing an untold amount of suffering and lost productivity for both children and their parents (Lewinsohn, Klein, & Seeley, 1995; Visser et al, 2014). Although federal government spending on antidrug measures increases each year and in 2014 totaled over $25 billion, more than 50% of high school seniors have experimented with an illicit drug, 25% have used an illicit drug within the past 30 days, and over 20% have engaged in binge drinking (e.g., consumed five or more alcoholic drinks in a row) within the past 14 days (Johnston, O'Malley, Miech, Bachman, & Schulenberg, 2013). Traumatic childhood experiences, such as being abused, witnessing abuse, or being raised in a home with a mentally ill member, affect over 50% of children and greatly increase the likelihood of later-onset substance abuse, mental illness, smoking, sexually transmitted disease, and obesity, all leading causes of death among adults (Felitti et al., 1998). Suicide, the most feared and tragic outcome of mental illness, has remained for many decades the third most common cause of death among adolescents and young adults, preceded only by accidents and homicide (R. N. Anderson & Smith, 2005; Centers for Disease Control and Prevention, National Vital Statistics System, National Center for Health Statistics, 2010).

In addition to simply documenting the epidemiology of mental illness and engaging in treatment, the field of child and adolescent psychiatry is currently making major strides in uncovering the etiology of some of the illnesses affecting our youth. Through basic scientific research and clinical investigation, our understanding of the neurobiological basis of mental illness has grown immensely over the past three decades. Putative genes have been identified for Tourette's syndrome, ADHD, and many syndromes resulting in intellectual disability, and advances in neuroimaging have allowed us to better understand many of the neural networks involved in ADHD, schizophrenia, autism, obsessive-compulsive disorder, and dyslexia (Abelson et al., 2005). As our understanding grows, so will our ability to target treatments for these illnesses. Concurrent with the research advances, the growth in evidence-based treatments, including medications and psychotherapies, has already advanced our ability to treat specific symptoms, such as psychosis, mania, tics, anxiety, hyperactivity, and depression, allowing many individuals to lead healthy, happy, and productive lives.

To be mentally ill in the United States is to be keenly aware of the lack of sufficient services and practitioners. In fact, an adult in the midst of a psychotic episode is three times more likely to end up in jail than in a hospital. It is estimated that more than 300,000 mentally ill people are in jails and prisons and another 500,000 are on court-ordered probation, where they generally do not receive the care they need. Perhaps most shocking, the largest public mental health facility in America is not a hospital, but rather the Los Angeles County Jail, which typically houses 3,000 mentally ill inmates on any given day (Earley, 2006). As previously noted, mental illness generally begins in childhood, and studies of youth in juvenile detention have found remarkably high rates of mental illness. Teplin, Abram, McClelland, Dulcan, and Mericle (2002) found that nearly two thirds of males and three quarters of females met diagnostic criteria for one or more psychiatric disorders, and others have shown similarly high rates (Duclos et al., 1998; McCabe, Lansing, Garland, & Hough, 2002; Wasserman, McReynolds, Lucas, Fisher, & Santos, 2002). Further complicating the lack of appropriate services is the lack of adequately trained practitioners.

Mental health practitioners who treat children and adolescents— including social workers, psychologists, educational specialists, and psychiatrists—are in short supply. The United States' Federal Bureau of Health Professions has named child and adolescent psychiatry as the most underserved of all medical subspecialties. The current workforce consists of approximately 8,300 child and adolescents psychiatrists, whereas the need has been estimated to be over 30,000 (American Medical Association, Physician Masterfile, 2012; W. J. Kim, 2003; Thomas & Holzer, 2006). Child and adolescent psychiatrists are not alone, however, as the national need for child and adolescent social workers, educational specialists, and psychologists is equally great. Even worse, the distribution of child and adolescent psychiatric services disproportionately favors those in urban areas with an elevated socioeconomic status (American Medical Association, Physician Masterfile, 2012).

The disparity in service delivery is also notable. While one in three Caucasian children receive the mental health care they need, the same is true for only one in five African American children and only one in seven Latino children nationwide. Many have advocated that we provide mental health care to our children by establishing clinics in public schools. Such clinics have repeatedly demonstrated themselves to be effective in accessing youth, yet fewer than 10% of our 80,000 public schools provide comprehensive mental health services at this time (U.S. Department of Health and Human Services, 1999). Equally concerning is the fact that although we have many effective treatments, only approximately 20% of youth with a diagnosable mental illness receive care, and of these individuals, only 2% receive a treatment known to be effective (Merikangas, He, Brody, et al., 2010).

In the face of service demands that overwhelm our ability to provide care for the many children and families in need, we face a potentially crippling trifecta—first, children represent an underserved and disenfranchised group with no voice of their own when it comes to policy and organizational decision-making; second, although our society has taken great strides, there remains significant stigma attached to those with mental illness and to families with a child who is ill; and finally, within the medical establishment itself, psychiatry (and particularly child psychiatry) suffers an undeserved reputation as an ineffectual and weak discipline couched within soft science. This book represents an effort to address these concerns and is aimed at an audience of first-line treatment providers.

Few texts currently exist that explain the core scientific knowledge and clinical application of this knowledge for an audience of primary care practitioners and psychotherapists. While the requirements for training child and adolescent psychiatrists are formally circumscribed by the Accreditation Council for Graduate Medical Education, the vast majority of child and adolescent mental health services worldwide are provided by primary care physicians, psychologists, and all manner of therapists, ranging from master's-level social workers to marriage and family therapists (Accreditation Council for Graduate Medical Education, 2007). In the United States, nearly 85% of all prescriptions for psychotropic medications for children, including stimulants, antipsychotics, antidepressants, anxiolytics, and mood stabilizers, are written by primary care practitioners, yet these individuals generally receive virtually no formal training in child and adolescent mental health (R. Goodwin, Gould, Blanco, & Olfson, 2001). Understandably, most primary care physicians and therapists do not feel comfortable treating child and adolescent mental illness, but given the paucity of trained specialists, they have little choice.

Consequently, this text has been written as a comprehensive but user-friendly guide for those practitioners who provide the vast majority of child mental health care but who have the least amount of training. This book describes the basics of child and adolescent mental health and psychopathology and the treatments that have been shown to work, including medications, psychotherapies, and psychosocial interventions. I am hopeful that it will have great value for a variety of health care practitioners, including pediatricians, family practitioners, nurse practitioners, general psychiatrists, psychologists, occupational therapists, speech and language therapists, social workers, and marriage and family therapists, who all too often find themselves confronted with a mentally ill child whom they feel ill equipped to help. This book also provides the core clinical knowledge necessary for entry-level child and adolescent psychiatry residents and psychology interns, and as such I am also hopeful that it will serve as a useful primer for these trainees as well. In addition, this book will have utility as a reference for schoolteachers, school counselors, and concerned parents. Finally, there are a host of undergraduate and graduate courses in child and adolescent psychopathology at colleges and universities nationwide for which this book could serve as a core text. My greatest wish for this book is that it be a "call to arms" of sorts, encouraging those who work with, care for, and treat mentally ill children and adolescents to utilize the material within these pages to advocate more research, expanded efforts at prevention, earlier screening, and better treatment of our children.

A Note About Clinical Studies

Throughout this book, numerous treatment studies will be referenced. To properly interpret these studies, it is important for the reader to have a grasp of various types of methodologies employed in clinical investigations.

Randomized, double-blind, placebo-controlled trials are the gold standard or best type of clinical intervention study, regardless of whether it is a medication, psychotherapy, or community intervention that is being investigated. In these studies, participants are randomly assigned to treatment groups. In one group, the subjects receive an active treatment—for example, a medication under study. In the other group, the subjects receive a placebo or sham treatment. Neither the subject nor the practitioner dispensing the treatment is aware of which treatment is being given, thus the "double-blind" component. There are numerous other types of studies that can be performed, but none provides us with data as reliable as the randomized, double-blind, placebo-controlled trial.

Sometimes a single randomized, controlled study does not provide adequate information about a treatment, and the best answer to the study question can be found by combining the results of numerous trials. Systematic reviews report the results from many studies. A meta-analysis combines many randomized, controlled trials and reanalyzes the data by putting it into summary form. Meta-analyses are limited in their utility by the "worst" or most limited study among the group, but the results from such pooled analyses often remain very useful.

When it is impossible, unethical, or too expensive to employ a blinded approach, we sometimes engage in treatment studies in an open-label fashion, such that both the subjects and the practitioner know which treatment is being delivered. Open-label studies do not employ a placebo, and therefore it is impossible to determine how many subjects improve simply because they are taking a medication or receiving a therapy, regardless of its effect. Still, open-label studies are often utilized for medications and treatments that are new to the market and provide useful results for the later construction of more detailed and sophisticated studies.

Randomized, controlled trials are expensive and take a great deal of time and effort. Consequently, researchers often use observational studies in which groups of people are followed or observed over time. Observational studies may take many forms, including case-control studies, cohort studies, chart reviews, and case reports. In a case-control study, two groups of individuals are viewed retrospectively to determine what caused the disorder or illness. The "cases" are those who have a certain disorder or illness under study, whereas the "controls" are an otherwise similar group who do not have the disorder or illness. By contrast, cohort studies prospectively follow a group of individuals who have experienced a similar exposure or share a common characteristic. They are followed over time to substantiate or refute an association between a given exposure or characteristic and a health outcome. Chart reviews and case reports similarly describe the experiences of individuals who have received certain treatments, but these analyses are highly subjective and open to numerous types of bias. Thus, while observational studies are often quicker to complete and are certainly less expensive, their results are generally not highly reliable.

Many studies will be discussed throughout this book. While our greatest power comes from multicenter randomized, double-blind, placebo-controlled trials, we have relatively few of these studies among children and adolescents. Consequently, we must often draw inferences from among the remaining open-label studies and observational data that are available to us, in addition to our clinical experience and evidence from studies of adults.

Foreword

As every primary care provider knows, the impact of mental illness on children, adolescents, and families is staggering. Diagnosable anxiety disorders affect one third of adolescents, disruptive behavior disorders affect one fifth, mood disorders affect one seventh, and substance dependence affects one tenth. Roughly 5% to 10% of children struggle with ADHD, and traumatic childhood experiences, which significantly increase the risk of substance abuse, mental illness, smoking, sexually transmitted infections, and obesity, affect over 50% of our children. Pediatricians are commonly the first line of defense for a child's mental health concerns, but they often lack sufficient training and experience in how to handle these problems. Similarly, therapists, another line of defense, are often not educated in the complexities and broad needs of children with psychiatric disorders.

If I suspect a child in my care has diabetes, I run a few simple blood tests. If I am concerned about strep throat, asthma, or an ear infection, I administer a few other tests. But when I visit with a child who is irritable, hyperactive or inattentive, sad, angry, shy or withdrawn, I have no blood test or other instrument to guide me. Unfortunately, this absence of straightforward psychological metrics is a daily problem for those of us caring for children. Study after study finds that between 25% and 50% of pediatric office visits involve an emotional, behavioral, or learning concern. Yet the training of pediatricians and family doctors is so focused on the many pressing medical problems they may face in practice that they end up receiving woefully little training in caring for the behavioral and emotional problems of the children and families they will care for in their communities. Equally concerning is the fact that most psychotherapists are not trained to work specifically with children and adolescents, even though they are often called on to do so in daily practice.

Enter Dr. Shatkin's *Child & Adolescent Mental Health: A Practical, All-in-One Guide.*

Flip through a few pages, and you will see that Dr. Shatkin, one of the leading child and adolescent psychiatry educators in the United States, has culled the most relevant and useful data from thousands of sources and over two decades of clinical experience to provide the reader with an up-to-date, accessible, and compelling understanding of not only what goes wrong for kids, but also how to fix it. This guide is intended for all first-line workers in the battle against child and adolescent mental illness—pediatricians, family docs, psychologists, social workers, school counselors, and teachers. Medical students and residents in pediatrics and psychiatry in particular will find a wealth of valuable information in these pages that will help them with each of their patients every single day.

In 2013, a new version of the *Diagnostic and Statistical Manual of Mental Disorders* was published by the American Psychiatric Association. This "bible" of psychiatric diagnostics, now in its fifth edition, is extremely helpful in identifying the symptoms that are typical in depression, ADHD, anorexia nervosa, and so forth. However, the *DSM* doesn't tell you how to take a patient from symptoms to wellness. Dr. Shatkin's book does.

Following two introductory chapters, Dr. Shatkin takes the reader on a tour through the most common disorders facing children, adolescents, and families, and what can be done about them. Evidence-based and extremely readable, *Child & Adolescent Mental Health: A Practical, All-in-One Guide* delivers exactly what it promises—a thorough, fascinating, and, most of all, essential toolkit for those who work with children, adolescents, and their families.

For the last five years, Dr. Shatkin's first edition of this book, *Treating Child and Adolescent Mental Illness*, has helped thousands of practitioners and families to understand what's gone wrong and how to get kids well. And it's no wonder—Dr. Shatkin leads the educational efforts of the Child Study Center at the NYU Langone Medical Center, one of the world's leading centers of clinical care, research, and education in the field of child and adolescent mental health. Dr. Shatkin spends his days teaching college and medical students, psychiatry and pediatric residents, and subspecialty fellows in child and adolescent psychiatry. He also engages in research in medical education, sleep, and mental health promotion and disease prevention. But most importantly, Dr. Shatkin provides clinical help to those who need it every single day, and he is sharing his "toolkit" with you here. Whether you read it cover to cover or use it as a case-by-case reference, this book will change how you clinically practice for the better.

—Harvey Karp, MD, FAAP

Child & Adolescent Mental Health

1

Introduction

Working with children, adolescents, and their families is an honor and a privilege, yet those of us who help youth struggling with difficulties related to their emotions, behavior, and cognition are few in number. The field of child mental health remains young. The American Academy of Child and Adolescent Psychiatry has been in existence for just over 60 years, and still the need for child and family mental health practitioners remains staggering. Given the paucity of child and adolescent psychiatrists and psychologists, there is an enormous demand upon other medical professionals such as pediatricians, social workers, general psychiatrists, and psychologists not trained directly to work with children, along with all manner of physicians, including family practitioners and internists, to help address the mental health needs of children and adolescents.

HISTORY

Prior to the 17th century, children were not generally considered deserving of basic human rights. Recognizing and demarcating childhood itself as a separate and necessary period of time to be cherished and during which time children should be nourished, encouraged, supported, and allowed to move through innate developmental phases appears to be a result of social changes emanating from the Victorian age. Between the 17th and 18th centuries, it is estimated that up to 70% of children died before reaching 5 years of age. In fact, it was not until the mid-1800s in Western societies that all children were presumed to have the right to some level of education and access to health care. This currently unimaginable situation becomes somewhat understandable when we recognize that because the child mortality rate was remarkably high until 200 years ago, families often did not emotionally invest fully in their children until they had lived past their fifth year, by which point many key developmental milestones had been passed.

Although mental illness was described in adults prior to the 18th century, professional and medical texts rarely discussed children's mental health problems. Essentially all recognized etiologies for disordered behavior in children were based on religious explanations and, perhaps to a lesser degree, magic. The separation between medicine, science, religion, and magic was virtually nonexistent, and mental health practitioners, psychiatrists who were sometimes known as "alienists" because the insane were thought to be estranged or alienated from their normal faculties, had very few tools by which to understand, diagnose, and treat mental illness.

Up until the mid-1800s, the predominant theory utilized to explain most health problems was humoral in nature. Humoral theories were based on the tradition of Galen, a second-century Greek physician who had suggested that disease occurred due to an excess in the production of any one of the four body "humors." As Galen defined them, the humors were blood, yellow bile, black bile, and phlegm. It was believed that the physiological imbalances that resulted from an excess in the production of one of these humors should be treated by nonspecific therapies, such as bleeding, purging, or vomiting.

In Europe the emergence of a social conscience and the effort to treat children with humane care and to provide social protection began to take root following industrialization. Industrialization brought modern thinking but also humanism, and social services became a new consideration. This change likely occurred due to the fact that as cities grew more quickly than their infrastructures could tolerate, injustice and the discrepancy between rich and poor became much more evident. The English philosopher and physician John Locke (1632–1704) advocated individual rights, asserting that children deserved to be cared for sensitively and raised with affection. Locke's ideas contrasted with the prevailing harsh and frequently indifferent childrearing culture of his time. He also suggested that children are born as a tabula rasa, or a blank slate without preformed mental content or innate ideas, upon which the environment plays a major role in the development of the personality. Without kindness and care, Locke proposed, children would suffer emotional damage. His ideas, drawn in part from numerous philosophers and probably originating in some form from Aristotle, later became a key tenant of psychoanalytic theory.

Jean-Marc Itard (1775–1838) is probably the first physician who documented his efforts to help a special-needs child. Victor of Aveyron was found in the French countryside at 11 or 12 years of age, having lived abandoned and alone since the age of 2 or 3. Victor could not speak, was inattentive, and was insensitive to many essential sensations, including temperature. Despite Itard's attempts to socialize Victor, the child was never able to fully rejoin society. Nonetheless, this well-publicized case of an exceptionally deprived child and the subsequent efforts to understand and heal his emotional and cognitive impairments placed an emphasis where heretofore one had not been noted in society.

At the same time, Philippe Pinel (1745–1826), known as the father of French psychiatry, discarded the long-held notion that mental illness was due to possession by demons and began to classify his observations of the mentally ill. He developed the concept of "moral treatment," the idea that the mentally ill should be provided psychosocially humane care and that an emphasis on moral discipline should accompany all treatment interventions. Pinel also made some of the first efforts into what we now consider to be psychotherapy. He worked solely with adults, but due to his efforts and those of others, such as the American Benjamin Rush (1745–1813), a physician, educator, writer, and humanitarian, the unique difficulties of the mentally ill began to be appreciated.

Benjamin Rush, who lived and practiced in Philadelphia and whose picture adorns the seal of the American Psychiatric Association, advocated the abolition of slavery and signed the Constitution of the United States of America. His practice was aimed at providing care for the poor, and his greatest contributions to medical science were the reforms he instituted in the care of the mentally ill during his 30 years as a senior physician at the Pennsylvania Hospital. He was known as a compassionate physician who replaced routine reliance on archaic procedures with more careful clinical observation and study. The year before he died, he published *Medical Inquiries and Observations Upon the Diseases of the Mind*, the first American textbook on psychiatry.

Also in America, Dorothea Dix (1802–1887) became an important teacher and social reformer for the treatment of the mentally ill. She established over two dozen benevolent mental hospitals for the treatment of mentally ill and disabled children and adolescents, who had previously been kept in asylums and in some cases cellars and cages. Although she did not contribute to our understanding of the nature of mental illness, she was a pioneer in addressing the inequities of care.

As infectious disease became increasingly treatable, physicians accepted the idea of a biological basis of disease, illness, and mental illness. Although the mental effects of some physical illnesses came to be recognized by the late 1800s—for example, syphilis and Huntington's disease—still little could be done for afflicted individuals. The first efforts at explaining mental illness from a biological vantage point focused on identifying a physical cause within the patient, and often resulted in blaming the individual for the illness. Consequently, attitudes toward the mentally ill and their treatment shifted yet again to contempt, fear, and negativity. During the late 19th and early 20th centuries, emerging ideas of public health and medicine—such as eugenics, sterilization, and institutionalization—were at times paradoxically used against the mentally ill, to prevent the "insane" from interacting with the rest of society (Mash & Wolfe, 2005).

PSYCHOANALYTIC THEORY

By this time, most mental health practitioners had become discouraged by their inability to treat mental illness in children. Although Sigmund Freud (1856–1939) believed that the origin of mental illness was largely biological, he also believed in the importance of experience in the shaping of psychopathology, and he was the first to imbue mental disorders with meaning by bridging them to childhood experiences. Although currently psychoanalysis does not inspire great faith in the majority of psychiatrists and psychologists, and most do not view psychoanalysis as a "hopeful" movement, in its time psychoanalysis and its theory gave true hope to a small and exhausted field that felt its work was, more often than not, futile. A working theory had been advanced that relied on psychotherapy as an innovative treatment and suggested that patients could improve, see relief from symptoms, and perhaps even be cured of mental illness.

While Freud's theory rested on the drive to develop and reach sexual maturity, other psychoanalytically oriented theories soon followed. Erik Erikson (1902–1994), for example, imagined a developmental theory that emphasized psychosocial development throughout the entire life cycle. Jean Piaget (1896–1980) developed a theory based on cognitive development. Others postulated theories that relied on a genetically determined capacity for the development of patterns or systems of behavior, in which a child acts on the environment from the very beginning of his or her life. The clinical implication of these structural theories is that some kind of reorganization within the child is required for him or her to grow and develop, such as the resolution of an intrapsychic conflict or an alteration of the family homeostasis. Another implication is that without having achieved a certain developmental milestone at a certain time of life, a child will not develop properly and may, therefore, develop mental illness.

Sigmund Freud's drive theory, the best known of the psychological development theories, suggested that aggressive and sexual drives are the primary motivating forces in our quest for pleasure. In Freud's theory, the end goal of development is sexual maturity. He identified five stages beginning in infancy and ending at puberty (see Table 1.1). Jean Piaget identified four stages, which start at infancy and conclude somewhere between 11 and 16 years of age, with the end goal of development being cognitive maturity or adultlike thinking (see Table 1.2). According to Erik Erikson's theory, "normal" development hinges on successfully traversing eight dichotomies beginning at birth and ending in old age. Perhaps most important, Erikson's model of development was the first to suggest that life is an ongoing process and that one is not fully "developed" simply because one has reached puberty, is able to think abstractly, or can effectively separate from one's parents (see Table 1.3).

Margaret Mahler (1897–1985) did not develop a new theory. Rather, she systematically observed and detailed the unfolding of object relations in children and infants (see Table 1.4). Object relations represents a more modern adaptation of psychoanalytic theory that places less emphasis on the drives of aggression and sexuality as motivational forces and more

Table 1.1   Freud's Drive Theory

Freud postulated that aggressive and sexual "drives" are the primary motivating forces in our quest for pleasure and that the end goal of development is sexual maturity. Freud defined five stages on the developmental pathway to sexual maturity:

1. Oral Phase (Infancy, birth to 18 months)
   Infants strive to obtain pleasure and relief from discomfort through the most immediate means possible. The greatest source of pleasure is the mouth.
2. Anal Phase (a.k.a. Sadistic Phase, 18–36 months)
   As infants develop, they acquire anal sphincter control. A sense of autonomy emerges and the infants derive pleasure from controlling their bowels.
3. Phallic-Oedipal Phase (3–6 years)
   Children work through the Oedipus complex. They have conflicting feelings about their sexual desires and fear of punishment for these feelings. Children will often repress these desires and identify with the same-sex parent instead. The greatest source of pleasure is the genitals.
4. Latency Phase (6–12 years)
   During the elementary school years, defense mechanisms, which bar from consciousness certain unacceptable impulses, are strengthened. The libido is transferred from parents to friends, and children enjoy being with members of the same sex.
5. Puberty and Adolescence
   Adolescents struggle to control sexual and aggressive urges, to separate from their families, to develop sexual relationships, and to achieve a sense of identity. Development is considered complete.

Table 1.2 Piaget's Cognitive Development Theory

Piaget identified four major stages of cognitive development:

1. Sensorimotor Stage (birth to 2 years)
   Infants' knowledge of the world is limited to their sensory perceptions and motor activities. Behaviors are limited to simple motor responses to sensory stimuli.
2. Preoperational Stage (2–7 years)
   Children develop language, although they do not yet understand concrete logic. They also become adept at using symbols while playing and pretending.
3. Concrete Operational Stage (7 years to adolescence)
   Children begin to think logically about concrete events but have difficulty understanding abstract concepts.
4. Formal Operational Stage (adolescence)
   Adolescents acquire the ability to think about abstract concepts.

Table 1.3 Erikson's Psychosocial Theory

Erikson's psychoanalytic theory comprised eight stages. "Normal" development hinges on successfully traversing dichotomies at each of these eight stages:

1. Basic Trust vs. Mistrust (Birth to 1 year)
   Infants develop the ability to trust based upon the consistency of their caregivers. If trust develops successfully, they acquire confidence and security. Unsuccessful completion of this stage can result in an inability to trust.
2. Autonomy vs. Shame and Doubt (1–3 years)
   Children begin to assert their independence. If encouraged, children become more confident in their ability to survive in the world. If overly controlled, children may doubt their own abilities.
3. Initiative vs. Guilt (3–5 years)
   Children assert themselves more frequently and develop a sense of initiative. If criticized, they develop a sense of guilt.
4. Industry vs. Inferiority (6–11 years)
   Children begin to develop a sense of pride in their accomplishments. If encouraged, they will become industrious. If restricted, children begin to doubt their own abilities.
5. Identity vs. Role Diffusion (11 years–end of adolescnece)
   Adolescents become more independent and begin to form their own identities.
6. Intimacy vs. Isolation (21–40 years)
   Young adults explore long-term relationships with individuals outside of their families. Avoiding intimacy can lead to isolation and loneliness.
7. Generativity vs. Stagnation (40–65 years)
   Middle-aged adults have established careers and settled down within relationships. If they have not achieved these objectives, they may become stagnant.
8. Integrity vs. Despair (over 65 years)
   Elderly adults reflect on their accomplishments and derive integrity from a successful life. If they perceive their lives as unproductive, the result is despair.

Table 1.4   Mahler's Observations on Separation and Individuation

Mahler's intent was not to add new theory but to systematically observe and detail the unfolding of object relations in children and infants.

Six stages of development lead to normal object relations, predicated upon a recognition of "separateness":

1. Normal Autism (birth to 2 months)
   Infants are detached and self-absorbed. (Mahler eventually abandoned this phase as research in child development disproved the existence of a normally "autistic" phase.)
2. Symbiosis (2–5 months)
   Infants are aware of their mother, but there is no sense of individuality.
3. Differentiation (5–10 months)
   Infants differentiate between themselves and their mothers. They demonstrate increased alertness and interest in the outside world.
4. Practicing Sub-Phase (10–18 months)
   As infants begin to crawl, they explore actively and become more distant from their mothers.
5. Rapprochement (18–24 months)
   Children desire to share their discoveries with their mothers and experience conflicting feelings about staying with their mothers or being more independent.
6. Object Constancy (2–5 years)
   Children understand that they have separate identities from their mothers. As a result, they internalize the representations that they have formed of their mothers. Deficiencies in positive internalization may lead to low self-esteem in adulthood.

emphasis on human relationships as the primary motivational force in life. In other words, object relations theory suggests that people seek relationships rather than pleasure (e.g., Freud). Mahler identified six stages leading to the development of normal object relations, beginning at birth and ending somewhere around 5 years of age.

Although most of the psychoanalytic or child development theories were focused on understanding adults, both Anna Freud (1895–1982) and Melanie Klein (1882–1960) were particularly important in applying analytic theories to children. The work of Anna Freud and Melanie Klein led to the development of the field of child psychoanalysis and a recognition of the importance of nonverbal communication such as play and drawing in understanding children.

BEHAVIORAL PSYCHOLOGY

The first evidence-based psychotherapies in mental health were rooted in behavioral theory and the early investigations of Ivan Pavlov (1849–1936), John B. Watson (1878–1958), and B. F. Skinner (1904–1990), whose research first described behavioral conditioning. While psychoanalysis sought to resolve unconscious conflicts, behavioral therapy aimed to shape behavior and improve individual adaptation (Mash & Wolfe, 2005). As the evidence supporting behavioral theory grew, the psychotherapeutic treatments applied in the early 20th century, such as psychoanalysis, became increasingly questioned. In fact, sparse data were generated during this time, other than case reports, which demonstrated the efficacy of psychodynamic treatment interventions in the care of both individuals and groups (e.g., children within group homes and orphanages). In addition, psychoanalytic approaches were acknowledged even by the primary theorists themselves to be most often of little utility for children with developmental disabilities and mental retardation, the very areas where behavioral theorists first demonstrated significant strides.

Throughout the past four decades, research supporting the utility of behavioral therapies has continued to mount, leading to the increased acceptance of behavioral treatments for all manner of difficulties, including anxiety, depression, substance abuse, personality disorders, and disruptive behavior. Since the 1970s, the use of behavioral methods in the treatment of children and adolescents has become and remained more the norm than the exception. Behavioral treatments currently in vogue, such as cognitive behavior therapy (CBT), parent management training (PMT), interpersonal therapy (IPT), dialectical behavior therapy (DBT), applied behavior analysis (ABA), motivational interviewing (MI), and habit reversal training (HRT), will be described in detail throughout this text.

NEUROBIOLOGY OF ATTACHMENT

We now recognize that the brain is hardwired for social learning from day one. Infants are drawn to particular faces, smells, textures, and voices by their own determination. Typically within the first six to eight weeks of life, infants develop a social smile in response to others; the social smile is so vital to our existence that even children born blind at birth develop a social smile in response to a parent's voice (Messenger & Fogel, 2007).

Children make choices from the very first moment of life and are not a tabula rasa or blank slate. At an early age, infants learn primarily through imitation, probably by employing mirror neurons, which are believed to be located in the inferior frontal cortex and superior parietal lobe. These neurons become active when someone performs an action or watches others perform an action, thus "mirroring" the behavior of another as if the observer were also doing the action. It has been suggested that mirror neurons are the neural substrate of not only action recognition, but also understanding others' intentions, which may be akin to empathy (Iacoboni et al., 2005).

Although brain development proceeds in an orderly fashion, it is different for different individuals. For example, some children develop motor skills early and show great proficiency in physical coordination but may lag somewhat behind in literacy skills, or vice versa. Generally, most children "catch up" so that normal milestones are achieved within a specified and typical developmental period (e.g., the vast majority of children walk independently between 10 and 14 months of age). Importantly, the process of attachment appears to promote this healthy neural development.

"Attachment" is a theoretical construct intended to describe a variety of neural systems and behavioral processes whose goal is to aid the infant in bonding or attaching to adult caregivers in order to support social and emotional development and, ultimately, survival of the infant. Attachment theory was proposed by John Bowlby, a British psychiatrist, who studied children orphaned by World War II. He observed that infants become well attached when caregivers are sensitive and responsive to their needs, allowing them to establish what Bowlby called a "secure base" in the world (Ainsworth, Blehar, Waters, & Wall, 1978). The interpersonal relationship or attachment between caregiver and child helps children organize themselves and manage emotion.

Infant attachment has been rigorously studied since the 1960s using the Infant Strange Situation. During this experimental design, the primary caregiver (usually the mother), is briefly separated from her 1-year-old, who is left in a new or strange environment with a stranger. It is believed that upon separation, an infant's attachment system is activated, allowing observation of the child's response at both separation and reunion (when the mother returns to the room). Two broad categories of attachment have been observed, secure and insecure, which are further broken down into four domains: secure, avoidant, resistant, and disorganized. An insecure attachment (e.g., avoidant, resistant, or disorganized) is believed to increase the risk of psychopathology, while a secure attachment is thought to provide an individual with some degree of resilience.

RISK AND RESILIENCE

As we begin to think more about psychopathology, we must consider the multitude of problems that can occur during childhood and interfere with normal child development. We must constantly ask ourselves:

What is normal? What is abnormal? When does an emotional issue or behavioral disturbance become a definable pathology? Which pathologies require clinical treatment and when? Which problems might children simply outgrow? Why do some children struggle more than others with the same symptoms or diagnosis? What accounts for the waxing and waning of symptoms over time? How can one help a child affected by psychopathology to become well? These are the core questions addressed in this book.

We speak frequently of risk factors in health care, and mental health is no different. A risk factor is defined as a variable (being physically abused as a child, growing up in poverty, etc.) that increases the likelihood of a negative outcome (psychopathology, disability, etc.). Epidemiological studies over the past 50 years have clarified a number of primary risk factors for child psychopathology, including poverty, inconsistent and deficient caregiving, parental mental illness, death of a parent, breakup of the family, homelessness, community disasters, early pregnancy, and neonatal complications. These risk factors are particularly damning in the absence of compensatory strengths and resources on the part of the child, family, and social environment. It is remarkable, however, how some children who have numerous risk factors and numerous psychiatric diagnoses seem to be in some way resilient and can traverse the pitfalls of their illness with success. A resilience factor, then, is a variable that decreases the likelihood of a negative outcome, despite the individual's being at risk for psychopathology. Resilience factors are much more difficult to categorize and may change over time depending on the child and the environment. They may typically include self-confidence, flexibility in one's approach to problem-solving, intelligence, coping skills, and emotional support from trusted family members and friends. Individual, family, and social factors all have an impact on the development of a child's resilience.

Although children are faring better today than in the past, still more than one in five children live in poverty in the United States (DeNavis-Walt, Proctor, & Smith, 2013). One third of youth in the United States experience poverty at some point during their childhood, which is of great concern, given that low income is correlated with many other difficulties that impact mental health, including lower salaries, decreased educational achievement, poor access to health care, inadequate nutrition, a single-parent home, limited resources, and an increased likelihood of exposure to violence. Clearly, poverty takes a tremendous toll on children. Low socioeconomic status confers nearly three times the rate of conduct disorder, two times the rate of chronic illness, and more than twice as high an incidence of school problems, hyperactivity, and emotional disorders as higher socioeconomic status. Furthermore, the worse the poverty, the greater the incidence of childhood violence, which increases three times in girls and five times in boys over standard rates for those who grow up in poverty (Brooks-Gunn & Duncan, 1997; Mash & Wolfe, 2005; McLoyd, 1998; Ross, Shillington, & Lockhead, 1994; Tremblay, Pihl, Vitaro, & Dobkin, 1994).

Another unfortunate but ubiquitous feature of childhood is abuse. Over 3 million child abuse reports involving more than 6 million youth are made in the United States each year. Over one third of children 10 to 16 years of age in the United States are physically or sexually assaulted during these years by family members or others they know. Unquestionably, abuse and trauma in their many forms (physical, sexual, and emotional) interfere with normal child development and predispose children and adolescents to psychopathology (Mash & Wolfe, 2005; Trocmé & Wolfe, 2001; U.S. Department of Health and Human Services, Administration for Children and Families, Administration on Children, Youth and Families, Children's Bureau, 2013).

SEX, RACE, AND CULTURE

Boys and girls commonly express psychopathology in different ways. Virtually all neurodevelopmental disorders—such as intellectual disability syndromes, autism spectrum disorders, Tourette's syndrome, and ADHD—are more common in boys than in girls for reasons that remain elusive. Some of the differences we see between boys and girls may have to do with the established definitions of these disorders. For example, while boys may demonstrate overtly aggressive behavior, such as fighting and property damage, girls may demonstrate aggression in more covert means, such as gossiping or spreading rumors. Consequently, girls may less commonly receive a diagnosis of conduct disorder or oppositional defiant disorder in part, at least, because the infractions made by boys are much more easily witnessed. In general, girls tend to internalize their distress, resulting more often in difficulties with anxiety, depression, somatization, eating disorders, and emotional withdrawal. Boys, in contrast, tend to demonstrate more externalizing problems, such as aggression, hyperactivity, and delinquency. Figure 1.1, which shows internalizing and externalizing behavior scores from the Child Behavior Checklist (a standardized rating scale of children's behavior), demonstrates that the developmental trajectories of boys and girls differ substantially. At a very early age, boys and girls have roughly the same rate of internalizing troubles, but as they age, females show a greater preponderance. By contrast, the

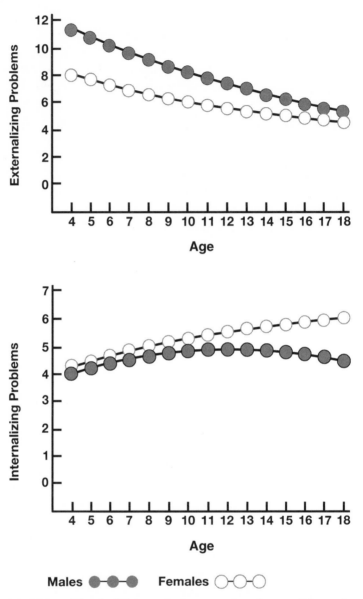

Figure 1.1 Male and female differences in the expression of externalizing and internalizing behaviors. Measures of externalizing disorders on the Child Behavior Checklist are greater for boys than girls at a young age. By adolescence, the differences between the sexes diminish. Internalizing problems, on the other hand, occur in roughly the same number of boys and girls at a young age, but by adolescence girls tend to demonstrate more internalizing problems than boys. Source: Adapted from Bongers, Koot, van der Ende, and Verhulst (2003).

externalizing disorders are more common in males at a younger age, but as children reach their late teen years, the proportion of males and females begins to equalize (Bongers, Koot, van der Ende, & Verhulst, 2003).

Understanding and employing resilience is key to preventing and tempering child mental illness. Some resilience factors are shared by the sexes and include positive same-sex role models and emotional support. Resilient girls are generally raised within households where risk-taking and independence are encouraged. These girls also have significant emotional support from a primary female caregiver, such as a mother, older sister, or grandmother. Resilient boys, similarly, are generally raised with a positive male role model, such as a father, older brother, or grandfather. In contrast to girls, however, boys appear to benefit more clearly from significant structure and rules within the home, along with encouragement to express their emotions (Werner, 1995).

There are other differences between males and females that emerge as early as infancy. It has been generally reported that men use far fewer words per day on average than women and that beginning in the teen years, females may receive a larger neurochemical (e.g., dopamine) "rush" from talking and gossiping than males. By 8 weeks in utero, testosterone produced by the testes in males begins to lead to enlargement of the amygdala, a brain structure where aggressive and fear-driven behaviors are believed to be housed. Male babies also generally show more interest in objects, while female babies show more interest in faces. In fact, female babies increase their visual interest in faces by 400% within the first 3 months of life, whereas males demonstrate virtually no change within this time period. In addition, girls' brains typically mature about 20% faster than boys' until the midteen years, which may explain why girls frequently tend to develop language quicker, toilet train earlier, and adjust their behavior to societal expectations and norms more rapidly (Brizendine, 2006).

Race and culture also have an impact on the development of child psychopathology. Minorities are overrepresented in many disorders such as substance use, delinquency, and teen suicide (Mash & Wolfe, 2005). These differences, however, are largely a result of coexisting conditions more commonly encountered by racial minorities, such as poverty, limited access to care, and the poor quality of care received by most minority groups. Consequently, once socioeconomic status, age, sex, and referral status are controlled for, few differences remain in the rate of psychological disorders among children of different races (Boney-McCoy & Finkelhor, 1995).

As noted, the barriers to receiving and accessing care are greater among racial minorities. We know, for example, that children without insurance receive less medical attention and that African American children with ADHD are less likely to receive stimulants than Caucasian children. The reasons for these discrepancies are not exactly clear, though there is no doubt that poor children and those from ethnic minorities reap far fewer benefits from society. To compound the problem, racial and ethnic minorities have historically been neglected in studies of child psychopathology, and most research has not been based on diverse populations. Thus, our understanding of risk and resilience factors, epidemiology, course of illness, and treatment strategies for child and adolescent mental illness is largely limited to the dominant, Caucasian population (Centers for Disease Control and Prevention, 2001; Children's Defense Fund, 2002).

ADOLESCENCE AND RISK TAKING

Adolescence, the period between childhood and adulthood, is the physically healthiest time of life. The improvements in strength, speed, reaction time, reasoning, and immune function, as well as increased resistance to the extremes of heat, cold, hunger, dehydration, and most types of injury, are truly phenomenal. Ironically, however, the overall morbidity and mortality rates increase by 200% between late childhood/ early adolescence (10 to14 years of age) and later adolescence (15 to 19 years of age). The primary reasons for this paradox (e.g., the increases in mortality and morbidity seen in adolescence) are the changes seen in behavior, cognition, and emotion that take place during these years.

The three most common causes of death in adolescence are accidents, homicide, and suicide (see Table 1.5). In addition, sickness or morbidity due to psychopathology increases greatly during this time. Depression, for example, increases from a prevalence of around 4% in school-age children to around 17% among adolescents. Rates of substance abuse, eating disorders, anxiety disorders, and psychotic disorders as well all rise greatly during the teen years and lead to major increases in morbidity, approaching or reaching adult levels in some cases. However, it is the sensation-seeking and risk-taking behavior that is of greatest concern during adolescence. For example, remember Romeo and Juliet. They were only 13 years of age and had known each other for only four days, yet they each committed suicide because they felt they could not live without each other. This type of erratic and emotionally charged behavior is characteristic of adolescents (Centers for Disease Control and Prevention, National Vital Statistics System, National Center for Health Statistics, 2010).

Table 1.5 Five Leading Causes of Death Among Persons Aged 15–19 Years, United States, 2010

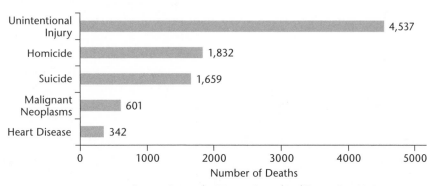

Source: Centers for Disease Control and Prevention, 2013

Why adolescents demonstrate such an increase in risk-taking behavior is not entirely clear. A Darwinian or evolutionary argument would posit that in order to become successful and to survive as one approaches adulthood, we must take more risks, become sensation seekers, and embrace adventure so that we are driven to strike out on our own and explore new food sources, mates, and living areas. In current society, there is also peer pressure, and then there is, of course, the growth and development of the brain itself.

We recognize now that cognitive development (i.e., planning, reasoning, problem-solving, logic, and organization) correlates more strongly with age and experience than with sexual and physical maturation. While early theorists postulated that child development is complete by the time of sexual maturity (e.g., Freud) or abstract cognition (e.g., Piaget), neuroscience now tells us otherwise. We currently believe that the brain develops in stages, such that not all structures mature at the same rate. Motor tracks responsible for physical movement and coordination, by example, are fully mature and networked by 15 to 16 years of age, which is why we see some of our best athletic performances in this age range (e.g., consider Olympic gymnasts). The social/emotional brain (or limbic system, involving such structures as the amygdala, hippocampus, and anterior thalamus) also develops early and reaches peak engagement by midadolescence, which explains why adolescents feel such emotions as fear, love, jealousy, and anger so intensely. However, the frontal lobe cognitive tracks (e.g., those associated with executive brain functions, such as planning, organizing, paying attention, problem-solving, and employing past experience in new situations) grow more slowly and are not fully developed and networked with the social/emotional brain structures until the late 20s (Keverne, 2004; J. C. Larson et al., 2007; Levin & Hanten, 2005; Yakovlev & Lecours, 1967).

Early on in adolescence, we see a great outpouring of emotionally driven behavior, which leads to the high rates of accidental injury and death, homicide, and suicide in this age range. It takes another 10 years or so, until we are in our late 20s, for our higher-level cognitive structures (e.g., the frontal lobe) to reign in our rapidly developing emotional brain (e.g., limbic system; Casey & Jones, 2010). The early development of the limbic system makes good evolutionary sense, because thousands of years ago when humans had a shorter life span, the need to reproduce early, fight others for territory, and explore new lands and sources of food was paramount. Only an animal driven by a strong emotional calling would take such risks. Certainly, many adolescent humans have died because they were driven to extremes by their emotions, and we owe a great debt to these risk-takers for allowing our species to live on. Without someone willing to kill a tiger for food or find new territory, we would have gone extinct long ago. Unfortunately, however, these same instincts and patterns of brain development that led us to be so successful long ago now threaten many of our adolescents today. The same emotions that drove us to explore new territories or fight a tiger thousands of years ago now push our youth to drive under the influence of alcohol or have early and unprotected intercourse. Let's think about these findings for a moment—they clearly help to explain why adolescents are so physically capable and can be such wonderful athletes, while also clarifying why they make such impulsive decisions and are extremely swayed by their emotions to the point of risking illness, injury, or death.

Consider the fact that major league baseball pitchers, the most important players on a team, averaged in age from a low of 27 years on the Houston Astros to a high of 31 years on the Boston Red Sox in 2014 (Statista, 2014). Even though a pitcher in his late 20s or early 30s does not throw a ball as consistently fast as a late teen or early 20s adult and takes longer to recuperate, his planning, problem-solving, focus, and patience are much greater by the time he hits 27 years and beyond. In other words, although a teenager can throw a ball with greater speed, the 30-year-old pitcher can rely on experience, use strategy better, anticipate what a batter is expecting, and ultimately deliver a more successful pitch. It is the older pitcher's ability to use the frontal lobe of the brain to control his limbic emotional centers that makes him a better pitcher and the man you want on your team. Likewise, National Football League quarterbacks, undoubtedly the most important players on the team, averaged 27 years of age in 2013 (Miglio, 2013). Here too, the team leader does best when he has attained a higher level of brain development even though he is past his physical prime.

The prefrontal cortex, the newest part of the brain and that which more than any other cerebral structure makes us truly "human," acts to inhibit impulsive and motivational drives. Yet this structure is still somewhat immature in adolescence. Thus, when dopamine increases in the nucleus accumbens (secondary to drug abuse or sexual activity) and a pleasure response occurs in the limbic system, an adolescent may have little ability to inhibit the motivation to continually seek out such pleasurable activities. Likewise, the degree of frontal lobe control needed to inhibit hyperactivity, sit still, and study instead of being distracted by anxiety, or take cognitive control of depressive thoughts, may be more than most adolescents can manage. Other factors also potently influence the adolescent brain, including the onslaught of new hormones, many of which are not understood and have not yet been characterized. The normative pruning of serotonin circuits in the adolescent brain may also lead to an increase in impulsivity, and common maladaptive behaviors of adolescence, such as a decrease in sleep and an increase in the use of caffeine and other substances, undoubtedly contribute to the impairments in judgment that we commonly see during these years.

PSYCHIATRIC DIAGNOSIS

Tolstoy opens *Anna Karenina* (1873–1877/2004) with this statement: "Happy families are all alike; every unhappy family is unhappy in its own way." While literate and wonderfully thoughtful, Tolstoy's statement, from a psychiatrist's point of view, is in error. In contrast to Tolstoy, who believes that happiness is all the same but that unhappiness is always unique, a psychiatrist accepts a great range of "normal" or "happy." In other words, there are many ways to feel good, many ways to be successful, and many satisfactory ways to experience one's emotions, behavior, and cognition. However, unhappiness or mental illness increasingly can be traced to specific causes or etiologies and most often expresses itself in characteristic patterns depending on the illness. For example, the symptoms of depression are reproducible in patient after patient and include difficulties with sleep, appetite, energy level, concentration, mood, pleasure-seeking behavior, hopelessness or guilt, slowed or agitated thinking or behavior, and suicidal thoughts. Virtually every individual who appears clinically depressed presents with a constellation of these symptoms. The same holds true for most psychiatric diagnoses, including anxiety, ADHD, schizophrenia, dementia, and so forth. While the causes of these illnesses have heretofore remained largely hidden, research into disease etiology is also increasingly demonstrating that these illnesses are perhaps more alike than they are dissimilar.

In defining a psychological disorder, we must look for a pattern of behavioral, cognitive, emotional, and physical symptoms demonstrated by an individual that result in some level of disability, a risk of suffering further harm, or distress. In the words of psychiatry, there must be an associated "functional impairment"; that is, a diagnosis is not valid, regardless of symptoms, without impairment or difficulty in achieving one's milestones or maintaining success in work, school, or relationships.

If an internist believes a patient may have diabetes, the physician takes a complete medical history and then requests a few simple blood and urine tests that can clarify the problem based on abnormal levels of glucose. However, the field of mental health has no such reliable biological tests to determine the presence, severity, or treatment response for mental illness. Consequently, we have had to develop a diagnostic classification system or nosology to help clinicians recognize the existence and severity of mental illness.

The most commonly employed diagnostic code book in the field of mental health is the *Diagnostic and Statistical Manual of Mental Disorders* (*DSM*) of the American Psychiatric Association. We are currently using the fifth edition of this manual, which was published in 2013. Although not without its faults, as described below, the *DSM* is a vital guidebook that aids us in the diagnosis of mental illness based on symptoms. However, being able to list important symptoms has not further clarified the etiology or our understanding of the origin of mental illness.

The *DSM* is phenomenological in that it builds diagnoses upon symptoms or phenomena, and a certain number of symptoms are required for an individual to meet diagnostic criteria. For example, *DSM-5* lists nine symptoms of depression: (1) depressed or irritable mood, (2) diminished interest or pleasure in nearly all activities, (3) recurrent thoughts of death or suicide, (4) insomnia or hypersomnia, (5) psychomotor agitation or retardation, (6) significant weight loss or gain or change in appetite, (7) difficulty concentrating or making decisions, (8) feelings of guilt or worthlessness, and (9) fatigue or a decrease in energy. While many individuals, perhaps the majority, may experience one or two of these symptoms on any given day, the *DSM* requires that five of these symptoms be present for at least a two-week period in order to establish a diagnosis of depression. Five of nine is not a magical combination of symptoms—it is simply the point at which significant impairment generally appears to result. It is, therefore, the number of symptoms selected as the diagnostic set point.

While extremely useful in helping us to understand or categorize which individuals suffer from which problems, it is important to remember that the diagnoses in the *DSM* are symptom driven and may be the result of biological, psychological, and social factors, many of which may be very difficult to ascertain. Throughout this book, we will refer to the *DSM* for diagnoses, but we will not reprint them here per se, as they are easily found in the *DSM*. This text, rather, will focus on providing the reader with an understanding of the clinical presentation, etiology, epidemiology, and natural history of each disorder, followed by an explanation of *how* to ascertain the diagnosis. This text comprises not simply symptom checklists, as in the case of the *DSM*, but a more thorough understanding of how to determine the presence of symptoms within affected individuals and the evidence-based treatments (including medication, psychotherapy, and psychosocial interventions) that can be utilized to treat each disorder.

Understanding the history of the *DSM* is instructive for the student of psychopathology. The first edition of the *DSM*, *DSM-I*, was published in 1952 (American Psychiatric Association, 1952). This slender volume considered all disorders that did not have a clearly defined cause to be "reactions" or psychologically charged responses to some emotional trauma. There were three primary categories of reaction: (1) schizophrenic reactions, (2) antisocial reactions, and (3) psychoneurotic reactions, which included the anxiety reaction, dissociative reaction, conversion reaction, phobic reaction, obsessive-compulsive reaction, and depressive reaction. The *DSM-I* was well couched within the predominant psychoanalytic theories of the day and upon Freud's emphasis on the importance of mastering anxieties generated by characteristic conflicts at particular stages of psychosexual development. The authors of *DSM-I* agreed that psychopathology was due to the failure of resolving these conflicts, and consequently it was implied, if not absolutely stated, that anxiety lay at the core of all psychiatric diagnoses. Sixteen years after the publication of *DSM-I*, *DSM-II* was released and provided, for the first time, signs and symptoms of the disorders themselves, although no formal diagnostic criteria were described (American Psychiatric Association, 1968).

Still following upon the leading psychological theories of the day, homosexuality was listed as a Sexual Deviation Disorder in both *DSM-I* and *DSM-II*. This category also included transvestism, pedophilia, fetishism, and sexual sadism (e.g., rape, assault, and sexual mutilation). In 1973, for the sixth printing of *DSM-II*, homosexuality was removed as a mental disorder but changed to Sexual Orientation Disturbance, a category for individuals whose sexual interests were aimed primarily toward those of the same sex and who were either disturbed by, were in conflict with, or desired to change their sexual orientation. *DSM-III*, published in 1980, further revised the diagnosis by removing Sexual Orientation Disturbance and adding Ego-Dystonic Homosexuality, intending to describe individuals who identified as homosexual but were distressed by their same-sex preference (American Psychiatric Association, 1980). Finally, *DSM-III-R* (revised edition) of 1987 removed all mention of homosexuality from the code book (American Psychiatric Association, 1987). Clearly, psychiatry has had an uneasy relationship with human sexuality.

Absolute symptoms and diagnostic criteria for the disorders were first described in *DSM-III*. This version of the *DSM* demonstrated better interrater reliability, indicating that different examiners were, for the first time, highly likely to arrive at the same diagnosis for the same patient when using these diagnostic parameters. *DSM-III* was also a landmark for child and adolescent mental health by including a group of disorders "usually first present in infancy, childhood, or adolescence," such as Reactive Attachment Disorder, Autistic Disorder, Separation Anxiety Disorder, Overanxious Disorder, and Avoidant Disorder. In addition, it was now permissible to apply adult anxiety diagnoses to children and adolescents. Finally, *DSM-III* introduced a much-flawed multiaxial system, such that individuals were coded according to five axes. Under Axis I, the primary clinical psychiatric disturbances were coded; Axis II represented personality disorders and mental retardation (e.g., conditions considered to be lifelong and impacting all aspects of an individual's functioning); Axis III listed the major medical diagnoses, such as asthma, hypertension, and diabetes; Axis IV provided an indication of psychosocial and environmental problems; and Axis V measured the individual's Global Assessment of Functioning (GAF), a numeric scale from 0 to 100 employed to rate social, occupational, and psychological functioning. The multiaxial system has never proven itself to be valid or necessary in the diagnosis of mental illness and therefore was dropped from *DSM-5* (American Psychiatric Association, 2013; J. B. W. Williams, 1985).

The most fundamental changes to the *DSM* occurred in 1980 with the publication of *DSM-III*. While both *DSM-III* and *DSM-III-R* were criticized by some researchers, particularly because of the inclusion of childhood diagnoses due to incomplete evidence of their validity at that time, *DSM-III* moved the pendulum far away from psychiatry's psychoanalytic history by taking an entirely atheoretical approach to the diagnosis of psychiatric illness and eliminating altogether the term *neurosis* from the lexicon. Given our incomplete understanding of the pathophysiology of most mental disorders, the authors of *DSM-III* chose to establish diagnostic criteria as the best possible description of how these disorders are expressed. *DSM-IV*, published in 1994, and *DSM-IV-TR* (the text revision of the fourth edition), published in 2000, largely provided a refinement of *DSM-III* nosology and added clinical significance criteria to over half the diagnoses, requiring that a mental illness cause significant distress in major life domains to meet criteria for diagnosis (American Psychiatric Association, 1994, 2000). Never at a standstill, American psychiatry is now embroiled in controversy surrounding the *DSM*'s most recent iteration, *DSM-5*.

The architects of *DSM-5* set themselves a lofty goal: to move away from categorical diagnoses and toward dimensional diagnoses. That is, *DSM-5* acknowledges that the distinction between various psychiatric diagnoses may not be as clear-cut or profound as was once believed. In other words, organized psychiatry has now recognized the limits imposed by the phenomenological approach of its classification or nosological system since the publication of *DSM-III*. *DSM-5* is intended to recognize the crossover between diagnoses or the "porous boundaries," such as the spectrum of autistic, anxiety, mood, psychotic, and other disorders (American Psychiatric Association, 2013). Such crossover is evident when evaluating the genetic and environmental risk factors shared by so many disorders (e.g., growing up in poverty is a risk factor for just about every psychiatric disorder); the heretofore high rate of "Not Otherwise Specified" (NOS) diagnoses (e.g., NOS is employed as a suffix for any given diagnosis when full symptom criteria are not met but the individual suffers some clinically meaningful and impairing symptoms); and the lack of treatment specificity (e.g., selective serotonin reuptake inhibitors work effectively for depression, anxiety disorders, bulimia nervosa, premenstrual dysphoric disorder, and premature ejaculation).

DSM-5 is organized developmentally, unlike past versions of the *DSM*, such that those diagnoses manifesting early in life appear earlier in the manual. Consequently, neurodevelopmental disorders, such as autism and intellectual disability, appear in the first pages of the text, whereas dementia appears toward the end of the book. Furthermore, disorders are clustered in *DSM-5* by "internalizing" and "externalizing" features. Mood and anxiety disorders, for example, in which individuals internalize their symptoms, are grouped closely together, as are disruptive behavior, addictive, and impulse control disorders, in which individuals externalize their symptoms.

DSM-5 incorporates a more objective measure of the disability caused by psychiatric illness by employing the World Health Organization's Disability Assessment Schedule (WHODAS) in contrast to the more subjective GAF scale coded on Axis V in *DSM-IV*. The WHODAS 2.0 is a 36-item questionnaire completed by self-report or interviewer administered. The WHODAS covers six domains, including cognition (understanding and communicating), mobility (moving and getting around), self-care (hygiene, dressing, eating, and staying alone), getting along (interacting with other people), life activities (domestic responsibilities, leisure, work, and school), and participation (joining in community activities). Although taking considerably more time to complete and score, the WHODAS produces a more standardized understanding of patient disability due to psychiatric, neurological, or addictive disorders (World Health Organization, 2014).

DSM-5 has expanded the cultural formulation and glossary of culture-bound syndromes (now referred to as "Glossary of Cultural Concepts of Distress") first included in DSM-IV. In the Cultural Formulation Interview (CFI), DSM-5 provides examples of questions to employ in the evaluation of individuals from outside Western culture. The CFI addresses the cultural definition of the problem the individual is having, cultural perceptions of cause, stressors and supports, cultural identity, coping skills, past efforts to seek help, barriers to care, preferences in care, and the clinician–patient relationship (American Psychiatric Association, 2013).

DSM-5 also makes an effort to provide more consistent data-gathering techniques that employ "cross-cutting symptom measures" to aid clinicians in carrying out comprehensive assessment (American Psychiatric Association, 2013). So-called Level 1 measures are general surveys available online and are intended to provide a review of 13 general psychiatric domains (12 domains in children and adolescents), such as anxiety, sleep, depression, self-injury, and substance abuse. Adults and youth aged 11 to 17 years can complete these forms themselves, while parents are expected to complete the assessment for children under 11 years of age. Depending on how an individual responds to the Level 1 rating scale, Level 2 cross-cutting symptom measures may be used, which are designed to evaluate the severity of symptoms identified in the Level 1 scale. The reliability of the cross-cutting symptom measures has been found to be "good to excellent" among most adults and parents reporting on their children. However, the reliability has not been generally good for child respondents and in assessing suicide in all age groups (Narrow et al, 2013).

Throughout its history, the DSM has been no stranger to criticism, and DSM-5 is no exception. Mental disorders present to us more as symptom complexes than discrete diagnoses whose pathophysiology has been fully elucidated. As a result, some believe that revamping the nosology at this point is premature, given that we do not fully understand the "dimensional" nature of the various psychiatric diagnoses. Beyond this primary concern, which goes to the root of the intended design of

DSM-5 (e.g., establishing dimensional diagnoses), a number of criticisms have been levied at the American Psychiatric Association for not allowing an outside review of the criteria before field-testing and for including new and inadequately substantiated diagnoses, such as Disruptive Mood Dysregulation Disorder, Mild Neurocognitive Disorder, and Binge Eating Disorder.

The National Institute of Mental Health (NIMH) shares concerns about *DSM-5* and is going so far as to move its research away from *DSM* categories and into broad-based "research domain criteria" (RDoC). These RDoC represent an effort to transform psychiatric diagnostic criteria by incorporating neuroimaging findings, genetics, and cognitive neuroscience. Although the NIMH recognizes that it is also far too early to rely on RDoC, it has begun a decade-long project to try to create valid criteria, which is truly what the field needs. The strengths of the *DSM* have increasingly been its high reliability (e.g., clinicians utilizing the same criteria to make the same diagnoses), while its weakness remains its low validity (e.g., the continued use of consensus criteria for establishing diagnoses instead of objective laboratory or other clinical measures). As a result, NIMH pledges to support research into, for example, the spectrum of mood disorders, instead of rigidly supporting studies of depression or bipolar disorder alone, given that we recognize that such a spectrum of diagnoses does exist clinically but is not well accounted for in the *DSM* (Insel, 2013).

However justified the criticisms may be, *DSM-5* is sure to replace its predecessor as the gold standard diagnostic codebook for mental health practitioners worldwide. For the present time, then, the *DSM* remains a necessary and highly useful tool to the practitioner that allows clinicians to agree more often than not on patient diagnoses, even if those diagnoses are not always valid. Flawed though it may be, the ultimate goal of the *DSM*, like any diagnostic system, gallantly remains determining the proper diagnosis so that the best treatment plan for each patient can be established.

2

Prevention

The preponderance of chronic and severe mental illness has its roots in childhood, adolescence, and early adulthood. ADHD, autism, learning disorders, disruptive behavior disorders, mood and anxiety disorders, schizophrenia, eating disorders, and substance use disorders are most often apparent by the mid-20s. Youth is characterized by not only an increase in psychiatric diagnoses, however, but also by an increase in illness, injury, and death driven by changes in the way that adolescents process information and experience emotions as well as in the behaviors in which they choose to engage. Chapter 1 noted that the top three causes of death in adolescents and young adults are accidents, homicide, and suicide, and that the rates of anxiety, depression, and other mental illnesses rapidly increase during these formative years. The rates of other disorders driven by adolescent emotions, impulsivity, and risk-taking behavior also increase during these years.

Nearly half the estimated 19 million new cases of sexually transmitted infections affect youth ages 15 to 19 years (Weinstock, Berman, & Cates, 2004). Twenty-six percent of new HIV infections occur in those 13 to 24 years of age (Centers for Disease Control and Prevention, 2010). Motor vehicle accidents are the leading cause of death for U.S. teens, and 32% of 15- to 20-year-olds killed in motor vehicle accidents have been driving under the influence of alcohol (National Highway Traffic Safety Administration, 2013). The vast majority of high school students rarely or never wear a bicycle helmet (87%), and nearly a third of high school students rarely or never wear a motorcycle helmet (32%). Large percentages of high school students have had sexual intercourse (47%), have smoked marijuana in the last 30 days (23%), have binge drunk in the last 30 days

(21%), have ridden in a vehicle driven by someone who has been drinking alcohol in the last 30 days (22%), have been cyberbullied (21%) or physically bullied on campus (20%), have felt sad or hopeless for at least two weeks (30%), have experienced physical dating violence (10%) or sexual dating violence (10%), have physically been forced to have sexual intercourse (7%), have seriously considered suicide (17%), have made a suicide plan (14%), or have made a suicide attempt (8%; Centers for Disease Control and Prevention, 2014a). Mental and physical health problems are commonly entwined during adolescence and early adulthood, leading to vast amounts of disability and making it imperative that we identify those at greatest risk.

In the simplest of terms, poverty, unemployment, and lower socioeconomic status are the most impactful risk factors affecting the mental and physical health of children, adolescents, and young adults. Chronic poverty before the age of 5 significantly predicts later childhood symptoms of anxiety and depression, independent of present poverty status. Unemployment and poverty are significantly associated with depressive symptoms among adults, and parent mental illness, as we will see in Chapter 12, leads to child mental illness. Populations that spend more time in poverty, such as blacks and Latinos, have higher rates of mental disturbance precisely because they spend more time in poverty. There is essentially no difference in the frequency of mental illness between the races when children are raised in the same socioeconomic environment (Mossakowski, 2008). Cigarette smoking, the most preventable cause of death in the United States, also disproportionately affects the poor; and those with less education, who also more often live in poverty, are more likely to smoke (Danaei et al., 2009).

People in poverty also tend to live in less healthy environments, and not surprisingly, neighborhood quality is known to impact both mental and physical health. Residential crowding and loud exterior noises elevate psychological distress, as does living in a high-rise apartment building, which has been shown to negatively impact children and mothers, presumably due to social isolation and lack of play space (Evans, 2003).

Just as poverty, unemployment, and lower socioeconomic status increase the likelihood of mental illness, mental illness and distress impact physical health. Among middle-aged female stroke survivors, for example, those who acknowledge feelings of apathy do not recover as well (Mayo, Fellows, Scott, Cameron, & Wood-Dauphinee, 2009); and hopelessness has been correlated to increased (averaging three times greater) thickening of neck arteries in otherwise healthy, middle-aged women (Whipple et al., 2009). We also know that heart attack sufferers whose jobs include a heavy workload and little chance to be creative or make decisions (both characteristics of high-stress jobs) are twice as likely to have a second heart attack after resuming work (Aboa-Eboulé et al., 2007).

Absolutely everything is health related. Consider something as simple as a leather shoe. At first glance, it does not seem to have anything to do with health, other than the fact that its design may have some impact on posture or the way one walks. If we delve a bit more deeply, however, and consider all aspects of how that shoe came to be, we find myriad health impacts. For example, the leather in the body of the shoe and the wood in the heel are natural resources, so how did those natural resources come about? In other words, how was that cow raised? Was it given corn feed so it would grow more quickly than it would if it were given grass to eat? Likely so, but corn invariably causes gastrointestinal ulcers in cows, thereby necessitating high doses of preventive antibiotics, which then run off into the groundwater when the cows urinate and defecate as well as enter the muscle that we eat as food. Did the wood in the heel come from a renewable source, and was a new tree planted in place of the one cut down for the shoe? What about the workers who quartered the slaughtered cow, cut the leather, and applied the (likely toxic) stains and dye? Were they wearing adequate protective clothing? Had they been trained in safe practices? Was the waste from all processes neutralized or stored safely so that it did not enter our groundwater and food chain? The same sort of complex web that impacts all aspects of our physical health surrounds our mental health.

Knowing that childhood, adolescence, and young adulthood are such vulnerable periods makes them ideal times to focus on prevention of mental illness and risk-taking behavior. If we can stop mental illness before it starts, or intervene early in its trajectory, perhaps we can change and even save some lives. Although prevention is often politically unpopular because it takes sometimes years to reap the benefits of health promotion efforts, studies increasingly demonstrate that mental health and substance use prevention efforts among children and adolescents have substantial returns on investment that far exceed the costs of the interventions themselves (D. Eisenberg & Neighbors, 2009).

Public health is defined as "the science and art of preventing disease, prolonging life and promoting health through the organized efforts and informed choices of society, organizations, public and private communities and individuals" (Winslow, 1920). In public health, we define three levels of prevention: (1) primary prevention—promoting wellness and healthy choices and behaviors (e.g., exercise, nutrition, and sleep education programs), along with efforts to prevent disease (e.g., vaccinations and wearing bicycle helmets); (2) secondary prevention—identifying illness early in its development and providing treatment; and (3) tertiary prevention—treating chronic and severe illness. Unfortunately, the vast majority of health care is provided directly to individuals when they are already ill, constituting a focus on tertiary prevention, which is more invasive and complicated for the patient (both medically and psychologically) and costly to both individuals and the health care system. Intensifying the problem is the fact that we have an inadequate number of services and practitioners to address the clinical need. Consequently, the only rational approach is to do everything within our power to stop mental illness before it starts.

A public health approach to mental health promotion and mental illness prevention is the only strategy that truly makes sense, given our resources. As described in Chapter 1, we will probably never have enough child and adolescent front-line mental health providers, but it's not only trained psychiatrists and psychologists we need—we also need programs to identify children who are at risk and then to implement change so that they never develop mental illness or substance dependence in the first place.

At first look, preventing mental illness may seem an untenable task. However, we now know a great deal about how to engage in primary and secondary mental health prevention. We know, for example, that broad-based programs work more effectively than single-focus programs; we know that those constructs that continually stand out in high-functioning programs include helping children and adolescents improve their competence, self-efficacy, and prosocial engagement; and we know that programs addressing more than one setting (e.g., school, church, home) and more than one level (e.g., the individual, the parents, the community) are more effective (Catalano, Berglund, Ryan, Lonczak, & Hawkins, 2004). Similarly, we know that the best public health programs offer more support, provide earlier intervention, and are more structured and sophisticated (C. Peterson, 2004).

Given what we know about the importance of the environment, socioeconomic status, and race and their impact on mental and physical health, we should undoubtedly be putting much of our effort into public health programs that address poverty. However, we are not generally able to take on the issue of poverty in a significant way when we build mental health programs, so we must continue to work at all levels of practice (individual, family, and community) and at each level of prevention (primary, secondary, and tertiary).

Imagine that we are designing a program to identify and treat adolescent depression. As seen in Table 2.1, primary prevention efforts for a high school depression program might include educating parents, teach-

Table 2.1 Depression Health Promotion Program Components

Intervention	Level of Practice	Type of Prevention
Educate youth about depression at school	Individual	Primary
Educate parents about depression	Family	Primary
Develop a mass media campaign about depression	Community	Primary
Delay school start time for high school	Community	Primary
Increase funding for exercise & nutrition programs in high school	Community	Primary
Advocate for research, clinical funding & school based programs	Community	Primary
Provide support & teach CBT skills to high-risk youth	Individual	Secondary
Assess all family members of high-risk youth	Family	Secondary
Refer depressed youth and family members to treatment	Individual/ Family	Secondary
Screen all youth in high schools	Community	Secondary
Provide treatment for all affected youth	Individual	Tertiary
Provide treatment for all affected family members	Family	Tertiary
Adequate inpatient, foster care, and residential treatment services	Community	Tertiary

ers, and youth about depression or developing a mass-media campaign about depression. Since we know that youth who do not receive adequate sleep are at increased risk for depression, delaying the school start time to 9 or 10 a.m. might also help (Owens, Adolescent Sleep Working Group and Committee on Adolescence, & Council on School Health, 2014). Similarly, exercise programs have been shown to improve symptoms of depression and may be an effective prevention tool, so supporting exercise and nutrition programs might decrease the risk of depression in youth. At a meta-level, we would want to advocate more funding for research, clinical care, and school-based programs, particularly given that fewer than 10% of America's 80,000 public schools have comprehensive mental health services (Goodman, 2014). Secondary prevention efforts might include identifying high-risk youth, such as those who have previously suffered an episode of depression or have family members with depression or come from a high-risk environment (e.g., have a chronically medically or mentally ill parent), who may benefit from additional support at school and learning cognitive behavioral skills (see Chapters 10 and 12). To expand the benefits of our program, we would screen the family members of high-risk youth, in addition to all high school students whether or not they are at identifiable risk, and make necessary referrals for further evaluation. Finally, at a tertiary level of prevention, we would treat all affected youth and their family members in addition to ensuring that adequate inpatient, foster care, residential treatment, and other services (e.g., child and family welfare) are available in the community.

To improve our prevention efforts, we also want to improve youth resilience, which we believe will help children and adolescents ward off or minimize the impact of mental illness. By identifying "what's right" with children and adolescents (not just "what's wrong") and promoting their strengths, we may find other ways to battle mental illness. Children and adolescents spend one third to one half of their days in school, where we infrequently teach resilience. Expanding our efforts to teach problem-solving skills, coping skills, empathy, effective communication, prosocial behavior, and emotion regulation may represent, in fact, some of our best efforts at preventing mental illness.

3

Attention-Deficit/
Hyperactivity Disorder

Attention-deficit/hyperactivity disorder (ADHD) is the most commonly diagnosed childhood behavioral disorder. Over the past two decades, our ability to diagnose and effectively treat ADHD has improved significantly, and we are now able to help children who would otherwise have long suffered without assistance. Children affected by ADHD more often than not suffer coexisting conditions, such as learning disorders and behavioral difficulties, that are equally if not more disruptive to their healthy development.

CLINICAL PRESENTATION

Throughout the first half of the past century, ADHD was thought to be the result of developmental problems in utero, and the diagnosis given to extremely hyperactive and impulsive children was *minimal brain damage*. As studies of affected children grew, it was recognized that these children were not technically brain damaged and that the concept of minimal brain damage, therefore, was in error. From approximately 1950 to 1970, children with severe hyperactivity and impulsivity were instead considered to suffer from a purely hyperkinetic or hyperactivity syndrome. *DSM-II* (American Psychiatric Association, 1968) recognized a diagnosis similar to what we now view as ADHD and labeled it within the psychiatric lexicon as the "hyperkinetic reaction of childhood."

During the 1970s, over 200 peer-reviewed publications brought to the forefront a frequently co-occurring symptom of children who suffered impairing hyperactivity and impulsivity, namely inattention. Based on this wealth of new scientific data, the entire concept of the disorder was reconsidered from one of hyperactivity to one of inattention by the time *DSM-III* (American Psychiatric Association, 1980) was published. The new diagnosis, "Attention Deficit Disorder (with or without symptoms of hyperactivity)," reflected this change. Attention deficit now became the cornerstone or sine qua non of the diagnosis itself. As researchers learned during the following decade that these three symptoms are most commonly intertwined and present in some combined fashion, attention deficit disorder (ADD) was once again renamed with the publication of *DSM-III-R* (American Psychiatric Association, 1987), this time as ADHD, with a series of mixed criteria. The diagnosis was now based on the presence of at least 8 of 14 symptoms, which could constitute a variety or intermingling of difficulties including hyperactivity, impulsivity, and inattention. With the publication of *DSM-IV* (American Psychiatric Association, 1994), the diagnosis became "ADHD (predominantly inattentive type, hyperactive/impulsive type, or combined type)," and it has remained essentially the same in *DSM-5* (American Psychiatric Association, 2013) with one small exception. *DSM-IV* mandated that some symptoms be present before age 7, whereas *DSM-5* now requires that several symptoms be present prior to age 12. As our understanding of the disorder has grown, so has our ability to diagnose it more accurately, which is reflected in each successive version of the *DSM* (Barkley, 1998).

Children diagnosed with ADHD can present clinically in myriad ways. The most easily recognizable children are remarkably physically active and almost always viewed by others as disruptive and extremely impulsive. Many of these children are falsely believed to be willfully dismissive of others' needs and desires, and as a result they are increasingly ostracized as they age. Preschool children are particularly forgiving of their peers' idiosyncrasies, but with age children become less forgiving, especially when one of them is always moving too quickly from topic to topic, rarely able to stay focused in a school or extracurricular activity, and distracting for others to be around. As a result, we commonly see affected children who have not been treated by their school-age years struggling with their self-esteem, as other children simply do not want to learn and play with them. Such social isolation, however, only compounds the feelings that these children already have about themselves, as they indeed also wonder why they cannot focus, stay seated, and control their impulses like their peers.

Another type of child affected by ADHD is simply inattentive but not generally hyperactive or impulsive. This child typically does better with peers but will also soon be filled with self-doubt as to why he cannot stay focused like his friends, be attentive on the ball field, and complete his schoolwork in the allotted time. As parents and teachers make fruitless but genuine efforts to help this child with his schoolwork (often employing tutors at home and special assistance at school), they become increasingly frustrated with his apparent lack of drive and determination. None of this dissatisfaction goes unnoticed by the child, who begins to view himself as an academic failure, incapable of succeeding in school and often with friends. After years of disappointment, he, just like the child affected by hyperactivity and impulsivity, is likely to lose faith in himself, undermine his own academic and social progress, and despair for his future.

ETIOLOGY

The etiology of ADHD is not clear, but research increasingly points to the cause of the disorder as neurological with limited environmental influence. Numerous brain structures have been implicated in some fashion, including the dorsolateral prefrontal cortex, the dorsal anterior cingulate cortex, the striatum, and the parietal cortex. Imaging studies have demonstrated that the caudate nucleus and globus pallidus (striatum), which contain a high density of dopamine receptors, are smaller in children affected by ADHD than in control groups. This research has also demonstrated that children with ADHD have smaller posterior brain regions (e.g., the occipital lobes), particularly in areas that coordinate the activities of multiple brain regions, such as the rostrum and splenium of the corpus callosum and the cerebellar vermis. Furthermore, we are now convinced that children with ADHD have smaller brain volumes in virtually all regions. Total cerebral volume, including cortical white and gray matter, is smaller by about 3%, and cerebellar volume is smaller by about 3.5%. These volumetric abnormalities persist with age, except those found within the caudate nucleus. There appear to be no gender differences, and the volumetric findings correlate with the severity of ADHD symptoms. Importantly, children who are unmedicated for ADHD show roughly the same differences in brain volume abnormalities as children who have been medicated or treated for ADHD, suggesting that the medication itself is not responsible for these changes (Castellanos et al., 2002).

Research has also begun to demonstrate that children suffering from ADHD have decreased cortical thickening in the anterior cingulate cortex, a key region involved in cognitive control (Makris et al., 2007). Some studies have found that children with a worse clinical outcome have a thinner left medial prefrontal cortex at baseline than children with a better outcome (Shaw et al., 2006). Taken as a whole, these studies increasingly point to neurological abnormalities in children diagnosed with ADHD.

Another potential cause of ADHD lies within the genetic code, and there are a number of genes that have been found to date to be associated with the disorder. Rare mutations in the human thyroid receptor beta gene on Chromosome 3 have resulted in symptoms suggestive of ADHD and are found in those with a general resistance to thyroid hormone (Hauser et al., 1993). The dopamine transporter gene on Chromosome 5 has also been implicated as a possible genetic cause of ADHD (Gill, Daly, Heron, Hawi, & Fitzgerald, 1997). When the dopamine presynaptic transporter (DAT), which is coded by Chromosome 5, is somewhat overly active and reabsorbs too much dopamine, the postsynaptic neuron cannot be fed adequate amounts of the neurotransmitter, which may result in an inability to maintain focus and attention (see Figure 3.1). Lastly, the dopamine receptor D4 gene on Chromosome 11 and the dopamine receptor D5 gene on Chromosome 4 have also been implicated, such that malfunction of these genes on the postsynaptic receptor does not allow transmission of dopamine (Swanson et al., 1998; see Figure 3.2). Malfunction at Chromosome 5, 11, or 4 and the resulting impairments at the dopamine transporter gene or D4 or D5 receptors would support the monoamine hypothesis of ADHD; that is, that a deficiency of dopamine and norepinephrine leads to clinical findings of ADHD. A number of other genes that code for enzymes that impact dopamine and norepinephrine, such as catechol-O-methyltransferase, monoamine oxidase, and tyrosine hydroxylase, have variably shown a modest association with ADHD (J. Eisenberg et al., 1999; Ernst et al., 1999; Hawi et al., 2001; Jiang et al., 2003; Lawson et al., 2003; Payton et al., 2001).

ADHD is a familial illness. Family studies have repeatedly demonstrated that a sibling's risk of having the disorder is two to five times greater than the general population risk. The parents are also at risk, and there is a three- to five-times-greater likelihood that if a child is affected, a parent is also affected. Twin studies have shown that ADHD is highly genetically bound. Monozygotes (identical twins) have about an 80% risk of suffering ADHD if the identical sibling is affected. ADHD is more tightly genetically bound among monozygotes than breast cancer, asthma, and schizophrenia (Faraone, 2000; Hemminki & Mutanen, 2001; Nikolas & Burt, 2010; Palmer et al., 2001).

A number of environmental factors with almost certain neurobiological impact are also likely to be implicated in the etiology of ADHD. Children with low birth weight, for example, are more likely to suffer ADHD symptoms as they age. The same is true for children who suf-

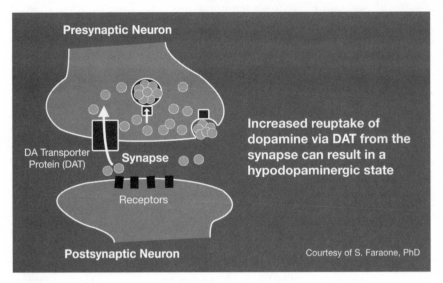

Figure 3.1 Significance of DAT dysfunction.

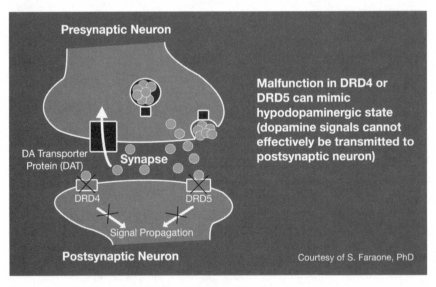

Figure 3.2 Significance of DRD4 or DRD5 dysfunction.

fer traumatic brain injury or experience excessive perinatal stress, whose mothers smoked during pregnancy, or who face severe early deprivation. The precise reasons for these findings are not clear, yet they appear to be more than simply correlational. Rather, it is likely that infants and children who face such environmental circumstances in conjunction with a genetic risk or predisposition suffer subsequent developmental and neurobiological damage, resulting in symptoms of inattention, hyperactivity, and impulsivity (Nigg & Casey, 2005; Nigg, Nikolas, & Burt, 2010).

Another area that has received much attention in recent years is the role of pesticides, toxins, and diet in the etiology of ADHD. Organophosphate pesticides have been studied minimally in relation to ADHD, with mixed and as yet unimpressive results. Among the industrial exposures, polychlorinated biphenyls (PCBs) and lead are both known to impair working memory, cognitive flexibility, and response inhibition, all characteristics of individuals affected by ADHD. It is plausible, and some studies have suggested but not yet proven, that these toxins could have a role in the development of ADHD. Certainly, there is adequate evidence to suggest that limiting early childhood exposure to these toxins is wise. Although it is clear that severe nutritional deficiency can result in neurodevelopmental impairment, it is not at all clear that mild to moderate deficiencies of various nutrients can lead to ADHD. Zinc, magnesium, iron, and polyunsaturated fatty acids have, perhaps, been studied to the greatest extent, but even here the data are insufficient to correlate cause and effect. Iron deficiency in particular is an attractive etiological hypothesis for ADHD, as iron is necessary in the processing of dopamine, one of the major neurotransmitters responsible for our ability to focus, sit still, and pay attention (Cortese, Angriman, Lecendreux, & Konofal, 2012; Thapar, Cooper, Eyre, & Langley, 2013). Food additives, such as colorings and preservatives, have been suggested as a cause of ADHD since Feingold prescribed a diet free of salicylates and synthetic colors and flavors (Feingold, 1975). To date, however, there is little data to suggest that food colorings and preservatives cause or aggravate ADHD, although one meta-analysis, with significant limitations, did find that approximately one third of children with ADHD may show symptom improvement with a dietary intervention limiting colors and preservatives and that up to 8% of children may experience symptoms of ADHD that are due to food coloring (Nigg, Lewis, Edinger, & Falk, 2012). Finally, there is virtually no convincing evidence linking dietary sugar intake with ADHD (Hoover & Milich, 1994; Millichap & Yee, 2012; Wolraich, Milich, Stumbo, & Schultz, 1985; Wolraich et al., 1994).

EPIDEMIOLOGY

Approximately 1 in 20, or 5%, of children worldwide are affected by ADHD. International research has demonstrated that between 3% and 9% of schoolchildren are affected, although in some studies the percent-

age of affected children is far greater (Goldman, Genel, Bezman, & Slanetz, 1998; Merikangas, He, Burstein, et al., 2010b). A recent random-
digit-dialing telephone survey of nearly 96,000 parents in the United
States, for example, found that 11% of children aged 4 to 17 years have
been given a diagnosis of ADHD, up from 7.8% in 2003, an increase of
42%. Furthermore, 6.1% of children are currently being given a prescription medication for the treatment of ADHD, up from 4.8% in 2007, an
increase of 27%, but nearly 20% of affected children are not receiving
either medication or counseling (Visser et al., 2013). As with virtually all
neurobehavioral disorders of childhood, males are more commonly
affected than females. In the past, when ADHD was viewed largely as a
disorder of hyperactivity and impulsivity, the vast majority of patients
diagnosed were male. However, our current understanding of ADHD as
not only a hyperkinetic disorder but also a disorder of inattention has led
us to study females more carefully. We now understand that the likelihood of boys and girls being affected is much less discrepant than we had
previously thought, such that we now believe males are probably affected
only about twice as often as females. Girls typically but not always show
less hyperactivity, exhibit fewer conduct problems and externalizing
behaviors, demonstrate symptoms a bit later than boys, and are more
often to be "politely inattentive" and not as overtly disruptive as boys.

Interestingly, we sometimes see a sex paradox with ADHD. That is,
since girls are less often afflicted by ADHD, when they do demonstrate
observable impairment, it may appear as clinically more severe than that
of the average boy with ADHD (Loeber & Kennan, 1994). The sex paradox
in ADHD is consistent with other multifactorial or polygenic conditions
(e.g., disorders where numerous factors or genes are acting as combined
causal agents). In other words, since girls are less commonly affected
by ADHD on a population level, it takes a greater accumulation of vulnerability and risk factors for them to develop the disorder. Even more
striking is the fact that girls with ADHD tend to have more functional
impairment than boys with ADHD, such as an increased risk of depression, suicide, and eating disorders (J. Gershon, 2002; Mikami, Hinshaw,
Patterson, & Lee, 2008). Furthermore, girls with ADHD, particularly the
inattentive subtype, have been shown to be bullied more often, to have
worse peer relationships, and to be more negatively affected in academics
than boys with ADHD (Elkins, Malone, Keyes, Iacono, & McGue, 2011).

Over 80% of children with ADHD demonstrate some sort of psychopathology as adults. Over half and perhaps as many as two thirds
continue to struggle with ADHD, but other impairments, such as mood,
anxiety, and learning disorders, commonly persist or develop (Cantwell,
1996). Furthermore, adults with ADHD face more problems maintaining

employment, an increase in sexual and reproductive risks, an increase in motor vehicle accidents and traffic violations, an increase in substance abuse, and a higher accident rate than those not affected by ADHD (Barkley, Murphy, & Kwasnik, 1996; Biederman, Petty, et al., 2008; Biederman, Wilens, Mick, Faraone, & Spencer, 1998). This increase in risk translates into higher associated medical costs and more outpatient medical care, inpatient hospitalizations, and emergency room visits for those with ADHD (Leibson, Katusic, Barbaresi, Ransom, & O'Brien, 2001).

Parents commonly ask about the risk of substance abuse among children who are treated for ADHD with stimulants. After much investigation, we now recognize that individuals with ADHD have a greater risk of substance abuse than the general population. In one longitudinal study, the hazard of developing any substance use disorder or alcohol dependence during the 10-year period was approximately 1.5 times greater among those with ADHD than among the general population, and even higher hazard rates were found for drug dependence (hazard ratio = 2.7) and cigarette smoking (hazard ratio = 2.4; Wilens et al., 2011). However, the data clearly show that children and adolescents with ADHD who are treated with stimulants are no more likely to become abusers of alcohol, tobacco, and illicit drugs than untreated youth with ADHD (Humphreys, Eng, & Lee, 2013). In fact, some studies have even found that those treated with stimulants for ADHD have lower rates of substance abuse than untreated adolescents who suffer ADHD, in addition to a host of other benefits (Wilens et al., 2008). In one study of 370 children with ADHD over 18 years, prescription stimulant treatment was associated with improved academic success, such as reading achievement, decreased absenteeism, and a decreased likelihood of grade retention (Barbaresi, Katusic, Colligan, Weaver, & Jacobsen, 2007). Another 10-year prospective study found that those treated for ADHD with stimulants had lower subsequent rates of depression, conduct disorder, oppositional defiant disorder, and anxiety disorders, in addition to lower rates of grade retention, than children with ADHD who never received stimulant treatment (Biederman, Monuteaux, Spencer, Wilens, & Faraone, 2009).

Primary care practitioners treat the vast majority of ADHD. ADHD-related outpatient visits to primary care practitioners increased from 1.6 million to 4.2 million between 1990 and 1993, along with an increase in the use of stimulant medications to treat the disorder (Swanson, Lerner, & Williams, 1995). Between 1991 and 2000, the annual production of methylphenidate rose by 740% in the United States. Production of amphetamine increased 25 times during this same time period (Diller, 2002). From 2000 to 2010, the number of physician outpatient visits in which ADHD was diagnosed increased by 66%, from 6.2 to 10.4 million visits.

Although pediatricians and family physicians continue to diagnose and treat most cases of ADHD, an increasing number of children and adolescents are being treated by psychiatrists, totaling 36% in 2010 (Garfield et al., 2012). The reasons for the increase in specialty care are unclear, particularly as the number of ADHD cases has continued to rise sharply while the number of specialists has risen only modestly. One reasonable hypothesis is that parents and practitioners are becoming increasingly aware of the potential hazards of prescription treatment for ADHD and prefer a specialist to be at the helm. A similar shift toward specialist care has been found in the case of antidepressants, where safety concerns have mounted and regulatory agencies have provided stricter recommendations for treatment of children and adolescents (Libby et al., 2007).

Although we find ADHD present within every culture studied, the United States uses the vast majority of stimulants. In 2000, America utilized 80% of the world's stimulants, while most other industrialized countries used about 10% the amount the United States used (Diller, 2002). Canada uses stimulants at about 50% of the U.S. rate. Hawaii has the lowest per-capita use of methylphenidate by a factor of about five. High stimulant utilization areas are found mostly in the eastern United States near college campuses and clinics that specialize in the diagnosis and treatment of ADHD (U.S. Drug Enforcement Agency, 2000). In 2008, approximately 2.8 million children and adolescents in the United States—3.5% of all youth in the United States—received a stimulant medication for ADHD, and sales of medications used to treat ADHD have now risen to over $4 billion from $759 million in the year 2000 (Food and Drug Administration, 2006; Scheffler, Hinshaw, Modrek, & Levine, 2007; Tcacik, 2011; Zuvekas & Vitiello, 2012). Finally, the Drug Enforcement Agency, which limits the amount of commercially manufactured amphetamine produced each year, has allowed increasing volumes to be produced in recent decades in line with the increased demand—in 1990, that number was 417 kg; in 2000, it was 9,007 kg; and in 2012, it was 25,300 kg (Kent, 2013).

Concurrent with an increase in the diagnosis and treatment of ADHD in children, adults have also been recognized to suffer from ADHD. The use of medications in adults increased 90% between 2002 and 2005, and the use of medications to treat ADHD in adults aged 20 to 44 rose 19% in 2005 alone. That same year, an estimated 1.7 million adults aged 20 to 64 years and 3.3 million children under 19 took a medication for ADHD (Okie, 2006).

With all of the increase in treatment, we would be remiss if we did not ask ourselves why the diagnosis has appeared more frequently in recent years. There are numerous possible explanations. Perhaps the most evident reason is that physicians and allied professionals are much better at recognizing ADHD today than they were in the past. Increasingly, not only child and adolescent psychiatrists but also neurologists, pediatricians, and primary care practitioners, including primary care physicians, nurse practitioners, and physicians' assistants, are being trained in the identification and treatment of ADHD.

Many wonder whether an increase in scholastic demands also accounts for some of the growth we have witnessed in the diagnosis and treatment of ADHD. This suspicion is impossible to fully substantiate, but many argue convincingly that the increased reliance on standardized testing within our schools and the consequent increase in focus required for students to perform on standardized exams has led to increasing parental anxiety about school performance and a greater likelihood that they will have their children evaluated for ADHD. As a result of the No Child Left Behind federal legislation, schools and teachers are also under increasing pressure for their students to perform well on standardized tests in order to maintain necessary funding. Parent and teacher pressure and a visit to a physician for an evaluation will not, in and of themselves, result in a diagnosis of ADHD, but we must also not forget the recent changes to our health care system (e.g., the influence of managed care), which have left physicians and therapists with less time to complete an evaluation and to arrive at a proper diagnosis. In addition, the availability of an increasing number of medications for the treatment of ADHD and the influence of the pharmaceutical industry on physicians have, no doubt, fostered an increase in the treatment of this disorder.

Finally, the 1991 amendments to the Individuals with Disability Education Act (IDEA) may have also inadvertently supported an increase in the diagnosis and treatment of ADHD by establishing the category of "other health impaired" (OHI). The OHI categorization now allows children with ADHD to receive special education services, whereas heretofore only children with a recognized learning disorder were given such supports. Consequently, a child with ADHD who is suffering academically can now also receive special assistance at school. While entirely justifiable and reasonable, the addition of OHI to the IDEA may have encouraged some parents and teachers to more readily identify ADHD in children who may have been left to struggle in silence in the not-too-distant past.

CLINICAL COURSE

The symptom of ADHD most often first reported is hyperactivity. In some cases mothers report that even in utero the child was active and kicking from nearly the moment of conception. More commonly, however, parents note a gradual onset of symptoms during the primary years. Parents will often report that by 2, 3, or 4 years of age, their children appeared very active and constantly "on the go." As children age and are able to make more choices for themselves, impulsivity is more easily spotted. As children age into their teen years, hyperactivity and impulsivity diminish in most cases. By midadolescence and into adulthood, it is much less common to experience proper hyperactivity, although some degree may remain and be described now as a sense of internal restlessness. Inattention, for those who are affected by this type alone or by combined-type ADHD, commonly persists to some degree well into adulthood, but often diminishes at least somewhat over time.

The natural history of ADHD is understood in general terms to follow the "rule of thirds," such that approximately one third of children demonstrate significant symptom resolution and are not terribly bothered in adulthood, about one third of children continue to experience inattention into adulthood, and about one third of children continue to experience symptoms in all domains (hyperactivity, impulsivity, and inattention) and to suffer other related difficulties, such as oppositional defiance, severe conduct-disordered behavior, excessively poor academic achievement, substance abuse, and perhaps even some antisocial traits as adults. Although one third of children appear to generally outgrow their ADHD, the majority of children affected by ADHD appear to maintain the diagnosis into adulthood, with the strongest predictor of a poor prognosis being prepubertal aggression (Cantwell, 1996).

Studies of specific age-related changes in children with ADHD indicate that preschool children, ages 3 to 5 years, are often identified as having hyperactive and impulsive symptoms. By school age, 6 to 12 years, children are often noted to suffer from a combination of symptoms (or inattentive symptoms alone in the case of inattentive type only). By adolescence, 13 to 18 years, youths complain of inattention, often with some restlessness and impulsivity, and adults likewise often complain of inattention with periodic restlessness and impulsivity.

DIAGNOSIS

Given the high prevalence of ADHD, it is uncommon to mistake the combined symptoms of hyperactivity, inattention, and impulsivity for another disorder. However, many other possible explanations for these symptoms (a.k.a. the "differential diagnosis") exist, including mood and psychotic disorders, anxiety disorders, learning disorders, intellectual disability and borderline intellectual functioning, oppositional defiant and conduct disorders, autism spectrum disorders, substance use disorders, and various personality disorders. Symptoms of hypervigilance and impulsivity are also sometimes found among children who have been physically or sexually abused or subjected to excessively harsh parenting. Finally, there are a number of general medical illnesses that can also result in a clinical picture that appears to be something like ADHD, including seizure disorders, chronic otitis media, hyperthyroidism, sleep apnea, various drug-induced inattentional syndromes, head injury, hepatic illness, toxic exposures, and narcolepsy.

DSM-5 diagnostic criteria for ADHD include two general symptom categories: (a) inattention and (b) hyperactivity and impulsivity. *DSM-5* demands that six of nine symptoms, in either or both domains, be present to meet diagnostic criteria. In addition to general inattention, symptoms within the inattentive domain include making careless mistakes, having difficulty following instructions and listening to others, being forgetful and poorly organized, losing things necessary for school or other required activities, being easily distracted, and avoiding tasks that require sustained focus. Within the hyperactive domain, symptoms include being always on the go and having great difficulty settling down, being extremely talkative, having difficulty quietly engaging in play or relaxing activities, having difficulty remaining seated for extended periods of time, being fidgety, and running or climbing about in locations where it is not appropriate to do so (e.g., the classroom, jumping on the furniture at home). Impulsive symptoms include blurting out responses to questions before they have been fully stated, having difficulty waiting one's turn, and interrupting and intruding on others. The *DSM* also demands that a series of so-called functional criteria be met for an individual to qualify for the diagnosis: The symptoms must have persisted for at least six months; at least some symptoms must have existed before 12 years of age; there must be impairment in two or more settings (home, school, church, ball field, etc.); and there must be social, academic, or occupational impairment (American Psychiatric Association, 2013).

Many parents ask about having their child "tested" for ADHD. As yet, there is no single test to identify ADHD. Assessing *DSM-5* symptoms to determine the degree of impairment is, at this time, the most useful measure of ADHD. The clinician must be careful, however, because ADHD should never be diagnosed in a one-to-one setting. Many, and perhaps most, children affected by ADHD are able to focus and contain their behavior when attention is focused solely on them, such as during a school tutorial, during a visit with a physician or therapist, or while playing video games. During these moments, all attention is focused entirely on the child, who is getting feedback to every statement, movement, and nuance. Rather, it is during shared or group activities, or when a child must wait his or her turn, that the symptoms of ADHD are most clearly evident. Consequently, the observations of not only the clinician, but also the parents, grandparents, or other caregivers; schoolteachers; coaches; Sunday school teacher; and so forth are vital in establishing a diagnosis.

Although there is no "test" to establish the diagnosis of ADHD, neuropsychological testing is often useful in measuring symptom severity. As would be expected, most children with ADHD have significant impairments in executive functioning, including their ability to maintain attentional vigilance, utilize working memory effectively, plan, organize, and inhibit impulsive responses. Neuropsychological testing of children with ADHD typically identifies impairment in spatial working memory, planning ability and ability with mazes, stop-task response suppression, and naming speed. Perhaps the most popular neuropsychological tests for ADHD are the continuous performance tasks. These instruments require a child to stay focused on a computerized task, such as pressing the space bar each time a certain letter or number appears on the screen, while the pace of the stimuli is varied and distractions are purposely added in. The tests, which include the Test of Variables of Attention (TOVA), the Conners' Continuous Performance Test (CPT), and the Intermediate Visual and Auditory Continuous Performance Test (IVA), are sometimes useful for monitoring symptoms and the changes that occur over time and with treatment (Nigg et al., 2005). However useful they may sometimes be, it is important to recognize that neuropsychological tests have not been found to be reliable diagnostic tools for ADHD.

The diagnosis of ADHD is multifactorial and relies on a thorough clinical interview, collateral interviews with individuals who see the child in numerous settings, an early age of onset of at least some symptoms, and symptoms in more than one setting. The clinical interview should include a diagnostic assessment of the primary complaint and a review of other possible explanations for the observed symptoms. More specifically, the clinician should assess not only inattention, hyperactivity, and impulsivity, but also general behavior (including oppositional and conduct difficulties), mood, anxiety, psychosis, trauma, vocal and motor tics, and substance abuse. A full medical history, including a detailed developmental, family, educational, and social history, should also be assessed.

Because children are often not the best historians and almost universally have trouble describing their symptoms of ADHD and other mental disorders (at least until adolescence), various objective rating scales have been designed for use by parents, teachers, and other collateral informants to help identify symptoms. Some of the better-known rating scales for ADHD include the Swanson, Nolan, and Pelham Questionnaire (SNAP) for parents and teachers; the Conners scales for teachers, parents, and affected adults; the ADHD Rating Scale (ADHD-RS); the Vanderbilt ADHD rating scales for parents and teachers, and the Swanson, Kotkin, Agler, M-Flynn, and Pelham Scale (SKAMP) for teachers. These rating scales are readily available as freeware or for purchase on the Internet.

Some individual practitioners will engage in a treatment trial with medication in order to establish or confirm the diagnosis. This approach is not advised, as the risk of adverse effects is not insignificant. Furthermore, many individuals, perhaps most, without ADHD will show some degree of improvement in their attention and focus, along with a decrease in impulsivity and general activity level, when treated with a stimulant medication. When an individual is affected by ADHD, however, the degree of improvement seen with treatment is remarkable and much greater than that typically seen by individuals who are unaffected. Although reliable indicators are not available, according to parent reports children with ADHD will commonly show greater than 50% improvement in their symptoms of inattention, hyperactivity, and impulsivity, whereas individuals unaffected by ADHD may show only small increases of 10% to 15% improvement in their ability to focus and pay attention.

Other practitioners will employ a placebo trial before initiating treatment with a stimulant. While placebo responses in many areas of medicine are high, they are moderate in ADHD (approximately 30%) but not sustained, thereby only further prolonging the effort at establishing a proper diagnosis (Sandler, Glesne, & Geller, 2008). Consequently, this method is also not recommended.

Approximately two thirds of children with ADHD present with one or more coexisting or comorbid psychiatric disorders (Biederman et al., 1996; Spencer, Biederman, & Wilens, 2000). The percentage of children with ADHD comorbid with another diagnosis varies greatly by study, but there is no denying that comorbidities remain a major concern for most children with ADHD. Anxiety disorders, behavioral disturbances such as oppositional defiant disorder and conduct disorder, mood disorders, tics, and learning disorders are extremely common comorbidities among children with ADHD.

TREATMENT

Treatment for ADHD typically involves three primary considerations: (a) medication; (b) behavioral therapy; and (c) educational support. The

Multimodal Treatment Assessment (MTA) Study of 1999 as well as numerous other studies have clearly demonstrated that medication is the most effective and reliable treatment for children suffering from the core symptoms of ADHD (MTA Cooperative Group, 1999). Although more recent iterations of organizational skills training have shown promise (see below), behavioral treatments have never demonstrated the efficacy that medications have for the primary symptom domains of ADHD (i.e., inattention, hyperactivity, and impulsivity). Behavioral treatments have, however, proven to be of great utility for commonly related impairments that beset children with ADHD, such as oppositional behavior and defiance. The MTA Study also found that more frequent and higher dosing of stimulant medication, along with increased physician contact (e.g., more frequent visits), leads to better treatment response and improved outcomes for children affected by ADHD.

Stimulants remain the most effective and most commonly employed treatment for ADHD, although a number of other medications are sometimes utilized. In 2010, 87% of outpatient prescriptions given for treatment of ADHD in the United States comprised stimulants, with the remaining 13% comprising alpha-2 agonists, atomoxetine, and antidepressants (Garfield et al., 2012). Although not entirely elucidated, the mechanism of action appears to involve the reuptake inhibition of dopamine and, to a lesser extent, norepinephrine (see Figure 3.3). In addition, stimulants cause an increase in the release of presynaptic norepinephrine and dopamine. Some stimulants are also mild inhibitors of monoamine oxidase (MAO), an enzyme that breaks down norepinephrine and dopamine, thereby leaving more active neurochemical in the synapse for a longer time. Amphetamine, but not methylphenidate, also promotes passive diffusion of norepinephrine and dopamine into the synaptic cleft and promotes the release of norepinephrine from cytoplasmic pools (Wilens & Spencer, 1998).

The response rate to stimulants is remarkably high and far greater than with most psychiatric medications. Regardless of the stimulant selected, typically 70% of children and adolescents with ADHD will respond favorably to the first medication trial (Spencer et al., 1996). If the first stimulant attempt is not effective, the second stimulant trial will usually pick up an additional 10% to 15% of individuals, such that 85% of those affected by ADHD will show statistically significant symptom improvement by the time they have tried two stimulants (Elia, Borcherding, Rapoport, & Keysor, 1991). This degree of efficacy is rarely found with treatments in any medical discipline. As implied, there is no significant difference in response rates when looking at large populations of youth treated with amphetamine, methylphenidate, or any of their

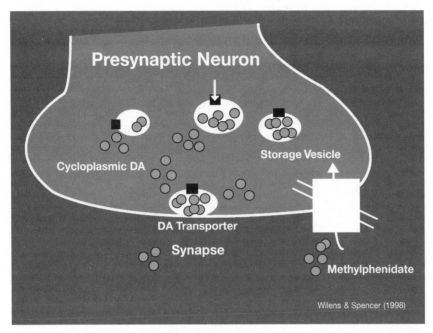

Figure 3.3   Probable mechanism of action of methylphenidate. Methylphenidate blocks the reuptake of dopamine into the presynaptic neuron, thereby increasing the amount of dopamine within the synapse that is free to interact with the postsynaptic neuron. Used with kind permission from Springer Science+Business Media: *Handbook of Substance Abuse*, 1998, pp. 501–503, Timothy Wilens.

derivatives, and numerous studies have demonstrated efficacy for these treatments in preschool children, school-age children, adolescents, and adults, although preschool children tend to show a less robust treatment effect (Arnold, 2000; Greenhill et al., 2006).

Historically, children and adults with ADHD were treated with immediate-release medications that were dosed numerous times throughout the day to maintain effect. The first long-acting stimulant medications for the treatment of ADHD were designed to result in a steady blood level of stimulant. These medications, however, such as Ritalin SR and Metadate ER, were found to be ineffective for many patients. We now realize that maintaining a steady blood level of a stimulant throughout the day does not effectively treat ADHD beyond a few hours for most individuals due to tachyphylaxis or the fact that the body's response to stimulants diminishes rapidly. Consequently, the blood level of a stimulant must be steadily increased throughout the day to maintain a continued response. Over the past decade, numerous long-acting medications have been developed that take advantage of our increasing knowledge of how these medications must be dosed (Swanson et al., 2003).

It is important to note that this method of treatment does not result in addiction or any habit-forming effect of the medication. Rather, because all individuals respond to the benefits of stimulants for only about as long as the half-life of the drug (presumably because of tachyphylaxis), another dose of the medication must be delivered at approximately every half-life to maintain clinical response. (See the Appendix for a thorough discussion of psychopharmacology, including drug half-lives.) As the half-life of methylphenidate is about two and a half to four hours and the half-life of amphetamine is about four to six hours, these medications must be dosed at those intervals if a sustained clinical response is to be achieved. The newer long-acting medications, such as Concerta, Adderall XR, Focalin XR, Metadate CD, Ritalin LA, Vyvanse, Daytrana, and Quillivant XR, take advantage of our understanding of tachyphylaxis, and by various mechanisms they increase the blood level of stimulant throughout the day, mirroring the effects of dosing an immediate-release medication numerous times throughout the day, thereby resulting in continual efficacy (see Figure 3.4).

Although doses vary considerably, the average dose of methylphenidate in the United States is typically about 30 mg per day and that of amphetamine about 20 mg per day. Body weight was historically utilized to determine the most effective dose for a given patient. Approxi-

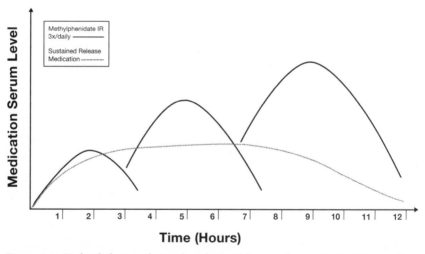

Figure 3.4 Tachyphylaxis and stimulant dosing. The use of a sustained-release medication (or one that maintains a steady blood level of stimulant throughout the day) does not result in an increase in blood levels and therefore is not effective after the first few hours of treatment. In contrast, repeated dosing of immediate-release medications does lead to increasing blood levels throughout the day and is the model for the newer and successful long-acting stimulant medications.

mately 1 mg/kg per day for methylphenidate and 0.6 mg/kg per day for amphetamine were the generally accepted values. However, we now realize that weight-based dosing is rarely accurate, as children, adolescents, and adults may require far lower or far higher doses, depending upon idiosyncratic features that have yet to be elucidated (Rapport & Denney, 1997). Consequently, we currently dose these medications to clinical response, lowering the dose or changing the medication if side effects develop.

In many cases children do not adequately benefit from stimulants because they are not properly dosed for a sufficient time. Compounding this problem is the fact that many practitioners are not comfortable prescribing stimulants and will therefore provide only a low dose, which will generally not result in notable benefit. For these reasons, practitioners are now often advised to follow a forced-dosage titration when starting a stimulant medication in a child diagnosed with ADHD. A forced-dosage titration takes place over a relatively short time and relies on increasing the dose every week or two until clinical benefit is achieved. For a child taking immediate-release methylphenidate, the practitioner may begin the dose at 5 mg three times a day for the first week, advance the dose to 10 mg three times a day for the second week, and advance the dose still further to 15 mg three times a day for the third week. A more conservative approach may involve dosing at 5 mg, then 7.5 mg, then 10 mg weekly. As long as rating scales are utilized during this period by the parents and teachers and side effects are well monitored by the family, the practitioner will typically know within three weeks if methylphenidate is helpful for this child.

Utilizing a long-acting methylphenidate product for the same child—Concerta, for example—the practitioner may prescribe 18-mg tablets in the morning for the first week, 36-mg tablets in the morning for the second week, and 54-mg tablets in the morning for the third week. If at any point significant side effects are encountered, the family is instructed to call the practitioner, stop the medication, and seek clarification on how to proceed. For a child prescribed Adderall XR, a long-acting amphetamine, a dose of 10 mg per day may be utilized for the first week, 20 mg for the second week, and 30 mg for the third week. Again, if impairing side effects are encountered, the family should contact the practitioner and clarify whether or not to continue.

The starting stimulant dosage and weekly increases are determined by the practitioner's clinical experience and perception of symptom severity. Although we do not rely on weight-based dosing any longer, sometimes practitioners will initiate treatment with some consideration of the child's weight. For example, a practitioner may start a child of 25 kg on a forced-dosage titration of Concerta of 18 mg for the first week, 27 mg for the second week, and 36 mg for the third week; while a child of 50 kg may be dosed at 18 mg for the first week, 36 mg for the second week, and 54 mg for the third week. Although this method is an imprecise science, as long as the child's caregivers understand the potential side effects of treatment, dosage increases in this fashion result in the most rapid assessment of medication efficacy.

Side effects of stimulants are common but rarely significant and insurmountable. The four most common difficulties are nausea, headaches, insomnia, and decreased appetite. Other less frequent side effects include the unmasking of motor and vocal tics, anxiety, hypertension, tachycardia, diaphoresis (sweating), tremors, and even psychosis. Insomnia and appetite suppression are generally the most distressing side effects for patients and can be so bothersome that the medication dose may need to be decreased or the medication itself changed. On some occasions, additional medication may be necessary to address these side effects. Relative contraindications to the use of stimulants include hypertension, symptomatic cardiovascular disease, glaucoma, hyperthyroidism, severe Tourette's syndrome, significant drug abuse, and psychosis. Depending on the nature and severity of these difficulties, the practitioner may decide to treat with stimulants or alternative medications (see below).

There have been increasing popular concerns about the cardiac safety of stimulants, and a number of patient advocacy groups and physicians have suggested that caution is demanded of those prescribing stimulants (Biederman, Spencer, Wilens, Prince, & Faraone, 2006). This issue has been explored in great detail by the American Academy of Child and Adolescent Psychiatry (AACAP), American Academy of Pediatrics (AAP) and the American Heart Association (AHA), among others, and it has been clearly determined that children with heart conditions have a higher incidence of ADHD than the general population (Vetter et al., 2008). It is also clear that, although rare, cardiovascular events (e.g., hypertension, arrhythmias, cerebrovascular disease) are more common in stimulant users than in those who do not use stimulants. In a nationwide study in Denmark of over 700,000 individuals followed for nearly 10 years, such occurrences were twice as likely among those using stimulants, particularly those with significant risk factors such as preexisting diabetes or cardiovascular disease, and those taking high doses of the stimulant (Dalsgaard, Kvist, Leckman, Nielsen, & Simonsen, 2014).

Current recommendations endorsed by these leading medical specialty organizations include the following: First, it is advised that all children who are diagnosed with ADHD be carefully evaluated for heart conditions prior to treatment. Second, the most important features of this assessment are a patient and family cardiovascular history along with a physical examination focused on cardiovascular risk factors. Acquiring an electrocardiogram (ECG) or echocardiogram is not mandatory or advised for all patients. However, it is recognized that obtaining an ECG or echocardiogram is reasonable if risk factors are identified, including a history of chest pain, dizziness, syncope (fainting), exercise intolerance, shortness of breath or a family history of sudden cardiac death in an individual under 40 years of age. Finally, treatment of patients with ADHD should not be withheld because an ECG is not performed unless further cardiac investigations are indicated. It is important to note that medications that treat ADHD have not been shown to cause heart conditions, nor have they been demonstrated to cause sudden cardiac death. However, stimulant medications that treat ADHD almost always result in modest increases in heart rate and blood pressure. While these side effects are not usually considered dangerous, blood pressure, heart rate, and cardiovascular symptoms should be monitored regularly in patients treated for ADHD. Most importantly, our best data indicate that there is no association between stimulant use in children and adolescents with ADHD and sudden cardiac death, myocardial infarction, stroke, or ventricular arrhythmia (Winterstein, 2013). The recommendations for cardiac monitoring prior to starting a stimulant medication in a child or adolescent, as put forth by the American Academy of Pediatrics and endorsed by the AACAP, Society for Developmental and Behavioral Pediatrics, and National Initiative for Children's Healthcare Quality, among others, appear in Figure 3.5.

The standard of care for treatment with stimulants includes the measurement of vital signs (e.g., blood pressure and heart rate) as well as a cardiac exam and a full family history. As previously discussed, the identification of cardiac concerns suggests the need for an ECG and a pediatric cardiology referral for possible echocardiogram prior to treatment. During treatment, height and weight measurements should be performed annually at a minimum and compared to published norms for age. If height for age decreases by more than one standard deviation while the patient is on treatment with stimulants, referral to a pediatric endocrinologist to evaluate possible growth hormone deficiency or hypothyroidism should be considered. Blood pressure and heart rate should be evaluated at least twice annually as well as prior and subsequent to any dosage increase. If the patient's medical history is unremarkable, laboratory and neurological testing are not indicated. Psychological and neuropsychological testing are not mandatory and should be performed only if the patient's history suggests general low cognitive ability or low

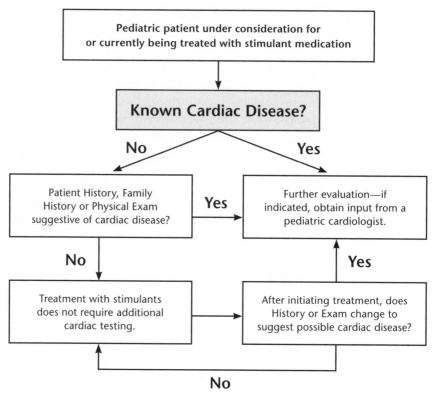

Figure 3.5 Cardiac evaluation of children and adolescents receiving or being considered for stimulant medications. Source: Perrin, Friedman, Knilans, American Academy of Pediatrics Black Box Working Group, and American Academy of Pediatrics Section on Cardiology and Cardiac Surgery (2008). Reproduced with permission from *Pediatrics, 122*(2), 451–453, Copyright © 2008 by the AAP.

achievement in language or mathematics relative to his or her intellectual functioning (AACAP Work Group on Stimulant Medications, 2002).

There are numerous pros and cons to the use of stimulants for the treatment of ADHD. As previously noted, stimulants are highly effective and have been utilized successfully for many years. However, their use results in a limited duration of action, and there are sometimes significant side effects and occasionally contraindications. Consequently, a variety of other medications have been developed for the treatment of ADHD.

Many children, perhaps over half of those who initiate treatment with a stimulant, may develop a transient motor tic (e.g., a repetitive, rhythmic motor movement, such as eye blinking or nose wrinkling; Borcherding, Keysor, Rapoport, Elia, & Amass, 1990; Tannock, Schachar, & Logan, 1995). Most tics diminish with time and are not a cause for great concern by the child or family (see Chapter 9). At this time, it is not clear that stimulants cause tics, although they may "unmask" them or make them more evident. The comorbidity or co-occurrence of tics in individuals with ADHD, whether or not they have been treated with stimulants, is quite high and generally noted at between 10% and 15%. Historically, it was believed that stimulants caused motor and vocal tics. We now realize that stimulants actually improve tics in many cases, so our understanding is not quite as simplistic as it once was (Gadow, Sverd, Sprafkin, Nolan, & Ezor, 1995).

For children who develop tics while taking stimulants, a slight decrease in the stimulant dose or a discontinuation or change of stimulant is often effective. At other times we are able to use habit reversal therapy, a behavioral therapy targeted directly at tics (see Chapter 9). If the tics are severe, we may consider other medications, such as atomoxetine (Strattera) for the treatment of ADHD, which may be less likely to cause tics, or alpha-2 agonists, such as clonidine (Catapres) or guanfacine (Tenex), or even antipsychotic medications. The mechanism of action of alpha-2 agonists is much less clear but may involve decreasing activity in the locus coeruleus noradrenergic cell bodies to improve attentional arousal and cognitive processes (Pliszka, McCracken, & Maas, 1996). Although alpha 2-agonists are frequently employed in children and adolescents, only the long-acting ones, Intuniv (extended-release guanfacine) and Kapvay (extended-release clonidine), are FDA approved for the treatment of ADHD; otherwise, the sole FDA indication for these medications is hypertension in adults.

More commonly, alpha-2 agonists have been utilized to decrease residual hyperactivity, impulsivity, and aggression, and to treat insomnia and treatment-emergent motor and vocal tics. Dosages of clonidine (Catapres) have typically been 0.1 to 0.3 mg per day and dosages of guanfacine (Tenex) have typically been 1 to 3 mg per day, although these dosages are sometimes doubled. In terms of the long-acting preparations, dosages of clonidine (Kapvay) are generally 0.1 to 0.4 mg per day, divided into morning and evening doses, and dosages of guanfacine (Intuniv) are generally 1 to 4 mg per day, given once daily. A routine physical examination and the assessment of vital signs should be performed prior to initiation of treatment. Contraindications to the use of alpha-2 agonists include coronary artery disease and impaired liver and renal function. Side effects most commonly include rebound hypertension and tachycardia, hypotension, sedation, dizziness, constipation, headache, and fatigue. When initiating treatment with an immediate release alpha-2 agonist, we generally begin with late afternoon or evening dosing and titrate toward the morning. With a child who is successfully utilizing a stimulant for the treatment of ADHD but suffering insomnia or late-afternoon rebound hyperactivity, we may begin with 0.05 mg (half a tablet) of clonidine (Catapres) or 0.5 mg (half a tablet) of guanfacine (Tenex) an hour before bedtime. This treatment may allow the child to relax, become less agitated and aggressive, and sleep better through the night. If the child continues to have afternoon difficulties after three or four days of this evening dose, we may add another dose of the same amount around 3 or 4 p.m. when he or she comes home from school. Should disruptivity, aggression, agitation, or tics persist, we may add yet a third dose toward the morning after three or four more days. If the initial dose is not sufficient, we may increase the dose to a full tablet, 0.1 mg of clonidine or 1 mg of guanfacine, in the evening, afternoon, and morning, using the same dosage titration.

Monitoring blood pressure is important, but the use of ECGs is not routinely necessary unless there is suspicion of cardiac concerns or impairment. Alpha-2 agonists have been shown to effectively reduce hyperactivity and impulsivity, both with and without methylphenidate, and in more recent studies they have even been found to improve inattention, although to a much lesser extent than stimulants (Biederman, Melmed, et al., 2008; Sallee et al., 2008; Tourette's Syndrome Study Group, 2002). For the treatment of ADHD, alpha-2 agonists are much less effective than stimulants.

Combining a stimulant with an alpha-2 agonist is a common and effective strategy for children with ADHD who also struggle with behavioral rebound in the afternoon, motor or vocal tics, comorbid aggression, or insomnia (Hazel & Stuart, 2003). A small number of physicians remain hesitant to prescribe these medications in conjunction with each other because of four reported deaths of children who were prescribed both methylphenidate and clonidine. In each of these cases, however, there were extenuating circumstances that better accounted for the death—an overdose of medication, an unrelated surgery, a history of syncope, and preexisting damage to the heart valves. At this time the Food and Drug Administration (FDA) places no limitations on the combined use of these medications and posts no advisories against their conjoint use. In addition, neither the American Academy of Pediatrics nor the American Academy of Child and Adolescent Psychiatry advises against their combined use nor recommends routine ECG monitoring, presuming there is no cardiac history (AACAP Work Group on Stimulant Medications, 2002).

Atomoxetine (Strattera) is another FDA-approved medication for the treatment of ADHD that works by a novel mechanism. Atomoxetine is a norepinephrine and dopamine reuptake inhibitor at the presynaptic neuron in the prefrontal cortex. Because atomoxetine does not have any effect on dopamine in the limbic system or striatum, the medication is typically associated with a lower risk of motor and vocal tics and has no abuse potential. Other advantages of atomoxetine include its 24-hour duration of action and the fact that it is not classified as a Schedule II medication by the Drug Enforcement Agency (DEA). As a result, atomoxetine prescriptions can be called in to pharmacies, and refills can be given on prescriptions. Unfortunately, however, it is quite clear to most practitioners that treatment of ADHD with atomoxetine does not result in as robust a response as treatment with stimulants. This clinical observation has now been confirmed in a series of studies as well (Gibson, Bettinger, Patel, & Crismon, 2006; Mano, Tom-Revzon, Bukstein, & Crismon, 2007; Newcorn et al., 2008). Side effects of atomoxetine most commonly include decreased appetite, dizziness, stomachaches, sedation, and mild changes in blood pressure and heart rate. There have been three reports of liver toxicity, each of which resolved when the medication was discontinued (Bangs et al., 2008), and some adults suffer anticholinergic side effects, such as dry mouth, constipation, urinary retention, and sexual dysfunction, such as decreased libido, erectile disturbance, and anorgasmia. Finally, atomoxetine has been serendipitously found to be effective in the treatment of enuresis, or bed-wetting (see Chapter 18).

The dosage of atomoxetine is entirely weight based. Typical starting dosages are between 0.5 and 1.0 mg/kg/day for up to 1 to 2 weeks; thereafter, the dose can generally be increased to 1.2 to 1.8 mg/kg/day, which is therapeutic for most individuals. Not infrequently, a higher dosage is administered, up to 2 or even 3 mg/kg/day, although studies have not demonstrated any increase in efficacy beyond 1.8 mg/kg/day. For children and adolescents who suffer excessive side effects due to stimulants but who require the efficacy of a stimulant, a common strategy is to combine a therapeutic dose of atomoxetine along with a lower dose of stimulant. Together, these medications sometimes result in therapeutic benefit with a decrease in side effects as compared to a higher dose of the stimulant alone.

There are a number of other treatments that have historically been utilized for the treatment of ADHD and are sometimes still employed for children and adolescents who have severe symptoms that are not adequately treated with stimulants, alpha-2 agonists, or atomoxetine. These medications are also used for the small number of children who cannot tolerate the side effects of stimulants and alpha-2 agonists.

The tricyclic antidepressants, particularly desipramine (Norpramin, Pertofrane), have been successfully employed for the treatment of ADHD. However, their use must be weighed carefully against the cardiac risk of treating a child with a tricyclic antidepressant due to the possible cardiac arrhythmia that can ensue with their use. Because of their cardiotoxicity, these medications should be prescribed only by an experienced practitioner and must be employed along with routine cardiac monitoring, including ECGs (see Chapter 12).

Bupropion (Wellbutrin) has been demonstrated to be effective in some studies, but the findings have been inconsistent (Conners et al., 1996; Daviss et al., 2001; Jafarinia et al., 2012). This medication is not approved for the treatment of ADHD by the FDA, indicating that the data supporting this treatment are not as yet adequately impressive. Furthermore, practicing clinicians rarely find bupropion to be of great use for the treatment of ADHD. Bupropion may be more of a consideration for a child suffering from comorbid depression and for whom the practitioner cannot ascribe the inattention and lack of focus entirely to ADHD but rather attributes it to some combination of ADHD and major depression. However, bupropion has little data to support its use as an antidepressant for children and adolescents as well (see Chapter 12). Another antidepressant, venlafaxine (Effexor) has shown some contradictory data, suggesting that it may have minimal utility for the treatment of adult ADHD, but it is rarely employed by physicians (Amiri, Farhang, Ghoreishizadeh, Malek, & Mohammadzadeh, 2012; Findling, Greenhill, et al., 2007).

A novel medication for the treatment of narcolepsy and excessive daytime sedation associated with sleep apnea and shift work sleep disorder, modafinil (Provigil), has also shown variable efficacy in the treatment of ADHD. Three randomized, double-blind, placebo-controlled trials at dosages of generally more than 300 mg per day have, however, yielded positive results (Biederman & Pliszka, 2008). Another study compared the performance of 28 children with ADHD on the TOVA after they were each given a one-time dose of either modafinil or methylphenidate, demonstrating no difference in improvement between the two drugs (Goez, Scott, Nevo, Bennett-Back, & Zelnik, 2012). Side effects to modafinil are relatively infrequent and include insomnia, headaches, and decreased appetite; there is also an extremely remote risk of severe dermatologic disorders, such as Stevens-Johnson syndrome.

Three relatively new stimulant formulations have recently arrived on the market. Lisdexamfetamine (Vyvanse) is an amphetamine pro-drug stimulant, which has a 12-hour duration of treatment. Because this medication is a "pro-drug," it is not metabolized to an active stimulant until it is digested. In patients with a history of drug abuse, the treatment has been shown to be less pleasurable and therefore may have utility among those at risk of drug abuse who require treatment for ADHD. Additionally, the methylphenidate patch (Daytrana), which is worn for nine hours a day, demonstrates 12-hour efficacy for the treatment of ADHD. Finally, an extended-release liquid form of methylphenidate (Quillivant XR) is a useful alternative for children who cannot swallow pills. Each of these various formulations appears to work as well as standard preparations of methylphenidate and amphetamine for the treatment of children and adolescents with ADHD.

As previously noted, behavioral treatments for the core symptoms of ADHD have not generally proven themselves to be effective. Various psychotherapies, including cognitive behavior therapy, parent management training, and social skills training, have not demonstrated consistent efficacy. These treatments are often effective, however, for a variety of common comorbidities, including oppositional defiant disorder and conduct disorder.

Organizational skills training represents a new approach to the behavioral treatment of ADHD. Organizational skills training involves the application of a manualized treatment, which is flexibly applied to individual needs and incorporates meetings with the child and the parents, consultation with teachers, and a focus on practical routines that children can repeatedly employ. Behavioral modification techniques, including rewards and reinforcement, are used to motivate change. Particular areas of focus typically include tracking assignments, organization of the settings in which children study and work, materials management (e.g., collection, storage, and transfer of their schoolwork), time management and scheduling, setting priorities, and planning for both short- and long-term projects. Studies of organizational skills training have identified major improvements in children's ability to organize, manage their time, and plan for tasks, all common problems among children with ADHD (Abikoff et al., 2013). While these treatments appear to be often useful, however, studies have not yet demonstrated their efficacy in the treatment of the core symptoms of ADHD (Langberg, Epstein, & Graham, 2008).

A variety of educational aids, including individual educational plans (IEPs) and various accommodations (e.g., 504 plans), are also often helpful for children with ADHD. These learning supports will be discussed in greater detail in Chapter 5.

4

Disruptive Behavior Disorders

While identifying disruptive behavior in children is simple, parents and teachers often have a much more difficult time deciding whether the observed behavior is "normal," typical, or socially acceptable. All children become angry and misbehave at times, but it is how they express their anger and manage their feelings that is important. In the words of Aristotle, "anyone can become angry, that is easy . . . but to become angry with . . . the right person . . . at the right time, and for the right purpose, and in the right way . . . this . . . is not easy."

CLINICAL PRESENTATION

What constitutes normal childhood behavior? This question is routinely asked by all parents and teachers. As is evident from even the most elementary of observations, the range of normalcy or what we might consider "typical" is quite large, particularly when it comes to disruptive behavior. "Normal" or "typical" children are often oppositional and defiant. There is not a single child who has reached his or her second birthday, who is gaining command of the language, who has not uttered the word *no* dozens upon dozens of times. "Normal" children have tantrums. "Normal" children are periodically mean-spirited in word, deed, and action. "Normal" children occasionally lie and cheat and are sometimes purposefully annoying. Most important, however, "normal" children generally grow out of these behaviors, and most children grow up to be responsible adults, even those who have suffered terrible misfortune growing up or who have been plagued by major psychiatric illnesses.

Consequently, any child who will meet diagnostic criteria for a disruptive behavior disorder, such as oppositional defiant disorder or conduct disorder, will suffer a degree of impairment that is quite profound and far beyond that which "normal" children experience. These affected children will not only occasionally lie or cheat and demonstrate disruptive, agitated, oppositional, and defiant behavior, but they will demonstrate these behaviors on a regular basis often without regard for the rights and concerns of others. These children will suffer impairments in all aspects of their lives, with family at home, with friends, and with teachers and other adults. Even without direct treatment, most children who are disruptive at a young age will become "civilized" with time, will show major improvements, and will not meet criteria for a disruptive behavior disorder as they age. For a significant minority of children, however, their behaviors will worsen, and they will become increasingly isolated from peers, family, and society.

ETIOLOGY

There are numerous biological, psychological, and social factors that are likely to contribute to the development of oppositional defiant disorder and conduct disorder in children and adolescents (Burke, Loeber, & Birmaher, 2002).

Biological

From the moment of conception, children are vulnerable to factors that may influence the later development of disruptive behavior, and potential links have been demonstrated between parental substance abuse, pregnancy and birth problems, and maternal smoking. What is not clear at this time, however, is whether these associations are due to an actual biological exposure in utero or simply due to being raised in a chaotic and disruptive environment.

A variety of neurophysiological and neuroanatomical findings have been identified in children, adolescents, and adults with a history of disruptive behavior disorders. Decreased frontal lobe glucose metabolism, for example, has been repeatedly shown to be connected with violent behavior. In addition, frontal lobe brain damage is associated with aggression and orbitofrontal damage with impulsive aggression. Furthermore, it has been suggested that amygdala malfunction is associated with problems interpreting social cues, such as facial expression, and that suppressing negative emotion may hinge in part on a connection between the amygdala and the prefrontal cortex, such that if either is damaged, the individual may become considerably more impulsive and aggressive.

Neurotransmitters have also been associated with the development of disruptive behavior in children and adolescents. Low levels of 5-hydroxyindoleacetic acid (5-HIAA), a serotonin metabolite, in the cerebrospinal fluid have been correlated with current and future aggression, yet higher serotonin blood levels have been found in boys with childhood-onset as opposed to adolescent-onset conduct disorder and are correlated with violence in adolescence. The meaning of these findings is not clear, but may suggest that a lower turnover of serotonin, or perhaps being a slower utilizer of serotonin, in the central nervous system is associated with disruptive behavior and aggression. Finally, low salivary cortisol levels are correlated with oppositional defiant disorder, while testosterone, interestingly, has only variably been associated with aggression.

The autonomic nervous system, which generally functions without our awareness but can be influenced by our purposeful behavior, exerts influence on such functions as heart rate, blood pressure, respiratory rate, and galvanic skin response. Severely disruptive children and adolescents have been repeatedly found to demonstrate altered autonomic nervous system function. For example, boys with oppositional defiant disorder generally maintain a lower heart rate at baseline but a higher heart rate when exposed to experimentally induced frustration. In addition, a lower galvanic skin response has been found in disruptive boys and a higher skin conductance has been noted among boys who do not engage in violent behavior.

A variety of neurotoxins may also possibly induce oppositional or agitated behavior in children, such as lead, which is a preventable risk factor. High levels of lead in children have been associated with increased aggression and higher delinquency scores on standardized rating scales. There remain a variety of other potential neurotoxins, such as organophosphate pesticides; food additives, including antibiotics and hormones; and other chemicals that are newly present in our food supply and environment. We have little understanding of their impact on a growing fetus and young child. Although there are no data to suggest that these factors are as yet impacting children's behavior, we must remain vigilant to this possibility (Burke et al., 2002).

Finally, although no specific gene or set of genes has been identified, a genetic predisposition or transmissible trait does seem a highly likely contributory factor to the development of many cases of externalizing disorders. Not only do children of antisocial parents have an increased risk of developing such traits themselves, but even children adopted out of homes with a violent or criminal parent have three to four times the average population rate of antisocial behavior (Keenan & Shaw, 2003).

Psychological

Research into child development has generally supported the notion that children are born with certain temperaments. In the original studies of temperament, nine characteristics were identified, including activity level, regularity, initial reaction, adaptability, intensity, mood, distractibility, persistence and attention span, and sensitivity. Taken together, the unique combination of these nine characteristics results in a child who is described as "easy," "difficult," or "slow to warm up" (Thomas, Chess, & Birch, 1968). Some mothers will say that they knew their child was aggressive from day one because the child kicked excessively in the womb or came out crying. Others will report that their child was always calm and easy to be with. Regardless of how it is labeled, an infant with a difficult temperament—that is, one who expresses a great deal of negative emotion, has a willful and impulsive way of responding, and is relatively inflexible—is more likely to be disruptive later in childhood (Sanson & Prior, 1999).

Another area of developmental psychology research, attachment theory, has also been investigated as a possible etiology of disruptive behavior. Attachment theory suggests that infants must establish secure relationships with adult caregivers in order to promote normal social and emotional development (Siegel, 1999). Although some of the research has been equivocal, insecure attachment has often been noted among children with early-onset conduct problems. Furthermore, some research has shown a connection between conduct-disordered children with callous-unemotional traits (i.e., those who are less responsive to others' affect and lack empathy) and an increased risk of disruption in parent–child attachment (M. T. Greenberg, Speltz, Deklyen, & Endriga, 1991; Pasalich, Dadds, Hawes, & Brennan, 2012).

Evidence of neuropsychological impairment has been found among some young children with severely disruptive behavior, but testing, while attractive in theory, has not yet been able to clearly parse out psychosocial factors from neuropsychological deficits as the etiological agent. While specific neuropsychological tests have consistently demonstrated that low intelligence is a possible predictor of disruptive behavior, most studies looking at IQ and its contribution to the development of oppositional defiant and conduct disorder have not controlled well for children with attention-deficit/hyperactivity disorder (ADHD), which itself greatly increases the likelihood of disruptive behaviors. Finally, although disruptive behavior in boys is a risk factor for the subsequent development of reading problems, in girls the opposite appears true; that is, early struggles with reading are predictive of later behavioral problems.

Behavioral inhibition, which can be viewed as the tendency to show fear and avoidance in unfamiliar social and nonsocial situations, is a research construct that can be demonstrated in children using a variety of rating scales and techniques. Behavioral inhibition subsumes shyness (e.g., social inhibition), indicating great hesitancy to engage in all or most situations that are novel to the child (Smoller et al., 2005). Children who are behaviorally inhibited tend to demonstrate a decreased risk of later delinquency. This effect may be related to anxiety, which has been shown to temper physical aggression even in boys who are already disruptive. In contrast, research findings also point to the fact that socially withdrawn boys, or those who do not relate well to peers but not because of behavioral inhibition or shyness, have a greater risk of delinquency.

Another important psychological research construct is that of social cognition, or the degree to which individuals are able to understand the behaviors and intentions of others around them. We sometimes informally refer to this factor as one's social or emotional IQ. Boys with disruptive behavior disorders tend to focus more on concrete and outward qualities of individuals and are self-centered in their description of peers; that is, they do not demonstrate an understanding of the other person's point of view. Boys with disruptive behavior disorders and boys with ADHD also commonly have problems understanding social cues and what others mean by their body language, eye contact, and general expressions. In addition, boys with disruptive behavior disorders tend to respond aggressively to problems. In research studies, these boys are more likely to misinterpret an awkward glance from a peer as an aggressive message. Furthermore, both boys and girls who suffer from conduct disorder demonstrate less empathy, an important finding considering that empathy is known to mediate and decrease aggressive behavior. Finally, early physical maturation is associated with increased behavior problems in girls but not in boys. The reasons for this finding are unclear, but they are consistent (Burke et al., 2002).

Social

There are a number of psychosocial factors that also may contribute to the development of oppositional defiant disorder and conduct disorder, perhaps the most impressive of which is parenting. Poor management of a child's behavior is related to an increase in disruptive behavior, while positive parenting may, in fact, be protective. Parental psychopathology or major mental illness in the parents, however, is probably even more predictive of the development of disruptive behavior disorders in children than bad parenting is. Aspects of bad parenting associated with disruptive behavior include poor monitoring of children's activities and behaviors, harsh and inconsistent or punitive discipline, differential treatment of siblings, and coercion. While severe and abusive physical punishment is strongly related, mild physical punishment is less so but still correlated with the development of disruptive behavior in children.

Assortative mating is another psychosocial risk factor for the development of disruptive behavior disorders. Female delinquents are more likely to have intimate relationships with male delinquents than vice versa. Consequently, females with a history of disruptive and agitated behavior are more likely to have a child who is the product of two offenders than are males with a history of disruptive behavior. The increased risk to the offspring, although not easily quantifiable, is likely to be significant for both genetic and environmental reasons.

Both physical and sexual abuse have been demonstrated to significantly increase the risk of conduct disorder. Furthermore, some data suggest that abused children have trouble with social processing and demonstrate hostile attribution biases, encoding errors, and positive evaluations of aggression (Dodge, Pettit, Bates, & Valente, 1995). These findings indicate that abused children may not understand social interaction in the same way as other children do and may misinterpret social cues as aggressive when they are not, in fact, intended to be so. As would be expected, sexually abused boys are less likely than sexually abused girls to suffer internalizing problems but are equally or more likely than girls to reveal conduct or externalizing problems.

Peers also directly and indirectly contribute to the development of oppositional defiant disorder and conduct disorder. For example, adolescents spend approximately one third of their time talking with peers versus less than 10% of their time talking with adults (Spear, 2000). As such, the peer group becomes highly important and influential in the life of an adolescent. While normal peers generally reject those with conduct disorder, simultaneously they often inadvertently reinforce the behavior by compliance and passivity. Association with like-minded deviant peers tends to concretize the behavior and social role of youth with conduct disorder. Chronically maltreated children are more aggressive and more commonly rejected by peers as early as grammar school. Aggressive girls appear to be more commonly rejected by peers, as aggressive boys are sometimes feared and looked up to by the general student population.

Finally, disruptive behavior in children is associated with growing up in poor and disadvantaged neighborhoods. A variety of factors appear to be important and predictive of later violence, including the increased availability of drugs, community disorganization, neighborhood adults involved in crime, poverty, and exposure to violence and racial prejudice (Burke et al., 2002).

EPIDEMIOLOGY

The epidemiology of disruptive behavior disorders varies a great deal depending on the study, where it was completed, and how many children were involved (Loeber, Burke, Lahey, Winters, & Zera, 2000). Rates of oppositional defiant disorder vary somewhere between 1% and 11%, but we generally accept that on average just over 3% of children suffer oppositional defiant disorder prior to their teenage years. The rate tends to decrease with age, and there is a great deal of diagnostic stability for both males and females, particularly when the expression is more severe. As previously noted, oppositional defiant disorder is more common among children from lower socioeconomic strata.

The rates of conduct disorder vary from around 2% to 10% in one-year population prevalence studies, with a median of 4% (American Psychiatric Association, 2013). Among children and adolescents diagnosed with conduct disorder, there is, of course, significant crossover with those first diagnosed with oppositional defiant disorder. In contrast to oppositional defiant disorder, the frequency of conduct disorder increases with age, and there is a great deal of diagnostic stability, depending on the study, ranging between 44% and 88% at three to four years following initial diagnosis (Lahey et al., 1995; Offord et al., 1992).

CLINICAL COURSE

Gender differences do not typically emerge until after 6 years of age in children with oppositional defiant disorder. From about 7 years of age until puberty, the disorder is more prevalent in males than females by a ratio of about 1.4:1 (American Psychiatric Association, 2013). After puberty, the male-to-female ratio equalizes. In general, symptoms of oppositional defiant disorder are evident by 8 years of age. Typically, symptoms emerge gradually over months or years, first at home with parents and other adults with whom the child is familiar. Over time, symptoms generalize to include other adults, such as teachers and coaches, and other settings in the child's life, such as school and camp.

Oppositional defiant disorder itself can be relatively benign, and even without formal treatment most children traverse the disorder naturally, growing out of it as they age. About 30% to 40% of individuals, however, will go on to develop conduct disorder, and about the same percentage of individuals with conduct disorder, 30% to 40%, will go on to develop antisocial personality disorder. Earlier age at onset typically predicts a worse prognosis and greater likelihood of progression to conduct disorder and antisocial personality disorder (Steiner, Remsing, & AACAP Work Group on Quality Issues, 2007).

The clinical course of conduct disorder is considerably more severe. Oppositional defiant disorder is a common but not necessary precursor, and less severe behaviors tend to emerge first, such as lying, shoplifting, and fighting. Onset of conduct disorder is rare after 16 years of age. In some cases the behaviors are adaptive or even protective. For example, in threatening, impoverished, or high-crime neighborhoods, children may join gangs to find some protection, solace, and a supportive peer group. A diagnosis in this environment may not be appropriate. In the majority of children, the disorder remits by adulthood, but as previously noted, a substantial proportion (30% to 40%) will go on to develop antisocial personality disorder.

While a theoretical model of delinquency has not been satisfactorily designed, some of the key factors in the development of delinquency include an early childhood characterized by poor parental monitoring and inconsistent or harsh parenting, along with a general lack of discipline. Children who are vulnerable may then go on to develop conduct problems. In middle childhood, conduct-disordered children are often rejected by normal peers and suffer academic difficulties, perhaps because of a comorbid learning disorder or perhaps because the children themselves have simply not been taught how to discipline themselves and properly learn. With repeated academic and social failures, the child may then become committed to a deviant peer group and by late childhood or early adolescence be engaging regularly in delinquent behaviors (see Figure 4.1).

DIAGNOSIS

The differential diagnosis for disruptive behavior disorders typically includes ADHD, mood disorders, adjustment disorders, and anxiety dis-

Early Childhood   **Middle Childhood**   **Late Childhood
                                                           and Adolescence**

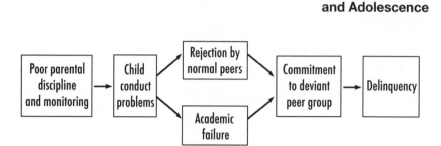

Figure 4.1   A developmental progression for antisocial behavior. This theoretical model of delinquency suggests that inadequate parental management in early childhood inadvertently supports the development of child behavior problems. By middle childhood, poorly behaved children are rejected by their peers and suffer academic failure, which leads these children to commit to deviant peer groups and furthers the likelihood of delinquency. Source: Patterson, DeBarshe, & Ramsey (1989).

orders. According to *DSM-5*, the criteria for oppositional defiant disorder require that four of eight symptoms be present for at least six months and that the symptoms be present "often" (American Psychiatric Association, 2013). This pattern of negativistic, hostile, and defiant behavior includes frequently losing one's temper, arguing with adults, actively defying or refusing to comply with rules, deliberately annoying others, blaming others for one's own mistakes or behavior, being touchy or easily annoyed by others, being angry and resentful, and being spiteful or vindictive. While almost all children will at times experience some of these symptoms, the *DSM* relies on the key word *often* to indicate that occasional difficulty is not adequate for a diagnosis.

Many children who meet diagnostic criteria for oppositional defiant disorder suffer low self-esteem; others, as if by a defense mechanism, demonstrate inflated self-esteem. Mood lability, low frustration tolerance, cursing, and the early use of alcohol and drugs are other commonly associated symptoms in children diagnosed with oppositional defiant disorder. The most common Axis I comorbidities include ADHD, learning disorders, and communication or speech disorders. Approximately 50% of children with ADHD also suffer oppositional defiant disorder or conduct disorder, while 70% of children with oppositional defiant disorder or conduct disorder suffer ADHD.

The diagnosis of conduct disorder is predicated upon three or more symptoms that have been present within the past 12 months from among four general categories; at least one symptom must have been present within the past six months to qualify an individual for the diagnosis.

Conduct disorder represents a more severe form of behavioral disruption because its diagnosis demands that the individual have a repeated pattern of behavior that ignores or violates the basic rights of others or major age-appropriate societal norms. The four primary categories are aggression to people and animals, property destruction, deceitfulness or theft, and serious rule violations.

Based on the child's age at onset of the disorder, two subtypes of conduct disorder have been recognized. They differ in their presenting symptoms, developmental course, prognosis, and gender. The childhood-onset or "unsocialized" type typically requires at least one criterion to be met before age 10. These individuals are usually male, are frequently aggressive, often demonstrate disturbed peer relations, often first suffered oppositional defiant disorder, may have concurrent ADHD, and are most likely to have persistent conduct disorder and later develop antisocial personality disorder. The second subtype is adolescent in onset, or the so-called "socialized" type. These youth demonstrate an absence of conduct disorder symptoms prior to age 10 and are more likely to have normal peer relationships, less likely to display aggressive behaviors, and less likely to suffer persistent conduct disorder and later develop antisocial personality disorder. While youths with this subtype are still more commonly male than female, the preponderance of males is far greater in the childhood-onset type.

Children diagnosed with conduct disorder face an increase in accident rates and generally lower self-esteem (although, as with oppositional defiant disorder, the self-esteem of these children is occasionally defensively inflated). In addition, conduct disorder is often associated with early sexual contact, the development of sexually transmitted diseases and pregnancy, and an increase in alcohol abuse, drug use, and risk-taking behavior. These children sometimes attend alternative schools and live in foster placement, and they attempt and complete suicide at a higher rate than other youth. The most common comorbidities include ADHD, learning disorders, communication or speech and language disorders, anxiety disorders, mood disorders, and substance use disorders. The best predictor of a later diagnosis of conduct disorder in a young child is cruelty to others and weapon use. Below age 13, cruelty, running away, and breaking and entering are also highly predictive of later conduct disorder.

Depression and conduct disorder are linked. For a sizable number of children, it appears that depression leads to conduct disorder. Depending on the study, children with depression are between three and nine times more likely to be diagnosed with a disruptive behavior disorder (Angold & Costello, 1993). Current research suggests that the correlation between conduct disorder and depression may rest most heavily on their shared causal or risk factors (Wolff & Ollendick, 2006).

Rating scales for the identification and classification of disruptive behavior disorders are not well established. The Swanson, Nolan, and Pelham Questionnaire (SNAP) and the Conners scale, both of which are used for diagnosing ADHD, include a number of disruptive behavior measures, as do most ADHD rating scales. Other instruments, such as the Disruptive Behavior Disorders Rating Scale, can be helpful in identifying the symptoms but also typically include many symptom questions for ADHD, given the high comorbidity between ADHD and the disruptive behavior disorders. Many of these scales are available as freeware and can be found on the Internet.

TREATMENT

Before addressing the treatment of oppositional defiant disorder and conduct disorder, it is worth considering protective factors. Unfortunately, our research in this area is not strong and does not provide clear guidance (Stouthamer-Loeber, Loeber, Wei, Farrington, & Wikström, 2002). All agree that controlling risk factors is probably the most effective step toward prevention. There is some evidence, however, that programs for preschool children, such as Head Start, may decrease later delinquency and oppositional defiant disorder and conduct disorder (Connor, 2002). Other early intervention programs have some supporting data as well. These programs either address the children directly, teaching improved interpersonal problem-solving skills and helping them to regulate their emotions (Conduct Problems Prevention Research Group, 1992); focus on the parents and teachers, helping them to strengthen the children's social support, improve parenting practices, and provide key proficiencies for children, such as anger management and social skills; or employ functional behavioral assessments to look beyond the disruptive behaviors themselves to determine "why" children misbehave and then design tailored interventions targeted at the root cause (Webster-Stratton & Reid, 2003; Dufrene, Doggett, Henington, & Watson, 2007). In general terms, relationships (e.g., good relations with at least one parent, good peer relations) and mentoring (e.g., consistent and attentive parental monitoring) appear to be at least somewhat protective against the development of oppositional defiant disorder. Community mentoring programs, such as Big Brothers Big Sisters, have also been shown to exert a protective effect by reducing drug and alcohol use, physical altercations, and school truancy while improving grades (Grossman & Tierney, 1998).

In addition to identifying prevention strategies, it is important to remember that comorbidities are more the rule than the exception with highly disruptive children. Therefore, addressing coexisting conditions is absolutely necessary for seeing sustained improvement. The most common concurrent diagnoses, including ADHD, anxiety and mood disorders, learning disorders, and communication disorders, must be identified and treated. The clinician should look closely for these problems even when they are not initially reported by the patient and family and have not previously been a focus of treatment.

Behavioral Parenting

By and large, treatment strategies aimed directly at affected children, such as psychotherapy, have not clearly demonstrated their utility regardless of the type (supportive, psychodynamic, play, cognitive behavior, etc.). To be fair, the effects and benefits of individual psychotherapy are difficult to measure, and many therapists continue to engage in psychodynamic approaches, whereby the child or adolescent builds an attachment to a therapist as the basis of behavior change. This therapeutic approach is nonspecific and almost always includes the parents in some fashion or other, as parents typically have their own conflicts and anxieties, which lead to poor parenting practices. There are, however, a number of short-term, evidence-based therapies designed specifically for parents and disruptive children.

Parent management training (PMT) is a very well established treatment that has demonstrated major and sustained reductions in the disruptive behavior of children aged 2 to 12 years (Kazdin, 1997, 2005). For younger children (2 to 6 years) whose symptoms are exceptionally severe, *parent–child interaction training* (PCIT) has also shown great utility (Herschell, Calzada, Eyberg, & McNeil, 2002). Both PMT and PCIT rely on basically the same behavioral modification principles, are highly therapist directed, and have a strong evidence base supporting their use. Both treatments are time limited, requiring generally somewhere between 4 and 20 weeks to teach to parents. Parent training approaches are so effective that even teaching this material to parents by means of a video in the absence of a therapist has been shown to result in significant and sustained efficacy (S. J. Bradley et al., 2003; Montgomery, Bjornstad, & Dennis, 2006).

Although most PMT techniques are timeworn and straightforward and incorporate much of what effective parents have been doing for years, for many parents such an approach is not intuitive. Virtually all children, whether diagnosed with a disruptive behavior disorder or not, demonstrate immense improvements in behavior after their parents have received PMT. The training is designed to help parents increase the behaviors they like and decrease the behaviors they dislike. Typically, the major topic areas covered include (a) effective commands, (b) tactful praise, (c) ignoring, (d) scheduling, (e) behavioral reward programs, (f) limit setting, (g) punishments, and (h) time-out. The emphasis in PMT is always on positive reinforcement, for which an unlimited number of strategies can be devised. Punishments are relatively few in number and are employed sparingly, as they quickly lose their power to change children's behavior if overutilized.

Two similar treatments, collaborative problem-solving (CPS) and problem-solving skills training (PSST), address children's cognitive distortions and teach them new ways of managing social situations. CPS has been shown to be effective in reducing seclusion and restraints in child psychiatric inpatient services (Greene et al., 2006; Martin et al., 2008). While early research into CPS suggests it to be at least as effective as PMT (Greene et al., 2004), it is still a relatively new treatment and has not been largely replicated in outpatient settings; and while PSST has been shown to be effective in altering children's cognitive perceptions, it is understood that altering cognition is not always a reliable means of improving behavior (Kazdin, 2003).

Psychosocial Interventions

Studies of foster care, often employed for youths with severely disruptive behavior, generally show only mild improvements in the behavior of children and adolescents who are placed within a foster home (Reddy & Pfeiffer, 1997). Some programs designed to reduce bullying at school, however, have strong empirical support, particularly when they address campus awareness, teach children and parents about the effects of bullying, employ a program of assertive monitoring of school behaviors, and intervene with specific individuals (Spivak & Prothrow-Stith, 2001).

Perhaps the most effective treatment for both children and adolescents who are severely disruptive, antisocial, and delinquent is multisystemic therapy (MST). MST is an intensive family and community-based behavioral intervention designed to address and treat the problems in every setting, including home and school, mitigating multiple risk factors simultaneously. MST adopts an integrated approach that commonly utilizes aspects of PMT, PSST, and marital and family therapy, along with other interventions targeted at substance abuse, bullying, classroom social skills, and improving communication between teachers and parents as well as special education services, legal services, and often pharmacological interventions. MST has been shown to be effective in reducing antisocial behavior for as long as five years following treatment and appears to be cost-effective in the long run by decreasing recidivism and persistent overutilization of psychiatric and social services (Henggeler & Lee, 2003).

Medication Treatment

There are a number of psychopharmacological interventions that have been utilized for many years, and new strategies are being applied regularly. However, it should be noted that the FDA has not yet "approved" any medication for the treatment of oppositional defiant disorder or conduct disorder. While sometimes useful, medications for the treatment of disruptive behavior should be considered adjunctive or palliative but not curative. Behavioral, family, school, and community-based interventions, as specified above, should be the main focus of treatment (Pappadopulos et al., 2003; Schur et al., 2003).

Antipsychotics are increasingly utilized for the treatment of disruptive behavior in children and adolescents (Olfson, Blanco, Liu, Moreno, & Laje, 2006). In fact, only a minority of children and adolescents who receive antipsychotic medications (around 30%) are given them for a diagnosis for which those drugs are approved by the FDA, such as schizophrenia, bipolar disorder, or autism (Crystal, Olfson, Huang, Pincus, & Gerhard, 2009). In the United States, the estimated number of office-based visits by children and adolescents that included antipsychotic treatment increased from approximately 201,000 in 1993 to 1,224,000 in 2002. From 2000 to 2002, the number of visits that included antipsychotic treatment was significantly higher for males than for females and for white non-Hispanic youth than for youth of other racial or ethnic groups. Overall, roughly 9% of mental health visits and 18% of visits to psychiatrists included antipsychotic treatment. Antipsychotics were most commonly used for diagnoses of disruptive behavior disorders (38%), mood disorders (32%), pervasive developmental disorders or mental retardation (17%), and psychotic disorders (14%). Medicaid-insured youth are about four times more likely to receive a prescription for an antipsychotic medication than those who are privately insured, and Medicaid now spends more on antipsychotic medication than on any other class of drugs (Crystal et al., 2009; Lagnato, 2013).

Although haloperidol (Haldol), molindone (Moban), chlorpromazine (Thorazine), and thioridazine (Mellaril) have been employed for many years, data supporting their use are scant, and the side effects are often significant, though rarely permanent (Campbell, Cohen, & Small, 1982; Campbell et al., 1985; Greenhill, Solomon, Pleak, & Ambrosini, 1985; Platt, Campbell, Green, Perry, & Cohen, 1981; see Chapter 15 for a thorough discussion of the side effects of antipsychotic medications).

In recent years, risperidone (Risperdal) has demonstrated efficacy in a number of randomized, double-blind, placebo-controlled trials in children with oppositional defiant and conduct disorder, some of whom also had a diagnosis of ADHD along with frequently aggressive behavior and most of whom had subaverage IQ. Dosages ranged between 1 and 3 mg per day, although most studies employed lower dosages of around 1 to 1.5 mg per day. By and large, these studies supported the efficacy of risperidone in the treatment of disruptive behavior disorders for short-term treatment (e.g., 10 weeks or less; Pringsheim & Gorman, 2012). Large-scale reviews of pilot, open-label, and larger clinical trials of over 800 children and adolescents with oppositional defiant disorder, conduct disorder, or disruptive behavior disorder not otherwise specified who were treated with risperidone at doses of 0.02 to 0.06 mg/kg per day found target symptom improvement compared with placebo and baseline functioning within one to four weeks of treatment (Pandina, Aman, & Findling, 2006). Although our best data among the antipsychotic medications for the treatment of disruptive behavior in children and adolescents lie with risperidone, a Cochrane Review found only limited evidence of its utility for aggression and conduct problems, and even then only among children with subaverage IQ (Loy, Merry, Hetrick, & Stasiak, 2012).

Much less data are available to support the use of quetiapine (Seroquel), olanzapine (Zyprexa), and aripiprazole (Abilify) in the treatment of disruptive behavior disorders. Although many clinicians find these medications effective at times, the scientific data supporting their use are minimal and largely based on open-label trials, chart reviews, pilot studies, and case reports (Findling, Reed, et al., 2006, 2007; Handen & Hardan, 2006; Masi et al., 2006). One small double-blind, placebo-controlled study of 23 children and adolescents found that aripiprazole led to reductions in aggression; two small double-blind, placebo-controlled trials of quetiapine found it to be superior to placebo on clinician-evaluated but not parent-rated measures of aggression; and one small double-blind, placebo-controlled study of 11 children with autism spectrum disorders found improvements in aggression (Lohr & Honaker, 2013).

The mood stabilizers, including lithium (Lithobid, Eskalith), divalproex sodium (Depakote), and carbamazepine (Tegretol), have also been employed for the treatment of disruptive behavior in children.

Two randomized controlled trials compared lithium with placebo and found that at therapeutic doses, lithium was efficacious and safe for the short-term treatment of aggressive inpatient children and adolescents with conduct disorder. Other studies as well have found lithium to be efficacious in the treatment of behavior disorders in children. One small randomized, double-blind, controlled study (Donovan et al., 2000); one randomized but open-label trial (Steiner, Petersen, Saxena, Ford, & Matthews, 2003); one small open-label trial (Saxena, Howe, Simeonova, Steiner, & Chang, 2006); and one randomized dosage study of incarcerated youth (Padhy et al., 2011) have demonstrated divalproex sodium to be effective for the treatment of aggression and explosive temper associated with oppositional defiant disorder and conduct disorder. It is likely, however, that divalproex sodium and carbamazepine are more likely to be effective for disruptive behavior among children and adolescents who are at risk for the development of a major mood disorder such as bipolar disorder.

Small randomized controlled trials have also demonstrated that clonidine (Catapres, Kapvay) may be useful for aggressive behavior in children with ADHD and comorbid oppositional defiant disorder and conduct disorder (Connor, Barkley, & Davis, 2000; Hazell & Stuart, 2003). In a meta-analysis of 11 double-blind randomized controlled studies from 1980 to 1999, clonidine demonstrated a moderate effect size (0.58) on symptoms of ADHD comorbid with conduct disorder, developmental delay, and motor tics (Connor, Fletcher, & Swanson, 1999). A number of other medications, such as beta blockers, benzodiazepines, buspirone (Buspar), and naltrexone (Revia, Vivitrol), have been demonstrated to be useful as adjunct agents in case series and case reports, but there is little impressive data to suggest their regular use for this population of children (Riddle et al., 1999).

Based on currently available data and clinical experience, a reasonable treatment approach for a child or adolescent with severely disruptive behavior first requires a clear psychiatric diagnosis. In addition, all coexisting psychiatric disorders should be identified and aggressively treated. Addressing concurrent problems, such as ADHD, depression, anxiety, and learning disorders, often considerably alleviates many of the disruptive behaviors. If direct treatment of the disruptive behaviors is necessary, all appropriate behavioral modification efforts, particularly those aimed at the parents, are clearly the first line of attack. If medications are to be employed, starting modestly—for example, with an alpha-2 agonist—would be a reasonable but not mandatory first step. If the behavior does not respond, the practitioner should revisit the diagnosis and make certain that other disorders are not unaddressed. If further medication efforts are necessary, then antipsychotics and mood stabilizers can be considered, but the practitioner and family must carefully weigh the considerable side effects of these medications. When absolutely necessary, the use of antipsychotics and mood stabilizers should be viewed as a short-term treatment effort to be employed while behavioral efforts are ongoing. Medications for disruptive behavior disorders are, at their best, treatments and not cures.

5

Learning Disorders

Learning disorders affect about 5% of American youth but are more commonly diagnosed among those with comorbid psychiatric disorders. New etiological research documents the neurobiological underpinnings of learning disorders with increasing clarity. These findings have direct relevance to novel treatment interventions. In addition, changes in government policy over the last 35 years have provided educational support and accommodations to children who struggle with learning disorders, helping to maximize their academic success.

CLINICAL PRESENTATION

Given the variety of ways in which learning disorders can present, they often go unrecognized (N. J. Cohen, Davine, Horodesky, Lipsett, & Isaacson, 1993). Fear of humiliation due to learning troubles may present as school refusal, somatic symptoms, or even oppositional defiant disorder. About half of children with a learning disorder also have a comorbid psychiatric disorder such as attention-deficit/hyperactivity disorder (ADHD), a speech or language disorder, or an anxiety or mood disorder. Even children who do not meet diagnostic criteria for another psychiatric disorder frequently suffer demoralization, depression, low self-esteem, and deficits in social skills (Kauffman, 1997; Kavale & Forness, 1995). Children with learning disorders typically have a long history of poor academic achievement and may have more difficulty than their peers in understanding others' moods, particularly in ambiguous situations (Bryan, 1991). The school dropout rate for children with learning disorders is more than twice that of students without such disabilities (Blackorby & Wagner, 1996). Thankfully, dropout rates have been coming down considerably in recent years as identification of affected children and access to services have grown. In 2000, 40% of students with a learning disability dropped out of school, but by 2009 that percentage had declined to 22% (Cortiella, 2011). However, that percentage is still considerably higher than the 7% drop-out rate among the general population (U.S. Department of Education, National Center for Education, 2011).

ETIOLOGY

Beginning in utero, the human brain grows actively by cell division. Cell migration occurs as developing neurons travel to preprogrammed areas where they will ultimately reside. In most cases, cell migration proceeds in expected ways. Alterations in cell migration, however, have been seen in the brains of adult dyslexics. Autopsies have shown that the planum temporale and Wernicke's area, parts of the brain believed to be important for understanding and interpreting speech and written language, are less organized and less well ordered. In fact, the neurons in these areas appear to be scattered, less dense in formation, and somewhat haphazardly assigned. The cause of this disorganization is not known, but presumably both prenatal and postnatal cell migration could account for these changes (Galaburda, Sherman, Rosen, Aboitiz, & Geschwind, 1985).

Other studies have suggested that there is a reversal or reduction in the normal leftward asymmetry of the planum temporale in dyslexia, but this finding has been disputed (Heiervang et al., 2000). Problems with phonological processing, or awareness of the sound and structure of words, along with a disruption in the white matter connections between posterior and frontal brain regions have been repeatedly found among those with dyslexia (Temple, 2002). Differences in brain activation have also been shown to occur in those suffering from dyslexia. Positron emission tomography (PET) scans have demonstrated altered activation in brain areas important for reading, which is associated with changes in the density of white and gray matter for those with dyslexia versus non-impaired readers (Silani et al., 2005).

Effective readers rely on posterior regions of the brain (e.g., the temporal and parietal lobes and the angular gyrus), which are involved in automatic word recognition and reading. Those without dyslexia can read most common words without even paying much attention to their meanings, allowing the brain to multitask. Studies of regional brain blood flow among dyslexic adults, however, demonstrate that dyslexics overuse the frontal areas of the brain and are unable to tap into the automatic fluent recognition of words in the posterior regions. Dyslexics appear to sound out the words they read each and every time they see them, as if they have never seen them before. This sounding-out approach is precisely what happens for all readers when they are confronted with new written words or similar stimuli. In this case, the frontal lobes of the brain are recruited to break down the word into phonemes or specific sounds and pieces in order to consciously read the word. For most readers who do not have dyslexia, common words do not call upon the frontal lobes to any great degree. The conscious and considerable effort that individuals with dyslexia must employ to read each and every word causes an increase in blood flow (as noted on functional magnetic resonance [fMRI] imaging) to the oral/motor speech areas and the frontal lobes, the site of executive function, organization, and planning (Shaywitz et al., 1998).

Because of the poor connectivity between the frontal lobes and posterior regions of the brain among those with dyslexia, the frontal lobes themselves may also be developmentally impaired in areas important for reading. Studies in remediation have demonstrated that with additional support and training, children can improve their reading abilities and functionality. Early but not widely replicated studies also suggest that with remediation there is a subsequent alteration in blood flow, as measured by fMRI, such that blood flow increases to the temporoparietal region, which is key for reading fluency, and away from the frontal lobes, which are overused in people with dyslexia (Temple et al., 2003).

Learning disorders tend to group in families, suggesting genetic and environmental factors, particularly in reading, math, and spelling. The relative risk of a learning disorder in reading is 4 to 8 times higher, and in mathematics 5 to 10 times higher, among first-degree relatives of individuals with one of these learning impairments (American Psychiatric Association, 2013). A family history of dyslexia and parent dyslexia predict literacy problems and learning disorders among offspring.

EPIDEMIOLOGY

The prevalence of learning disorders ranges greatly in studies from 2% to 15%. This range has largely to do with the fact that there are few population-based epidemiologic studies that have applied strict diagnostic criteria. Among the studies that have been completed, inconsistencies in the ages of children evaluated and the populations selected for study (e.g., clinically referred as opposed to a more general population of children) have contributed to the varying range in prevalence.

We generally accept that approximately 5% of children in the United States suffer from a learning disorder. Boys are more commonly affected than girls by a ratio of 2:1 to 3:1, although as with ADHD and other externalizing disorders (e.g., oppositional defiant disorder and conduct disorder), boys are more likely to be identified because they are more often disruptive and therefore more easily noticed by teachers (Beitchman & Young, 1997). Approximately 50% of children who receive special services at public schools throughout the country are learning disordered.

Reading disorder, or dyslexia, is essentially the sine qua non of learning disorders. That is, reading disorder is the most common learning disorder, and it is relatively rare to find an individual who suffers a mathematics or writing disorder in the absence of reading disorder. Sixty percent to 80% of those who suffer from reading disorder are male, and the prevalence is estimated at 4% of school-age children in the United States. Reading disorder aggregates in families, such that 35% to 40% of those with reading disorder have a first-degree relative who is also affected (Beitchman, Cantwell, Forness, Kavale, & Kauffman, 1998).

Mathematics disorder makes up the vast bulk of the remaining children who suffer a learning disorder. The prevalence is roughly 1% of school-age children in the United States. Mathematics disorder frequently co-occurs with reading disorder. *Disorder of written expression*, or *writing disorder*, is much more difficult to categorize and diagnose because standardized tests have not to date demonstrated themselves to be particularly useful. It is uncommon to find a child with a disorder of written expression who is not also suffering from dyslexia.

CLINICAL COURSE

As previously noted, the course of learning disorders is commonly severe. Although estimates vary from 25% to 97%, a large percentage of juvenile delinquents and incarcerated adults suffer from learning disorders (Grigorenko, 2006). Although learning disorders do not result in incarceration directly, they do account for a great deal of lost school and work time and, as previously described, are commonly associated with other psychiatric disorders, in addition to low self-esteem, poor social functioning, and an increase in school dropout.

DIAGNOSIS

There are a variety of ways in which learning disorders are identified. Traditionally, a learning disorder is diagnosed when an individual's achievement on individually administered standardized tests in reading, math, or written expression is substantially below that expected for age, schooling, and level of measured intelligence. The phrase "substantially below" is usually defined as a discrepancy of more than two standard deviations between one's performance on an achievement test—for example, in reading or math—and one's score on an IQ test. This discrepancy of two standard deviations demonstrates a clear difference between one's given ability (IQ) and one's demonstrated functioning (achievement). In many cases, learning disorders are defined not strictly by IQ and achievement test scores, but rather by correlation with one's expected level of functioning, given the age of the child or grade level in school. Because we now understand the typical patterns in performance among children with learning disorders, however, problems can often be identified by neuropsychological testing even if the discrepancy between grade, age, or IQ and academic functioning or achievement is not readily evident. A child who struggles with reading, for example, regardless of whether he or she meets standardized testing criteria, will typically show characteristic problems with phonological coding and rapid word retrieval, a pattern indicative of a reading disorder.

Reading disorder, or dyslexia, is an unexpected difficulty with reading in children who otherwise have the intelligence to learn to read. It is characterized by distortions, substitutions, or omissions in reading. Both oral and silent reading are typically slow, with frequent comprehension errors. Reading disorder is thought to arise from a left hemisphere deficit, or defect, in the planum temporale, which, as previously noted, is found to be lacking in expected asymmetry. More disorganized and smaller cell bodies have also been noted in the visual magnocellular system. These changes typically persist into adolescence and adulthood if not effectively remediated. Even though we can now visualize some discreet brain changes among those with reading disorder, such means are not useful for diagnosis, which still rests upon clinical observation. The best predictors of adult reading levels are believed to be an individual's general intelligence and initial severity of the reading disorder.

Mathematics disorder usually becomes apparent by the second or third grade, as mathematics principles become increasingly important at school. Many skills may be effected, including linguistic skills, which are important for understanding mathematical terms, operations, concepts, and decoding; perceptual skills, which are important for recognizing and reading numerical symbols, mathematical signs, and grouping objects; attentional skills, which are necessary for writing numbers and figures correctly, remembering to "carry" numbers, and minding operational signs; and mathematical skills, which involve following steps, counting objects, and learning multiplication tables (American Psychiatric Association, 2000). Mathematics disorder is associated with a pattern of deficits in neurocognitive and adaptive functions generally attributed to the right hemisphere, which include spatial recognition and visuoperceptual/simultaneous information processing. When concurrent problems in social and emotional functioning accompany problems with general mathematical abilities, this characteristic cluster of symptomatology is referred to as a *nonverbal learning disorder* (NVLD).

NVLD generally persists into adulthood and may worsen over time. Those with NVLD face an increased risk for internalizing disorders, such as anxiety and depression, along with social and emotional difficulties. The abnormal language characteristics, such as poor prosody and pragmatic use of language, coupled with a good vocabulary and the pronounced social difficulties that these children evidence, have led to questions about a connection between Asperger's disorder, schizoid personality disorder, and mathematics disorder. (For more information on NVLD, see Chapter 8.)

The third category of learning disorders comprises disorders of written expression. Their prevalence, as previously reported, is unknown, and they are difficult to diagnose because standardized tests are not particularly useful. Generally, disorders of written expression involve a combination of difficulties with composing written text, such as grammar and punctuation errors, poor paragraph organization, multiple spelling errors, and poor handwriting.

There is a great overlap between many psychiatric disorders and learning disorders. Those diagnoses most commonly comorbid or co-occurring with learning disorders include conduct disorder, oppositional defiant disorder, ADHD, anxiety, and depression.

Educational Testing

To understand the utility of the IQ score, one must understand the distribution of IQ within the general population. Intelligence tests, along with virtually all commonly utilized educational and achievement tests, are scored on a standard scale, such that a score of 100 points is the defined

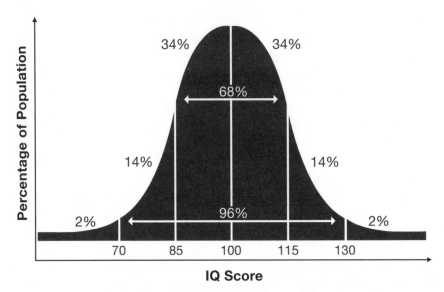

Figure 5.1 IQ score distribution. The IQ score distribution follows a typical bell-shaped curve where the vast majority of individuals in the population lie within the normal range between 85 and 115. Approximately 16% of the population falls to the left of the normal range, indicating below-average IQ, and 16% falls to the right, indicating above-average IQ.

"normal" or average. The typical standard deviation is 15 points. Plotted on a curve, then, the grid looks something like a bell, where the precise center is at 100 and 50% of the population is captured between a score of 90 and 109 (see Figure 5.1).

IQ tests correlate with and predict school achievement, and as such they are a good measure of academic intelligence. IQ tests are relatively stable, and their stability increases with age, but they are not unchanging. Heredity and environment influence IQ scores, and no test is free from cultural influences. Some questions on IQ tests rely on knowledge of facts and recognition of material that individuals must have been exposed to in order to perform well.

Scores on IQ tests are descriptive but not explanatory. The IQ score tells us where an individual does well and where she struggles but not why she struggles. The IQ test also fails to measure many factors that are important to individual success and happiness, such as creativity, perseverance, discipline, and one's social ability. In summary, IQ tests are very useful for measuring academic intelligence and predicting school achievement, but they otherwise have little utility.

There are numerous tests of intelligence available today, all of which do essentially the same thing and typically score children on the same scale. The most commonly utilized scales are the Wechsler scales and include the Wechsler Preschool and Primary Scale of Intelligence (WPPSI, now in its third edition) for children 2:6 to 7:3 years of age; the Wechsler Intelligence Scale for Children (WISC) for children 6 to 16:11 years of age; and the Wechsler Adult Intelligence Scale (WAIS, now in its fourth edition) for individuals 16 to 89 years of age. Other commonly utilized scales include the Stanford-Binet Intelligence Scale, which is typically employed for individuals whose intelligence is thought to reside at the upper and lower ends of the IQ scale; the Kaufman Assessment Battery for Children; and the Woodcock-Johnson Tests of Cognitive Abilities.

The WISC recently entered its fourth edition. Previously, the WISC-III gave summary scores for verbal IQ, performance IQ, and full-scale IQ. The WISC-IV provides a more comprehensive understanding of one's academic potential by providing summary scores or indices in verbal comprehension, perceptual reasoning, working memory, and processing speed. The WISC-IV also adds a number of new domains to IQ testing, such as word reasoning, matrix reasoning, letter and number sequencing, and symbol search and cancellation. In contrast to the WISC-III, the WISC-IV has been normed on typical or normal student populations as well as students receiving special education services, such as those affected by ADHD, learning disorders, intellectual disability, and so forth.

In addition to the standard IQ tests, there are a number of special-purpose educational tests that address particular populations. The Gesell Developmental Scales and the Denver Developmental Screening Test are designed for infants and toddlers; the Vineland Adaptive Behavior Scale and American Association on Mental Retardation (AAMR) Adaptive Behavior Scale are both designed to determine the degree to which individuals with intellectual disability are able to function independently within society (an up-to-date version of this scale, The American Association of Intellectual and Development Disabilities [AAIDD] Diagnostic Adaptive Behavior Scale, is scheduled to be released in 2015); and the Hiskey-Nebraska Test of Learning Aptitude is designed for the hearing impaired, while the Leiter International Performance Scale is designed for those with limited reading abilities.

A variety of tests are commonly employed to evaluate academic achievement or abilities within a specific domain, such as reading, writing, and arithmetic. Some achievement tests are administered to large groups of students in public school systems in an effort to monitor not only individual progress, but also how well the schools are teaching the students. The instruments most commonly utilized are the Stanford Achievement Test (Stanford 9), the California Achievement Test (CAT), and the Iowa Tests of Basic Skills. There are also a number of individually administered achievement tests, which are most commonly used along with an IQ test to determine a potential learning disorder. The most common individually administered achievement tests are the Wide Range Achievement Test, fourth edition (WRAT4); the Wechsler Individual Achievement Test (WIAT); and the Woodcock-Johnson Psycho-Educational Battery, Revised (WJ-R).

Neuropsychological testing is performed in an effort to understand the behavioral expression of brain dysfunction and is utilized to aid in diagnosis and treatment planning. There are a number of standard neuropsychological test batteries utilized in children, such as the Halstead-Reitan, the Luria-Nebraska, and the NEPSY. These tests constitute a broad range of components that measure all manner of functioning, including general motor function, visual–motor integration, perceptual ability, language, memory, and various executive functions.

A number of specialized-component neuropsychological tests exist as well. Those that specifically measure motor function include the Purdue Pegboard Test and the Dynamometer Grip Strength Test. The Reitan-Klove Sensory-Perceptual Examination, an element of the Halstead Reitan, is commonly utilized to measure sensory perception on various sides of the body. The Bender Gestalt and the Developmental Test of Visual Motor Integration are both designed to measure visual–motor integration. Common tests of expressive and receptive language as well as phonology include the Peabody Picture Vocabulary Test and the Boston Naming Test, and tests of short-term, long-term, verbal, and visual memory and memory storage include the Wide Range Assessment of Memory and Learning (WRAML) and the Buschke Selective Reminding Test. Finally, the tests of executive functioning, or those that directly measure frontal lobe activity involved in organization, attention, and planning, include the Stroop Color and Word Test, the Wisconsin Card Sorting Test, the Trail Making Test, the Continuous Performance Test, and the Tower of London.

Projective testing is yet another category of neuropsychological testing occasionally employed with children in whom we are concerned about the presence of a thought disorder or perceptual disturbance, such as psychosis. Projective tests present the examinee with vague or ambiguous stimuli, such as drawings, written or visual scenarios, or sentences with various words left out that the patient must complete. In theory, these tests demand that the patient "project" his or her unconscious thoughts, feelings, perceptions, and emotions onto the scenario presented, revealing something about the patient that he or she is unable or unwilling to speak about. For example, a child is presented with a vague drawing of a scene and asked to describe what is happening. Children will give various responses to this type of stimulation, and it is often difficult to score these tests. However, a great deal of useful clinical information can be gleaned from this exercise, such as a child's perception of herself and others, a sense of her internal emotional state, and a sense of her values. Various commonly utilized projective tests include the Rorschach Test, Human Figure Drawing Test, Kinetic Family Drawing Test, Thematic Apperception Test (TAT), and Sentence Completion Test.

TREATMENT

No medications have been demonstrated to be useful specifically for learning disorders. Many children with learning disorders, as previously described, suffer from comorbid psychiatric disorders, particularly ADHD. For those with ADHD, the use of stimulants is often helpful in improving attention and memory, with subsequent benefits in academic achievement. However, stimulants are not advised or recommended for the general population who simply would like to stay awake to study throughout the night or to get "an edge" in studying for exams or writing papers. Stimulant medications should be given only to those with an established diagnosis of ADHD. These medications can have significant side effects and are readily abusable.

A number of studies of alternative medications and treatments have been published. One small study of the use of ginkgo biloba demonstrated benefit for a small group of children with learning disorders; however, no control group, randomization, or subject/examiner blinding was employed, and the sample size and duration of the study were limited (Donfrancesco & Ferrante, 2007). Other studies have evaluated the effects of omega-3 fish oils (two of them were randomized, double-blind, placebo-controlled studies) but have shown no benefit for learning disabilities (Kairaluoma, Narhi, Ahonen, Westerholm, & Aro, 2009; Richardson & Puri, 2002). One small neurofeedback study that employed a double-blind, placebo-controlled approach found benefit on IQ and WISC scores among five children (Fernández et al., 2003). One randomized, controlled trial employing chiropractic and herbal remedies found benefit only for academic and reading self-esteem and not for performance, while another prospective study reported improvement on numerous psychometric tests (Bull, 2007; Cuthbert & Barras, 2009). Finally, a prospective nonrandomized study of music therapy with a very small sample size noted improvement in word decoding, word knowledge, and reading comprehension (Register, Darrow, Standley, & Swedberg, 2007).

Other treatment avenues for learning disorders have included the use of tutors and various learning specialists. There are a number of specific methods to help children suffering from dyslexia to gain strategies in reading, such as the decoding of words. Specific proprietary methodologies include those sponsored by Lindamood-Bell, Orton Gillingham, and Preventing Academic Failure. Fast ForWord is a computer-based program designed to help children blend speech sounds in an effort to speed the normal process of phonological manipulation. Although each method undoubtedly has its merits, head-to-head studies have not been completed, and therefore we do not know if one is more beneficial than another.

A variety of accommodations and modifications are provided by federal law and are often of great benefit for children with learning disorders. The Rehabilitation Act of 1973 (Public Law 93-112) protects those with disabilities from discrimination (physical, mental, and emotional) in federally funded programs, which include public schools. This law established the 504 Plan, which demands that students receive "reasonable accommodation" for their disabilities. An "accommodation" allows a student to complete the same assignments or tests as other students but with changes in timing, formatting, setting, scheduling, response, and/or presentation (as indicated for each child). A "modification" is an adjustment to an assignment or test that changes the standard or the way in which the test or assignment measures a student's learning.

Typical 504 accommodations and modifications include providing students with alternative books that are easier to read but that teach similar concepts; providing audiotapes of textbooks and/or chapter summaries; giving shorter assignments focused on mastering only the key concepts; substituting alternatives for written assignments, such as clay models, posters, or collections; and providing a computer or a word processor, such as an AlphaSmart, for written work. In addition, alternative seating; using both oral and printed directions; providing visual aids; providing time for transitions between activities; allowing additional time for tasks, such as homework, without a penalty; using worksheets that require minimal handwriting; reading test questions aloud; grading spelling separately from content; and allowing the use of a calculator for math are also commonly utilized accommodations and modifications.

A law of even greater importance for children with learning disabilities was passed in 1975. Public Law 94-142, the Education for All Handicapped Children Act (later renamed the Individuals with Disabilities Education Act, or IDEA), which established the IEP, or individual educational plan, guarantees a free and appropriate education to each child with a disability in every state and locality across the country and requires schools to provide a customized educational environment for children with learning disabilities. In 1991, the Individuals with Disabilities Education Act Amendments and Reauthorization added the category

DATE

(*Principal's name*)
(*Child's school*)
(*School address*)
(*City, State, Zip Code*)

Re: (*Child's name, date of birth*)

Dear (*Principal's name*):

I am writing to request an assessment for special education for (*child's name*), a student in the (*child's grade*) grade at (*child's school*) School. (*Child's name*) lives at (*child's address*), which is within the (*school district name*) School District. I am (*child's name*)'s (*your relationship to child*).

I believe my child has a (*name of learning disability if known*) disability impacting (*his/her*) ability to learn in school. (*Describe child's educational performance, including grades, behavior, and disciplinary history, if any. Include reports of primary-care physicians, psychiatrists, psychologists, social workers, teachers, or therapists, if any. Explain why you believe these behaviors result from a learning disability.*) Because of (*his/her*) learning disability, I believe (*child's name*) would benefit from special education services. (*Explain which services the child needs if known.*)

Additionally, I am requesting that the (*school district name*) School District evaluate (*child's name*) for any program modifications or services for which (*he/she*) is eligible under Section 504 of the Rehabilitation Act and the Americans with Disabilities Act.

Thank you for consideration of my request. I look forward to hearing from you within the next 15 days.

Sincerely,

(*Your signature/your full name*)

cc: School District Superintendent

Figure 5.2   Sample IEP request letter.

of "other health impaired," which extended the purview of the law to include children with physical and emotional illnesses, such as ADHD and anxiety disorders, whose academic work suffers as a result of their primary illness.

The process of receiving learning support is standardized through-

Table 5.1 Timing of the IEP Process

1. 15 working days from request to school response.
2. 10 workweeks to complete testing and evaluation.
3. 10 working days to meet with the parents and IEP team upon completion of testing.
4. 10 working days for the parents to respond to the IEP meeting.
5. If the parents are unsatisfied, they can try to reach agreement with the school.
6. Parents can then request mediation.
7. Parents can then request due process.
8. Parents can write a letter of complaint to the State Department of Education.

out the country. To obtain an evaluation for a possible IEP, a parent simply needs to write a letter to the school district requesting an evaluation of his or her child's learning. A typical IEP request letter is modeled in Figure 5.2. Generally, a parent requests an IEP, although this request may also be initiated by a concerned teacher, school principal, or psychologist with the approval of the parent. Once the referral is made, the child is evaluated. The testing utilized will vary depending on the difficulties the child appears to face and may include some combination of IQ and achievement testing, additional language or academic testing, and neuropsychological and projective testing. After the testing is completed and analyzed, a meeting is held with concerned personnel from the school along with the parents. If an IEP is deemed necessary, a formal document is written, services are provided, and follow-up meetings to assess progress are held each year. Children receiving IEP services are typically reevaluated every three years. The timing of the IEP process is described in Table 5.1.

The process of receiving support through 504 services is generally less formal. Many teachers, in fact, will automatically provide learning accommodations and modifications, particularly for younger children, before even consulting the parents. It is important, however, for parents to understand these changes in their child's learning environment and to have them formally written down. Otherwise, these supports may not accompany their child through different grades and schools.

The content of a typical IEP will include the child's current performance and functioning, annual goals for the child, any special education and related services, participation with nondisabled children, participation in state and district testing, dates and places of services, transitional services, and how progress will be measured. Members of the student's IEP team will include the student (as appropriate), the regular education teachers, any special education teachers or providers, a school system representative, the parents, and an individual who can evaluate and interpret the test results, such as a school psychologist. Representatives from various service agencies from which the student may require support (e.g., foster care) and those who have special knowledge of the child or special expertise in an area of the child's difficulties (e.g., a physician or therapist) may also be invited to the meeting.

Children with IEPs may require a variety of related services, depending on the severity of their impairments. Those listed under the IDEA and commonly indicated include audiology services, counseling services, early identification and assessment of disabilities, medical services, occupational therapy, orientation and mobility services, parent counseling and training, physical therapy, psychological services, recreation, rehabilitation counseling services, school health services, social work services in school, speech and language pathology services, and transportation. Special factors to consider include the child's behavior, proficiency in English, blindness or visual impairment, deafness or hearing impairment, and any special communication needs.

6

Communication Disorders

Over 50% of children diagnosed with a speech and language disorder are believed to suffer social, emotional, and/or behavioral problems (Prizant & Meyer, 1993). Communication deficits are perhaps most common among those with autism spectrum disorders, but approximately one third of children referred to psychiatric clinics for the treatment of conduct disorder and other behavioral problems have associated speech and language difficulties. In addition, more than two thirds of children with attention-deficit/hyperactivity disorder (ADHD) have language problems (Giddan, 1991), and children with communication disorders are more likely to experience maltreatment and abuse (Knutson & Sullivan, 1993).

CLINICAL PRESENTATION

The presentation of speech and language disorders varies greatly depending upon the precise difficulty. The communication disorder diagnostic categories identified by *DSM-5* include language disorder, speech sound disorder, childhood-onset fluency disorder (stuttering), and social (pragmatic) communication disorder (American Psychiatric Association, 2013). While there is much overlap and similarity between these conditions, each disorder has its unique characteristics.

Language disorder is characterized by difficulties in understanding and/or expressing both spoken and written language. The *DSM-5* diagnosis of language disorder combines two prior *DSM* diagnoses, *expressive language disorder* and *mixed receptive-expressive language disorder*. The new diagnosis requires that affected individuals demonstrate a reduced vocabulary, limited sentence structure, and impairments in discourse. In practice, these symptoms are generally of two sorts: Children have difficulty expressing speech and language, evincing a paucity of speech, a restricted vocabulary, problems learning new words, difficulty with word finding, vocabulary mistakes, problems with phraseology, little variety in sentence structure, and odd ordering of words; and/or they have difficulty understanding speech and language, demonstrating confusion with certain types of terminology or complicated sentences, struggling with basic vocabulary, and experiencing deficits in auditory processing, such that they are unable to differentiate sounds, build associations between sounds and symbols (e.g., letters), or are unable to remember and classify language. Many children with language disorder also have trouble maintaining a conversation and following commands and may appear as if they are inattentive or confused when spoken to. Children with language disorder are typically slow to develop language in general and have a limited grasp of grammar, often not comprehending specific types of words and their contexts.

Speech sound disorder (previously known as *phonological disorder*) is the most prevalent type of speech and language disorder, accounting for up to 80% of clinical speech referrals (Edwards, 1984). It is defined as impairment in the ability to use the speech sounds appropriate for one's age, resulting in difficulties with speech intelligibility or preventing verbal communication. The disorder may be due to difficulties with either phonology (i.e., knowledge of the various speech sounds in language) or articulation (i.e., the ability to coordinate the physical movements necessary for speech). The term *verbal dyspraxia* is sometimes used to describe these difficulties. Affected children's speech is characterized by misarticulations, such that, for example, the /s/ sound is pronounced with a lisp. Alternatively, certain sounds may be omitted from words such that, for example, "place" is pronounced as "pace," lacking the /l/ sound. Other children may incorrectly substitute one sound for another, such that, for example, "car" is pronounced "dar." Speech sound disorder cannot be attributed solely to deficits or abnormalities in intelligence or hearing. For some affected children, the substitutions and misarticulations may be idiosyncratic or atypical, such that certain sounds are oversimplified, avoided, reversed, or misordered. In other cases the errors follow a prescriptive pattern. Most children's speech is intelligible by others at age 4, and most speech sounds and words should be clearly pronounced by age 7. Some commonly misarticulated sounds (i.e., the "late eight," which are /l/, /r/, /s/, /z/, /th/, /ch/, /dzh/, and /zh/) may not be mastered until age 8 (American Psychiatric Association, 2013).

Childhood-onset fluency disorder or stuttering is characterized by impairment in speech fluency or frequent repetitions or prolongations of various sounds, syllables, or words. Other interruptions in speech, such as sound blocking, hesitations, word substitutions, or tense pauses, may also be present. Typically, the words will begin with fragmentation of syllables or words will be followed by repetition of single sounds or syllables, prolongations, or forceful articulation. Stuttering is generally more severe when there is pressure to communicate, high stress, or anxiety, such as when interviewing for a job or giving a report at school, and is often absent during reading aloud, singing, or speaking with inanimate objects or pets. Stuttering is not to be confused with normal speech repetitions, which occasionally occur when children repeat whole words or phrases (e.g., "I need I need to go to the bathroom") or speak in incomplete sentences or only with interjections or parenthetical remarks.

Although often unaware of the problem at onset, children who stutter eventually may try to decrease the problem by changing the rate of their speech, avoiding certain situations (e.g., speaking in public), or not using troublesome words or sounds. Stuttering is sometimes accompanied by motor tics, eye blinking, tremors, or other body movements. Untreated children may eventually complain of social troubles because of the anxiety, shame, and frustration they feel secondary to the embarrassment of stuttering.

DSM-5 also includes one entirely novel diagnosis, social (pragmatic) communication disorder. This diagnosis aims to identify individuals who have difficulties with the practical use of verbal and nonverbal communication for social purposes but who are not autistic. The communication problems described by the diagnosis (e.g., difficulties with greeting others and sharing information; modulating one's speech to match the context of the environment, such as speaking differently to children than adults; and following implicit rules of conversation and storytelling, such as taking turns and employing and understanding nonverbal signals) are most commonly seen among individuals affected by autism spectrum disorders. However, in the case of autism, restricted and repetitive patterns of behavior, interests, or activities must also be identified (American Psychiatric Association, 2013).

ETIOLOGY

Language disorders can be acquired or developmental in nature. In the acquired type, problems develop after a period of normal development, typically as a result of a neurological or medical complication, such as encephalitis, traumatic brain injury, brain irradiation, or damage from tumors or seizures. Focal lesions generally affect language in children if they are unilateral to the left side of the brain. Children younger than 10 years of age often recover completely from aphasias. Prenatal exposure to drugs and alcohol, or parental behavior disorders such as abuse and neglect, may also lead to language disorders in children. Developmental language disorders are not associated with a known postnatal neurological insult or physical insult and persist from the earliest of ages.

The developmental type of language disorder is more likely to occur in families where a first-degree relative is affected or where there are other family members with a communication or learning disorder. The acquired type does not aggregate in families. Some types of speech sound disorder are more common in families, as is the case with stuttering.

As previously noted, anxiety and stress have been shown to aggravate stuttering but do not play a role in the disorder's etiology. Those who stutter show laryngeal behavior that is different from that of typical speakers, even during fluent speech (Conture, Schwartz, & Brewer, 1984). Based on family and twin studies, there is significant evidence of a possible genetic linkage, as the risk of stuttering among first-degree relatives is more than three times the general population risk. Among men who have a history of stuttering, approximately 10% of their daughters and 20% of their sons will stutter. Theoretical causes include biological vulnerability, environmental demands and expectations, and temperamental characteristics of the speaker.

Medications—such as tricyclic antidepressants, monoamine oxidase inhibitors, and phenothiazines—have also been reported to cause stuttering (Brady, 1991). PET (positron emission tomography) studies indicate left-hemisphere dysfunction with compensatory right-hemisphere responses in some cases of stuttering, such that motor regions involved in speech production are more active in stutterers.

EPIDEMIOLOGY

The prevalence of communication disorders varies by type (American Psychiatric Association, 2000, 2013). Language delays are noted in about 10% to 15% of children under 3 years of age. Language disorders are generally more common in males than females and are believed to affect about 7% of children. Expressive language difficulties occur in about 3% to 7% of school-age children, with the developmental type being more common than the acquired type. A combination of receptive and expressive difficulties is thought to occur in up to 5% of preschool children and 3% of school-age children.

Speech sound disorder affects the largest number of children, although in most cases its impact is mild. Only about 2% of children 6 to 7 years of age experience moderate to severe difficulties. The prevalence of phonological disorder among preschool children ranges from 3% to 25% (Law, Boyle, Harris, Harkness, & Nye, 2000). Prevalence drops to about 0.5% by 17 years of age.

Stuttering is about three times more common in males than females and affects approximately 1% of prepubertal children. By adolescence, the prevalence drops below 1%.

The prevalence of social (pragmatic) communication disorder is unknown, in part, at least, as a result of its being a new diagnosis and there being inconsistency in its definition.

CLINICAL COURSE

The clinical course of speech and language disorders varies by diagnosis. Most speech problems are evident by 3 or 4 years of age. If a child's speech is significantly delayed beyond that point, one must seriously consider other diagnoses that could result in a delay in speech, such as an autistic spectrum disorder or intellectual disability.

Language disorder is also typically noted by age 3 or 4, although milder forms may not be evident until adolescence, when language demands become more complex. Those affected by the developmental type typically attain relatively normal language capabilities by late adolescence, although slight difficulties may endure, sometimes even into adulthood. Those affected by the acquired type vary greatly in speech and language impairment and improvement depending on the nature and site of the insult. Although full recovery is common, the prognosis is generally worse for those who have receptive language difficulties. Children affected by more severe forms of language disorders are more likely to suffer comorbid learning disorders.

Most cases of speech sound disorder are identified by the time a child enters preschool or kindergarten, when his or her speech is found to be unintelligible to teachers and other children. However, children as young as age 3 are sometimes diagnosed if the speech is incomprehensible even to family members. The clinical course is variable and dependent on the etiology and degree of impairment. A significant number of children who are afflicted require special services throughout their elementary school years. Most children whose speech sound disorder is not due to a medical condition show spontaneous resolution by age 6 (American Psychiatric Association, 2000), but up to 75% of children with delayed speech development in their preschool years may suffer an associated language disorder later in life (Shriberg & Kwiatkowski, 1988).

Stuttering almost always begins by 6 years of age. The onset is typically slow, occurring over many months, often starting with long words or the beginnings of sentences and only becoming evident over time. The disorder tends to wax and wane in frequency and severity. As the child ages and becomes increasingly aware of the problem, he may develop means for avoiding the use of certain difficult words, phrases, and emotional responses that tend to elicit the stuttering. Somewhere between 65% and 85% of individuals who stutter recover by late adolescence. The severity of the disorder at 8 years of age is the best predictor of recovery (American Psychiatric Association, 2013).

As with its epidemiology, the clinical course of social (pragmatic) communication disorder is as yet unknown.

DIAGNOSIS

If a communication disorder is suspected, other syndromes or causes of speech and language difficulties should be ruled out, particularly problems understanding language, which are the least evident and most difficult to identify. These disorders include hearing impairments (sometimes secondary to a history of chronic ear infections), intellectual disability, autism spectrum disorder, and any organic causes of speech and language problems, such as cleft palate, apraxia, cerebral palsy, or an acquired aphasia. In addition, psychiatric comorbidities, which can complicate learning and speech, such as ADHD, learning disorders, and anxiety disorders, should be ruled out.

Communication disorders are typically identified through careful speech and language testing and occasionally neuropsychological testing. Diagnostic instruments include individually administered standardized examinations that test nonverbal intelligence, receptive language skills, and expressive language skills. In the case of language disorder, the demonstrated nonverbal intelligence is generally significantly higher than test results of both expressive and receptive language.

Speech sound disorder is often identified without excessive neurological or speech and language testing and is determined by a child's inability to use expected speech sounds appropriate for his or her age. Errors in creating, using, depicting, and organizing sounds, along with sound replacements or exclusions, are clear indicators. Speech and language testing remains useful and often necessary for these children, however, as other language impairments are often present and will not be identified without a thorough evaluation.

Stuttering is also often evident under clinical observation alone. As previously described, stuttering is characterized by problems with speech fluency or frequent repetitions or prolongation of sounds, syllables, or words.

Social (pragmatic) communication disorder is generally identified by screening those children with demonstrated difficulties in the use of practical, social, idiomatic language. For example, children who are confused by age-appropriate common sayings, such as "Catch you later" or "What's up?," would warrant evaluation. The first step in assessment involves parent and teacher reports, interviews and observations, and hearing screening. If no better explanation is found for the difficulties, the child should be referred to a speech and language therapist for a thorough evaluation. If cognitive, behavioral, or emotional difficulties accompany the language problem, then a referral should also be made to a child and adolescent psychiatrist or psychologist.

In order for *DSM-5* criteria to apply to any of the communication disorders, difficulties with speech and language must interfere with academic or occupational achievement or with social functioning (American Psychiatric Association, 2013).

TREATMENT

There is a great deal of overlap among the treatments for most communication disorders that affect children and adolescents. The choice of treatment is best determined by a certified speech and language therapist, who may recommend individual treatments and/or small-group therapy. Children commonly receive both types of treatment with varying frequency. A complete psychiatric evaluation is generally also advised to rule out common comorbidities, such as learning disorders and ADHD, along with any possible medical or neurological causes for the impairments. Social skills training and parent management training are also sometimes helpful for both the child and parent, respectively, for associated educational, social, and behavioral problems.

The behavioral approach to the treatment of communication disorders varies by practitioner. Some use behavioral modification approaches while others use more child-centered approaches, such as indirect language stimulation. With this method, the parent and therapist use "self-talk," describing each thing they are doing out loud and in detail, such as, "I hold the key. I unlock the door. I get inside the car." Other indirect language stimulation techniques include parallel talk, where the adult describes out loud what the child is doing; description, where the adult uses labeling and explanatory phrases to identify and describe the child's experiences (e.g., "that dog is a Chihuahua" or "that car is long and blue"); and expansion, where the adult repeats the child's words but with proper enunciation and grammar.

Another commonly employed technique is whole-language instruction, which was initially applied to children with reading disorder. Because readers tend to grasp the whole meanings of words and children tend to speak words in their entirety, not broken down into their parts, it was reasoned that children should be taught to read by the same mechanism, that is, by whole words, not by reading words in their component parts. Speech therapists apply this intervention by creating a rich communicative environment that leads to incidental learning. Numerous play opportunities and focused stimulation are employed to elicit language targets.

By and large, those specific speech and language therapies that have been tested demonstrate efficacy (Enderby & Emerson, 1996). Still, few treatments have been tested, and as is evident from this chapter, major problems remain regarding the terminology and classification of communication disorders among children. Additionally, most children do better over time regardless of intervention, and most communication disorders appear to spontaneously resolve by early school age. Further scientific efforts must be put into identifying those affected children whose impairments will not improve independently and are in need of more intensive intervention.

Psychopharmacological interventions are not routinely effective or helpful in the treatment of communication disorders. More commonly, medications and psychotherapy are used to treat the psychiatric comorbidities that may be interfering with the child's ability to function and use language effectively. For example, some stutterers who have been treated for anxiety related to speaking have shown an improvement in symptoms (Van Riper, 1973), but treating anxiety per se has not typically been found effective.

7

Intellectual Disability

Many currently unfavorable terms have been used in the past to describe the cognitive impairments and behavioral delays that characterize individuals with intellectual disability. In their day, the terms *idiot, moron, feebleminded*, and until publication of the *DSM-5, mental retardation*, were all readily accepted. While most causes of intellectual disability remain elusive, we can now categorize the cognitive deficits that individuals face and identify risk factors and certain behavioral characteristics that are typical of affected individuals. In recent years, we have also become better at distinguishing intellectual disability from the commonly comorbid psychiatric conditions that these individuals often face.

CLINICAL PRESENTATION

The clinical presentation of intellectual disability is as varied as are the causes. In the first edition of this book, it was reported that over 500 etiologies of mental retardation had been identified. A keyword search for "mental retardation" in the Online Mendelian Inheritance in Man database (www.omim.org) reveals nearly 3,000 entries to date. Still, we are unable to identify an organic cause in the vast majority of cases (Dykens, Hodapp, & Finucane, 2000; B. H. King, State, Shah, Davanzo, & Dykens, 1997). Skills and impairments suffered by children and adults with intellectual disability often correlate to their IQs, but problems with adaptive functioning, such as communication, self-care, and social skills, are also always evident. Among those affected by certain well-defined or "classic" intellectual disability syndromes, such as Down syndrome or fragile X syndrome, we observe a typical profile of impairments. As we learn more about the etiology of each syndrome of intellectual disability, we become better able to predict the impairments that affected individuals will suffer.

The more severely affected the child, the earlier in life intellectual disability is generally diagnosed. For the vast majority of children, however, the impairments are considered "mild," and therefore are often not immediately evident. Consequently, those children who are not identified on the basis of speech, cognitive, or motor delays early in life may not be recognized until they enter preschool or even kindergarten, when it becomes clear that they cannot keep up with their peers.

ETIOLOGY

The three most common causes of intellectual disability are, in order, Down syndrome, fragile X syndrome, and fetal alcohol syndrome (B. H. King et al., 1997). Together, these three disorders account for up to 30% of all identified cases of intellectual disability (Batshaw, 1993). Of the hundreds of known causes of intellectual disability, over 300 have been related to the X, or female, chromosome to date (Ropers & Hamel, 2005; Skuse, 2005). Fragile X accounts for 40% of all X-linked syndromes and is the most common inherited cause of intellectual disability.

Although we are aware of hundreds of intellectual disability syndromes, still no clear etiology or explanation for the clinical symptoms observed is found in about three quarters of those affected by mild intellectual disability and about one third of those affected by severe intellectual disability (McLaren & Bryson, 1987). The specific etiologies that have been identified are more commonly observed among the most severe, yet rare, syndromes. Although intelligence as measured by IQ appears to be somewhat heritable, such that somewhere between 45% and 80% of the variability seen in IQ scores is due to genetic factors (A. T. Russell & Tanguay, 1996), no evident and reliable familial pattern of inheritance of intellectual disability has been established. However, certain specific illnesses that result in intellectual disability are heritable. Tay-Sachs and phenylketonuria (PKU), for example, are autosomal recessive genetic disorders that lead to inborn errors of metabolism that cause intellectual disability. A variety of single-gene aberrations following strict Mendelian inheritance with variable manifestations, such as tuberous sclerosis, have also been demonstrated to cause intellectual disability, as can hereditary chromosomal aberrations, such as fragile X.

Intellectual disability can also result from early problems during embryonic development. Chromosomal changes as seen in Down syndrome, for example, or prenatal damage due to toxins such as maternal alcohol ingestion or infections during the prenatal period, can cause intellectual disability. Environmental deprivation during the neonatal period, characterized by inadequate social, emotional, and linguistic nurturance, can also predispose a child to intellectual disability. While such severe environmental deprivation is not typical, we clearly recognize that there are critical developmental periods during which key brain structures are established. In the same way that patching the eye of a newborn monkey for the first months of life will result in permanent blindness in that eye because of the lack of visual stimulation necessary for neuronal growth, we believe that a lack of social, emotional, and cognitive stimulation can result in brain damage in developing children.

A variety of problems can occur during pregnancy and the perinatal period that also can predispose a child to intellectual disability or act as a causal agent, including fetal malnutrition, prematurity, hypoxia, viral and bacterial infections, and trauma. Numerous medical conditions acquired during infancy or childhood can also cause intellectual disability. Examples include neonatal infections, trauma, and lead or other heavy metal poisoning. Finally, a large proportion of children diagnosed with an autism spectrum disorder, particularly more severe forms, suffer from intellectual disability. In the not-too-distant past, when we did not always appreciate the milder forms of autism, at least 75% of autistic children were also diagnosed with intellectual disability. Regardless of the precise percentage, the two disorders often run hand in hand, but it remains unclear how these disorders are bound and which, if either, causes the other.

EPIDEMIOLOGY

The prevalence of intellectual disability is about 1% worldwide and typically ranges from 1% to 3% in developed countries. The prevalence of intellectual disability due to biological factors is similar among children of all socioeconomic classes. However, certain etiologic factors are linked to lower socioeconomic strata, such as lead poisoning and premature birth. Children born to a family at the lower end of the socioeconomic spectrum, then, are more likely to suffer intellectual disability.

Intellectual disability is more common among males; the male-to-female ratio is approximately 1.6:1 for mild impairment and 1.2:1 for severe impairment (American Psychiatric Association, 2013). As previously described, in cases where there is no specifically identified organic or biological cause, the intellectual disability is usually milder.

CLINICAL COURSE

The course of intellectual disability varies depending upon the etiology and level of impairment. Children diagnosed with mild intellectual disability, previously referred to as "educable," constitute the largest number of those affected, approximately 85% of all cases. Generally speaking, these children develop social skills and language capabilities by 5 years of age, suffering minimal sensory and motor impairments, and are often indistinguishable from typical children until elementary school. By adolescence, these youths can develop academic skills equivalent to the sixth-grade level. By adulthood, they are usually able to support themselves, and many lead independent lives. In fact, the diagnosis may not hold throughout one's entire life, as adaptive functioning may improve adequately so that diagnostic criteria are no longer met in adulthood (B. H. King et al., 1997). Others require more social and vocational support, along with assistance and supervision, particularly at times of high stress (American Psychiatric Association, 2013).

Children diagnosed with moderate intellectual disability, previously referred to as "trainable," constitute about 10% of those affected. Most of these children develop the ability to communicate by speech and other means as youngsters. They generally benefit greatly from social and vocational training and, with some supervision, are able to manage their own personal care. Peer relations suffer, particularly by adolescence, as they struggle with social skills and convention. Academically, they are unlikely to surpass the second-grade level. As adults, they often do well in supervised venues within the community, performing unskilled or semiskilled work (American Psychiatric Association, 2013).

Children diagnosed with severe intellectual disability constitute about 3% to 4% of those affected. These children struggle with communication but may eventually learn to speak and engage in simple self-care. They often benefit from basic education, such as learning the alphabet and how to count, and can be taught to recognize important "survival" words and objects, such as stop signs. They require a great deal of supervision as adults but can often learn to perform simple duties. Most of these individuals remain with their families or in group homes unless they suffer from a comorbid medical condition that demands specialized care (American Psychiatric Association, 2013).

The most severely affected children are those with profound intellectual disability, constituting 1% to 2% of the total population of those affected. Most of these individuals suffer from a recognized neurological or medical condition that accounts for their symptoms and have severe impairments in sensory and motor function. Extensive supervision, training, and a highly structured environment are required for the development of maximum speech, motor, and self-care capacities (American Psychiatric Association, 2013).

Individuals with intellectual disability present with a broad variety of personalities, behaviors, and temperaments. As expected, those who struggle more with communication skills may tend to evidence more disruptive, impulsive, and aggressive behaviors. The prevalence of comorbid psychiatric disorders in these individuals is estimated to be three to four times that of the general population. A review of representative studies found a prevalence of psychiatric disorders among intellectually disabled persons ranging from 27% to 71% (Bregman, 1991), yet the presentation and symptoms of the disorders appear to be much the same, such that attention-deficit/hyperactivity disorder (ADHD), depression, and anxiety look the same in an individual who is intellectually disabled as they do in an individual who is not (American Psychiatric Association, 2013). Similarly, individuals with intellectual disability and comorbid psychiatric disorders are generally thought to respond to medications in much the same way as those without intellectual disability, although, as we shall see, there is very little data to support this assertion.

DIAGNOSIS

According to *DSM-IV*, the diagnosis of mental retardation demanded impairment in IQ as well as adaptive functioning (i.e., how well the individual functions in his or her daily life). An IQ score of 70 or below had to be determined by an accepted test of intelligence, such as the Wechsler, Stanford-Binet, Woodcock-Johnson, or Kaufman. (See Chapter 5 for a detailed description of these tests.) Impairments in adaptive functioning are generally measured using either the American Association on Mental Retardation (AAMR) Adaptive Behavior Scale or Vineland Adaptive Behavior Scale. The Vineland and AAMR are designed to assess how well individuals cope within the social environment, manage typical life demands, and meet the standards of independence expected of their age. These tests should always be administered by a qualified neuropsychologist. The American Association on Intellectual and Developmental Disabilities (AAIDD), the new name for the AAMR, is planning to release a new Diagnostic Adaptive Behavior Scale in 2015.

DSM-IV defined the severity of mental retardation (mild, moderate, severe, or profound) by the individual's IQ score, but, as previously described, adaptive functioning was also viewed as a core component to be considered as well. According to *DSM-IV,* mild mental retardation corresponded to an IQ of 50–55 to approximately 70. Moderate mental retardation corresponded to an IQ of 35–40 to 50–55. Severe mental retardation corresponded to an IQ of 20–25 to 35–40, and profound mental retardation corresponded to an IQ of less than 20–25. These numbers were given in ranges for two reasons: (1) Each IQ test has a certain standard error, which recognizes that an individual's IQ score may be slightly different, although not profoundly different, on any given day depending on how the person is feeling, how rested the person is, and so forth; and (2) these numbers must leave room to take into account an individual's level of adaptive functioning, such that even if the IQ is a bit lower, for example, his or her adaptive functioning may be high enough to place the individual in a less-impaired category of mental retardation, and vice versa (American Psychiatric Association, 2000).

DSM-5 adopts many but not all of the criteria of *DSM-IV* for the diagnosis of intellectual disability. *DSM-5* persists in requiring that both deficits in intellectual and adaptive functioning be present and continues to categorize individuals as mildly, moderately, severely, or profoundly impaired. Consistent with *DSM-5*'s emphasis on a dimensional approach to diagnosis (see Chapter 1), the new version of the manual does not pair IQ levels with degree of impairment. Instead, the specifiers *mild, moderate, severe,* and *profound* are based entirely on an individual's adaptive functioning, which is further broken down into three domains: (1) *conceptual* or *academic,* which addresses cognitive domains such as memory, language, reading, writing, math reasoning, problem-solving, and judgment; (2) *social,* which addresses awareness of others' thoughts and feelings, empathy, communication and social skills, and social judgment; and (3) *practical,* which addresses self-care, money management, recreation, job capability, and school or work task organization (American Psychiatric Association, 2013).

The American Association on Intellectual and Developmental Disabilities (AAIDD) shares the conceptual, social, and practical domains of adaptive functioning with *DSM-5* in its understanding of intellectual disability but defines severity based on the intensity of supports needed as opposed to the degree of impairment observed. As a result, what *DSM-5* would call mild intellectual disability, the AAIDD classification system would define as intellectual disability with the need for intermittent support. Likewise, moderate intellectual disability would be characterized by needing limited support; severe intellectual disability would require extensive support; and pervasive intellectual disability would require pervasive support.

Borderline intellectual functioning is yet another category listed within *DSM-5*, although not considered a proper diagnosis. This descriptor is applied to an individual whose IQ lies somewhere between 71 and 84 but does not have any particular or stereotyped challenges with adaptive functioning. Technically speaking, *DSM-5* lists borderline intellectual functioning as a V code (i.e., not a formal diagnosis but an area requiring clinical attention because it may impact the care an individual receives).

The most commonly comorbid psychiatric conditions among those with intellectual disability include ADHD, mood disorders (both depression and bipolar disorder), autism spectrum disorders, anxiety disorders, stereotypic movement disorders, impulse control disorders, and various mental disorders secondary to general medical conditions.

There are a variety of specific intellectual disability syndromes that bear discussion given their prevalence, their classic behavioral presentations, and the genetic lessons that they so clearly illustrate; these include Down syndrome, fragile X syndrome, fetal alcohol syndrome, Prader-Willi syndrome, Angelman syndrome, and Williams syndrome.

Down Syndrome

As previously described, Down syndrome is the most common known cause of intellectual disability and the most common chromosomal (e.g., genetic) abnormality that leads to intellectual disability. Occurring in approximately 1.2 per 1,000 births, Down syndrome is due to the nondisjunction, or inadequate separation, of Chromosome 21 during early embryonic cell division. These individuals have relative strengths in their visual processing (versus auditory processing) and their social functioning. Relative weaknesses include language expression and pronunciation. Most individuals with Down syndrome are well engaged socially and require very little psychiatric care, and in fact, people with Down syndrome are generally recognized to suffer less severe psychopathology than other developmentally delayed groups (State, King, & Dykens, 1997). Unfortunately, given coexisting problems that result from nondisjunction of Chromosome 21, by 40 years of age affected individuals nearly always demonstrate postmortem neuronal defects that are indistinguishable from Alzheimer's disease and contribute to deteriorating cognitive function early in life.

Females with Down syndrome are believed to have better cognitive abilities and speech production than males with the syndrome, who generally have more behavioral troubles. ADHD symptoms are often seen in childhood across gender, and depression is diagnosed more often in adults with mild to moderate intellectual impairment than among those with more severe intellectual impairment. Autistic behavior is more common in those with major intellectual impairment, and, as previously noted, the elderly commonly demonstrate declines in adaptive behavior that are consistent with a diagnosis of Alzheimer's disease (Määttä, Tervo-Määttä, Taanila, Kaski, & Iivanainen, 2006).

In addition to the social, emotional, and psychiatric features of Down syndrome, there are a variety of physical features that are well recognized and occur in most cases, including a flattened face, straight hair, small ears, and protrusion of the tongue. In addition, these individuals commonly have a single crease on their fifth finger, are hypotonic, and have slanted palpebral fissures or eyelid openings (K. L. Jones, 1997).

Fragile X Syndrome

Fragile X syndrome is, again, the most common inherited cause of intellectual disability, affecting approximately 1 in 4,000 males and 1 in 8,000 females. Fragile X syndrome is due to a trinucleotide repeat of DNA, a group of over 200 trinucleotides of the CGG base pairs on the FMR-1 gene found at the X chromosome, region Q27.3. Some degree of CGG repeat is normal, and only as the base pairs expand past 50 repeats, in some cases reaching over 3,000 repeats, does the syndrome express itself. Fragile X syndrome illustrates two genetic principles: (1) dynamic mutation, meaning that more mutations occur with successive generations; and (2) anticipation, meaning that the severity of the disorder increases with successive generations. General problems include intellectual disability, mild connective tissue dysplasia, and macroorchidism. Only about half of females with the full mutation have IQs in the borderline or mild intellectually disabled range versus over 95% of males, as males do not have another X chromosome to compensate for the damage to their single X chromosome (Garber, Visootsak, & Warren, 2008).

Fragile X syndrome increases the risk for ADHD and social phobia. In addition, somewhere between 10% and 25% of individuals with fragile X may meet criteria for an autism spectrum disorder or show significant autistic-like symptoms, although numbers as high as 60% have been reported (Dykens et al., 2000). Individuals with fragile X syndrome suffer increasing deficits in adaptive and cognitive functioning with age, with a predictable decrease in IQ beginning around puberty. Their relative strengths include verbal long-term memory, while their relative weaknesses are in the areas of short-term memory, visual–motor integration, sequential processing, mathematics, and attention (State et al., 1997).

The characteristic physical signs of fragile X syndrome include macrocephaly, prognathism (enlarged and protruding chin), thickening of the nasal bridge, large ears, dental crowding, and epicanthal folds (a skin fold from the upper eyelids that covers the inner or medial corner of the eyes). Features occasionally noted include nystagmus (slow rhythmic eye movements in one direction and saccade-like, quick movements in the other direction), strabismus (a wandering eye), epilepsy, hypotonia, flat feet, and mitral valve prolapse, among others (K. L. Jones, 1997).

Fetal Alcohol Syndrome

Fetal alcohol syndrome has an incidence of 0.5 to 2 cases per 1,000 births and is the most preventable environmental cause of intellectual disability. By some estimates, as many as 1% of children in the United States may suffer fetal alcohol spectrum effects (Wattendorf & Muenke, 2005). The precise amount of alcohol required to induce the full syndrome is unclear, but we do know that even 7 to 14 alcoholic beverages per week results in growth deficits, an increase in disruptive behavior, and neurocognitive problems, such as difficulties with math, language, and memory. Visual-spatial ability, attention, and processing speed may also be impaired. Binge drinking (more than five drinks at a time) and drinking more than seven drinks per week are both known to put children at significantly higher risk for the full syndrome (U.S. Surgeon General, 2005).

Given that alcohol is a known and potent teratogen, complete abstinence prior to conception and during pregnancy makes the most sense. From a public health perspective, no amount of alcohol consumption during pregnancy can be considered safe. Certainly, drinking alcohol during the first few weeks after conception seems to carry no clear risk, as it takes about two weeks for the fertilized egg to implant in the uterine wall, and during this time the egg is feeding off its own yolk supply, which is not dependent on maternal blood. However, by Week 3 following conception, as the egg embeds in the uterine wall, the source of nutrition comes directly from the mother, and alcohol use in moderate to large amounts will now have a direct impact on the developing fetus.

The full syndrome is characterized by intellectual disability (average IQ of 63), fine motor difficulties, irritability, joint abnormalities, and heart murmur with ventricular septal defect. The characteristic facial features include macrocephaly, shortened palpebral fissures, bilateral ptosis (drooping of the upper eyelid), a thin upper lip, a small mandible, a flattened nasal bridge, a smooth philtrum, and protruding ears. Other problems may include cleft lip with or without cleft palate, central nervous system deformities such as meningomyelocele and hydrocephalus, neck deformities such as mild webbing, cervical vertebrae and rib abnormalities, cardiac deformities such as the tetralogy of Fallot and coarctation of the aorta, and hypoplastic labia majora and strawberry hemangiomas (K. L. Jones, 1997).

Prader-Willi Syndrome

Prader-Willi syndrome results from a deletion in the long arm of Chromosome 15 between Sections 11 and 13 (15Q11-13) and has a prevalence of about 1 case in 15,000 births. Sixty percent to 80% of affected individuals have a microscopic deletion on paternal Chromosome 15. The remaining cases of Prader-Willi syndrome have two copies of the maternal chromosome with no paternal chromosome, resulting in uniparental disomy. That is, these individuals have a section of chromosome that is only from the mother and not from the father, thus uniparental.

In contrast to those with fragile X syndrome, where we observe a deterioration of cognitive performance and adaptability with age, there is relative stability in the adaptive functioning of those affected by Prader-Willi syndrome during adolescence and early adulthood (B. H. King et al., 1997). Their relative strengths include expressive vocabulary, long-term memory, visual-spatial integration, and visual memory. It has been noted that many children with Prader-Willi syndrome have an unusual interest in jigsaw puzzles. Their relative weaknesses are in areas that include sequential processing and visual and motor short-term memory (State et al., 1997).

Behaviorally, these children commonly suffer temper tantrums, emotional lability, and mood symptoms. They are also known to be particularly anxious, as evidenced by frequent skin picking and obsessive-compulsive symptoms. Over 50% of those affected, in fact, are diagnosed with obsessive-compulsive disorder, and one of the most common expressions is compulsive overeating and the hoarding of food (State et al., 1997).

Children born with Prader-Willi syndrome suffer from infantile hypotonia, hyperphagia (i.e., an expansive appetite), morbid obesity, and small hands and feet; two thirds of those affected have mild intellectual disability, while one third have moderate disability. These children typically have a notably almond-shaped cranium, small genitalia, and often scoliosis, osteoporosis, high pain tolerance, and temperature instability (K. L. Jones, 1997).

Angelman Syndrome

Chromosomally similar to Prader-Willi, yet vastly different in expression, is Angelman syndrome. These children suffer from severe intellectual disability and are commonly plagued by seizures and a lack of speech but episodes of laughter. Ataxia, along with jerky arm movements and paroxysms of laughter in the absence of speech, has led to those with Angelman syndrome being described in the literature as "happy puppets." Like individuals with Prader-Willi syndrome, these children suffer from an error in Chromosome 15Q11-13. However, in the case of Angelman syndrome, all identified cases of deletion are traced to the mother's Chromosome 15. Angelman syndrome and Prader-Willi syndrome, then, illustrate the genetic concept of genomic imprinting, or the fact that the parent of origin of the deletion at the same locus impacts the phenotype or expression of the disorder. Consequently, while deletion of paternal 15Q11-13 results in Prader-Willi syndrome, deletion of maternal 15Q11-13 results in Angelman syndrome (K. L. Jones, 1997).

Williams Syndrome

Williams syndrome has received a great deal of attention from researchers in recent years because, even though it is extremely rare, those affected show unique strengths and weaknesses. While always resulting in global mild to moderate intellectual disability, these individuals often show great strength in linguistic functioning. Their relative strengths include a remarkable facility for recognizing facial features, increased interest and talent in music, and a loquacious, pseudomature "cocktail party speech," which allows them to speak fluidly and easily. Relative weaknesses include an increased risk for ADHD and high rates of anxiety, fears, and phobias. Physically, these individuals suffer from cardiovascular anomalies, protruding lips, infantile hypercalcemia, hoarse voice, renal anomalies, and growth deficiency. Affected individuals typically show major impairments in visual-spatial abilities. Williams syndrome is due to the deletion of the elastin gene 7Q11.23 (Dykens et al., 2000; K. L. Jones, 1997; State et al., 1997).

TREATMENT

There are no specific therapies or medications for intellectual disability. Treatments are typically symptom specific and include pharmacological interventions, behavioral therapies, and psychoeducation for the family, teachers, and other caregivers. Treatments tend to focus on social support, parent training, social skills training, and engaging the patient in the community to the greatest degree possible. Much effort is placed on managing the living situation of the patient and helping him or her find a meaningful life filled with valued activities. Addressing the individual needs of the child is paramount in establishing a robust treatment plan.

While no medications have specifically been designed or identified to treat intellectual disability, nor to address specific associated symptoms, medications are commonly employed for many of the comorbidities and behavioral disturbances that children and adults with intellectual disability face, such as agitation, aggression, irritability, and self-injurious behavior. Rates of psychotropic medication use vary from study to study but are commonly 15% to 40% in institutions and 20% to 30% in community settings, excluding anticonvulsants, which are commonly employed for comorbid seizure disorders that plague so many children with intellectual disability (Singh, Ellis, & Wechsler, 1997).

Stimulants

ADHD is the most widely diagnosed psychiatric disorder among children and adolescents with intellectual disability. This finding is not surprising, given that ADHD is the most common behavioral disorder in childhood. Prevalence rates are estimated at 8% to 16% (Emerson, 2003; Stromme & Diseth, 2000), but symptoms of inattention, hyperactivity, and impulsivity have been reported among up to 80% of children with developmental delays (Frazier et al., 2001). At least 20 randomized, double-blind, placebo-controlled trials have been published involving the use of methylphenidate (Ritalin) with individuals with intellectual disability. Positive response rates range from 45% to 65% in these studies (Aman, Collier-Crespin, & Lindsay, 2000), notably lower than the rates found within the non-intellectually-disabled population, which approach 80% (Greenhill et al., 2001). As expected, positive response to medication is predicted by a higher IQ (greater than 50) and higher scores at baseline on parent and teacher ratings of activity and inattention (Handen & Gilchrist, 2006). Given the global neurological deficits that many children with intellectual disability face, these individuals may be more susceptible to side effects from stimulants. As a result, some practitioners may choose to initiate treatment for ADHD with a nonstimulant, such as an alpha-2 agonist (e.g., clonidine [Catapres] or guanfacine [Tenex]) or atomoxetine (Strattera). Studies of these treatments are fewer in number but have generally demonstrated modest improvements among patients (Rowles & Findling, 2010). Furthermore, these treatments may be less likely to result in agitation than stimulants.

Antidepressants

Antidepressants have commonly been employed in the treatment of children with intellectual disability who suffer from depressive mood disorders, anxiety, self-injurious behavior, and stereotypic movement disorders. Antidepressants include both the selective serotonin reuptake inhibitors (SSRIs), such as fluoxetine, sertraline, paroxetine, and citalopram, and the tricyclic antidepressants, such as clomipramine. Among 15 published case reports and four prospective open-label trials involving children and adults with intellectual disability and/or autism spectrum disorders, decreases in self-injurious behavior, irritability, or depressive symptoms were noted for most patients treated with fluoxetine (Prozac), except in two studies (Aman, Arnold, & Armstrong, 1999). However, among the negative studies, fluoxetine led to increased aggression, agitation, and hypomanic behavior for a number of individuals.

There are no studies of sertraline (Zoloft) for the treatment of children with intellectual disability. Luiselli, Blew, and Thibadeau (2001) noted a case of one adult with severe intellectual disability who showed improvement in self-injurious behavior with sertraline. In addition, among adults with intellectual disability and autism spectrum disorders, sertraline has been found to reduce self-injurious behavior and aggression (Hellings, Kelley, Gabrielli, Kilgore, & Shah, 1996). Similarly, there are no studies of fluvoxamine (Luvox) for the treatment of intellectual disability and any of its comorbidities for children and adolescents. One open-label study of 60 adults with intellectual disability who were treated with 200 to 300 mg per day of fluvoxamine reported a significant reduction in aggression after three weeks of treatment (La Malfa, Bertelli, & Conte, 2001). No significant side effects were reported.

Paroxetine (Paxil) has been studied in small numbers of adults and children with intellectual disability for the treatment of self-injurious behavior, aggression, and depression. By and large, these open-label, retrospective, and case studies demonstrated brief, time-limited effects or benefits for only a small number of individuals (Handen & Gilchrist, 2006). In a nine-week depression study of seven adolescents, four no longer met criteria for depression following treatment with paroxetine at dosages of 20 to 40 mg per day (Masi, Marcheschi, & Pfanner, 1997). Side effects varied in these trials, but in some cases individuals discontinued treatment because of an increase in agitation, aggression, and hypomanic behavior.

Other antidepressant studies in adults have been conducted with both clomipramine (Anafranil) and citalopram (Celexa). Six of 10 patients treated with clomipramine in a double-blind, placebo-controlled fashion demonstrated reductions in the intensity and frequency of hyperactivity, irritability, and stereotyped behaviors (Lewis, Bodfish, Powell, & Golden, 1995). In a subsequent study by the same group, clomipramine led to a 50% or greater reduction in the intensity of self-injurious behavior as compared to placebo (Lewis, Bodfish, Powell, Parker, & Golden, 1996). In the second study, one patient suffered a seizure and another tachycardia and agitation. One retrospective review of 38 institutionalized, intellectually disabled adults found reductions in aggression, self-injurious behavior, depression, and disruptive behavior among those treated with SSRIs or clomipramine (Janowsky, Shetty, Barnhill, Elamir, & Davis, 2005), as did a review of 241 impaired adults who received SSRIs, SNRIs (selective serotonin and norepinephrine reuptake inhibitors), or tricyclic antidepressants for depression, anxiety, or obsessive-compulsive disorder (Rai & Kerr, 2010). Finally, citalopram was studied in 20 intellectually disabled adults at dosages of 20 to 60 mg per day in an open-label fashion. Sixty percent of patients demonstrated moderate to marked improvement in depression for one year (Verhoeven, Veendrik-Meekes, Jacobs, van den Berg, & Tuinier, 2001a).

Antipsychotics

Antipsychotics or neuroleptics are commonly employed in the treatment of those with intellectual disability. First-generation, or so-called "typical," antipsychotic medications have a long history of use among the intellectually disabled for disorders other than psychosis, such as hyperactivity, antisocial behavior, stereotypies, self-injurious behavior, and aggression (Handen & Gilchrist, 2006). Second-generation, or "atypical," antipsychotics are now being increasingly prescribed to this population in the hope that they will cause fewer side effects, which is particularly important given the likely increased vulnerability of these individuals to medication side effects.

Among the atypical antipsychotics, clozapine (Clozaril) has demonstrated efficacy in the treatment of resistant psychosis among individuals with intellectual disability (Antochi, Stavrakaki, & Emery, 2003). However, the side effect profile of clozapine can be so egregious and difficult to manage (e.g., agranulocytosis, excessive weight gain, seizures, Type 2 diabetes) that we rarely employ this medication unless absolutely necessary.

Risperidone (Risperdal), another atypical antipsychotic, has been found effective in managing aggression, irritability, and self-injurious and repetitive behaviors in both children and adults with intellectual disability in numerous studies (Aman et al., 1999; Handen & Gilchrist, 2006). Aman, De Smedt, Derivan, Lyons, and Findling (2002) demonstrated a beneficial response in 53.8% (versus 7.9% for placebo) of children 5 to 12 years of age in a large multicenter double-blind, placebo-controlled trial. Differences among those on active medication were evident within the first week of this six-week study. Snyder et al. (2002) also found risperidone better than placebo for the treatment of disruptive behaviors in a randomized, controlled trial of children with intellectual disability. Zarcone et al. (2001) found reductions in self-injurious behavior, aggression, property destruction, and stereotypies in 20 children and adults treated with risperidone. Finally, Gagiano, Read, Thorpe, Eerdekens, and Van Hove (2005) found significant benefit for intellectually disabled adults treated with risperidone versus placebo in a randomized, controlled trial, 52.8% versus 31.3%. Like clozapine, all atypical antipsychotic medications can cause significant side effects that must be monitored closely, including weight gain, sedation, extrapyramidal side effects and movement disorders, prolactin elevation, and liver damage. (See Chapter 15 for a thorough discussion of the side effects and monitoring of antipsychotic medications.)

Olanzapine (Zyprexa), another atypical antipsychotic, has been utilized somewhat less in the treatment of children with intellectual disability, perhaps because of the excessive weight gain commonly associated with this medication. While no placebo-controlled studies of olanzapine exist in this population, a number of chart reviews and open-label trials of adolescents and adults with intellectual disability suggest that it is often useful in decreasing aggression, irritability, and self-injurious behavior (Handen & Gilchrist, 2006). Of great concern is the fact that olanzapine, probably more so than the other atypicals, has a great propensity to induce significant weight gain, which can result in insulin resistance and Type 2 diabetes, among other side effects that are common to all atypical antipsychotics.

Little data is available on quetiapine (Seroquel), another atypical antipsychotic. Quetiapine has been reported to quiet hyperactivity, inattention, and conduct problems among children and adolescents with intellectual disability in a retrospective chart review, but no other published data are available (Handen & Gilchrist, 2006). Aripiprazole (Abilify), another atypical antipsychotic, was found to have the highest overall response rate (71%) among atypical antipsychotics for individuals with fragile X syndrome who required treatment for distractibility, anxiety, mood instability, aggression, and aberrant social behaviors (Hagerman et al., 2009). In an open-label study, eight subjects from 11 to 21 years of age who received 12 weeks of aripiprazole were rated as "very much improved" or "much improved" (Erickson, Stigler, Posey, & McDougle, 2010), and another small open-label study demonstrated aripiprazole's significant utility for the treatment of aggression, hyperactivity, impulsivity, and self-injurious behaviors (Valicenti-McDermott & Demb, 2006). No published data on the use of ziprasidone (Geodon) exist as yet.

Mood Stabilizers

Mood stabilizers, such as lithium and the anticonvulsants divalproex sodium (Depakote), carbamazepine (Tegretol), topiramate (Topamax), and lamotrigine (Lamictal), have also been employed in the treatment of those with intellectual disability. Lithium is typically indicated for the treatment of bipolar disorder but has been shown effective for mood lability, aggression, and disruptive behavior among the intellectually disabled in numerous studies (Antochi et al., 2003). Furthermore, lithium has demonstrated benefit for the treatment of self-injurious behavior in at least two double-blind, placebo-controlled studies (Craft et al., 1987; Tyrer, Walsh, Edwards, Berney, & Stephens, 1984). Lithium has also been found in one open-label trial of 15 individuals with fragile X syndrome, aged 6 to 23 years, to improve aberrant behavior and adaptive functioning (Berry-Kravis et al., 2008). Given the low therapeutic index and high potential toxicity of lithium along with this population's increased vulnerability to medication side effects, however, lithium requires close monitoring if utilized.

Divalproex sodium has sometimes been employed for the treatment of self-injurious behavior and aggression in intellectually disabled children and adults with demonstrated efficacy (Antochi et al., 2003). A review of 17 reports of 164 patients treated with divalproex sodium for aggressive and violent behaviors found a composite response rate of 77% (Lindenmayer & Kotsaftis, 2000). One prospective (Verhoeven & Tuinier, 2001) and one retrospective (Ruedrich, Swales, Fossaceca, Toliver, & Rutkowski, 1999) study, both uncontrolled, found benefit for divalproex sodium for over two thirds of adults for symptoms of self-injurious behavior, hyperactivity, impulsivity, and aggression. While there may be benefit for some patients with intellectual disability, the side effects of divalproex sodium are not insignificant and can include liver failure, pancreatitis, thrombocytopenia, birth defects, and possibly polycystic ovary syndrome, in addition to milder side effects, such as weight gain, sedation, alopecia, and tremor. Consequently, this medication must be utilized with great care.

Other anticonvulsants, such as carbamazepine and lamotrigine, have no supporting data for their use in children with intellectual disability. Studies of carbamazepine in adults with intellectual disability are weakly supported (Aman et al., 2000). Finally, a retrospective open-label study of topiramate in children with severe intellectual disability found that 74% of the sample of 22 demonstrated improvement (Janowsky, Kraus, Barnhill, Elamir, & Davis, 2003).

Other Treatments

Numerous other medications, such as propranolol, buspirone (Buspar), and naltrexone, have been employed for the treatment of aggressive, anxious, disruptive, and self-injurious behavior among those with intellectual disability. The data supporting these medications, which include primarily open-label, retrospective, and case studies, yield contradictory results. One review of five small double-blind, placebo-controlled trials of naltrexone for the treatment of self-injurious behavior in adults with intellectual disability concluded that there was "weak evidence" to demonstrate that the drug is any better than placebo (Rana, Gormez, & Varghese, 2013). Virtually no data exist on the use of antihistamines and sedative-hypnotics, which may lead to confusion in some patients.

Although there is little data, electroconvulsive therapy (ECT) has been used in the intellectually disabled and developmentally delayed population subsequent to failed behavioral and pharmacological interventions. R. J. Kessler's 2004 review of 16 successful case reports between 1968 and 2001 demonstrates a potential role for ECT, particularly given that none of these individuals suffered significant side effects or further cognitive deterioration.

8

Autism Spectrum Disorders

Autism spectrum disorders (ASD) are characterized by severe impairment in several areas of development and functioning, including reciprocal social interaction, verbal and nonverbal communication, and the normal range of behaviors, interests, and activities. These disorders are generally observed within the first few years of life and are often associated with intellectual disability and an assorted group of medical conditions, such as chromosomal abnormalities, congenital infections, and structural abnormalities of the central nervous system. While *DSM-IV* (American Psychiatric Association, 2000) described five disorders under the rubric of pervasive developmental disorders, including autistic disorder, Asperger's disorder, Rett's disorder, childhood disintegrative disorder, and pervasive developmental disorder not otherwise specified (NOS), *DSM-5* has done away with individual diagnoses for each of these disorders. Instead, *DSM-5* (American Psychiatric Association, 2013) has grouped autistic disorder, Asperger's disorder, childhood disintegrative disorder, and pervasive developmental disorder NOS under the single diagnosis of *autism spectrum disorder*, given the scientific consensus that these four diagnoses represent a single disorder with varying levels of impairment. Rett's disorder was removed entirely from *DSM-5* because it is now known to be an X-linked disorder due to mutations in the MeCP2 gene, and *DSM* diagnoses to date, at least, have incorporated only disorders whose manifestations are behavioral, emotional, or cognitive and whose etiology is not wholly genetic.

The inclusion of Asperger's disorder as a *DSM-IV* diagnosis was controversial in 1994 when *DSM-IV* was published. The initial intention of the *DSM-IV* committee was to make Asperger's disorder a research criterion or tentative diagnosis, but due to outcry from parents, clinicians, activist groups, and a number of research scientists, Asperger's was ultimately included as a separate and independent diagnostic category (Klin, Volkmar, & Sparrow, 2000). In the intervening years between the publication of *DSM-IV* and *DSM-5*, it became clear that Asperger's disorder could not be reliably differentiated from high-functioning autistic disorder, and that pervasive developmental disorder NOS and Asperger's disorder were often used interchangeably as well. Due to this lack of specificity and sensitivity in diagnostics, the *DSM-5* committee settled instead on one diagnosis with three levels of severity.

CLINICAL PRESENTATION

Before we understood autism to be a unique problem of its own, children with autism were often thought to be schizophrenic. Therefore, much of the early research and data on autistic children is muddied by diagnostic uncertainty. Consequently, case examples and histories of children with schizophrenia and severe mental illness, such as psychotic depression and bipolar disorder, from prior to the 1940s and 1950s are very difficult to take at diagnostic face value.

In 1943, Leo Kanner of the Johns Hopkins Medical Center described 11 cases of what he termed *early infantile autism*, noting the ways in which this presentation was distinctive from psychosis and schizophrenia. Kanner's unfortunate choice of the word *autism* was meant to convey the unusual egocentric quality of these children, following upon Bleuler's description of schizophrenia. Paul Eugen Bleuler was a Swiss psychiatrist who, in 1912, defined the four "As" of schizophrenia. Bleuler noted that schizophrenics demonstrate **a**mbivalence, display a flattened **a**ffect, speak with loose **a**ssociations, and are **a**utistic, a term he coined to describe the self-centered nature of these individuals. He derived the word from the Greek term *autos*, or "self," and the suffix *–ismos*, or "action or state." Kanner's use of the term *autism* to describe these individuals inadvertently contributed to the ongoing confusion between autism and schizophrenia. Many of Kanner's original observations have persisted over time. However, his speculations about certain aspects of the illness—for example, that these children generally have normal intelligence, that there is a lack of association with other medical conditions, and that poor parenting and education could result in an autistic syndrome—have been proven incorrect.

Coincidentally, Asperger's disorder was defined at about the same time that Kanner was making his observations on autism. In Austria in 1944, Hans Asperger proposed a novel diagnostic concept, which he termed *autistic psychopathy*, based upon his observations of four children. Ironically, he borrowed the same term from Bleuler that Kanner did, and his understanding of these children, too, resembled Kanner's concept in many ways. Neither Asperger nor Kanner was aware of the other, however, and so these two diagnostic constructs grew in parallel. In 1981, Lorna Wing in England coined the term *Asperger's* to describe a group of children who had numerous autistic symptoms but who did not meet full criteria for autistic disorder. She also was hoping to avoid the use of the word *psychopathy* and to separate this group of children from the general grouping of children with autism. To date, Asperger's syndrome has been better described in the European literature, and in the United States these children have generally been diagnosed with high-functioning autism.

There are a number of historical myths about autism that many practitioners still rely on. For example, we have been led to believe that children with autism never make eye contact, show affection, or smile; that inside a child with autism is a normal child or a genius waiting to emerge; that children with autism do not speak, but they could if they wanted to; that children with autism never relate well to peers and adults and do not want friends; that children with autism are manipulative and selfish; that autism is an emotional disorder; and that autism can be outgrown, or that progress means a child is not autistic. These myths have been perpetuated because, like most stereotypes, there is some truth to these statements for some individuals. However, we have now come to understand that the diversity of clinical presentations among autistic children is quite broad and encompasses children with a wide range of impairments. Although a small number of these children may be gifted in remarkable ways—the so-called "idiot savants," as they were previously described and as most notably displayed in the film *Rain Man*—the vast majority of autistic individuals display no such special skills.

Autism formally entered the psychiatric diagnostic lexicon in 1980 with the publication of *DSM-III*. *DSM-III* placed three diagnoses under the pervasive developmental disorder category: childhood-onset pervasive developmental disorder, infantile autism, and atypical autism. *DSM-III-R* rewrote the diagnoses to include only autistic disorder and pervasive developmental disorder NOS. *DSM-IV* revised the diagnosis still further to include autistic disorder, Asperger's disorder, childhood disintegrative disorder, Rett's syndrome, and pervasive developmental disorder NOS; and finally, *DSM-5* has abridged the diagnosis to only autism spectrum disorder. Heretofore, more consistent definitions and diagnoses were hindered by continuity with other disorders, the broad range of syndrome expression, changes in syndrome expression with age, a high frequency of autistic-like symptoms in those with intellectual disability, and the relative infrequency of this disorder. In most cases there is no period of unequivocally normal development, although in many cases, perhaps as high as 20%, parents report normal development for the first year or two of life, followed by a sudden onset of symptoms.

ETIOLOGY

We now know that autism is a biological disorder with multiple etiologies. Clearly there is no single cause, nor is there a single cure. As yet, no biological marker or single test can establish a diagnosis of autism. There is no evidence of parenting defects or emotionally induced autism. The so-called "refrigerator mother" theory, a psychoanalytic paradigm from the 1950s and 1960s that proposed autism to be the result of frigid and withholding mothers, is now thankfully discredited. Currently, the view is that some factor or factors act through one or more mechanisms to produce a final common pathway of central nervous system insult that results in the behavioral syndrome of autism.

Research into the causes of ASD presently abounds and focuses on a number of unique areas. Genome abnormalities, mechanisms underlying the expression of genes during brain development, structural and functional abnormalities in the brain, and behavioral expressions of ASD are all active areas of current inquiry.

Genetics

More than 100 genomic changes have been found among individuals with ASD, and numerous candidate genes have been proposed as possible areas for investigation (Schaefer & Mendelsohn, 2013). The fragile X gene, FXR1, for example, has been studied extensively, given that approximately 10% to 25% of children with fragile X syndrome demonstrate significant autistic symptoms (Dykens et al., 2000). The same is true of Chromosome 15, due to the recognition that many children with Chromosome 15 duplications (e.g., Angelman syndrome, Prader-Willi syndrome) demonstrate autistic-like symptoms or a "Chromosome 15 phenotype." A possible speech and language region at Chromosome 7q31-q33 may also be linked to autism, along with other candidate genes, including FOXP2, RAY1/ST7, IMMP2L, and RELN, at 7q22-q33 (Muhle, Trentacoste, & Rapin, 2004). Alternate expressions (or alleles) of the serotonin transporter gene (5-HTT) on Chromosome 17q11-q12 are more frequent among individuals with ASD, and Chromosome 22 (Shank 3 gene) has also been suggested. Because genes are essentially the blueprints of life, the hope that a single gene or series of inherited genes will lead to a clear etiology of ASD is very attractive yet too simplistic an approach, as genes are likely to be only one component of what ultimately accounts for ASD.

The suggestion that ASD may be due to random and spontaneous errors in DNA replication rather than directly inherited genes has recently become somewhat popular. *Copy number variations*, or errors that involve the addition or loss of large DNA sequences that occur during replication, may be responsible. DNA variations are often benign. Genes are constantly being duplicated as cells in the body are repaired and replaced. Redundancy and natural rejection of imperfect duplications protect the body from genetic errors that can result during this process. However, genetic mistakes may also result in disease. Though copy number variations have been known about for some time, they have more recently been suggested as a possible etiology for a wide variety of disorders, including ASD. In fact, a single genetic locus (16p11.2) has been reported to have copy number variants in 0.5% to 1% of all individuals with ASD (Schaefer & Mendelsohn, 2013). This theory is particularly provocative, given that perhaps as many as 90% of ASD cases appear to be sporadic and show no clear familial pattern or inherited pathway (Sebat et al., 2007).

Mirror Neurons

Another attractive etiological theory of ASD involves mirror neurons. In monkeys, mirror neurons are found in the inferior frontal gyrus and inferior parietal lobe. These neurons become active when monkeys watch someone perform a task. A similar system is theorized to exist in the human brain, where these neurons are thought to be important for understanding the actions of others and for learning new skills by imitation. This proposed mirror system may also contribute to our *theory of mind*, a theoretical construct that allows us to empathize and understand others' beliefs, desires, and intentions and is generally impaired in those with ASD. Stated another way, *theory of mind* is often defined as an understanding that others have their own beliefs, desires and intentions that may be different from our own (Rizzolatti & Fabbri-Destro, 2010). Electroencephalographic studies have now demonstrated less activity compared to controls, presumably due to decreased mirror neuron activity, in the inferior frontal gyrus (specifically the pars opercularis) in children and adults with ASD (Oberman et al., 2005), but these findings have not been consistently replicated (Y. T. Fan, Decety, Yang, Liu, & Cheng, 2010).

Amygdala

The amygdala, or "almond," (so named because of its physical appearance in the brain), has many important roles, including fear conditioning, memory consolidation, and the generation of emotional responses. The amygdala has long been suspected to be a source of some concern in ASD, and there are a variety of findings related to the amygdala that at present time appear to be somewhat contradictory. More recent neuroimaging studies have demonstrated fewer neurons in the amygdala among those diagnosed with ASD. However, prior amygdala research found larger structures among children with autism (Schumann et al., 2004), and larger right amygdala volume has been associated with more severe social and communication impairments in autistic 3- and 4-year-olds, which are predictive of a more severe clinical course and outcome (Munson et al., 2006). In addition, early postmortem evaluation studies of adult autistic brains reported higher cell density in the amygdala (Rapin & Katzman, 1998). Consequently, the role and importance of the amygdala is not clear at this time, but it does appear to be altered in some way in autism. More recent theories suggest that social fear in autism may cause an early rapid increase in amygdala growth, which over time leads to a toxic response that results in the death of amygdala cells and structural shrinking (Nacewicz et al., 2006).

Other studies have revealed that individuals with ASD who have smaller amygdalae have more difficulty identifying facial expressions and spend the least amount of time looking at the eyes relative to other, less emotionally salient parts of the face. This same result has been found, perhaps not surprisingly, among individuals without autism who have suffered unilateral or bilateral amygdala damage, leading to great difficulty recognizing complex mental states in faces, such as sadness, happiness, flirtatiousness, or guilt (Adolphs, Baron-Cohen, & Tranel, 2002). Similar results in terms of gaze fixation and brain response to human faces have been noted among well siblings of people with ASD (Dalton et al., 2005). One study found that it took individuals with ASD and small amygdalae 40% more time than those with larger amygdalae to identify and label facial expressions (Dalton, Nacewicz, Alexander, & Davidson, 2007). This study also found that those individuals with the largest amygdalae spent about four times longer looking at the eyes than those with the smallest. In addition, those with small amygdalae reported more nonverbal social impairment as children. Finally, it has been repeatedly demonstrated in these and other studies that the amygdala among those with ASD is hyperresponsive to facial expressions and that these individuals perceive a higher level of threat when shown "neutral" faces. It may indeed be, therefore, that limiting eye contact is a means for those with ASD to manage these negative interpretations (Tottenham et al., 2014).

To lay the responsibility for autism on any single brain structure would be folly. Although the amygdala is one of the most networked structures in the brain, there are inconsistencies among the many findings. Perhaps, then, the key brain abnormality in autism is not the amygdala itself but rather the functional neural connectivity of the various social circuits within the brain. One study, in fact, has identified not only decreases in neural connectivity in the brains of adolescents with autism, but also more severely impaired neural connections between the limbic or emotional brain regions involved in social processing and the language and sensorimotor areas that are also very important for social functioning (Gotts et al., 2012).

Basal Ganglia

Another area of the brain that has received some attention is the basal ganglia. The basal ganglia represents a variety of structures including the globus pallidus, thalamus, putamen, and caudate nucleus. Evolutionarily speaking, the basal ganglia is a very old part of the brain and among other things is involved in regulating and managing body movement. Furthermore, the basal ganglia, most particularly the caudate nucleus, is known to be an important structure that is very active among those who engage in repeated behaviors, such as obsessive thinking and compulsive behavior, as in obsessive-compulsive disorder (OCD), or repetitive motor and vocal tics, as in Tourette's disorder (Bloch, Leckman, Zhu, & Peterson, 2005; Mazziotta, Phelps, & Pahl, 1988). Among his original 11 cases, Kanner described "an anxiously obsessive desire for the preservation of sameness" (Kanner, 1965). This "sameness" has come to be described in modern parlance as the stereotyped ritualistic and perseverative motor behaviors, interests, and activities in which children with ASD engage. Given the staunch demand for routine and repetition, some have wondered about a possible phenomenological similarity between ASD, OCD, and Tourette's syndrome.

Whereas individuals with Tourette's or OCD feel compelled to engage in what they recognize to be distasteful ritualistic behaviors or to obsess upon certain subject matters, individuals with ASD typically experience passion about their particular interests or behaviors and express a desire to engage in repetitive activities. In the language of psychoanalysis, we would describe the desire for sameness among those with ASD as *ego-syntonic* or in sync with the needs of the ego, whereas individuals with OCD and Tourette's syndrome find their repetitive behaviors and thoughts to be *ego-dystonic* or at odds with their ego or self-image. In other words, those with OCD and Tourette's syndrome feel compelled to worry or behave as they do but do not desire to be engaged in these activities. While the caudate nucleus and other structures within the basal ganglia have been implicated in all three disorders based upon imaging studies, both structural and functional abnormalities in this area have been demonstrated among those with ASD. In some studies, larger caudate nucleus volumes have been correlated to an increase in repetitive and stereotyped behaviors among these children (Hollander, Anagnostou, et al., 2005), while in other studies a smaller basal ganglia volume has been associated with these behaviors (Estes et al., 2011; Sears et al., 1999). Still other work has found that basal ganglia shape abnormalities are associated with social, communication, and motor difficulties among children with ASD (Qiu, Adler, Crocetti, Miller, & Mostofsky, 2010).

Oxytocin

Oxytocin (from the Greek for "quick birth") is a peptide synthesized in the hypothalamus and released into the bloodstream by the pituitary gland. Oxytocin acts both peripherally as a hormone by promoting uterine contractions and milk letdown and centrally as a neuromodulator along with arginine vasopressin, where it has a role in promoting bonding and sexual behaviors. Some data point to lower levels of oxytocin in the blood of children with autism, and other work has identified a decrease in repetitive behaviors among children with autism when oxytocin is administered intravenously (Green & Hollander, 2010). A number of studies have also found that intranasal oxytocin improves emotion recognition among both adults and youth diagnosed with ASD (Domes, Heinrichs, Michel, Berger, & Herpertz, 2006; Guastella et al., 2010; Hollander et al., 2006), and one study to date has found that a single dose of intranasal oxytocin enhances brain activity in areas associated with reward and emotion recognition in children with ASD who are engaged in social tasks (I. Gordon et al., 2013). Although not available as a treatment, oxytocin or some derivation may one day be useful as a tool in helping children with ASD improve their social functioning (Preti et al., 2014).

Visual Tracking

The data available on visual tracking are fascinating and highly illustrative of some of the social and emotional challenges that individuals with ASD face. It has long been known that autistic individuals have trouble with facial recognition, and studies over the past decade have looked carefully at the eye movements of individuals with ASD when presented with faces (Dawson et al., 2002). In virtually all cases, individuals with ASD do not follow the most salient features when viewing faces or watching other individuals. Whereas a person without autism would typically watch the eyes for the greatest amount of information, a person with autism may wander in his or her gaze to the mouth (where there is movement) or to the shoulder or to the clothes to gather information (Klin, Jones, Schultz, Volkmar, & Cohen, 2002).

Observations of visual tracking correspond nicely to data obtained from studying the fusiform gyrus, which lies under the temporal lobe. For a number of years, we have known that the fusiform gyrus has a special role in facial recognition. In nonautistic individuals, the *fusiform facial area* becomes very active when looking at faces. In autistic individuals, this area seems to become active only when they look at faces they recognize very well, such as their mothers and fathers. One debate in the scientific literature has centered on whether the fusiform gyrus is only a facial recognition area or whether it is a general recognition area for things that people enjoy or like (Gauthier, Skudlarski, Gore, & Anderson, 2000). Regardless, it does appear that for experts in a certain subject area, and perhaps for an autistic child who is passionate about trains, for example, the area is stimulated when the child sees trains in the same way that the area is stimulated or excited when the child sees the face of his mother or father.

Most information, as previously noted, obtained from personal interaction comes from watching the eyes of the individual with whom one is speaking. As already noted, however, people with ASD have a great deal of difficulty with visual tracking, and those who make more eye contact are better at recognizing emotions (Kirchner, Hatri, Heekeren, & Dziobek, 2011). The most impaired individuals seem to look haphazardly at everything and anything in the field of vision and appear highly disorganized. Moderately impaired individuals appear to look at objects within a room, and the higher-functioning individuals tend to look at the mouth, where there is movement. Even toddlers with ASD as young as 14 months of age show a preference for viewing dynamic geometric images over viewing children in high action, such as dancing; this finding is so robust that in one study, if a toddler spent more than 69% of the time observing the geometric images instead of the active children, the positive predictive value for accurately diagnosing that child with ASD was 100% (K. Pierce, Conant, Hazin, Stoner, & Desmond, 2011). It is abundantly clear, then, that the vast majority of individuals with ASD, when engaged in a personal conversation or simply observing others, do not gather information from the eyes, thereby missing the most salient social information (Klin et al., 2002).

By 6 months of age, most individuals are better at recognizing faces when they are presented right side up as opposed to upside down. This *facial inversion effect*, as it is known, appears never to be achieved by many with ASD or, at the least, to be seriously impaired (Bookheimer, Ting Wang, Scott, Sigman, & Dapretto, 2008). Consequently, these individuals tend to recognize faces equally poorly, be they right side up or upside down. Imaging studies of the *fusiform facial area* indicate that among individuals with ASD, the area is less stimulated, less active, and receives less blood than a typical or normal individual when interacting with others and observing the faces of others (Schultz et al., 2000). In nonautistic children, the fusiform gyrus is activated in response to any human face. In autistic children, this activation is normal only when they are shown pictures of their mothers but diminished when they are shown pictures of strangers (Sterling et al., 2008). It is suggested that autistic individuals, therefore, may be trained to learn better facial recognition skills, thereby improving their social skills.

Brain Size

For years it was believed that the brains of autistic individuals were larger than those of nonautistic individuals. Many now suspect that at birth children with autism have slightly smaller heads but then show sudden and excessive growth within the first two years of life (Courchesne, 2004). Brain structures growing at the most deviant rate are believed to be those that are vital for cognitive, social, emotional, and language functioning, and include cerebral, cerebellar, and limbic areas. The increase in brain size appears to be due to an increase in the quantity of gray matter (Petropoulos et al., 2006). Although the implications of this alternate growth pattern have yet to be elucidated, a delay in neuronal development and maturation or specification of brain tissue in children with autism has been suggested. More recent data suggest, however, that many reports of early brain overgrowth in ASD may have been influenced by biased norms, and that we cannot, therefore, make any clear claims about brain size in ASD (Raznahan et al., 2013). Regardless, by adolescence, brain sizes have typically been reported to normalize, further confusing the issue of whether damage has been done during early growth and development.

Vaccines

In 1998, Wakefield et al. published a highly controversial report in which they suggested that childhood vaccinations might be the cause of autistic disorder, particularly in children with comorbid gastrointestinal sensitivities. The measles, mumps, and rubella (MMR) vaccine came under particular scrutiny in large part because of thimerosal, a mercury-containing preservative used in the vaccine. Wakefield's hypothesis was that the MMR vaccine causes intestinal inflammation, which leads to a loss of intestinal integrity and a weakening of the barrier wall, which then allows proteins into the bloodstream that damage the brain, resulting in autism. Although an appealing theory, subsequent analyses in Europe and the United States have shown that the number of cases of ASD has continued to grow regardless of vaccine exposure (Schechter & Grether, 2008; Stehr-Green, Tull, Stellfeld, Mortenson, & Simpson, 2003). Even with the subsequent removal of thimerosal, ASD rates have remained on the rise. Honda, Shimizu, and Rutter (2005) found that even though the MMR vaccine has essentially not been used in Yokohama, Japan, since 1992, the number of cases of ASD has continued to grow. A large retrospective cohort study of all children born in Denmark between 1991 and 1998, over half a million children, found no correlation between the administration of the MMR vaccine and ASD (Madsen et al., 2002). Finally, a 2004 report by the Institute of Medicine confirmed, based on all the available data, that there was no connection between MMR and ASD (Institute of Medicine, Board on Health Promotion and Disease Prevention, Immunization Safety Review Committee, 2004).

A population study from southern England also demonstrated the same finding (Baird et al., 2008). This study looked not at behavioral symptoms of ASD, but at blood samples for the presence of persistent measles infection or an abnormal immune response. The authors suggested that if the MMR vaccine or one of its component parts was causing autism, we would expect to see a significant antibody response among children who have autism. The results of the blood sample analysis showed that there was no difference in circulating measles virus or antibody levels between children who developed ASD and those who did not. In summary, then, it is quite clear that vaccines are not a cause of ASD. Wakefield's original report was based on 12 cases. Even though most of his coauthors subsequently retracted their support and disavowed the findings, concern over the possible connection between autism and MMR has led many parents to withhold the MMR and other vaccines from their children.

Diet

Another popular theory is that autism is caused by diet and nutrition. This theory suggests that some children with ASD will show symptom improvement when gluten, which is found in wheat products, or casein, found in dairy products, is removed from their diet. The hypothesis is that these two proteins are difficult for these children to digest and that the undigested metabolites of these proteins "leak" through the gut (ergo the "leaky gut" hypothesis of autism) and into the blood circulation, where they have an opioid-like effect on the central nervous system. The leaky gut theory hypothesizes that vaccines like MMR or proteins like gluten damage the gut, causing an increase in various peptides, such as casein, to flow into the bloodstream and central nervous system, where they can then lead to deleterious effects on brain opioid receptors, resulting in autistic symptoms (Hunter, O'Hare, Herron, Fisher, & Jones, 2003). Opioids can be tested for in the urine, and some individuals with ASD and self-injurious behavior have, in fact, been found in a few small studies to have higher levels of opioids in their urine (Sher, 1997). These data have recently been refuted, however, with more sophisticated screening techniques (Cass et al., 2008). Still, the theory is particularly attractive when considering autistic children who suffer from self-injurious behavior, as these children appear to be relatively immune to self-induced pain. One potential flaw with this theory is that naltrexone, an opioid-blocking agent, has not been proven to be particularly helpful for those individuals with autism who suffer self-injurious behavior.

A number of modified diet studies in children with ASD have been published, many of which have suggested that a gluten-free, casein-free diet (GFCF-D) is beneficial for children with autism. The vast majority of this data, however, has been in the form of case reports and observational studies and is of poor quality (Millward, Ferriter, Calver, & Connell-Jones, 2008). In one review of eight studies of a GFCF-D among children with ASD (six of which were open, one of which used a single-blind approach with 10 children, and one of which used a double-blind approach with no placebo and included only 15 children), all open- and single-blinded studies reported improvement when casein and gluten were removed from the children's diet (Christison & Ivany, 2006). The double-blind study demonstrated no group effect, although some parents reported improvement in their children's disruptive behaviors when they followed the diet (Elder et al., 2006). The possibility that these proteins, casein and gluten, or other dietary factors, may improve or worsen ASD is certainly possible, but larger randomized, double-blind, placebo-controlled trials are needed in order to ascertain any true benefit.

EPIDEMIOLOGY

Autism is ubiquitous and occurs all over the world. The incidence ranges considerably depending upon the study, but conservative estimates from the 1980s and 1990s typically reported autistic disorder to occur at a rate of about 5 per 10,000 in the general population (American Psychiatric Association, 2000). Being a relatively new diagnosis not initially intended for inclusion in *DSM-IV*, the prevalence rates of Asperger's have gone largely uncharacterized. With the development of improved diagnostic measures, however, and the recognition of the broad "spectrum" of disorders subsumed under the umbrella term of *autism* or ASD, we now recognize that many more children are affected than had previously been thought.

According to the Centers for Disease Control, which gathers data from the Autism and Developmental Disabilities Monitoring (ADDM) Network (a group of programs funded by the Centers for Disease Control and Prevention [CDC] to estimate the number of children with ASD), the number of affected children grows each year. Among 8-year-old children, the national frequency of ASD has risen from 6.7 per 1,000 children (1 in 150) in the 2000, to 14.7 per 1,000 children (1 in 68) in 2010. Among the 11 states sampled in 2010, rates varied from a low of 5.7 per 1,000 in Alabama to a high of 21.9 per 1,000 in New Jersey (CDC, 2014a). Even higher numbers have been reported in a well-designed large population study of over 55,000 seven- to twelve-year-old Korean children, where the prevalence of ASD was estimated to be 2.64% (Kim et al., 2011).

Many individuals wonder if the increase in the prevalence of ASD represents a true increase in cases or whether we are simply seeing some diagnosis switching between those children who were previously diagnosed with attention-deficit/hyperactivity disorder (ADHD), learning disorders, intellectual disability, or other psychiatric impairments and are now being diagnosed with ASD. While we currently do not have a clear answer to this question, national data do not show decreases in the prevalence of intellectual disability and speech and language disorders concurrent with the increases in ASD diagnoses, suggesting that these disorders do not account for any diagnostic reclassification or shifting (Newschaffer, Falb, & Gurney, 2005).

As with virtually all neurodevelopmental disorders, males are more commonly affected than females. The male-to-female ratio of ASD is about 5:1 in the CDC studies, representing frequencies of about 1 in 42 boys and 1 in 189 girls (CDC, 2014a). According to *DSM-5*, ASD is diagnosed four times more often in males than in females (American Psychiatric Association, 2013). Familiar patterns are now well established yet still account for only a relatively small number of cases. Twin studies show a 60% to 96% concordance for identical twins with autistic disorder versus a 5% to 24% concordance for fraternal, or nonidentical, twins, but these percentages run even higher when one looks at the full range of ASD symptoms and cognitive impairment (Bailey et al., 1995; Ritvo, Freeman, Mason-Brothers, Mo, & Ritvo, 1985; Rutter, 2000; Steffenburg et al., 1989). Studies also suggest that each subsequent child born into a family with one autistic child has between a 2% and 14% chance of having an ASD, or a risk about 3 to 22 times that of the general population (Newschaffer et al., 2007; Sumi, Taniai, Miyachi, & Tanemura, 2006).

CLINICAL COURSE

The prognosis and course of ASD is highly dependent on the level of functioning at any given time. By school age, the most severely affected children (e.g., those who would have been diagnosed with *DSM-IV* "autistic disorder" or, as we shall see below, what *DSM-5* now calls autism spectrum disorder Level 3) can be divided into three general groups. Those who are low functioning have a verbal and nonverbal IQ of less than 70. These children are considered intellectually disabled and constitute about 50% of affected children. The second group includes those who are midfunctioning and whose nonverbal IQ is greater than 70 but whose verbal IQ is less than 70. These children will meet criteria for a diagnosis of either intellectual disability or borderline intellectual functioning, depending upon their full-scale IQ score. Midfunctioning individuals constitute about 25% of affected children. The third group is high functioning and includes those whose verbal and nonverbal IQs are greater than 70 and who are not intellectually disabled; they constitute about 25% of affected children (Howlin, Goode, Hutton, & Rutter, 2004).

Many children with ASD Level 3 will show improvement by adolescence, which predicts a better adult outcome. Their activity level or hyperactivity tends to decrease, their behavior becomes more manageable, and their self-help skills improve. Communication continues to develop and becomes more robust. Although the IQ usually remains stable, these individuals often become more social and more adept at using social skills as they age. A large percentage, perhaps as many as 35% of children, will develop seizures of all types as they age (Deykin & MacMahon, 1979; Olsson, Steffenburg, & Gillberg, 1988; Parmeggiani et al., 2007).

Because prior versions of the *DSM* have forbidden numerous other diagnoses, such as ADHD, in the presence of autism, investigators have not always looked for these disorders among affected individuals. We now recognize, however, that comorbidities are more often than not the rule with autism. Although we have only recently begun to identify comorbid psychiatric disorders among those with ASD, it is believed that over 70% of individuals are likely to suffer at least one co-occurring mental disorder, and 40% may have two or more co-occurring mental disorders (American Psychiatric Association, 2013). The most common comorbidities identified include anxiety, depression, ADHD, motor skill deficits, self-injurious behavior, and disruptive behavior disorders (Simonoff et al., 2008).

There are a number of other illnesses commonly associated with the most severe forms of autism. These illnesses include, most notably, intellectual disability, the most common coexisting disorder, which affects somewhere between 50% and 75% of those with ASD Level 3. Fragile X is likely the most common cause of intellectual disability among those with ASD Level 3, accounting for perhaps as many as 15% to 25% of cases (Dykens et al., 2000). Down syndrome is also not uncommon. Other associated illnesses include epilepsy, various developmental syndromes such as Turner syndrome, tuberous sclerosis, and metabolic disorders such as phenylketonuria.

Few prognostic indicators are recognized for autism. Those predictors known to be related to outcome are IQ and communication skills by age 5, along with additional mental health problems (Gillberg & Steffenberg, 1987; Newschaffer et al., 2007). Epilepsy, a common comorbidity, is associated with lower verbal ability, more severe intellectual disability, and more impaired functioning (American Psychiatric Association, 2013). Among those factors not known to be related to outcome are family history of neuropsychiatric disorders, adequacy of parenting, and the family environment or atmosphere.

As expected, the natural history of Asperger's disorder or higher-functioning forms of autism (e.g., what *DSM-5* would call autism spectrum disorder Level 1 or 2) is somewhat different from the most severe form. Asperger's is also a lifelong disorder, yet the improvements among those with Asperger's may be more significant than among those with

ASD Level 3. By adolescence, some individuals may learn to apply explicit verbal rules or routines in stressful social situations, which help them to negotiate difficult interactions and minimize their anxiety. Children and adolescents with Asperger's disorder will commonly establish relationships with older individuals because these friendships are often more comfortable for them, as adults tend to be more understanding and permissive of odd or idiosyncratic behavior. Given these individuals' difficulties with managing social conventions, establishing peer relations is quite difficult.

Asperger's disorder has a better prognosis than the more severe forms of autism (Szatmari et al., 2000). As with ASD Level 3, the best predictors of improved outcome are intellectual level and communicative speech (Klin et al., 2000). Adults are often capable of gainful employment and self-sufficiency. As with more severe forms of autism, there is an increased frequency of ASD among first-degree relatives, and an increased risk of general social problems is also suspected (American Psychiatric Association, 2000).

The *phenotype* or expression of ASD Level 3 is reliable. Younger children often express little outward interest in establishing relationships. As they age, they may develop greater social interests, but they still generally lack an understanding of the social conventions required for successful friendships and intimate relationships. Those more severely affected are often unable to demonstrate an understanding of the needs and interests of others and cannot identify important emotions, such as happiness, sadness, distress, and anger, even among those closest to them.

Communication among those with ASD Level 3, including not only speech but also body language and other nonverbal forms of interaction, is characterized by delays and sometimes a complete lack of functional ability. When speech is present, individuals often demonstrate atypical intonation or prosody. The grammatical and syntactical structures of speech are often delayed, and these individuals may repeat stereotyped phrases, jingles, and commercials that they have overheard elsewhere. Comprehension, too, is often delayed, and imaginative play involving language is often absent or markedly impaired. Perhaps of greatest impact are the weaknesses in the pragmatic and social use of language, such as the inability to understand humor and irony.

The behavioral phenotype of ASD Level 3 is characterized by stereotyped behaviors, interests, and activities. Nonfunctional routines and rituals, an "insistence on sameness" as described by Kanner (1965), obsession with certain odd interests and activities, strange motor mannerisms, and a fixation on parts of objects further characterize these individuals.

The phenotypic expression of Asperger's disorder or higher-functioning ASD (e.g., Levels 1 and 2) is similar to that of ASD Level 3 but less severe. While individuals demonstrate odd social and emotional functioning, their communication is typically better, although not normal. In addition, the stereotyped behaviors, interests, and activities seen in ASD are often seen as more "quirky," idiosyncratic, or odd among those with Asperger's disorder in contrast to ASD Level 3, where those symptoms are almost always severely impairing.

DIAGNOSIS

The assessment of a child with suspected ASD must be broad ranging and incorporate virtually all aspects of the child's life and functioning. Motor skills, including both gross and fine motor, should be evaluated, along with verbal and nonverbal communication. The emotional assessment of a child with possible ASD should include a review of social skills as well as family attachments, friendships, self-concept, and mood. Academic and cognitive ability must be explored with standardized measures, and a behavioral and family assessment should also be completed.

ASD is clinically identified long after it begins, with some studies reporting as long as 80 months from the first symptoms noted by parents to the first diagnosis by a clinician (Oslejskova, Kontrová, Foralová, Dusek, & Némethová, 2007). Even when brought to the attention of a clinician, the diagnosis commonly still takes over a year to establish (Wiggins, Baio, & Rice, 2006).

At this time, there remains no good measure of how "autistic" someone is. Although we frequently employ a variety of rating scales to help us clarify the degree of symptomatology (see below), we remain unable to determine how biologically or neurologically impaired by autism one individual is as compared to another. Typically, we measure the severity of autism in part by the level of intellectual functioning or IQ and communication skills. Among those with severe intellectual impairment or intellectual disability, the relationship between cognitive abilities and adaptive functioning, as determined by a Vineland or AAMR inventory (see Chapter 5), is vital and often a useful starting point for determining clinical interventions.

Autism is typically a retrospective diagnosis for which the developmental history is essential. There are no reliable measures by which to diagnose the illness before onset of symptoms. Because the natural course of ASD is generally toward improvement, we may misdiagnose affected adolescents and adults if we do not obtain an adequate history. One of the greatest hallmarks of the diagnosis is inconsistency in development, which results in regressions, spurts, delays, and greater variation than would be expected in transition from one developmental stage to the next.

It is important to remember that there are numerous developmental oddities that typical or normal children who are not autistic do experience. These normal behaviors include spinning, toe-walking, enjoying the effect of strobe lighting, having odd or rigid food preferences, and disliking labels and seams in their clothing. The difference between typical or normal children and autistic children is that normal children generally grow out of these oddities. Thus, the emphasis upon developmental delay in the diagnosis of ASD is warranted.

Among children with more severe forms of autism, there are two types of onset generally reported. In the greatest number of cases, symptoms are present in the first year of life. Many of these children will fail to initiate baby games with parents at 4 to 6 months, such as peek-a-boo or giggling and other interactions. These children may not communicate common emotions well, such as hunger and pain, and parents may wonder why their children do not shout out for them and do not seem to connect with them. In another series of cases, perhaps as many as 20%, development is apparently normal until approximately 12 to 24 months of age, when symptoms appear. It is unclear whether the symptom onset is actually sudden in these 20% of cases, or if these parents simply do not know the signs of normal development, consequently not recognizing their child's impairments until he or she is nearly 2 years of age, when the delays become much more pronounced and obvious. A common referral from such a family notes, "He began to speak and then stopped."

Medical Evaluation

Each child with a suspected diagnosis of autism must be medically evaluated. This evaluation will vary depending upon the child and his or her needs but should start with a full medical history. At a minimum, each child should also receive a complete physical examination, including auditory and visual screening, a speech and language evaluation, and an occupational and physical therapy evaluation. Growth milestones, such as head circumference, should be followed, and neuropsychological testing should be completed, particularly IQ and achievement testing. The utility of neuroimaging, such as a magnetic resonance imaging or computed tomography scan, and electroencephalography (EEG) is less clear. With an adequate index of suspicion, the physician may order EEG to rule out a seizure disorder, including Landau-Kleffner syndrome (acquired epileptic aphasia), and neuroimaging to rule out tuberous sclerosis and various leukodystrophies, which may result in autistic-like symptoms.

The laboratory assessment of a child with suspected ASD will also depend on the individual clinical presentation. Without any clear indication, laboratory analyses are often not necessary. When employed, specific testing may include cytogenic and molecular screening for the fragile X DNA probe and DNA for MeCP2 for Rett's syndrome. A karyotype or general chromosomal analysis is rarely done, but specific chromosomal testing for DiGeorge or velocardiofacial (VCF) syndrome (22Q11), Williams syndrome (7Q11.23), and Prader-Willi syndrome and Angelman syndrome (15Q11-13) will sometimes be considered if signs or symptoms suggestive of these disorders are present. Fluorescence in situ hybridization (FISH) is a specific tool sometimes used to identify the presence or absence of particular DNA sequences on suspected chromosomes, such as 15Q11-13. Finally, laboratory assessment may also include obtaining ASO (antistreptolysin O) titers and anti-DNase B, which could indicate a recent streptococcal infection and PANDAS ("pediatric autoimmune neuropsychiatric disorders associated with streptococcal infections") syndrome (see Chapter 9), and metabolic screening of a 24-hour urine for uric acid, calcium and phosphorus, magnesium, homovanillic acid, and creatinine. Various purine and calcium disorders, lactic acidosis, phenylketonuria, and infectious causes, such as herpes or cytomegalovirus (CMV), may be identified through these processes.

DSM Diagnostic Criteria

The signs and symptoms of ASD often depend upon chronological and mental age. The diagnostic criteria of autistic disorder have been established by the American Psychiatric Association and are found in *DSM-5*. Whereas *DSM-IV* required six symptoms from among the three primary domains of impairment—social and emotional functioning, communication, and restricted behaviors, activities, and interests—*DSM-5* has collapsed two of those categories and describes the symptom domains as (1) social communication and social interaction and (2) restricted and repetitive behaviors, interests, or activities. Although not a fundamental change by any means, the new grouping of symptoms represents a recognition that social/emotional functioning and communication both rest on one's ability to engage directly with others.

DSM-5 describes two primary domains of difficulty for children with ASD: (1) social and communication problems and (2) a restricted realm of

behaviors, interests, and activities. The social and communication challenges are characterized by difficulties with establishing and managing
interpersonal relationships; trouble demonstrating empathy and carrying out emotional interchange or "reciprocity" with others (i.e., difficulty
sharing emotions, experiences, and interests and struggling to start or
maintain a conversation or social interaction); and impairment in the use
of nonverbal behaviors to promote social interaction, such as body language and eye contact. Stereotyped or restricted behaviors, interests, and
activities are characterized by a preoccupation with a particular interest, behavior, or activity to the exclusion of others; inflexible adherence
to nonfunctional rules, rituals, or routines; repetitive motor movements,
speech, mannerisms, or use of objects; and preoccupation with certain
aspects of the physical surroundings or excessive or minimal reactivity
to sensory input (e.g., pain, temperature, sound, light). Many children
with ASD also experience a delay in the development of language itself
and struggle with creativity and make-believe play, but the *DSM* does not
include these features as diagnostic criteria. *DSM-5* requires that all three
social communication and social interaction deficits be present for a diagnosis, in addition to at least two deficits in the realm of restricted behaviors, interests, and activities. *DSM-5* also requires that some symptoms
must be present in the early developmental period but does not give a
specific age at which symptoms must be evident.

ASD Severity Level

Nowhere does *DSM-5* live up to its intention to provide a dimensional
approach to diagnosis (see Chapter 1) as well as it does with ASD. By
doing away with numerous subdiagnoses, such as Asperger's and pervasive developmental delay NOS, *DSM-5* establishes one diagnosis, ASD,
with varying levels of severity. *DSM-5* specifies Level 3 as the most severe,
"requiring very substantial support." These individuals are severely
impaired and limited in verbal and nonverbal communication and social
interaction, may have few or no words, and behave in a very atypical way
with others. Their behavior is characterized by inflexibility, great difficulty tolerating change in their environment, and severely restricted and
repetitive behaviors and interests. Level 2 ASD requires "substantial support" per *DSM-5*. These individuals will be verbal but will have many
notable deficits in both verbal and nonverbal social communication.
They will demonstrate limited interests, speak in simple phrases, and
demonstrate oddities in nonverbal engagement. These individuals will
also have trouble coping with change and demonstrate moderately

restricted and repetitive behaviors that are obvious to others. Finally, Level 1 ASD requires "support" per *DSM-5* and is more in line with what had previously been called high-functioning autism or Asperger's disorder in *DSM-IV*. These individuals, as discussed below, are atypical in many ways that interfere with their functioning.

Asperger's Disorder

Although technically no longer a *DSM* diagnosis, a more thorough review of Asperger's disorder bears discussion, as many individuals currently hold the diagnosis and undoubtedly will continue to identify their disorder as Asperger's. In *DSM-5* nosology or parlance, most of these individuals will be diagnosed with ASD Level 1, although some may qualify for Level 2, depending on their abilities and level of impairment. *DSM-IV* diagnostic criteria for Asperger's made no mention of communication difficulties. Yet perhaps one of the most obvious facets of the presentation of an individual with Asperger's disorder is, in fact, severe deficits in the social and pragmatic use of language in spite of relative strengths in formal language domains (Klin et al., 2000). Primary difficulties include impaired use of social language, as evidenced by these individuals' often verbose and egocentric speech about their particular areas of interest, which may appear to outsiders as a monologue; lack of socially reciprocal speech or failure to invite others into the conversation; and often monotone speech with little inflection and normal alteration in prosody. In addition to the evident language impairments, these individuals generally demonstrate difficulties in nonverbal areas, such as visual–motor skills, which also cause them social difficulty. Consequently, while early speech development, such as vocabulary and rote memorization, is often not noted to be a problem in Asperger's or *DSM-5* ASD Level 1, major troubles in the pragmatic and conversational use of language become evident with maturation (Volkmar & Klin, 2000).

Another frequent area of impairment among these individuals is motor function, most commonly described as clumsiness and awkwardness. Even Asperger himself in his initial case descriptions noted that his subjects had delayed motor skills and were somewhat uncoordinated. While the difficulties are generally mild, they are likely to contribute to peer rejection, particularly for males for whom athletic ability as a child is a cornerstone of social acceptance.

Although affected individuals are often interested in establishing friendships and intimate relationships, they simply do not know how to do so. They often approach peers in peculiar ways, by telling about a particular interest or passion in a one-sided and pedantic fashion, for example, which is virtually guaranteed to annoy others. Furthermore, the concrete interpersonal style of these individuals makes it difficult for them to assess the emotional states of others, impairs their understanding of social cause and effect, limits their appreciation of humor and irony, and leads to misinterpretations of others' behaviors and intentions. Repeated social failures can lead to clinical depression and anxiety, which are not uncommonly seen among those affected (Volkmar & Klin, 2000).

Since Asperger's disorder entered the psychiatric lexicon in the United States only about 20 years ago (in the early 1990s), it is presumed that impaired individuals who received a diagnosis of Asperger's disorder in recent years were previously, and are likely to be still, diagnosed with alternative disorders. Affected adults seeing a general psychiatrist, for example, may be diagnosed with a schizoid personality disorder due to their lack of close relationships, emotional detachment, odd communication style, and rigid thoughts and behavior. Those individuals seeing a learning specialist may be diagnosed with a nonverbal learning disorder because of their impairment in tactile perception, psychomotor coordination, visual-spatial organization, and nonverbal problem-solving, while maintaining rote verbal abilities. Those seeing a neurologist may be diagnosed with a so-called developmental learning disability of the right hemisphere; those seeing an occupational therapist may be diagnosed with a sensory integration disorder; and those seeing a speech pathologist may be diagnosed with a semantic-pragmatic disorder because their speech is sufficient in appearance (grammar and sound) but damaged in content and use (effective communication; Volkmar & Klin, 2000).

Asperger's disorder or ASD Level 1 is often not evident until school age, when academic and social demands first become apparent. Affected individuals may feel victimized and socially isolated with age, as they feel further removed from peers. Although intellectual disability is not observed, ADHD is often a first diagnosis, given the frequent hyperactivity and inattention that many of these children tend to display. In addition, Tourette's syndrome and obsessive-compulsive disorder may be more common among these individuals. Certainly, anxiety and mood disorders, as previously noted, are common with age as individuals develop an increased self-awareness of their poor social insight and abilities and become repeatedly frustrated in their attempts to establish satisfactory social relationships.

Because of the disproportionate reliance upon language as a means of relating socially, gathering information, and relieving anxiety, these individuals are limited in their learning strategies. Facts gathered through rote memorization may be learned relatively easily, but higher-

level concepts are much more difficult, such as what is meant by the concept of "number," "more or less," "greater than and less than," "fraction,"
and so forth.

Most of these individuals will experience significant nonverbal
learning problems, but the converse is not always the case. The primary
assets among individuals with nonverbal learning disorders are proficiency in rote verbal skills and, in some, simple motor and psychomotor
skills. The primary deficits include bilateral tactile perceptual problems;
bilateral psychomotor coordination deficiencies; visual perceptual organizational deficiencies; poor adaptation to novel and otherwise complex
situations; deficits in nonverbal problem solving, concept formation,
and hypothesis testing; a distorted sense of time; much verbosity in a
repetitive and straightforward manner; relative deficiencies in mechani-
cal arithmetic, as compared to proficiencies in reading, word recognition, and spelling; and significant deficits in social perception, judgment,
and interaction with maintenance of well-developed verbal capabilities.
These deficits can and should be determined by routine neuropsychological testing.

Rating Scales

Rating scales are often employed to aid in the assessment of symptoms of
those with ASD. Some of the available scales include the Gilliam Autism
Rating Scale (GARS), the Gilliam Asperger's Disorder Scale (GADS), the
Childhood Autism Rating Scale (CARS), the Social Communication
Questionnaire (SCQ), the Social Responsiveness Scale (SRS), and the
Autism Spectrum Quotient. Each of these scales has its weaknesses, but
each can also be effectively utilized by the practitioner to aid in the clinical diagnosis and treatment response. The current "gold standards" of
evaluation are the Autism Diagnostic Observation Schedule (ADOS), a
clinical survey performed directly with the child by a trained examiner,
and the Autism Diagnostic Interview, Revised (ADI-R), a survey of the
parent(s) or caregiver(s) of the child. The ADOS and ADI-R are currently
the best-validated rating scales.

In addition to the diagnostic rating scales, there are a number of
brief screening tools that should be utilized by primary care providers to
identify early signs of ASD. The Checklist for Autism in Toddlers (CHAT)
and the Modified Checklist for Autism in Toddlers (M-CHAT) are tools
designed to assist primary care providers in identifying the early signs of
autism (Baron-Cohen, Allen, & Gillberg, 1992; Baron-Cohen et al., 1996;
Robins, Fein, Barton, & Green, 2001). The CHAT is a five-item checklist

Table 8.1 Checklist for Autism in Toddlers (CHAT)

Observations by primary care practitioner:
1. Look for sustained eye contact.
2. Get child's attention; then point out an interesting object in the room. The typical child should look to where the physician points.
3. Ask the child to point out something in the room (e.g., "show me the light"). The absence of pointing by 18 months is a cardinal sign of ASD.
4. Show the child a doll and a cup and ask, "Can you give the baby some juice?" An autistic child will have difficulty engaging in pretend play.
5. Ask the child to build a tower of three blocks. (The purpose of this task is to assess social interaction).
Children who fail items 2, 3, & 4 are at risk of ASD and warrant further evaluation.

Questions for parents:
1. Does your child enjoy being swung or bounced on your knee?
2. Does your child take interest in other children?
3. Does your child like climbing on things such as stairs?
4. Does your child play peek-a-boo or hide-and-seek?
5. Does your child ever pretend?
6. Does your child ever use his index finger to point to or ask for something?
7. Does your child ever use your index finger to point and indicate an interest in something?
8. Can your child play appropriately with small toys without just mouthing, fiddling, or dropping them?
9. Does your child ever bring objects to you to show you something?
Children who fail items 5 and 7 are at risk of ASD and warrant further evaluation.

for primary care practitioners and a nine-item checklist of questions for parents that is recommended at the 18-month pediatric evaluation (see Table 8.1).

The M-CHAT (see Table 8.2) is a more detailed but better-validated screening tool for toddlers between the ages of 16 months and 30 months of age to assess risks for ASD. The M-CHAT is quick to administer and can be employed as part of a well-child checkup. Because the goal of the M-CHAT is to identify as many cases as possible, the instrument is very sensitive and has a high false-positive rate, meaning that not all children who appear to be at risk for ASD will actually meet diagnostic criteria when further evaluated.

Finally, the American Academy of Neurology has enumerated five early warning signs of ASD (Filipek et al., 2000). A child's inability to reach any of these developmental milestones is suggestive of the need for an evaluation to rule out ASD:

- No babbling by 12 months
- No gesturing, pointing, or waving good-bye by 12 months

Table 8.2   Modified Checklist for Autism in Toddlers (M-CHAT)

Instructions: Please fill out the following about how your child usually is. Please try to answer every question. If the behavior is rare (e.g., you've seen it once or twice), please answer as if the child does not do it.

1. Does your child enjoy being swung, bounced on your knee, etc.?	Yes No
2. Does your child take an interest in other children?	Yes No
3. Does your child like climbing on things, such as up stairs?	Yes No
4. Does your child enjoy playing peek-a-boo/hide-and-seek?	Yes No
5. Does your child ever pretend, for example, to talk on the phone or take care of a doll or pretend other things?	Yes No
6. Does your child ever use his/her index finger to point, to ask for something?	Yes No
7. Does your child ever use his/her index finger to point, to indicate interest in something?	Yes No
8. Can your child play properly with small toys (e.g., cars or blocks) without just mouthing, fiddling, or dropping them?	Yes No
9. Does your child ever bring objects over to you (parent) to show you something?	Yes No
10. Does your child look you in the eye for more than a second or two?	Yes No
11. Does your child ever seem oversensitive to noise (e.g., plugging ears)?	Yes No
12. Does your child smile in response to your face or your smile?	Yes No
13. Does your child imitate you (e.g., you make a face—will your child imitate it?)?	Yes No
14. Does your child respond to his/her name when you call?	Yes No
15. If you point at a toy across the room, does your child look at it?	Yes No
16. Does your child walk?	Yes No
17. Does your child look at things you are looking at?	Yes No
18. Does your child make unusual finger movements near his/her face?	Yes No
19. Does your child try to attract your attention to his/her own activity?	Yes No
20. Have you ever wondered if your child is deaf?	Yes No
21. Does your child understand what people say?	Yes No
22. Does your child sometimes stare at nothing or wander with no purpose?	Yes No
23. Does your child look at your face to check your reaction when faced with something unfamiliar?	Yes No

A child fails the M-CHAT when two or more critical items are failed or when any three items are failed. Yes/No answers convert to pass/fail responses. The "critical" items are numbers: 2, 7, 9, 13, 14, and 15. Among typically developing children, the answers to all questions above should be "yes," except for numbers 11, 18, 20, and 22.

- No single words spoken by 16 months
- No two words spoken together spontaneously by 24 months that are not echolalic
- Any loss of previously acquired language or social skills at any time

TREATMENT

The first step in the treatment of ASD is to identify and address all comorbid disorders, which commonly include ADHD but may also include anxiety, depression, and even psychosis. Coexisting psychiatric conditions are highly common in ASD, as previously noted, and it is believed that over 70% of affected individuals have one additional diagnosis and 40% have two or more (American Psychiatric Association, 2013; Simonoff et al., 2008). The same medications utilized for the treatment of these disorders in typical or normal individuals are utilized in the treatment of those with ASD.

The treatment of ASD must be comprehensive and involve all aspects of the patient's life. We increasingly recognize that early intervention is vitally important for the best outcome (Rogers, 1996). Individuals who are diagnosed and treated early will have improved chances of living a satisfying and productive life and are likely to show the greatest amount of symptom improvement with age (Paul, 2008). Family and caretaker psychoeducation is another linchpin of early intervention. Academic support, speech and language therapy, and occupational and physical therapy as indicated are all standard but nonspecific measures commonly employed in the treatment and support of children with ASD. Although many treatments exist for children with ASD, the two best-established treatments at this time are *applied behavior analysis* (ABA) and medication (Foxx, 2008).

ABA is the bedrock of effective treatment for ASD. ABA is the umbrella term for a variety of behavioral modification therapies, including *discreet trials training* and the *Lovaas method*. In comparison to the many other treatments available for children with ASD, the data supporting ABA is overwhelmingly positive, particularly when it is delivered early in the life of an affected child (Foxx, 2008; Peters-Scheffer, Didden, Korzilius, & Sturmey, 2010). ABA focuses on teaching small, measurable units of behavior in a systematic manner. Problematic target behaviors are chosen, antecedents are identified, and corrective behaviors are then taught. Typically, the patient is given a stimulus, such as a question or an activity that must be completed, along with a hint or cue, if necessary, as to what the correct response should be. If the patient responds correctly, he or she is rewarded with something simple, such as praise, a small candy, or a "high five." All other responses are ignored or corrected in a neutral fashion. As the patient's responses become more reliable and accurate, the cues become withdrawn until the individual is responding independently. It is through this type of behavioral shaping that ABA is typically employed. ABA therapy is not simply discreet trial training, however, as an ABA therapist or program utilizes a comprehensive series of interventions aimed at every setting and every possible moment in order to shape the behavior of a child.

Although the data supporting ABA is far superior to that supporting other treatments, there are a number of other therapies that have some data supporting their effectiveness in the treatment of ASD. The Picture Exchange Communication System (PECS), for example, utilizes symbols to teach communication strategies to those with ASD and severe language deficits. When used regularly, PECS has been shown effective for children and adults in initiating interaction, in promoting short-term word acquisition, and in communicating in the classroom, but studies to date have not shown durability nor demonstrated maintenance and generalization of gains to venues outside the classroom once formal intervention has ceased (Howlin, Gordon, Pasco, Wade, & Charman, 2007; Warren et al., 2011).

While lacking a firm evidence base, social skills training appears to hold promise and should be utilized to teach social norms and expectations and to improve empathy (Laugeson, Frankel, Mogil, & Dillon, 2008). Many forms of social skills instruction are available, including social stories, video modeling, social problem-solving, pivotal response training, scripting procedures, priming and prompting procedures, self-monitoring, and computer-based interventions (Bellini & Peters, 2008). Another social skill lacking in many children with ASD is "joint attention," the ability to share focus with another individual. Joint attention skills correlate with communication and social skill development and may provide an avenue for building such skills among those with ASD (E. A. Jones, 2009). Imitation is sometimes used to strengthen joint attention. Studies have shown that children with ASD who are imitated show greater social engagement for longer periods of time (Tiegerman & Primavera, 1981). Furthermore, therapeutic activities focused on adults following the lead of an ASD child and imitating their behaviors have led to increases in joint attention and more active social participation by affected children (C. E. Stephens, 2008).

TEACHH, or Treatment and Education of Autistic and Related Communication Handicapped Children, comprises a series of nonspecific and highly individualized methodologies designed to help the child with ASD to communicate and develop autonomy. Educational means are utilized, along with basic behavior modification methodologies, such as scheduling, establishing clear expectations, arranging activities in a predictable fashion, positioning materials to promote independence from adult direction, and reorganizing the physical environment, to promote success. The results of studies evaluating TEACHH vary greatly because of the highly individualistic means of the interventions, but some studies have been favorable (Ospina et al., 2008). One meta-analysis of 13 TEACHH studies among children and adults found moderate to large gains in social behavior and maladaptive behavior but only negligible to small gains in communication, activities of daily living, cognitive skills, and motor functioning (Virues-Ortega, Julio, & Pastor-Barriuso, 2013).

Although scattered and inconsistent data exist on many other therapies, those that are most effective clearly employ a behavioral approach. Cognitive behavioral therapy (CBT) for comorbid anxiety among children with ASD is a recognized approach with good supporting data, which may also prove to be useful for other co-occurring psychiatric disorders (Wood et al., 2009). While some therapies, such as *Greenspan's floortime*, emanate from a staunch theoretical perspective, others, such as alternative diets or secretin therapy, are generally vague in their rationale. Regardless, it must be emphasized again that the most effective therapeutic treatments for children with ASD are behavioral in nature. In addition to educational and psychotherapeutic treatments, however, medications have also proven themselves useful.

Although few randomized, double-blind, placebo-controlled trials exist, virtually all psychiatric medications have been tried for the treatment of ASD. The antipsychotics risperidone (Risperdal) and aripiprazole (Abilify) have both demonstrated efficacy in the treatment of ASD and have been approved by the Food and Drug Administration for children and adolescents with autism. Both medications have demonstrated decreases in the irritability that many of these children suffer, along with other behavioral problems such as aggression, deliberate self-injury, and temper tantrums (Marcus et al., 2009; McCracken et al., 2002; Owen et al., 2009; Shea et al., 2004). Risperidone has also shown efficacy in small numbers of preschool children as young as age 2 years in separate randomized, double-blind, placebo-controlled studies (Luby et al., 2006; Nagaraj, Singhi, & Malhi, 2006).

The dosage of risperidone will vary by practitioner, but typically the lowest dose of 0.25 mg is applied once daily, usually in the evening to start, because of the common sedative side effect that follows. Over time, the dosage may be increased and may reach as high as 2 to 4 mg per day. Risperidone is also available as a liquid of 1 mg/ml, and smaller doses can be given in that fashion, particularly for children who cannot swallow a tablet.

Aripiprazole is often initiated at 1 to 2 mg per day, generally administered in the evening to start because of its possible sedative effect in some children. The smallest tablet available is 2 mg, which can be broken in half, and there is also a liquid form available of 1 mg/ml. Dosages in the efficacy studies of aripiprazole varied between 2 and 15 mg per day among children 6 to 17 years of age, with each dosage demonstrating benefit but higher dosages generally causing more side effects.

The side effects of antipsychotic medications can be significant and may include weight gain, insulin resistance, liver function abnormalities, elevations in cholesterol, hyperprolactinemia, hypersalivation, movement disorders, and sedation. Long-term studies of antipsychotic side effects are hard to come by, but a review of over 800 children who were treated with risperidone for disruptive behavior disorders found that weight increases stabilized after six months and that initial increases in prolactin often came down to normal limits within about three months (Pandina, Aman, & Findling, 2006). Still, most practitioners would agree, and most studies would support the idea, that so-called atypical antipsychotics (see Chapter 15), such as risperidone and aripiprazole, are commonly associated with some degree of side effects and very often weight gain.

Other antipsychotic medications have also shown benefit in open-label trials and case studies. Although scant data are available, small numbers of children and adolescents with ASD have benefited from treatment with olanzapine (Zyprexa), ziprasidone (Geodon), and quetiapine (Seroquel) for the treatment of irritability, anxiety, hyperactivity, and aggression (Kemner, Willemsen-Swinkels, deJonge, Tuynman-Qua, & van Engeland, 2002; Posey, Stigler, Erickson, & McDougle, 2008). In general, then, the use of antipsychotics is common but not always recommended because of side effects. Prior to using such intensive medications, a full trial of behavioral therapy should be employed.

A more typical psychopharmacological treatment approach for a child with ASD will include addressing the psychiatric comorbidities, such as ADHD. Although *DSM-IV* prohibited a diagnosis of ADHD in the presence of a pervasive developmental disorder, most clinicians see these disorders as separate entities and treat them as such. Others believe that the inattention, hyperactivity, and impulsivity of children with ASD are different from those typically seen in children with ADHD, and that these symptoms are a part of ASD as opposed to comorbid ADHD. Furthermore, stimulants are sometimes agitating for children with ASD. For these reasons, it may be wise to start treatment of these symptoms with an alpha-2 agonist, such as guanfacine (Tenex) or clonidine (Catapres), followed by atomoxetine (Strattera) and then a stimulant if necessary. Extensive clinical experience and small clinical trials have demonstrated benefit from guanfacine and clonidine in the treatment of hyperactivity, inattention, motor tics, and insomnia in children and adolescents with ASD (Frankhauser, Karumanchi, German, Yates, & Karumanchi, 1992;

Handen, Sahl, & Hardan, 2008; Ming, Gordon, Kang, & Wagner, 2008; Posey, Puntney, Sasher, Kem, & McDougle, 2004). (See Chapter 3 for a complete discussion of these medications for the treatment of ADHD.)

Antidepressant medications are also sometimes used for comorbid anxiety and depression or simply to help decrease agitation and perseveration among those with ASD. Clomipramine, an older and less commonly used antidepressant due to frequently difficult-to-tolerate side effects, has shown modest benefit over placebo and desipramine (another antidepressant) in one small single-blind study (Gordon, State, Nelson, Hamburger, & Rapoport, 1993) and equal benefit to haloperidol (an older antipsychotic medication) for stereotyped and repetitive behaviors, but more severe side effects, resulting in a high study dropout rate (Remington, Sloman, Konstantareas, Parker, & Gow, 2001). Results for fluvoxamine (Luvox) have been mixed, with some double-blind, placebo-controlled trials in both children and adults showing benefit for symptoms of repetitive thoughts and behavior (McDougle, Kresch, & Posey, 2000; McDougle et al., 1996) and at least one open-label study showing no benefit (Martin, Koenig, Anderson, & Scahill, 2003). The only other two placebo-controlled, double-blind published studies of an antidepressant for the treatment of ASD in children involve fluoxetine (Prozac), which was found to be beneficial for the treatment of repetitive behaviors (Hollander, Phillips, et al., 2005), and citalopram (Celexa), which was not found to be beneficial in general nor specifically for the treatment of repetitive behavior (B. H. King et al., 2009). A meta-analysis of published and unpublished trials of antidepressants for the treatment of repetitive behaviors, including many of the aforementioned studies, found a small but significant benefit for the medications, but there was significant evidence of publication bias (e.g., only those trials showing benefit had been published; Carrasco, Volkmar, & Bloch, 2012). In open-label studies, sertraline (Zoloft) was found to be beneficial in helping children adjust to transitions (Steingard, Zimnitzky, DeMaso, Bauman, & Bucci, 1997), and fluoxetine was noted to be helpful in decreasing some of the core symptoms of autism (DeLong, Ritch, & Burch, 2002). The remaining studies are few in number and comprise mostly case reports and retrospective chart reviews, which provide little guidance in the treatment of children and adolescents with ASD (Posey, Erickson, Stigler, & McDougle, 2006).

ASD are extremely perplexing and devastating for the families of affected children. As our understanding of ASD grows, so will our ability to provide effective treatments. In the meantime, however, families will understandably often grasp at anything within their reach to help their children. Although testimonials supporting virtually all therapies can be found, with the exception of the treatments described above there is little that a clinician can confidently offer a family at this time. Some alternative treatments, such as chelation therapy, have even proven themselves deadly (A. J. Baxter & Krenzelok, 2008), while others, such as porcine secretin hormone, have been shown convincingly not to work (K. Williams, Wray, & Wheeler, 2012). Other unproven methods, such as holding therapy, dietary and vitamin regimens, anti-yeast therapy, brushing therapies, and Higashi daily life therapy, among others, may someday demonstrate utility, but at this time they are viewed through a scientific lens as being benign at best. At the end of the day, parents and practitioners must make their own judgments about how to help children affected by ASD.

9

Tourette's and Tic Disorders

The history of Tourette's disorder is fascinating and a study in how our understanding of behavioral disorders has changed over time. The first case of what is now known as Tourette's was reported by a French physician, Jean-Marc Itard (1775–1838), in 1825 (see Chapter 1 for a description of Itard's work with Victor of Aveyron). He described the case of the Marquise de Dampierre, a woman of notability and great importance. The marquise suffered motor tics, coprolalia (uncontrollable offensive speech), and echolalia (repetition of the words of others) from the age of 7 years. Itard wrote,

> In the midst of a conversation that interests her extremely, all of a sudden, without being able to prevent it, she interrupts what she is saying or what she is listening to with bizarre shouts and with words that are even more extraordinary and which make a deplorable contrast with her intellect and her distinguished manners. These words are for the most part gross swear words and obscene epithets and, something that is no less embarrassing for her than for the listeners, an extremely crude expression of a judgment or of an unfavorable opinion of someone in the group. (1825, p. 405)

The more she herself was troubled by her own words, explained Itard, "the more she [was] tormented by the fear that she [would] utter them, and this preoccupation [was] precisely what [put] them at the tip of her tongue where she [could] no longer control it" (Kushner, 1995). Itard was describing the sense of premonitory urge that often precedes the expression of a tic in just the same way as we understand it today.

In 1885, George Gilles de la Tourette described nine cases of the syndrome that now carries his name. One of his cases was the Marquise de Dampierre, who by then was in her 80s. Throughout much of the 20th century, Tourette's disorder was believed to be of psychogenic origin. More recent research, however, has resulted in a return to Tourette's original impression of the disorder as a nonprogressive hereditary neurological condition. This final point is illustrative of many recognized psychiatric conditions, which as little as 40 years ago were believed to be entirely psychogenic in origin, but in their original descriptions and case studies were thought to be neurological, genetic, or somehow physical in nature.

CLINICAL PRESENTATION

A *tic* is defined as a sudden, rapid, repetitive, involuntary, nonrhythmic and stereotyped motor movement or vocalization (American Psychiatric Association, 2013). Tics may be simple, thereby implicating only a few muscles or simple sounds, or complex, in which case they involve multiple groups of muscles, resulting in more fluid and larger movements that may include uttering words and sentences. Both motor and vocal tics can be simple or complex. A *simple motor tic* is very brief, generally lasting fewer than several hundred milliseconds. Examples include blinking the eyes, jerking the head, sucking the lips, opening the mouth, wrinkling the nose, shrugging the shoulders, or contorting the face. Some simple motor tics are more difficult to observe, such as crunching the toes.

A *complex motor tic* lasts longer than a simple motor tic, typically seconds or even longer; examples include crouching, jumping, touching, pulling at clothes, skipping, sticking out the tongue, gesturing with the hands, tensing muscle groups, repeatedly smelling things, pounding the chest, holding the body in an unusual position, and retracing one's steps or weaving while walking. Both *copropraxia* (sudden, uncontrollable offensive gestures made in a tic-like fashion, such as "flipping someone off" or grabbing one's genitals) and *echopraxia* (an involuntary mirroring of another's movements) are considered complex motor tics.

Vocal tics can also be simple or complex. Simple vocal tics are typically brief sounds that have no meaning and are not related to the situation at hand. They may include snorting, barking, honking, coughing, spitting, sniffing, grunting, laughing, or, perhaps most commonly, throat clearing. Complex vocal tics are clearly language based; examples include making unusual changes in volume or pitch, stuttering, and blurting out words or phrases.

There are a number of so-called "lalias," all of which are considered complex vocal tics. *Palilalia* is the repeating of one's own sounds or words; *echolalia* is the repeating of others' sounds or words; and *coprolalia* is the involuntary utterance of socially objectionable words or phrases and may include cussing, blasphemy, or racial slurs. Although coprolalia is perhaps the most recognizable of the vocal tics, it is found in fewer than 10% of individuals who suffer from tic disorders.

Tourette's disorder typically begins with a simple motor tic on the face, such as blinking. The tics persist and generalize to other parts of the body, waxing and waning over time. Eventually explosive vocalizations, such as throat clearing, hiccupping, or uttering nonsense or intelligible words, ensue.

Most affected individuals report that their tics are irresistible but that they can suppress them at times. Children, particularly at onset, are sometimes oblivious to their tics, but with age they become only too aware of their symptoms, in large part due to the responses of others. Many individuals who suffer from tics and Tourette's describe a premonitory urge or an increasing tension or physical feeling that is relieved when the tic bursts forth. One patient notes,

> I guess it's sort of an aching feeling in a limb or a body area, or else in my throat if it proceeds a vocalization. If I don't relieve it, it either drives me crazy or begins to hurt (or both)—in that way it's both mental and physical. (Leckman, Walker, & Cohen, 1993)

Another patient reports,

> A need to tic is an intense feeling that unless I tic or twitch I feel as if I'm going to burst. Unless I can physically tic, all of my mental thoughts center on ticking until I am able to let it out. It's a terrible urge that needs to be satisfied. (Leckman et al., 1993)

Individuals affected by Tourette's and tic disorders may feel the need to perform a tic repeatedly or in a specific way until it has been done "just right" and the person feels as if it is no longer necessary to repeat it. Tics often occur in short groupings and may be separated by minutes or hours without tics. Tics generally disappear during sleep and during intense sexual arousal, and they often change in severity over the course of the day. Commonly, they also change in location and intensity, coming and going with time. Tics also fluctuate in their rate of recurrence and in how much they disrupt one's life. Affected individuals are often better at suppressing tics when in public than when they are alone. In fact, tics are quite common when an individual is relaxed, such as when listening to music or watching television, and less frequent when an individual is engaged in directed purposeful activity, such as reading. Tics are also commonly aggravated by stress, such as school and work pressures.

ETIOLOGY

As yet, no clear etiology for tics and Tourette's disorder has been elucidated. Current research implicates numerous factors, including certain brain structures and the circuits that interconnect these structures, neurotransmitters, perinatal insults and infections, and immune response, all of which are likely to contribute to the ultimate expression of the disorders. Although the brains of those affected by tics and Tourette's are grossly normal, certain morphological abnormalities have been found in magnetic resonance imaging (MRI) studies of those with Tourette's; these include a loss or reversal of normal asymmetries of the putamen and lenticular nucleus; variation in corpus callosum morphology among males; decreases in the density and number of GABAergic neurons in the basal ganglia; and decreases in the volume of the caudate nucleus (Faridi & Suchowersky, 2003; Kalanithi et al., 2005; B. S. Peterson et al., 2003).

Single-photon emission tomography (SPET) studies have found hypoperfusion in the basal ganglia bilaterally, anterior cingulate cortex, left dorsolateral prefrontal cortex, and orbital and anterior medial regions of the frontal and temporal lobes. Similarly, positron emission tomography (PET) studies have shown decreased metabolic activity in the prefrontal cortices and the striatum, implying abnormal interconnections between these areas. Functional magnetic resonance imaging (fMRI) studies have found an increase in the activation of the supplemental motor cortex, which may suggest an alteration of motor pathway organization among affected individuals. Such fMRI studies have also revealed variable brain activity when affected individuals try to suppress a tic, resulting in a bilateral decrease in globus pallidus and putamen activation, or when they allow a tic, resulting in abnormal signals in the primary motor and speech (e.g., Broca's) areas, along with striatal activity (Faridi & Suchowersky, 2003).

Neurotransmitters also appear to have a role in Tourette's disorder. The clearest evidence of this association rests on the fact that dopamine blockade suppresses tics, and dopamine-releasing drugs tend to exacerbate them. Other data also suggest the importance of dopamine in tics. For example, Tourette's patients have been found to release more dopamine in response to amphetamine than normal controls, and increased innervation of dopamine neurons has been found in the striatum of affected individuals (Swain, Scahill, Lombroso, King, & Leckman, 2007).

Tourette's disorder has also been tied to a variety of perinatal insults and environmental factors. Perinatal hypoxia is associated with an increased risk of developing Tourette's, as is prenatal maternal smoking. Individuals with Tourette's also report higher levels of psychosocial stress and have higher levels of corticotropin-releasing factor (CRF) in the cerebrospinal fluid than normal controls (Swain et al., 2007).

Yet another possible cause of Tourette's disorder is infection with group A beta-hemolytic streptococci (GABHS). Known in the scientific parlance now as PANDAS (pediatric autoimmune neuropsychiatric disorders associated with streptococcal infections), this proposed infectious etiology of Tourette's disorder and obsessive-compulsive disorder (OCD) in all likelihood accounts for a relatively small number of cases. The theory suggests that GABHS infection in a select group of individuals may induce neuron damage and an autoimmune response, leading to the production of autoantibodies that attack certain nerves in the brain, which results in the characteristic tics of Tourette's along with obsessive thinking and compulsive behavior. Evidence for this association is based on the fact that rats demonstrate an increase in total and daily oral stereotypies when their brains (e.g., striatum) are infused with sera from patients with Tourette's disorder containing high levels of GABHS antibodies. In contrast, rats injected with sera from normal controls and Tourette's patients with low levels of antibodies demonstrate no such changes in behavior (Swedo et al., 1998; Yeh et al., 2006).

Children affected by PANDAS typically experience the rapid onset of symptoms following a GABHS infection, such as strep throat. Symptoms may include not only Tourette's but also symptoms of obsessive-compulsive disorder. The autoimmune response triggered by strep causes the production of autoantibodies that attack the host—specifically, it appears, the basal ganglia, which is highly important in managing body movement and behavior. This same process is known to cause rheumatic fever when these autoantibodies attack the mitral valve, arthritis when these autoantibodies attack joints, and abnormal movements when these autoantibodies attack the basal ganglia, resulting in Sydenham's chorea or St. Vitus' dance.

Finally, tics and Tourette's disorder are known to have a genetic basis. Family studies have found that Tourette's syndrome is inherited and that first-degree relatives of a proband or affected individual are at increased risk by a factor of 10- to 100-fold when compared to the general population (Faridi & Suchowersky, 2003; O'Rourke, Scharf, Yu, & Pauls, 2009). Chronic and transient tics are also found at increased rates among first-degree relatives, suggesting alternate expressions of Tourette's (Faridi & Suchowersky, 2003). Twin studies have found a much higher concordance rate among monozygotic (identical) twins (up to 53%) than among dizygotic (nonidentical) twins (up to 8%; Price, Kidd, Cohen, Pauls, & Leckman, 1985). If chronic motor tics are included in the count, monozygotic twin pairs are nearly 90% concordant, and dizygotic twin pairs are nearly 30% concordant (Leckman & Cohen, 1996). Although tic disorders are not passed consistently and reliably from generation to generation, an autosomal dominant pattern of inheritance with variable penetrance has been indicated by studies to date, suggesting that other factors, such as genomic imprinting, may be at play (see Chapter 7). Regardless, family members of an affected individual are clearly at significant risk (Faridi & Suchowersky, 2003).

Abelson et al. (2005) identified a Chromosome 13 inversion in a patient with Tourette's disorder. The gene SLITRK1 was suggested to be responsible for the expression of Tourette's in the identified patient and a small number of other unrelated individuals (O'Rourke et al., 2009). With rare exceptions such as SLITRK1, however, Tourette's disorder is most often likely due to multiple genes (Swain et al., 2007).

EPIDEMIOLOGY

Tics and Tourette's disorder have been found in all racial and ethnic groups studied. Due to misdiagnosis, underreporting, and the fact that most data have emanated from clinical samples, the precise prevalence is unknown. While motor tics are quite routinely observed, Tourette's is an uncommon phenomenon. One large study of over 28,000 Israeli Army recruits aged 16 to 17 years identified an overall rate of 4.3 per 10,000, slightly higher in males (4.9) than females (3.1; Apter et al., 1993). A Swedish screening study of 11-year-old children that utilized both a survey and a physical examination reported a 1.1% incidence among boys and a 0.5% incidence among girls (Kadesjö & Gillberg, 2000). By contrast, a lifetime prevalence of Tourette's disorder of 0.39% was found in a population study that utilized structured diagnostic interviews from 1975 to 1992 in upstate New York (B. S. Peterson, Pine, Cohen, & Brook, 2001). This same study identified a nearly 18% prevalence of tics in early childhood, which fell to 2% to 3% by adolescence. Zohar et al.'s (1999) review of population studies reported rates of Tourette's disorder ranging from 0.05% to 0.1% among children. Finally, DSM-5 reports the prevalence at 3 to 8 per 1,000 in school-age children, and the prevalence among males in the United States is estimated to be three times that of females (American Psychiatric Association, 2013; Bitsko et al., 2014).

CLINICAL COURSE

About 20% to 25% of children will develop transient tics or what the *DSM* calls a provisional tic disorder at some time before age 18 (Pringsheim, Davenport, & Lang, 2003). To meet *DSM-5* diagnostic criteria, these tics may be single or multiple motor and/or vocal and persist for less than one year (American Psychiatric Association, 2013). Eye blinking, snout reflex, throat clicking or clearing, sniffing, and a facial grimace are perhaps the most common expressions, which are likely to wax and wane, become exacerbated with stress, and then dissipate over time. Tics usually begin between 3 and 8 years of age.

Tourette's disorder generally starts with a simple motor tic and then later generalizes to both motor and vocal tics. Tics may begin as early as 2 years of age but typically start between 6 and 7 years. A prepubertal exacerbation is common with Tourette's, as is a postpubertal attenuation, followed by stabilization of symptoms in adulthood (Faridi & Suchowersky, 2003). Although Tourette's was once considered a lifelong disorder, one retrospective cohort study demonstrated that approximately 50% of patients were asymptomatic by 18 years of age (Leckman et al., 1998). Tourette's symptoms typically stabilize in adulthood, with up to 65% of patients showing no changes in symptoms over five years (de Groot, Bornstein, Spetie, & Burriss, 1994).

DIAGNOSIS

The diagnosis of Tourette's disorder rests on the presence of persistent motor and vocal tics. By *DSM-5* criteria, the tics must have been present for at least one year following first onset (American Psychiatric Association, 2013). Tics rarely begin after age 18, and the *DSM* relies upon this criterion as well for the diagnosis of Tourette's disorder.

The differential diagnosis of Tourette's disorder is broad and includes a variety of movement disorders, infectious etiologies, perinatal insults, traumas, toxins, and medications as well as drug abuse. By establishing the time criterion for the diagnosis (i.e., both motor and vocal tics must have been present for at least one year), one can rule out a diagnosis of provisional tic disorder, or what *DSM-IV* called transient tic disorder (American Psychiatric Association, 2000). Other disorders, such as Huntington's disease, Lesch-Nyhan syndrome, Sydenham's chorea, and multiple sclerosis, commonly result in movement disorders that can be mistaken for Tourette's disorder. Congenital central nervous system conditions and various birth defects can also result in tics and should be considered. A complete birth and developmental history will assist the clinician in assessing these variables. In addition to GABHS, as described above, postviral encephalitis, HIV infection, and Lyme disease can cause both motor and vocal tics. Head trauma and seizure disorders must also be considered, and the onset of tics should be measured against any known history of injury. Toxins such as carbon monoxide and gasoline; prescription medications such as antipsychotics, L-dopa, stimulants, and lamotrigine; and withdrawal from drugs of abuse, such as amphetamines and opiates, can also cause tics and should be ruled out.

Genetic disorders, such as Hallervorden-Spatz disease, Wilson's disease, hyperekplexias, Rett's syndrome, and neuroacanthocytosis, can result in tics, as can various chromosomal abnormalities, such as XYY, XXY, and fragile X syndrome. Finally, both children and adults diagnosed with autism spectrum disorders (ASD) often demonstrate repetitive and stereotyped movements (Faridi & Suchowersky, 2003). In extreme cases, these actions may include hand flapping, head wagging, body rocking, odd posturing, and spinning, but in less affected individuals these movements may simply include blinking, sticking out the tongue, or other repetitive motor movements that may be misinterpreted as a tic. To distinguish between ASD and true tics or Tourette's, the clinician should remember that tics have an involuntary quality and occur in bouts, whereas autistic stereotypies appear self-soothing and intentional.

Comorbidities are more commonly the rule than the exception when it comes to both tics and Tourette's disorder, with nearly 95% of children with moderate Tourette's and 100% of those with severe Tourette's qualifying for another psychiatric diagnosis (Coffey et al., 2000). Somewhere between 50% and 90% of clinically referred children and adolescents with Tourette's disorder carry a comorbid diagnosis of attention-deficit/hyperactivity disorder (ADHD), oppositional defiant disorder, or conduct disorder (Leckman, 2003). Comorbid ADHD is also commonly associated with aggression, low frustration tolerance, explosive behavior, and noncompliance (Swain et al., 2007). Similar clinically derived samples show a high co-occurrence of ADHD and Tourette's disorder, ranging between 8% and 80% (Lebowitz et al., 2012; Towbin & Riddle, 1993), and ADHD and discreet tic disorders, ranging between 8% and 34% (Biederman et al., 1996; Spencer, Biederman, & Wilens, 1999). Regardless of the precise frequency, it is apparent that ADHD and Tourette's syndrome frequently co-occur in those patients who seek medical attention. ADHD also occurs at an increased rate in the families of patients with Tourette's disorder, suggesting a shared group of genes (Faridi & Suchowersky, 2003).

OCD is also strongly associated with Tourette's disorder, with as many as 60% of clinically referred children and adolescents demonstrating significant symptoms or full diagnostic criteria (Lebowitz, et al., 2012; Schapiro, 2002). In the opposite direction, up to 7% of referred children with OCD have comorbid Tourette's disorder and 20% have comorbid tics (Coffey & Park, 1997). Some data suggest a difference between the obsessions and compulsions in Tourette's patients with comorbid OCD and those in patients with pure OCD. Tourette's patients tend to have more obsessions focused on symmetry and doing things until they are "just right," along with more aggressive and sexual obsessions (Faridi & Suchowersky, 2003). In addition, these individuals may have an earlier age of onset, are more commonly male, and may be less responsive to treatment with selective serotonin reuptake inhibitors (SSRIs; American Psychiatric Association, 2000). Furthermore, individuals affected by comorbid Tourette's and OCD may engage in more touching and counting behaviors, whereas OCD patients without Tourette's report more contamination obsessions, washing compulsions, and hoarding (American Psychiatric Association, 2000; Faridi & Suchowersky, 2003).

A number of other comorbidities have also been reported among those with Tourette's disorder. As with any disorder where the impairment is entirely apparent to others, those affected may suffer any number of psychosocial difficulties. Symptoms of anxiety (especially phobias and separation anxiety) and depression may be due to the stress and public humiliation that individuals with Tourette's often feel or perhaps due to some shared genetic roots between anxiety disorders and Tourette's (Swain et al., 2007). Impairments in peer relations and social skills have also been reported (Bawden, Stokes, Camfield, Camfield, & Salisbury, 1998; A. S. Carter et al., 2000). As many as one third of children with Tourette's and ADHD may be diagnosed with a learning disorder, although this finding may rest more on the ADHD than the Tourette's (Faridi & Suchowersky, 2003). Finally, migraine headaches are also up to four times more common among those with Tourette's disorder (Swain et al., 2007).

There are a number of rating scales available for assessing tics, including the Tourette Syndrome Global Scale (TSGS), the Yale Global Tic Severity Scale (YGTSS), and the Tourette's Disorder Scale (TODS). These simple tracking devices are useful for determining the nature and severity of tics and for following them over time. Probably the most commonly utilized scale is the YGTSS, which allows the clinician and family to rate tic symptoms upon a Likert scale from "not at all present" to "almost always present."

TREATMENT

At the outset, education and support of the child as well as his or her peers, family, and school are vital. Because tics and Tourette's cause the child to stand out, everyone in his or her circle of family and friends should be taught about the disorder. Not infrequently, parents will come to the child's school and instruct the teachers and other children about the disorder, often resulting in great success. The Tourette Syndrome Association (http://www.tsa-usa.org) has many online resources, including instructional material and videos that families can use to educate themselves, teachers, and the child's peers. Although not a direct treatment for the tics themselves, supportive counseling and family therapy are also often helpful for the child and family, respectively, in dealing with the stress of the disorder, enhancing coping skills, and supporting self-esteem and adjustment at school. Diet, exercise, and other lifestyle changes may be helpful as well by decreasing overall stress, which may lessen the tics.

Given the overwhelming prevalence of comorbid psychiatric disorders, their treatment must also be one of the clinician's first considerations. The treatment of ADHD, OCD, and other coexisting disorders often leads to improvement in the tics as well (Swain et al., 2007). OCD should be treated with cognitive behavior therapy (CBT) along with an SSRI antidepressant (e.g., fluoxetine, sertraline, fluvoxamine, paroxetine, citalopram, or escitalopram) or clomipramine if indicated (see Chapter 10). Because some children with OCD and comorbid Tourette's disorder do not seem to respond as well to SSRIs as children with OCD who do not have Tourette's, augmenting the treatment with an antipsychotic medication, which appears to enhance the effect of the SSRI, is often useful and not uncommon (Bloch et al., 2006).

Historically, there was great concern that stimulants would "unmask" tics or cause them to worsen. Psychiatrists were hesitant to prescribe stimulants for the treatment of ADHD in an individual suffering from a tic or Tourette's disorder given anecdotal reports of deterioration. However, numerous recent studies, including double-blind, placebo-controlled trials, have found that stimulants do not cause a significant worsening of tics among these patients (Erenberg, 2005; Kurlan, 2003). These same studies have also demonstrated that ADHD responds equally well to stimulants among those who have tics and Tourette's. While no statistically significant group effects have been demonstrated, there is no doubt that some individuals will at least acutely experience an increase in the severity of their tics when they are treated with a stimulant. However, because of the natural waxing and waning of tics, which can be coincident with medication changes, the practitioner must not rush to judgment that a certain medication either relieved or worsened the tic symptoms. Rather, a thoughtful and measured approach to medication changes will serve the patient best by giving each treatment an adequate trial before labeling it beneficial or detrimental.

Although no medications have been approved by the Food and Drug Administration for the treatment of tics, pharmacological treatments are frequently employed and very often helpful. The older antipsychotic medications—haloperidol (Haldol) and pimozide (Orap)—have been approved by the FDA for treatment of Tourette's, and along with risperidone (Risperdal) have the best evidence of efficacy, with numerous randomized, double-blind, placebo-controlled trials supporting their use (Swain et al., 2007). While their mechanism of action in the treatment of tics and Tourette's is not known, it is thought that dopamine receptor blockade of the basal ganglia is foremost in their beneficial effects. Although adequate long-term safety studies of these medications have not been performed and would likely prove them to be equally troublesome, albeit in different ways, risperidone is now more commonly employed than haloperidol, given its relative ease of use. Prior to treatment with an antipsychotic, the practitioner should consider the safety guidelines laid out in Chapter 15 and collect adequate baseline patient data. If starting with risperidone, an initial dosage of 0.25 to 0.5 mg per day would be typical, perhaps given in divided doses. In the aforementioned studies, dosages of risperidone have ranged between 1.0 and 3.5 mg per day. Pimozide is now used less frequently, given its greater likelihood of causing cardiac disturbance via extending the QTc rhythm (Zemrak & Kenna, 2008).

Other antipsychotic medications have also shown promise in the treatment of tics and Tourette's. In one small double-blind, placebo-controlled trial, ziprasidone (Geodon) demonstrated efficacy (Sallee et al., 2000). Because of its novel mechanism of action as a mixed dopamine agonist/antagonist, there is also a great deal of interest in aripiprazole (Abilify), which has proven beneficial for the treatment of tics and Tourette's in case studies and open-label trials (Seo, Sung, Sea, & Bai, 2008; Davies, Stern, Agrawal, & Robertson, 2006; Wenzel, Kleimann, Bokemeyer, & Muller-Vahl, 2012). Finally, olanzapine (Zyprexa), quetiapine (Seroquel), and clozapine (Clozaril), three additional antipsychotics, have also demonstrated efficacy in open-label trials, chart reviews, and case reports for the treatment of tics and Tourette's (Copur, Arpaci, Demir, & Narin, 2007; Jaffe, Trémeau, Sharif, & Reider, 1995; McCracken, Suddath, Chang, Thakur, & Piacentini, 2008; Mukaddes, & Abali, 2003; R. J. Stephens, Bassel, & Sandor, 2004; Van den Eynde, Naudts, De Saedeleer, van Heeringen, & Audenaert, 2005).

More-benign and commonly utilized first treatments are the alpha-2 agonists, clonidine (Catapres) and guanfacine (Tenex), which have also shown benefit in case studies and single- and double-blind studies (Eddy, Rickards, & Cavanna, 2011). These medications are generally prescribed for adults with hypertension, where they act centrally in the brain by decreasing norepinephrine tone. They are thought to resolve tics by essentially the same mechanism of action at dosages of 1 to 2 mg two to three times a day for guanfacine or 0.1 to 0.2 mg two to four times a day for clonidine. When starting an alpha-2 agonist, it is wise to begin dosing in the evening, such as 0.05 mg of clonidine or 0.5 mg of guanfacine about an hour before bedtime. If well tolerated and a higher dosage seems necessary after three to four days, adding another pill about four to six hours prior to the first, and later a third tablet in the morning by the same titration, is common practice. When discontinuing clonidine or guanfacine, the taper should be done in the same way and with the same pacing but in reverse order (see Chapter 3). Offering another medication delivery system for children, a large multicenter, randomized, double-blind, placebo-controlled study of over 400 children and adolescents with mixed tic disorders in China employed the clonidine patch at doses of 1 to 2 mg per week and found a statistically significant reduction in tics among those treated with the patch (Du et al., 2008).

A number of other medications have been employed for the treatment of tics and Tourette's, some of which have reasonable data to support their use. Desipramine, a tricyclic antidepressant, for example, has been shown in a double-blind, placebo-controlled study to reduce symptoms of ADHD by 42% and tics by 30% from baseline (Spencer et al., 2002). Practitioners are advised, however, to proceed cautiously with tricyclic antidepressants when treating children and adolescents, given their potential for cardiac toxicity (see Chapter 12). Pergolide (Permax), a dopamine agonist that is used in the treatment of Parkinson's disease, has also been shown in double-blind studies to be moderately effective but has been removed from the U.S. market because of its potential to cause cardiac valvular disease (Gilbert et al., 2003; Gilbert, Sethuraman, Sine, Peters, & Sallee, 2000). Given promising case reports, pramipexole (Mirapex), another dopamine agonist used in the treatment of Parkinson's and restless legs syndrome, was investigated in a multicenter, randomized, double-blind, placebo-controlled study and found to be ineffective (Kurlan et al., 2012). Numerous other medications, including flunarizine, naloxone, baclofen, opiates, delta-9-tetrahydrocannabinol, baclofen, buspirone, tetrabenazine, sulpiride, tiapride, botulinum toxin, nicotine, L-dopa, odansetron, metaclopramide, topiramate, levetiracetam, donepezil, selegiline, and benzodiazepines, have limited supporting data from small trials and case studies but would generally only be attempted after failure of numerous other treatments with more evidence of efficacy (Eddy et al., 2011; Faridi & Suchowersky, 2003; Kurlan, 2014; Swain et al., 2007).

Should a child present in the context of a recent strep throat infection with a case of rapid-onset tics, Tourette's, and/or obsessive-compulsive symptoms suggestive of PANDAS, the child should receive a throat culture. Blood work for ASO (antistreptolysin O) titer and anti-DNase B should also be performed. If the index of suspicion remains high, a full course of antibiotics should be employed, such as penicillin V potassium or amoxicillin, at therapeutic dosages for 10 to 14 days. Should symptoms continue, immunomodulatory therapies, such as intravenous immunoglobulin and therapeutic plasma exchange, have both proven useful in a placebo-controlled trial (Swedo, Garvey, Snider, Hamilton, & Leonard, 2001). However, at present these treatments should only be performed within the context of a research trial or by an experienced clinician.

While often effective, medications should be attempted for the treatment of tics and Tourette's disorder only after other treatments have failed because of their potential to cause side effects. Mild difficulties are unlikely to require medication, as many affected individuals can hide their tics or do well without any major disruption in their lives. If education, relaxation, and supportive therapies are not adequately effective, a trial of a more specific therapy is indicated prior to the use of medication.

Behavioral therapies in general have not resulted in remarkable benefits for most patients (R. A. King, Scahill, Findley, & Cohen, 1999). However, in recent years a more precise treatment for tics has emerged that has supporting data from case studies and randomized trials (Swain et al., 2007). Habit reversal training (HRT) is a behavioral treatment designed to treat repetitive behavior disorders, such as tics, nail biting, trichotillomania, skin picking, and thumb sucking. HRT relies on five aspects: (1) awareness training, (2) competing response training, (3) contingency management, (4) relaxation training, and (5) generalization training. In the treatment of tics and Tourette's, these five components are designed to increase the awareness of one's tics and then to allow for the development of a competing response that the individual will perform instead of the tic. For example, when the patient feels the urge to tic, instead of shouting out he or she will learn to stomp a foot lightly, squeeze a hand into a fist, and so forth. These competing responses are more socially acceptable and less disruptive. In order for HRT to be effective, the patient must have a premonitory urge or a sensation of some sort that occurs prior to the tic. When applicable, HRT is an acceptable and durable treatment for tics that has been found effective in controlled trials (Hwang, Tillberg, & Scahill, 2012; Piacentini & Chang, 2006).

10

Anxiety Disorders

All children experience anxiety. Thus, while approximately 10–32% of children and adolescents suffer from a diagnosable anxiety disorder, many more children, in fact, experience significant anxiety that does not technically meet diagnostic criteria (Merikangas, He, Burstein, et al., 2010; Walkup et al., 2008). For example, studies have found that approximately 40% of grade-school children have fears of separation from their parents; 40% of children aged 6 to 12 years have seven or more specific fears that trouble them; 30% of children worry about their competence and require considerable and regular reassurance; and 20% of grade-school children are afraid of heights, shy in new situations, or anxious about public speaking and social acceptance (Bell-Dolan, Last, & Strauss, 1990). Girls typically report more anxiety and stress than boys, although this finding may be an artifact of social expectations, as boys are encouraged to be "tough" and not to share their worries. Thankfully, children outgrow most of their worries as they age and mature.

As most of us recognize, some anxiety is useful and even necessary in order to motivate us to action. In 1908, Yerkes and Dodson proposed the curve seen in Figure 10.1 to explain the relationship between the level of arousal or stress and performance. As described by Yerkes and Dodson, one's performance typically increases as one's arousal, anxiety, or stress increases, up to a certain optimal level. At some point, however, when the level of arousal or anxiety gets too high, one's performance becomes impaired. Research as well as practical experience suggests that the Yerkes-Dodson correlation does exist, but the reasons for the relationship have yet to be elucidated (J. R. Anderson, 2000; K. J. Anderson, Revelle, & Lynch, 1989; Broadhurst, 1957; E. Duffy, 1957).

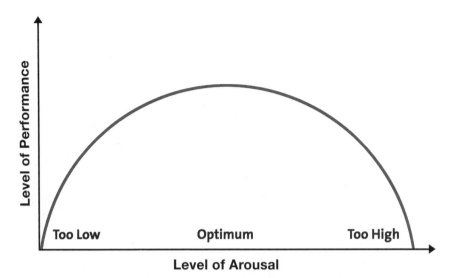

Figure 10.1 Yerkes-Dodson correlation. As proposed by Yerkes and Dodson, performance improves at an optimal level of arousal. Both minimal and maximal arousal result in impaired performance. Source: Adapted from Yerkes and Dodson (1908).

A number of questions help us to distinguish normal or typical anxiety from pathological anxiety in children and adolescents. We must first wonder about the object of worry. Is this issue something a child this age should be worrying about? Second, we must ask ourselves whether the degree of distress is reasonable or realistic given the child's developmental stage. We then look at the degree of impairment. Is the anxiety interfering with the child's life on a daily basis? How is the child's social, academic, and family functioning affected by the anxiety? Finally, we want to know about the child's coping skills. Is the child still bothered even when the stressor is not present? Does the child worry about future occurrences, and is the anxiety present across multiple settings?

Given that fear and worry are normative experiences, the clinician must be able to distinguish developmentally normal from abnormal fears and worries. Infants, for example, are commonly fearful of loud noises, surprises, and strangers. Toddlers may be fearful of imaginary creatures or monsters, darkness, and separation from their parents and siblings. While some degree of worry is normal, children with high levels of anxiety early in life are more likely to continue to suffer from anxiety as they age. Children who are confident and eager to explore novel situations at 5 years of age are less likely to manifest anxiety in later childhood and adolescence, yet children who are passive, shy, or fearful, and avoid new situations at the same age, are more likely to exhibit anxiety later in life (Caspi,

Henry, McGee, Moffitt, & Silva, 1995). In general, younger children tend to report more normative anxiety symptoms than older children.

School-age children often worry about injury and natural events and disasters, such as storms, lightning, earthquakes, and volcanoes. These children may also interpret ambiguous or vague situations in a negative way and underestimate their own competency or ability to handle themselves in such situations. For example, they may misread another's facial expression or view a remark made by a peer as a criticism, which only acts to reinforce their anxiety. These children are not being paranoid in a psychotic sense, but they are likely to experience *attribution bias*, an error in cognition based on incomplete evidence and their own high anxiety, which causes them to be more suspicious of others' intentions.

As children age, their anxiety often tends to diminish, but in some cases the anxiety simply finds a new expression (Last, Perrin, Hersen, & Kazdin, 1996). While separation anxiety diminishes in frequency, for example, panic disorder tends to increase with age (Ollendick, 1998). By adolescence, normative fears tend to mirror those of adults more closely and are typically related to school, social capabilities, and issues of physical and mental health.

CLINICAL PRESENTATION

Young children commonly have difficulty recognizing and describing their emotions. It is no surprise, then, that preschool and school-age children suffering from an anxiety disorder often present with physical or somatic symptoms, such as headaches, stomachaches, and nausea. Adolescents are much better at identifying their feelings but still may present, as may younger children, with oppositionality or disruptive behavior when feeling anxious. Although there is much crossover among the anxiety disorders, there are some differences in how children with different disorders present.

Separation Anxiety

Children suffering from separation anxiety experience excessive fear when separated from home or primary attachment figures. The anxiety can be quite severe and commonly occurs not only during separation, but also in anticipation of separation. Children typically worry about their own safety and health or that of their parents. Symptoms may include bedtime resistance and refusal to sleep alone, dreams and nightmares of separation, school refusal, physical or somatic complaints, and disobedience whenever separation is perceived as a possibility.

Specific Phobia

Phobias are fears of particular objects or situations that are either avoided or tolerated with great discomfort. Phobic children and adolescents often have more than one specific fear. Adolescents and adults typically recognize that their fears are unreasonable, but younger children most often do not. Children will commonly avoid situations in which they feel phobic, which can be particularly disruptive and lead to a host of developmental difficulties.

Social Phobia

Some children are particularly scared in social or performance situations. They fear that they will embarrass themselves and have trouble speaking in class, reading aloud, conversing with people they do not know, and attending parties and social gatherings. Whereas children with phobias usually feel better when they are removed from the dreaded objects or situations, children suffering from other anxiety disorders tend to struggle most of the time.

Panic Attacks

Panic attacks, uncomfortable as they are, are a normative experience characterized by brief, intense fear in the absence of a genuine threat or danger along with a number of somatic and cognitive symptoms, such as shortness of breath, palpitations, sweating, dizziness, tremor, derealization, and a fear of going crazy, losing control, or dying. Attacks usually last 10 minutes or less, and individuals often report a desire to flee when they experience an episode. Most individuals will have at least one panic attack in their lifetime. Although uncommon in children, panic attacks are most often seen among those who suffer separation anxiety and social phobia.

Generalized Anxiety

Some children suffer from chronic, excessive, but nonspecific anxiety about many things. Unlike phobias, the anxiety these children experience is a moving target, shifting every so often from one thing to another. These children have trouble managing their anxiety and experience numerous manifestations and somatic symptoms, such as difficulty sleeping, irritability, muscle tension, difficulty concentrating, and restlessness.

Obsessions and Compulsions

Children who experience obsessive thoughts feel unable to control their worries and the compulsive behaviors they employ to neutralize their anxiety. These children and adolescents are universally very private about their thoughts and behaviors, which even they experience as strange and out of the ordinary. In fact, these children are so secretive and ashamed of their thoughts and behaviors that symptoms commonly exist for years before reaching clinical attention, if ever. Parents often unwittingly collude with their children in worsening the symptoms by providing constant reassurance, which only tends to invigorate and perpetuate the anxiety.

ETIOLOGY

The etiology or cause of anxiety is highly complex and has roots in our genes, neuroanatomy, endocrine function, neurotransmitters, and environment. One measureable temperamental construct, *behavioral inhibition*, has been helpful in understanding the development of child and adolescent anxiety. Behavioral inhibition is defined as the tendency to be unusually withdrawn or timid and to show fear and avoidance in novel or unfamiliar social and nonsocial situations (Smoller et al., 2005). Those who are withdrawn only in social situations are simply considered shy. Both behavioral inhibition and shyness are associated with anxiety disorders in children and adults (Van Ameringen, Mancini, & Oakman, 1998), and the tendency to approach or withdraw from novel situations appears to be an enduring temperamental trait (Moehler et al., 2008) that may have its roots in our genetic code (Smoller et al., 2008).

Behaviorally inhibited children demonstrate a host of physiological signs often associated with anxiety, including enhanced sympathetic nervous system tone (e.g., elevated resting heart rate and salivary cortisol), increased tension in the vocal cords and larynx, and elevations in urinary catecholamines (Kagan, Reznick, & Snidman, 1988). Children who demonstrate behavioral inhibition in laboratory settings are more likely to suffer multiple psychiatric disorders and two or more anxiety disorders, particularly social phobia, separation anxiety disorder (SAD), and agoraphobia (Biederman et al., 1993; Hirshfeld et al., 1992; Kagan & Snidman, 1999). These children have also been found to be at higher risk for panic disorder and phobias as they age (Smoller et al., 2005). Behavioral inhibition is also associated with a family history of anxiety, and children of parents with panic disorder with agoraphobia are at increased risk for behavioral inhibition (Rosenbaum et al., 1993). In summary, studies of behavioral inhibition demonstrate that these traits are heritable and predict the later onset of anxiety disorders. Whether behavioral inhibition is due to genes or the environment, however, remains unclear.

The neurobiology of anxiety is under active investigation, and numerous neural structures and networks appear to have important roles. In order to promote survival, the brain has many redundant mechanisms for sensing threat and responding rapidly. The reticular activating system, a group of neural systems involved in arousal, appears to be at the center of these networks. The locus coeruleus, the seat of noradrenergic neurons that project throughout the brain, is important in mobilizing the body in response to a perceived threat. The dorsal raphe nucleus, which houses the serotonin neuron cell bodies, can affect the sensitivity of the locus coeruleus. Cholinergic neuron projections, found within the lateral dorsal tegmentum, constitute yet another component of the reticular activating system, as do the dopamine neurons emanating from the substantia nigra, which project into mesolimbic and mesocortical areas, playing a vital role in the brain's sensation and interpretation of threat (Perry, 1998). Finally, varying expressions or genetic polymorphisms of gamma-aminobutyric acid, or GABA (the major inhibitory neurotransmitter in the central nervous system), cortisol (a potent steroid hormone released in response to stress), adenosine receptors (which act to slow metabolic activity within the brain), and catechol-O-methyltransferase, or COMT (an enzyme that degrades catecholamines, such as dopamine, epinephrine, and norepinephrine), have been implicated in anxiety disorders. Various drugs and medications that affect these brain structures, including the alpha-2 agonists, the selective serotonin reuptake inhibitors (SSRIs), tricyclic antidepressants, and stimulants, have major effects on anxiety by modulating these systems.

The limbic system, the brain's emotional processing hub, is a complicated network of subcortical structures, which include the amygdala, hippocampus, cingulate gyrus, hypothalamus, fornix, and thalamus. The amygdala receives neural projections from many areas (e.g., the sensory thalamus, the hippocampus, the entorhinal cortex) and plays a central role in orchestrating the brain's response to this sensory input by sending projections to motor, autonomic, and neuroendocrine systems. Although anxiety is believed to be recognized at the site of the amygdala, the hippo-campus is likely to be the storage site of cognitive and emotional memories. The hippocampus itself is highly sensitive to stress, which impairs its ability to accurately store certain types of information and may promote some of the cognitive distortions associated with anxiety disorders (Perry, 1998).

The human brain is designed to allow for pairing of cues, such as the honk of a car's horn and fear of harm. Once the horn is heard, the brain rapidly assesses for any real threat and responds. It is precisely this amazing ability of the brain to generalize from a common event, such as a horn honking, to a specific action, such as jumping out of the way, however, that makes us vulnerable to false associations and over-generalizations. The brain is evolutionarily primed to make associations between threats and outcomes to promote survival, but once these cues (e.g., heights) become paired with emotions (e.g., anxiety), it is up to the individual's limbic sensitivity and cortex-mediated subjective appraisal to determine the appropriate response (Perry, 1998).

Family studies demonstrate that anxiety disorders tend to run in families. However, as yet, few twin studies have been completed (Kendler, 2001), and candidate genes for anxiety disorders are few (Donner et al., 2008). Heritability estimates exist for some illnesses, such as panic dis-order at 48% and generalized anxiety disorder (GAD) at 32% (Hettema, Neale, & Kendler, 2001). Given these estimates, it is clear that genes account for only some portion of the increase in risk among family mem-bers of an affected individual. Environmental factors, then, such as peri-natal exposures and developmental experience, must play a major role.

Some anxieties may be due to genetically fixed patterns developed over eons of evolution. For example, it is likely that many humans are afraid of snakes because fear of snakes or fear of slithering reptiles has been passed down and has become a part of our genetic code. Children mirror their parents' responses when interpreting internal states of pain, arousal, and anxiety. Consequently, children who grow up in a home with snakes or with parents who are comfortable handling snakes themselves will quite likely have no difficulties in this regard. Thus, it appears that while some anxiety is learned or easily built upon a genetically vulnerable substrate, anxiety can also be unlearned. Over time, children may come to pair a host of external cues, such as snakes, to anxiety following upon their parents' worries. When exposed to these cues, the child will perceive the situation as potentially threatening and will experience symptoms of anxiety. This learned response hypothesis is thought to be important in many cases of specific phobias, some types of posttraumatic stress disor-der (PTSD), and GAD (Ronan & Kendall, 1990).

In an effort to put these various etiological perspectives together, let us consider obsessive-compulsive disorder (OCD) as a modal anxiety disorder. First, we recognize a genetic component, given the elevated concordance between monozygotes, or identical twins (vs. dizygotes, or nonidentical twins), and the increased rates seen among first-degree relatives of affected individuals or probands (Towbin & Riddle, 1996). Physiologically, we know that individuals with OCD have increased brain metabolic activity in the orbitofrontal cortex and caudate nucleus when they actively obsess, as demonstrated by positron emission tomography (PET) scans (Baxter et al., 1992). We also know that the endocrine system is somehow involved in OCD, as affected individuals have been shown to have elevated levels of cerebrospinal oxytocin, a hormone that is typically released in large amounts when a woman is breastfeeding and that appears to increase bonding behavior between mother and child (Towbin & Riddle, 1996). Some of the behaviors associated with OCD are similar to the behavioral effects of oxytocin, such as repetitive grooming and obsessive worrying (Leckman et al., 1994). Finally, the neurotransmitter serotonin figures prominently in our understanding of OCD, as moderate to high dosages of medications that promote serotonin are highly effective in the treatment of this disorder.

EPIDEMIOLOGY

Anxiety disorders may be the most prevalent mental illness affecting children and teens. Various large epidemiological studies tell us that somewhere between 6% and 20% of children suffer at least one major anxiety disorder prior to age 18 (Costello, Egger, & Angold, 2004). The largest prevalence study to date among youth found that anxiety disorders are the most common psychiatric condition in adolescents, affecting 32% of 13- to 18-year-olds with a median age of onset at 6 years (Merikangas, He, Burstein, 2010b). While impressive, these numbers are themselves somewhat deceiving because we know that many additional children experience subclinical anxiety not meeting formal *DSM-5* criteria but causing significant impairment and disability (Angold, Costello, Farmer, Burns, & Erkanli, 1999). In a study of nearly 800 eleven-year-olds, J. C. Anderson, Williams, McGee, and Silva (1987) reported that 3.5% suffered from separation anxiety disorder (SAD), 2.9% from overanxious disorder (a *DSM-III* diagnosis for what we now call GAD), 2.4% from specific phobia, and 1% from social phobia. Other studies have found similar rates (Bowen, Offord, & Boyle, 1990). In a study of over 5,000 fourteen- to seventeen-year-olds, the lifetime prevalence of panic disorder was 0.6% (Whitaker et al., 1990).

Although anxiety disorders often lessen over time, one disorder may simply substitute or replace another (Last et al., 1996). Untreated anxiety leads to an increased risk of additional anxiety disorders, depression, educational underachievement, and substance abuse in childhood (Connolly & Bernstein, 2007) and an increased risk of anxiety and depression in adulthood (Pine, Cohen, Gurley, Brook, & Ma, 1998). Girls are more commonly affected by anxiety than boys (U.S. Department of Health and Human Services, 1999), and anxiety in the first grade has been shown to predict anxiety and low academic achievement in reading and math by fifth grade (Ialongo, Edelsohn, Werthamer-Larsson, Crockett, & Kellam, 1995).

Risk factors for the development of anxiety disorders include shyness and behavioral inhibition (Biederman et al., 1993; Van Ameringen et al., 1998) and parental anxiety disorder (Biederman et al., 2001). Anxious, critical, and overprotective parenting styles also increase a child's risk for anxiety, as does an insecure attachment to the primary caregivers (Connolly & Bernstein, 2007). Sophisticated coping skills, such as distraction and problem-solving strategies rather than avoidance, are considered protective for children (Ayers, Sandler, West, & Roosa, 1996).

CLINICAL COURSE

Children with anxiety disorders are often overwhelmed by their anxiety and do not recognize their fears as unreasonable. Given that they are still in the early stages of cognitive development and it is difficult for them to think in an abstract manner, it is also very difficult for them to reason their way through the worries they experience. Since younger children may not be even aware of their anxiety and often cannot articulate their feelings easily, they most frequently present with physical expressions of their anxiety, such as stomachaches, headaches, diarrhea or constipation, dizziness, chest pain, fear of choking, a lump in the throat (globus hystericus), fatigue or exhaustion, or sleep disturbance. Clues that a child is struggling with anxiety include physical aches and pains, difficulty falling or staying asleep, avoidance of activities outside the home (school, parties, camp, slumber parties, safe strangers, etc.), an excessive need for reassurance (particularly in new situations, at bedtime, during storms, etc.), inattention and poor school performance, and irritability or explosive outbursts. These symptoms or expressions of anxiety may not be pervasive in that some areas of the child's functioning may remain entirely intact, particularly in situations where the child is comfortable and secure.

Generally speaking, childhood anxiety disorders do not readily remit, and the majority of affected adults report retrospectively that they suffered significant difficulties with anxiety as children (Angst & Vollrath, 1991). Given that adolescents often report a greater severity of anxiety than children with the same diagnosis, it is likely that without treatment, symptoms persist and worsen over time (Kendall, Safford, Flannery-Schroeder, & Webb, 2004).

The usual course of most anxiety disorders is chronic, with waxing and waning. As the months and years go by, some individuals will improve, but many may simply "trade" one anxiety disorder for another. Children with a prior anxiety disorder appear to be more likely to suffer not only another anxiety disorder in the future, but also other nonanxiety psychiatric disorders (Last et al., 1996).

Depression, suicidal ideation and suicide attempts, and substance abuse have all been linked to a childhood history of anxiety disorders (Brent et al., 1986; Last, Hersen, Kazdin, Finkelstein, & Strauss, 1993). Studies suggest that anxiety commonly precedes the development of depression and substance abuse and that in at least some cases, drugs and alcohol are used to self-medicate the anxiety (Kendall et al., 2004; Manassis & Monga, 2001). The lifetime comorbidity estimates of substance use and anxiety disorders are quite high, ranging from 33% to 45% (R. C. Kessler et al., 1996; Regier et al., 1990). In addition to these comorbidities, we must also consider the demoralization and damage to one's self-esteem that anxiety sufferers commonly endure. The frustration that these children and adolescents feel often negatively impacts their peer and family relationships and academic functioning (Kendall et al., 2004).

DIAGNOSIS

There is typically low concordance between child and parent reports of anxiety (Barbosa, Tannock, & Manassis, 2002; Choudhury, Pimentel, & Kendall, 2003). While parents tend to overreport symptoms of externalizing or disruptive behavior disorders, children tend to overreport symptoms of internalizing disorders, such as anxiety and depression (Kenny & Faust, 1997). Nonetheless, the best evidence comes from observation of the child and a series of collateral reports on his or her behavior. Older children can report more objectively on their own symptoms, but rating scales are often helpful as well. Two scales commonly used for general anxiety include the Screen for Child Anxiety Related Emotional Disorders (SCARED) and the Multidimensional Anxiety Scale for Children

(MASC). For children with obsessive-compulsive symptoms, the most commonly employed scale is the Children's Yale-Brown Obsessive-Compulsive Scale (CY-BOCS). The Leyton Obsessional Inventory is sometimes used as well for these children.

DSM-III-R (*Diagnostic and Statistical Manual of Mental Disorders*, 3rd edition, revised) included only three childhood anxiety disorders—separation anxiety disorder, overanxious disorder (now known as generalized anxiety disorder), and avoidant disorder (now known as social phobia; American Psychiatric Association, 1987). As our knowledge of childhood anxiety has increased in recent years, the *DSM* has allowed for an expansion of childhood diagnoses into areas previously reserved only for adults, including panic disorder, specific phobia, OCD, and acute stress and PTSD. *DSM-5* has stratified many of the anxiety disorders into subcategories. Separation anxiety disorder, selective mutism, specific phobia, social anxiety disorder, panic disorder, agoraphobia, and generalized anxiety disorder are the primary anxiety disorders; and obsessive-compulsive disorder, body dysmorphic disorder, hoarding disorder, trichotillomania (hair-pulling), and excoriation (skin-picking) are the core of a new *DSM* category, obsessive-compulsive and related disorders. Although grouping the disorders in this way makes some sense due to their nature, by and large these disorders all respond to the same treatments, both psychotherapeutic and psychopharmacologic, and are therefore grouped in the anxiety disorders chapter of this book. Another new diagnostic grouping, trauma- and stressor-related disorders, will be addressed in the next chapter.

Separation Anxiety Disorder

Given that some degree of separation anxiety is normative for most children prior to 3 years of age, separation anxiety disorder (SAD) is understandably the earliest anxiety disorder usually observed. *DSM-5* defines SAD as developmentally inappropriate and unwarranted anxiety regarding separation from home or major attachment figures. Three or more additional symptoms are required for the diagnosis, including excessive distress on separation; extreme worry about losing, or harm coming to, an attachment figure; fears of somehow being separated from an attachment figure, such as by kidnapping or getting lost; refusal to attend school or anywhere else due to fear of separation; refusal to sleep alone at home or away from home; fear of being alone at home or in new situations without attachment figures present; continual nightmares of being separated from attachment figures; and frequent physical complaints upon separation or when planning such events. Finally, *DSM-5* requires at least four weeks of symptoms (American Psychiatric Association, 2013).

Children with SAD often grow up within closely knit families. Upon separation, however, they become sad, withdrawn, and apathetic and have difficulty concentrating. The specific fears that children with SAD report commonly mirror their developmental level, such that younger children may fear monsters and older children airplanes or natural disasters. Death or dying is a frequent concern among these children as well, who are often viewed as demanding because of their need for constant reassurance. Adults with SAD are generally fearful of changes, such as starting a new job or moving, and are overly worried about their children and spouses.

SAD may develop after a major life change or stress, such as the death of a family member or move to a new home. Approximately 4% of children aged 6 to 12 years, 1.6% of adolescents, and 1% to 2% of adults are believed to be affected. SAD is more common among first-degree relatives and in children of mothers with panic disorder than in the general population. Adolescent onset is rare. Girls appear to be affected somewhat more frequently than boys. Typically, the anxiety waxes and wanes over time, with most children being free from anxiety by adulthood. However, some individuals appear to be at greater risk of depression and dysthymia, and SAD may precede the onset of panic disorder with agoraphobia, among other anxiety disorders (American Psychiatric Association, 2013).

Panic Disorder

Panic attacks per se are not considered a psychiatric diagnosis, given the preponderance of individuals who experience at least one such episode in their lifetime. Furthermore, panic attacks are ubiquitous among a host of medical and psychiatric conditions, including mood, substance use, and anxiety disorders, as well as cardiac, respiratory, vestibular, and gastrointestinal disorders.

Two types of panic attacks are typically described, those that are unexpected or uncued and those that are situationally bound or cued. In the former, the attacks are always unexpected and occur "out of the blue," as opposed to the latter, which generally occur during or in anticipation of a feared situation, such as a school examination or flying in an airplane. Unexpected panic attacks are required for a *DSM-5* diagnosis of panic disorder. Cued or situationally bound panic attacks are also common in panic disorder but do occur in the context of other anxiety disorders, such as social phobia and PTSD. In addition to recurrent, unexpected panic attacks, *DSM-5* requires that at least one of the panic attacks be followed by one month or more of persistent fear of having additional attacks, fear of the implications of the attack (e.g., having a heart attack or going insane), or a major behavior change following the attack (American Psychiatric Association, 2013). Agoraphobia, literally a "fear of the open marketplace" but in actuality a fear of being in a place or situation from which one cannot easily exit or escape, may also accompany panic disorder.

The 12-month prevalence of panic disorder with or without agoraphobia is somewhere between 2% and 3% in adolescents and adults. Higher rates are generally found in clinical samples, with up to 10% of psychiatrically referred adults and up to 6% of psychiatrically referred children demonstrating diagnostic symptoms (Biederman et al., 1997). These numbers are considerably higher among adults in respiratory, vestibular, and gastrointestinal clinics, where up to 30% are affected, and cardiology clinics, where up to 60% are affected. Up to one half of community samples demonstrate comorbid agoraphobia, but the rate among clinical samples is higher. Panic attacks, on the other hand, are much more common, affecting over 10% of the U.S. population of adults annually (American Psychiatric Association, 2000, 2013).

Panic attacks are uncommon prior to puberty. Onset in most cases is between late adolescence and approximately 30 years of age. Affected children may complain of physical symptoms, appear frightened or upset without explanation, be unable to articulate the intense fears they are experiencing, demonstrate behavior that is confusing to onlookers, and explain their symptoms as a response to external triggers. Adolescents are generally much better able to describe what they are experiencing. First-degree relatives are up to 8 times more likely to develop panic disorder; this number increases to up to 20 times more likely if the age of onset of the proband or index case is under 20 years old. Panic disorder is often viewed as a chronic condition, although longitudinal studies have primarily been performed in psychiatric treatment centers where recidivism is generally elevated, and prevalence decreases greatly with age (e.g., down to 0.7% in adults over the age of 64 years; American Psychiatric Association, 2000, 2013).

As previously noted, comorbidity with other anxiety disorders is high. Social phobia and generalized anxiety disorder affect 15% to 30% of individuals with panic disorder, specific phobia affects 2% to 20%, and obsessive-compulsive disorder affects as many as 10%. PTSD may occur in 10% or more of those affected, and SAD and hypochondriasis are common. Rates of coexisting major depressive disorder are also high, and studies vary, with somewhere between 10% and 65% of panic sufferers being affected. In most individuals the depression co-occurs with or follows the panic. In a minority of cases the depression precedes the panic. Finally, some individuals with panic disorder misuse alcohol and drugs in an effort to treat their anxiety (American Psychiatric Association, 2000, 2013).

There are no diagnostic laboratory tests, although a number of abnormalities have been consistently found among groups of individuals with panic disorder. Most notably, some individuals demonstrate a compensated respiratory alkalosis (e.g., decreased carbon dioxide and bicarbonate levels in the presence of a nearly normal pH), and some are easily provoked into an attack with sodium lactate or carbon dioxide inhalation. Debate remains as to the role of mitral valve prolapse and thyroid disease in panic. Certainly, many individuals with panic disorder are hypersensitive to physical cues and medication side effects for fear of experiencing an attack (American Psychiatric Association, 2000, 2013).

Specific Phobias

A phobia is characterized by severe unreasonable and continual anxiety brought on by the presence or anticipation of a feared situation or object. In order for the *DSM-5* definition to hold, the individual must always experience excessive anxiety, perhaps even a panic attack, after exposure to the feared object or situation or in anticipation of it. Children, however, may respond with a tantrum or by crying or clinging to an adult. Phobic adults generally recognize their fears as excessive, but this is often not the case with children. At the very least, the *DSM* demands that the anxiety be out of proportion to the real danger of the situation or object. Affected individuals generally avoid those situations or objects that bother them but in some cases may suffer through exposure to the feared stimulus with great discomfort (American Psychiatric Association, 2013).

DSM-5 defines the four most common types of phobia as animal type (cued by animals or insects, with onset generally in childhood); natural environmental type (cued by naturally occurring objects in the environment, such as lightning or heights, with onset generally in childhood); blood-injection-injury type (cued by fear of injury, blood, injection, or venipuncture, often running in families and associated with a vasovagal response); and situational type (cued by feared situations, such as driving over a bridge or in a tunnel, flying, or being in an elevator). Other phobias not uncommonly observed in children include fear of vomiting, choking, costumed characters, loud sounds, or getting sick (American Psychiatric Association, 2013).

Fears are common among children and adolescents but rarely cause enough difficulty to warrant a diagnosis of specific phobia. Community samples show 12-month prevalence rates as high as 9% and lifetime prevalence rates as high as 11%, with decline among the elderly to 3% to 5%. Prevalence rates are about 5% in children and 16% in 13- to 17-year-olds. Females are affected about twice as often as males, and phobias tend to aggregate in families. The first symptoms usually occur in childhood or early adolescence but may not show up, particularly for situational phobias such as one brought on by experiencing an extremely turbulent flight, until the mid-20s. Comorbidities are common, affecting as many as 80% of individuals. Typically the comorbid conditions cause more distress than the phobias themselves, which rarely bring individuals to treatment (American Psychiatric Association, 2000, 2013).

Social Anxiety Disorder (Social Phobia)

Social phobia is characterized by consistent fear of social or performance situations in which the individual fears embarrassment or judgment by others. Affected individuals worry that they will be humiliated in performance situations or demonstrate symptoms of anxiety. *DSM-5* requires that children have an established capacity for age-appropriate social relationships and that the anxiety occur with peers as well as adults. As with specific phobia, the individual must always experience excessive anxiety, perhaps even a panic attack, after exposure to a feared social situation. Other common physical signs of anxiety include palpitations, sweating, tremors, and gastrointestinal symptoms such as diarrhea or vomiting. Children, however, may respond only with a tantrum or by crying or clinging to an adult. Socially phobic adults generally recognize their fears as excessive, but this is often not the case with children. At the very least, the *DSM* demands that the anxiety be out of proportion to the real danger of the social situation. Affected individuals generally avoid situations that bother them but in some cases may suffer through exposure to the social situation with great discomfort. *DSM-5* requires a symptom duration of at least six months prior to diagnosis. Socially phobic individuals are often passive, are often hypersensitive to criticism or rejection, and tend to demonstrate low self-esteem and feelings of inferiority (although these tendencies are not diagnostic; American Psychiatric Association, 2013).

Although the ratio is not entirely clear, women tend to suffer more often than men. The 12-month prevalence is about 7% in the United

States but generally much lower in other countries, 0.5% to 2%, even when using the same diagnostic measures. Like other anxiety disorders, social phobia typically occurs more frequently among first-degree relatives (American Psychiatric Association, 2013).

Obsessive-Compulsive Disorder

OCD is characterized by repeated obsessions and/or compulsions that require extensive time (more than one hour each day) or cause severe distress or impairment. Obsessions are defined as intrusive and inappropriate thoughts, impulses, or images that cause significant anguish. Affected individuals typically try to ignore or suppress the troubling obsessions, generally but not always maintaining good insight, realizing that these thoughts are due to anxiety. Unlike most adults, children with OCD may not realize that the obsessions and compulsions are excessive or unreasonable. Compulsions, on the other hand, are the behavioral corollary of obsessions. They are defined as repeated behaviors, such as hand washing and checking, or mental acts, such as counting or praying, that an individual feels forced to do in response to an obsession or according to some rules that s/he feels must be followed. The compulsive behaviors or mental acts are consciously or unconsciously designed to prevent or reduce the stress that the individual feels but are not linked in any real way to the thoughts, images, or impulses they are trying to counteract or stop (American Psychiatric Association, 2013).

The most common obsessions are related to contamination (e.g., dirt, germs, or illness), aggression (e.g., fear of hurting oneself or others), hoarding, sexual content (e.g., having "forbidden" or perverse sexual thoughts), superstitions, and scrupulosity. As expected, the most common compulsions are behavioral manifestations of these same obsessions, designed to neutralize the thoughts, and include excessive cleaning and hand washing, checking to make sure that nothing is wrong, repeating, counting, ordering, arranging, hoarding, and engaging in superstitious acts. Unfortunately, these compulsive behaviors, the very acts designed to counteract the obsessions and relieve the anxiety (which they often very briefly do), rapidly become problems in their own right as the individual feels unable to stop them. In contrast to autism spectrum disorders, the obsessive thoughts and compulsive behaviors of OCD are *ego-dystonic* (see Chapter 8).

Epidemiological studies of children and adolescents worldwide estimate a 12-month prevalence of roughly 1% to 2%. OCD typically begins in adolescence or early adulthood but may begin in childhood. Modal age at onset for males, 6 to 15 years of age, is typically earlier than for females, 20 to 29 years of age. In adults, the disorder is equally common in males and females, but in childhood the disorder is more common in boys. OCD has a higher concordance among monozygotic (identical) as opposed to dizygotic (fraternal) twins. As with other anxiety disorders, there is a greater risk of OCD among first-degree relatives of affected individuals (American Psychiatric Association, 2013).

Onset is typically gradual, but acute onset can occur. Children often do not seek help, as the symptoms may not be as ego-dystonic or as uncomfortable as they are in adults. Some women experience new-onset OCD after pregnancy and childbirth, which may have to do with elevated levels of oxytocin. PANDAS (pediatric autoimmune neuropsychiatric disorders associated with streptococcal infections), as described in Chapter 9, may also be a cause of OCD.

Comorbidities are common among those with OCD. Coexisting conditions among adults may include a mood disorder (lifetime prevalence of 63%, with depression being the most common at 41%), another anxiety disorder (lifetime prevalence of 76%), eating disorders, and obsessive-compulsive personality disorder (lifetime prevalence of 23% to 32%); among children, OCD is more commonly associated with other anxiety disorders, learning disorders, and disruptive behavior disorders. As noted in Chapter 9, OCD is strongly linked with Tourette's disorder, with up to 7% of referred children with OCD having comorbid Tourette's and 30% having comorbid tics. Comorbid obsessive-compulsive spectrum disorders such as trichotillomania, body dysmorphia, and habits, such as nail-biting, are not common but not rare among affected children. Finally, among those with schizophrenia or schizoaffective disorder, OCD is present in up to 12% (American Psychiatric Association, 2000, 2013).

Like other anxiety disorders, OCD generally has a waxing and waning course, with the vast majority of patients showing a continuous course of illness and about 15% of affected individuals showing progressive deterioration (Rasmussen & Tsuang, 1986). A review of long-term outcome studies comprising over 500 individuals with OCD first diagnosed in childhood found that 41% of individuals had full OCD and 60% had full or subthreshold OCD between 1 and 16 years following diagnosis (Stewart et al., 2004).

Generalized Anxiety Disorder

GAD is characterized by extreme anxiety and apprehension about numerous events or activities, such as work or school, more days than not for at least six months. The *DSM-5* diagnosis demands that an affected individual find it difficult to manage the anxiety and have a number of symptoms (only one symptom is required in children), such as restlessness, fatigue, impairment in attention and concentration, irritability, muscle tension, or sleep disruption. Many affected individuals also suffer from other physical symptoms of anxiety, such as sweating, nausea, or diarrhea, in addition to being easily startled. Symptoms characteristic of panic, such as shortness of breath and palpitations, are not common in GAD (American Psychiatric Association, 2013).

The lifetime prevalence of GAD is about 9%. Epidemiological studies have found that roughly two thirds of those affected are women. GAD is frequently comorbid with mood disorders, other anxiety disorders, and substance use disorders. Most affected individuals report having experienced symptoms of anxiety since childhood, but the median age of onset is 30 years, later than that of all other anxiety disorders (American Psychiatric Association, 2013).

Among children and adolescents, the worries experienced are usually developmentally age appropriate. Children commonly express concerns about school, athletics, peer relations, and catastrophic events such as plane crashes or hurricanes. Affected children may place a great deal of pressure on themselves, be perfectionistic, and seek reassurance from adults and teachers, for whom they can be quite taxing (American Psychiatric Association, 2013).

Selective Mutism

Although not an anxiety disorder according to *DSM-IV*, selective mutism has long been considered by many in the field to represent a subtype of social phobia (Black & Uhde, 1992; Yagenah, Beidel, Turner, Pina, & Silverman, 2003). More recent data, however, suggest that while social anxiety is a prominent feature of selective mutism, affected children may also express communication delays and/or mild behavior problems (Cohan et al., 2008). Although its prevalence is not well established, affecting certainly fewer than 0.5% of the population, the diagnosis has been added to *DSM-5*. The clinical presentation of selective mutism is reliable and characterized by repeated refusal to speak in social situations where speaking is expected, such as at school. Children with selective mutism do speak readily, however, with family members and familiar contacts. Affected children are generally shy, socially isolated, and withdrawn; sometimes teased by peers; fearful of embarrassment; and often oppositional at home. Selective mutism is usually evident by 5 years of age (American Psychiatric Association, 2013).

Trichotillomania

Trichotillomania, or chronic hair-pulling, is categorized under the new obsessive-compulsive and related disorders chapter in *DSM-5*. Most cases begin in childhood or adolescence. As with motor and vocal tics, affected individuals commonly report a buildup of tension before hair-pulling or when trying to resist hair-pulling, along with a sense of satisfaction, release, and happiness while pulling or after pulling the hair. The eyebrows, eyelashes, and head are the most common sites of hair-pulling, but all areas of the body can be affected. Hair pulling is typically scattered throughout the day. As with tics, it generally occurs more often when individuals are alone, relaxing, reading, or watching television, although stress can also exacerbate the behavior. Some affected individuals may eat their hair, known as *trichophagia*, which can result in hairballs or bezoars. Examination of the affected areas typically shows damage to the hair follicles and short, broken hairs (American Psychiatric Association, 2013).

Trichotillomania is equally common among boys and girls, but more common among women than men by a ratio of 10:1. The prevalence is unknown, but estimates vary greatly from a high of 4% to a low of 0.6%, with most researchers accepting a prevalence of about 1% (Diefenbach, Reitman, & Williamson, 2000).

TREATMENT

Given the large variety of anxiety disorders, it is notable that the effective treatments are much the same regardless of diagnosis. Treatment should begin with psychoeducation. Parents and children often blame themselves for the anxiety they feel and are ashamed to discuss their symptoms for fear of ridicule, embarrassment, or sounding "crazy." The most important first step, then, is for the clinician to normalize the anxiety and remove the blame. With both children and adults, this phase of treatment includes teaching about the brain, neurochemistry, and the body's response to anxiety. Patients are taught that they have a "supercharged" fight-or-flight response, which would have been helpful for our evolutionary ancestors on the African savanna who were vulnerable to lions but, unfortunately, sometimes gets in their way in the modern world. It is also often helpful to externalize the anxiety by giving it a name. Children, in particular, enjoy naming their anxiety, such as calling it "bully" or any other name they choose. When bothered by their anxiety, they can say, either out loud or to themselves, "Leave me alone, bully!" Such seemingly simple approaches can sometimes make all the difference to a struggling patient. Second, the clinician should inform the patient and family that anxiety disorders are extremely common, that the patient is not alone, and that these disorders are highly responsive to treatment.

Sometimes education and supportive counseling, oftentimes including a brief stint of family therapy, are all that is needed to improve the relationship between family members and relieve the anxiety. For infants and preschool children struggling with separation and other worries, an insecure bond between child and parent might lie behind the anxiety, and all efforts at strengthening this connection should be considered (Bernstein, Borchardt, & Perwien, 1996). Such interventions may be best achieved by working directly with the parents, who are likely to be anxious themselves, or with the parent and child together to strengthen their relationship. This method is generally more effective than working with the child alone (Bernstein et al., 1996). When a child or adolescent meets full diagnostic criteria for an anxiety disorder, however, or the child's function is significantly impaired, more intensive treatment is warranted.

The treatment of anxiety disorders in children and adolescents may incorporate psychotherapy, medication, or both. Psychodynamic psychotherapy, often termed "play therapy" with children, was previously utilized a great deal in the treatment of child anxiety disorders, but we have only a few small studies to support its use (Heinicke & Ramsey-Klee, 1986; Target & Fonagy, 1994). Although these studies have demonstrated improvements in adaptation and interpersonal relationships among the children receiving this treatment, the therapy is labor intensive, time consuming, and highly idiosyncratic. Furthermore, while these treatments often have great value, they are nonspecific and nearly impossible to replicate in a reliable fashion for a wide variety of patients because they are fraught with subjectivity by virtue of the unique nature of the therapist–child relationship, which will vary for each patient and practitioner.

Cognitive Behavior Therapy

In contrast to psychodynamic psychotherapy, cognitive behavior therapy (CBT) is an easily replicable form of psychotherapy that has been proven useful, expedient, and cost-effective in the treatment of a wide variety of child and adolescent anxiety disorders. In a large multistudy review, CBT was effective for 56% of children and adolescents suffering from an anxiety disorder versus 28% who improved in control groups (James, Soler, &

Weatherall, 2005). Most studies report remission rates of anxiety disorders at 60% to 70% with the use of CBT (Hannesdottir & Ollendick, 2007), with rates as high as 85% for OCD (P. M. Barrett, Farrell, Pina, Peris, & Piacentini, 2008) and 84% for panic disorder (Landon & Barlow, 2004).

CBT rests on the assertion that if one's thoughts and behaviors are changed, then one's feelings will follow suit. When treating anxiety disorders, the primary emphasis is on the behavioral component of CBT, and homework is always employed, in contrast to traditional psychotherapy. Behavioral therapy techniques for anxiety disorders can be likened to a vaccine or inoculation. Through a gradual process, the patient is exposed to toxic stimuli, precisely the things that cause distress. Over time, he or she becomes "immune" to the insult and is bothered to a much lesser extent, if at all. Essentially, this method relies on the concept of *habituation*.

The theory of exposure and response prevention (ERP) emanates from the work of Victor Meyer (1966). He suggested that a prolonged confrontation with a feared "exposure," along with corresponding response prevention, would lead to a significant decrease in subjective distress. Meyer's initial conceptualization still forms the basis of ERP—the live or in vivo exposure to the feared object or situation must be extensive. The exposure must also be functional, in that the feared situation must be reenacted accurately in order to reflect what the patient really feels. For example, if an individual with OCD fears driving alone because he thinks he may hit a pedestrian with the car, then driving with the therapist present is of little utility and does not truly simulate the real condition. Meyer's concept of response prevention incorporates stopping the individual from performing any act that would "undo" or lower his anxiety. For example, for an individual with a phobia of germs, one would therapeutically stop her from washing after a germ "exposure." Finally, since some fears simply cannot be acted out (e.g., an individual may fear leaving the stove on and burning down the house), *imaginal exposures* allow for certain scenarios to be thought through.

ERP works because we can only stay intensely anxious for so long before our body tires and relaxes. With habituation, one's anxiety level comes down by itself. In the same way that only so much of a neurochemical (e.g., dopamine) can be released from a neuron before the neuron has to "recharge," our anxiety must reload before we can experience another intensive burst. A nice way of understanding this concept is to use a Subjective Units of Distress Scale, or SUDS, as in Figure 10.2.

In this example, an individual with OCD has a fear of germs. In the first curve (Curve 1) the individual is exposed to a stressor at time

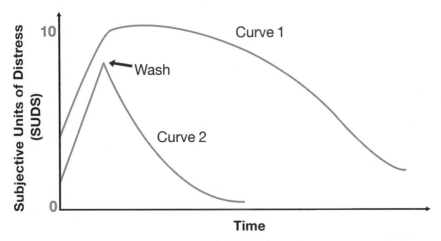

Figure 10.2 Subjective Units of Distress (SUDS) Scale. As shown in Curve #1, exposure to a stressful situation (e.g., perceived contamination) at time zero results in a high
level of distress that diminishes slowly over time. In Curve #2, the stress is relieved rapidly by compulsively washing.

zero (e.g., she touches a toilet seat in a public bathroom). She worries and
worries, and her anxiety stays elevated for a considerable period of time,
perhaps 30 to 90 minutes, before she calms down. In the second curve
(Curve 2), she washes her hands compulsively (perhaps three to five
times) shortly after the exposure, allowing the anxiety to decrease relatively rapidly, perhaps in 10 minutes. Repeatedly washing her hands has
the immediate effect of calming her down, but it also provides a positive
reinforcement, which inadvertently helps to perpetuate the germ phobia.

The CBT intervention is to stop the patient from washing her hands
each time she experiences a given exposure. For example, ERP homework for this patient might be to touch a toilet seat in a public place
three times each day and not wash her hands for 60 minutes after each
exposure. What happens to the anxiety curve? As seen in Figure 10.3, the
anxiety curve repeats itself but at a decreased level with each exposure
because she becomes "habituated" to the exposure.

One of the first behavioral techniques employed in CBT is to
develop a fear hierarchy. Without knowing one's fears, we cannot effectively design exposures. An added benefit of developing a hierarchy is
that we learn more about the individual's anxiety and what causes him
or her concern. This investigation is itself a therapeutic tool and often
an opportunity for the therapist to challenge many of the cognitive distortions and assumptions of the patient (see Chapter 12). Various scales
may be utilized for assessing what precisely increases an individual's

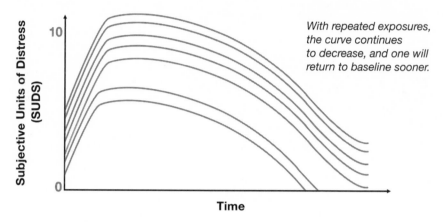

Figure 10.3 Exposure and response prevention (ERP).

anxiety, such as the Reiss-Epstein-Gursky Anxiety Sensitivity Index for
Panic Disorder or the CY-BOCS for OCD. These tools can also be used
to grade the intensity of the anxiety and how much it interferes with the
patient's life. Furthermore, the instrument can be used to monitor treatment progress over time.

Once a list of fears has been compiled, they are placed in order of
intensity. We often use numbers (e.g., on a scale of 1 to 10) to indicate the
degree of distress that a certain exposure might cause for a given individual. A number value can be assessed by asking the individual questions,
such as, "How much distress would you feel if you did not wash after
touching a toilet seat? Would you call that a 7? Would you call that an
8?" Alternatively, one could ask, "Which of these items we've discussed is
the most difficult? We'll call that a 10." A child with a needle phobia may
create the fear hierarchy seen in Table 10.1.

**Table 10.1 Example of a Needle Phobia Fear
Hierarchy for a Child**

Action	Level of distress
Driving past a hospital	0
Walking into a doctor's office	2
Holding an alcohol swab	4
Rubbing an alcohol swab on the arm	6
Holding a syringe with needle attached	8
Receiving an injection	10

Table 10.2 Example of an HIV Fear Hierarchy for a Male Teen

Action	Level of distress
Being anywhere someone with HIV may have been	20
Touching shopping carts	25
Using public phones	30
Opening doors	45
Shaking hands	50
Leaving the house without bandages on cuts	55
Bumping into people	60
Eating at restaurants	65
Touching something in my house with dirty hands	65
Sitting down without checking what I sit on	70
Drinking from a public fountain	80
Wearing shorts or a bathing suit and touching someone	80
Kissing a girl	85
Taking food from anyone	90
Using a public toilet	95
Touching anything that appears to be blood	99

In an effort to work through to the upper levels of anxiety and not to rush the patient, one may need to add many steps in the hierarchy. This process is often creative and even enjoyable for both the patient and the clinician. For the above individual, we may add "walking into a doctor's office and asking directions to a nearby store" (distress level = 1), "drawing a picture of a syringe" (distress level = 3), "watching a medical drama on television" (distress level = 5), and so forth. Many examples may be needed in order to keep the therapy moving along until the higher levels of intensity can be reached. A male teenager with a fear of HIV may develop the fear hierarchy in Table 10.2.

Although some patients will move through their fear hierarchies quickly, it is important not to push the patient too hard in order to maintain adherence to the treatment plan. The lower the patient starts on the hierarchy, the greater the chances of initial success, and the more likely he or she will be to complete the therapy. Many therapists create their own scales or develop fear thermometers to help children rate the degree of discomfort they feel from a given exposure (see Figure 10.4).

For an individual with panic disorder, it should first be determined whether the panic attacks are cued or noncued. If they are cued, then an exposure hierarchy similar to those provided in Tables 10.1 and 10.2 can be produced. For example, if panic attacks are cued by being alone, a variety of scenarios can be created whereby the individual spends more and more time alone (e.g., alone in his room for five minutes, alone in a grocery store for five minutes, etc.). If the panic attacks are random,

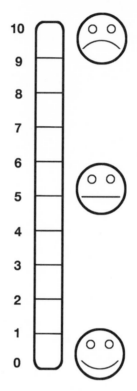

Feels the Worst/Very Scary

Feels the Best/Not Scary at All

Figure 10.4 Fear thermometer. Fear thermometers and other similar tools are useful in helping children to describe their anxiety.

then the focus of treatment should be on the symptoms that the panic attacks produce (e.g., shortness of breath, elevated heart rate, sweating, dizziness), as these are often the most frightening for the patient. These symptoms can be reproduced on a fear hierarchy scale by engaging in activities such as running in place, being spun in a chair, breathing through a straw, and so forth. Once the fear or anxiety hierarchy is complete, the in vivo therapy can commence.

Each CBT therapy session using ERP should start with a discussion of the past week. The clinician should ask if any new anxieties or problems arose, review the last week's homework, identify strengths and successes from the past week, provide positive reinforcement, and determine how to make the sessions and homework more functional and directly related to the fears the individual is having. The therapist and patient should then engage in some ERP together, selecting tasks from the fear hierarchy that may be perceived as too difficult for the patient to accomplish alone. The therapist should monitor closely for obstacles and provide adequate positive feedback. Finally, the session ends with the assigning of new homework for the coming week. Assigning homework is a collaborative effort between the therapist and patient and should constitute just enough of a challenge without overwhelming the patient.

Imaginal exposures are considerably more difficult to create but are often effective for those situations that are impossible to re-create. After it has been determined that certain fears are not amenable to in vivo exposure, a hierarchy of all anxieties requiring imaginal exposure should be created. Once the starting point on the hierarchy is determined, a scene for the imagined fear is developed, and the patient records the scene in his own voice on audiotape. The patient then listens to the scene repeatedly until he is able to tolerate the anxiety that the imagined exposure creates within him. As with in vivo exposures, the method is repeated until the most feared item on the hierarchy produces only minimal anxiety.

There are numerous potential pitfalls and problems with implementing ERP. Commonly, for example, patients report that they experienced too much anxiety to follow through on the homework. In this case, the therapist should make certain that the homework is adequately functional and addresses the correct exposure. Perhaps the assignment needs to be reworked, or perhaps this exposure is one that the therapist and patient should do together during a session. The therapist should make certain that the patient is not simply stalling or trying to use a subtle avoidance technique. Conversely, the therapist may need to consider decreasing the use of relaxation techniques or even anxiolytic medications so that the patient feels adequate distress during the exposures. Only by feeling a significant degree of anxiety during exposures will ERP ultimately work.

Another common problem with ERP occurs when the patient reports that the anxiety does not adequately decrease during the exposure, thereby not allowing habituation to the anxiety. In this case, the therapist should consider increasing the length of the exposure, or, if the obsession is future oriented, using imaginal exposure. Perhaps better still is choosing an item lower on the fear hierarchy.

For patients who do not practice their exposures enough, consider additional sessions with the therapist or involving a significant other, such as a parent, older sibling, or babysitter, in helping to make sure the exposures are practiced. The therapist should always exercise caution when incorporating family members, however, as this technique may lead to more conflict between the patient and parents. Sometimes meeting with the patient more often, such as twice weekly, will speed the therapy and may, in fact, be more effective for some individuals. If the child still refuses to engage in treatment, a day or after-school treatment program may be necessary. Alternatively, for children who will engage in exposures only with the therapist, decreasing therapy sessions and further incorporating parents or other family members may be useful.

CBT should be employed for as long as necessary, but in the vast majority of cases, CBT is a time-limited therapeutic approach. For the treatment of anxiety, patients typically receive 12 to 16 weeks of treatment with periodic boosters thereafter if necessary. For particularly difficult cases, the therapy may be extended for many more weeks or months.

Psychopharmacological Treatment of Anxiety

Medications are commonly employed to treat anxiety in children and adolescents when therapy is unavailable or only partially effective. Some children and their families prefer medication to psychotherapy, which may be reasonable at times but should be carefully considered. While medication may address the symptoms of anxiety, without therapy the patient may never learn to manage the anxiety on his or her own, and medication may always be necessary. There are certainly many cases where medication is a key part of the treatment plan. However, we hope that by engaging in CBT, the patient will learn to recognize the signs of anxiety and to employ these skills when necessary.

There is little data to suggest that tricyclic antidepressants (TCAs), the "older" antidepressants, are effective for most child and adolescent anxiety disorders. While clomipramine (Anafranil) is one of the gold-standard treatments for OCD and is approved by the Food and Drug Administration (FDA) for the treatment of OCD in children down to age 11 years (DeVeaugh-Geiss et al., 1992; Flament et al., 1985; Leonard et al., 1989), studies of TCAs for other anxiety disorders have yielded mixed results. Randomized, double-blind, placebo-controlled studies of imipramine (Tofranil) combined with behavioral therapy for school refusal and SAD have been contradictory (Bernstein et al., 2000; Bernstein, Garfinkel, & Borchardt, 1990; Gittelman-Klein & Klein, 1973; R. G. Klein, Koplewicz, & Kanner, 1992). One study of clomipramine (Anafranil) found no benefit for the treatment of school phobia (Berney et al., 1981), and questions have been raised about the stability of treatment gains with TCAs for these children (Bernstein, Hektner, Borchardt, & McMillan, 2001). Furthermore, there are a variety of reasons that TCAs may not be as effective in children as they are in adults, and the safety concerns of these medications are significant and sufficiently concerning to limit their use (see Chapter 12). In general, TCAs should be prescribed for children and adolescents only by an experienced practitioner and, even then, under very limited circumstances.

More commonly utilized for anxiety disorders are the selective serotonin reuptake inhibitors (SSRIs). These medications have a safety profile preferable to that of the TCAs and are relatively easy for practitioners to prescribe and patients to tolerate. Three of these medications have been approved by the FDA for the treatment of OCD in children and adolescents—sertraline (Zoloft) has been approved down to age 6, fluoxetine (Prozac) has been approved down to age 7, and fluvoxamine (Luvox) has been approved down to age 8. The FDA approval for these medications is based on randomized, double-blind, placebo-controlled studies (D. A. Geller et al., 2001; Liebowitz et al., 2002; March et al., 1998; Pediatric OCD Treatment Study Team, 2004; Riddle et al., 2001; Riddle et al., 1992). Paroxetine (Paxil) has also demonstrated efficacy in the treatment of pediatric OCD but generally causes more side effects and has not been FDA approved for the treatment of anxiety in children and adolescents (D. A. Geller et al., 2003; D. A. Geller et al., 2004).

Though the data supporting SSRIs in the treatment of non-OCD anxiety disorders is not as robust, these medications have shown utility in treating a broad range of adult and child anxiety disorders and are frequently employed for this purpose (Ipser, Stein, Hawkridge, & Hoppe, 2009; Kodish, Rockhill, & Varley, 2011; Uthman & Abdulmalik, 2010). A handful of randomized, double-blind, placebo-controlled studies support the use of SSRIs for SAD, GAD, social phobia, and selective mutism. Fluvoxamine is supported by at least one study (Research Units for Pediatric Psychopharmacology [RUPP] Anxiety Study Group, 2001); fluoxetine is supported by at least two studies (Birmaher et al., 2003; Black & Uhde, 1994); paroxetine is supported by at least one study (Wagner, Berard, et al., 2004); and sertraline (Zoloft) is supported by at least two studies (Rynn, Siqueland, & Rickels, 2001; Walkup et al., 2008).

The most recent and largest of these investigations, the Child/Adolescent Anxiety Multimodal Study (CAMS), published its first data in 2008 (Walkup et al., 2008). This study sought to determine whether CBT, medications, or their combined action is the preferred treatment for pediatric anxiety disorders. The study randomly assigned 488 children and adolescents with SAD, social phobia, or GAD, aged 7 to 17 years, to one of four treatment groups for 12 weeks. The first group received CBT for 14 sessions; the second group received sertraline up to a dosage of 200 mg per day; the third group received both CBT and sertraline (Zoloft); and the fourth group received only placebo. Over 80% of children who received combined treatment, medication plus CBT, improved, as opposed to 60% receiving CBT only and 55% receiving medication only, although there was no statistical separation between the CBT and medication groups, and the 5% difference in efficacy between these two treatments could be due to chance. All treatments were statistically more effective than placebo, which led to improvement in only 24% of subjects. Consequently, the CAMS Study demonstrates that medication and CBT both work well for pediatric anxiety disorders and that their combination is the best form of treatment.

SSRIs are generally viewed as safe for children, adolescents, and adults, though recent concerns about their ability to induce depression and suicidal thoughts have been raised (these issues are addressed fully in the Appendix). As yet, there are no direct head-to-head studies comparing different SSRIs for the treatment of anxiety. Consequently, the practitioner has few guideposts by which to choose the specific SSRI an anxious child should take. These decisions are commonly made by weighing the various side effect profiles of the medications. Many practitioners will select an SSRI based on family members who may have taken and successfully tolerated one of these medications. However, we have no evidence to support this metric as a means of making this decision.

Another area for which we have little guidance is the dosage of SSRIs in children and adolescents with various anxiety disorders. In general, we titrate these medications to the highest and most beneficial dose that is well tolerated with minimal or no side effects. For panic disorder and particularly nervous children, we must often titrate the dosage upward very slowly, and a low dose is frequently sufficient because some of the potential side effects of the medications themselves (e.g., sweating, tremor, and derealization, for example) can be misinterpreted as physical symptoms of anxiety. For those with OCD, by contrast, the best clinical response typically occurs at a high dosage.

As above, three SSRIs have an FDA indication for the treatment of OCD in children and adolescents, in addition to one TCA, clomipramine. Unfortunately, CBT along with an SSRI or clomipramine is still too often insufficient to adequately treat OCD. Studies vary, but only about 50% of all individuals with OCD treated with an SSRI or clomipramine demonstrate an adequate response, and many of these individuals continue to suffer significant impairment. In addition to aggressive CBT and high-dose SSRI treatment, augmentation of the medication regimen with an antipsychotic results in significant symptom improvement in about one third of individuals (Bloch et al., 2006). It is not entirely clear at this time which antipsychotic should be utilized, but the most impressive data lie with haloperidol (Haldol) and risperidone (Risperdal). For a complete discussion of antipsychotic medication in children and adolescents, see Chapter 15.

In addition to the antipsychotic medications, clonazepam (Klonipin) and lithium may be effective for augmenting SSRIs and clomipramine (Anafranil) in the treatment of OCD (Leonard et al., 1994; Rasmussen, 1984). However, the supporting studies for these interventions are only case reports. The data at the present time favor antipsychotic medications for augmentation. Nonetheless, no augmentation should be attempted until an adequate treatment trial of an SSRI or clomipramine at a sufficient dose has been attempted, because a significant minority of patients will not respond until they have received 8 to 12 weeks of treatment with the initial agent.

For the treatment of GAD in children and adolescents, extended-release venlafaxine (Effexor XR) has demonstrated efficacy. Rynn, Riddle, Yeung, and Kunz (2007) reported on two separate multicenter randomized, double-blind, placebo-controlled trials involving more than 300 children aged 6 to 17 years with GAD who were treated with extended-release venlafaxine for 8 weeks. The first study showed improvement in specific GAD symptoms, but the second study showed improvement only on secondary measures. The combined response rates for the studies were 69% for the active drug versus 48% for placebo. While positive overall, more data are needed before we can presume that extended-release venlafaxine is truly effective for GAD. The remarkably high placebo rate, the relatively small difference between response rates among those taking the active drug versus those taking a placebo, and the fact that only when combined did the two studies show statistical significance suggest that extended-release venlafaxine may not be a robust treatment for GAD in children and adolescents.

Extended-release venlafaxine has also been found effective in the treatment of social phobia in a randomized, double-blind, placebo-controlled study of children and adolescents aged 8 to 17 years (March, Entusah, Rynn, Albano, & Tourian, 2007). In this large sample of nearly 300 subjects who were treated for 16 weeks, 56% of children responded to the active drug versus 37% who responded to the placebo. While statistically significant, once again the split between active treatment and placebo is not particularly large.

Other medications utilized for children and adolescents with anxiety disorders have historically included barbiturates and benzodiazepines. Barbiturates, however, are concerning because of their safety profile and toxicity in overdose and are rarely used for treating childhood anxiety any longer. Benzodiazepines, which inhibit the nervous system by their action on gamma-aminobutyric acid (GABA) receptors, are much safer and highly effective for anxiety in adults, but in children and adolescents they not infrequently cause paradoxical disinhibition and irritability. The agitation so commonly seen among children taking benzodiazepines is believed to be due to the fact that children do not have a full complement of GABA receptors until the late teen years and therefore cannot properly utilize these treatments.

Data supporting the use of medications for the treatment of panic disorder, selective mutism, and specific phobias is generally lacking for children and adolescents, but a sufficient number of studies have yet to be completed. Due to the paucity of empirical studies from which to draw upon, we have little to guide us. CBT remains the treatment of choice for these disorders, but when medications are necessary, we must draw upon our experience with adults and extrapolate to children and adolescents.

Anxiety disorders are perhaps the most common psychiatric problems in children and adolescents. While we have some wonderful psychotherapeutic and medication treatments, nowhere is our lack of knowledge of child mental health as tragically evident as it is with anxiety disorders. OCD, one of the best-recognized anxiety disorders, remains one of the top 10 causes of disability worldwide, and at present we are effective in treating only about half of all cases when gold-standard treatment is even available (Murray & Lopez, 1996). The ubiquitous nature of these problems demands that we invest more resources into educating the public, researching etiology, and identifying effective treatments.

For those who continue to struggle even with therapy and medication treatment, sometimes acceptance therapy or mindfulness is helpful. Mindfulness is often viewed as the "third wave" of anxiety treatments (after psychodynamic therapy and CBT). Because we recognize that most anxiety emanates from fears related to the future (e.g., "What if I get nervous when I give my presentation in class?") or the past (e.g., "What if I failed my exam?"), we use mindfulness techniques to help individuals live "in the moment," where thoughts of anxiety are less likely to cause them problems. Teaching patients mindfulness techniques, such as belly breathing, progressive muscle relaxation, guided imagery, meditation, and yoga, often helps them to accept the anxiety that they cannot change and keep them focused on their life and activities so that their worries are less bothersome.

11

Trauma

Historically, traumatic stress has been considered a type of anxiety disorder. Clinicians, however, have long recognized that traumatic stress reactions may present as a veritable cornucopia of psychiatric diagnoses, including anxiety, mood, behavioral, learning, and psychotic disorders. With good reason, then, *DSM-5* has now placed these disorders into a separate diagnostic domain.

Our understanding of traumatic stress has changed much over the past century. During World War I, "shell shock," or combat fatigue, became a well-recognized phenomenon. With the publication of *DSM-I*, the diagnosis of *gross stress reaction* was described, whereby after exposure to combat or catastrophe, such as explosions or earthquake, some individuals develop an extreme and disordered response (American Psychiatric Association, 1952). In *DSM-II*, under the category of transient situational disturbances, *adjustment reactions* were defined as temporary difficulties occurring in individuals without a major underlying psychiatric diagnosis who had been exposed to an overwhelming environmental stressor (American Psychiatric Association, 1968). The diagnosis of *posttraumatic stress disorder* entered the psychiatric nomenclature with the publication of *DSM-III* in 1980 and has remained relatively stable since that time (American Psychiatric Association, 1980). *DSM-5* now incorporates a number of other diagnoses in the chapter on trauma- and stress-related disorders, including reactive attachment disorder, acute stress disorder, adjustment disorders, and the newly added disinhibited social engagement disorder (American Psychiatric Association, 2013). This chapter will focus on the most common and relevant of these diagnoses for children and adolescents, *posttraumatic stress disorder* (PTSD).

CLINICAL PRESENTATION

As above, posttraumatic stress reactions can present in myriad ways among children and adolescents representing a wide variety of emotional, cognitive, behavioral, and physical symptoms. Young children will commonly demonstrate symptoms of separation anxiety, avoidance, nightmares, somatic symptoms (e.g., stomachaches), behavioral agitation and irritability, and difficulty learning. Older children and adolescents may express some of these symptoms in addition to difficulty sleeping, negative cognitions, social withdrawal, and high-risk behavior. Symptoms of PTSD typically occur within three months of the trauma but may be delayed in some cases. Partial symptoms are common, as are comorbid conditions. Girls generally tend to be more symptomatic than boys.

Given the developmentally typical egocentric point of view of children and adolescents, they may also express feelings of guilt and personal responsibility for the traumatic events or their outcome. Guilty feelings often lead to irrational thoughts and beliefs (e.g., "I was beaten by my father because I didn't score a goal in soccer"). Unabated negative cognitions may lead to depression, self-injury, risk-taking behavior (drinking and driving, unprotected sexual intercourse, etc.), and suicide attempts, all of which are more common in adolescents than children.

"Complex trauma" is typically defined as that which develops after repeated exposure to traumatic events and affects numerous domains of a child's life. Not only may the child express symptoms of PTSD, but affective dysregulation, impaired academic performance, troubling interpersonal relationships, worsening self-esteem, and high-risk behavior may also ensue.

ETIOLOGY

Although we are not born with PTSD, there appear to be conditions which make some individuals more vulnerable than others. Precisely which factors are most important in establishing vulnerability remains a matter of debate, but it does seem that those individuals with an increased propensity towards anxiety and depression are at risk. In addition, the amount or "dose" of traumatic exposure, the time period for which one is exposed, and the specific type of trauma may strongly influence the way we respond to stress and the impact it has upon our brains.

Biologically, there are a number of factors that influence the etiology of PTSD. The neuroendocrine system, acting via the hypothalamic-pituitary-adrenal (HPA) axis, has been shown in numerous studies of those who have been exposed to traumatic stress to be affected, resulting in alterations in various hormone levels. Decrease in the stress hormone cortisol, for example, which is believed to result in atrophy or shrinking of the brain's hippocampus, a major structure within the limbic system or emotional brain, is a ubiquitous finding among adults who were traumatized as children. Some studies have also suggested that preexisting low levels of cortisol may predispose certain individuals to PTSD upon exposure to traumatic stress. Though seemingly counterintuitive, initial increases in cortisol upon exposure to trauma become attenuated with chronic stress exposure. In other words, one long-term result of childhood trauma appears to be a down-regulation in baseline cortisol levels in nonstressful situations by adulthood (Sherin & Nemeroff, 2011).

Thyroid abnormalities can also be caused by exposure to trauma, with some data suggesting that elevated T3 hormone in relation to T4 hormone levels may increase the sense of subjective anxiety among certain exposed individuals. Oxytocin, a hormone important in the regulation of social interactions, including empathy and attachment, is also affected by stress, and lower levels have been found among women exposed to childhood maltreatment (De Bellis & Zisk, 2014; Sherin & Nemeroff, 2011).

A number of neurochemical abnormalities have also been suggested to play a key role in the development of PTSD. Increased dopamine levels, for example, have been found in the mesolimbic area among some individuals with PTSD and may interfere with fear conditioning. Elevated norepinephrine levels have been found as well and are suggested to increase arousal, startle response, and the encoding of fearful memories. In addition, an increase in norepinephrine can trigger the autonomic nervous system's fight-or-flight response, which leads to an increase in blood pressure and heart rate, the latter of which has been independently associated with an increase in the propensity to develop PTSD among those exposed to traumatic stress. Decreases in serotonin in numerous brain areas have also been suggested to interfere with the interaction between the amygdala (the "fear hub" of the brain) and the hippocampus (a structure important for the consolidation of memory and emotion); lower concentrations of serotonin may also impair the ability to tolerate anxiety while increasing vigilance, impulsivity, startle response, and intrusive memories. Furthermore, some individuals with PTSD have been found to have fewer neuronal binding sites for the brain's chief inhibitory neurotransmitter, gamma-aminobutyric acid (GABA) which decreases our response to stress, suggesting impaired anxiolytic ability among those affected. Glutamate, in contrast to GABA, is the brain's primary excitatory neurotransmitter. Levels of glutamate increase upon exposure to stress and bind to N-methyl D-aspartate (NMDA) receptors throughout the brain, where they are believed to promote derealization, dissociation, and interfere with learning and memory by damaging hippocampal neurons. Finally, both elevated endogenous opioids, which can promote emotional numbing and dissociation, and decreased neuropeptide Y, which can cause an increase in the HPA stress response, have been found among some individuals diagnosed with PTSD (Sherin & Nemeroff, 2011).

Three key brain areas are known to be affected by traumatic stress. A classic feature of PTSD is the reduction in hippocampal volume, which has been found in most MRI studies and is a sign of impaired neuronal cell formation and growth. The volume reduction is thought to be either a preexisting feature of vulnerable individuals or due to chronic glutamate exposure. Regardless, reduced hippocampal volume appears to alter the brain's ability to terminate stress responses and distinguish accurately between safe and unsafe environmental situations. The amygdala, by contrast, appears to be hyperresponsive in PTSD, making it important not only because of its relationship to the hippocampus but also because it may impair an individual's ability to accurately assess threat. An overly active amygdala will lead to hypervigilance, a key symptom of PTSD. Finally, a reduction in the volume of the medial prefrontal cortex, including the anterior cingulate area, which is known to inhibit stress responses and emotional reactions via its impact on the amygdala, has been found among individuals with PTSD (Sherin & Nemeroff, 2011).

Though most of the neurological data on traumatic stress is based on studies of adults, data in children and adolescents are emerging. Children who are exposed to physical and sexual abuse in the first five years of life, for example, are more likely to suffer symptoms of anxiety and depression along with HPA axis dysregulation than children who are exposed to trauma after 5 years of age. More extreme traumatic exposure is also associated with greater HPA dysfunction. In addition, lower IQ scores and difficulties with language and academic achievement have been found among abused children, and studies of maltreated children have identified numerous morphological brain differences in comparison to normal children, even after controlling for socioeconomic status (De Bellis & Zisk, 2014).

EPIDEMIOLOGY

The lifetime risk of PTSD in the United States by age 75 is nearly 9%. About 3.5% of adults in the U.S. are affected each year (American Psychiatric Association, 2013). As noted in Chapter 1, over 3 million reports of child abuse, involving more than 6 million youth, are made in the United States each year, and over one third of children 10 to 16 years of age in the United States report having been physically or sexually assaulted by family or others they know (Mash & Wolfe, 2005; Trocmé & Wolfe, 2001; U.S. Department of Health and Human Services, Administration for Children and Families, Administration on Children, Youth and Families, Children's Bureau, 2013).

A number of factors determine who develops PTSD. Some individuals may be biologically predisposed, such as those with a smaller hippocampus or a hyperresponsive amygdala, as described above. Those with preexisting psychiatric conditions are also at risk. Lower socioeconomic status, less education, prior exposure to trauma, general adversity, lower intelligence, family psychiatric history, and racial minority status also increase the likelihood of PTSD. Additional factors, such as closer physical proximity to a traumatic event, increased media exposure to traumatic events (which serve as reminders to those previously traumatized), and interpersonal factors, such as temperament and locus of control, appear to be important. The risk of PTSD is increased with the amount of trauma to which one is exposed, the intensity of the trauma, the degree of physical injury, the degree to which the trauma is interpersonal in nature, and the degree of threat to one's life. Although exposure to trauma before age 5 portends a worse outcome, a lower prevalence of PTSD has generally been reported among children and adolescents, including those under 5 years of age, after exposure to trauma. However, this finding may be an artifact of inadequate diagnostic criteria and improperly trained practitioners (American Psychiatric Association, 2013).

CLINICAL COURSE

By definition, PTSD can occur any time after 1 year of age. Initial symptoms may meet criteria for an acute stress disorder, and posttraumatic symptoms are usually evident within three months of the cardinal event. A full recovery is typical for about 50% of adults, although some individuals remain symptomatic for many years (American Psychiatric Association, 2013). A child or adolescent's response to trauma appears to depend in large part on his or her developmental level. For younger children exposed to acute trauma, their response appears to be largely mediated by their parents' reaction. If the parents manage the stressor well, the children typically do well (J. A. Cohen, Mannarino, & Deblinger, 2006). As has been noted previously, however, the earlier the traumatic exposure and the longer it continues, the more likely it is to interfere

with the child's development. Older children and adolescents may tolerate acute or chronic trauma well if they are resilient, but without support
they may suffer a great deal.

While some individuals are remarkably resilient, others appear
more vulnerable to the effects of traumatic stress. Social support, both
prior to and after the event(s), is at least somewhat protective (American Psychiatric Association, 2013), as are effective coping strategies, feeling good about one's actions when faced with danger, and feeling able
to act effectively even when experiencing fear (Charney, 2004). Children
and adolescents who have been traumatized may present clinically with
a great variety of symptoms and disorders, as previously mentioned,
making PTSD somewhat of a psychiatric "imposter." A child may be
depressed, anxious, acting out, or wetting the bed, but the underlying
cause is traumatic stress. The symptoms typically wax and wane but generally worsen when the child is confronted with any reminders or situations reminiscent of the trauma he or she experienced.

As has been described, chronic and untreated childhood trauma
appears to cause more negative outcomes than adult trauma. Individuals
who were sexually abused as children and again as adults, for example,
have a greater risk of affect dysregulation, suicide attempts, and dissociative behavior than those individuals who were only sexually abused
as adults. Individuals who were abused as children and again as adults
have more interpersonal problems as they age and more difficulties being
assertive, sociable, responsible, and intimate. These individuals also have
more difficulties with emotional control and are more likely to be sub-
missive than those who were abused only as adults (Cloitre, Scarvalone,
& Difede, 1997).

Traumatic childhood experiences are a significant risk factor for
the development of later-onset psychopathology and physical illness.
Children and adolescents who are psychologically, physically, or sexually abused or who have witnessed their mother being abused, or who
are raised in a household with a member who suffers substance abuse or
major mental illness or is imprisoned, face major increases in health risks
as adults—up to a 12-fold increase in alcoholism, drug abuse, depression,
and suicide attempts; a two- to fourfold increase in smoking and sexually transmitted disease; and a 1.4- to 1.6-fold increase in obesity. As the
number of adverse childhood experiences increases, so do the risks these
individuals face as adults (Felitti et al., 1998).

PTSD is most often comorbid with other mental health conditions.
People with PTSD are 80% more likely to have a co-occurring mental
disorder, most commonly a mood, anxiety, or substance use disorder.
Substance use disorders and conduct disorder are more common comor-

bidities among males than females. Children also most often meet criteria for at least one comorbid diagnosis, usually oppositional defiant disorder or separation anxiety disorder (American Psychiatric Association, 2013).

DIAGNOSIS

The sine qua non for a posttraumatic stress reaction is exposure to a traumatic stressor. Classic traumatic events include war, torture, kidnapping, and direct physical and sexual assault. However, many other exposures may be traumatic for individuals, including motor vehicle accidents, fires, natural disasters, life-threatening illness, medical events (e.g., anaphylactic shock), witnessing similar events in others, or learning about similar events in those to whom one is very close. When these events involve serious injury, death, or the threat of injury or death, the likelihood of a traumatic response increases.

Subsequent to the traumatic event, there are four requirements for a *DSM-5* diagnosis of PTSD. First, the individual must regularly reexperience the event via, for example, flashbacks, nightmares, and recurrent thoughts, or have an overwhelming emotional or physiological response upon exposure to cues that symbolize or resemble the traumatic event. Individuals may experience dissociative episodes, such as flashbacks, during which time they feel that the traumatic event is occurring again. Children may demonstrate these symptoms by repetitive play with themes related to the trauma, frightening dreams unrelated to the content of the trauma, or trauma-specific reenactments. Second, the traumatized individual must avoid anything related to the trauma, including people, thoughts, and locations, that arouses memories of the traumatic event. Third, individuals must experience negative thoughts and moods, characterized by difficulty with memory recall related to the event, thoughts of guilt or self-blame, less interest in routine activities, feeling detached from others, appearing emotionally blunted, expressing a sense of doom for the future, or feeling unable to enjoy positive feelings. Fourth, affected individuals must experience some symptoms of irritability, anger, high-risk self-destructive behavior, attentional impairment, hypervigilance, exaggerated startle response, or trouble sleeping. *DSM-5* also requires that the symptoms last for at least one month before a diagnosis is given (American Psychiatric Association, 2013). Finally, *DSM-5* provides a minimally altered set of diagnostic criteria for children 6 years and younger in an effort to be more developmentally sensitive.

Bereavement and grief are usually uncomplicated and proceed

through typical stages. Children and adolescents sometimes experience symptoms akin to a time-limited major depressive disorder. However, traumatic grief in childhood, upon witnessing an unexpected, violent, or gruesome death; exposure to graphic details; or being the first to find the body of a family member or caretaker, can result in symptoms of unresolved grief and PTSD. Symptoms of PTSD among grieving children can not only interfere with the normal grief process, but also place them at risk for later depression, substance use, and borderline personality disorder (J. A. Cohen et al., 2006).

When assessing children and adolescents for PTSD, the practitioner is advised to begin by establishing rapport. Understanding the child's history and functioning prior to the trauma is key, along with an assessment of coping skills. Asking the child to give a detailed account of a positive or neutral event prior to being asked about the traumatic event has been shown to result in a more detailed description of the traumatic event when it is later addressed. Finally, starting with open-ended questions followed by reflective and clarifying statements will help the child get started on forming the trauma narrative that is often helpful in treatment (J. A. Cohen et al., 2006).

Finally, it is always necessary to assess the parent's level of traumatic exposure (both current and past), general psychological functioning, and coping skills in order to understand how to best help a child or adolescent. In addition to interviews, a number of scales and measures are available to help assess parents, including the Impact of Events Scale (Joseph, Williams, Yule, & Walker, 1992), the Parent Emotional Reaction Questionnaire (Mannarino & Cohen, 1996), and the UCLA PTSD Reaction Index for *DSM-5* (Steinberg & Beyerlein, 2014).

TREATMENT

The most evidence-based psychotherapeutic treatment for PTSD is trauma-focused cognitive behavior therapy (TF-CBT), which has shown benefit in both individual and group application. In addition to numerous clinical studies, functional MRI has demonstrated that CBT can relieve dysregulation of the fear response and the negative emotions correlated with anxiety (De Bellis & Zisk, 2014). TF-CBT is a flexible treatment approach that is family focused and modular, where the therapeutic relationship is central and emphasis is placed on self-efficacy. The treatment, fully described elsewhere (J. A. Cohen et al., 2006), typically runs for 10 to 18 sessions and relies on psychoeducation and parenting skills, teaching relaxation and stress reduction techniques, helping to manage affect and mood, improving coping skills, establishing a trauma narrative (as a method of exposure), mastering in vivo reminders of the trauma, working with both parents and children together and individually, and taking steps to augment the child's future safety and development.

Some clinicians suggest that psychotherapy can only be effective if employed alongside body therapy techniques, such as eye movement desensitization and reprocessing (EMDR). Studies of EMDR have demonstrated benefit as an effective therapeutic treatment for adults, and small controlled studies suggest at least moderate efficacy in children (Dyregrov & Yule, 2006; Rodenburg, Benjamin, de Roos, Meijer, & Stams, 2009). Although we lack neuroimaging and other biological data to distinguish any possible brain differences after treatment with TF-CBT alone versus in conjunction with EMDR, the efficacy of TF-CBT as a stand-alone therapeutic treatment is not in question.

Debriefing, a technique employed in TF-CBT, is commonly utilized with trauma survivors. This popular approach helps the child transform his or her self-concept from that of victim to that of survivor. Interventions often involve helping the child focus on recovery, leading to an eventual sense of mastery. Revenge fantasies commonly complicate the emotional resolution of symptoms and are discouraged.

Clinicians are advised to address sleep hygiene early in treatment. Recent studies have suggested that sleep may function by eliminating potentially neurotoxic waste from the brain, such as beta amyloid, and that catecholamine inhibition improves this process (e.g., high levels of catecholamine, as is commonly found in trauma victims, may inhibit this process; Xie et al., 2013). This theory is based on studies of adult mice. If the same holds for humans, then correcting sleep with behavioral means and/or medications is strongly indicated. Regardless, sleep is often impaired in trauma survivors, and aggressively addressing insomnia and nightmares will help the child feel better and more able to engage in the process of recovery.

As the psychotherapy progresses, some clinicians will add a medication to treat the persistent arousal that sometimes hinders the therapy and sleep hygiene efforts. Selective serotonin reuptake inhibitors (SSRIs) and/or an antihypertensive, such as propranolol (Inderal), prazosin (Minipress), guanfacine (Tenex), or clonidine (Catapres), are the typical first-line treatments. While these medications work by different mechanisms, they have each been successfully utilized at times for both adults and children with PTSD, although controlled studies are needed in children and adolescents. Both sertraline (Zoloft) and paroxetine (Paxil) have been approved by the Food and Drug Administration (FDA) for the treatment of PTSD in adults. Gabapentin (Neurontin), D-cycloserine, and various antipsychotic medications are sometimes reportedly useful in adults as well, but studies in children are as yet unimpressive or lacking (Scheeringa & Weems, 2014).

Finally, Trauma Systems Therapy (TST) is a treatment model that recognizes the place of children within a larger family and societal system and incorporates all the aforementioned treatment elements. The treatment addresses the child's individual emotional needs in addition to the social environment in which he or she lives and the systems of care in which he or she receives treatment. TST views trauma within a schema that incorporates the affected child along with the social environment and/or system of care that is unable to sufficiently help the child regulate his or her emotional state. TST represents a multitiered team approach to treatment that enhances the child's ability to regulate emotions while decreasing the stressors and threats in the social environment. The TST program incorporates four elements—skill-based psychotherapy, family and community based care, advocacy, and psychopharmacology. TST is an effective treatment for children with PTSD (Saxe, Ellis, Fogler, Hansen, & Sorkin, 2005; Saxe, Ellis, & Kaplow, 2007).

12

Depression

Case reports of childhood depression date to the early 17th century. Melancholia was first reported in children in the middle of the 19th century. Still, the existence of depression in children prior to 1960 was seriously doubted because it was felt that a child's immature *superego* would not permit the development of mood disorders. To Freud and other psychoanalysts of his day, the superego was understood to be the part of the psyche that, among other things, punished bad behavior with feelings of guilt (Reber, 1985). Psychoanalysis held that the superego was formally in place only after resolution of the Oedipus complex (e.g., the desire of a child to sexually possess the opposite-sex parent), which is theorized to initiate during Freud's third stage of sexual development, around 3 to 6 years of age, but not resolve until adolescence (see Chapter 1, Table 1.1). Thus, psychoanalytic theory suggested that children were unable to feel profound intrapsychic conflict, such as guilt, shame, and a sense of absolute right and wrong, and were, therefore, unable to develop clinical depression. Research from Europe and the United States in the 1960s and 1970s, however, led to an increasing awareness of precisely how children and adolescents experience depression and express its symptoms. We now clearly recognize that children and adolescents are vulnerable to depression, although the symptom expression often differs somewhat from that seen in adults.

CLINICAL PRESENTATION

According to *DSM-5*, the criteria for major depressive disorder (MDD) do not differ appreciably for children, adolescents, and adults. In place of depressed mood, *DSM-5* suggests that children and adolescents may experience an irritable mood, which may be expressed as temper tantrums and oppositional behavior; and in place of a significant decrease in weight, *DSM-5* suggests that children and adolescents may simply fail to make expected weight gains (American Psychiatric Association, 2013). Though not described in the diagnostic criteria, depressed children and adolescents also tend to suffer fewer neurovegetative problems or impairments in sleep, appetite, energy, and concentration than do depressed adults. In addition, there are other differences in child and adolescent depression not fully appreciated by *DSM-5* criteria.

Young children tend to demonstrate more symptoms of anxiety when depressed, commonly expressed as phobias, separation anxiety, or somatic complaints, such as headache and stomachache. Though not common, these children may also experience auditory hallucinations, such as hearing their own named being called (Chambers, Puig-Antich, Tabrizi, & Davies, 1982). Describing their depression and labeling the symptoms is often difficult for prepubertal children, particularly given their relative inability to think in an abstract fashion and report upon their own mood state in an introspective and reflective manner. Rather, children may simply recognize the detachment, boredom, anger, and anxiety they feel. Unlike depressed adults, their negative mood may not entirely consume them, and they may still be able to enjoy numerous activities, engage with peers effectively, and complete their work relatively well at times, while demonstrating severe discomfort and behavior problems at other times. This inconsistency in mood is often confusing to parents, friends, and teachers, who may wonder about the validity of the diagnosis.

Mood lability, which is not uncommon among normally developing children and is particularly frequent among those with attention-deficit/ hyperactivity disorder (ADHD), disruptive behavior disorders, anxiety disorders, bipolar disorder, and MDD, is not a good marker of depression in children. By midchildhood, or ages 8 through 12 years, depressed children may begin to experience preoccupations with death, lowered self-esteem, social withdrawal, peer rejection, and poor school performance (Mitchell, McCauley, Burke, & Moss, 1988; Ryan et al., 1987), yet depressed children under the age of 15 years express few delusional beliefs and rarely attempt suicide (Centers for Disease Control and Prevention, 2010.)

Depressed adolescents look considerably more like their adult counterparts. Adolescents typically demonstrate more cognitive components to their depression than do children. Guilt and hopelessness now become apparent. Major behavioral changes, such as a decrease in academic performance, loss of friends, and lack of motivation and interest in formerly pleasurable activities, may also be indicative of mood changes or speak to the severity of an adolescent's depression. Adolescents, like adults, demonstrate more sleep and appetite disturbances, are more likely than children to experience psychotic symptoms, and may express significant suicidal ideation and make bona fide suicide attempts. Despite our advances in recognition and treatment, suicide remains the third leading cause of death in adolescents in the United States (Centers for Disease Control and Prevention, 2013). Compared to adults, however, adolescents still demonstrate more behavior problems and fewer neurovegetative difficulties associated with their depression.

ETIOLOGY

The cause of depression remains unclear, but numerous theories have proven themselves useful to clinicians in considering their approach to the patient. Psychodynamic theory, for example, suggests that those who are depressed suffer from a severe and unrelenting superego and are extremely critical and prohibitive of their own fantasies, feelings, and actions. By contrast, attachment theory asserts that those with depression had insecure early attachments, were never adequately bonded to their primary caregivers, and as a result feel adrift and alone. Behavioral theorists believe that depressed individuals never learned to obtain adequate reinforcement and, therefore, cannot gain pleasure from life. Cognitive theorists argue that depressed individuals struggle with a negative or depressive mindset and see the world in a distorted fashion. Others view self-control as the crux of depression, suggesting that deficits in self-monitoring and self-evaluation cause depression. Most would agree that environmental and social stressors, such as loss of a spouse, parent, or job, along with other negative circumstances, can, at the very least, predispose one to depression. Finally, there are a host of biological theories, ranging from neurochemical to endocrine, suggestive of an etiological explanation.

Regardless of which approach or theory one finds most attractive and useful in treating patients, at this time we do not have a unifying explanation for why people get depressed. Still, these theoretical constructs are often useful in helping the clinician to consider which aspects of an individual and his or her life may be worth focusing on in psychotherapy and amenable to change. Of note, these theories apply largely to adults, as relatively little work has been done with children and adolescents.

A number of biological markers have been identified which, while not explanatory, are suggestive of a biological cause of depression. Perhaps as many as 70% of adult patients suffering from severe depression do not show normal suppression of cortisol secretion following an infusion of dexamethasone, known as the Dexamethasone Suppression Test (DST), suggesting an alteration in their stress response. This test is not, however, a useful tool for diagnosing depression, as there are relatively high rates of DST nonsuppression in other psychiatric conditions, such as anorexia nervosa, dementia, and substance abuse (Díaz-Marsá et al., 2008; Murialdo et al., 2000; Sher, 2006). In addition, the data on children and the DST are not as impressive (Dahl et al., 1992). Both depressed children and adults, however, have a blunting of the normal growth hormone release in response to insulin challenge and a blunted production of thyroid-stimulating hormone in response to thyroid-releasing hormone (Dinan, 1998; Trimble, 1996). In addition, depressed girls secrete significantly more prolactin than girls who are not depressed (Hardan et al., 1999). The neuroendocrine abnormalities in depression are evident across various endocrine organs (e.g., adrenals, pancreas, and thyroid). Given this finding, the true neuroendocrine abnormality is likely at the level of the hypothalamus, a region largely regulated by monoamine neurotransmitters, such as serotonin, dopamine, and norepinephrine.

The biogenic amine or catecholamine hypothesis of mood disorders suggests that too much neurotransmitter causes mania and too little causes depression. While we realize that this explanation is an oversimplification, it is supported to some degree by the observation that medications that induce biogenic amine neurotransmitters, such as dopamine, norepinephrine, and serotonin, often improve depression and, likewise, worsen mania. There are, however, many limitations to this hypothesis, including the fact that direct precursors of amines, such as L-dopa and tryptophan, generally have no effect on mood, and compounds that block amine reuptake, such as cocaine and amphetamines, do not generally improve depression.

Studies have shown that typical changes found in the electroencephalogram (EEG) recordings of depressed adults, such as decreased slow-wave sleep, decreased REM latency (e.g., entering REM more quickly after falling asleep), and longer periods of REM sleep, occur less often in depressed children and adolescents (Ivanenko, Crabtree, & Gozal, 2005). Studies of adolescents and adults do, however, share the finding that those with pervasive suicidal thoughts and intent have less of the major serotonin metabolite, 5-hydroxy-indoleacetic acid (5-HIAA), in their central nervous system, suggesting that the serotonin system may be impaired (Mann, Oquendo, Underwood, & Arango, 1999). Although there is a certain lack of precision, it is currently estimated that one third of the risk for developing depression is genetically inherited and two thirds of the risk is environmental (Saveanu & Nemeroff, 2012).

Adults with one or two copies of the short allele of the serotonin transporter gene exhibit more depressive symptoms, diagnosable depression, and suicidality in response to stressful life events than adults with two copies of the long allele (Caspi et al., 2003). The reasons for this observation are not entirely clear, but it may be that individuals carrying the short allele serotonin transporter gene are less able to employ their cingulate cortex (i.e., a part of the brain's limbic system important for processing emotion) to "control" or manage the negative emotions expressed by their amygdala, the fear hub of the brain (Pezawas et al., 2005). Family studies suggest a moderate genetic influence on the heritability of depression based upon investigations of identical twins, 35% to 75% of whom will share the diagnosis (Eley & Stevenson, 1999; Glowinski, Madden, Bucholz, Lynskey, & Heath, 2003). In order to quantify the precise genetic influence, identical twin adoption studies would need to be completed, but even without these studies we have impressive data supporting the familial transmission of depression. In one study, children whose parents suffered depression as children, for example, were up to 14 times more likely than controls to become depressed prior to age 13 (Weissman, Warner, Wickramaratne, & Prusoff, 1988). This relationship also moves in the opposite direction, as mothers of children with MDD are themselves about 50% to 75% likely to develop the disorder at some point in their lifetimes (Kovacs, Devlin, Pollock, Richards, & Mukerji, 1997).

A family history of depression is a major risk factor for the development of depression in other family members. First-degree relatives of a child with MDD, for example, are more likely to suffer depression, and prevalence rates vary between 30% and 50% (Harrington et al., 1997; Wickramaratne, Greenwald, & Weissman, 2000). In addition, children of parents with depression are two to three times more likely to suffer depression themselves, and these children have an earlier age of onset for their depression by approximately three years (Beardslee, Versage, & Gladstone, 1998; Weissman, Warner, Wickramaratne, Moreau, & Olfson, 1997). A 20-year follow-up of offspring of depressed and nondepressed parents found that the risks for anxiety disorder, major depression, and substance dependence were about three times higher in the offspring of depressed parents versus nondepressed parents. These children also suffered greater social impairments. All of these difficulties became much more evident when the children were about 15 to 20 years of age, particularly among females. The data also suggested higher rates of medical problems and mortality among the children of depressed parents as the children enter middle age (Weissman, Wickramaratne, et al., 2006b).

Most studies comparing children and their parents utilize mothers, largely because mothers generally are the primary caregiver and live with their children. One large study of nearly 22,000 parents utilized Medical Expenditure Panel Survey data from 2004 to 2008 constituting a nationally representative sample of mothers and fathers of 5- to 17-year-old-children in the United States to assess for a broad variety of mental health factors. This survey found that the risk of a child having emotional or behavioral problems was much greater if the mother, rather than father, has such problems. While paternal mental health problems were independently associated with a 33% to 77% increased risk of mental health problems among the children, maternal mental health problems were associated with a 50% to 350% increased risk. Of even greater concern is the fact that 25% of the children who were living in a home where both parents suffered mental illness demonstrated emotional or behavioral problems (Weitzman, Rosenthal, & Liu, 2011).

EPIDEMIOLOGY

Varying prevalence rates of MDD in children and adolescents have been reported, and as yet there is no definitive study. We generally accept the prevalence to be about 1% for preschool children, 2% for school-age prepubertal children, and 4% to 8% for adolescents. The gender ratio is about 1:1, male to female, during childhood, reaching approximately 1:2 by mid to late adolescence and somewhere between 1:1.5 and 1:3 from adolescence onward (American Psychiatric Association, 2013; Fleming & Offord, 1990; Kashani & Carlson, 1987; Kashani et al., 1987; Lewinsohn, Clarke, Seeley, & Rohde, 1994; Lewinsohn, Hops, Roberts, Seeley, & Andrews, 1993). The prevalence of MDD increases each year during adolescence such that by 18 years of age the lifetime prevalence (or the chance that a child will have experienced an episode of MDD by this point in his or her life) is approximately 12% (16% among girls and 8% among boys), with 9% suffering severe impairment (Kessler & Walters, 1998; Kessler et al., 2005a; Merikangas, He, Burstein, et al., 2010b).

Hospitalized children and adolescents and those with certain comorbidities demonstrate particularly high rates of MDD. As many as 40% of children on neurology wards with unexplained headaches have been diagnosed with depression (Ling, Oftedal, & Weinberg, 1970) as have 7% of general pediatric inpatients (Kashani, Barbero, & Bolander, 1981), 28% of child psychiatry outpatients (Carlson & Cantwell, 1980), 59% of child psychiatry inpatients (Petti, 1978), and 27% of adolescent inpatients (Robbins, Alessi, Cook, Poznanski, & Yanchyshyn, 1982).

Dysthymic disorder, or persistent depressive disorder as it is called in *DSM-5*, a chronic, low-grade depression which can be just as severely disruptive for a child as MDD, has a wide range in prevalence depending upon the study. The frequency of occurrence in prepubertal children ranges from 0.6% to 1.7% and in adolescents from 1.6% to 8% (Garrison, Addy, Jackson, McKeown, & Waller, 1992; Kashani et al., 1987; Lewinsohn et al., 1993; Lewinsohn et al., 1994). Such variation in prevalence is not uncommonly seen in epidemiological studies, the discrepancy being largely due to study design and the patient population sampled.

The prevalence of depression increases during adolescence for reasons that are not entirely clear. We assume that hormonal and other maturational changes have something to do with the adolescent increase in depression, even though we do not fully understand the effect of puberty on the psyche of a developing child. Environmental factors, such as increased social and academic expectations, also presumably play a role, as these youths are preparing for life in the adult world. It is also true that the longer one lives, the more likely it is that one will encounter negative life events, such as friends and family getting sick, injured, or dying; witnessing the effects of poverty and injustice; and so forth. These experiences are sometimes too much for teens to process and understand with ease and can have an impact upon mood.

As teens age, they embrace increasing freedoms while struggling with establishing independence and a sense of who they are and wish to be. Erikson termed this stage of development *identity vs. role diffusion* and noted that as adolescents develop their unique identities, they are often preoccupied with appearance, hero worship, and ideology (Erikson & Erikson, 1997). Piaget viewed adolescence in terms of cognitive development and the ability to establish "formal operations" and abstract thought (Flavell, 1963). Once a child can think abstractly, in many ways the world becomes a much more frightening place. The adolescent now begins to see much of the inequity and brutality within society and realizes that he or she must advance further in his or her education, learn a skill, eventually earn a living, and possibly raise a family. Without proper adult guidance and support, this realization can be overly daunting and may contribute to the increase in depression.

CLINICAL COURSE

Among clinically referred children and adolescents, the median duration of depression is somewhere between seven and nine months. For samples drawn from the community, the median duration is about one to two months. These numbers suggest that the most severe and recalcitrant cases—those that last longer—find their way to specialty clinics and that those found within the community either get better on their own or receive treatment from a local therapist or physician. Approximately 90% of MDD episodes remit within one to two years of onset, where "remission" is defined as a two-week to two-month period with only one or fewer clinically significant symptoms. Approximately 6% to 10% of MDD episodes become chronic. Predictors of a longer episode of MDD include increased severity of depression, comorbidities, negative life events (e.g., academic troubles, family conflict, abuse, or neglect), parental psychiatric illness, personality disorder, and poor psychosocial functioning (Birmaher & Brent, 1998).

About 50% of children and adolescents who suffer from MDD will experience a relapse or second episode after acute treatment during a period of remission, indicating the need for close observation and ongoing treatment after the initial episode has remitted. Given that up to 60% of children relapse in some studies, it may simply be the nature of depression to return, particularly with early childhood onset, which presumably indicates that the illness is more virulent in these cases. Factors likely to predict relapse include lack of treatment adherence and increased negative life events (Birmaher & Brent, 1998).

A patient is considered to be in "recovery" after an asymptomatic period of at least two months. "Recurrence" is defined as the reemergence of major depressive symptoms during a period of recovery; in other words, a recurrence is essentially a new episode of MDD. Both clinical and community samples have found the probability of recurrence to be somewhere between 20% and 60% within one to two years following remission and approximately 70% after five years. These numbers are higher than those found in adults and likely reflect the virulence of early-onset MDD. Recurrence is predicted by earlier age at onset, greater number of prior episodes, severity of the initial episode, presence of psychosis, psychosocial stressors, coexisting dysthymic disorder or other comorbidities, and treatment noncompliance (Birmaher & Brent, 1998).

The risk of ultimately developing bipolar disorder for children with a first episode of depression is extraordinarily high, as a depressive episode commonly heralds what will later prove to be bipolar disorder (i.e., comprising both depression and mania). Depending on the study, somewhere between 20% and 40% of children and adolescents initially diagnosed with MDD will subsequently be diagnosed with bipolar disorder within five years. Risk factors among these children for developing bipolar disorder Type I include early-onset MDD, psychomotor retardation, psychosis, pharmacologically induced hypomania, a family history of bipolar disorder or psychotic depression, and a significant family history of mood disorders (Birmaher & Brent, 1998).

DIAGNOSIS

DSM-5 requires five of nine symptoms to be present for two weeks to establish a diagnosis of MDD (American Psychiatric Association, 2013). At least one of these symptoms must be either a depressed mood or anhedonia (i.e., loss of pleasure or motivation). Additional symptoms may include changes in sleep, appetite, energy level, and concentration as well as hopelessness or guilt, slowed or agitated thinking or behavior, and suicidal thoughts. The diagnosis for children and adolescents differs only slightly from adults; as previously noted, irritability can substitute for depressed mood, and failure to make expected weight gains can substitute for significant weight loss.

Dysthymic disorder, as previously described, is a chronic, low-grade form of depression that also takes a great toll on those affected. The word *dysthymia* comes from the Greek, meaning "bad state of mind" or "ill humor," and draws upon the antiquated idea that mood is controlled and balanced by the thymus gland. Though considerably milder than depression, symptoms of dysthymic disorder can be every bit as disruptive as MDD in the life of a child or adolescent and are often a precursor to MDD. *DSM-5* diagnosis of dysthymic disorder (which is now also referred to as *persistent depressive disorder*) requires a depressed or irritable mood on most days for at least one year in children and adolescents or at least two years in adults, in addition to two or more of six symptoms, which include changes in appetite, insomnia or hypersomnia, fatigue, poor self-esteem, difficulty with concentration or being decisive, and hopelessness.

Depression can present in many different guises, and *DSM-5* has defined a number of depressive variants. These include bipolar depression, psychotic depression, anxious depression, melancholic depression, peripartum depression, seasonal depression, and atypical depression (characterized by mood reactivity, weight gain, hypersomnia, leaden paralysis, and interpersonal rejection hypersensitivity). Most commonly, however, children and adolescents are diagnosed simply with MDD or dysthymic disorder.

Complicating matters somewhat, *DSM-5* has added a new diagnosis to the depression nosology specifically for children, *disruptive mood dysregulation disorder* (DMDD). DMDD represents the *DSM's* effort to more accurately classify the increasing numbers of children and adolescents who have been mistakenly diagnosed with bipolar disorder in recent years (see Chapter 13). DMDD is intended to provide a diagnosis for those children who present with the primary symptoms of chronic and severe irritability and frequent temper outbursts, the so-called "diagnostic orphans" (Carlson, Pine, Nottelmann, & Leibenluft, 2004). These children are often difficult to classify, as they typically demonstrate symptoms of ADHD, learning disorders, oppositional defiant disorder or conduct disorder, mood instability, anxiety, and posttraumatic stress disorder. Because many of these children have a mix of symptoms across many diagnostic domains and because they are often difficult to treat, many have, in recent years, been given a presumptive diagnosis of bipolar disorder, even though they do not meet the full *DSM* criteria for bipolar disorder.

These children present the practitioner with three diagnostic dilemmas. First, most individuals with bipolar disorder have clear symptoms of euphoria or elation when in a manic state, not just irritability. By contrast, these children are almost wholly irritable when not feeling well. Second, these children almost always demonstrate symptoms of multiple coexisting conditions (e.g., ADHD, learning disorders, etc.), making it difficult to assess their core problem. By contrast, among affected adults, "pure" bipolar disorder (true manias and depressions meeting *DSM* criteria) can be observed, even though bipolar disorder is often comorbid in adults as well. Third, the typical episode length of a manic or depressive mood in the case of bipolar disorder is many days to months. By contrast, these children are often described as having extremely brief episodes of mania and depression, often lasting only hours. Further complicating our understanding of these children's difficulties is the fact that among the research there is almost a complete absence of investigation into these children's history of emotional attachment, abuse, neglect, maltreatment, and trauma, all of which could explain these children's troubling behavior (Parry, 2012).

DSM-5 categorizes DMDD as a depressive disorder, but the symptoms described are largely related to temper tantrums and irritability. Criteria demand that children have recurrent temper outbursts with behavioral and/or verbal manifestations that are much worse than would be expected in a given situation; the temper outbursts are worse than would be expected for the child's age; the outbursts occur three or more times per week on average; the child's mood when he or she is not in the midst of a temper outburst is primarily irritable; the symptoms have been present for 12 months or more; and the symptoms are present in two or more settings. Finally, the diagnosis cannot be made before 6 years of age or after 18 (American Psychiatric Association, 2013).

Thankfully, an increasing number of practitioners now recognize that those children with severe irritability, temper tantrums, and mood dysregulation are not generally bipolar. Longitudinal studies to date (as reviewed in Chapter 13) also demonstrate that these children by and large do not grow up to have a diagnosis of bipolar disorder as adults. Studies of these children instead generally reveal that they are more likely to develop depression and/or anxiety disorders as adults (Leibenluft, 2011). Consequently, practitioners should be extremely cautious when considering a diagnosis of pediatric bipolar disorder and employ great patience is following the patient for a sufficient period of time in order to observe and record true manic and depressive episodes.

Comorbidities are more often the rule than the exception in childhood-onset depression. Although studies vary greatly, somewhere between 40% and 90% of children and adolescents with depression have a second psychiatric disorder, and 20% to 50% have two or more comorbid disorders (Birmaher, Ryan, Williamson, Brent, & Kaufman, 1996; Merikangas, He, Burstein, et al., 2010b). Even though the ranges are great, predictably, dysthymic disorder (30% to 80%), anxiety disorders (30% to 80%), disruptive behavior disorders (10% to 80%), and substance use disorders (20% to 30%) affect the largest numbers of youth (Birmaher & Brent, 1998). MDD usually sets on after the commencement of other psychiatric disorders with the exception of substance abuse and occasionally conduct disorder, where the latter disorders may follow the onset of MDD.

The differential diagnosis of depression in children and adolescents includes a number of mood disorders, such as adjustment disorder with depressed mood, bipolar disorder, dysthymic disorder, seasonal affective disorder, and bereavement. There are also, however, a number of non-mood psychiatric conditions that should be considered and ruled out when depressive symptoms are present, including ADHD, anxiety disorders, disruptive behavior disorders (e.g., oppositional defiant disorder and conduct disorder), learning disorders, substance use disorders, eating disorders, personality disorders, and premenstrual dysphoric disorder. One of the most common causes of depression in young children under 7 years of age is severe neglect and abuse, which should be screened for in every young child with depressive symptoms (Elliott & Smiga, 2003). General medical conditions, such as HIV infection, anemia, hypothyroidism, seizure disorders, cancer, lupus, chronic fatigue syndrome, and diabetes, are also associated with higher-than-expected rates of depression (Birmaher & Brent, 1998). Finally, stimulants, antipsychotics, corticosteroids, and contraceptives, among other medications, may induce or contribute to depression. Consequently, the clinician must consider other potential causes of depression in the evaluation of any child or adolescent and should consider ordering a complete blood count (to rule out anemia), a thyroid-stimulating hormone and free T4 (to rule out hypothyroidism), a urine drug toxicology screen of adolescents to rule out drug abuse, and any additional testing that is suggested by the history and clinical examination.

In recent years, there has been considerable debate about the role of vitamin D in depression. As a result many clinicians are assessing vitamin D levels in patients and encouraging vitamin D supplementation where indicated. Based on current studies in adults, vitamin D supplementation may be helpful for reducing depressive symptoms among those adults with clinically significant depression who are already taking a standard antidepressant. However, there is insufficient evidence to suggest that vitamin D alone can treat depression, and there are no reliable data in children and adolescents (J. A. Shaffer et al., 2014).

Rating scales can be employed to assist in the management of childhood depression. Although numerous scales are available, due to their low specificity, they are more useful for assessing symptoms and severity of depression, along with monitoring change in mood over time, than they are for diagnosing MDD. The Children's Depression Rating Scale, Revised (CDRS-R) is the most commonly utilized scale in studies of depression and is considered the gold standard. This scale must be administered by a trained examiner and does not have great relevance for the practicing clinician. The most commonly utilized scale by clinicians is the Children's Depression Inventory (CDI), a 27-question, self-administered scale that takes about 5 to 10 minutes to complete and score (Kovacs, 1985). Other scales designed for self-report in adults, such as the Beck Depression Inventory (BDI) and the Center for Epidemiologic Studies Depression Scale (CES-D), are sometimes used with adolescents and appear to be reasonably reliable (Sawyer Radloff, 1991; Teri, 1982). Additional scales sometimes employed in studies of childhood depression include the Global Assessment of Functioning (GAF), Children's Global Assessment Scale (CGAS), or Clinical Global Impression (CGI) Scale, all of which are nonspecific to depression and limited in their utility by their highly subjective nature.

TREATMENT

At present we cannot define a single best approach to the treatment of depressed children and adolescents. Too few studies of both medication and psychotherapy have demonstrated adequate efficacy. Consequently, our treatment approach is founded upon the limited data we have from studies of children and adolescents, our clinical experience, and evidence inferred from studies of depressed adults. Treatment should always begin in the least restrictive setting and take into consideration the duration and intensity of the patient's symptoms. The more chronic and severely affected children should receive both psychotherapy and medication, while those mildly affected and not suicidal may warrant a trial of psychotherapy and close monitoring first before a medication is employed. Educating the patient, family, and other important figures in the child's life, such as teachers, friends, and coaches, is critical in helping to build adequate support for the ill child. As depression is known to cluster within families, the clinician should make all efforts to identify and treat, or refer for treatment, other family members, particularly parents and siblings, who may themselves be depressed or suffering from another psychiatric condition.

Mothers with MDD and their children have been studied extensively, and we now know that effective treatment of such mothers is associated with a reduction in anxiety, depression, and disruptive behavior in their children. In one study of 151 mother–child pairs, such diagnoses dropped by 11% in those children whose mothers were successfully treated for MDD, as opposed to an 8% increase in diagnoses among those children whose mothers did not respond to medication treatment. Of the children with MDD themselves at baseline, remission occurred in 33% of those whose mothers' MDD remitted versus 12% of those whose mothers' MDD did not remit. Finally, of the mothers who did not respond to treatment, 17% of their children without a diagnosis at baseline later developed a psychiatric condition within 3 months, as opposed to none of the children whose mothers responded to treatment (Weissman et al., 2006a). As these data demonstrate, it is absolutely necessary to address the entire family in the treatment of a child with MDD.

Treatment studies of both medications and psychotherapies for MDD typically begin with a rarified sample of children and adolescents. In other words, the youths studied are screened very carefully to make sure that they are relatively free from comorbidities that would hinder or obscure the effect of the treatment being studied. For example, when treating a child with MDD and comorbid posttraumatic stress disorder (PTSD), it may be difficult to discern how much symptom improvement is due to the effect of the treatment under study, either psychotherapeutic or pharmacologic, on the MDD or on the PTSD. Even though these are different disorders, there is considerable symptom overlap between them, and the same psychiatric treatments are often effective for different disorders. As seen in Table 12.1, the numerous typical exclusion criteria

Table 12.1 Typical Exclusion Criteria for Pediatric Depression Studies

- Attention-deficit/hyperactivity disorder
- Posttraumatic stress disorder
- Bipolar disorder
- Autism spectrum disorders
- Intellectual disability
- Disruptive behavior disorders
- Psychosis
- Any recent medication treatment (within 2–4 weeks)
- Current alcohol or drug abuse
- Eating disorder
- Recent initiation of psychotherapy
- Recent suicide attempts (past year)

limit to some degree our ability to interpret and generalize the data from treatment studies of depression because it is more commonly the exception rather than the rule to find a child or adolescent with MDD who does not also have one of these comorbid conditions.

Placebo responses in MDD are quite high, particularly among children and adolescents where in randomized, double-blind, placebo-controlled studies of antidepressants they have ranged between 33% and 57% (Bridge, Birmaher, Iyengar, Barbe, & Brent, 2008). In adult studies, approximately 25% to 35% of depressed subjects will experience a response to placebo. Overall response rates to antidepressants in adult trials of MDD are usually about 65% to 70% and in trials of children and adolescents sometimes no more than 55%. Consequently, only about half of individuals responding to an antidepressant in most drug trials are responding because of the medication itself. In other words, the true antidepressant response rate is usually around 25% to 35%, and the placebo response rate is about 25% to 35%, so the total response rate is about 50% to 70%. Because children and adolescents tend to have a very high placebo response rate for the treatment of depression, it is extremely difficult to demonstrate drug efficacy.

Tricyclic Antidepressants

Tricyclic antidepressants (TCAs) are typically thought of as the "older" antidepressants, as they were the first established group of effective medications for MDD. Although not commonly employed in children and adolescents any longer, a discussion of their history and usage remains valuable in understanding both the depressive disorders and the more modern treatments.

The TCAs were found serendipitously, subsequent to the synthesis of chlorpromazine in 1950 from synthetic antihistamines, which themselves were first discovered in the 1940s. Initially designed to be an antihistamine, chlorpromazine was found in 1952 to have profound antipsychotic effects. By 1955, chlorpromazine, also known as Thorazine, was widely accepted, and its ubiquitous use in asylums and psychiatric hospitals helped to pave the way for the reintegration of many chronically ill schizophrenic and bipolar patients back into society. Imipramine, the first TCA, is an analog of chlorpromazine, not initially designed for the treatment of depression but rather for psychosis. The drug's tendency to induce manic effects and generally worsen psychosis in schizophrenia, however, led to its testing with depressed patients. The first trial of imipramine, also known as Tofranil, took place in 1955, and the first report of its antidepressant effects was published in 1957. The second member of the tricyclic family, amitriptyline (Elavil), was introduced in 1961. There are numerous other TCAs available today, and those best known include desipramine (Norpramin), clomipramine (Anafranil), nortriptyline (Aventyl, Pamelor), and doxepin (Sinequan).

TCAs are presumed to exert their positive effects by blocking the reuptake of norepinephrine, serotonin, and dopamine to varying degrees by neuronal presynaptic receptors (see Figure 12.1). This effect thereby causes these neurochemicals to remain within the synapse longer. By increasing the amount of time that serotonin and norepinephrine stay in the synapse, we increase the likelihood that these neurochemicals will stimulate a postsynaptic receptor. Although we understand this mechanism of action, it is still unclear why antidepressants take many weeks to demonstrate any clinical benefit. In all likelihood, the beneficial effects are due to alterations in neuron receptors and cell proteins, which typically take four to six weeks for the body's DNA and RNA to transcribe and synthesize. Thus, the true effect of an antidepressant is probably many steps downstream from the simple mechanism demonstrated in this figure.

While highly effective for adult depression, TCAs have unfortunately shown little utility in the treatment of pediatric MDD. Open-label trials of TCAs have reported that up to 80% of children and adolescents respond positively. However, among at least 11 published randomized, double-blind, placebo-controlled trials, five in adolescents and six in children, only one study of 30 depressed children ages 6 to 14 years treated with imipramine demonstrated a positive result (Birmaher et al., 1996; Preskorn, Weller, Hughes, Weller, & Bolte, 1987). In addition, a meta-

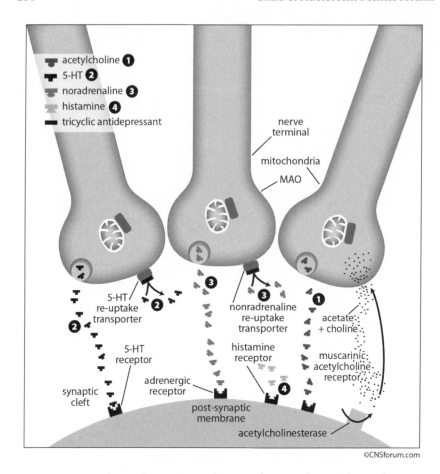

©CNSforum.com

Figure 12.1 Tricyclic antidepressant mechanism of action. The tricyclic antidepressant blocks the 5-HT (serotonin) re-uptake transporter and the noradrenaline re-uptake transporter, thereby leaving more serotonin and noradrenaline within the synapse to stimulate the post-synaptic neuron.

analysis of numerous studies likewise found no beneficial effect for TCAs in the treatment of MDD in children and adolescents (Hazell, O'Connell, Heathcote, Robertson, & Henry, 1995).

Numerous factors may have negatively biased the TCA studies of pediatric depression that have been performed. Small sample sizes with a great deal of diagnostic heterogeneity and levels of symptom impairment, the incorporation of patients with depression secondary to other primary psychiatric conditions (who may have had higher placebo response rates), and short trials of six to eight weeks are but a few of the features that may have limited the data. Furthermore, lower doses of these medications were used because of understandable concerns about cardiac safety, yet children and adolescents may require higher dosages because of their more effective hepatic metabolism of drugs (see Appendix). Additionally, noradrenergic or secondary amine TCAs (see below) were most often employed in these studies, which are likely to be less favorable treatments for children. Since noradrenergic brain receptors may not be fully developed until early adulthood, children and adolescents may simply not be ready for noradrenergic (as opposed to serotonergic) antidepressants. Another potential factor is that more depressed children and adolescents than adults make the eventual transition into bipolar disorder, and TCAs are generally less effective for bipolar depression. Finally, the high prevalence of comorbid conditions in these studies may have interfered with ascertaining their true potential for the treatment of pediatric MDD (Birmaher et al., 1996).

Tricyclic antidepressants are classified as secondary or tertiary amines. Amines are organic compounds whose functional group contains a nitrogen atom with a loan pair of electrons. A primary amine has one of the three hydrogen atoms replaced by a carbon group, a secondary amine has two hydrogen atoms replaced by carbon groups, and a tertiary amine has three hydrogen atoms replaced by carbon groups. In general, the tertiary amines boost serotonin as well as norepinephrine and produce more sedation, anticholinergic effects (e.g., dry mouth and eyes, confusion, sedation), and orthostatic hypotension. The secondary amines act primarily on norepinephrine and tend to have a lower side effect profile. The tertiary amines include amitriptyline (Elavil), imipramine (Tofranil), trimipramine (Surmontil), doxepin (Sinequan), clomipramine (Anafranil), and lofepramine (Gamanil); the secondary amines include nortriptyline (Pamelor), desipramine (Norpramin), protriptyline (Vivactil), and amoxapine (Asendin).

TCAs have demonstrated efficacy in the treatment of depression and anxiety in adults, obsessive-compulsive disorder (OCD) in children and adolescents (particularly clomipramine), ADHD (particularly desipramine), analgesia for migraine headache prevention and neuropathic pain (particularly amitriptyline), and enuresis (particularly imipramine). For children and adolescents with these comorbidities, TCAs may be a reasonable treatment.

The most common side effects of TCAs are a result of their antimuscarinic and anticholinergic activity. Side effects include dry mouth, eyes, and nose, blurred vision, decreased gastrointestinal motility and constipation, urinary retention or hesitancy, sedation, and hyperthermia. Tolerance to these side effects often develops if treatment is continued. Side effects may also be less troublesome if the treatment is initiated at low dose and then gradually increased, although this approach will certainly delay the clinical effect. Other side effects of TCAs may include anxiety, restlessness, cognitive and memory difficulties, confusion, dizziness, akathisia (a sense of internal restlessness), increased appetite with weight gain, sweating, a decrease in sexual ability and desire, muscle twitches, weakness, nausea, vomiting, hypotension, tachycardia and, rarely, irregular heart rhythms.

There have been at least eight cases of sudden death reported in children and adolescents who have taken therapeutic doses of TCAs for the treatment of depression (Varley, 2001). More cases of sudden death have been reported among children and adolescents who took these medications in overdose (Amitai & Frischer, 2006). QT prolongation and subsequent *torsade de pointes* is the suggested cause of death in each case. The level of risk, however, remains unclear, as in many cases the children were taking other medications and their cardiac status had not been routinely monitored prior to treatment. Although infrequent, sudden death does occur in children regardless of medication treatment. Consequently, only experienced practitioners should prescribe TCAs, and even then only when all other reasonable alternatives have been exhausted. If a TCA is employed, the child and parents should be interviewed carefully. A history of sudden cardiac death in a first-degree relative and any symptoms of chest pain, exercise intolerance, syncope, shortness of breath, or dizziness in the child should be further explored and considered a possible contraindication to the initiation of treatment with a TCA. If a TCA is started, the child's cardiac status should be monitored before initiation of treatment, with each dosage adjustment, and regularly thereafter. (For a more extensive review of cardiac evaluation procedures prior to initiating potentially cardiotoxic medications, see Chapter 15.)

Monoamine Oxidase Inhibitors

Monoamine oxidase inhibitors (MAOIs) are a class of powerful antidepressants. The first MAOI, iproniazid, was designed to treat tuberculosis but was serendipitously found to improve patients' moods. Subsequent research led to its marketing in 1958 as an antidepressant, although it was later replaced by less hepatotoxic medications, including isocarboxazid (Marplan) in 1959. MAOIs are believed to work by decreasing the function of monoamine oxidase, an intracellular enzyme that metabolizes neurotransmitters. By decreasing the effect of this enzyme, the neurotransmitters, including norepinephrine, dopamine, and serotonin, are allowed to stay in the synapse longer and stimulate the postsynaptic neuron to a greater extent. Due to potentially lethal dietary and drug interactions, however, MAOIs have been reserved as a later line of defense to be used only when other classes of antidepressant drugs have been unsuccessful.

In recent years, a patch form of the drug selegiline (Emsam) was developed. When applied transdermally in low dosages, the drug does not enter the gastrointestinal tract as it does when taken orally, thereby decreasing the dangers of dietary interactions associated with MAOIs taken orally. The four available MAIOs in the United States are isocarboxazid (Marplan), phenelzine (Nardil), tranylcypromine (Parnate), and selegiline (available as Eldepryl in tablet form and, as mentioned, Emsam in patch form). In the past MAOIs were prescribed for those resistant to TCAs, but the newer MAOIs are now sometimes used as a first-line treatment by some practitioners for adult depression, social anxiety, smoking cessation, and atypical depression. Still, there remain no convincing studies of these medications in depressed children and adolescents.

The side effects of MAOIs can be significant and lethal. Of greatest concern is the hypertensive crisis that can occur when foods containing the amino acid tyramine are consumed. Monoamine oxidase typically degrades this protein, but if this enzyme system is inhibited by an MAOI, tyramine is free to enter the bloodstream where it is taken up by sympathetic nervous system terminals where it can lead to release of endogenous catecholamines, such as norepinephrine and dopamine; these, in turn, can lead to hypertension, hyperpyrexia, tachycardia, diaphoresis, tremors, and cardiac arrhythmias. Similarly, when used in combination with selective serotonin reuptake inhibitors (SSRIs), clomipramine (Anafranil), or other serotonin-promoting drugs or foods high in tryptophan, the serotonin syndrome can result, characterized by tachycardia, hypertension, and fever. Both serotonin syndrome and tyramine ingestion can result, in the worst-case scenario, in coma, seizures, and death. For these reasons, MAOIs are infrequently used in children and adolescents, particularly given some data suggesting that 80% of adolescents do not follow the required diet (Ryan, Meyer, Dachille, Mazzie, & Puig-Antich, 1988). There is also great risk associated with MAOI use and over-the-counter medications, illicit drugs, and certain supplements, such as St. John's wort.

Selective Serotonin Reuptake Inhibitors

SSRIs are much safer for use in children and adolescents, easier to prescribe, and generally better tolerated. The six available SSRIs include fluoxetine (Prozac), sertraline (Zoloft), paroxetine (Paxil), fluvoxamine

(Luvox), citalopram (Celexa), and escitalopram (Lexapro). The presumed mechanism of action is similar to that with the TCAs, yet these medications exert their effects more specifically at the serotonin presynaptic receptors. By blocking the reuptake of serotonin at the presynaptic nerve, the SSRIs increase the amount of serotonin in the synapse to further stimulate the downstream neuron.

While generally useful for pediatric anxiety disorders, the SSRIs are perhaps less effective in treating pediatric depression. Although open-label studies have reported a 70% to 90% response rate in the treatment of adolescents with depression, more rigorous studies have not been as impressive (Birmaher et al., 1996). Two large randomized, double-blind, placebo-controlled studies demonstrated the superiority of fluoxetine over placebo leading to Food and Drug Administration (FDA) approval of fluoxetine as the best supported treatment for pediatric depression in children ages 8 to 17 years (Emslie et al., 2002; Emslie, Rush, et al., 1997). Similar studies of escitalopram for the treatment of adolescents with depression have also been sufficiently convincing to warrant FDA approval of the medication for the treatment of adolescents with depression, ages 12 to 17 years (Emslie, Ventura, Korotzer, & Tourkodimitris, 2009; Wagner, Jonas, Findling, Ventura, & Saikali, 2006). Studies of the remaining SSRIs, however, have shown mixed results. Although most have demonstrated significant benefit in open-label studies, the randomized, double-blind, placebo-controlled studies that have been performed have not been robust (Berard, Fong, Carpenter, Thomason, & Wilkinson, 2006; Emslie et al., 2006; Keller et al., 2001; von Knorring, Olsson, Thomsen, Lemming, & Hultén, 2006; Wagner et al., 2003; Wagner, Berard, et al., 2004; Wagner, Robb, et al., 2004). Consequently, at this time fluoxetine is best supported by the research for the treatment of pediatric depression along with escitalopram for adolescents, but other SSRIs have little evidence to suggest they are better than placebo.

Most common side effects of SSRIs tend to occur during the first few weeks of treatment, often becoming less apparent or bothersome thereafter. Sexual side effects, however, such as ejaculatory delay, anorgasmia, and decreased libido may set on after many weeks of treatment, although they generally improve over time. The transient side effects of SSRIs may include nausea, vomiting, diarrhea, drowsiness, headache, teeth clenching, vivid and strange dreams, dizziness, changes in appetite, weight loss or gain, increased feelings of depression and anxiety, tremors, autonomic dysfunction (including orthostatic hypotension or sweating), akathisia, hyponatremia, liver or renal impairment, and photosensitivity. Suicidal ideation has also been reported among children and adolescents taking SSRIs and is discussed at length in the Appendix.

The practitioner is always advised to proceed cautiously with dosing antidepressants in children and adolescents. When treating with fluoxetine, most youth can be started on a dose of 10 mg or even 5 mg, advancing to 10 mg within a few weeks. Practitioners should always follow up with their patients within one to two weeks of starting an antidepressant to encourage adherence to the treatment regimen, answer questions, provide further education, and address any side effects. Many children and adolescents will respond adequately to 10 mg of fluoxetine for the treatment of depression. Although advancing the dosage of antidepressants beyond an initial therapeutic target (typically 20 mg of fluoxetine for adults with depression) has not generally been demonstrated to lead to improved efficacy, clinical experience dictates that if the treatment response is only partial, the dosage should be increased. Because it takes two weeks at a minimum and perhaps as many as 12 weeks at a maximum to see any benefit from the treatment, the prescribing physician is advised to be patient and advance the dosage cautiously.

Mixed Antidepressants

The serotonin-norepinephrine reuptake inhibitors (SNRIs) have yet to demonstrate efficacy for the treatment of pediatric depression. Open-label studies and case reports support the use of bupropion (Wellbutrin), nefazodone (Serzone), and mirtazapine (Remeron), but no randomized, double-blind, placebo-controlled studies have been completed (Daviss et al., 2001; Findling et al., 2000; Haapasalo-Pesu, Vuola, Lahelma, & Marttunen, 2004; Wilens, Spencer, Biederman, & Schleifer, 1997). Venlafaxine (Effexor) has been studied in two randomized, double-blind, placebo-controlled trials, but neither has demonstrated treatment efficacy (Emslie, Findling, Yeung, Kunz, & Li, 2007; Mandoki, Tapia, Tapia, Sumner, & Parker, 1997).

Antidepressant Augmentation

When a patient is partially but not fully responding to antidepressant treatment, augmenting medications are sometimes employed. A number of medications have proven themselves at least partially useful for this purpose in adults, including lithium, triiodothyronine (T3 thyroid hormone), stimulants, pindolol (Visken), and buspirone (Buspar; Nelson, 2007). Antipsychotic medications as well have been employed more frequently in recent years, including risperidone (Risperdal) and aripiprazole (Abilify), the latter of which is approved by the FDA for the augmentation of treatment-resistant unipolar, nonpsychotic depression in adults (Philip, Carpenter, Tyrka, & Price, 2008; Reeves et al., 2008). One additional strategy sometimes employed for treatment-resistant depression, but without supportive data other than clinical experience, is combining antidepressants, particularly those that act within different neurochemical systems; a common example is bupropion (Wellbutrin), which acts primarily in the norepinephrine system, with an SSRI. In children and adolescents, however, other than lithium, which has only scant data, there is no evidence to support antidepressant augmentation, although in practice it happens frequently (Ryan, Meyer, Dachille, Mazzie, & Puig-Antich, 1988; Strober, Freeman, Rigali, Schmidt, & Diamond, 1992; Walter, Lyndon, & Kubb, 1998).

Atypical Agents

The use of atypical pharmacological agents and strategies, including complementary and alternative medications and vitamins, has been increasing in recent years. Memantine, riluzole, inositol, s-Adenosylmethionine (SAMe), omega-3 fatty acids, and St. John's wort have all demonstrated varying but generally modest benefit in studies of adults with depression, but scant data in children are available (Shatkin & Janssen, 2012).

As previously noted in this chapter, vitamin D augmentation of a standard antidepressant is another consideration in adults and unlikely to be harmful to children, although there is no solid evidence to suggest the use of vitamin D alone for the treatment of depression. In the case of documented vitamin D deficiency co-occurring with depression, supplementation is reasonable. Dosage will depend upon age and whether or not one is truly deficient or simply augmenting antidepressant treatment with vitamin D. For the treatment of vitamin D deficiency in children and adolescents, typically 2,000 units by mouth per day is given for six weeks; in adults, 6,000 units are given for eight weeks. There are many caveats to these dosage strategies, however, including obesity and difficulties absorbing vitamins. In the case of antidepressant augmentation among adults, studies have commonly employed 400 to 600 units per day but sometimes up to 5,000 units per day have been given. Importantly, because vitamin D is fat-soluble, it should always be taken with food containing at least some fat so that it is adequately absorbed. Finally, although some debate remains, at this time vitamin D3 is the preferred form of the supplement for antidepressant augmentation (Shaffer et al., 2014).

Electroconvulsive Therapy

Case reports of children and adolescents receiving electroconvulsive therapy (ECT) for treatment-resistant depression date back to 1942. Most case reports, however, suffer from a lack of diagnostic clarity, small sample sizes, and heterogeneous diagnoses. Retrospective studies have reported the success of ECT in adolescents with a variety of psychiatric disorders, primarily MDD, some acute psychotic states, catatonia, and mania associated with bipolar disorder. ECT has not demonstrated efficacy for the treatment of anxiety, substance abuse, personality disorders, or dysthymia. Response rates vary from 51% to 100% in studies of adolescents with higher response rates noted among those with mood disorders (Ghaziuddin et al., 2004). Only one study has compared adolescents treated with ECT with those who refused ECT. Kutcher and Robertson (1995) found significant improvements noted among those who received ECT. Treated patients had shorter hospital stays, averaging 74 versus 176 days.

International estimates of ECT utilization are nearly impossible to assess, and even in the United States no mandatory reporting system exists. However, a study by the National Institutes of Mental Health revealed that about 1.5% of all ECT performed in 1980 in the United States, or about 500 cases, was for children and adolescents ages 11 to 20 years (J. W. Thompson & Blaine, 1987).

ECT is generally viewed as a remarkably safe and effective treatment for adults. Remission rates are usually greater than those reported for antidepressants, averaging at least 60% to 70% and in some studies quite a bit higher (U.S. Department of Health and Human Services, 1999). A single case series of four adolescents who received ECT found that only one teen responded favorably, and three had prolonged seizures of greater than 4 minutes each (Guttmacher & Cretella, 1988). This finding, however, has not been replicated, and all other studies suggest ECT to be effective in children and adolescents with no greater side effect profile than in adults (Rey & Walter, 1997).

Medication Treatment Algorithm

Upon establishing a proper diagnosis that warrants antidepressant treatment, the treating practitioner is advised to consider the use of fluoxetine as a first measure in children and adolescents and escitalopram in adolescents, given their FDA approval and demonstrated efficacy. Beyond this point in treatment, the practitioner is essentially left with only clinical experience to guide decision-making. Other SSRIs may be

Table 12.2 Suggested Antidepressants Treatment Algorithm

*Step 1:	Fluoxetine (Prozac®) or escitalopram (Lexapro®)
*Step 2:	SNRI or alternate SSRI
*Step 3:	TCA
Step 4:	MAOI
Step 5:	ECT

*Augmentation for partial responders can be considered at any of these three steps.

perfectly acceptable as a starting point as well, but the research data do not strongly support this approach at present time. If fluoxetine or escitalopram are ineffective, a second SSRI or an alternate antidepressant, such as an SNRI, may be considered. If fluoxetine or escitalopram are partially effective, the practitioner should consider a dosage increase. If the dosage increase is ineffective, the practitioner should consider an alternate antidepressant of a different mechanism, such as an SNRI. If either the first or the second antidepressant is partially effective, augmentation may be considered and may include lithium, an antipsychotic, or another antidepressant. T3 thyroid hormone, pindolol, a stimulant, or buspirone may also be considered at this time, even though we have no objective data to support this strategy in children and adolescents. Should augmentation fail, treatment with a TCA is advised, followed by augmentation of the TCA. If the TCA is ineffective, an MAOI without augmentation followed by ECT should be considered (see Table 12.2). Only experienced and skilled practitioners are advised to treat beyond the first two steps, particularly if augmentation is involved. If the practitioner has any questions, he or she should refer to an experienced specialist for consultation.

Psychodynamic Psychotherapy

Psychotherapy for the treatment of child and adolescent depression was historically psychodynamic or analytic in nature, often focusing on play as a means of getting to know the inner experience of the child. While often useful, the practice of such therapies, however, is highly idiosyncratic, and the utility of the treatment depends largely upon the therapist's skills and the fit between the therapist and patient. Although there are no absolute inclusion or exclusion criteria for patients entering psychodynamic psychotherapy, there are some generalizations that can be made. First, the ability to think abstractly helps considerably. For children in play therapy, abstract conceptualization is not a requirement, but in the absence of play as a primary technique, the ability to think outside of oneself is of great utility. Second, the patient should have reasonably good *ego strength* or an ability to withstand observations of his or her behavior and thoughts and to receive criticism from both himself or herself and the therapist. Third, psychologically minded, introspective individuals tend to do better in psychodynamic psychotherapy. Finally, patients without an overwhelming *superego* tend to do better, as they do not feel excessively restricted by external values and morays to the point that they are incapable of questioning their natural inclinations, principles, and ideas. Cognitive behavior therapy (CBT), by contrast, does not make such demands on the patient. CBT only demands that the patient be willing to do homework and be in enough distress to be motivated to change his or her thinking and behavior.

Cognitive Behavior Therapy

In recent years CBT has moved to the forefront of depression treatment. Initially described by Aaron Beck for the treatment of adults with depression, CBT has since been successfully applied to depressed children and adolescents (Beck, Rush, Shaw, & Emery, 1979). Other therapies derived in part from CBT, including interpersonal therapy (IPT) and dialectical behavior therapy (DBT), have also demonstrated some degree of efficacy in treating both adults and youth with depression. These therapies have the distinct advantage of being "manualized" or designed for application in a straightforward, almost algorithmic fashion, which allows them to be rationally structured, reliably taught, and effectively replicated.

CBT has been found more effective than a wait-list condition or non-CBT psychotherapy for the treatment of depression in children and adolescents (Curry, 2001). Harrington, Whittaker, and Shoebridge's (1998) review of CBT in depressed children and adolescents reported benefit for 62% of treated patients versus 36% in placebo groups. Most studies have also found CBT better than other manualized treatments, such as relaxation training and family and supportive therapy, and CBT results in more rapid symptom remission than family or supportive therapy (Brent et al., 1997). Unfortunately, CBT follow-up studies have found high rates of relapse, which suggests the need for continued treatment (Birmaher & Brent, 1998). While clearly a more effective acute treatment, long-term follow-up studies of depressed adolescents have shown no superiority for CBT over other psychotherapies (Birmaher et al., 2000; Curry, 2001). In other words, while CBT generally results in a more rapid resolution of symptoms, years after the initial episode of depression, it is not clear that

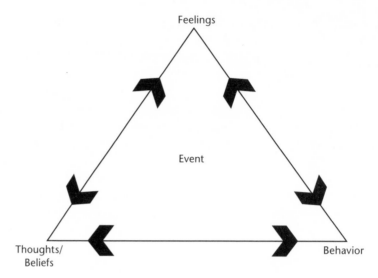

Figure 12.2 The Cognitive Triangle

CBT is more effective than other types of psychotherapy. Finally, no form of CBT has as yet shown superiority over others.

The cognitive triangle is illustrated in Figure 12.2. At the center of the triangle lies an "event," something that triggers the complex interplay between thoughts, feelings, and behaviors. If a patient is feeling depressed, it does us little good to tell him or her not to feel depressed. However, since feelings, thoughts, and behaviors all influence one another, as depicted by the double-headed arrows on each line, influencing one of these factors will also influence the others. For patients who are feeling depressed, then, we strive to help them change their thoughts and behaviors in an effort to improve their feelings.

Both cognitive and behavioral strategies are employed when treating depression with CBT. CBT is based on the idea that learned thoughts and behavioral patterns lead to feelings. The cognitive model presumes that the way in which we interpret and think about the things around us and the way in which we behave determines the way we feel and react. We know, for example, that different individuals often have different reactions to precisely the same event. Imagine a child waiting to be picked up from school by her parent. The child waits and waits; all of the other children have already been picked up by their parents, and now she stands alone. Our child may fear that her mother and father have died, thereby leading to feelings of sadness, abandonment, or panic. Conversely, our child may believe that her dad simply got caught at work, which may lead to feelings of neglect or anger. Or perhaps our child has not even been paying much attention to the fact that she is the last one waiting, and she's turned her attention to a book that she is excited about, leading to feelings of relief or happiness. The basic tenant of cognitive therapy is "the thoughts create the feelings."

Similarly, we know that changing our behaviors often makes us feel better, even when nothing else in our lives has changed. Let us revisit the child in prior paragraph. She is the last child waiting for her father to pick her up, and she now stands alone. In addition to the thought patterns described above that influence her feelings, the behaviors in which she engages can also impact her mood. She may choose to read while waiting, essentially distracting herself from her worries. Alternatively, she may choose to practice deep breathing, meditation, or engage in some exercise and stretching while waiting; or she may challenge herself to come up with a game counting all the red cars that go by, or identifying 10 unique things that she has never noticed before in the spot where she is waiting. Engaging in these activities may make her feel happy, involved in her environment, and pleasantly distracted from her sadness. The basic tenant of behavioral therapy is "the behaviors create the feelings."

CBT is generally brief and time-limited, typically no more than 12 to 16 weeks. Homework is stressed and viewed as a necessary component of the therapeutic work. The patient is encouraged to stay focused on the homework as part of the therapy, to employ time management, and to focus on solvable problems. Handouts, tapes, and other materials are often used. A good therapeutic relationship is important for CBT, but in contrast to traditional psychodynamic psychotherapy, the therapist may even use self-disclosure at times and share his or her own thoughts and behavioral responses with the patient. CBT is collaborative, and there is no hidden agenda. The patient may even be encouraged to read about CBT to help him or her understand the process. CBT often employs the Socratic method, using questions to examine patients' thoughts and suggesting that they substitute less troublesome thoughts for those they feel are bogging them down. CBT is therapist directed and problem focused. Finally, teaching is actively used by the therapist as indicated, as is an inductive model of experimenting and searching for facts (e.g., actively questioning the patient's theories about his or her behavior and thoughts).

In order to evaluate a patient's thoughts, CBT utilizes a number of methodologies. Using record keeping, a patient can keep tabs on his or her thoughts or "activating experiences" throughout the day. These thoughts, often distorted by depression, can be reviewed with the therapist during sessions. One can also have patients act out certain activities or problems that cause them stress and then evaluate how they think about them. Another therapeutic method is "thought listing," whereby

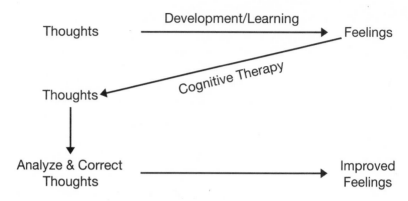

Figure 12.3 Model of CBT for treatment of depression. Cognitive behavior theory hypothesizes that thoughts dictate feelings. Cognitive behavior therapy works by helping patients to analyze and correct their thoughts, which then leads to improved feelings.

patients describe what they were thinking prior to an activating experience in an attempt to recognize cues or precursors to the feelings that are experienced. Some therapists use audio or video recordings to observe a patient during a particularly difficult activity or role-play. The tapes can then be played back during therapy, where the therapist and patient can focus on the patient's thoughts at that time. Relaxation techniques are also used at times to help patients who have difficulty expressing their thoughts. Using these and other methods, the therapist makes an effort to push "feelings" back into thoughts, which can then be analyzed and "corrected," resulting in improved feelings (see Figure 12.3).

For example, the adolescent may state, "I feel bad about myself in these situations." The proper therapist response using CBT techniques is not one of pure empathy (e.g., "You must have felt very sad."); further probing (e.g., "How did it feel to you to recognize that you cannot possibly do everything?"); or simple acknowledgment (e.g., "Tell me more."). Rather, the therapist's appropriate response using CBT is to focus on the evidence for the patient's feelings. A proper response might be, "Why do you *think* that you are bad?" The therapist may then help the patient to weigh the evidence and decide whether there really are enough data to suggest that the thoughts are accurate or whether they are, rather, distorted. Finally, the therapist may ask the patient what advice he or she would give to a friend in the same situation. Individuals with depression are generally much more generous and forgiving of their friends than they are of themselves. The "what advice would you give to a friend" strategy often helps adolescents to blame themselves less and feel better.

One of the key tenants of CBT for depression is to address patients' distorted thoughts. There are a number of so-called cognitive distortions to which depressed individuals commonly fall prey. These thought patterns are addressed directly in CBT. They include:

- *Filtering*—magnifying the negative details from a situation while filtering out all of the positive aspects.
- *Polarized thinking*—viewing everything as "good" or "bad" in an overly dogmatic fashion; believing that one must be perfect or a failure, allowing for no middle ground.
- *Overgeneralization*—coming to a conclusion about one's capabilities based upon a single incident or piece of evidence; when something bad happens once, the expectation is that it will happen over and over again.
- *Mind-reading*—presuming to understand how others feel and to know why they act as they do; particularly believing that one knows how others feel about one.
- *Catastrophizing*—expecting disaster from every interaction or situation.
- *Personalization*—thinking that everything people do or say is a reaction to oneself; constantly comparing oneself to others and trying to determine who is smarter, better looking, and so forth.
- *Fallacy of control*—some individuals feel helpless and externally controlled by others, a victim of fate; alternatively, some individuals have a fallacy of internal control, which makes them feel as if they are responsible for the happiness and pain of everyone around them.
- *Fallacy of fairness*—feeling resentful because one thinks one knows what is fair but others will not agree.
- *Fallacy of change*—expecting that others will change or respond if one only pressures or cajoles them adequately; one feels the need to change others because one feels that one's happiness depends entirely upon them.
- *Heaven's reward fallacy*—expecting all one's sacrifices and self-denial to pay off as if someone were keeping score; feeling bitter and angry when the reward does not come.
- *Blaming*—holding others responsible for the pain one feels, or blaming oneself for every problem in oneself and others.
- *Shoulds*—having a list of restrictive rules about how one and others should act; becoming angered when others break these rules or feeling guilty if one violates them.
- *Emotional reasoning*—believing that what one feels must be automatically true, such that if one feels bored or not intelligent in a given situation, then one must actually be "boring and stupid."

- *Global labeling*—generalizing one or two qualities into a negative global judgment.
- *Being right*—feeling continually on trial to prove that one's opinions and actions are correct; being wrong is impermissible and therefore going to great lengths to demonstrates one's correctness.

Behavioral efforts in CBT typically include activation and relaxation strategies. By reengaging individuals in the activities of their life, they often feel better. This strategy can take many forms and may simply include pushing oneself to get back to old hobbies and friendships that have been interrupted by the depression. Another common strategy involves "opposite action" or acting the opposite of how one would normally behave in a given situation. For example, if a friend asks the depressed child to go to a movie and the child does not feel up to the activity, she might do the opposite of how she feels, in effect "forcing" herself to attend the movie. Likewise, if a child is feeling left out of a group and these feelings are contributing to the depression, the therapist might work with the child to develop active strategies to help him make entry into the group in a socially acceptable way. This type of practical strategizing and problem solving is common in CBT and often very helpful. Behavioral relaxation strategies are also helpful and may include belly breathing, progressive muscle relaxation, giving oneself affirmation statements, journaling, meditating, yoga, exercising, and identifying the positive aspects of any situation. In general, prepubertal children tend to do better with more of the behavioral aspects of CBT, as questioning one's cognition is usually difficult for younger children. With age, adolescents show an increasing ability to incorporate the cognitive components into their CBT.

Interpersonal Therapy

Interpersonal therapy (IPT), another manualized therapy, has been shown to be more efficacious than a wait-list condition or minimal clinical management in a number of treatment studies of depressed adolescents (L. Miller, Gur, Shanok, & Weissman, 2008; Mufson, Weissman, Moreau, & Garfinkel, 1999; Rosselló & Bernal, 1999). Like CBT, IPT is a time-limited psychotherapy that uses a highly structured approach, along with homework assignments. IPT is based on Harry Stack Sullivan's interpersonal theory, which suggests that individual relationships and interactions with others can provide the necessary insight into the causes and cures of mental dysfunction. IPT in its current form was developed by Gerald Klerman and Myrna Weissman in the 1980s for use in treatment studies of adult depression. IPT has since been modified for treatment of anorexia nervosa, bipolar disorder, PTSD, and anxiety disorders. The focus of IPT is generally on one or two personal issues or relationships most closely related to the depression. As with CBT, the therapist is the patient's advocate, not a neutral party.

IPT asserts that depression has three main features—symptom formation, social functioning, and personality contributions. IPT intervenes specifically in the realm of social functioning with the direct goal of alleviating symptoms. Problems in social functioning are hypothesized to occur in four ways—interpersonal disputes, role transitions, grief, and interpersonal deficits. IPT takes a very concrete approach by working with the patient to "solve" one specific problem with the belief that by so doing, the depression is likely to improve.

Both IPT and CBT have demonstrated efficacy in the treatment of adolescent depression when delivered either individually or in groups, making these treatments highly cost-effective and portable (David-Ferdon & Kaslow, 2008). Yet, given the wealth of data supporting CBT for the treatment of adolescent depression, it remains the gold standard by which other psychotherapies should be judged (Rosselló, Bernal, & Rivera-Medina, 2008).

Dialectical Behavior Therapy

Dialectical behavior therapy (DBT), designed initially for the treatment of individuals with borderline personality disorder, has been effectively utilized for the treatment of suicidal and nonsuicidal self-injurious behavior in adults (Harley, Sprich, Safren, Jacobo, & Fava, 2008; Linehan, 1993; Stanley, Brodsky, Nelson, & Dulit, 2007). Although adequate scientific studies have not yet been performed in youth, DBT also appears to hold great promise for treating adolescents with MDD who are chronically suicidal or who self-injure (Fleischhaker, Munz, Böhme, Sixt, & Schulz, 2006; James, Taylor, Winmill, & Alfoadari, 2008; Miller, Rathus, & Linehan, 2006; Perepletchikova et al., 2011). At its core, DBT attempts to help individuals integrate opposing points of view or *dialectics* in an effort to become whole individuals. In addition to a reliance upon CBT strategies, DBT leans heavily upon Zen Buddhist philosophy, emphasizing the interrelatedness of opposing forces. From this perspective, typical borderline defenses, such as "splitting" and "projective identification," are viewed as a response to one's inability to allow contradictory feelings, such as love and anger, to exist side by side. DBT aims to help affected individuals learn to regulate their emotions, tolerate distress without harming themselves, believe in their own interpersonal effectiveness, and engage in mindful ways of thinking. For those adolescents with MDD who self-injure or are chronically suicidal, referral for group or individual DBT is worth considering.

Combining Psychotherapy and Medication

Numerous studies have attempted to determine which treatment is "best" for child and adolescent depression—CBT, SSRIs, or a combination of the two. These large, federally funded multisite studies have compared CBT with various SSRIs and placebo for extended periods of time.

The Treatment for Adolescents with Depression Study (TADS) is a multicenter, randomized clinical trial of 12- to 17-year-old adolescents with MDD, which enrolled over 430 youth. TADS compared the efficacy of fluoxetine at dosages of 10 to 40 mg per day, CBT, their combination, and placebo for up to one year. Those receiving a medication were blinded, as were the treating physicians. Response rates at 12 weeks were 71% for combined treatment (fluoxetine plus CBT), 61% for fluoxetine alone, 43% for CBT alone, and 35% for placebo. Fluoxetine alone was superior to CBT alone, which did not itself separate from placebo. Remission rates totaled 23% for the study and included 37% of those receiving combined treatment, 23% of those receiving fluoxetine only, 17% of those receiving placebo, and 16% of those receiving CBT. Adolescents who were younger, were less chronically depressed, were higher functioning, were less hopeless with fewer indications of suicidal ideation, had fewer melancholic features and comorbid diagnoses, and those with greater expectations for improvement were more likely to benefit from treatment (March et al., 2004).

After 36 weeks of continued treatment, the TADS data look different (March, Silva, et al., 2007). By this time, 86% of those receiving combined treatment, 81% receiving fluoxetine, and 81% receiving CBT improved. Thus, most adolescents with depression who had not improved during acute treatment did so during the continuation and maintenance phases of the study. This continuation study also suggests that CBT is as effective as fluoxetine but takes somewhat longer to work. Furthermore, by 36 weeks, patients treated with fluoxetine alone were twice as likely as patients treated with combined fluoxetine and CBT to report clinically significant suicidal ideation or to engage in a suicidal behavior, suggesting a protective effect on suicidality from adding CBT to medication.

The adolescents in TADS were followed naturalistically for one year after the formal study ended, confirming and revealing further important observations. First, combined treatment (fluoxetine plus CBT) achieves its maximum benefit earlier (by week 18) than either fluoxetine alone (30 weeks) or CBT alone (36 weeks). Second, 36 weeks (nine months) of treatment was superior to 12 weeks (three months). Third, even when active treatment was discontinued and patients were followed naturalistically for up to one year, most patients experienced sustained and clinically meaningful improvement with a lower relapse rate than is typically found in medication only treatment studies (Treatment for Adolescents with Depression Study [TADS] Team, 2009).

Because only about 60% of adolescents demonstrate an adequate therapeutic response to SSRI treatment alone, the National Institutes of Mental Health sponsored the Treatment of Resistant Depression in Adolescents (TORDIA) Study. This multisite clinical trial compared the efficacy of fluoxetine, paroxetine, citalopram, and venlafaxine alone and in combination with CBT for 12- to 18-year-old adolescents with treatment-resistant depression. The study utilized a randomized, double-blind, placebo-controlled methodology by offering adolescents with MDD who did not respond to two months of initial treatment with an SSRI: (a) 12 additional weeks of a second, different SSRI (e.g., fluoxetine, paroxetine, or citalopram at 20 to 40 mg per day); (b) a switch to a second SSRI in addition to CBT; (c) a switch to venlafaxine alone at 150 to 225 mg per day; or (d) a switch to venlafaxine in addition to CBT. The study found that switching to an alternate medication plus CBT resulted in a higher response rate (55%) among these treatment-resistant adolescents than simply a medication switch alone (41%). While there were no differences in the response rates among those adolescents switching to a second SSRI versus venlafaxine, more side effects were noted among those taking venlafaxine, including slight blood pressure and heart rate increases, along with skin rashes (Brent et al., 2008).

When treating pediatric depression, the clinician is advised to evaluate all possible causes and comorbidities. If treatment for depression is indicated, CBT or IPT should be initiated for mild to moderate cases without suicidality. In the presence of chronic depression, suicidality, or moderate to severe symptoms, fluoxetine or escitalopram should be considered. Should this combination not result in significant symptom remission, an augmenting strategy and/or second medication (as above) should be considered, along with a referral to a child and adolescent psychiatrist for consultation.

13

Bipolar Disorder

Emil Kraepelin was among the first to comment on bipolar disorder in children and adolescents. In his observations of over 900 patients with manic depression (the prior term for bipolar disorder) in 1917, he reported that the illness most frequently set on between 15 and 20 years of age. Kraepelin also reported that onset prior to 10 years of age was rare and mild, if it occurred at all (A. Duffy, 2007). As happened with pediatric depression, psychoanalytic theory, which held great clout in American psychiatry through the 1970s, suggested that children lack the higher level cognitive structures required for a diagnosis of bipolar disorder. Thanks to research over the past three decades, however, we now once again recognize, as did Kraepelin, that bipolar disorder can affect children and adolescents. Nearly 60% of bipolar adults recall having some symptoms prior to age 19 (Lish, Dime-Meenan, Whybrow, Price, & Hirschfeld, 1994), and up to 20% of adults recall having significant prodromal symptoms prior to age 10 years (Egeland, Hostetter, Pauls, & Sussex, 2000).

CLINICAL PRESENTATION

The classic adult presentation of bipolar disorder Type I (BP-I), with discrete episodes of mania and depression with clear onset and offset, is rare in children and younger adolescents (F. K. Goodwin & Jamison, 1990). In contrast, we more commonly see episodes of long duration characterized by rapid or continuous cycling and mixed mania among children. Among adolescents, BP-I more frequently resembles the adult presentation with euphoria, grandiosity, paranoid ideation, and flight of ideas, whereas younger children more frequently present with irritability, excitability, aggression, explosiveness, and significant mood lability. Those children with extensive mood disturbance who do not meet specific criteria for BP-I or bipolar disorder Type II (BP-II), characterized by episodes of hypomania alternating with depression, and whose symptoms are predominantly irritable and aggressive, are commonly and often mistakenly diagnosed with bipolar disorder not otherwise specified (BP-NOS); now renamed *unspecified bipolar disorder* in *DSM-5*. The diagnosis of cyclothymia, which is rarely used for children and adolescents, describes a mood disorder with alternations between hypomania and low-grade depression.

The atypical presentation of bipolar disorder in prepubertal children has led many investigators and clinicians to doubt once again the existence of the illness in preadolescents. It has, after all, not yet been established that preteens currently diagnosed with bipolar disorder will develop the adult form (Chang, 2007), as characterized clearly in *DSM-5* (American Psychiatric Association, 2013). Perhaps the predominant irritability and aggression seen in these children is due to a different disorder or combination of disorders, such as attention-deficit/hyperactivity disorder (ADHD), learning disorders, oppositional defiant or conduct disorder, and posttraumatic stress disorder along with poor parental monitoring. Because prepubertal children are simply not developmentally capable of expressing some of the classic *DSM-5* symptoms of bipolar disorder (such as "engaging in unrestrained buying sprees, sexual indiscretions, or foolish business investments"), some parents, clinicians, and researchers have been seen as zealots, embracing the disorder fervently to the exclusion of other reasonable explanations for a child's disruptive behavior. Certainly, irritability, aggression, and mood lability are frequent symptoms of many childhood psychiatric conditions and are most often not indicative of bipolar disorder (Stringaris & Goodman, 2008). In an effort to more accurately categorize these "diagnostic orphans," who commonly express a great deal of irritability along with anxiety, oppositional behavior and inattention/hyperactivity and who grow up to more commonly have troubles with anxiety and depression rather than bipolar disorder, *DSM-5* has created a new diagnosis within the depressive disorder spectrum, *disruptive mood dysregulation disorder,* as discussed in Chapter 12.

In order to properly diagnose bipolar disorder as we currently understand it, clear *DSM-5* symptom criteria must be present, but the symptoms in children will differ at least somewhat from those seen in adolescents and adults. Some investigators have argued that a bipolar elated mood may present in a child as repeated giggling in inappropriate places with an inability to stop; grandiosity may present as stealing and a child believing that rules do not apply to him or her; decreased need for sleep may present as staying awake late and keeping very busy, then needing only a few hours of sleep and awakening filled with energy for the day ahead; and risk-taking behavior may present as hypersexuality, including provocative speech, gestures, and inappropriate touching of oneself and others in public (B. Geller, Zimerman, Williams, DelBello, Frazier, et al., 2002). Such symptom variants should be considered potentially diagnostic only if they are consistent with an overall clinical picture of bipolar disorder.

To further muddy the diagnostic water, rapid or complex cycling has been described in over 80% of children diagnosed with bipolar disorder in some studies (B. Geller et al., 2000). *DSM-5* defines "rapid cycling" bipolar disorder as four or more distinct episodes of either mania, hypomania, or depression per year with each episode meeting full diagnostic criteria for duration (e.g., two weeks for a major depressive episode, one week for a manic episode, and four days for a hypomanic episode) and separated by either full or partial remission of at least two months or a switch to a mood episode of the opposite polarity. Although rapid cycling occurs in only about 10% to 20% of adults with bipolar disorder, it has generally been the rule in childhood manifestations of the disorder. In fact, investigators have termed the phrase "ultra rapid cycling" for those who have more than 4 but fewer than 365 cycles per year and "ultradian" for those who have numerous cycles every day or more than 365 per year (B. Geller, Tillman, & Bolhofner, 2007). While these terms may not prove to be diagnostically valid in the years to come, researchers do agree that bipolar disorder in children is typically chronic with long, predominantly mixed symptoms of mania and depression and less clearly defined episodes than in adults.

ETIOLOGY

We currently envision the mood disorders as lying on a spectrum, with bipolar disorder being the most severe expression. Although not an etiological theory per se, the idea of *kindling*, generally applied to seizure disorders, has also been suggested as a way of understanding bipolar disorder (Mazza et al., 2007). Kindling theory suggests that repeated subthreshold stimulation of a nerve cell, or kindling a nerve cell, just as one would a campfire, eventually causes that nerve to activate or fire. Once this pattern of nerve activation is set in motion, repeated episodes of mood instability continue to stimulate those same tracts or pathways, resulting in a greater likelihood of repeated stimulation of these same nerve pathways over time, leading to repeated manic episodes (Post, 2007). Kindling is believed to be a function of the temporal lobes in bipolar disorder.

There are a number of interesting biological findings, which, taken as a whole, suggest a number of contributing etiological factors. Smaller hippocampal and total cerebral volumes have been found among children and adolescents with bipolar disorder (Frazier et al., 2005), although the meaning of these findings is unclear. Abnormalities have been found within the hypothalamic-pituitary-adrenal (HPA) axis among adults with bipolar disorder. Excess cortisol is suggested to contribute to depressive symptoms and neurotoxicity resulting in cognitive deficits, while mania has been proposed to be secondary to an increase in both ACTH and cortisol (Daban, Vieta, Mackin, & Young, 2005). Various gene mutations or associations have also been suggested as possible etiologies of bipolar disorder. A mutation in the G protein receptor kinase 3 (GRK3) gene may be responsible for up to 10% of cases. This GRK3 mutation is thought to lead to dopamine hypersensitivity, which in turn may cause mood swings (T. B. Barrett et al., 2003). Still, other research suggests that the portion of the genome that encodes diacylglycerol kinase eta (DGKH), an important protein in the lithium-sensitive phosphatidylinositol pathway, may be involved in the genesis of bipolar disorder (Baum et al., 2008). Clearly, numerous biological factors are at play, and the genetic transmission of bipolar disorder is multifactorial.

Inheritance of bipolar disorder is most certain to be polygenic with no single responsible gene. Genetic transmission is probably greater for bipolar disorder than for major depressive disorder (MDD), with numerous studies suggesting an approximately 80% or greater concordance for monozygotic (identical) twins as opposed to about a 20% concordance for dizygotic (fraternal) twins (Cardno et al., 1999; Kieseppä, Partonen, Haukka, Kaprio, & Lönnqvist, 2004). In addition, the vast majority of children and adolescents with bipolar disorder have a relative with a major mood disorder, and a family history of bipolar disorder is a major risk factor for the same in children.

EPIDEMIOLOGY

BP-I has generally been thought to affect about 1% or slightly more of the adult population. When all forms of bipolar disorder are taken into account, that percentage may be as high as 3% (Angst, 1999). BP-I is diagnosed among adults considerably less than BP-II, BP-NOS (unspecified), and cyclothymia. Among children and adolescents, this same pattern is followed, as establishing a clear diagnosis of BP-I in children is riddled with complications. In one large trial of older adolescents 14 to 18 years of age, the lifetime prevalence of bipolar disorder, primarily BP-II and cyclothymia, was 1%, but an additional 5.7% reported periods of abnormally and continually elevated, expansive, or irritable moods that never met criteria for BP-I or BP-II (Lewinsohn, Klein, & Seeley, 1995). In the present day, this group would undoubtedly be diagnosed by many with unspecified bipolar disorder (National Institute of Mental Health, Research Roundtable on Prepubertal Bipolar Disorder, 2001).

Family studies of parents with bipolar disorder have found that offspring have nearly a three times greater risk for developing any psychiatric condition and a four times greater risk for developing a mood disorder (Chang, Steiner, & Ketter, 2003). One study of children with at least one bipolar parent found a prevalence of 55% for any psychiatric disorder, 15% for depressive disorders, and 15% for bipolar disorder or cyclothymia among the offspring (Chang, Steiner, & Ketter, 2000). E. S. Gershon et al. (1982) found a 24% risk of developing a mood disorder for first-degree relatives of individuals with bipolar disorder, increasing to 27% if one parent has bipolar disorder and to 74% if both parents do. These studies suggest a high concordance among family members with bipolar disorder. By contrast, a Dutch study reported a prevalence of 44% for any psychiatric disorder and 23% for depressive disorders but only 4% for bipolar spectrum disorders in offspring of adult bipolar patients (Wals et al., 2004). The reason for this discrepancy in bipolar disorder rates between the United States and Holland is not clear.

The United States has been leading the effort to understand pediatric bipolar disorder in recent years, and the epidemiological statistics have sometimes been contradictory and controversial. One very large study of ambulatory medical care in the United States identified a 40-fold increase in the percentage of total office visits for those under 19 years-of-age with a diagnosis of bipolar disorder between 1994–1995 and 2002–2003 from 25 cases per 100,000 to 1,003 cases per 100,000. By contrast, the increase among adults over 20 years of age during this same time period was only 1.8-fold from 905 per 100,000 to 1,679 per 100,000 (Moreno et al., 2007). It can certainly be argued that practitioners are becoming better diagnosticians and more sensitive to the symptoms of bipolar disorder in children and adolescents. However, we would generally expect to see the same trend in other Western countries, which use the same diagnostic criteria; yet in England and Ireland, for example, a far lower prevalence is reported, 1.7 and 2.2 cases per 100,000, respectively (Scully, Owens, Kinsella, & Waddington, 2004; Sigurdsson, Fombonne, Sayal, & Checkley, 1999).

Numerous other studies have also found greatly increasing rates of bipolar disorder among child and adolescent inpatients. One study identified an increase of over 500% in diagnoses among children and adolescents between 1990 and 2000 (from 2.9% to 15.1%), while another found a 300% increase in diagnoses among children (from 10.3% to 34.1%) and a 250% increase in diagnoses among adolescents (Blader & Carlson, 2007; Case, Olfson, Marcus, & Siegel, 2007). Certainly, psychiatrically hospitalized children are more likely to receive a diagnosis of bipolar disorder than children in the community, but the increase has been swift and remarkable.

Given these statistics, and the observable increase in bipolar diagnoses in clinical practice, it is clear that our epidemiological understanding of this diagnosis among children and adolescents is far from perfect. Furthermore, well-executed, large, community-based epidemiological studies using standardized diagnostic tools have continued to identify low and stable rates of bipolar disorder among those 9 to 24 years of age, averaging well under 1.5% (Costello et al., 1996; Lewinsohn et al., 1995; Wittchen, Nelson, & Lachner, 1998). Consequently, the diagnosis of pediatric bipolar disorder should always be viewed with great skepticism by practitioners, who should judge the diagnosis for themselves based on a thorough history and longitudinal familiarity with the patient.

Finally, early age at onset of bipolar disorder appears to confer several risks. Children with earlier onset have more frequent suicidal ideation and attempts, substance use disorders, and rapid cycling (Carlson, Bromet, & Sievers, 2000; T. D. Carter, Mundo, Parikh, & Kennedy, 2003). In addition, younger age at onset confers a greater risk of bipolar disorder among first-degree relatives of an affected child (B. Geller et al., 2006).

CLINICAL COURSE

The onset of bipolar disorder generally occurs between 15 and 20 years of age. Males may present slightly earlier than females. In the largest study of children and adolescents with bipolar disorder to date (the Course and Outcome of Bipolar Illness in Youth, or COBY), approximately 25% of subjects converted to a more severe form of the disorder during the initial two-year follow-up, such that children initially diagnosed with BP-II, for example, were later diagnosed with BP-I. This finding held at four-year follow-up by which time 38% of those with Bipolar NOS (unspecified) had converted into Bipolar I or II (Birmaher et al., 2009). Younger age at onset or longer duration of illness, BP-NOS, low socioeconomic status, and psychotic symptoms predicted a worse outcome among these youth (Birmaher et al., 2006).

Most children (80%) recover from their first or index episode within 2.5 years. Among those who do recover, approximately 60% will have at least one recurrence within 1.5 years (Birmaher, 2007; Birmaher et al., 2009). The polarity of the first episode of mood disorder also may predict the polarity of later mood episodes. A smaller naturalistic study of children and adolescents found that rate of recovery varied by polarity of the first episode, such that a more rapid recovery was observed in those with pure mania or mixed mania as opposed to those with pure depression at first presentation (Strober et al., 1995). Virtually all longitudinal studies in adults indicate that bipolar disorder is chronic, relapse is the rule, and fewer than 10% fully recover (American Psychiatric Association, 2013). Similar findings in children and adolescents are suggested but not yet substantiated.

Studies of bipolar adults suggest that over time episodes occur more frequently. Left untreated, the length of each cycle tends to decrease for each of the first four or five episodes until it stabilizes. As previously noted, cycling is a recognized characteristic of bipolar disorder and is a diagnostic specifier in *DSM-5*. Cycling may be transient or chronic. Risk factors for rapid cycling in adults include female gender, antidepressant use, thyroid disease, intellectual disability, certain neurological conditions (e.g., multiple sclerosis), and head injury. The rapid cycling subtype in adults has a poorer prognosis (American Psychiatric Association, 2013). Risk factors for rapid cycling in children and adolescents are not known at this time, but, as previously noted, rapid cycling has been suggested to affect 80% or more of youth with bipolar disorder (B. Geller et al., 2000).

"Mixed episode" is another specifier for bipolar disorder and can be understood as a combination of mania and depression present at the same time. Affected individuals may laugh and cry simultaneously, expressing both sadness and glee with equal intensity. Others may speak rapidly, be highly distractible, and make grandiose or euphoric statements, while reporting depression with suicidal ideation and paranoia. Mixed states appear to happen more commonly in children and adolescents with bipolar disorder than adults (Staton, Volness, & Beatty, 2008). However, we must remember that mixed emotional presentations are more common in children than adults even in the absence of psychopathology and that elevated and mixed emotions alone are not diagnostic.

The likelihood of "switching" diagnoses from MDD to bipolar disorder decreases with age. That is, the longer an individual has suffered from depression, the less likely he is to transition into bipolar disorder. The risk of conversion is greatest for children and adolescents (Othmer et al., 2007). Among adults, the risk of diagnostic conversion is greatest during the first five years after the onset of MDD, and about 10% to 15% of adults are affected. Risk factors for switching among adults include early onset, severity of MDD, family history of bipolar disorder, psychosis, and psychiatric comorbidity (Holma, Melartin, Holma, & Isometsä, 2008). The risk of converting to bipolar disorder from MDD probably increases with the number of these risk factors, such that those with two or more risk factors may be 50% or more likely to convert (Othmer et al., 2007).

As discussed in Chapter 12, a significant minority of children and adolescents, somewhere between 20% and 40%, who are initially diagnosed with MDD are believed to subsequently develop bipolar disorder within five years. Risk factors include early-onset MDD, psychomotor retardation, psychosis, pharmacologically induced hypomania, a family history of bipolar disorder or psychotic depression, and a significant family history of mood disorders (Birmaher & Brent, 1998).

Given the relatively small numbers of children and adolescents who are diagnosed with bipolar disorder and the controversies surrounding the diagnosis in this age group, predicting the course and prognosis of the illness is remarkably difficult (Strober et al., 2006). Based on the COBY and other studies, however, we do know that 20% to 30% of bipolar youths make at least one medically significant suicide attempt within 2 to 5 years of diagnosis (T. R. Goldstein et al., 2005; Strober et al., 1995), 20% suffer physical and/or sexual abuse (Romero et al., 2009), and 16% of adolescents suffer substance use disorders (B. I. Goldstein et al., 2008). In addition, the COBY study found that 80% of subjects utilized mental health services in a six-month period, illustrating only one of the many costs to our society of this illness (Rizzo et al., 2007).

Studies of both adults and children indicate severe psychosocial impairments among those with bipolar disorder. During episodes of mania and depression, all individuals suffer. However, between episodes, approximately one third of adults with bipolar disorder continue to suffer major mood difficulties, and two thirds struggle with chronic interpersonal and occupational troubles (American Psychiatric Association, 2000). The same appears true for children and adolescents, where even those in partial remission or full recovery continue to struggle interpersonally and with academic functioning. Predictors of impairment include adolescence (as opposed to childhood), symptom severity, psychosis, and comorbid conduct disorder (T. R. Goldstein et al., 2008). Unquestionably, bipolar children and children of bipolar parents are more likely to be exposed to negative life events and psychosocial stressors because of their upbringing. Families with bipolar children, as well as families with bipolar parents, are characterized by poor cohesion and high conflict (Belardinelli et al., 2008; Chang, Blasey, Ketter, & Steiner, 2001).

DIAGNOSIS

DSM-5 describes a number of bipolar variants, including BP-I, BP-II, BP-NOS (unspecified), and cyclothymia. Both BP-I and BP-II have a characteristic manic phase alternating with periods of major depression. In addition, various specifiers, including "mixed episode" and "rapid cycling," are described. BP-I, the most virulent form of the illness, is characterized by at least one week (or less if hospitalization is required) of an abnormally elevated, expansive, or irritable mood. During this time, at least three of the following symptoms are present (four symptoms are required if the mood is only irritable): (a) decreased need for sleep; (b) grandiosity; (c) excessive talkativeness or pressured speech; (d) excessive risk-taking behavior; (e) excessive goal-directed behavior; (f) excessive distractibility; or (g) racing thoughts. BP-II, or hypomania, is considered a more modest form of the disorder, where only four days of symptoms are required without hospitalization or psychosis. Cyclothymia, by contrast, demands at least two years (one year in children and adolescents) of numerous hypomanic and depressive symptoms, never meeting criteria for MDD or bipolar disorder.

As previously noted, many of the hallmark symptoms of bipolar disorder are difficult to assess in children and adolescents. Grandiosity, for example, is developmentally normal in prepubertal children until about 8 years of age. Young children who report, and truly believe, that they can beat their father at chess or in a wrestling match are not grandiose in the psychotic sense. In fact, even as children age, grandiosity may still be viewed as somewhat more boastful or oppositional rather than delusional, as is more common with adolescent-onset and adult-onset bipolar disorder. The examiner, then, must use many data points and be extremely cautious about the interpretation of symptoms. When they are adequately assessed, some investigators feel that grandiosity, hypersexuality, and an elated, euphoric mood are the most reliable indicators of true mania (B. Geller, Williams, et al., 1998).

We must understand that it is quite rare to see true *DSM-5* bipolar disorder in children under 12 years of age. That is, we may witness true bipolar disorder, but its appearance is somewhat different than expected. Rapid mood fluctuations or lability, hyperactivity, disinhibition, and aggression are evident, but these are not the typical euphoria, grandiosity, or increase in goal-directed behavior seen in the adult presentation of bipolar disorder. Many of the symptoms reported by children and their families sound rather more like ADHD than bipolar disorder, and this differential must be fully explored. Studies report that at least half and perhaps over 80% of bipolar children and adolescents suffer from comorbid ADHD symptoms and that over two thirds have comorbid symptoms of conduct disorder (Borchardt & Bernstein, 1995; Faraone, Biederman, Jetton, & Tsuang, 1997; Kovacs & Pollock, 1995; Milberger, Biederman, Faraone, Murphy, & Tsuang, 1995; S. A. West, McElroy, Strakowski, Keck, & McConville, 1995). Anxiety disorders are also highly comorbid with child and adolescent bipolar disorder, and studies typically show coexisting rates of 20% to 70% (Jolin, Weller, & Weller, 2008). However, whether these symptoms truly represent comorbid conditions or prodromal symptoms, current symptoms, or simply an overlap in *DSM-5* diagnostic symptoms remains unclear. Certainly, this confusion appears to be a greater problem with younger children, as adolescent-onset bipolar disorder has less reported comorbidity with ADHD and disruptive behavior disorders, appearing more like the adult form (Faraone, Biederman, Wozniak, et al., 1997; B. Geller & Luby, 1997). As seen in Table 13.1, among the hallmark symptoms of bipolar disorder, only racing thoughts, grandiosity, and euphoria are not also symptoms of ADHD. However, irritability, another common feature of both disorders, further contributes to the confusion in making the diagnosis.

The centrality of irritability, or aggression and agitation, as a core symptom of bipolar disorder has taken main stage in the child bipolar controversy. Some clinicians support a diagnosis of bipolar disorder if a child meets *DSM-5* criteria with irritability as a core symptom, even in the absence of elation and/or euphoria. Other clinicians believe that unmodified *DSM-5* criteria should always be followed for a diagnosis of bipolar disorder in both children and adults. Another aspect of the con-

Table 13.1   Symptom Crossover Between ADHD and Bipolar Disorder

DSM-5 Symptoms of Mania	Occurrence in ADHD
Elevated/expansive mood	No
Irritability	Common
Grandiosity	No
Decreased need for sleep	Common but relatively mild
Excessive talkativeness	Criterion for diagnosis
Racing thoughts/flight-of-ideas	No
Excess goal-directed behavior	Hyperactivity criteria are similar
High-risk activities	Common
Distractibility	Criterion for diagnosis

troversy involves the high comorbidity among children suspected to have bipolar disorder (e.g., ADHD, learning disorders, oppositional defiant and conduct disorder, posttraumatic stress disorder), thereby making it very difficult to discern if bipolar disorder is truly present. Finally, the abbreviated length of mood episodes in children, sometimes only hours, contrasts with what is universally observed in adults.

It has become increasingly clear that most prepubertal children who have received the diagnosis of BP-NOS (unspecified) or cyclothymia will not go on to develop strictly defined *DSM-5* bipolar disorder as adolescents or adults; and as we have seen, *DSM-5* would now characterize most of these children on the depression spectrum, applying the disruptive mood dysregulation disorder diagnosis. Still, these children represent a greater conundrum to the clinician than simply a child with ADHD, disruptive behavior, poor social support, and learning disabilities. For while these features are extremely common among this cohort of children, regardless of how they are ultimately diagnosed, the fact remains that extensive treatments, including antidepressants, mood stabilizers and antipsychotics, along with intensive family, social, and individual psychosocial therapies, are often necessary to manage their symptoms (S. E. Meyer et al., 2009).

A thorough diagnostic assessment of a child or adolescent with bipolar disorder will include more than one clinical interview. Parents and the child should be seen both together and separately. Mood episodes should be assessed for their quality, duration, and the degree of functional impairment they cause. Precipitants, aggravating and alleviating factors should be considered. Collateral information from teachers, coaches, tutors, and afterschool care providers is essential. All comorbid diagnoses must be considered, along with the child's symptoms during periods of euthymia. Finally, any residual confusion about the diagnosis suggests that expert or additional consultation should be requested, such as referral to a child and adolescent psychiatrist.

The differential diagnosis for bipolar disorder is extensive and includes psychotic, mood, anxiety, externalizing, and personality disorders. Schizophrenia and schizoaffective disorder, while equally difficult to diagnose in children as bipolar disorder, should be considered. Posttraumatic stress disorder, among other anxiety disorders such as obsessive-compulsive disorder, can also present with symptoms similar to bipolar disorder. ADHD, as already discussed, oppositional defiant disorder, and conduct disorder run so highly comorbid that these disorders are often difficult to distinguish from bipolar disorder. Finally, other mood and personality disorders should also be ruled out.

In addition to other psychiatric conditions, there are a number of general medical conditions that mimic mania. Although uncommon, neurologic conditions, including brain tumors, central nervous system infections, multiple sclerosis, temporal lobe epilepsy, and Kleine-Levin syndrome, can make children appear manic. Systemic conditions, including hyperthyroidism, uremia, Wilson's disease, and porphyria, while also infrequent occurrences, can present like bipolar disorder. Finally, numerous medications can induce a manic state, including antidepressants, stimulants, steroids, and various substances of abuse, such as amphetamines, cocaine, phencyclidine (PCP), inhalants, and ecstasy.

There are a number of rating scales that can be helpful in diagnosing child and adolescent bipolar disorder, but none should be relied upon as an absolute diagnostic tool. Perhaps the most useful method of determining if the presenting symptoms do, in fact, represent bipolar disorder is by maintaining a daily mood chart (see Table 13.2). Parents can be taught to log the fluctuations in their child's daily moods on a simple grid designed to follow extreme highs and lows. Parents should also be encouraged to enter how many hours of sleep the child received each day, any significantly stressful events that might explain mood changes, and any psychotic symptoms. Such mood charts allow the clinician to more accurately assess parent and child reports, determine the longitudinal course of the illness, clarify the diagnosis, and assist with tracking treatment response. Perhaps most important, a mood chart can help the clinician decide when to refer to a specialist. Mood charts are typically completed by parents, but collateral sources, such as teachers, and adolescents themselves can also maintain separate charts. Prior to employing a mood chart, the clinician must be certain to explain clearly what is meant by a "high" or manic and "low" or depressed mood to minimize inaccurate recordings.

The Parent Version of the Young Mania Rating Scale, an 11-question survey for parents about their child's mood, offers another method to help clinicians determine when to refer to specialist care. The scale, which is readily available on numerous Internet sites for free, is not intended to diagnose bipolar disorder and does not follow strict *DSM-5* criteria for bipolar disorder. Average scores among manic children are approximately 25 and among hypomanic children approximately 20. Scores above 13 are considered suggestive of bipolar disorder, and scores over 21 are considered probable (Gracious, Youngstrom, Findling, & Calabrese, 2002).

Finally, the Children's Mania Rating Scale (see Figure 13.1) can also aid in diagnosis and be particularly helpful in distinguishing bipolar disorder from ADHD. In research trials, scores over 21 were considered suggestive of a bipolar diagnosis as opposed to ADHD (Pavuluri, Henry, Devineni, Carbray, & Birmaher, 2006).

Table 13.2 Mood Chart

Day #	1	2	3	4	5	6	7	8	9	10	11	12	13	14	15	16	17	18	19	20	21	22	23	24	25	26	27	28	29	30	31
Agitated/manic																															
Hypomanic																															
Euthymic																															
Dysthymic																															
Depressed																															
Sleep (hours)																															
Psychosis																															
Stressful events																															

Child's name	Date of Birth (mm/dd/yy)	Case #/ID #

INSTRUCTIONS

The following questions concern your child's mood and behavior in the **past month**. Please place a checkmark or an "x" in a box for each item. Please consider it a problem if it's **causing trouble** and is beyond what is normal for your child's age. Otherwise, check "rare or never" if the behavior is not causing trouble.

Does your child . . .	NEVER/ RARELY	SOMETIMES	OFTEN	VERY OFTEN	
1. Have periods of feeling super happy for hours or days at a time, extremely wound up and excited, such as feeling "on top of the world"	0	1	2	3	____
2. Feel irritable, cranky, or mad for hours or days at a time	0	1	2	3	____
3. Think that he or she can be anything or do anything (e.g., leader, best basket ball player, rap singer, millionaire, princess) beyond what is usual for that age	0	1	2	3	____
4. Believe that he or she has unrealistic abilities or powers that are unusual, and may try to act upon them, which causes trouble	0	1	2	3	____
5. Need less sleep than usual; yet does not feel tired the next day	0	1	2	3	____
6. Have periods of too much energy	0	1	2	3	____
7. Have periods when she or he talks too much or too loud or talks a mile-a-minute	0	1	2	3	____
8. Have periods of racing thoughts that his or her mind cannot slow down, and it seems that your child's mouth cannot keep up with his or her mind	0	1	2	3	____
9. Talk so fast that he or she jumps from topic to topic	0	1	2	3	____
10. Rush around doing things nonstop	0	1	2	3	____
11. Have trouble staying on track and is easily drawn to what is happening around him or her	0	1	2	3	____
12. Do many more things than usual, or is unusually productive or highly creative	0	1	2	3	____
13. Behave in a sexually inappropriate way (e.g., talks dirty, exposing, playing with private parts, masturbating, making sex phone calls, humping on dogs, playing sex games, touches others sexually)	0	1	2	3	____
14. Go and talk to strangers inappropriately, is more socially outgoing than usual	0	1	2	3	____

Does your child . . .	NEVER/ RARELY	SOMETIMES	OFTEN	VERY OFTEN	
15. Do things that are unusual for him or her that are foolish or risky (e.g., jumping off heights, ordering CDs with your credit cards, giving things away)	0	1	2	3	____
16. Have rage attacks, intense and prolonged temper tantrums	0	1	2	3	____
17. Crack jokes or pun more than usual, laugh loud, or act silly in a way that is out of the ordinary	0	1	2	3	____
18. Experience rapid mood swings	0	1	2	3	____
19. Have any suspicious or strange thoughts	0	1	2	3	____
20. Hear voices that nobody else can hear	0	1	2	3	____
21. See things that nobody else can see	0	1	2	3	____

TOTAL SCORE _____

*Used with permission of Mani Pavuluri, MD

Figure 13.1 Children's mania rating scale, parent version.

TREATMENT

The first step in treatment is education about the disorder for the affected individual, family, and important collaterals, such as teachers, friends, and coaches. An enormous amount can be gained by teaching youth with bipolar disorder and their families about associated risks and the need for adherence to the treatment regimen. Much of this instruction can be accomplished by individual supportive psychotherapy and family therapy. Helping a child or adolescent to reckon with the diagnosis is, perhaps, the most difficult part of treatment and can take months or even years. Once achieved, however, acceptance of the diagnosis is immensely useful because it allows the individual to identify the warning signs of an impending mood episode and to address the problems immediately.

Mood hygiene is also an extremely important component of treatment, and those with bipolar disorder must learn how fragile their moods can be. Even small changes in their sleep cycle, nutrition, and stress can cause imbalance and agitation, and can predispose them to a major mood episode. To this end, children, adolescents, and their parents should keep mood charts, as described above, particularly when establishing the diagnosis and making major changes in treatment. The data gathered will aid in maintaining mood hygiene and further educating the child and family about the disorder.

In establishing a treatment plan, it is vital to understand the factors that interfere with symptom resolution. While we have little data to guide us in this regard at present time, we do recognize that effective treatment should address all comorbidities. ADHD, conduct disorder, anxiety, and aggression have clearly been shown to interfere with treatment efficacy and must be addressed within a comprehensive treatment plan (Jolin et al., 2008; Masi et al., 2004; Papolos, Hennen, & Cockerham, 2005). In addition, low socioeconomic status, ADHD, anxiety, and poor adherence to medication treatment are associated with delayed recovery. More rapid symptom recurrence is observed among those who abuse alcohol and do not receive psychotherapy (DelBello, Hanseman, Adler, Fleck, & Strakowski, 2007). Finally, we recognize that early onset, long illness duration, mixed episodes, rapid cycling, psychosis, negative life events, untreated subsyndromal symptoms, and family psychopathology are associated with worse long-term outcomes (Birmaher, 2007). Given these factors, treatment should address each of these areas and commence immediately upon suspected diagnosis.

Among bipolar adults with even mild symptom impairment, delays in necessary medication treatment are correlated with worse psychosocial functioning, more hospitalizations, and a greater likelihood of making a suicide attempt (Goldberg & Ernst, 2002). Though parallel data in children and adolescents are not yet available, we suspect the same to be true. Furthermore, children diagnosed with ADHD and/or MDD who have a significant family history of bipolar disorder may be experiencing a prodromal bipolar state. For such children, we anticipate that early psychotherapeutic and medication interventions may even help prevent the more severe manifestations of the illness (Chang, Howe, Gallelli, & Miklowitz, 2006).

If the disease course can be altered by recurrence (e.g., kindling), then repeated episodes of the illness are likely to affect gene expression. If we presume that the kindling theory is valid, then it follows that illness progression can also be altered by rapidly halting a manic episode, and, in fact, this pattern is precisely what we see in clinical practice. The more rapid and aggressive our treatment, the longer the individual is likely to stay well. Lack of treatment or rapid discontinuation of treatment may then, alternatively, promote advancement of the illness, leading to longer episodes with greater frequency. It is quite clear that one's risk of recurrence is increased with inadequate treatment and decreased with proper treatment.

Finally, a note of caution: Because pediatric bipolar disorder is often difficult to diagnose and infrequent, some or perhaps many of the children and adolescents in the studies discussed below may not have actually had bipolar disorder. Both the chosen assessment tools and the willingness of the researchers to stray from formal *DSM* criteria impact the diagnosis. Some of these children are undoubtedly bipolar, but others, perhaps, have ADHD, learning disorders, posttraumatic stress disorder, oppositional defiant disorder or conduct disorder, or depression and anxiety disorders. Once again, it is important to view every study related to the diagnosis and treatment of pediatric bipolar disorder with caution.

Psychotherapeutic Treatment of Bipolar Disorder

As noted above, psychotherapy may be useful early in the course of illness to provide patient education and support acceptance of the diagnosis. Therapy can also help the affected individual to recognize episode triggers, identify symptoms early before a full-blown mood episode ensues, and help family members to reduce "expressed emotion," or excessive criticism expressed toward the affected individual. As yet, no single type of psychotherapy or other psychosocial treatment has emerged as superior to others. Some methods have, however, shown early promise.

Family-focused therapy (FFT), which emphasizes psychoeducation, communication enhancement, and problem-solving skills, has been shown to prolong time to relapse in randomized clinical trials of adults. One small open trial of FFT in bipolar adolescents (FFT-A), who were also receiving mood-stabilizing medications, demonstrated improvements in subjects' symptoms of depression, mania, and general behavior problems over one year (Miklowitz et al., 2004). In a follow-up to this study, teens treated with mood stabilizers were randomly assigned to 21 sessions of FFT or 3 sessions of "enhanced care," a relapse prevention, treatment adherence, and psychoeducation program. Here again, those in FFT had more rapid recovery from depression, shorter episodes of depression, and lower scores on depression ratings for two years (Miklowitz et al., 2008). FFT has also been adapted for children and adolescents at high risk of developing bipolar disorder (FFT-HR) as a 12-session treatment for youths age 9 to 17 years with the goal of intervening early in mood episodes and improving communication and problem-solving skills. One randomized trial for 40 youths found that in combination with pharmacotherapy and compared to a psychoeducation control, those in FFT-HR recovered from initial mood symptoms more quickly, spent more time in remission, and had greater improvement in hypomania over the one-year study (Miklowitz et al., 2013).

Multifamily psychoeducation groups have been explored for children ages 8 to 11 as an adjunctive therapy (Fristad, Goldberg-Arnold, & Gavazzi, 2003). Two randomized controlled trials have evaluated the multifamily psychoeducation-based psychotherapy (MF-PEP) and one randomized controlled trial has evaluated the individual format psychoeducation-based psychotherapy (IF-PEP). Compared to those with treatment as usual, families in the psychoeducation groups reported greater knowledge about their child's mood symptoms, more positive family interactions, greater parental support as perceived by children, and increased utilization of appropriate services by the families. The second and larger of the two group trials also found improvements in mood symptoms (Fristad, Verducci, Walters, & Young, 2009). IF-PEP also resulted in an improvement in mood symptoms and family climate with effects lasting until a one-year follow-up (Mendenhall, Fristad, & Early, 2009).

Pavuluri, Graczyk, et al. (2004) designed a child- and family-focused CBT (CFF-CBT) intended to be used along with adjunctive medication treatment for children 8 to 12 years of age. This treatment incorporates both CBT and family-focused therapy, also incorporating mindfulness techniques, positive psychology, and aspects of interpersonal therapy. After 12 sessions, participants who engaged in the therapy, which focuses on the specific problems that bipolar children face and the role of environmental stressors, demonstrated improvements in mood symptoms, psychosocial functioning, and medication adherence. A second preliminary study of the same treatment in groups found that CFF-CBT was feasible, acceptable to families, and led to significant improvements in manic, but not depressive, symptoms and in the children's psychosocial functioning (A. E. West et al., 2009).

T. R. Goldstein, Axelson, Birmaher, and Brent (2007) developed a modified dialectical behavior therapy (DBT) for adolescents with bipolar disorder. The initial small, open trial consisted of a one-year intervention focused on family skills training and individual therapy as an adjunct to medication treatment. The treatment was well accepted by participants who demonstrated decreases in suicidal ideation, nonsuicidal self-injurious behavior, depressive symptoms, and emotional dysregulation. A second randomized, small pilot study by the same group found similar results with DBT participants nearly three times more likely to show improvement in suicidal ideation (T. R. Goldstein et al., 2014). Particularly given the high comorbidity of bipolar disorder with conduct disorder among teens and personality disorders among adults (A. H. Fan & Hassell, 2008), this study should pave the way for further investigations of DBT. (For a review of DBT, see Chapter 12.)

Two additional treatments for adolescents with bipolar disorder that incorporate interpersonal therapy and CBT have also shown some promising data. Interpersonal and social rhythm therapy (IPSRT) has been found effective for the treatment of bipolar disorder in adults and has been adapted for adolescents. IPSRT-A was studied in a small open trial of adolescents, revealing improvements in mania, depression, general psychiatric symptoms and global psychosocial symptoms (Hiastala, Kotler, McClellan, & McCauley, 2010). Finally, Feeny, Danielson, Schwartz, Youngstrom, and Findling (2006) have reported the successful development of a manualized cognitive behavior therapy (CBT) for adolescents with bipolar disorder receiving adjunctive psychopharmacological treatment. In their small open study, those receiving CBT focused on psychoeducation, medication compliance, mood and sleep management, altering negative thoughts, and family communication demonstrated more symptom improvement than those teens in the matched group who did not receive any psychosocial treatment. (For a complete review of CBT, see Chapters 10 and 12.)

Psychopharmacological Treatment of Bipolar Disorder

Medications have proven themselves remarkably helpful in the treatment of bipolar disorder. Though we have much more data on effective treatments for adults, emerging data suggest parallel findings for the same medications among children and adolescents. The sine qua non of bipolar treatment is the mood stabilizer, which is often augmented with an antipsychotic and/or antidepressant. Lithium and divalproex sodium (Depakote) are the two mood stabilizers approved by the Food and Drug Administration (FDA) for the treatment of acute mania in adults, and aripiprazole (Abilify), olanzapine (Zyprexa), risperidone (Risperdal), quetiapine (Seroquel), ziprasidone (Geodon), and chlorpromazine (Thorazine) are all FDA-approved antipsychotics for the same indication. Both lamotrigine (Lamictal) and olanzapine are approved for maintenance therapy of adult bipolar disorder, and the combination of olanzapine and fluoxetine (Symbyax) and quetiapine extended release (Seroquel XR) are approved for the treatment of adult bipolar depression.

A mood stabilizer is essentially any psychiatric medication that is used to treat bipolar disorder. We think of mood stabilizers as something akin to Dolby Sound—these medications take out some of the extreme highs and extreme lows in one's mood. The mood stabilizers consist of lithium carbonate, various anticonvulsants, and a number of antipsychotics. Most mood stabilizers are pure antimanic agents, but both lithium and lamotrigine (Lamictal) have notable antidepressant effects often employed in the treatment of bipolar depression (Patel et al., 2006). Beyond bipolar disorder, mood stabilizers are sometimes used as augmenting medications for aggression, irritability, anxiety, borderline personality, depression, conduct disorder, and ADHD.

Lithium Carbonate

Lithium carbonate, available under many trade names, is the "classic" and first mood stabilizer described. Lithium is highly effective for the treatment of mania associated with bipolar disorder, for bipolar depression, and as an augmenting medication for treatment-resistant MDD. Lithium has a narrow therapeutic index, meaning that its therapeutic dose is not far afield from its toxic dose. Consequently, lithium should only be prescribed by an experienced practitioner, who follows blood levels and other lab values regularly.

Prescreening for lithium treatment includes a complete blood count, thyroid panel, kidney panel, and electrolytes, along with an electrocardiogram to rule out sick sinus syndrome in the elderly or anyone with cardiac risk factors. Lab values should be followed every three to six months and after every dosage adjustment. Therapeutic blood levels of lithium in children and adolescents are generally the same as those for adults. Excessive fluid loss, as by strenuous exercise, diarrhea, or vomiting, can result in a rapid increase in blood lithium to potentially toxic levels. The use of nonsteroidal anti-inflammatory medications, such as aspirin and ibuprofen, can also lead to an increase in lithium blood levels. Thus, the medication must be carefully monitored over time. Side effects can include tremor, sedation, weight gain, various gastrointestinal effects, acne, white blood cell count elevation, and thyroid and kidney damage.

Lithium is presumed to work by blocking the synthesis of inositol from glucose and the recycling of inositol phosphates, thereby inhibiting the neurons from creating the second messengers, diacylglycerol and inositol triphosphate. This mechanism dampens the ability of a rapidly firing neuron (e.g., an overactive or "manic" neuron) to respond to further stimulation.

Dozens of studies have established the efficacy of lithium for the treatment of adult bipolar disorder (Fountoulakis & Vieta, 2008). Far fewer studies have been completed in bipolar youth, and most of these have been case series and open-label studies (DeLong & Nieman, 1983; Strober, Morrell, Lampert, & Burroughs, 1990; Varanka, Weller, Weller, & Fristad, 1988) along with a few small and short-term double-blind efforts (B. Geller, Cooper, et al., 1998; Kafantaris et al., 2004). A one-year small open-label study found lithium (0.92 mEq/l) to be an effective monotherapy for obtaining and maintaining response and relapse prevention in nearly half of patients (Pavuluri, Henry, Carbray, et al., 2006); and a 16-week study which allowed concurrent medications to be given for residual symptoms reported that lithium (1 ± 0.3 mEq/l) was effective in maintaining treatment response and attaining remission in half of patients who responded during acute treatment with lithium (Findling et al., 2013). Given the benefits of lithium in randomized, double-blind, placebo-controlled studies of adults with bipolar disorder and the benefits suggested for youth in the aforementioned trials, lithium has been approved by the FDA for the treatment of adolescent bipolar disorder down to age 13. In addition, guidelines published by the American Academy of Child and Adolescent Psychiatry recommend lithium for the treatment of manic or mixed-episode pediatric bipolar disorder (Kowatch et al., 2005). Given the promise of lithium for bipolar youth but the many uncertainties regarding it use, including dosage, monitoring, short- and long-term efficacy, safety, and pharmacokinetics, large multi-site studies would be beneficial.

Antipsychotics

In addition to lithium, the FDA has approved four antipsychotics, aripiprazole (Abilify), risperidone (Risperdal), quetiapine (Seroquel), and olanzapine (Zyprexa), for the acute treatment of bipolar mania down to age 10. Each medication has demonstrated efficacy in treating manic and mixed-episode symptoms in children and adolescents suffering from bipolar disorder in multisite, randomized controlled trials. The data supporting aripiprazole and risperidone are more robust. Studies of risperidone have demonstrated separation from placebo by week one in a three-week study of over 150 children within two dosage ranges, 0.5–2.5 mg and 3–6 mg per day (Pandina et al., 2007). Of note, those taking the higher dose did no better than those within the lower dosage range, although they did experience more side effects. Aripiprazole separated from placebo by the end point in a four-week study of nearly 300 children also at two different dosages, 10 and 30 mg per day (Chang et al., 2007). A 30-week extension of this study found continued efficacy (Wagner, Nyilas, & Johnson, 2007).

Quetiapine has also been studied in acute mania versus placebo at dosages of 400 and 600 mg per day in nearly 300 subjects. Results show separation of drug from placebo by day four for the higher dose with maintained efficacy throughout the length of the three-week study (DelBello, Findling, Earley, Stankowski, & Acevedo, 2007). Likewise, olanzapine has been found efficacious, at dosages of 2.5 to 20 mg per day, in a three-week blinded, placebo-controlled study of just over 100 bipolar teens for the treatment of acute mania and mixed episodes (Tohen et al., 2007). Two 4-week randomized, placebo-controlled trials have also found quetiapine effective for the acute treatment of youth with BP-I, and gains were held in a 26-week open label extension. Similar results were found for an open-label extension of ziprasidone (Geodon) after a 4-week double-blind, placebo-controlled treatment trial (DelBello, Findling, Wang, Gundapaneni, & Versael, 2008; Díaz-Caneja et al., 2014).

We now have considerable evidence that numerous atypical antipsychotic medications are effective at suppressing acute manic and mixed episodes of pediatric bipolar disorder. Furthermore, there are numerous open label extension studies that suggest these medications may have additional use in maintenance therapy. However, they have yet to be studied for long-term safety and efficacy. Practitioners prescribing antipsychotic medications to children and adolescents should always start with modest doses and proceed cautiously because of the potential for significant side effects (see Chapter 15 for a complete discussion of antipsychotic medications).

Anticonvulsants

Anticonvulsants have also proven useful for the treatment of bipolar disorder in adults, where they are presumed to function via cellular membrane stabilization. Most frequently used for rapid-cycling bipolar disorder, divalproex sodium (Depakote) and to a lesser extent carbamazepine (Tegretol) have strong supporting data in adults and are used routinely, but as expected, studies in children and adolescents are few in number. Open-label trials, case reports, and retrospective chart reviews have found divalproex sodium and carbamazepine to be effective for acute manic and mixed episodes in children and adolescents (Davanzo et al., 2003; McClellan, Kowatch, & Findling, 2007; Papatheodorou, Kutcher, Katic, & Szalai, 1995; Wagner et al., 2002). Two open-label studies of divalproex sodium found six-month response rates in excess of 50%. By contrast, one 4-week double-blind, placebo-controlled acute phase trial of divalproex sodium versus placebo found no benefit from the medication and nor did a six-month follow-up (Díaz-Caneja et al., 2014). There is also some support for lamotrigine in the treatment of adolescent bipolar depression (Carandang, Robbins, Mullany, Yazbek, & Minot, 2007; Chang, Saxena, & Howe, 2006). One randomized, double-blind, placebo-controlled trial of oxcarbazepine (Trileptal) for manic or mixed episodes of over 100 children and adolescents found no benefit at an average dose of 1,500 mg per day for seven weeks (Wagner, Kowatch, et al., 2006).

Few comparison studies between medications have been completed. A moderate-sized randomized, double-blind trial of risperidone versus divalproex sodium found that risperidone led to a more rapid improvement and greater reduction in manic symptoms; in addition, risperidone was better tolerated and led to fewer youth dropping out of the study (Pavuluri et al., 2010). Another randomized, double-blind controlled study comparing risperidone, lithium, and divalproex sodium in children 6 to 15 years of age also found risperidone to be more efficacious than both lithium and divalproex sodium with no statistical difference between the latter two (Geller et al., 2011). A randomized, double-blind study of 50 hospitalized adolescents with BP-I in a manic or mixed episode compared quetiapine at dosages of 400 to 600 mg per day with divalproex sodium at therapeutic serum levels of 80 to 120 mcg per milliliter for 28 days. Both groups showed statistically significant improvements in functioning, although quetiapine may have acted more rapidly (DelBello et al., 2006). One open-label comparison among lithium, divalproex sodium, and carbamazepine found no statistically significant difference between the three after eight weeks in 42 youth with BP-I or

BP-II in a manic or mixed episode. The effect sizes were more robust than the response rates—for divalproex sodium, the response rate was 53% (effect size of 1.63); the response rate to lithium was 38% (effect size of 1.06); and the response rate to carbamazepine was 38% (effect size 1.00; Kowatch et al., 2000). Another study comparing lithium and divalproex sodium for maintenance treatment in a double-blind fashion for up to 18 months found no differences in survival time until relapse or until patients discontinued their medications for any reason (Findling et al., 2005). Finally, one double-blind study compared lithium, divalproex sodium, and placebo in over 150 subjects for eight weeks and found that only divalproex sodium separated from placebo (Kowatch, Findling, Scheffer, & Stanford, 2007).

Combined treatment with an antipsychotic and a mood stabilizer is a common strategy for both adults and youth with bipolar disorder who are in a manic or mixed episode, but scant data are available to guide this practice in children and adolescents. One 12-month open-label trial of risperidone augmentation in lithium nonresponders with preschool onset bipolar disorder found that 86% of the 21 subjects demonstrated a greater than 50% improvement from baseline. Predictors of inadequate response to lithium monotherapy included ADHD, severity at baseline, history of sexual or physical abuse, and young or preschool age (Pavuluri, Henry, Carbray, et al., 2006). Another study looked at augmenting both divalproex sodium and lithium with risperidone. Both augmented treatments were highly effective with very large effect sizes and response rates in excess of 80% (Pavuluri, Henry, et al., 2004). Finally, another 20-week prospective study of lithium and divalproex sodium found the combination to be effective for slightly more than half of the 90 youth and well tolerated (Findling et al., 2003).

Selecting between an antipsychotic or alternate mood stabilizer for the acute treatment of a manic or mixed episode is not always an easy task. Given our current data, however, it is reasonable to begin treatment of a manic or mixed episode of BP-I or BP-II with an antipsychotic, particularly if psychosis is present. Although some data support lithium and anticonvulsants for this practice, the preponderance of studies supporting the use of antipsychotics strongly suggests that treatment should start here. Augmentation with a second mood stabilizer is entirely reasonable, especially for a severe episode. Once the manic episode is stabilized, the patient may be transitioned over to lithium or an anticonvulsant, either alone or in combination with an antipsychotic. Lamotrigine or an antidepressant may be added later if the mood subsequently becomes depressed.

Medication Monitoring

The use of mood stabilizers requires significant safety precautions and monitoring. Prior to treatment with lithium, thyroid function, kidney function, electrolytes including calcium, and a complete blood count including white cells should be ordered. In addition, the patient should undergo a 12-lead electrocardiogram (ECG) to rule out sick sinus syndrome or any sinus node abnormalities that would contradict treatment with lithium if the patient is elderly or at any cardiac risk. The practitioner should also be aware that lithium can induce benign T-wave flattening in the ECG over time. As lithium can impact both the thyroid and parathyroid glands, it may alter the set point at which the gland responds to the presence of calcium by an internal feedback mechanism. Thus, treatment with lithium raises the risk of increasing calcium beyond safe levels and must be monitored. During treatment with lithium, the use of nonsteroidal anti-inflammatory medications, such as aspirin and ibuprofen, should be discontinued or severely limited, given the propensity for these medications to elevate the blood level of lithium. There are numerous other medications that are contraindicated with lithium treatment, and these must be reviewed carefully with the patient. Thyroid function and calcium should be rechecked at two and six months after initiating treatment and annually thereafter. Lithium should be discontinued if calcium levels surpass 11.5 mg/dl. Renal function should be monitored every six months, and the complete blood count should be checked annually. Lithium levels should be followed at six-month intervals and before and after any dosage adjustments. ECGs should be followed annually if indicated.

Prior to treatment with an anticonvulsant, a complete blood count, including platelets and white cells, electrolytes and a chemistry panel including fasting glucose and lipids, liver function, amylase, lipase, and thyroid tests should be performed. For divalproex sodium, a menstrual history is necessary, along with a pregnancy test in any female of reproductive age, given the risk of birth defects to a developing fetus. Sexually active females taking anticonvulsants should be advised to use two forms of contraception, such as condoms along with oral contraception, an intrauterine device, or a diaphragm. During treatment, divalproex sodium and carbamazepine levels should be checked every 6 to 12 months and before and after any dosage adjustments. Other laboratory values as noted above should be followed annually. Given concerns about the possibility of a relationship between divalproex sodium and the development of polycystic ovary syndrome (PCOS), practitioners should regularly monitor for irregular menses, hirsutism, and acne and refer to an endocrinologist should any concern arise. Lamotrigine is generally well tolerated, but a small number of individuals will suffer dermatitis and in rare cases Stevens-Johnson syndrome, which can be fatal. The practitioner should carefully review all additional medications the patient is taking and pay particular attention to potential drug–drug interactions. For safety precautions and monitoring of atypical antipsychotics, see Chapter 15.

Given the frequent comorbidity of ADHD with bipolar disorder among children and adolescents, it is reasonable to wonder about the possibility of inducing mania or mood instability by giving stimulant treatment to a bipolar child. However, as numerous studies have shown, bipolar children and adolescents with ADHD generally respond favorably to stimulants and are not likely to be pushed into a manic episode (Carlson, Loney, Salisbury, Kramer, & Arthur, 2000; Craney & Geller, 2003; Galanter et al., 2003; B. Geller, Zimmerman, Williams, DelBello, Bolhofner, et al., 2002). The clinician is advised, however, to treat comorbid ADHD only in children and adolescents who are already receiving adequate mood-stabilizing treatment.

In conclusion, when evaluating children and adolescents for bipolar disorder, we must remember to apply *DSM-5* criteria in a developmentally sensitive manner. Irritability is a core feature of the illness, but in and of itself is not sufficient to warrant a diagnosis. The high comorbidity with ADHD, anxiety, depression, posttraumatic stress disorder, oppositional defiant disorder, and conduct disorder must be appreciated and treated as necessary. A number of psychotherapies show promising data, and at least lithium, risperidone, aripiprazole, quetiapine, and olanzapine have adequate evidence to support their use. Most importantly, the child and family must be educated about the mood disorder, and a close working relationship must be established between the clinician and family.

14

Suicide and
Self-Injurious Behavior

Suicide and nonsuicidal self-injurious behavior are not psychiatric diagnoses, but they are an all too common co-occurrence of mood, anxiety, disruptive behavior, substance use, personality, and psychotic disorders. Suicide is the most feared outcome for mental health practitioners. Nonsuicidal self-injury, such as self-inflicting cutting, is sometimes associated with suicidal behavior but is most often altogether different. This chapter will provide an understanding of these behaviors, their relationship to one another, and sensible efforts aimed at prevention and treatment.

Nearly 40,000 people die by suicide each year in the United States, accounting for 1.4% of all deaths. Worldwide, approximately 1 million take their lives annually (American Foundation for Suicide Prevention, n.d.; Nock et al., 2008). Suicide is the third leading cause of death among adolescents and young adults, after accidents and homicides, making it more common than the next eight leading causes of death combined (Centers for Disease Control and Prevention, National Vital Statistics System, National Center for Health Statistics, 2010). Seventeen percent of high school students report having seriously considered suicide, 14% of students have made a plan of how they would commit suicide, and 8% of students have made a suicide attempt (Centers for Disease Control and Prevention, 2014a). Although not usually resulting in a completed suicide, at least 15% of adolescents engage in nonsuicidal self-injury at least once, and rates among college students are even higher, ranging from 17% to 35%. Among adolescents with a diagnosed psychiatric disorder, the rates are higher still, ranging from 40% to 80% (P. L. Kerr, Muehlenkamp, & Turner, 2010).

Suicidal behavior is differentiated from self-injurious behavior in a number of ways. Although some individuals who self-injure report thoughts of suicide while engaging in the behavior, and half of more of individuals who self-injure have attempted suicide at least once, individuals who self-injure generally report that they do not intend to cause death while engaging in the behavior. Rather, the intent of self-injurious behavior for most individuals is to decrease distress and negative emotions. Furthermore, cutting, the most common form of self-injury, accounts for only 2% or fewer of completed suicides. Upwards of 90% or more attempted and completed suicides, in fact, are due to gunshots, hanging, overdose, poisoning, and jumping from heights, methods that are never employed in self-injury. Finally, individuals who self-injure typically report feeling better after engaging in the behavior, relief, a decrease in negative emotions, and sometimes positive feelings. By contrast, nonlethal suicide attempts often result in more severe depressive symptoms and continued suicidal behavior (P. L. Kerr et al., 2010).

SUICIDE

Although ebbing and flowing slightly, the suicide rate in the United States has changed relatively little over the past 20 years from 12.5 per 100,000 in 1990 to 12.3 in 2010. Middle aged individuals between the ages of 45 and 64 years are at greatest risk and have the highest rate (18.6), followed by those over 85 years (16.9). Although teenagers and young adults have lower rates (those age 15 to 24 years have a rate of 11.0), as noted above suicide is the third most common cause of death among individuals in this age group (American Foundation for Suicide Prevention, 2014).

Adolescent boys are more likely than females to die by suicide. Although females are six to nine times more likely to attempt suicide, males are five times more likely to complete suicide. Males tend to use more lethal means, such as firearms, hanging, or poisoning, while females tend to employ less lethal methods, such as medication overdose or cutting. Most adolescent attempts, in fact, are by overdose (76%), but most completed suicides among this age group are due to firearms (72%; Freda, 2010).

There are many known risk factors for suicide, which should be assessed when interviewing all adolescents and young adults but particularly those who present with psychosis, mood, severe anxiety, externalizing disorders (especially males with conduct disorder), and substance use disorders. More than 90% of youth who complete suicide have at least one psychiatric diagnosis, depression being the most common. Hopelessness, anhedonia, impulsivity, and high emotional reactivity are the psychological factors of greatest concern. Prior suicide attempts are one of the key predictors of future attempts (D. Shaffer et al., 1996). Other risk factors include male gender, non-Hispanic white and Native American ethnicity, access to a gun, chronic or terminal illness, sexual minority youth (e.g., gay, lesbian, and bisexual), and stressful life events. A family history of suicide confers additional risk and is doubled for those with a first degree relative who completed suicide. Adolescents whose parents suffer from depression and substance abuse, as well as those who have been physically or sexually abused, are also at increased risk (Freda, 2010; Nock et al., 2008).

Bullying and peer victimization, including "cyberbullying," have recently come to light as important risk factors for adolescent and young adult suicide (Epstein & Spirito, 2009). Adolescents threatened or injured by peers are 2.4 times more likely to acknowledge suicidal ideation and up to 3.8 times more likely to report suicidal behavior than those who are not victimized (Kaminski & Fang, 2008). In addition, suicide contagion or "copycat" behavior is a well-recognized risk factor for youth suicide; in fact, a "dose response" relationship between the quantity, duration, and prominence of media exposure and a subsequent increase in suicides has been established (Gould, Jamieson, & Romer, 2003). Gay, lesbian, and bisexual adolescents are especially vulnerable, particularly when learning about the suicides of other sexual minority youth (Freda, 2010).

Though fewer in number, some protective factors have been elucidated. Religious beliefs and practices, as well as a general sense of spirituality, are associated with a decreased likelihood of suicide attempts. The social support and moral objection to suicide that typically accompany religious and spiritual beliefs and practices are likely to be the most important factors in this relationship. The perception of family support is also associated with a reduction in suicidal behavior (Nock et al., 2008). Other possible protective factors have less empirical data support but make intuitive sense, such as academic achievement, strong peer relations, good coping skills, impulse control, having responsibilities for others (e.g., pets, younger siblings), help-seeking behaviors (e.g., asking advice from others), and access to mental health care.

As the review of risk and protective factors makes abundantly clear, a suicide attempt is influenced by many factors, including access to a means by which to complete the suicide, the presence of medical and/or mental illness, substance abuse, family history, prior suicidal behavior, gender, sexual orientation, physical or sexual abuse, religious and/or spiritual beliefs and practices, and family support. Most youth who attempt suicide have experienced some psychiatric symptoms for over a year before the attempt (Shaffer et al., 1996).

Common warning signs of depression in children and adolescents include changes in eating and sleeping habits, a worsening in school performance, impaired concentration, feelings of worthlessness or guilt, overreaction to criticism, hopelessness, sadness, low self-esteem, lack of enthusiasm and motivation, drug or alcohol use, thoughts of death or suicide, and withdrawal from friends, family, and regular activities. Stressful events may precede a suicide attempt, such as the death of a family member or close friend, loss of a good friend or romantic relationship, loss of a parent through divorce or separation, loss of a pet or treasured object, fear of punishment, physical or sexual abuse, unwanted pregnancy, poor academic performance, embarrassment or humiliation, and confusion about one's sexuality. Clinicians and caregivers must be alert to the aforementioned conditions and risk factors, given that many teens act impulsively and provide no warning of an impending suicide attempt.

During the assessment of a child or adolescent, a number of direct questions relating to suicide should be asked. Examples include:

- Do you ever wish you were never born?
- Do you ever wish you would go to sleep and never wake up?
- Do you ever have thoughts of death or dying?
- Do you ever think about killing yourself?
  - If so, have you ever made a plan?
  - If so, what is your plan?
- Have you ever made an attempt to kill yourself?
- Do you have a current plan to kill yourself?

An assessment of a child or adolescent's strengths and coping skills is also useful. In addition to speaking with the child's parents or caregivers, additional questions for the child might include:

- Have you coped well with serious problems and stressful situations in the past?
  - If so, what skills have you used?
  - Can you use those skills again now?
- Do you have anyone to speak with about your feelings?
  - If so, who might that be?
  - Can you reach out to them?
  - Can I contact them to share my concerns?
- How can we make things better right now?
- How can I help?

There has been much discussion in the field of mental health for many years about so-called "no-suicide contracts" and "no-harm contracts," or agreements made between a healthcare provider and a patient at risk of suicide. These "contracts" generally take the form of a written or handshake agreement, whereby a potentially suicidal individual consents not to harm himself or herself. Unfortunately, there is little evidence to suggest that such agreements are effective. Still, however, these contracts are commonly employed and may give the clinician a false sense of security.

One alternative to the no-suicide contract is the "commitment to treatment statement," which requires individuals to pledge to regular treatment instead of pledging not to harm themselves. In other words, commitment to treatment statements emphasize not what a suicidal person will not do, but rather what a suicidal person will do. Conceptually, this approach is more positive. Typical components of a commitment to treatment statement include an agreement to attend sessions, set treatment goals, express thoughts and feelings honestly, be actively involved in sessions, complete therapeutic homework assignments, take medication as prescribed, try new behaviors, consider alternative cognitions, and implement the crisis response plan when necessary (Rudd, Mandrusiak, & Joiner, 2006). Such plans can be collaboratively written during treatment sessions, signed, and agreed to by both the patient and therapist.

Safety or crisis plans can be embedded within commitment to treatment statements or can stand alone. Safety plans include a list of coping skills and sources of support that individuals are reminded to access when they are in a moment of distress. Typical components include behavioral relaxation techniques (such as deep breathing and progressive muscle relaxation), physical activities to reduce stress (such as exercise, taking a walk, or yoga), mental exercises (such as challenging one's cognitive distortions), enjoyable activities (such as listening to a favorite "play list" or drawing), and reaching out for emotional support from family, peers, or one's therapist. Safety plans should be written down and easily accessible for patients in multiple locations (e.g., a written card in their wallet or purse, a "note" in their cellphone, etc.). The final aspect of a safety plan is what to do in case of an imminent risk of a suicide attempt (let someone know you're in distress, call 911, etc.).

Finally, there are a few specific treatments, which have shown benefit in suicide prevention. Psychotherapeutically, both cognitive behavior therapy (CBT) and dialectical behavior therapy (DBT) have proven utility in experimental studies. Both treatments are described in Chapter 12. The only medication approved by the Food and Drug Administration

(FDA) to reduce suicide risk is clozapine (Clozaril) for use with individuals with schizophrenia. Although not all studies of lithium among individuals with depression and bipolar disorder agree, most data suggest that lithium has some protective effect against suicide, and one meta-analysis reported a 60% reduction in the risk of death and suicide among those taking lithium in comparison to placebo (Cipriani, Hawton, Stockton, & Geddes, 2013).

SELF-INJURIOUS BEHAVIOR

Nonsuicidal self-injurious behavior is defined as the purposeful destruction of body tissue without suicidal intent. Based upon studies of patient populations, the average age of onset is 13 to 14 years. The most common form of self-injury is skin cutting, which is employed by more than 70% of adolescents who self-injure. Most youth who self-injure use other methods in addition to cutting, such as scratching the skin, burning, hitting oneself, biting, and head banging. The most commonly injured areas of the body are the arms, hands, wrists, thighs, and stomach. Most youth who engage in self-injury do so only once or a few times, and only a minority of youth continue to self-injure chronically (Klonsky & Muehlenkamp, 2007).

About 4% of adults in the United States acknowledge a history of engaging in self-injurious behavior, and 1% report a severe history. As noted at the outset of this chapter, a minimum of 15% of adolescents engage in nonsuicidal self-injury at least once, and rates among college students range from 17% to 35%. Although assumed to occur more frequently among women, similar rates of this behavior exist among men and women with women more likely to cut and men more likely to burn or hit themselves. Self-injury is higher among whites than nonwhites, and, not surprisingly, higher among individuals who experience frequent negative emotions, have difficulties expressing their emotions, and are self-critical (P. L. Kerr et al., 2010; Klonsky & Muehlenkamp, 2007).

The general goal of self-injurious behavior is to relieve distress and decrease negative emotions. In seeming contrast, however, a smaller number of patients report that they often feel so "numb" and apart from themselves and others that they engage in self-injury in order to feel "something." Consequently, self-injurious behavior seems to have an effect at both increasing and decreasing emotion. Self-injury also results in varying levels of reinforcement. Individuals are reinforced immediately after engaging in the behavior because it relieves distress or gives them a positive feeling. Individuals are reinforced later as well if they receive attention from others for the behavior or if they are allowed to avoid punishment or doing something unpleasant because of the self-mutilating behavior (Nock & Prinstein, 2004).

Meaningful risk factors for self-injurious behavior are difficult to ascertain because those individual features correlated with self-injury (e.g., frequent negative emotions, difficulty expressing emotions, self-critical nature, parental divorce, past history of sexual or physical abuse, living with family members who suffer from substance use issues or mental illness, etc.) are also correlated with many psychiatric disorders, particularly mood and anxiety disorders. What is missing from our understanding of self-injurious behavior is an understanding of why people choose to self-injure as a way of regulating their emotions and social interaction. A number of untested theories have been presented by Nock (2010), which may have some bearing on this question. The social learning hypothesis would suggest that individuals engage in behaviors they observe among others; the self-punishment hypothesis suggest that people engage in self-injury for affect regulation because it concurrently provides a means of punishing oneself for some perceived wrongdoing or self-hatred; the implicit attitude/identification hypothesis suggests that our inherent attitudes and identifications predict our behaviors (e.g., people engage in self-injury because they have a more favorable attitude toward self-injury); the social signaling hypothesis suggests that people self-injure as a way to signal or demonstrate distress to others, given that it is more effective for them than speaking or crying; the pain analgesia/opiate hypothesis emanates from the observation that those who self-injure appear to be less sensitive to pain which may be due to higher than normal levels of endorphins (endogenous opiates) that are released upon injury and lead to emotional relief; and the pragmatic hypothesis suggests that people choose self-injury as a coping strategy because it is a quick, effective, portable, and easy way to regulate their emotions.

All teens should be assessed for self-injurious behavior during a clinical evaluation. Asking to see physical evidence of self-injury is one of the best ways to assess the intensity of the behavior and how recent it is, while establishing a baseline so that further self-injury can be monitored. Adolescents will sometimes wear long-sleeved shirts or other forms of concealing clothing to cover up their injuries, and so examiners will almost always have to be explicit in their request to see the mutilation. Example questions include:

- Have you ever purposefully or deliberately harmed yourself physically in any way?
  - If so, how?

  - – Are there any scars left?
  - – May I see them?
- Does it help to self-injure?
  - – If so, how?
- What situations or stressors make you want to self-injure?
- What do you tend to feel before and after you self-injure?
- Who knows that you self-injure?

As previously discussed, even though most individuals who self-injure are not intending to commit suicide, suicide is more frequent among those who self-injure; furthermore, suicide has been reported to occur 10 times more often among those who self-injure than among those in the general population (Hawton & Harriss, 2007). As a result, questions related to suicide (as described earlier in this chapter) should also be addressed.

The treatment of self-injurious behavior has historically hinged upon treating the primary psychiatric diagnoses that accompany the self-injury (e.g., depression, anxiety, etc.). Dialectical behavior therapy (DBT) is an effective treatment for adults with borderline personality disorder who frequently self-injure. Numerous small, nonrandomized trials have also demonstrated the efficacy of DBT for adolescents, although data from larger, randomized trials are forthcoming (Salsman & Arthur, 2011). There are no studies demonstrating direct benefit from medications for the treatment of self-injurious behavior. Again, however, medications, such as antidepressants and antipsychotics, are commonly employed for the comorbid psychiatric conditions that these individuals suffer, and a decrease in self-injury is sometimes observed.

15

Schizophrenia and Psychosis

Psychosis is not a distinct disorder, but rather a symptom found among many disorders, both psychiatric and medical. The core symptoms of schizophrenia and schizoaffective disorder are psychotic in nature, in contrast to bipolar disorder, major depressive disorder, posttraumatic stress, and other anxiety disorders, where psychotic symptoms sometimes occur. Even though schizophrenia and schizoaffective disorder are the primary psychotic illnesses, mood and anxiety disorders are, in fact, the most common causes of psychotic symptoms in children and adolescents. Psychosis can also occur in the context of drug and alcohol abuse, seizure disorders, metabolic illnesses, central nervous system tumors and infections, dementia and delirium.

The second edition of the Diagnostic and Statistical Manual of Mental Disorders of the American Psychiatric Association (*DSM-II*) grouped all psychoses in childhood under the rubric of childhood schizophrenia, thus obscuring both our understanding of schizophrenia and psychosis itself. At that time psychosis was a highly inclusive term that included any mental disorder that grossly interfered with one's ability to meet life's typical demands; psychosis was also meant to indicate a loss of ego boundaries or profound difficulties with reality testing (American Psychiatric Association, 1968). As a result, much of the early work on childhood schizophrenia was muddied by overlap with autism and other disorders that are sometimes characterized by these broadly defined psychotic symptoms. It was not until publication of *DSM-III* in 1980 that the criteria used to diagnose adult schizophrenia were applied to child and adolescent schizophrenia.

Psychosis is best defined as a loss of contact with reality that can take many forms. Delusions (e.g., false beliefs, including paranoia and grandiosity) and hallucinations (e.g., false perceptions, including auditory, visual, olfactory, tactile, and gustatory) may be the two best recognized types; but disorganized speech and behavior, along with severely constricted affect, limited speech, and lack of motivation or engagement are also commonly observed. Psychosis is often viewed as a constellation of symptoms that include both the so-called positive symptoms (e.g., hallucinations, delusions, disorganized speech, and grossly disorganized or catatonic behavior) and the negative symptoms (e.g., affective blunting, poverty of thought and speech or alogia, and difficulty initiating goal-directed behavior or avolition). Illusions or the misinterpretation of a genuine phenomenon or occurrence (e.g., briefly "seeing" a recently deceased relative in the distance) are considered normal and commonly occur at stressful moments among both children and adults.

The impact of psychosis on children and adolescents is profound, but thankfully such symptoms are relatively rare. In order to help those affected children, the clinician must be able to distinguish developmentally normal from psychotic behavior and cognition. At the same time, one must be sensitive to the frequently subtle nuances in mood, cognition, and behavior that indicate psychosis. Furthermore, the practitioner must be knowledgeable about antipsychotic medications as they are now commonly used for a variety of child and adolescent mental disorders, psychotic and nonpsychotic alike.

CLINICAL PRESENTATION

In order to understand psychosis in a child or adolescent, it is first necessary to understand what is developmentally "normal." As already stated, most children and adolescents who experience psychotic symptoms are not schizophrenic. Transient hallucinations are sometimes seen in preschool children, visual and tactile being the most common, and are prognostically benign. These symptoms are generally exacerbated by stress or anxiety. Hypnogogic hallucinations (e.g., false perceptions experienced while falling off to sleep) or hypnopompic hallucinations (e.g., false perceptions upon awakening) are normal and occur in both children and adults. Loosening of associations and illogical thinking decrease considerably after about age 6 or 7 years in children but are common and expected before that time (Volkmar, 1996a).

Psychotic thought content among children tends to reflect their developmental stage and concerns. For example, a grade-school child may experience hallucinations relating to monsters or toys, while an adolescent may experience command auditory hallucinations that tell her to harm herself, reflecting the increased cognitive capacity of her age. The onset of schizophrenia is usually insidious, and in addition to hallucinations and delusions, the attendant signs of psychosis may include bizarre or unusual thinking and behavior, moodiness, paranoia, poor peer relations and social withdrawal, and decline in personal hygiene. Auditory hallucinations are common in childhood schizophrenia, but delusions are less frequent, affecting only about half of diagnosed children. Other psychotic symptoms may be congruent with the cause of the primary illness. For example, a child suffering from bipolar disorder is more likely to experience psychosis in the context of his mood, such that during a manic episode he may exhibit extreme grandiosity and, during a depressive episode, suicidal ideation and paranoia.

During the premorbid phase of schizophrenia before any illness is evident, there may be nonspecific concerns until school age. By this time, impairments in attention and behavior, along with behavioral problems and developmental delays in language and motor skills, may be noted. Interpersonal relations and problem-solving skills may begin to suffer, and lower IQ, solitary play, and excessive anxiety may be observed. During the prodromal phase, just prior to the onset of illness, psychosis will gradually develop. The best predictor of outcome in childhood-onset schizophrenia is premorbid functioning (Schaeffer & Ross, 2002).

Schizophrenia and schizoaffective disorder are extremely rare in preteens. There may be at least two clinical phenotypes or presentations of schizophrenia, one characterized by long-standing neurobehavioral difficulties of early onset and the other that occurs in a previously "normal" person. Age at diagnosis distinguishes very early onset schizophrenia (VEOS; prior to age 13) from early-onset schizophrenia (EOS; between 13 and 18 years). Those children at increased risk of VEOS may show abnormalities of gait, posture, and muscle tone, the so-called neurological soft signs. Hallucinations, disordered thinking, and a flattened or blunted affect are other common features and are generally more easily detected. Children with VEOS tend to show characteristic communication deficits, including loose associations, illogical thinking, and impaired discourse skills. They may also be unaware that they are experiencing psychotic phenomena and soon disengage socially or are ostracized by peers, particularly if they share their thoughts with others. Among children with VEOS, it is commonly the behavior of the child that is more telling of the psychotic disorder than any overtly delusional thinking. For example, these children may regularly start fights with much larger peers, or consistently confuse television and dreams with reality. Such repeated displays of reckless judgment and bizarre behavior may be more indicative of a psychotic thought disorder than anything a young child actually reports. EOS, by contrast, tends to mirror much more closely the late teen and adult presentations of schizophrenia with which most clinicians are much more familiar.

ETIOLOGY

Numerous theories and associations have been suggested as possible etiological factors in the development of schizophrenia. A history of obstetrical complications at birth, for example, appears to be more common among those with schizophrenia (Preti et al., 2000). It remains unclear, however, which birth events and which factors, genetic or otherwise, account for these findings. There are mixed reports of increased frequency of schizophrenia among offspring of mothers who were pregnant during influenza epidemics, received poor nutrition, experienced high prenatal stress, or suffered intrapartum maternal infections (A. S. Brown et al., 2004; Clarke, Harley, & Cannon, 2006; Susser & Lin, 1992). Other associated risk factors include advanced paternal age (A. S. Brown et al., 2002) and birth in late winter (Messias & Kirkpatrick, 2001). While each is compelling in its own way, none of these findings or theories has adequately clarified the etiology of schizophrenia.

A number of neurobiological findings in the brains of schizophrenics further clarify some aspects of the illness. The best recognized and replicated neurological finding is increased size of the cerebral ventricles and overall decreased brain volume, which were first observed in the 1800s (R. Brown et al., 1986; Hecker, 1871). One review found that lateral ventricular enlargement, third ventricular enlargement, and cortical changes occur in 67% to 83% of subjects across numerous studies (Shelton & Weinberger, 1986). Studies of first-break schizophrenia among twins suggest that these findings are not due to medication treatment or hospitalization (Cardno et al., 1999; Nybäck, Wiesel, Berggren, & Hindmarsh, 1982; Reveley, Reveley, Clifford, & Murray, 1982). Magnetic resonance imaging (MRI) studies have also now validated these findings (McDonald et al., 2006). Some investigators have reported clinical correlations between larger ventricles among schizophrenics and poor premorbid adjustment, cognitive impairment, increased severity of negative symptoms, poor response to antipsychotics, and more frequent movement disorders, although these reports are disputed by others (Cleghorn, Zipursky, & List, 1991).

MRI brain scans of adolescent schizophrenics reveal the same neurological changes observed in adults. Abnormally enlarged ventricles are seen as early as 9 years of age (Sowell et al., 2000). As the ventricles increase in size, these children lose about four to five times as much cortical gray matter as do normal teens. The gray-matter loss progressively engulfs the brain from back to front, beginning in parietal structures involved in visuospatial and associative thinking and eventually moving forward to the temporal and dorsolateral prefrontal cortices involved in sensorimotor and visual function. The loss of tissue in these areas corresponds directly to clinical impairments, mirroring the neuromotor, auditory, visual search, and executive functioning (e.g., organization, planning, and attention) deficits found in schizophrenics. This research has controlled for the effects of antipsychotic medication, IQ, and gender, and the findings hold. While healthy teens lose an average of 1% of cortical gray matter per year, these schizophrenic teens lost 5% per year, with the greatest loss occurring among individuals with the most severe symptoms. By age 18, these teens had lost up to 25% of their gray matter in certain brain regions (P. M. Thompson et al., 2001).

A number of additional, sometimes contradictory, neuroanatomical findings have been observed among the brains of schizophrenics. Reduced cell size and total neurons, along with altered volume, have been reported in the basal ganglia. Abnormalities of the medial temporal lobe have also been reported and are not surprising, given the deficits in memory on neuropsychological testing commonly evidenced among schizophrenics. In addition, reduced amygdala, hippocampal, and parahippocampal volume has been widely noted. Finally, reduced prefrontal activity, thalamic abnormalities, and a reduction in the size of the cerebellar vermis have also been reported (Knable, Kleinman, & Weinberger, 1998).

The structural abnormalities in the brains of schizophrenics are suspected to have their foundation in fetal development, because of the noted lack of gliosis. Gliosis is a normal inflammatory response to cell damage that begins to take place by the third trimester of pregnancy. Neuronal damage after this time results in a classic pattern of observable inflammation. The fact that gliosis is not found in postmortem studies of schizophrenic brains suggests that any neuroanatomical damage occurs during the first and second trimesters (Fruntes & Limosin, 2008).

In addition to neuroanatomical data, there are a number of neurochemical findings in schizophrenia suggestive of etiology. Decreased metabolism in the prefrontal cortex, particularly during cognitive tasks, has been noted by many researchers, suggesting a "hypofrontality" in schizophrenia (Ben-Shachar et al., 2007). Additionally, the neurotransmitters dopamine, glutamate, serotonin, norepinephrine, and gamma-aminobutyric acid (GABA) have all been implicated for different reasons.

Dopamine and norepinephrine agonists, such as cocaine and amphet-amine, can potentiate or even induce psychosis. The same is true for the glutamate receptor (N-methyl D-aspartate, NMDA) antagonists, phen-cyclidine (PCP) and ketamine. The so-called dopamine hypothesis of schizophrenia has been particularly attractive for the past 40 years, given the fact that dozens of studies have identified elevated levels of dopamine D2 receptors in the caudate nucleus, putamen, and nucleus accumbens of schizophrenic brains and the fact that virtually all effective antipsychotic medications antagonize dopamine in some fashion (Knable et al., 1998). However, we now realize that while dopamine is a key player in schizo-phrenia, the dopamine hypothesis is an oversimplification.

Decreased prefrontal brain activity has been consistently found in schizophrenic patients as compared to normal controls, in addition to associated deficits in cognitive performance (Andreasen et al., 1992). Auditory and visual working memory, attention, and eye-tracking are the most typical impairments seen among schizophrenics, but emotional perception, verbal abilities, perceptual-motor speed, and visuospatial skills have also been found to be impaired in schizophrenic children and their otherwise well siblings (Davalos, Compagnon, Heinlein, & Ross, 2003; Niendam et al., 2003). Related alterations in glucose metabo-lism and irregular autonomic nervous system arousal, as noted in adult schizophrenics, have also been found in children with schizophrenia (Jacobsen et al., 1997; Zahn et al., 1997).

Family studies of schizophrenia have generally reported about a 50% concordance rate for monozygotic (identical) twins and a 15% concor-dance for dizygotic (nonidentical) twins (Cardno et al., 1999). Additional-ly, the risk for a first-degree relative of an affected individual is about 10 times that of the general population (American Psychiatric Association, 2000). The rate of schizophrenia among parents of an affected child is about 10%, also considerably greater than the population base rate (Volk-mar, 1996b). These findings indicate that schizophrenia is highly geneti-cally bound but also highly susceptible to environmental influences, such as drug abuse, head injury, birth complications, paternal age at concep-tion, and stressful life events (Sagud et al., 2008). Heritability estimates vary greatly but suggest that over 80% of the risk of becoming schizo-phrenic may be due to genetics (Cardno & Gottesman, 2000). Genetic studies have increasingly found copy number variations (primarily dele-tions in the DNA) along with common single nucleotide polymorphisms (difference in a single DNA nucleotide base) among alleles connected to schizophrenia. Regardless of risk, we now recognize that schizophrenia is a polygenetic disorder and is not inherited in simple Mendelian fashion. Furthermore, the current data suggest that there may be genetic overlap between schizophrenia, bipolar disorder and autism (Gejman, Sanders, & Duan, 2011).

Finally, evidence has consistently shown that marijuana, *cannabis sativa*, is a risk factor for the development of psychosis. Although clearly not a causal agent in the vast majority of cases, strong evidence suggests that cannabis both worsens existing psychotic disorders and increases the likelihood of chronic psychosis among those individuals predisposed to developing a psychotic disorder. Similarly, numerous synthetic cannabinoids, such as "spice" and "mojo," have been described as causing psychosis in case reports (Pierre, 2011).

EPIDEMIOLOGY

Fewer than 1 in 10,000 children will develop schizophrenia or schizoaffective disorder. The rate then steadily increases during adolescence until hitting a peak incidence of 1% among adults. The lifetime prevalence of schizophrenia is roughly 0.3% to 0.7%, with small variations being reported among different ethnicities, across countries, and immigrants and their children. Schizoaffective disorder is about one-third as common, affecting approximately 0.3% of the population (American Psychiatric Association, 2013). About 4% of all cases of schizophrenia present prior to age 15. The average age of onset is 18 to 25 years for men and 23 to 35 years for women (Gorwood, Leboyer, Jay, Payan, & Feingold, 1995). A second but much smaller peak in incidence after 40 years of age, considered late-onset schizophrenia, occurs among females, accounting for as many as 10% of all female cases. Affected females tend to experience more psychotic symptoms, such as paranoid delusions and hallucinations, with relative conservation of social functioning and affect. Consequently, there is some question as to whether or not late-onset schizophrenia, as currently diagnosed, is actually the same condition as the schizophrenia diagnosed in those prior to mid-life (e.g., 55 years; American Psychiatric Association, 2013).

Women generally have a better prognosis than men, based upon length of hospital stay and rehospitalizations, although this finding is quite possibly due to the fact that males generally experience earlier onset of symptoms which leads to greater disruption in their lives, such as lower academic achievement and worse premorbid functioning (American Psychiatric Association, 2013). Males are more commonly diagnosed in childhood and throughout the teen years. There is a 2:1 male to female ratio in children under 14 years of age, but by midadulthood the gender ratio equalizes. Although men and women are believed to be equally affected by schizophrenia, a diagnostic bias may result in more psychotic females being diagnosed with a mood disorder or schizoaffective disorder (depressive type) and more psychotic males with schizophrenia (Beauchamp & Gagnon, 2004).

Risk factors for the later development of psychosis have been suggested. Cannon et al. (2008) followed nearly 300 teens deemed to be at high risk of psychosis based on experiencing prodromal symptoms in one or more of the following five categories in the 12 months prior to study entry: (a) unusual thought content, (b) suspicion/paranoia, (c) perceptual anomalies, (d) grandiosity, and (e) disorganized communication. At the end of 30 months of observation, the team identified five factors assessed at baseline that contributed to the prediction of psychosis: (a) a genetic risk for schizophrenia with recent deterioration in functioning; (b) higher levels of unusual thought content; (c) higher levels of suspicion/paranoia; (d) greater social impairment; and (e) a history of substance abuse. Algorithms combining two or three of these factors were 68% to 80% predictive of psychosis as compared to the prodromal risk criteria alone. This multisite North American study represents the largest prodromal population followed to date worldwide and suggests strongly that clinicians should be assessing these predictive risk factors.

CLINICAL COURSE

Early-onset schizophrenia more commonly occurs among males with poor premorbid adjustment, lower academic achievement, and significant negative psychotic symptoms. These individuals also display more signs of neuroanatomical abnormalities and cognitive impairment and suffer a worse outcome. By contrast, those with later-onset illness are more commonly female, have fewer signs of neuroanatomical abnormalities and cognitive impairment, and have a better outcome (American Psychiatric Association, 2000). A number of additional prognostic indicators for schizophrenia have been identified, as seen in Table 15.1.

Up to 75% of schizophrenics may develop the neurological soft signs previously mentioned either early in the course of the illness or over time. These tests primarily call upon the cerebellum and parietal lobes, which, as noted above, suffer deterioration early in the developmental course of the illness. These include abnormalities in stereognosis, the ability to perceive the form of an object with only the sense of touch; graphesthesia, the ability to recognize writing on the skin purely by the sense of touch; balance, often measured by impairment in tandem gait; ocular abilities, such as eye-tracking; and proprioception, a sense of the relative position-

Table 15.1 Prognostic Indicators for Schizophrenia

Good	Bad
Acute onset	Insidious onset
Short duration of illness	Long duration of illness
Lack of prior psychiatric history	Psychiatric history
Presence of affective symptoms, confusion, or mood symptoms	Poor insight
	Obsessive-compulsive symptoms
Good premorbid adjustment	History of violence
Steady work history	Poor insight
Marriage	Premorbid personality disorder
Older age at onset	Poor work history
Female	Celibacy
	Young age at onset
	Family history of schizophrenia

ing of various parts of the body, most commonly measured by closing one's eyes and bringing the index finger to the nose or following and tapping another's finger in the visual plane. Mood-disordered patients, particularly those with periodic psychosis, also experience these difficulties at times but less so, by and large, than those with schizophrenia. Some studies also report a reduction in Stage 3 (deep) sleep in schizophrenics, and a lack of interest in sex is common.

Schizophrenia is virtually always a chronic illness with variable periods of exacerbation and remission. Over time the illness may stabilize but is unlikely to ever fully remit. Most clinicians concur that EOS, particularly VEOS, has a poor prognosis. The longitudinal course of the illness, as classically described by Bleuler, is believed to follow a cyclic pattern of acute psychosis, followed by longer periods of recuperation, and then remission. Bleuler described increasing deterioration with each cycle, leading to an eventual burnout around 10 years into the active phase of the illness, leaving individuals with various degrees of disability and predominately negative residual symptoms (Bleuler, 1978). Affected individuals may occasionally find satisfying work and relationships but virtually always require extensive assistance. Most schizophrenics live with their families of origin as long as possible or in assisted group homes. Perhaps a smaller number will progressively deteriorate, becoming increasingly disabled and necessitating long-term inpatient treatment and institutional support. A high level of "expressed emotion" within the family of origin, a measure of hostility, emotional overinvolvement, and criticism, is known to be damaging for affected individuals (M. J. Goldstein, 1989).

Suicide, the most feared outcome of mental illness, is unfortunately quite common among those with psychotic disorders. About 5% to 6% of individuals with schizophrenia or schizoaffective disorder die by suicide, and about 20% of these individuals attempt suicide one or more times. The risk of suicide remains elevated throughout the lifetime of both males and females with schizophrenia, but it may be particularly high among young males with coexisting substance abuse. Suicide attempters often later report having heard command auditory hallucinations telling them to kill themselves. Additional risk factors include depressive mood, hopelessness, lack of employment, and when emerging from a psychotic episode or discharging from a hospital (American Psychiatric Association, 2013).

DIAGNOSIS

Emile Kraepelin, a German psychiatrist, first named dementia praecox (early dementia) in 1887, distinguishing it from manic depression (now bipolar disorder). Paul Eugen Bleuler, a Swiss psychiatrist, renamed dementia praecox, given his observation that it was not a dementia and did not exclusively affect the young. He coined the term *schizophrenia* (from the Greek, meaning literally "to split the mind") in 1912 to emphasize the cognitive impairments, which he conceptualized as a "splitting" of the psychic processes. Bleuler believed that the characteristic symptoms could be described by what he labeled as the 4 As of schizophrenia: (1) affective blunting; (2) loosening of associations (speech characterized by shifting between topics that are only minimally related to one another, a feature indicative of cognitive disorganization); (3) autism, another term he invented to describe the self-centered nature of these individuals (see Chapter 8); and (4) ambivalence or indecisiveness. Bleuler believed that the negative symptoms of schizophrenia, the 4 As, were the true defining features of the illness and regarded positive symptoms of schizophrenia, such as delusions and hallucinations, as accessory because they occurred in other disorders, such as bipolar disorder and psychotic depression (Bleuler, 1978).

Kurt Schneider, another German psychiatrist, followed upon the heels of Kraepelin and Bleuler and was also interested in differentiating schizophrenia from other psychotic illnesses. Unlike Bleuler, however, he felt that it was the unique positive symptoms of psychosis—or first-rank symptoms, as they came to be known—that were the true hallmark of schizophrenia. Schneider felt that all first-rank symptoms involved ego boundaries and did not regularly occur in patients with mood disorders. The symptoms he described included hearing one's own thoughts, hearing voices arguing in one's head, hearing voices commenting on one's behavior, and believing that an external force is acting upon one's body.

Other first-rank symptoms include "thought withdrawal," or the idea that thoughts can be taken out of one's head; "thought insertion," or the idea that others' thoughts can be placed inside of one's head; "thought broadcasting," or the idea that one's thoughts can be broadcast out loud for others to hear; and ideas of reference, the idea that unrelated phenomena refer directly to the affected individual (e.g., believing that radio broadcasts, media articles, and television programs are produced especially for or about them; K. Schneider, 1959). Although Schneider's work was influential in its time and had the effect of placing the diagnostic focus of schizophrenia on the positive symptoms, mental health practitioners today incorporate both positive and negative symptoms into the diagnostic understanding of schizophrenia.

DSM-5 requires at least two of the following symptoms in order to meet criteria for a diagnosis of schizophrenia: (a) delusions (false beliefs); (b) hallucinations (false sensations); (c) disorganized speech, sounding confused and disjointed; (d) grossly disorganized or catatonic behavior; and (e) negative symptoms, such as affective blunting, poverty of thought and speech (alogia), or difficulty initiating goal-directed behavior (avolition). *DSM-5* also requires that the illness be functionally impairing and extend for at least 6 months before a diagnosis is given (American Psychiatric Association, 2013).

Five subtypes of schizophrenia were previously described in *DSM-IV*. Although *DSM-5* has discontinued use of all but one of these specifiers (because of diagnostic instability, poor validity, and low reliability), they still warrant discussion, given the large numbers of individuals who have been diagnosed in this fashion. The most common specifier is the chronic paranoid type, which characterizes about 85% of those with schizophrenia. Chronic paranoid schizophrenics suffer troublesome paranoid delusions and auditory hallucinations, while maintaining relatively intact cognitive function and affect. Disorganized type schizophrenia is characterized by disorganized speech, behavior, and an affect that is flat or inappropriate to the situation. Catatonic type schizophrenia, the one specifier that remains in *DSM-5*, is characterized by psychological and motor impairments affecting movement and speech. Affected individuals may be immobile or cataplectic and exhibit odd movements and posturing, excessive and purposeless motor activity, extreme negativism or mutism, and echolalia and echopraxia. Those individuals who suffer at least one episode of schizophrenia but who subsequently only suffer negative symptoms or negative symptoms with only mild and minimally impairing positive symptoms are described as having residual type schizophrenia. Finally, those affected individuals whose schizophrenia is not better characterized by paranoid, disorganized, or catatonic types are considered to be of the undifferentiated type (American Psychiatric Association, 2000).

Upon presentation, children with psychotic symptoms should receive a full medical and neurological evaluation. Any evidence of neurological impairment should be followed with specific testing, including an electroencephalogram and neuroimaging studies. Delirium, seizure disorders, central nervous system lesions (e.g., tumors, malformations, and head trauma), neurodegenerative disorders (e.g., Huntington's chorea), metabolic disorders (e.g., Wilson's disease), infectious diseases (e.g., encephalitis, HIV, meningitis), and toxic encephalopathies (e.g., substances of abuse, industrial chemicals, toxins) should be ruled out as potential causes. Rates of comorbid substance abuse among adolescents presenting with psychotic symptoms are as high as 50% in some studies. In fact, first-break psychotic episodes commonly occur in the context of substance abuse, which may exacerbate or trigger the psychosis, even if it is not the primary etiological factor (McClellan & Werry, 1997).

The differential diagnosis of schizophrenia includes a broad range of disorders. Schizoaffective disorder, bipolar disorder, and major depressive disorder can all present with psychosis and must be considered. Following the patient longitudinally and obtaining collateral information is absolutely vital in establishing this differential, along with establishing a complete family history. Conduct and other disruptive behavior disorders can also present with psychotic-like symptoms, although these youths tend to have lower rates of delusions and thought disorder. Autism spectrum disorders are best differentiated by their early age at onset and transient psychotic symptoms, if present at all. Anxiety disorders, particularly obsessive-compulsive disorder (OCD), can be difficult to differentiate because schizophrenics themselves can also display significant obsessive-compulsive symptoms; however, most often those affected by OCD recognize their anxieties as unreasonable and excessive. Other anxiety disorders, such as posttraumatic stress disorder, can present with psychotic features, particularly among those children who have been physically and sexually abused. Here again, it is the history and longitudinal course that provides the greatest help in differentiating this disorder from a primary psychotic process. Various speech and language disorders, which can present with disordered speech, and personality disorders, which can present with paranoia and mildly psychotic behavior, must also be ruled out (McClellan & Werry, 1997).

Because young children are concrete in their cognition and cannot easily abstract, they may misunderstand direct questions about psychotic phenomena during an interview. As expected, questions regarding rare occurrences, such as psychosis, typically have the highest rates of false-positive responses in structured interviews. From a child's perspective, normal thought and memory processes may include hearing internal voices and experiencing odd or false beliefs. Consequently, assessing and understanding a child's symptoms are particularly difficult, and in many cases it is virtually impossible to obtain a reliable answer to a direct question about hallucinations or delusions. Obtaining collateral information about the child's behavior at home, at school, and with friends from parents, teachers, and other individuals in the child's life, therefore, is absolutely necessary. As previously noted, behavioral observations are often more useful than direct interview questions when assessing childhood psychosis. In addition, the clinician should interact more loosely with the child, playing if indicated, or discussing popular culture, friendships, hobbies, and interests. Such interactions can provide great insight into a child's psyche.

When asking children directly about psychotic phenomena, the questions should be couched in developmentally appropriate language. Asking questions about hallucinations and delusions successfully is tricky for even the most seasoned examiner. Some good examples of specific questions that clinicians might employ follow[*]:

- "Sometimes when it's quiet or when people are alone, they see or hear things that other people cannot see or hear. Has that ever happened to you? Will you tell me about it?"
- "Do you sometimes hear your own thoughts or hear yourself thinking? Lots of people say they do. But have you ever actually heard, like with your own ears, voices that other people could not hear? What did they say?"
- "Have you ever heard your name being called when no one else was around?"
- "Have you ever seen things that other people cannot see? What did you see?"
- "Do you know what imagination is? Can you tell me? Has your imagination ever played tricks on you? What was that like?"
- "Have you ever felt like anybody else knew just what you were thinking? Did it ever feel like they could take thoughts out of your head or put thoughts into your head?"
- "Does it ever feel like songs on the radio or shows on the TV are being put there just for you?"
- "Have you ever had thoughts that you were afraid to tell other people about, even your parents? Can you tell me about that?"

*Adapted from the K-SADS-PL, a semistructured diagnostic interview frequently employed in research studies

- "Do you sometimes believe things that nobody else seems to believe?"
- "Do you ever worry that someone is trying to hurt you? Do you ever feel like someone is following you around?"
- "Do you ever worry that people might be talking about you or saying bad things about you?"
- "What do you want to be when you're a grown-up? Do you ever think that you're destined to be a great or really special person?"

Affirmative responses to these questions do not provide absolute confirmation of psychosis, but with some practice the clinician will get a sense of which responses are typical or "normal" and which are aberrant. Depending upon the child's age, self-report of psychotic symptoms can be fraught with confusion. The validity of self-report should be questioned when the details are inconsistent and when there is no documented evidence to support the assertion (e.g., no observed odd behavior) other than the child's statement. Self-report should also be questioned when the nature of the report is not typical of psychosis, such as highly detailed descriptions of delusions and hallucinations that are more suggestive of fantasy, imagination, or attention-seeking. Finally, self-report should be questioned when the symptoms occur only at specific times or are reinforced by current circumstances, such that, for example, one hears voices only when angry or after an argument or fight.

Neuropsychological testing can also sometimes be useful in evaluating psychosis. Schizophrenics tend to do poorly on most psychological tests but have particular difficulty with tests of frontal lobe function that assess problem-solving, judgment, working memory, attention, concentration, and eye-tracking. Temporal lobe function is also typically impaired, as evidenced by the language and thought disorders identified by testing, and deficient long-term memory functioning, which is thought to be both medial temporal lobe and hippocampal in nature (Knable et al., 1998). Finally, as described in Chapter 5, projective tests are often useful for assessing hidden and unconscious thoughts and emotions.

TREATMENT

The interval between onset of psychosis and initiation of treatment varies greatly but generally averages one to two years. The duration of untreated psychosis depends upon a variety of factors. Those who are more severely affected and those with more social support tend to receive services sooner, but other factors influencing when people begin to receive treatment remain unknown (Ho & Andreason, 2001). Increasing evidence indicates that a delay in treatment exerts at least a modest negative influence upon clinical outcome and that earlier treatment leads to a better prognosis and treatment response (Addington, Van Mastrigt, & Addington, 2004; Marshall et al., 2005; Novak Sarotar, Pesek, Agius, & Kocmur, 2008). Among schizophrenics in one study, delays in treatment resulted in greater negative, positive, and general psychopathological symptoms, along with global functioning deficits, 15 years after the first psychiatric admission, even after other factors possibly related to long-term outcome were controlled for (Bottlender et al., 2003). Even Kraepelin identified more persistent symptoms and worse outcomes among those who had a longer duration of illness (Kraepelin, Barclay, & Robertson, 1919). Given the studies described above regarding the rapid and expansive brain deterioration of adolescents diagnosed with schizophrenia (see Etiology) along with post-mortem and structural MRI studies, it is thought that early treatment may slow both neurological and clinical deterioration. Presumably, treatment with an antipsychotic would be the most reasonable for adolescents or young adults with premorbid or prodromal schizophrenia, but some studies have suggested that antidepressants may also have a role here (Larson, Walker, & Compton, 2010). Prolonged untreated psychosis commonly creates profound psychosocial problems as well.

The role of early psychosocial treatment is paramount because it leads to far lower relapse rates. One study of integrated services for adults with schizophrenia found that when given case management and medication only, 54% of individuals with schizophrenia relapsed within one year. However, when given family education in addition to medication and case management, the relapse rate dropped to 27%; and when problem-solving skills were added, the one-year relapse rate dropped still further to 23%. Finally, when also given social skills training, the one-year relapse rate dropped to 14% (Falloon, Held, Coverdale, Roncone, & Laidlaw, 1999).

Historically, the neurological deficits associated with psychosis were thought to be due to toxicity associated with the psychosis itself; however, more recently it has been suggested that those parts of the brain involved in the production of psychotic symptoms may become somewhat hypertrophic whereas other areas that are not utilized during these times of intense symptomatology become somewhat atrophic. The result of this combined overuse hypertrophy and disuse atrophy might be a net loss in brain interconnectivity, synaptic plasticity, and cognitive capacity (McGlashan, 2006). It is becoming increasingly clear, therefore, that clinicians should take great pains to identify and aggressively treat psychotic symptoms from the moment they are evident.

The Food and Drug Administration (FDA) has approved various antipsychotic medications in children and adolescents for the treatment of schizophrenia, acute mania associated with bipolar disorder, irritability associated with autistic disorder, and Tourette's disorder in children and adolescents. The FDA has not validated the efficacy of these medications for the treatment of aggression, anxiety, attention-deficit/hyperactivity disorder (ADHD), personality disorders, oppositional defiant and conduct disorder, and major depressive disorder in children and adolescents, yet we often use them for these indications as well. Practitioners vary in their degree of comfort in prescribing antipsychotics for off-label purposes, either as primary or adjunctive medications, but all practitioners agree that the antipsychotics do have a place in the treatment of many conditions for which they do not have an FDA indication, as is shown by prescribing practices.

Antipsychotics have been increasingly prescribed for the treatment of a wide variety of conditions in children and adolescents over the past decade. The number of children prescribed antipsychotics increased five times between 1995 and 2002, to an estimated 2.5 million children per year by 2002; or from 8.6 per 1,000 children in 1995 to 39.4 per 1,000 in 2002. The rate of increase in the use of antipsychotics has also been greater among children in recent years than among adults. Antipsychotic use saw a 73% increase between 2001 and 2005 in those under 18 years of age, as opposed to a 13% increase among adults during this same time. Fifteen percent of all antipsychotics are now prescribed to those 18 years and younger, most often for disorders of mood and behavior (Cooper et al., 2006).

By 2009, the frequency of antipsychotic use had continued to climb. Between 1993 and 1998, 0.24% of child, 0.78% of adolescent, and 3.25% of adult visits to outpatient physicians included antipsychotic treatment. By 2005 to 2009, however, the rate among children had increased to 1.8%, among adolescents to 3.8%, and among adults to 6.2%. Boys are more commonly prescribed these medications than girls, in contrast to adults where women are more likely to receive them than men (Olfson, Blanco, Liu, Wang, & Correll, 2012). Among youth, Medicaid-insured children and adolescents are about four times more likely than those who are privately insured to fill a prescription for an antipsychotic medication. Furthermore, only a minority of privately insured (32.6%) and Medicaid-insured (26.9%) youth are prescribed these medications for a diagnosis of schizophrenia, bipolar disorder, or autism spectrum disorder (Crystal, Olfson, Huang, Pincus, & Gerhard, 2009). In other words, most children and adolescents for whom these medications are being prescribed are receiving them for a diagnosis for which antipsychotics have not yet been proven to be effective and for which they are not FDA approved in children and adolescents (Pathak, West, Martin, Helm, & Henderson, 2010).

Previously described as neuroleptics, which quite literally means to "seize the neuron," antipsychotics work by antagonizing dopamine-mediated synaptic transmission by blocking postsynaptic dopamine receptors. The primary effect of most antipsychotics is to block the dopamine D2 receptor, although other dopamine receptors, such as D3 and D4, and a host of serotonin, histamine, muscarinic, and other receptors are often purposefully and inadvertently blocked by these medications. The medications are hypothesized to exert their effects via depolarization inactivation; that is, chronic treatment is believed to push the dopamine neurons in the substantia nigra and ventral tegmental area beyond their physiological limits and drive them into quiescence secondary to excessive membrane depolarization (Mereu et al., 1995). The clinical potency of most, but not all, antipsychotics correlates well with their relative blocking of the D2 receptor. The first generation or typical antipsychotics exert their beneficial effects by acting exclusively on dopamine. The second generation or atypical antipsychotics are unique in that they act on both dopamine and serotonin.

Risperidone (Risperdal), an atypical antipsychotic, has been approved by the FDA for the treatment of irritability associated with autistic disorder in children age 5 to 16 (McCracken et al., 2002; Shea et al., 2004). Risperidone has also been approved for the acute treatment of schizophrenia in adolescents age 13 to 17 and bipolar mania in youth age 10 to 17 (Pandina et al., 2007). The two studies of risperidone in schizophrenia lasted six and eight weeks, respectively, and included over 400 subjects. Dosages ranged from 0.25 mg per day to 6 mg per day. Dosages higher than 3 mg per day did not increase efficacy but did increase the number of side effects. Aripiprazole (Abilify), another atypical, has also been FDA approved for the treatment of irritability associated with autistic disorder in children age 6 to 17 years (Marcus et al., 2009; Owen et al., 2009), as well as for the acute treatment of schizophrenia in adolescents age 13 to 17 and bipolar mania in youth ages 10 to 17 (Chang et al., 2007). The aripiprazole study of schizophrenia lasted six weeks and included over 300 subjects, and both dosages utilized, 10 mg and 30 mg, were efficacious.

Quetiapine (Seroquel), an atypical, has been FDA approved for the acute treatment of schizophrenia in adolescents age 13 to 17 and bipolar mania in youth age 10 to 17. At dosages of 400 and 800 mg per day, quetiapine demonstrated equal benefit in a six-week trial of adolescents with schizophrenia (Findling, McKenna, Earley, Stankowski, & Pathak, 2012). Finally, olanzapine (Zyprexa), an atypical, has also been FDA approved for the acute treatment of schizophrenia in adolescents age 13 to 17 and bipolar mania in youth age 10 to 17 (Kryzhanovskaya et al., 2009).

Although the medications described above are the most frequently prescribed for the treatment of schizophrenia and bipolar disorder in children and adolescents, numerous other randomized and nonrandomized studies of antipsychotics have been performed in children and adolescents. Based upon one meta-analysis of all published randomized and controlled trials, clozapine (Clozaril) was superior to all other antipsychotics, followed by second generation antipsychotics and then first generation antipsychotics (see below; Sarkar & Grover, 2013).

Unfortunately, there is no hard and fast rule to guide us in prescribing one antipsychotic over another in youth or adults. Both the Clinical Antipsychotic Trials of Intervention Effectiveness (CATIE) Study in adults and the Treatment of Early-Onset Schizophrenia Spectrum (TEOSS) Study in children and adolescents compared first and second generation antipsychotics and found, by and large, disappointing results. While CATIE concluded that olanzapine was a somewhat superior treatment, this finding was entirely due to the fact that olanzapine had the lowest discontinuation rate, allowing study subjects to stay on the medication longer and receive the benefit of more treatment. Other atypical antipsychotics in the trial did not separate from one another or from the typical antipsychotic used in the study. The discontinuation rate averaged 74% in the CATIE study, largely due to side effects and lack of treatment benefit. Likewise, the TEOSS study had an even larger dropout rate of 88% for similar reasons as the CATIE trial; and as with CATIE, there was essentially no difference in efficacy between typical and atypical antipsychotic treatment (Findling et al., 2010; Lieberman et al., 2005). As stated, the primary reason that these medications did not show benefit in both trials had to do with the preponderance of individuals who discontinued treatment due to side effects or lack of benefit. Practice parameters for the treatment of schizophrenia and psychosis in youth, however, vehemently confirm antipsychotic medication as the most robust treatment (McClellan & Stock, 2013). As a result, practitioners must make every effort to improve treatment adherence, which will demand frequent appointments with treated individuals and extensive psychosocial supports.

First-Generation Antipsychotics

The first typical antipsychotic invented was chlorpromazine (Thorazine) in 1950, released for general distribution in 1955. Medications in this class are highly lipophilic—membrane- or protein-bound—and accumulate in the brain, lung, and other highly vascularized tissues. The usual half-life of the typical antipsychotics is about 20 to 40 hours, depending on the medication. Consequently, the biological effects of a single dose can last 24 hours or more.

Dopamine neurons project throughout the brain from the substantia nigra and ventral tegmentum, the primary dopamine hubs. Dopamine neurons follow four main pathways, each of which is blocked to some degree by antipsychotic medications. The typical antipsychotics exert their beneficial clinical impact by blocking dopamine D2 receptors in the mesolimbic pathway, which is highly involved in emotion. Because these medications are not particularly selective, however, they also block dopamine receptors in other areas of the brain, such as the mesocortical area, where they can interfere with memory, cognition, and motivation; the tuberoinfundibular pathway, where they can interfere with hormonal regulation and lead to increases in prolactin; and the nigrostriatal pathway, where they can interfere with physical movement and motor control, resulting in tremors, stiffness, dyskinesias, and dystonias.

The first-generation antipsychotics are described as either low or high potency, depending on the strength of their dopamine D2 binding. The best-known high-potency medications are haloperidol (Haldol) and fluphenazine (Prolixin). Higher-potency antipsychotics are given in dosages of a few milligrams, induce less sedation than low-potency antipsychotics, but lead to more extrapyramidal side effects or difficulties with movement because they block dopamine more severely. Lower-potency antipsychotics, such as thioridazine (Mellaril) and chlorpromazine, are given in dosages of several hundred milligrams and induce greater sedation and calming because of their increased anticholinergic and antihistaminergic activity, which can counteract some of their dopamine blockade–related side effects.

Second-Generation Antipsychotics

The second-generation antipsychotics, or "atypicals," arrived in Europe in 1971. Clozapine was initially introduced in Europe but was withdrawn from the market in 1975 because it was shown to sometimes cause agranulocytosis (resulting in a severe drop in white blood cells that could result in death). The broad acceptance of the atypicals began in 1993 with the release of risperidone, a much safer and more easily tolerated medication for most individuals. These drugs are unique in that they not only block dopamine D2 receptors, but they also block or partially block sero-tonin receptors, particularly 5HT2A, 5HT2C, and 5HT1A. One of these medications, aripiprazole, also stimulates or agonizes dopamine recep-tors, in addition to blocking them. Still other atypicals, such as olanzap-ine, also block dopamine D1, D3, and D4 receptors, in addition to D2. When initially released, these medications were believed to be at least equally effective to the first-generation antipsychotics for the treatment of positive symptoms but of greater utility for negative symptoms, in large part, it was thought, because of their effects on serotonin (Stahl, 2002). Head to head trials among both psychotic adults and children and adolescents, however, have demonstrated no significant difference in effi-cacy between the first- and second-generation antipsychotics in at least the acute treatment of psychosis (Lieberman et al., 2005; Sikich et al., 2008). Because the atypical antipsychotics cause fewer extrapyramidal side effects, they are sometimes initially easier for patients to tolerate. However, no medication is free from side effects, and what the atypicals lack in the extrapyramidal domain, they often make up for in metabolic complications, including weight gain and insulin resistance.

Clozapine

Clozapine was introduced into the United States in 1989, following stud-ies that found it was effective for treatment-resistant schizophrenia (Kane, Honigfeld, Singer, & Metlzer, 1988). Unlike most other antipsy-chotics, with the exception of olanzapine, clozapine has little effect on dopamine D2 receptors, which may explain why it rarely causes extrapy-ramidal side effects or interferes with prolactin. In fact, clozapine exerts a 10-times-greater blockade of D4 receptors than D2 receptors, while also exerting influence on 5HTC, muscarinic, and alpha-1 adrenergic recep-tors. Because clozapine can have such severe side effects, it carries five FDA "black-box warnings" for agranulocytosis, myocarditis, seizures, increased mortality in elderly with dementia-related psychosis, and adverse cardiovascular and respiratory problems. A black-box warning is the strongest caution the FDA can place on a medication, signifying that the drug carries a major risk of serious or potentially life-threatening complications. Because of its extreme side effect potential, clozapine is generally selected after numerous other antipsychotics have been tried, even though in studies of adults and children with schizophrenia it is generally more effective than other treatments (Citrome, 2012; C. Schnei-der, Corrigall, Hayes, Kyriakopolous, & Frangou, 2014).

Antipsychotic Side Effects

Antipsychotics can cause numerous adverse effects, many of which are a nuisance and not a cause for discontinuation. Sedation, dry mouth, tremor, dizziness, and nausea, for example, are relatively common, albeit troubling, side effects; yet many, perhaps most, children and adolescents quickly become accustomed to these disturbances, particularly if mild or time limited, and may continue on the medication without complaints. Other side effects, however, are more significant and may necessitate medication adjustments or discontinuation.

The most common difficulties with the first-generation antipsychotics are the extrapyramidal side effects, so named because the "extrapyramidal" motor neuron network lies outside of the motor tracts that travel through the "pyramids" of the medulla. The extrapyramidal system modulates motor activity in areas of the brain highly vulnerable to antipsychotic medications but does not directly innervate motor neurons. There are four primary extrapyramidal problems that can arise secondary to the use of antipsychotics—dystonias, akathisia, Parkinsonism, and dyskinesias. Dystonias are movements in which sustained muscle contractions cause bending or twisting, recurring movements, or abnormal postures. Some of the more common dystonias include torticollis (a rotation of the neck), blepharospasm (rapid eye-blinking), and oculogyric crisis (an upward deviation of the eyes). Dystonias are extremely uncomfortable at the least but can be painful and incapacitating. Akathisia is characterized by a sense of internal restlessness and an inability to sit still and is often confused with anxiety. Parkinsonism represents a series of side effects that mirror the effects of Parkinson's syndrome, including stiffness, rigidity, tremor, and an unsteady posture. Parkinsonism is so called because the hypodopaminergic state induced by some antipsychotics mirrors that found in Parkinson's syndrome. Finally, dyskinesias are repetitive, involuntary, and purposeless movements of the lips, face, legs, or torso.

Dyskinesias are similar to tics and are more likely to happen with repeated exposure to antipsychotics over time. When they set on after chronic exposure to an antipsychotic, they are termed tardive dyskinesia (TD), tardive being derived from the French word for late. The risk of developing TD is not clearly established but is estimated to be about 3% to 5% per year, at least for the first five years of treatment. Untreated schizophrenics have a significant risk of developing TD as well, although antipsychotic treatment clearly increases that risk. The atypical antipsychotics were initially thought to result in less TD, although some studies now dispute this assumption (Kane, 2006). The most common expression of TD among antipsychotic users is movements of the mouth and tongue.

Children are generally more vulnerable than adults to extrapyramidal side effects, particularly with the first-generation antipsychotics (Correll & Kane, 2007; Nasrallah, 2006). Both the first-generation and atypical antipsychotics can also cause cardiac toxicity, prolactin elevation, and weight gain. The atypicals, however, are particularly troublesome in this regard.

Finally, antipsychotic medications can also rarely induce fatal side effects, including seizures and neuroleptic malignant syndrome (NMS). NMS is the most severe of the antipsychotic side effects with a mortality rate approaching 30%. The presentation of NMS is characterized by muscular rigidity, elevated body temperature, unstable vital signs, elevations in creatine phosphokinase, and eventually altered consciousness (Marder, 1998). When caught early, NMS is highly treatable.

Medication Monitoring

Any child or adolescent taking an antipsychotic medication requires extensive and continued monitoring. Baseline blood work should include a fasting glucose and lipid profile, complete blood count, electrolytes (including calcium and magnesium), BUN (blood urea nitrogen), creatinine, liver function tests, thyroid function tests, and prolactin, in addition to height, weight, and a urine drug screen if there is even a remote possibility of substance abuse. The body mass index (BMI) should be calculated from the height and weight, as it represents a highly reliable measure of body fat. A physical examination should have been performed in the past 12 months, and an electrocardiogram (EKG) is also advised.

There are a number of features of the heart rhythm that antipsychotics can alter. In most cases, these alterations, when they occur, are mild and cause no notable concerns. However, in rare cases they can result in arrhythmias and death. Virtually all of the antipsychotics can extend the time it takes for the ventricles of the heart to both depolarize and repolarize, a gap known as the QT interval or the QTc when corrected for heart rate. The QT duration is the single best parameter for assessing unstable ventricular depolarization. A QTc of less than 450 milliseconds is considered normal (Zareba & Lin, 2003). EKGs should be assessed both before and during treatment with an antipsychotic, and any increases beyond 450 milliseconds or greater than 10% over baseline suggests the need for further investigation. In addition, hypokalemia, hypermagnesemia, or hypercalcemia should be treated prior to starting a child or adolescent on an antipsychotic, as these abnormalities can cause prolongation of the QT interval. Finally, delayed cardiac conduction, as observed by a PR interval of greater than 200 milliseconds or a QRS interval of greater than 120 milliseconds, may necessitate a dosage or medication change (Kaplan & Sadock, 2007).

Given that excessive weight gain and Type 2 diabetes can result from antipsychotic use, practitioners sometimes struggle with how to monitor their patients. The American Diabetes Association, along with a number of other professional groups including the American Psychiatric Association, has endorsed recommendations for monitoring individuals taking second-generation antipsychotics (American Diabetes Association, 2004). Although these guidelines were designed for adults taking antipsychotics over extended periods of time, they are also reasonable for children and adolescents, as the antipsychotics have a similar and often immediate metabolic impact on youth (see Table 15.2). In addition, the practitioner should regularly inquire about clinical signs of diabetes, such as unintended weight loss, polydipsia, and polyuria.

Prior to treating a female, a menstrual history should be ascertained. During treatment, it is also important to inquire regularly about menstruation and amenorrhea among females, as antipsychotic-induced prolactin elevation can have severe long-term consequences. Among both males and females, nipple discharge, sexual dysfunction, and pubertal development should be regularly assessed as well. If serum prolactin is elevated in a female, pregnancy or oral contraceptives could be the culprit, in addition

Table 15.2 Monitoring Protocol for Patients on Second-Generation Antipsychotics

Lab Value	Baseline	4 weeks	8 weeks	12 weeks	Quarterly	Annually	Every 5 years
Personal/ family history	X					X	
Weight (BMI)	X	X	X	X	X		
Waist circumference	X					X	
Blood pressure	X			X		X	
Fasting plasma glucose	X			X		X	
Fasting lipid profile	X			X			X

Source: American Diabetes Association, "Consensus Development Conference on Antipsychotic Drugs and Obesity and Diabetes," 2008. Copyright and all rights reserved. Material from this publication has been used with the permission of American Diabetes Association.

to the antipsychotic, and all possibilities should be evaluated. Additionally, thyroid-stimulating hormone (TSH) and serum creatinine should be rechecked because both hypothyroidism and renal failure can result in an increase in prolactin. Sexually active females taking antipsychotics should be advised to use two forms of contraception, such as condoms along with oral contraception, an intrauterine device, or a diaphragm, given the risk of possible birth defects to a developing fetus. If the prolactin is repeatedly over 200 ng/ml or does not decrease even after changing to a prolactin-sparing antipsychotic such as quetiapine, aripiprazole, or clozapine, then a brain MRI of the sella turcica should be performed to rule out a pituitary adenoma or a parasellar tumor. Because prolactin levels may rise early in response to antipsychotic treatment and then taper off to normal levels over 12 months, it may be prudent to follow levels for 6 to 12 months before making major changes in regimen unless side effects are troubling (Pandina, Aman, & Findling, 2006).

Psychosocial Treatments for Psychotic Disorders

Multimodal psychosocial treatment approaches that incorporate medication management, family and collateral psychoeducation, vocational rehabilitation, and supportive psychotherapy are effective in reducing relapse rates and morbidity due to psychosis among adults (McClellan & Werry, 1997). In contrast, insight-oriented psychotherapy by itself has not proven useful for psychotic individuals, and it would be rare indeed to find a psychiatrist or therapist these days providing such treatment as the sole intervention (M. J. Goldstein, 1989).

Most psychotherapeutic approaches to the treatment of psychosis have been studied in adults and will generalize reasonably well to older adolescents but perhaps not as well to children. High-functioning rehabilitation programs that support social and vocational skills training have proven useful. These programs are particularly necessary for those diagnosed with EOS and VEOS because the earlier one is affected by a chronic psychotic illness, the greater not only the morbidity from the psychosis itself, but also from the resulting deviations in normal development (McClellan & Werry, 1997).

Most psychotic children and adolescents will not do well in a regular academic setting and will require specialized supports. For those who are unable to continue academically beyond a certain point for whatever reason, training in problem-solving, life skills, and independent living has proven remarkably helpful. Other program components, such as vocational counseling, job training, educational support, money management skills, use of public transportation, and social skills training are all key components that have been shown to be effective for those with schizophrenia (Kopelowicz, Liberman, & Wallace, 2003). These approaches are typically community centered and attempt to provide patients with the skills necessary to lead productive lives outside of hospitals and chronic care facilities.

Cognitive behavior therapy (CBT) has proven useful with schizophrenic adults (Lecomte et al., 2008). In addition, family therapy focused on improving family interactions and reducing "expressed emotion," or excessive criticism expressed toward the affected individual, has been shown to decrease relapse rates among schizophrenic adults (M. J. Goldstein, 1989; McClellan & Werry, 1997). Neither CBT nor family therapy, however, has been adequately tested in children and adolescents (Muñoz-Solomando, Kendall, & Whittington, 2008).

Family education is vital and must begin the moment the diagnosis is established. The family should be taught about the illness itself and how to support the affected member. Most important, all efforts to support the family in maintaining relapse prevention must be employed. Teaching coping strategies and problem-solving skills to both the patient and the family is also a major tenant of family education. Families can also help the affected individual by supporting adherence to the medication regimen and regular visits with the treating physician.

Self-help groups have sometimes been used effectively for those with schizophrenia and are becoming more common. These groups can provide support and comfort for patients and may serve other important functions by acting, for example, as a surrogate family and source of friendships. Community-based clubhouse programs for those with chronic mental illness provide a gathering place and a setting in which to teach social and life skills. Finally, intensive case management and assertive community treatment (ACT) programs, which provide community-based mobile mental health treatment, have been shown to decrease recidivism among adults with severe and persistent psychotic illness (Weisbrod, 1983). The ACT service delivery model uses a team of clinical professionals from various disciplines, including psychiatry, nursing, addiction counseling, and vocational rehabilitation, to provide treatment, rehabilitation, and support services on a 24-hour, seven-day-a-week basis. Regardless of the therapeutic approach selected, it is important to remember that psychosocial treatment approaches are not a substitute for medication, which is clearly the first-line treatment for those with psychosis.

Substance Use Disorders

Gambling, eating, sex, and drug and alcohol use are all normal behaviors. When done in excess, however, each can cause major impairments. Though rarely a problem in children, drug and alcohol use among adolescents and adults takes a tremendous toll on the affected individuals, their families, and society. We might rather think of these behaviors as lying on a spectrum, where engaging in some drug and alcohol use is typical but engaging in excessive use is impairing. Clinicians and physicians must ask themselves the difficult question of what constitutes normative substance use in adolescents before they can effectively diagnose and treat these disorders.

As humans we have a universal desire to alter our consciousness, which is evident from childhood. Some children hold their breath or spin in circles to make themselves feel dizzy. Recall the merry-go-rounds in parks and playgrounds and the thrill of swinging. Consider how much children enjoy amusement parks and fast rides. Adults also enjoy mind-altering experiences, as clearly seen by their extensive use of alcohol and drugs. Far from benign, coffee is the second most frequently traded commodity in the world (after oil) and an over $100 billion industry worldwide (Avery, 2009; Goldschein, 2011).

CLINICAL PRESENTATION

To help children or adolescents who are struggling with *substance use disorders (SUDS)*, we must first identify the problem. Given that some level of use is normative, particularly during adolescence when many teens experiment, it can be particularly difficult to determine when use becomes abuse. Furthermore, most adolescents who abuse drugs and alcohol with any regularity tend to deny it and will not seek help unless forced to do so (Indig, Copeland, & Conigrave, 2008).

The clinical presentation of SUDS may take many forms and will vary to some degree, depending upon which substance(s) the adolescent is using. The most apparent feature is a child or adolescent's failure to meet academic, occupational, and social expectations and mandates. These persistent and recurrent social and interpersonal problems that occur as a result of alcohol and substance use, or are exacerbated by the effects of substances, are commonly the first features noted. Still, parents and other family members, peers, teachers, and clinicians must maintain some degree of vigilance and suspicion in order to detect substance abuse early.

ETIOLOGY

Before we can effectively diagnose and treat SUDS, it helps to understand why individuals abuse alcohol and substances. There are numerous theories, none of which fully explains the issue in its entirety, but each of which contributes something to our understanding and perspective. Many individuals use drugs and alcohol in order to fit in with their peers (Pilkington, 2007). Some children and adolescents try drugs and alcohol to relieve boredom, feel good, challenge parental authority, escape parental pressure, forget their troubles, relax, satisfy their curiosity, have fun, ease physical or emotional pain, or take a risk. Others insist that the media is at least partially responsible.

Numerous well-known celebrities and popular music stars, whom many adolescents view as role models, are known to have used drugs and alcohol. In addition, many popular films portray images of alcohol, drugs, and tobacco. Sixteen of the most popular R-rated films in the mid-1980s, for example, contained alcohol use and averaged 16 episodes of use per film (B. S. Greenberg, Siemicki, & Dorfman, 1993). Ninety-three percent of the 200 most popular video rentals from 1996 to 1997 depicted alcohol use, and 22% depicted illicit drugs (Roberts, Henriksen, & Christenson, 1999). Over one quarter of these films depicted graphic portrayals of drug preparation and/or ingestion. Few of these movies gave any indication as to the reason for drug use among the characters. Fewer than 50% of the films portrayed short-term consequences of substance abuse, and only 12% depicted long-term consequences. Films between 1960 and 1990 showed characters smoking at a rate of three times the national average for American adults (Hazan, Lipton, & Glantz, 1994). Among the 25 top-grossing films each year between 1988 and 1997, over 75% of them contained tobacco use. Likewise, nearly 90% of the 200 most popular movie rentals from 1996 to 1997 depicted tobacco use (Roberts et al., 1999). Even with federally mandated tobacco package warnings, total tobacco incidents per movie rose by 7% from 2010 to 2011 (Glantz, Iaccopucci, Titus, & Polansky, 2012). These films tend to portray smoking in a positive fashion, and the characters who smoke are sexier and more romantic than other characters in the films (McIntosh, Bazzini, Smith, & Wayne, 1998). Another study reviewed all G-rated animated feature films released between 1937 and 2000 and found that 47% portrayed alcohol use and 43% portrayed tobacco use (Thompson & Yokota, 2001); and smoking incidents in movies with a G, PG, or PG-13 rating increased by 34% per movie from 2010 to 2011, but the movies are not alone (Glantz et al., 2012).

Primack, Dalton, Carroll, Agarwal, and Fine (2008) analyzed 279 of the most popular songs of 2005, according to *Billboard* magazine, and found that 33% contained explicit references to drug or alcohol use. This percentage translates into 35.2 substance references per hour of listening to music. Given that adolescents listen to an average of nearly 2.5 hours of music per day, the typical teen is exposed to approximately 84 references to explicit substance use daily in songs. The number of references varied by genre—about 9% of pop songs,14% of rock songs, 20% of rhythm and blues and hip-hop songs, 36% of country songs, and 77% of rap songs had lyrics relating to drugs or alcohol. Only 4% of songs contained explicit antidrug-use messages, and none portrayed refusal of substance use. The authors also found that the substance use depicted in popular music was generally motivated by a desire for peer acceptance and sex and usually had positive associations and consequences. While there is no doubt that the media's influence is important in the equation of why adolescents use substances, these data are correlative only and are clearly not the only causal factor (Petraitis, Flay, Miller, Torpy, & Greiner, 1998).

Still, it is generally accepted that advertising may be responsible for up to 30% of teen alcohol and tobacco use (Atkin, 1995; J. P. Pierce et al., 1998). For example, middle school students who report more exposure to alcohol advertising are more likely to drink alcohol in high school than those who report less exposure (Scull, Kupersmidt, & Erausquin, 2014). As a result, the American Academy of Pediatrics has issued a policy statement recommending a ban on all tobacco advertising in all media, strong limitations on alcohol advertising, and avoiding substance-related exposures on television and in PG-13- and R-rated movies (Council on *Communications and Media*, 2010).

Since virtually all children and adolescents struggle with peer acceptance, periodic boredom, parental pressure, and are exposed to the media, yet only a minority become dependent upon drugs and alcohol, additional factors must be at play. Research supports the assertion that emotional vulnerability makes some children and adolescents more susceptible to the influence of peers and may help to explain why at least some portion of adolescents become drug dependent (Nuño-Gutiérrez, Rodriguez-Cerda, & Alvarez-Nemegyei, 2006). We must ask ourselves, however, why some children and adolescents are more emotionally vulnerable than others. Various risk factors, including family strife, psychopathology, early sexual maturation, academic troubles, and even neurobiology, may hold the answer (Rumpold et al., 2006).

From a neurobiological perspective it appears that the use of drugs and alcohol increases dopamine in the limbic system, the emotional center of the brain. As a neurotransmitter, dopamine helps to regulate the motivation of behaviors necessary for survival. Food intake increases dopamine, which gives us a good feeling and leads us to seek it out; sexual behavior increases dopamine, which gives us a good feeling and leads us to seek it out; and social interaction also increases dopamine, leading us to seek that out as well. Drugs of abuse, by nature of their dopamine effects, also make us feel good, which is crucial to their reinforcing and addictive effects (Volkow, 2004).

We now understand that individuals who use drugs, such as cocaine, amphetamines, heroine, and alcohol, generally have a lower number of dopamine receptors, particularly D2 dopamine receptors, in their brains in key limbic areas that appear to be involved in addiction. We can even watch as individuals continue to abuse drugs and alcohol over time, observing their dopamine D2 receptors decrease with increased abuse.

Dopamine D2 receptor density appears to matter because, as already noted, dopamine neurons turn our attention to what is salient, fun, sad, aversive, and important for survival. If the dopamine D2 density is naturally lower among those who abuse drugs and alcohol, they may experience less of a signal from the firing of dopamine neurons in a given situation. For example, natural reinforcers, such as food, sex, and getting an A on an exam, may be less rewarding for some than for others because the increase in dopamine is simply not enough to signal them as salient stimuli. Drugs of abuse, however, provide a much more powerful dopamine signal that triggers the D2 receptors, making drugs and alcohol highly reinforcing.

It is difficult to know which came first among those who abuse drugs and alcohol—the low D2 dopamine receptor density or the addiction. In studies of randomly selected individuals who do not abuse drugs, those with a low compliment of dopamine D2 receptors at baseline typically experience drugs, such as intravenous stimulants, as pleasurable, whereas those with high levels of dopamine D2 receptors experience drugs as unpleasant. One possible conclusion, then, is that low levels of dopamine D2 receptors may make individuals more vulnerable to taking drugs because the experience is pleasant, which increases the probability of trying it again. Conversely, high levels of receptors may protect against drug abuse because the reaction to the drugs tends to be aversive, which decreases the probability of trying it again.

Increases in dopamine within the dopamine neuron synapses are 5 to 10 times greater with drugs of abuse than with natural reinforcers, such as food and sex. Moreover, drugs like cocaine, amphetamines, and methamphetamine block the reuptake transporter so that dopamine stays in the synapse longer than with natural reinforcers. Thus, despite the fact that the number of dopamine D2 receptors may be decreased among drug abusers, the probability of interaction between dopamine and the receptors is increased by the drugs themselves and because the drugs force dopamine to stay in the synapse longer. For the drug abuser, natural reinforcers no longer generate a salient "feel-good" signal, but abusing drugs does. This fact perpetuates addictive behavior (Volkow, 2004).

Still, dopamine is not enough to explain addiction. If you were to give drugs to an individual who is not addicted, you would see an increase in dopamine in the brain that would be equal to or even larger than that seen in the brain of an addicted individual, yet most individuals who experiment with drugs do not become addicted. Thus, dopamine in and of itself is not a sufficient explanation (Volkow, 2004).

Most would agree that the environment in which children are raised has a major impact upon their personality development and behavior. Studies of macaque monkeys have found that dominant monkeys have higher levels of dopamine D2 receptors than subordinate monkeys, yet these dopamine levels are not predetermined. That is, the D2 levels appear to rise among the dominant monkeys only once they enter a social group and establish their hierarchy. Consequently, it appears that the environment somehow triggered higher dopamine D2 receptor levels in the dominant monkeys. It is also notable that the subordinate animals not only had lower D2 receptor density, but also readily self-administered high doses of cocaine, whereas the dominant monkeys had relatively no interest in the drug (Morgan et al., 2005).

EPIDEMIOLOGY

Approximately 9% of adolescents ages 12 to 17 are considered in need of treatment for alcohol and substance abuse. About 10% to 20% of indi-

viduals will at some point be addicted to a drug or alcohol in their lifetime. Over 22 million Americans—nearly 9% of the total population age
12 and older—meet criteria for substance dependence or abuse; 2.8 million are dependent on or abuse both alcohol and illicit drugs; 4.5 million
are dependent on or abuse illicit drugs but not alcohol; and 14.9 million
are dependent on or abuse alcohol but not illicit drugs (Substance Abuse
and Mental Health Services Administration [SAMHSA], 2008b, 2013a).

Illicit drug use peaks in late adolescence and early adulthood with
nearly 22% of 18- to 20-year-olds reporting use in the past month and
similarly high percentages of 16- to 17-year-olds (16%) and 21- to 25-year-
olds (nearly 19%) reporting the same. Nearly 12% of 12- to 17-year-olds
used an illicit drug in the past month, with marijuana being the most
common (over 6%). Abuse of prescription medications (3.3%), inhalants
(1.2%), and hallucinogens (0.7%) follows behind (SAMHSA, 2008b). The
majority of teens who abuse prescription drugs get them easily and for
free, primarily from friends and relatives (University of Michigan, 2008).
The prescription drugs most commonly abused by teens are stimulants,
painkillers, sedatives, and tranquilizers.

The Monitoring the Future Study surveys approximately 50,000
8th-, 10th-, and 12th-graders annually to determine their drug and alcohol use patterns. In 2013, 50% of 12th-graders, 39% of 10th-graders, and
20% of 8th-graders reported having used an illicit substance on at least
one occasion in their lifetime; and 26% of 12th-graders, 19% of 10th-
graders, and 9% of 8th-graders reported using an illicit substance within
the past month. Daily cigarette use was reported by nearly 9% of 12th-
graders, 4% of 10th-graders, and 2% of 8th-graders. Alcohol was used
by 39% of 12th-graders, 26% of 10th-graders, and 10% of 8th-graders in
the past month, and 2% of 12th-graders, 1% of 10th-graders, and under
1% of 8th-graders reported daily use; while 52% of 12th-graders, 34%
of 10th-graders, and 12% of 8th-graders reported having been drunk at
least once in their lifetime (University of Michigan, 2013). In 2011, more
than 23% of high school seniors acknowledged driving under the influence of marijuana or with a drugged driver in the two weeks prior to the
survey, and 19% reported driving drunk or with a drunk driver. Females
as well as individuals who earn good grades, have a strong religious commitment, and have two parents in the home are less likely to drive after
alcohol or marijuana use (O'Malley & Johnston, 2013).

Over 10 million people reported driving under the influence of an
illicit drug in 2012 or 4% of the population 12 years and older. The rate
was highest (12%) among young adults, ages 18 to 25. Driving under
the influence is associated with age—nearly 5% of 16- to 17-year-olds
drove under the influence, but nearly 22% of 21- to 25-year-olds did.

Rates decline beyond this age. Males are nearly twice as likely as females (15% versus 8%) to drive under the influence of an illicit drug or alcohol (SAMHSA, 2013a).

Marijuana is the most widely used illicit drug but rarely the first substance used (Gfroerer, Wu, & Penne, 2002). Over 90% of new marijuana initiates have first used cigarettes and/or alcohol before trying marijuana, making cigarettes and alcohol true gateway drugs (SAMHSA, 2003).

Teens are also using over-the-counter drugs with increasing frequency, mostly cough and cold remedies containing dextromethorphan (DXM), a cough suppressant. In 2006, approximately 3.1 million people, or 5.3% of the population, aged 12 to 25 years reported a lifetime history of using an over-the-counter cough or cold medicine to get high, and nearly 1 million had done so in the past year (SAMHSA, 2008a). In 2008, 6% of 12th-graders, 5% of 10th-graders, and 4% of 8th-graders abused a cough or cold medicine at some point during the past year (University of Michigan, 2008). Products with DXM are found in more than 140 over-the-counter cough and cold preparations, including Nyquil, Coricidin, and Robitussin. Prescription drugs too are becoming an increasing problem. In 2011, nearly 16 million people 12 years of age and older had used a prescription drug for nonmedical purposes, and 6.7 million had done so in the past month (SAMHSA, 2013b).

The younger one is at initiation of drug and alcohol use or experimentation, the greater the risk for adult abuse and dependence (Chen, Storr, & Anthony, 2009). Other risk factors include early aggressive behavior, lack of parental supervision, drug availability, and poverty. Association with peers who abuse drugs is perhaps the most robust predictor of adolescent substance abuse (National Institute on Drug Abuse, 2008; Rowe, Liddle, Caruso, & Dakof, 2004). Difficult temperament, lack of self-control, and aggressive behavior are risk factors that can be noted as early as infancy. Family conflict, lack of nurturing and attachment, and caregiver drug abuse are also frequently cited as risk factors for later substance abuse. In addition, individuals who abuse alcohol and drugs have high rates of physical, sexual, and emotional abuse; often live in disorganized and violent neighborhoods; have frequent psychiatric diagnoses; and experience high rates of chronic pain and disability. Education level is also associated with drug abuse. Regular illicit drug use is lower for college graduates (5.1%) than for those who do not graduate from high school (9.3%), high school graduates (8.6%), and those with some college (8.9%). By contrast, college graduates are more likely to try illicit drugs in their lifetime than adults who have not completed high school (52% vs. 36%; SAMHSA, 2008b).

As noted above, those with mental illness use substances at an even higher rate than the general population. Among youth 12 to 17 years of age, 34% of those with a diagnosis of major depressive disorder use illicit drugs compared to 16% without depression. Likewise, 16% of youth 12 to 17 years of age with depression also meet diagnostic criteria for drug or alcohol dependence or abuse in comparison to only 5% of youth without depression (SAMHSA, 2013a). Statistics of this sort further clarify the vulnerability of those with mental illness and the great need for prevention, early detection, and treatment.

CLINICAL COURSE

Most individuals experiment with drugs and alcohol to some degree, but most do not become addicted. For those who do become addicted, they often struggle for many years, and effective treatment programs typically describe these individuals as perpetually "in recovery." Among the greatest risk factors for chronicity are early onset and childhood vulnerabilities, as has been found in studies of adult alcoholics.

Two stereotyped groups of chronic alcoholics, Type A and Type B, have been described (Babor et al., 1992). Type A alcoholics have a later onset, fewer childhood risk factors, less severe dependence, less psychopathological dysfunction, and better treatment outcomes than Type B. By contrast, Type B alcoholics have more childhood risk factors, a family history of alcoholism, early onset of alcohol-related problems, more severe dependence, polydrug use, a more chronic treatment history, greater psychopathological dysfunction, and more stress. This typology has been replicated with adult drug abusers, suggesting the same impact with early-onset drug abuse. Similarly, the earlier an adolescent begins abusing substances, the greater the likelihood of conduct problems and family dysfunction and the more likely one is to experience chronic problems into adulthood (Zucker, 1996).

Long-term follow-up studies of alcoholics have found that 20% or more eventually become permanently abstinent, generally after a major life stressor, such as incarceration or life-threatening complications related to alcohol abuse. Relapse rates are particularly high during the first 12 months of abstinence (American Psychiatric Association, 2000). Recovery among adolescent drug and alcohol abusers varies greatly and is impacted by many factors, including motivation to change, access to resources, and severity of abuse and dependence. A 25-year longitudinal study of adolescents who began using marijuana prior to 21 years of age found that high levels of cannabis use in adolescence were related to worse educational outcomes, lower income, greater welfare dependence and unemployment, and less relationship and general life satisfaction (Fergusson & Boden, 2008). All manner of risky behavior, including early sexual activity, accidents and motor vehicle accidents, violence, and school dropout, are more common among teens who abuse drugs and alcohol (Weinberg, Rahdert, Colliver, & Glantz, 1998).

We are increasingly aware of the health consequences of drug and alcohol abuse as well. Methamphetamine, for example, is known to cause cell damage and even dopamine neuron cell death in animals. Methamphetamine addicts are known to have significant reductions in dopamine transporters, and the lower the number of dopamine transporters, the worse addicts tend to perform on neuropsychological tests of gross memory speed and fine motor and memory function. After detoxification and sustained abstinence, many addicts appear to recover roughly their full complement of dopamine transporters. There may be a less marked trend, however, toward recovery of motor and memory function, and in some cases there appears to be permanent damage (Volkow, 2004). The most important drug to prevent our children from trying is, however, tobacco. Smoking leads to the greatest numbers of preventable deaths in the United States—nearly 500,000 per year (Danaei et al., 2009); and more than 16 million Americans suffer from smoking related illness and disability (U.S. Department of Health and Human Services, 2014).

DIAGNOSIS

DSM-5 identifies 10 categories of drugs (alcohol, caffeine, cannabis, hallucinogens, inhalants, opioids, sedatives/hypnotics/anxiolytics, stimulants, tobacco, and other/unknown) to which individuals may have a substance use disorder. Gambling disorder is also included within the section on substance-related disorders in *DSM-5*, given that gambling is believed to activate the same neural reward pathways and results in similar behavioral patterns among those who are addicted. Other frequently discussed so-called behavioral addictions, such as video game addiction, internet addiction, sex addiction, exercise addiction, and shopping addiction, were not included in *DSM-5* due to lack of sufficient peer reviewed evidence to include them as disorders at this time (American Psychiatric Association, 2013). Prior *DSM-IV* diagnoses, such as substance dependence, substance abuse, substance intoxication, substance withdrawal, polysubstance dependence, and substance-induced psychiatric disorders, have been replaced in *DSM-5* with subcategory specifiers, such as *use disorder, intoxication, withdrawal, other,* and *unspecified.*

In order to diagnose, we must first define the terms. Addiction is generally viewed as a cluster of cognitive, affective, behavioral, and physiologic signs that indicate compulsive use of a substance and inability to control intake, despite negative consequences, such as medical illness, failure in life roles, and interpersonal difficulties. Having previously referred to *dependence*, *DSM-5* now describes drug or alcohol *use* to be a maladaptive pattern of substance use, which results in more use and for a longer period of time than intended and when discontinued causes an individual to experience pathological signs and symptoms, such as tolerance and withdrawal. Pathological drug use (or dependence) is demonstrated by individuals engaging in extensive but unsuccessful efforts to control their use; spending a great deal of time and effort trying to procure the substance; experiencing cravings; using the substance in physically hazardous situations; failing to fulfill role obligations at work, home, and school; and experiencing major impairment in their social, occupational, or recreational commitments, despite their awareness of the detrimental effects of the substance. Tolerance is defined as a need for increased amounts of the substance to achieve the desired effect or diminished effect with use of the same amount; and withdrawal is defined by a characteristic drug discontinuation syndrome or taking more of the substance or a similar substance to avoid the discontinuation symptoms. Finally, substance intoxication is defined as a reversible substance-specific syndrome due to drug use (American Psychiatric Association, 2013).

Psychiatric comorbidities abound among adolescents with SUDS. In one study of over 200 adolescents at an inpatient drug treatment program, over 80% had an additional psychiatric disorder, and 75% had more than one additional disorder. Among the disorders identified, 61% had a mood disorder, 54% had conduct disorder, and 43% had an anxiety disorder (Stowell & Estroff, 1992). Another study found that among over 150 adolescents on an inpatient dual-diagnosis unit, 71% had conduct disorder and 31% had a major depressive disorder (Bukstein, Glancy, & Kaminer, 1992). Attention-deficit/hyperactivity disorder (ADHD) has been frequently noted to be comorbid with SUDS as well, although its association may have more to do with its mutual association with conduct disorder than a true relation to SUDS (Weinberg et al., 1998).

Assessing substance use is difficult. For those individuals who abuse drugs and are engaged in inpatient or outpatient treatment programs or individual treatment, urine drug toxicology screens are commonly employed to monitor progress. However, most drugs dissipate within about one to three days, after which time finding traces of their presence is very difficult, with the exception of marijuana, which can be accurately measured for up to seven weeks after the last use.

Table 16.1   CRAFFT Screening Protocol

C Have you ever gotten into a *car* driven by someone including yourself who was high or using alcohol or drugs?

R Do you ever use alcohol or drugs to *relax*?

A Do you ever use alcohol or drugs while you are by yourself or *alone*?

F Has a *friend, family member*, or other person every thought you had a problem with alcohol or drugs?

F Do you ever *forget* (or regret) things you did while using?

T Have you ever gotten into *trouble* while using alcohol or drugs, or done something you would not normally do—for example, break the laws, rules, or curfew, or engage in risky behavior?

Fewer than half of pediatricians screen adolescents for tobacco, alcohol, and drug use, and fewer than one-quarter report that they are comfortable asking about these issues (Kulig, 2005). Yet simply asking about the frequency and quantity of alcohol and drug use has not shown great validity as a screening tool. Yes/no questions about substance use can be useful, but these questions do not address the quantity of use. Although there are a number of well-designed and validated self-report measures available for purchase, one of the most clinically relevant tools is the CRAFFT Screening Test (Griswold, Aronoff, Kernan, & Kahn, 2008). This six-item verbally administered screening tool is quick, easy to employ, and effective in identifying children and adolescents at risk (see Table 16.1). If a child or adolescent answers in the affirmative to two or more questions, then further investigation into substance use patterns (or referral to a specialist) is advised.

TREATMENT

Parents differ greatly in their levels of tolerance for their children's use of drugs and alcohol. While some parents maintain staunch opposition to all drug and alcohol use among their underage minors, others are more liberal in their approach and take a "what I don't know won't hurt me" approach. As is evident from the epidemiology of substance use, it is normative for many minors to experiment with drugs and alcohol. If children and adolescents continue to meet all of their expected social and academic milestones, then it is likely that whatever their level of experimentation, they are probably managing it well. However, parents should be encouraged to remain vigilant in supervising their children in this regard; and whenever any significant changes are observed (e.g., sudden changes in peer group, truancy, a drop in grades, an increase in irritability, changes in physical appearance, any criminal or misdemeanor behavior, disinterest or lack of motivation in previously enjoyable activities, or changes in mood, anxiety, sleep, appetite, energy level or focus and concentration), a direct approach in dealing with the concern is strongly advised.

The first step in understanding the problem will certainly be confronting the child in a supportive but strong manner. Many children, adolescents, and adults lie or minimize when confronted directly about their substance use. As a result, parents may need to check their children's laundry for evidence of drug paraphernalia, place limits on unsupervised time, limit Internet use by withholding smart phones and requiring that all computer use happen in common areas of the home, such as the kitchen or family room, follow their children's activities on Facebook and other Internet social networking sites, speak with their children's friends' parents to verify concerns, and perhaps even initiate random drug screening in consultation with their pediatrician or a child and adolescent psychiatrist. These steps may seem radical and difficult to accept for some parents. However, we know that drug use by 13 years of age triples the odds of drug dependence as compared to those who begin use at age 21 years or after and that alcohol use by 15 years of age increases the rate of subsequent abuse or dependence sixfold (SAMHSA, 2003).

Some parents will begin offering their children alcohol, and perhaps other drugs or tobacco, early in life in an effort to teach them responsible use. Sometimes alcohol or other drugs are part of a family's culture, where they are not typically associated with abuse. Nonetheless, parents should be aware that each year alcohol drinking is delayed, there is a 14% reduction in the likelihood of eventual dependence (SAMHSA, 2003). Furthermore, drug dependence ratings are very high in the United States, and 32% of those who try nicotine will become dependent; the same is true for 23% of those who try heroin, 17% of those who try intranasal cocaine, 15% of those who try alcohol, 9% of those who try cannabis, 9% of those who try anxiolytics, 8% of those who try analgesics, 5% of those who try psychedelics, and 4% of those who try inhalants (Anthony, Warner, & Kessler, 1994).

For those who argue that in places with a lower drinking age, such as Europe, adolescents learn to drink responsibly, the statistics prove otherwise. In the last 30 days, most 15- to 16-year-old European adolescents used alcohol at a rate far exceeding that of American teens. In Denmark, for example, 76% used alcohol, and in France 67%, Italy 63%, Greece 72%, and the United Kingdom 65%. Binge drinking, defined as five or more drinks on one occasion (e.g., a two-hour period), was acknowledged by 56% of those in Denmark, 44% of those in France, 35% of those in Italy, 45% of those in Greece, and 52% of those in the United Kingdom. On average, 57% of 15- to 16-year-olds in Europe have drunk alcohol in the past 30 days, and 39% have binge drunk (European School Survey Project on Alcohol and Drugs, 2012). By contrast, in the United States, 26% of tenth grade students (generally 15 to 16 years of age) have drunk alcohol in the past 30 days, and 21% of all high school students have binge drunk (Centers for Disease Control and Prevention, 2014b; University of Michigan, 2013). Therefore, if we follow the statistics, prevention of drug and alcohol abuse rests largely upon delaying exposure.

Numerous medications exist for helping adults with addiction. None of these has been approved by the Food and Drug Administration for use in children or adolescents, although they are sometimes employed. These medications include acamprosate (Campral) for alcohol abstinence, which decreases cravings; buprenorphine (Subutex) for opioid dependence; disulfiram (Antabuse) for the maintenance of sobriety; methadone (Dolophine or Methadose) for opioid dependence; naltrexone (Revia, Depade, or Vivitrol) for alcohol and opioid dependence; bupropion (Zyban or Buproban) and varenicline (Chantix) for smoking cessation; and buprenorphine plus naloxone (Suboxone) for opioid dependence. There are numerous nicotine replacements available, including nicotine gum (Nicorette), a nicotine inhalation system (Nicotrol inhaler), a nicotine lozenge (Commit), a nicotine nasal spray (Nicotrol NS), electronic cigarettes or e-cigarettes, and a nicotine patch (Habitrol, NicoDerm, and Nicotrol). All of these products are designed to replace nicotine and thereby decrease cravings; or in the case of e-cigarettes, the goal is simply to make smoking more acceptable and less intrusive upon others, although by removing tobacco it may also reduce some health risks.

Although adolescents experiment a great deal with drugs and alcohol, we are fortunate that most do not require intensive medication treatment for the addiction itself. More commonly, children and adolescents will require treatment for comorbid psychiatric conditions, such as conduct disorder, anxiety, depression, and ADHD. These treatments often include medications and therapeutic interventions aimed at the individual, family, peer, and social network.

The five key steps in the treatment of addiction include: (a) detoxification; (b) inpatient hospitalization; (c) therapeutic community; (d) outpatient treatment; and (e) self-help programs. If detoxification is necessary, it is best performed during an inpatient hospital stay. Depending upon the drug, the level of addiction, and the patient's social support, however, outpatient detoxification is sometimes possible. Thankfully, for most adolescents who abuse drugs and alcohol, detoxification is not generally required.

Inpatient hospitalization is commonly employed for those who have severe drug or alcohol dependence. Hospitalization typically begins with a thorough assessment of all presenting problems and may include neuropsychological testing to identify cognitive impairments that preceded or were caused by the substance abuse. Inpatient programs are generally administered by physicians, drug counselors, therapists, and psychologists, who can provide multimodal care to the drug-dependent individual. Along with general medical care, psychiatric comorbidities are a key focus of treatment during an inpatient hospitalization, as are individual drug counseling and peer group and family education. There are no standard inpatient admission criteria for adolescent drug addiction. Admission is generally based upon the severity of comorbid psychiatric conditions, a clear determination that the individual will continue to use unabated without hospitalization, or the belief that the individual is at great risk to herself or others.

Therapeutic communities are designed to isolate an addicted individual from the influence of his or her peer group and place him or her in a drug-free, supportive environment. The goal of a therapeutic community is to teach individuals how to cope, function, and socialize without drugs. These programs are commonly based upon mutual help or self-help philosophies and are often staffed by prior addicts. Treatment may take months or even more than a year, although the dropout rate is often quite high, as individuals frequently relapse. Therapeutic communities are supportive and emphasize intensive therapy, counseling to build self-esteem, the establishment of social skills, education, and job training. As these programs are not standardized in their treatment approach, it is difficult to accurately assess outcomes, although some adolescent programs have shown remarkable success in decreasing substance abuse, improving psychological functioning, and reducing crime (Morral, McCaffrey, & Ridgeway, 2004). Families also anecdotally often report that these programs are effective.

A more modern form of the therapeutic community, and one often employed with adolescents, is a wilderness camp or retreat in which a child is separated from his or her family and peer group to live in relative isolation. Length of stay for these programs is generally about 30 days but may extend to three or four months or even longer in some cases. Wilderness programs lack the intensive group process that takes place in treatment programs with a longer length of stay; additionally, the family is largely unable to be involved in these programs. Consequently, a child may go off to a wilderness program, have a good experience, but then come home to an unchanged family, home life, and peer group. Regardless of their efficacy, adolescent admissions to substance abuse treatment programs have increased greatly in recent years. Between 1995 and 1998, for example, admissions increased by 46%, almost entirely due to referrals from the criminal justice system (SAMHSA, 2001).

Whereas therapeutic communities emphasize mutual self-help, behavioral consequences, and shared values regarding "right living," another community-based adolescent treatment approach, the Minnesota Model, takes a slightly different theoretical perspective. The Minnesota Model derives its approach from Alcoholics Anonymous and incorporates techniques of both individual and group psychotherapy (Morral et al., 2004). The Minnesota Model has also proven useful among adolescents and leads to higher rates of abstinence among those who complete the program as opposed to those who drop out or are placed on a wait list (Winters, Stinchfield, Opland, Weller, & Latimer, 2000). While the therapeutic community views substance dependence as a behavioral and personality problem and the community as the effective change agent, the Minnesota Model views substance dependence as a disease and the counselor as the treatment director. As yet, no head-to-head studies comparing these treatment programs for adolescents exist, although studies of adult alcohol and substance abuse treatment programs suggest that the differences between the models are now most often minimal and that the key "constant" is the reliance upon the peer-group process (Borkman, Kaskutas, & Owen, 2008).

The vast majority of adolescent substance abuse treatment programs are outpatient. These programs generally incorporate individual and group counseling, aftercare services for those who have already been to a residential treatment program or therapeutic community, structured day treatment as an alternative to inpatient care, and family therapy. Adolescents without major medical or psychiatric comorbidities and who are motivated and cooperative are good candidates for outpatient treatment programs. In addition, willingness to submit to random urine drug testing and a family commitment to engage in treatment and therapy are vitally important. Outpatient programs often employ a variety of therapeutic interventions, including individual and group, family, and behavioral therapy, crisis and emergency services, and sometimes even hypnosis and biofeedback.

A number of specific therapies are currently utilized for the treatment of adolescent substance abuse. Numerous family therapies, including multidimensional family therapy, brief strategic family therapy, multisystemic therapy, Purdue brief family therapy, and various forms of family therapy integrated with cognitive behavior therapy (CBT) have proven efficacious (Deas, 2008; Liddle, Rowe, Dakof, Henderson, & Greenbaum, 2009; Santisteban, Suarez-Morales, Robbins, & Szapocznik, 2006). Perhaps more than the specific details of the therapies themselves, these findings point to the importance of the family in understanding and treating adolescent substance abuse.

Much recent attention has been paid to motivational enhancement therapy, also known as motivational interviewing (MI). MI is a brief treatment designed to increase an individual's motivation to make changes about substance abuse and aspects of his or her life that trigger or perpetuate substance abuse. This treatment has been successful with teens and adults, in part because substance abusers benefit from efforts to motivate their engagement in treatment as they have difficulties motivating themselves. There are four major therapeutic principles that encompass the fundamental tenants of MI: (a) employ empathy to listen and accept the individual; (b) develop discrepancy between the patient's behavior and their greater values and goals as a way to motivate change; (c) roll with resistance and do not argue with the patient or directly oppose the resistance; rather reframe the resistance to create a new perspective; and (d) support self-efficacy by encouraging the patient's belief in himself or herself.

The final strategy in the treatment of substance abuse and dependence, self-help, may be employed as a stand-alone treatment but is also commonly integrated into the aforementioned venues, including inpatient and outpatient care and therapeutic communities. The prototypical self-help program is Alcoholics Anonymous, but many 12-step and similar programs exist today. Self-help programs rely in large part on the idea that one's participation is willing and voluntary. However, this core tenant lies in opposition to the reality of many adolescents, whose participation is often mandatory and at the discretion of their parents or the criminal justice system. Another roadblock to the success of self-help programs is the fact that the first and fundamental step of a 12-step program is to acknowledge that one is helpless or powerless in the face of substance abuse. This principle lies in contrast to the natural striving for independence that is developmentally normative at this age. The 12-step idea, that of hitting "rock bottom" before one can recover, also may not be easily accepted by an adolescent who feels he has his whole life ahead of him. Consequently, although 12-step programs can be used successfully with adolescents, expectations and structure must often be redesigned or developmentally adapted (Dusenbury, Khuri, & Millman, 1992).

While many of the aforementioned treatment interventions are helpful, we do not yet know when it is absolutely best to employ each modality. We also do not know which types of addictions and which types of teens and families benefit most from each type of treatment. We do know, however, that particular therapeutic skills are helpful and that treatment must address not only the child, but also the family, peer group, and community. Regardless of the ultimate treatment plan, we also know that across all types of treatment programs, both inpatient and outpatient, slightly more than one-third of adolescents maintain abstinence at 6 months and slightly less than one third after 12 months. The factors most closely related to good outcome include completing the treatment program, low pretreatment substance use, and peer, parent, and social support of nonuse (R. J. Williams & Chang, 2000).

In working with adolescents, it is vital to remember that the majority will use alcohol and drugs at some time but that most will not develop SUDS. Delaying initiation of drug and alcohol use, however, is clearly beneficial and will lead to lower rates of abuse. Most important is close parental and societal monitoring while helping adolescents to establish guidelines for reasonable choices. Paracelsus (1493–1541) stated, "All substances are poisons; there is none which is not a poison. The right dose differentiates a poison and a remedy." Paracelsus's words ring as true today as they did 500 years ago.

17

Eating Disorders

The modern obsession with body weight and dieting is stunning: 40% to 60% of normal-weight adolescents see themselves as overweight; up to 60% of teens regularly diet to lose weight; over 50% of teens report that they exercise in order to improve their shape or lose weight; nearly 50% of teens periodically smoke cigarettes to lose weight; the majority of teens acknowledge being preoccupied with how much they eat; and roughly 70% of girls report that their body shape is important to their self-esteem (Strober & Schneider, 2005).

Although often thought to be a product of modern society, eating disorders have a long history. In Western Europe in the 12th and 13th centuries, "miracle maidens," or women who starved themselves, were highly regarded, and their behavior was imbued with religious interpretations. Catherine of Siena (1347–1380), whose complete control over her food intake was seen as a sign of religious devotion, was regarded as a saint (Heywood, 1996). This period of "holy anorexia" was, however, short-lived, and in the 16th century the Catholic Church began to disapprove of asceticism. Some anorexics were subsequently viewed as witches and burned at the stake (Brumberg, 2000).

The English physician Richard Morton described two cases, one male and one female, of a "wasting" disease of nervous etiology in 1689 that may mark the first clinical portrayal of anorexia nervosa (AN) in a medical text (Gordon, 2000). The first formal description of AN, however, is credited to Sir William Gull, physician to Queen Victoria, who in 1868 named the disorder anorexia hysterica, emphasizing what he believed to be its psychogenic origins. He later changed the name to anorexia nervosa to avoid confusion with the psychological umbrella term *hysteria* (Hepworth, 1999). Although quite descriptive, the word *anorexia* is a misnomer, as the term literally means "lack of appetite," which is, in fact, rare.

Bulimia nervosa (BN), by contrast, was first clinically described in 1979, although by historical accounts it, too, does not appear to be a new disorder (G. Russell, 1979). The word *bulimia* is derived from the Greek and means "ravenous hunger," quite the opposite of anorexia. Bulimic behavior is noted in case reports as far back as 1398 when "true boulimus" was described in an individual having an intense preoccupation with food and overeating at very short intervals, terminated by vomiting (D. Stein & Laakso, 1988). Regardless, much less has been historically made of bulimic behavior, and consequently, we have significantly less knowledge of this disorder.

Binge eating disorder (BED) previously fell under the category of eating disorder not otherwise specified in *DSM-IV*. BED has received increasing attention in recent years, as its prevalence has been found to be significant among both men and women. Although relatively little is known about how the disorder develops, binge eating itself is common among adolescents and young adults, and there remains question as to how often BED is a precursor to other eating disorders.

CLINICAL PRESENTATION

One of the most notable features of individuals affected by AN is the number and variety of odd and self-destructive behaviors in which they willingly engage in order to lose weight. Extreme diets, refusing to eat with others or in public places, radically changing their eating patterns, and adopting unusual food choices are but a few examples. Perhaps paradoxically, affected individuals show an extraordinary interest in food that belies their fear of gaining weight. They may, for example, prepare elaborate meals for others, hoard food, develop an interest in nutrition, and collect recipes. Many patients ultimately abuse laxatives, diuretics, and stimulants in an effort to lose weight. Others develop an intense interest in exercise and maintain strict workout regimens. All eating-disordered patients tend to carry on these behaviors in secrecy or privacy if at all possible.

Both AN and BN tend to have a stereotypic clinical presentation, age at onset, and gender distribution (Kaye, Klump, Frank, & Strober, 2000). Anorexic children tend to come from families that are characterized as nonconflictive and intrusive. By example, the parents may tend to be overprotective and answer for the children, maintaining rigid and inflexible rules at home. The anorexic temperament is classically risk averse, emotionally restrained, socially constricted, obsessional, compli-

Table 17.1 Anorexia vs. Bulimia

Anorexia	Bulimia
Denies abnormal eating behavior	Recognizes abnormal eating behavior
Introverted	Extroverted
Turns away from food in order to cope	Turns to food in order to cope
Preoccupation with losing more weight	Preoccupation with attaining an ideal but often unrealistic weight

Source: U.S. Department of Health and Human Services, womenshealth.gov.

ant, conventional, and perfectionistic. Affected children are not typically resilient and prefer order and routine in an effort to maintain control of their environment and emotions. These children are often academically successful but have poor social and sexual adjustment.

While anorexics restrict their food intake, bulimics typically over-eat foods high in carbohydrates. The binge may bring with it feelings of relief, but it is almost always followed by feelings of self-disgust and guilt, which lead to the compensatory purging. In addition to abusing laxatives, diuretics, and stimulants, some patients use Ipecac or other emetics in order to promote vomiting.

The bulimic temperament is classically impulsive and affectively unstable. Substance abuse, nonsuicidal self-injurious behavior, and shoplifting are not uncommon, as are personality disorders. Whereas the families of children with AN tend to be highly rigid and inflexible, the families of children with BN are characterized by a notable lack of control; low levels of parental affection; negative, hostile, and disengaged interactions between members; and parental impulsivity, alcoholism, obesity, and even chaos (see Table 17.1).

Binge eating occurs in both normal and overweight individuals. One study of binge eating disorder in a clinical sample found that 87% of the affected patients were obese (Villarejo et al, 2012). However, binge eating disorder is not the same as obesity, and most obese individuals do not regularly engage in binge eating. Furthermore, in laboratory studies, those with binge eating disorder consume more calories and have greater emotional disturbance, psychiatric comorbidity, and impairment in meeting daily demands as well as lower quality of life than obese individuals (American Psychiatric Association, 2013).

ETIOLOGY

Early psychological theories proposed that AN represented a phobic avoidance of food (Crisp & Bhat, 1982). Psychoanalytic formulations suggested that anorexic patients avoid food because they have fantasies of oral impregnation (Masserman, 1941). Self-psychology suggested that the disorder arose when a child subordinated her needs to those of her mother (Geist, 1985), and still others have argued that AN is the result of an undue emphasis upon female independence and autonomy (Steiner-Adair, 1986).

More modern psychological theory on the etiology of AN began with the work of Hilda Bruch (1962), who viewed self-starvation as a representation of an effort to gain control. She posited that the mother's failure to recognize and confirm a child's independence produced difficulties in three areas: (a) a propensity to overestimate body size; (b) an inability to correctly identify internal sensations, such as hunger, satiety, mood, and sexual feelings; and (c) a general sense of feeling ineffective in one's life and a loss of control. Bruch's observations and writings were timely and coincided with greater societal recognition of eating disorders.

Current psychological theories stress that anorexics are avoidant of normal maturational challenges, which are perceived as insurmountable. Concretization and avoidance of psychological discord follow thereafter. These children aim for the antithesis of puberty. They feel unprepared for adolescence and adulthood and exert control by not eating, thereby staying young, immature, and prepubescent. They experience profound self-loathing along with the illusion of competence because of their ability to follow rules, dietary and otherwise (Crisp, 1980).

Other points of influence are also worthy of exploration and include the role of the family, cognition, and social influences. Minuchin, Rosman, and Baker (1978) have suggested that anorexia amounts to a cry for help from a child who is enmeshed within a conflicted and dysfunctional family. Furthermore, they suggest that family members unconsciously collude to perpetuate the child's symptoms because focus on the child defuses the parental conflicts. Cognitive behavior theory, meanwhile, proposes that individuals are rewarded by peers and society for being slender, which for some can be sufficiently powerful to maintain the illness despite the health risks. Finally, the social and cultural emphasis upon being thin and the associated pressures that are overtly and covertly placed upon children by the fashion industry and reflected in every aspect of media are believed to contribute in some way to the genesis of eating disorders (Brumberg, 1988). The stress to conform to the American ideal of youth, beauty, and slimness is an enduring characteristic of our society.

It is no wonder that the media has been targeted in the war on eating disorders. Ninety percent of all girls aged 3 to 11 years in the United States own a Barbie doll. If Barbie were a real woman, her measurements would be 38″-18″-34″ (Brownell & Napolitano, 1995). This body shape portrayed in toys and advertising as the ideal for women is possessed naturally by only about 1 in 100,000 women (Norton, 1996). Consequently, most women in our society maintain a body shape that is very different from that which is idealized, and through media images they are constantly reminded of this fact. There is no doubt that these images have an effect on girls and boys. The degree of impact, however, remains unknown.

Over 60 years ago it was proposed that AN had a biological basis and might be the result of a pituitary or hypothalamic disturbance. More recently, the role of neurotransmitters in both AN and BN has been studied with some interesting results. A number of neuroendocrine abnormalities have been observed in both disorders, including alteration in the hypothalamic-pituitary-gonadal axis, hypothalamic-pituitary-adrenal axis, thyroid system, growth hormone, fluid conservation, metabolism, and autonomic nervous system (Kaye et al., 2000). Most of these observed changes, however, appear to occur as a result of the malnutrition of the eating disorder itself and normalize readily once nutrition is restored. The occurrence of amenorrhea, or loss of the menstrual period, also suggests a hypothalamic disturbance. Most commonly, amenorrhea appears to occur as a consequence of weight loss. However, in about 20% of patients the amenorrhea occurs before the onset of dietary restriction (Kaplan, Sadock, & Greb, 1994).

Studies of the cerebrospinal fluid of anorexic patients have found an increase in corticotropin-releasing factor (CRF). When administered to rats, CRF leads to a reduction in food intake, feeding time, and feeding episodes. CRF also leads to an increase in grooming time, decreased sexual activity, and hyperactivity, all of which are also noted among anorexics (Kaye et al., 2000). Another hormone, leptin, appears to play a key role in anorexia as well, as several symptoms of anorexia, including amenorrhea and semistarvation-induced hyperactivity, are related to low levels of circulating leptin. Leptin is secreted by adipose tissue, and once the body fat drops precipitously low, no more leptin is released; this, in turn, leads to down-regulation of the hypothalamic-pituitary-gonadal and thyroid axes and an up-regulation of the hypothalamic-pituitary-adrenal axis (Müller, Föcker, Holtkamp, Herpertz-Dahlmann, & Hebebrand, 2009). Other peptides, including adiponectin, resistin, ghrelin, peptide YY (PYY), the neurotrophin brain-derived neurotrophic factor (BDNF), and endocannabinoid substances may also play some as-yet-unidentified role in the etiology of both AN and BN (Monteleone, Castaldo, & Maj, 2008).

Other evidence supports neurotransmitter system dysregulation in eating disorders, which affects serotonin, norepinephrine, and dopamine. Serotonin pathways are important in the pathological behaviors generally observed in people with eating disorders, such as obsessionality and disturbance in mood, eating, and impulse control. Numerous studies have shown altered levels of serotonin among those with eating disorders, and it appears that these disturbances persist even after recovery (Kaye et al., 2000). While theories of serotonergic hyperfunctioning in AN and serotonergic hypofunctioning in BN are attractive, they do not explain why selective serotonin reuptake inhibitors (SSRIs) can be helpful for both disorders. Additional evidence suggests that reduced norepinephrine activity and turnover play a role in eating disorders, resulting in hypotension, bradycardia, hypothermia, and depression (Pirke, 1996). Finally, vomiting leads to an increase in dopamine levels in the area postrema, which ironically rewards and reinforces vomiting behavior.

Eating disorders are familial. The risk of AN among mothers and sisters of probands is estimated at 4% or about eight times the rate among the general population (Strober, Freeman, Lampert, Diamond, & Kaye, 2000). A large twin registry study appears to confirm that BN and AN are related. This study found that the co-twin of a child with AN was 2.6 times more likely to have a diagnosis of BN than were co-twins of children without an eating disorder (Walters & Kendler, 1995). Twin studies confirm a genetic link. Studies of identical or monozygotic twins show concordance of up to 90% for AN and 83% for BN (Kaye et al., 2000). Nearly all women in Western society diet at some point in adolescence or young adulthood, yet fewer than 1% develop AN. While not entirely causal, a genetic predisposition must play a significant role.

EPIDEMIOLOGY

While the prevalence of AN lies somewhere between 0.3% and 0.8%, the annual incidence or number of new cases per year is less than 0.1%. The prevalence of BN is considerably higher, affecting somewhere between 1% and 1.5% of the population, but with an annual incidence of also less than 0.1% (American Psychiatric Association, 2013; Kaye et al., 2000). These figures demonstrate that eating disorders are highly chronic, because even though only small numbers of new cases occur each year, much higher percentages of affected individuals maintain their disorders. The prevalence of both disorders among men is about one-tenth that of women. Binge eating disorder, by contrast, is only about twice as common among women as men and is thought to affect approximately 1.6% of females and 0.8% of males over 18 years of age at any given time and about 3.5% of women and 2% of men over the course of a lifetime (American Psychiatric Association, 2013; Westerberg & Waitz, 2013).

The symptoms of eating disorders, such as binge eating, purging, fasting, use of laxatives, and excessive exercise, are much more common than the disorders themselves. In fact, most individuals who employ these behaviors at one time or another do not go on to develop a full-blown eating disorder. The typical age of onset for AN is 14 to 18 years; for BN, it is late adolescence and early adulthood. The developmental course of BED is not known at this time. AN is more prevalent in industrialized societies where food is abundant and the cultural norm links beauty to thinness. Immigrants who move from countries with low rates of AN to Western cultures increase their vulnerability to the disorder as they assimilate to the new culture (American Psychiatric Association, 2000).

The onset of puberty is a major risk factor for AN. Other risks include a perfectionistic personality; a history of mood disorder, obsessive-compulsive disorder, or another anxiety disorder; impaired family interactions; and stressful life events, such as a history of sexual abuse or moving away from home for the first time. Risk factors for BN include dieting, puberty, and transitions, such as starting college, a new job, or the breakup of a relationship. Certain jobs and activities carry a particularly high risk of bulimia. Athletes who must maintain their weight class, such as wrestlers and ballerinas, and actors and models are prime examples. A history of AN, impulsivity, and anxiety are also risk factors for the development of BN. Risk factors for BED are less well established. Based on a small number of studies among teens and young adults, negative affect, pressure to be thin, emotional eating, overvaluation of one's appearance, dissatisfaction with one's body, increased body mass index, increased dieting, symptoms of depression, childhood maltreatment and abuse, bullying, and poor social support were associated with increased rates of BED (Pull, 2004).

CLINICAL COURSE

Long-term follow-up studies show varying rates of recovery for both AN and BN, much of which has to do with the design of each study and the length of follow-up. Studies referenced here ranged from two months to 20 years. Approximately 50% of anorexics achieve a normal weight, and fewer than 10% are overweight at follow-up. Consequently, only about half of anorexics eventually achieve a normal weight, defined as within 10% to 15% of ideal body weight. Also unfortunate is the fact that only about one third of anorexics maintain a normal diet upon follow-up, whereas one half avoid high-calorie foods and up to one half display evidence of bulimic behaviors, including binge eating, vomiting, and laxative abuse. Menstrual functioning returns in about 40% to 90% of affected women but typically only after 90% of ideal body weight is attained. Psychosocial impairments are common at follow-up, including difficulties with educational, vocational, psychological, social, and sexual functioning. Even among those who improve, many continue to display characteristic symptoms of the illness, such as a distorted body image. Within the first five years of the illness, as many as 30% of anorexics begin to engage in bulimic behavior. Finally, mortality has generally been accepted to be 5% to 10% after 10 years, but longer-term studies now suggest higher rates of up to 15% after 20 years. AN, therefore, has the highest mortality rate in psychiatry. About 50% of deaths are due to complications from the illness, 25% die by suicide, and 25% die of unrelated causes (American Psychiatric Association, 2000, 2013; M. Fisher, 2003). In general terms, those who are doing poorly at 5- to 10-year follow-up most often continue to do poorly or die within the following years.

BN typically begins in the context of a diet. In most cases the illness continues for years after onset and may take a waxing and waning course. We have considerably less long-term follow-up data available on BN, but behaviors often persist, such as vomiting (28% to 77%), binge eating (29% to 67%), and laxative abuse (3% to 13%). Furthermore, depression commonly affects somewhere between 15% and 36% at follow-up, and the risk of suicide is elevated (M. Fisher, 2003).

Again, less is known about the clinical course of BED. However, among the eating disorders, BED clearly has the best outcome data. One prospective study found that by five-year follow-up, only 18% of patients maintained the diagnosis; in another study, half the women in a community sample no longer met diagnostic criteria at six-month follow-up (Pull, 2004). These studies notwithstanding, *DSM-5* likens the severity and duration of BED to be similar to that of BN (American Psychiatric Association, 2013). BED most often begins during the teen and young adult years but may set on later. Dieting often follows episodes of binge eating, but neither AN nor BN is a common outcome for those with BED.

Poor outcome in AN is generally associated with a longer duration and greater severity of illness, lowest weight achieved, duration of inpatient admissions, number of readmissions, and comorbid bulimic behaviors. In addition, psychiatric comorbidity, particularly borderline personality disorder, and, to a lesser extent, depression and anxiety, predict a worse outcome. Very early onset AN, under 12 years of age, predicts a bad outcome, as would be expected for a highly virulent disorder that sets on so early. Paradoxically, however, onset between 12 and 18 years of age is better than adult onset, as measured by long-term outcome, normalization of body weight, menstruation, eating behaviors, and psychiatric comorbidity. Outcome is better for adolescents because they are still minors, and families can mandate treatment for them (M. Fisher, 2003).

Though we know considerably less about the prognosis of BN, certainly the long-term outcome is better than that of AN. Approximately one half of affected individuals recover, one quarter improve but still suffer bulimic symptoms, and one quarter remain chronically ill. After 10 years, about two thirds to three quarters of bulimics are in at least partial recovery. Relatively few bulimics cross over into AN, with rates no higher than 15% at long-term follow-up. Comorbid psychiatric conditions, particularly borderline personality disorder but also depression, anxiety, and alcohol abuse, have a negative impact on outcome. Social adjustment and personal relationships tend to normalize over time for bulimics, but many women continue to suffer from social and sexual impairments. Finally, the mortality of BN ranges from 1% to 6% after many years of follow-up (Steinhausen, 2009).

AN wreaks havoc on the entire body. Weight loss is not the only outcome, although most secondary effects are due to the malnourished state. Hypothermia, dependent edema, anemia, impaired renal function, bradycardia, hypotension, cardiac arrhythmias, lanugo (soft downy hair on the skin), osteoporosis, and even brain atrophy are common for those who are chronically ill. Hormonal abnormalities may include elevated growth hormone and plasma cortisol levels, along with reduced gonadotropin, follicle-stimulating hormone, luteinizing hormone, and estrogen levels (testosterone in males). Triiodothyronine (T3 thyroid hormone) is often decreased, although T4 and TSH (thyroid-stimulating hormone) levels are often normal. In addition to amenorrhea, physical symptoms commonly include constipation, abdominal pain, cold intolerance, lethargy, and excessive energy (see Figure 17.1).

BN, by contrast, frequently results in many symptoms secondary to the purging behaviors, such as calluses on the dorsal surface of the hands from self-induced vomiting and the biting or clamping down of the jaw that follows a gag reflex. Additionally, dental caries due to corrosion of the enamel from stomach acid are often observed, along with esophageal erosion and a risk of rupture, which, while rare, can be fatal. Enlarged parotid glands and a resultant "chipmunk" face are due to the increased amylase released from the parotid glands, which accompanies vomiting. Bradycardia, hypotension, and cardiac arrhythmias secondary to hypokalemia (low potassium) may follow. Bulimic patients may also develop lanugo hair, as in AN. Medical complications include hypocalcemia (low calcium), hypochloremia (low chloride), hypokalemia, metabolic alkalosis, electrolyte disturbances, serum transaminase increases reflecting fatty degeneration of the liver, lethargy, and seizures (see Figure 17.2).

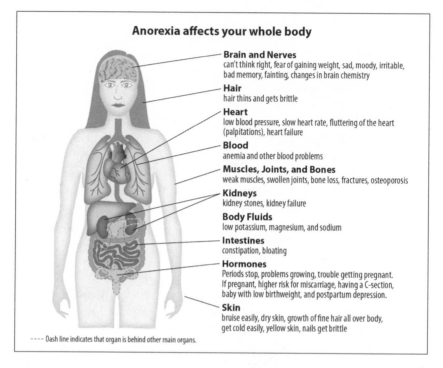

Anorexia affects your whole body

Brain and Nerves
can't think right, fear of gaining weight, sad, moody, irritable, bad memory, fainting, changes in brain chemistry

Hair
hair thins and gets brittle

Heart
low blood pressure, slow heart rate, fluttering of the heart (palpitations), heart failure

Blood
anemia and other blood problems

Muscles, Joints, and Bones
weak muscles, swollen joints, bone loss, fractures, osteoporosis

Kidneys
kidney stones, kidney failure

Body Fluids
low potassium, magnesium, and sodium

Intestines
constipation, bloating

Hormones
Periods stop, problems growing, trouble getting pregnant. If pregnant, higher risk for miscarriage, having a C-section, baby with low birthweight, and postpartum depression.

Skin
bruise easily, dry skin, growth of fine hair all over body, get cold easily, yellow skin, nails get brittle

---- Dash line indicates that organ is behind other main organs.

Figure 17.1 Impact of anorexia nervosa on the body. Anorexia nervosa literally starves the body of needed protein and calories, resulting in a plethora of impairments to virtually all major body systems. Source: U.S. Department of Health and Human Services, womenshealth.gov.

DIAGNOSIS

DSM-5 further subcategorizes AN into *restricting type* (e.g., those who only restrict their food intake) and *binge-eating/purging type* (e.g., those who restrict food intake but also engage in binge-eating and/or purging behaviors, such as self-induced vomiting or the misuse of laxatives, diuretics, or enemas). Binge-eating/purging type anorexics often demonstrate many of the typical eating behaviors, personality characteristics, and family troubles of "classic" bulimics. *DSM-5* no longer subcategorizes BN into *purging type* (e.g., those who self-induce vomiting and/or misuse laxatives, diuretics, or enemas to purge) and *nonpurging type* (e.g., those who use other compensatory behaviors after binge eating, such as excessive exercise or fasting), but individuals can meet criteria for BN by engaging in either or both types of behavior.

    DSM-5 diagnosis of AN requires three features: (a) self-induced food restriction resulting in markedly low body weight in comparison to what

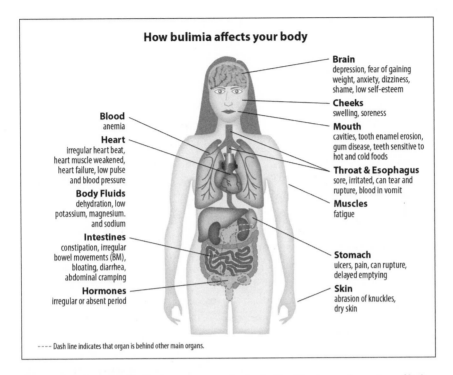

How bulimia affects your body

Brain
depression, fear of gaining weight, anxiety, dizziness, shame, low self-esteem

Cheeks
swelling, soreness

Mouth
cavities, tooth enamel erosion, gum disease, teeth sensitive to hot and cold foods

Throat & Esophagus
sore, irritated, can tear and rupture, blood in vomit

Muscles
fatigue

Stomach
ulcers, pain, can rupture, delayed emptying

Skin
abrasion of knuckles, dry skin

Blood
anemia

Heart
irregular heart beat, heart muscle weakened, heart failure, low pulse and blood pressure

Body Fluids
dehydration, low potassium, magnesium. and sodium

Intestines
constipation, irregular bowel movements (BM), bloating, diarrhea, abdominal cramping

Hormones
irregular or absent period

---- Dash line indicates that organ is behind other main organs.

Figure 17.2   Impact of bulimia nervosa on the body. The binging and purging of bulimia nervosa commonly result in damage to many major body systems. Source: U.S. Department of Health and Human Services, womenshealth.gov.

is expected for one's age, sex, development, and health; (b) an intense fear of weight gain or becoming fat, despite being underweight, or engaging in behavior that impedes weight gain; and (c) a fundamental disturbance in the way in which one perceives one's body weight or shape, such that one feels overweight despite evidence to the contrary, and harshly evaluates oneself based on body weight or shape, along with a lack of acknowledgment of the seriousness of the problem. Endocrine changes resulting in amenorrhea in females for at least three consecutive months and a lack of sexual interest, virulence, and potency in males had previously been a criterion for AN in *DSM-IV* but was discontinued in *DSM-5* (American Psychiatric Association, 2000, 2013). *DSM-5* has also added severity criteria to the diagnosis based upon body mass index (BMI), such that a BMI over 17 kg/m^2 reflects mild impairment, 16 to 16.99 kg/m^2 moderate impairment, 15 to 15.99 kg/m^2 severe impairment, and less than 15 kg/m^2 extreme impairment.

The discrepancy between body weight and perceived body image is key to the diagnosis of AN. Anorexics take great joy in their weight loss and feel highly competent as dieters. Even at subnormal weights, anorexics perceive themselves as fat and are driven to lose more weight. They are intensely fearful of gaining weight and becoming fat and are extraordinarily preoccupied with body shape and size. All their efforts are aimed at lowering their body weight still further, and the illness entirely distorts their self-perception and takes all of their time. Sexual development is also commonly delayed, and physical growth slows or ceases entirely due to lack of nutrition and altered hormone levels.

DSM-5 diagnosis of BN requires recurrent episodes of binge eating, which is defined as eating more than one normally would within a discrete period of time and feeling a lack of control during eating. The diagnosis also requires repeated compensatory behaviors in an effort to counteract the weight gain, such as vomiting; misusing laxatives, diuretics, enemas, or other medications; fasting; or exercising excessively. The binge eating and compensatory behaviors must occur on average at least once a week for at least three months. As with AN, diagnostic criteria require that one's self-evaluation be overly influenced by body weight and shape. *DSM-5* has added severity criteria to the diagnosis of BN as well, defining mild impairment as 1 to 3 episodes of bulimic behavior per week, moderate impairment as 4 to 7 episodes per week, severe impairment as 8 to 13 episodes per week, and extreme impairment as 14 or more episodes per week (American Psychiatric Association, 2013).

Bulimics feel overwhelmed by the urge to binge and often only stop eating when they become too physically uncomfortable to continue. Although binge eating may briefly elevate one's mood, the episodes are generally triggered by stress and dysphoria, and after the binge these feelings immediately return. Subsequent feelings of guilt, anxiety, and depression follow because of the individual's perceived inability to control her or his intake and appetite. In an effort to regain control over the prior eating episode, the compensatory behaviors take hold. The most common method is vomiting, but as previously noted, laxatives, diuretics, appetite suppressants, enemas, fasting, stimulants, and excessive exercise are not uncommon.

DSM-5 diagnosis of BED requires recurrent episodes of binge eating, as defined above, that are associated with three or more of the following: (1) eating more rapidly than usual; (2) eating until feeling unpleasantly full; (3) eating large amounts when not hungry; (4) eating alone for fear of embarrassment; and (5) feeling disgusted, depressed, or guilty afterward. The individual must feel great distress while binge eating, and, as with BN, it must occur at least once a week for at least three months (American Psychiatric Association, 2013).

Individuals with a diagnosis of unspecified eating disorder generally represent either those who have been effectively treated for their eating disorder but maintain some residual symptoms or those who are on the way toward the development of a full-blown eating disorder. Additionally, this category may represent those who vomit after eating small amounts of "guilty" foods (e.g., a cupcake), eat at night, or chew their food and then spit it out before swallowing (American Psychiatric Association, 2013).

According to *DSM-5*, obesity is not an eating disorder. The National Institutes of Health (2014) defines obesity in adults as a body mass index (BMI) of greater than or equal to 30 kg/m^2 and in youth as a BMI of greater than the 95th percentile. By this definition, 35% of American adults are obese, more than a doubling in prevalence since 1980 (Hedley et al., 2004; Ogden, Carroll, Kit, & Flegal, 2014). Approximately 17% of American youth are obese and another 17% are at risk of being overweight, as defined by a BMI greater than the 85th percentile, representing a tripling in prevalence over the past 30 years (Hedley et al., 2004; Ogden et al., 2006; Ogden et al., 2014). Although not an eating disorder per se, obesity is associated with a greatly increased rate of not only many medical and physical complications (e.g., diabetes, cardiovascular disease, sleep apnea, hypertension, stroke, and even some cancers), but also depression and lowered self-esteem (Bean, Stewart, & Olbrisch, 2008).

The differential diagnosis of AN includes a number of psychiatric and medical illnesses. Obsessive-compulsive disorder (OCD) is not only a potential alternate diagnosis, but also a common comorbidity, particularly given the ritualistic eating behaviors so often in evidence. Some have even argued that AN may be a variant of OCD, as obsessive-compulsive symptoms are so common among anorexics and the ritualistic eating behaviors seen among anorexics can be experimentally induced in lab animals by starvation (Herpertz-Dahlmann, 2009). Major depressive disorder (MDD) is also characterized by weight loss, and given the seemingly delusional aspects of AN, schizophrenia is sometimes considered in the differential as well. However, in both mood and psychotic disorders, the weight loss is not desired, nor is there a fear of gaining weight. Aspects of both social phobia and body dysmorphic disorder (BDD) are frequently present in AN. BDD can be distinguished from AN by the presence of distortions unrelated to body weight and shape. Anorexics may be socially phobic, but this diagnosis is only valid if the individual is phobic about a variety of social behaviors and situations and not just eating in public. Numerous other disorders can also cause excessive weight loss, including HIV, cancer, substance use disorders, and gastrointestinal disease. In each case, however, the weight loss is not desired, and the affected individuals do not typically have a distorted body image.

The differential diagnosis for BN includes anxiety and mood disorders, particularly MDD with atypical features, along with borderline personality disorder. Important general medical conditions to rule out include Kleine-Levin syndrome, which is characterized by periodic hyperphagia, hypersomnia, and irritability in male adolescents and typically has a self-limiting course; and Klüver-Bucy syndrome, a limbic system dysfunction with resulting visual and auditory agnosia, placidity, hyperorality, hypersexuality, and hyperphagia. Klüver-Bucy is sometimes seen in Pick's disease, HIV encephalopathy, herpes encephalitis, and brain tumors.

The differential diagnosis for BED includes primarily BN, obesity, mood disorders, and borderline personality disorder. Regarding BN, the compensatory purging behaviors are absent in BED, and there is a higher improvement rate among those with BED. Mood disorders often coexist with BED, and the criteria for atypical depression include overeating. Finally, binge eating is one of the impulsive behaviors sometimes observed among individuals with borderline personality disorder.

Psychiatric comorbidities are extremely common among eating disorders, and the majority of affected individuals will meet criteria for another disorder during either the acute stage of the illness and/or over the long-term course. Up to 80% of adolescents with AN suffer MDD, and similar rates have been found among bulimics. Up to 20% of anorexics and 35% of bulimics acknowledge having attempted suicide, there being a greater likelihood among those who engage in binge/purge behavior. Suicidal behavior is associated with the severity of the eating disorder and the presence of Cluster B personality disorders. Up to 60% of anorexics and 75% of bulimics have a comorbid anxiety disorder, social phobia, panic disorder, agoraphobia, generalized anxiety disorder, and posttraumatic stress disorder being particularly common. Studies of adults with both AN and BN indicate a 40% lifetime comorbidity of OCD, while studies of adolescents reveal rates of about 20%. Alcohol and substance abuse affect upwards of 25% of all individuals with eating disorders, 30% of binge/purge anorexics and bulimics. Personality disorders, particularly Cluster C disorders among restricting anorexics and Cluster B disorders among binge/purge anorexics and bulimics, are also elevated among individuals with eating disorders (Herpertz-Dahlmann, 2009). Considerably less is known about comorbid conditions among those with BED, but mood disorders (affecting roughly one half), substance abuse (affecting roughly one quarter to one third), and anxiety disorders (affecting roughly one quarter to one third) have been observed in at least two studies (Myers & Wiman, 2014).

Both AN and BN commonly lead to a variety of endocrine changes, which are generally a result of starvation or abnormal eating behavior. By definition, amenorrhea is no longer a core symptom of anorexia but is common. In addition, other endocrine changes affecting the adrenal and thyroid glands as well as neuropeptides such as leptin and ghrelin are well established. Adolescents with eating disorders are at increased risk of osteopenia and osteoporosis, as most bone mass is built up during adolescence, and this process cannot be adequately achieved in the presence of starvation (Herpertz-Dahlmann, 2009).

WARNING SIGNS OF AN EATING DISORDER

There are numerous warning signs that indicate a child may be at risk of developing an eating disorder. These include dissatisfaction with body shape, weight, or size; skipping meals; fasting for 24 hours; losing weight to the bottom of the healthy range for age and size; exercising excessively; preferring to eat in private and not in public; demonstrating a tendency toward perfectionism; developing odd eating habits, such as chewing each bite for extensive periods of time or cutting food into very small pieces; vomiting after an occasional large meal; most often choosing low-fat or low-carbohydrate foods or becoming a vegetarian; demonstrating sudden episodes of binging; overeating and then starving in regular cycles; studying food labels for nutritional content; rigidly applying diet plans such as Weight Watchers, Jenny Craig, South Beach, or Atkins; and being physically and emotionally uncomfortable after eating because of anxiety about the calories ingested. For AN specifically, additional signs include excessive weight loss; odd food rituals; lack of menstrual cycles; lanugo hair on the face, arms, and torso; wearing baggy clothing; exercising vigorously at odd hours; appearing pale or dizzy; and fainting. Additional signs of BN include missing food around the house (for household members); fluctuating weight; secret eating; cuts or scrapes on the back of the hand from purging; tooth decay from vomiting; using the bathroom after meals; taking diet pills or abusing laxatives, emetics, or enemas; self-disparaging talk related to food intake; and swollen glands, puffy cheeks, or broken blood vessels under the eyes (Strober & Schneider, 2005).

During a clinical evaluation, questions may include:

- Do you constantly think about food?
- Do you find it hard to concentrate because you are thinking about food and your weight?
- Do you worry about how the food you eat is affecting your body?

- Do you feel guilt and shame after you eat?
- Do you find it hard to eat in public? Do you prefer eating alone?
- Are you constantly counting calories?
- Do you feel fat regardless of what others say about your body?
- Even if you're thin, do you find that you still obsess about parts of your body and how they look (stomach, hips, thighs, etc.)?
- Do you feel as if you're constantly weighing yourself?
- Does your mood change with the number on the scale?
- Do you punish yourself with more exercise and food restriction if you don't like the number on the scale?
- Do you exercise more than one hour five times each week with the goal of burning calories?
- Do you exercise even if you are ill or injured?
- Do you think of foods as "good" and "bad?"
- Do you vomit after eating or use laxatives or diuretics?

TREATMENT

Anorexia Nervosa

The treatment of AN must focus on three primary issues: (1) restoring weight, (2) modifying distorted eating behavior, and (3) addressing the psychological and family issues. Treatment methods typically include nutritional rehabilitation, psychotherapy, and medication. Many individuals with an eating disorder can be treated on an outpatient basis, which sometimes includes periods of intensive day treatment, but in the United States about half of all patients with AN who seek treatment are hospitalized (Herpertz-Dahlmann & Salbach-Andrae, 2009). Hospitalization is typically encouraged when the patient is severely malnourished, dehydrated, suffering from an electrolyte imbalance, or facing other physically threatening complications. Hospitalization is also indicated when outpatient treatment has not been effective, there is a risk of suicide, psychosis is present, or there is a major lack of motivation toward resolving the eating disorder. The benefits of inpatient versus outpatient treatment remain unclear, however, and as yet we have no evidence-based criteria for inpatient admission. Additionally, adequate controlled studies comparing day treatment to inpatient programs have not been performed (Herpertz-Dahlmann & Salbach-Andrae, 2009).

Although systematic studies are lacking, there is general support for a multimodal treatment approach that incorporates nutritional rehabilitation, nutritional counseling, individual psychotherapy to help correct cognitive distortions and improve self-esteem, group therapy, and family or parent therapy. Comorbid medical and psychiatric conditions should also be addressed concurrently.

The goals of nutritional rehabilitation are to restore weight, normalize eating patterns, reestablish normal perceptions of hunger and satiety, and correct the biological and psychological sequelae of malnutrition. The treatment plan should establish clear goals for target weight gain, which are generally accepted to be 1 to 2 pounds per week for inpatients and 0.5 to 1 pound per week for outpatients. Nutritionists and pediatricians are often involved in this phase of treatment, and routine lab parameters must be followed. Physical activity must be monitored as well and restricted if it interferes with weight gain. All reasonable steps should be taken to avoid forced feeding, but severely malnourished patients who refuse to eat must be aggressively managed (American Psychiatric Association, 2006).

Nutritional counseling involves the establishment of meal plans, proper food choices, and balanced nutrition. Both individual and group psychoeducation are often employed, as are group cooking sessions and meals in order to combat the shame that many anorexics feel when eating with others. Involving the family in this process is also important, as is supporting parents in their efforts to speak with their children about food.

Many different types of individual psychotherapy have been evaluated among adults with AN, but no controlled studies have been performed in children and adolescents. Cognitive behavior therapy (CBT), interpersonal therapy (IPT), cognitive analytic therapy, focal psychoanalytic therapy, and specialist supportive clinical management have all shown utility in adults, and it is not clear that any one method is superior to others. Regardless of the technique, the establishment of a trusting and accepting relationship with the therapist is vital. Additionally, therapists are generally more effective with anorexics when they actively engage the patient and directly address body image and concept, growth and development, and family and peer interactions. Typical cognitive distortions affecting those with anorexia should also be addressed in therapy and include personalization, polarized thinking, mind reading, catastrophizing, "shoulds," overgeneralizing, and global labeling (see Chapter 12).

Group psychotherapy is also a mainstay of treatment for AN in both inpatient and outpatient settings. Still, only one randomized, controlled trial has examined the efficacy of group therapy for anorexia, and no studies have compared individual versus group psychotherapy. Pilot studies of dialectical behavior therapy (DBT) in adolescents suggest utility in the treatment of both AN and BN, but further study is required (Herpertz-Dahlmann & Salbach-Andrae, 2009).

Finally, family-based therapy (FBT), which grew out of the work of Minuchin and was developed at the Maudsley Institute in London, is a problem-focused therapy that aims to change behavior through unified parental action. The family in FBT is not viewed as the cause of the disorder, but rather as a positive resource in the adolescent's weight restoration and return to normal eating and health. In fact, FBT takes no stance on disease etiology and tries instead to separate the pathology of AN from the adolescent herself or himself. FBT posits that figuring out the strengths of the family and finding new solutions are much more helpful than pursuing the search for an etiology of the illness within the family. The first phase of treatment supports the parents in their efforts to restore their child's weight. The second phase begins when the child has reached 90% of ideal body weight and is eating without much resistance; at this point the parents are supported in returning the responsibility for their child's eating back to the child. The final phase generally begins when the adolescent has achieved a healthy weight for his or her age and height and focuses on the general issues of adolescent development and how the eating disorder affected this process. There are few contraindications to FBT, but in families where there is significant parental psychopathology or a very critical environment, family therapy has been found less useful (le Grange & Eisler, 2009). FBT, or the so-called Maudsley Method, has been shown effective in 50% to 75% of adolescents, who in randomized trials achieved weight restoration by the end of treatment and maintained it for up to five years. In one trial of adolescents with a short history of illness, the response rate reached 90% (Eisler et al., 1997).

Medication Treatment

Medications have not generally proven themselves to be remarkably effective for the treatment of AN. However, tricyclic antidepressants (TCAs), monoamine oxidase inhibitors (MAOIs), trazodone (Desyrel), and the selective serotonin reuptake inhibitors (SSRIs) have demonstrated benefit in the treatment of binge/purge behavior in BN. The greatest evidence of benefit lies with fluoxetine (Prozac), which has been approved by the FDA for the treatment of adults with BN in both acute and maintenance treatment at a dosage of 60 mg per day (Fichter et al., 1991; Fluoxetine Bulimia Nervosa Collaborative Study Group, 1992). Follow-up studies suggest that fluoxetine should be continued for at least one year among those who respond positively to the medication within the first eight weeks, as it extends the time to relapse. Much less data supports the use of fluoxetine and other antidepressants for children and adolescents with BN. The most impressive study is an open-label investigation, which treated adolescents for eight weeks with 60 mg of fluoxetine per day, along with supportive psychotherapy. The study found decreases in binge/purge episodes, and 70% of subjects were rated as improved or much improved by study's end (Kotler, Devlin, Davies, & Walsh, 2003). While fluoxetine can also be used to treat comorbidities, such as depression and OCD among patients with eating disorders, the medication appears to treat binge/purge behavior regardless of the presence of comorbid depression (D. J. Goldstein, Wilson, Ascroft, & al-Banna, 1999). Although other medications may be employed to treat the comorbidities of BN, no other medications are indicated in the treatment of BN itself. Certainly, bupropion (Wellbutrin) is contraindicated, given the elevated risk of seizures in patients with BN.

Medications considered for the treatment of AN have generally included antidepressants and antipsychotics. Scant data, however, support their use in adults, and virtually nothing other than a few case reports suggests their utility in children and adolescents (Couturier & Lock, 2007). Both TCAs and SSRIs have shown little promise in the treatment of adult AN. Kaye et al. (2001) did find an increased time to relapse with fluoxetine compared to placebo in 35 patients, but a larger randomized, controlled trial of 93 adults found the opposite (Walsh et al., 2006).

As with antidepressants, there is little data to support the use of antipsychotics among patients with AN. Case reports of olanzapine (Zyprexa) among children and adolescents and risperidone (Risperdal) have reported greater treatment compliance and weight gain, along with decreased anxiety and agitation (Boachie, Goldfield, & Spettigue, 2003; Newman-Toker, 2000). Among adults, one small randomized trial compared 10 mg of olanzapine with 50 mg of chlorpromazine (Thorazine) and found decreases in rumination with olanzapine but no differences in weight gain (Mondraty et al., 2005). Two other small placebo-controlled trials using olanzapine in adults with AN also revealed favorable results on weight gain, and one of them led to reductions in depressive symptoms (Bissada, Tasca, Barber, & Bradwejn, 2008; Brambilla et al., 2007). Consequently, limited data suggest that olanzapine and perhaps other atypical antipsychotics may be helpful in reducing eating-related anxiety and depression and supporting weight gain. There is a small amount of evidence supporting the use of SSRIs for relapse prevention, but in general medications for AN should be targeted at treatment comorbidities. The practitioner must be cautious, however, as symptoms of depression and OCD often resolve independently once the AN is treated and weight is restored.

Bulimia Nervosa

Although medications can have a significant role in the treatment of BN, as with AN, effective treatment is largely psychotherapeutic. The main issues of concern in the treatment of BN are (a) reducing or eliminating binge eating and purging, (b) modifying distorted eating behavior, and (c) addressing the psychological and family issues. Hospitalization is less commonly necessary than with AN but is sometimes employed, particularly for those affected individuals who have comorbid conditions that are interfering with recovery from the BN.

Nutritional rehabilitation in the case of BN generally involves the design of structured meal planning to reduce episodes of dietary restriction and the urge to binge, along with adequate nutrition to promote satiety and reduce craving. Simply being of normal or expected BMI or weight for age and size does not equate to adequate nutrition or normal body composition. Finally, nutritional counseling is helpful for all affected individuals to assist with food restriction, expand the variety of foods eaten, and encourage healthy exercise habits (American Psychiatric Association, 2006).

CBT has demonstrated efficacy for the treatment of adults with BN in both individual and group settings, with little difference between the two approaches. Preliminary evidence suggests that DBT, too, may be effective for BN in adults (Herpertz-Dahlmann & Salbach-Andrae, 2009). CBT has been modified specifically for the treatment of BN (CBT-BN) by emphasizing bulimic behaviors and cognitions, such as distortions about weight, shape, and appearance (Fairburn, Marcus, & Wilson, 1993). Among adults with BN, CBT-BN is at least as effective as other psychotherapies if not superior in producing recovery. The National Institute for Health and Clinical Excellence of the United Kingdom now recommends CBT-BN as the treatment of choice for BN and binge eating disorder. After a course of treatment, 30% to 40% of patients are free of symptoms and maintain these gains at long-term follow-up. Studies of CBT-BN in adolescents, however, are few in number and supported only by anecdotal report and case studies (Schmidt, 2009). Although data continue to emerge, family-based therapy (FBT) has also been successfully employed among adolescents with BN and found to be superior to supportive psychotherapy (le Grange, Crosby, Rathouz, & Leventhal, 2007).

Other psychotherapy studies of adolescents have reported mixed results. One randomized, controlled study compared family therapy with a manualized form of CBT. Results indicate that CBT leads to earlier improvements in bingeing but few other differences in clinical outcomes compared to family therapy. Another group adapted CBT for individual

Internet access by adolescents and found after eight interactive online sessions that the treatment was acceptable and effective in reducing bingeing, vomiting, global eating disorder problems, and service contacts at three and six months following treatment (Schmidt, 2009). For patients who do not respond to CBT, both IPT and family therapy have shown some, although generally less, utility (American Psychiatric Association, 2006).

Binge Eating Disorder

Studies for the treatment of BED are now emerging, and a number of investigations in adults have demonstrated benefit, particularly for psychotherapy. Studies of CBT and IPT have found reductions in binge eating lasting two years (Wilson, Wilfley, Agras, & Bryson, 2010) and four years (Hilbert et al., 2012). Additional benefits of treatment have included reductions in associated psychopathology and stability in BMI (Hilbert et al., 2012). Two studies have compared fluoxetine (Prozac) alone and in conjunction with CBT and placebo among adults in a randomized, double-blind, placebo-controlled fashion and found that CBT plus placebo was superior to treatment with fluoxetine alone and fluoxetine in conjunction with CBT (Grilo, Crosby, Wilson, & Masheb, 2012; Grilo, Masheb, & Wilson, 2005). The most potent predictor of binge remission was lack of overvaluation of body shape and weight (Grilo, Masheb, & Crosby, 2012b).

Medications for BED have generally failed to show significant benefit with one exception. Topiramate (Topamax) resulted in remission of binge eating in 58% of women in a placebo-controlled study of nearly 400 patients versus 29% who responded to placebo. Zonisamide (Zonegran) has also shown benefit in a 12-week open-label study (Marazziti, Corsi, Baroni, Consoli, & Catena-Dellosso, 2012).

Unspecified Eating Disorder

Given the variety of symptoms and presentations that can accompany a diagnosis of unspecified eating disorder, the most sensible approach is to treat the patient for the disorder that most closely approximates her or his symptoms (National Institute for Clinical Excellence, 2004). Consequently, if the patient is binge eating or purging, then a treatment protocol for BN may be most appropriate. Alternatively, if food restriction is the greatest problem, then treating for AN is suggested.

18

Sleep Disorders

Although we have some general understanding of the biochemical, neurophysiological, and neuroendocrine activities during sleep, we still do not entirely understand the function of sleep. Certainly, sleep appears to be both restorative and homeostatic, helping us to conserve energy and maintain our body temperature. Sleep is also important in the consolidation of learning and memory and for healthy neurocognitive functioning (Brawn, Fenn, Nusbaum, & Margoliash, 2008). It has been suggested that the programming of species-specific behaviors occurs during sleep, such that animals and humans rehearse instinctual behaviors during sleep (Tauber & Glovinsky, 1987). Regardless of its function, problems with sleep are ubiquitous and sometimes a cause for great concern. Although individuals with diagnosable sleep problems generally have higher rates of mood and anxiety disorders than the general population, the vast majority do not suffer major psychiatric impairments.

CLINICAL PRESENTATION

Most parents struggle to help their infants, children, and adolescents establish habits of good sleep hygiene. Parents must teach infants to self-soothe and put themselves back to sleep in the middle of the night, for no child truly sleeps through the night. Infants awaken every few hours, as do children and adults, simply to roll over and fall back to sleep. If we do not teach our infants to fall asleep on their own, they will never be able to soothe themselves back to sleep during these normal nighttime awakenings.

Some parents prefer a family bed, where all members co-sleep in the same bed or sleep separately but share the same room. Unlike our psychoanalytic forefathers, psychiatrists today have no reason to suspect that sleeping in the same bed or room is damaging in any way to our children's psyche. Yet children must still learn the skill of falling asleep on their own even in a family bed. Without this training, our children's sleep will be disrupted by their awakenings, during which time they will search out a parent to soothe them back down, which leads to even more awakenings and fracturing of a normal night's sleep. The only situation in which sleeping with an infant or child is potentially dangerous is when the parent has been drinking alcohol or taking medications or drugs that can impair his or her ability to awaken easily. In these situations, the risk of sudden infant death syndrome (SIDS) is increased, as the parent may roll over on top of the infant and suffocate the child without awakening.

Children and adolescents have many additional issues with sleep. Children may wet the bed or experience nightmares, narcolepsy, sleep terrors, or insomnia; others may sleepwalk, talk in their sleep, grind their teeth, or suffer breathing difficulties during sleep; still others may simply refuse to go to bed. Adolescents may experience these difficulties as well, in addition to a delayed sleep phase, such that their sleep cycle becomes shifted to later in the evening. Sleep-phase disorders can lead to severe difficulties with awakening on time for school or other activities.

Infants, children, and adolescents traverse most sleep problems without seeking professional consultation. Still, most parents will benefit from learning about sleep and proper sleep hygiene, which will allow them to teach their children good sleep habits, and that in turn will promote a more refreshing night's sleep and better daytime energy and concentration (Weiss, Wasdell, Bomben, Rea, & Freeman, 2006).

Sleep Problems Associated With Psychiatric Conditions

Sleep difficulties are common in a number of psychiatric disorders and a core *DSM-5* symptom among other psychiatric conditions. Disrupted sleep has long been recognized as a feature of children diagnosed with attention-deficit/hyperactivity disorder (ADHD), for example. The *Diagnostic and Statistical Manual of Mental Disorders*, third edition (*DSM-III*), in fact, considered excessive movements during sleep to be a criterion for hyperactivity in children (American Psychiatric Association, 1980). Children with ADHD usually show greater variation in sleep onset time, wake time, and sleep duration; significantly more bedtime struggles with parents than other children; an increase in the frequency of habitual snoring to three times that among the general population; and a greater frequency of periodic leg movement disorder (PLMD) and sleep-disordered breathing (SDB) (Sung, Hiscock, Sciberras, & Efron, 2008).

Children, adolescents, and adults diagnosed with autism spectrum disorders also commonly experience sleep difficulties. The clinical presentation of these children may include difficulties falling asleep, frequent awakenings with difficulty returning to sleep, early-morning awakening, irregular sleep–wake patterns, a shortened duration of sleep, and dyssomnias and parasomnias (Johnson & Malow, 2008).

The clinical presentation of children with mood disorders may include bedtime resistance or anxiety, early and middle insomnia, a desire to co-sleep with parents because of fears or bad moods, enuresis, nightmares, sleepwalking, early-morning awakening, and excessive daytime sleepiness. Over 50% of depressed adolescents report difficulties falling and staying asleep with extended evening awakenings, excessive daytime sleepiness, and unrefreshing sleep, while a much smaller percentage report hypersomnia (Liu et al., 2007). Adolescents who report sleep problems are also much more likely to report symptoms of depression, anxiety, poor self-esteem, lethargy, irritability, and emotional lability even in the absence of a proper mood disorder (Ivanenko, Crabtree, & Gozal, 2005). Adolescents who report sleep problems are also much more likely to consume caffeine, nicotine, alcohol, and drugs, which themselves cause difficulties with sleep (Roane & Taylor, 2008). Consequently, sleep problems should be viewed as a potential early marker for adolescents at risk of developing some sort of psychopathology.

The clinical presentation of anxiety in children includes nighttime fears that commonly take the form of animals and age-appropriate fictitious characters, such as witches and monsters. Children may also fear being kidnapped or being teased by peers. Anxiety also appears to predispose children to parasomnias and nightmares (Muris, Merckelbach, Gadet, & Moulaert, 2000).

ETIOLOGY

Electroencephalography (EEG) provides a reliable and reproducible measure of brain waves during sleep and allows us to define various sleep stages. While awake and alert, the brain is predominantly generating beta waves. As seen in Figure 18.1, beta waves are of low amplitude and are the fastest of the four types of brain waves, running at a frequency of 15 to 40 cycles per second (Hz). The presence of beta waves indicates an active and engaged mind. Someone in conversation would be producing lots of beta waves; during an argument, an individual would be in high beta. When

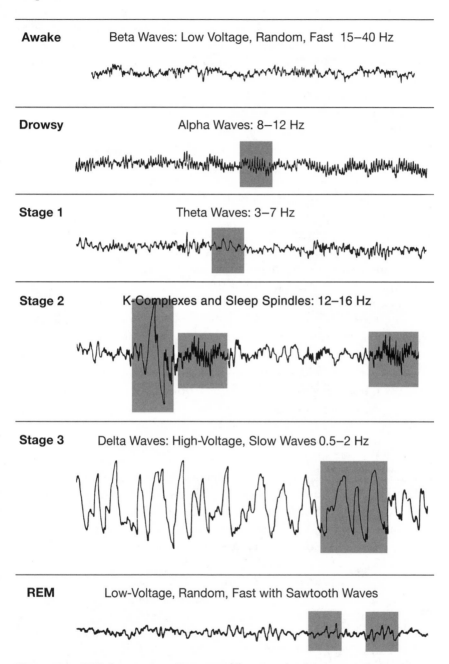

Awake   Beta Waves: Low Voltage, Random, Fast 15–40 Hz

Drowsy   Alpha Waves: 8–12 Hz

Stage 1   Theta Waves: 3–7 Hz

Stage 2   K-Complexes and Sleep Spindles: 12–16 Hz

Stage 3   Delta Waves: High-Voltage, Slow Waves 0.5–2 Hz

REM   Low-Voltage, Random, Fast with Sawtooth Waves

Figure 18.1   EEG sleep patterns. Figure 18.1 illustrates the characteristic brain waves of each sleep stage. Source: Harold I. Kaplan, Benjamin J. Sadock, and Jack A. Grebb, *Kaplan and Sadock's Synopsis of Psychiatry*, 7th edition, Williams & Wilkins, 1994.

the eyes are shut and there is a subsequent lack of visual processing, the EEG shows a slightly higher voltage and slower (8- to 12-Hz) brain wave pattern, characterized by the presence of alpha waves. Alpha waves appear regardless of drowsiness and represent a relative lack of focus and decreased visual processing. Alpha waves emanate from the occipital lobe of the brain, where the visual centers are housed. Alpha waves are less prevalent in the blind, particularly those who have been blind since birth. Alpha waves occur during the waking state and will appear in every sleep stage at various times, particularly during dream sleep. Someone resting or relaxing will experience an increase in alpha waves.

Sleep begins in Stage 1 and by definition begins at the moment alpha waves disappear from the EEG. Stage 1 sleep is characterized by brain waves of still greater amplitude and lower frequency, around 3 to 7 Hz. Theta waves are the predominant EEG brain wave pattern evident during this stage of sleep. Theta waves appear during daydreaming, while drowsy, or even when engaged in a repetitive task, such as freeway driving. As opposed to city driving, where one is always concentrating on the traffic and beta waves are largely in evidence, freeway driving often brings on theta waves because the task requires a lower level of concentration and is sometimes performed while in a trancelike state. At any time that one is involved in an automatic task from which one can mentally disengage while still performing the task (e.g., brushing teeth, taking a shower, jogging, swimming laps, meditation, yoga), the predominant theta waves are hypothesized to place one in a state of "flow," in which many individuals report the generation of good ideas and mental well-being (Csikszentmihalyi, 1991; Wachsmuth & Dolce, 1980). Theta waves emerge from the cortex and hippocampus. Jerking movements or sudden twitches, known as positive myoclonus, along with hallucinations upon drifting off to sleep, known as hypnagogic hallucinations, are common during Stage 1, as is some degree of muscle tone loss and decreased conscious awareness of the external environment. Stage 1 sleep occupies about 2% to 5% of total sleep time in children.

Stage 2 sleep is notable for high-amplitude waves at 12 to 16 Hz, along with sleep spindles, which are characteristic jagged runs on the EEG. In addition, larger spikes, known as K-complexes, are present. Sleep spindles originate in the thalamus and are thought to represent efforts by the brain to inhibit processing in order to keep the sleeper tranquil. K-complexes originate widely in the cortex and are brief, high-voltage peaks, usually followed by bursts of sleep spindles, which may occur in response to both internal (e.g., digestive) and external (e.g., auditory or tactile) stimuli during sleep. K-complexes are thought to suppress cortical arousal and aid in sleep-based memory consolidation. Stage 2 sleep is notable for reduced muscle tone and decelerations in respiration and heart rate. Children can move about freely and reposition themselves during Stage 2, which occupies about 50% of total sleep time.

Stages 3 and 4 are characterized by high-amplitude slow delta waves occurring at 0.5 to 2 Hz. Previously distinguished by the predominance of delta waves (e.g., in Stage 3 delta waves accounted for less than 50% of the total wave patterns and in Stage 4 more than 50%), the American Academy of Sleep Medicine has now eliminated this distinction from their staging system. Currently, all delta wave, slow-wave, or deep sleep is categorized as Stage 3, and Stage 4 no longer exists (Schulz, 2008). Delta waves emanate from the cortex and thalamus and aid in declarative memory formation, consolidation, and hormone release. Parasomnias, such as night terrors, sleepwalking, sleep talking, and bruxism, commonly occur during deep sleep, which accounts for about 20% of total sleep time.

Finally, REM sleep, commonly thought of as dream sleep, is the final sleep stage. So named because of the frequent flickering of the eyelids observed as the eyes move underneath, REM sleep is characterized by low-voltage random waves emanating from throughout the cortex, causing a periodic sawtooth pattern. More than at any other sleep stage, the brain waves during REM sleep look a great deal like those during the awake state. REM constitutes the greatest proportion of sleep in infants (approximately 55%), declining to about 25% by 5 years of age. The high proportion of REM during the first year of life is thought to be important for brain stimulation and rapid neural growth. Both REM and Stage 3 are homeostatic, meaning that when deprived of sleep, the body will preferentially "rebound" into these stages once sleep is allowed. This observation suggests that both deep sleep and REM are essential. Although certain brain waves predominate at different stages of sleep, alpha, beta, theta, and delta are all present, if only in trace amounts, throughout the day and in each sleep stage.

In order to understand sleep pathology, one must first understand some basic terms utilized in the study of sleep:

- *Sleep latency* is the period of time required to fall asleep, typically taken as the amount of time it takes to enter Stage 1.
- *REM latency* is defined as the amount of time between the onset of sleep and the first REM period.
- *REM density* is defined as the number of eye movement bursts or frequency of eye movements per minute of REM sleep.
- *REM rebound* describes the body's preference for REM when in a sleep-deprived state and the fact that the body will more rapidly "rebound" into REM when the individual is underslept.

- *Sleep-onset REM* occurs when one lapses immediately into REM upon falling asleep, bypassing Stages 1, 2, and 3, as occurs with narcolepsy.

For purposes of understanding sleep physiology and pathology, it is useful to think of sleep as being subdivided into REM and non-REM (Stages 1 through 3). During non-REM, there is generally reduced physiological activity, as evidenced by slowing of the heart rate and respiration, decreased metabolic function, and a decrease in the activation of the autonomic nervous system, yet the body maintains a steady internal temperature. During non-REM sleep, one can move about freely and may pull up the blankets if too cold or kick off the sheets if too warm. Non-REM is also notable for episodic involuntary and sometimes jerky movements. Finally, during non-REM there is a slowing of blood flow, few penile erections, and little vaginal lubrication. REM sleep physiological changes, by contrast, are the opposite of those in non-REM sleep.

REM sleep is notable for increased physiological activity and autonomic nervous system activation. Altered thermoregulation, such that the body does not maintain a steady internal body temperature, and partial or full penile erections and significant vaginal lubrication are also characteristic. Skeletal muscle paralysis and numerous REMs are also evident. It is theorized that skeletal muscle paralysis is necessary during REM sleep because we would otherwise stand up and act out our dreams, which tend to occur in greatest density during REM.

During REM sleep, cells in the preoptic/anterior hypothalamus, which are responsible for maintaining a steady body temperature, cease firing, causing us to experience poikilothermia or to respond like cold-blooded animals. Since our thermoregulatory cells stop functioning during REM, our body temperatures tend to approach the temperature of the ambient environment. Interestingly, when the ambient temperature is at an extreme of hot or cold, REM sleep is lost, as if the body is refusing to let such an uncomfortable temperature be imposed upon itself. Likewise, animals kept in thermoneutral zones during sleep, or temperature ranges of greatest comfort for their species, show a maximal amount of REM (Alam, McGinty, & Szymusiak, 1995; Buguet, 2007).

The cyclical nature of sleep is reliable. REM periods occur about every 90 to 120 minutes. The first REM period is the shortest. Most deep sleep, Stage 3, occurs early in the evening, while most REM sleep occurs later. The normal sleep cycle for children is portrayed in Figure 18.2. In contrast to adult sleep, the density of deep sleep early in the evening is somewhat greater during childhood. In the elderly population, there is little Stage 3 sleep, particularly after age 70. Sleep becomes more frag-

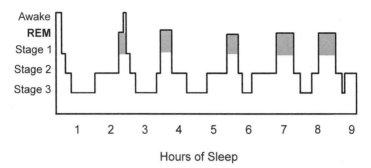

Figure 18.2   Normal sleep cycle in children. Figure 18.2 illustrates the relative time spent in each sleep stage throughout a typical evening.

mented by this age, and there are numerous awakenings throughout the evening, particularly toward the morning. It is this relative lack of deep sleep that often causes the elderly to feel sleepy throughout the day and accounts for their frequent naps.

There is no clear single center that regulates sleep, but we do recognize numerous brain structures, neurochemicals, and hormones that are involved. The neurochemicals serotonin, norepinephrine, dopamine, histamine, glutamate, aspartate, acetylcholine, and gamma aminobutyric acid (GABA) all play a role. The suprachiasmatic nucleus, located within the hypothalamus, is responsible for controlling endogenous circadian rhythms. The suprachiasmatic nucleus contains several cell types and releases several different peptide hormones, including vasopressin (antidiuretic hormone) and vasoactive intestinal peptide. Numerous other hormones are also involved in sleep, such as growth hormone, cortisol, thyroid hormone, leptin, and ghrelin.

Orexin, a pair of excitatory neuropeptide hormones, so named because of their orexigenic (appetite-stimulating) activity, are synthesized in the hypothalamus and involved in narcolepsy. Dogs lacking an orexin receptor have narcolepsy, while people and other animals lacking the orexin neuropeptide itself also have narcolepsy. Another hormone, melatonin, is synthesized by the pineal gland and is released at night and inhibited by ambient light. While exogenous administration increases total sleep time and decreases sleep latency, the exact role of melatonin in sleep has yet to be elucidated. Growth hormone is released during Stage 3 sleep in children. Consequently, children who do not obtain adequate deep sleep are at risk of growth retardation.

The onset of sleep is associated with a dramatic reorganization of thermoregulatory control. Core body temperature falls at sleep onset aided by a variety of heat loss mechanisms, such as sweating and vasodilation at the periphery; as the core body temperature drops, the peripheral body temperature heats. The fall in core body temperature and slowed metabolism presumably contribute to energy conservation, which may be one of the most important roles of sleep. In general, we sleep best at night when our core body temperature is low and our melatonin levels are elevated. In fact, mounting evidence suggests that sleeping medications and melatonin tend to decrease our core body temperature and that caffeine tends to increase it. Anything that heats our core in the evening generally has the effect of fracturing or delaying our sleep, such as a long hot shower or bath before bed. Our reaction time and alertness are at their peak when our core body temperature is at its normal level, approximately 98.6 degrees Fahrenheit. The core body temperature hits its nadir about four hours before our usual wake time, at which point our alertness and reaction time are also at their lowest.

Given the timing of our physiological processes to sleep and wake periods, it is clear that humans have evolved in line with the day and night cycles of our universe. For each hour we are awake, we incur a sleep debt of about 30 minutes. Sleep debt builds throughout the day, eventually becoming so overwhelming that we sleep. Borbély (1982) proposed a "two-process model" of sleep, as shown in Figure 18.3. Process S repre-

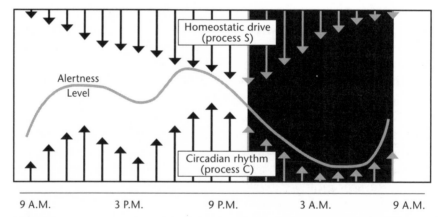

Figure 18.3 The Two Process Model of sleep. The Two Process Model explains the variation in our alertness over a 24-hour period. Process C, or the circadian drive, rises in the morning, decreases midday (corresponding to an increase in melatonin and timed to a midday siesta), and then increases throughout the late day and early evening in opposition to the increasing homeostatic sleep drive, or Process S. After typically about 16 hours in adults, the sleep drive, which has been building all day, becomes too much for our bodies to oppose, and we fall asleep (represented by the darkened area of the graph). Our alertness varies throughout the day in response to the relative drives of Process C and Process S.

sents the homeostatic, internal sleep drive which builds throughout the day, placing increasing sleep pressure on the individual. Process C represents the circadian rhythm or our wake-promoting drive, which varies in strength throughout the day. In the midafternoon, coincident with a rise in melatonin, Process C drops; later in the day, Process C reaches its peak in order to help us stay awake just as our sleep debt is reaching its greatest point. The interaction between Process C and Process S represents a theoretical but probable model that dictates our alertness throughout the day.

Perhaps the purpose of sleep is to dream. Until just recently, we believed that dreams occurred only during REM sleep. This observation was founded upon the fact that when individuals were awoken during REM, they could rapidly and easily recount their dreams, whereas when awoken in other stages of sleep, dreams were not easily recalled. In recent years we have come to understand that individuals do, in fact, dream during non-REM sleep, but these dreams are often brief, fragmented, and not as vivid and well remembered.

Neurocognitive Effects of Sleep Disruption

We have limited data on the neurocognitive effects of sleep disruption on children's attention and memory. Most of our information is based on studies of the daytime performance of children with sleep-disordered breathing (SDB). The most common cause of SDB is sleep apnea, which can affect both children and adults. When an individual is apneic, the brain does not receive sufficient oxygen, and sleep is interrupted. These individuals generally do not reach deep sleep or REM and are constantly awoken throughout the night as they gasp for air (Gozal, O'Brien, & Row, 2004). Sleep restriction in experimental settings causes daytime inattention and changes in cortical EEG responses even after only one hour of restriction the night before (Randazzo, Muehlbach, Schweitzer, & Walsh, 1998). Data are inconsistent regarding the effects of sleep disruption on memory performance, yet children suffering from obstructive sleep apnea (OSA), periodic limb movement disorder (PLMD), and restless legs syndrome (RLS) with resulting sleep fragmentation have been shown to suffer academic deficits, learning problems, and symptoms that mirror attention-deficit/hyperactivity disorder (ADHD). In the case of OSA at least, symptoms are generally reversible after treatment (Chervin & Archbold, 2001; Chervin et al., 2002).

Neuropsychological testing has been useful in demonstrating the acute effects of sleep restriction on children and adolescents. Sleep restriction and total sleep deprivation reduce computational speed, impair verbal fluency, and decrease creativity and abstract problem-solving ability (Engleman & Joffe, 1999; Fallone, Acebo, Arnedt, Seifer, & Carskadon, 2001). Severe sleep fragmentation, as seen in OSA, may even result in reduced IQ scores. Sleep disruption can also have clear effects on academic achievement (Gozal, 1998). In fact, children with OSA suffer lower academic achievement even when age, race, gender, socioeconomic status, and school attended are controlled for. Furthermore, just one additional hour of sleep in children aged 8 to 12 years over one week results in parent and child reports of improved emotional functioning and objective improvements in memory, attention, and math fluency (Vriend et al., 2013). Likewise, in children 7 to 11 years old, one additional hour in bed, averaging 27 minutes of additional sleep, leads to improvements in teachers' blinded ratings of emotional lability and impulsivity (Gruber, Cassoff, Frenette, Wiebe, & Carrier, 2012).

The treatment of OSA results in significant improvement in school performance. Even children who snore loudly and consistently in their early years are at a greater risk for academic delays in later years, suggesting some residual effects on learning that continue even after resolution of symptoms (Blunden, Lushington, Kennedy, Martin, & Dawson, 2000). Animal models show increased locomotor activity and neuron cell loss in the hippocampus and prefrontal cortex in rats exposed to intermittent hypoxia, along with decreases in special task acquisition and retention compared to controls (O'Brien & Gozal, 2004).

EPIDEMIOLOGY

Approximately 25% of youth will suffer a sleep problem at some point during childhood (Owens & Witmans, 2004). Complaints range from bedtime resistance and anxiety to primary sleep disorders, such as OSA and narcolepsy. Research is remarkably consistent, with parents reporting about 50% of preschool children (S. Kerr & Jowett, 1994), 30% of school-age children (M. A. Stein, Mendelson, Obermeyer, Amronin, & Benca, 2001), and 40% of adolescents as having sleep difficulties (Smedje, Broman, & Hetta, 2001). Self-reports among adolescents reveal that up to one third complain of frequent or extended nighttime awakenings, excessive daytime sleepiness, unrefreshing sleep, trouble falling asleep, or a subjective need for more sleep (Patten, Choi, Gillin, & Pierce, 2000; Saarenpää-Heikkilä, Laippala, & Koivikko, 2001).

Perhaps the most frightening sleep disorder, SIDS, has seen a worldwide decline in the past decade. The incidence is estimated at about 0.77 per 1,000 live births in Great Britain. The incidence in the United States has dropped more than 50%, from 1.53 per 1,000 live births in 1980 to 0.56 per 1,000 live births in 2001 (Arias, MacDorman, Strobino, & Guyer, 2002; Leach et al., 1999). Still, SIDS accounted for 8% of all infant deaths in the United States in 2002 and ranks as the third leading cause of infant death in the United States (Hoyert, Mathews, Menacker, Strobino, & Guyer, 2006). In the United States, the SIDS rate for African and Native American infants remains at more than twice that of Caucasian infants, reflecting a long-standing racial disparity.

Narcolepsy occurs at a rate of about 1.37 per 100,000 and has a prevalence of 56 per 100,000 in the United States (Kotagal, 2008). Narcolepsy most commonly sets on during the second decade of life but is not uncommonly diagnosed in the third and fourth decades. Cataplexy, or the sudden loss of muscle tone, which commonly occurs secondary to an emotional trigger such as anger or laughter, affects 50% to 70% of those with narcolepsy.

The prevalence of pediatric insomnia is estimated at between 1% and 6% in the general pediatric population but considerably higher among those children with neurodevelopmental delays and chronic medical and psychiatric conditions (Ivanenko et al., 2004; Manni et al., 1997; M. A. Stein et al., 2001). A study of children aged 5 to 16 years found that 50% of those presenting to a pediatric sleep center for insomnia had a preexisting psychiatric diagnosis, while the remaining 50% had elevated psychiatric impairment scores on psychometric measures and diagnostic interview. Perhaps the majority of children with pediatric insomnia, then, may have at least psychiatric symptoms, if not an actual disorder (Ivanenko, Barnes, Crabtree, & Gozal, 2005).

The prevalence of snoring among children is somewhere between 7% and 12%, while OSA is much less frequent, with a prevalence of 1% to 2% (Ersu et al., 2004; Gozal, 1998). The frequency of upper airway resistance syndrome, a relatively newer category of SDB, has been as yet difficult to ascertain.

Enuresis occurs in approximately 30% of 4-year-olds, 10% of 6-year-olds, 5% of 10-year-olds, 3% of 12-year-olds, and about 1% of those 15 years of age and over (Byrd, Weitzman, Lanphear, & Auinger, 1996; Essen & Peckham, 1976; Feehan, McGee, Stanton, & Silva, 1990; Fergusson & Horwood, 1994; Hellström, Hanson, Hansson, Hjalmas, & Jodal, 1990; Kalo & Bella, 1986; Klackenberg, 1981; Rahim & Cederblad, 1986). Although not satisfying *DSM-5* criteria for a diagnosis, between 10% and 20% of 5-year-olds continue to have at least one episode of nocturnal enuresis per month (N. J. Klein, 2001).

Non-REM parasomnias are common among children and adolescents. As an example, *sleep terrors* affect somewhere between 3% and

7% of children and 1% to 3% of adults (American Psychiatric Association, 2000). Sleepwalking is a much more common occurrence, with a prevalence of somewhere between 6% and 17% in children and a lifetime incidence of as high as 40% in the general population. The prevalence in adults is about 1% to 2% (Mahowald & Rosen, 1990). Although not a formal *DSM-5* diagnosis, *confusional arousals* are described in the International Classification of Sleep Disorders (American Sleep Disorders Association, 2007). Confusional arousals are essentially sleepwalking episodes during which an individual becomes confused and disruptive. The epidemiology of such events is unclear. In one Stockholm study, a 4% incidence was noted (Klackenberg, 1981).

Sleep Problems Associated With Psychiatric Conditions

All varieties of sleep disorders are about five times more common among children with ADHD than healthy controls, controls with other psychiatric disorders, and healthy siblings (Corkum, Tannock, & Moldofsky, 1998). It is estimated that up to 25% of children with severe sleep problems in infancy will later meet criteria for a diagnosis of ADHD (Thunström, 2002). Up to 83% of children with a diagnosis of frank autistic disorder are reported to suffer sleep difficulties, as are up to 86% of children with autism spectrum disorders (Patzold, Richdale, & Tonge, 1998; Richdale & Prior, 1995; Wiggs & Stores, 1996). Younger children and those with more significant cognitive delay or disability tend to demonstrate increased problems. Sleep problems are often long-standing. A study of adults with Asperger's syndrome, for example, demonstrated that 90% continue to complain of frequent insomnia (Tani et al., 2003).

Mood disorders too are commonly comorbid with sleep problems. Up to two thirds of children with a diagnosis of major depressive disorder have early and middle insomnia, and half of these children also report late insomnia or early-morning awakening (Puig-Antich et al., 1982). Nearly 90% of depressed adolescents report sleep disturbances, usually insomnia, with up to 25% of these teens reporting hypersomnia (Goetz et al., 1987). About 10% experience continued insomnia even after the depression is lifted (Goetz et al., 1983). One study of bipolar children found that 40% had a dramatically reduced need for sleep versus controls and those with ADHD (B. Geller, Zimerman, Williams, Delbello, Bolhofner, et al., 2002).

Anxiety and sleep are intimately tied in childhood. Sleep problems by age 4 are correlated with later-onset depression and anxiety by age 15

(Ivanenko et al., 2004). Nighttime fears are common and are reported by up to 75% of typical children (Muris et al., 2000). Sleep problems generally follow for those children with diagnosed anxiety disorders. Occasional nightmares occur in 80% of children; 15% report frequent nightmares (e.g., more than one a month); and up to 70% of children report that the content of their nightmares is influenced by frightening material viewed on television or at the movies (Hawkins & Williams, 1992; Muris et al., 2000). This statistic should not go unheeded by clinicians and parents. It is vital to acknowledge that the media has a major impact on children's thoughts and subsequent behavior and that parents must carefully monitor their children's media exposure, limiting that which frightens them or is not age appropriate.

CLINICAL COURSE

Most sleep disorders in children and adolescents are developmental and dissipate with time as the children outgrow them. Only a fraction of affected children, as already noted, continue to sleepwalk, wet the bed, or experience sleep terrors as adults, and the same is true with nightmares. SDB in children is most often due to enlarged tonsils and will generally be less troublesome as children age and their tonsils naturally shrink. Alternatively, tonsillectomy and adenoidectomy are almost always effective in treating the problem immediately. By contrast, narcolepsy is generally a lifelong condition with a stable course over time.

Primary insomnia is typically of sudden onset with continuation due to negative conditioning and the development of maladaptive sleep patterns. Individuals who have a series of nights or weeks where they have difficulty falling or staying asleep become rapidly conditioned into fearing that they will have difficulty falling or staying asleep; they then often develop a series of maladaptive behaviors, such as watching television in bed, sleeping on the couch, reading in bed, or drinking alcohol before sleep, all of which ultimately interfere further with their ability to maintain a good night's sleep.

DIAGNOSIS

Sleep is best studied by observation in a sleep lab, where the patient stays overnight. The gold standard of sleep studies is the polysomnogram (PSG). PSG is simply a term for describing the conglomeration of tests employed to study an individual during sleep. These measures usually include videotaped observation, EEG, electromyography (which monitors muscle movements), electrooculography (which monitors eye movements), vital signs, and any other physiological parameters that may be relevant, such as electrocardiography to follow heart rate and rhythm.

Newer methods for studying sleep allow investigators to observe patients not simply in a sleep lab, but also in their home. The most common ambulatory technique involves actigraphy. This method was developed in the early 1970s and has come into increasing use in both research and clinical practice. Actigraphy allows for the study of sleep–wake patterns and circadian rhythms via the assessment of body movements. The device is worn on the wrist like a watch and can easily be adapted for home use. It is reliable and valid for the study of sleep in normal healthy populations but less reliable for detecting disturbed sleep.

A number of survey instruments, such as sleep diaries and questionnaires, also exist for detecting problematic sleep in children and adolescents. Self-report measures, such as the Sleep Disturbance Scale for Children, the Child Sleep Questionnaire, and the Child and Family Sleep History Questionnaire, along with parent report forms, are frequently helpful (Blader, Koplewicz, Abikoff, & Foley, 1997; Corkum, Moldofsky, Hogg-Johnson, Humphries, & Tannock, 1999).

Sudden Infant Death Syndrome

The most widely accepted definitions of SIDS require that all other possible causes of death be ruled out by death scene investigation, review of the clinical history, and autopsy prior to accepting SIDS as the diagnosis (Krous et al., 2004). Intentional or nonintentional injury and suffocation must also be considered.

DSM-5 Sleep Disorders

DSM-5 defines 11 general categories of sleep disturbances in the chapter on sleep–wake disorders. These include insomnia, hyperinsomnolence, narcolepsy, breathing-related sleep disorders, circadian rhythm sleep–wake disorders, parasomnias, nightmare disorder, REM sleep behavior disorder, restless legs syndrome, substance/medication-induced sleep disorder, and a generic series of "other" and "unspecified" forms. As with all *DSM-5* diagnoses, in order to be considered a "disorder," significant functional impairment must be present.

Insomnia

Insomnia among adults most commonly occurs in the early and mideve-ning hours. Affected individuals have difficulty falling and staying asleep. In the vast majority of individuals with a diagnosis of insomnia, PSG studies are negative. Although many of these individuals display subclin-ical symptoms of psychiatric illness, most do not have another primary psychiatric diagnosis but are at greater risk than the general population (American Psychiatric Association, 2013).

Although insomnia has long been recognized among adults, no clear definition for pediatric insomnia existed until 2005. According to the International Classification of Sleep Disorders, pediatric insomnia is now defined as "frequent problems with sleep initiation, duration, con-solidation, and/or quality that occurs despite adequate opportunity for sleep, resulting in daytime functional impairment for the child and/or family" (American Sleep Disorders Association, 2007, p. 26).

Behavioral insomnia is another diagnostic category recently intro-duced to describe the sleep difficulties resulting from inadequate parental limit-setting or sleep associations, such as rocking a child to bed at night, allowing a child to fall asleep in the parent's bed, or allowing children to watch television to fall asleep. Behavioral insomnia is characterized by the inability of the child to fall asleep in the absence of these conditions at both bedtime and following nocturnal awakenings.

Narcolepsy

Narcolepsy is diagnosed by nocturnal PSG, sleep history, and the multi-ple sleep latency test, which measures how long it takes the patient to fall asleep in a sleep lab during repeated nap opportunities. Symptoms of narcolepsy may set on all at once or gradually over a series of years.

Breathing-Related Sleep Disorders

Many children and adolescents snore. As long as there are no changes in sleep architecture, alveolar ventilation, or blood oxygenation and the child is not awakening frequently and experiencing difficulties through-out the day, there is generally no major concern. Still, however, snoring is not considered "normal." OSA is the most impairing of the sleep breath-ing difficulties faced by children and is characterized by frequent awakenings, blood oxygen desaturations, and poor sleep quality, resulting in excessive daytime sleepiness and many of the neurocognitive impairments previously noted. Upper airway resistance syndrome, which causes frequent awakenings, does not result in blood oxygen desaturations and is therefore less impairing.

Parents whose child suffers from sleep-disordered breathing (SDB) will commonly complain of hearing their child snore and also recount frequent awakenings, excessive daytime sleepiness, poor academic performance, irritability, poor executive functioning, and general inattention or cognitive impairment. Lab results for children who are severely affected by SDB will demonstrate a reduction in air flow and lowered hemoglobin oxygen saturation along with an increase in total hemoglobin. Sinus arrhythmias, premature ventricular contractions (PVCs), atrioventricular (AV) block, sinus arrest, and a preponderance of Stage 1 sleep signify severe impairment. Physical examination may show adenotonsillar enlargement, pectus excavatum, obesity, hypertension, and cor pulmonale or right heart enlargement.

Circadian Rhythm Sleep–Wake Disorders

Circadian rhythm sleep-wake disorders is a broad category for a variety of difficulties in which regular sleep disruption is due to a misalignment of the circadian rhythm and sleep–wake schedule. Examples include delayed sleep phase type, advanced sleep phase type, irregular sleep–wake type, non-24-hour sleep–wake type, and shift work type. Delayed sleep phase type is the most commonly encountered form among adolescents, as their natural circadian rhythm tends to drift later after puberty and remains delayed through early adulthood. In all cases, circadian rhythm disorders must result in excessive sleepiness and/or insomnia.

Parasomnias

Parasomnias can occur during REM and non-REM sleep. Non-REM parasomnias include somnambulism (sleepwalking), sleep terrors, somniloquy (sleep talking), and sleep-related involuntary movement disorders such as PLMD, body rocking, and bruxism (jaw clenching or tooth grinding throughout the night). The non-REM sleep disorders have many features in common. They are of short duration, lasting somewhere between 1 and 30 minutes; affected individuals do not recall the events subsequently upon awakening due to retrograde amnesia; there is a high potential for injury to oneself or others; and there is often a personal or family history of such events. Non-REM parasomnias occur during slow-wave deep sleep (e.g., Stage 3). As already discussed, they are more common in childhood than adulthood. Psychopathology among affected children is rare. Precipitating factors include a preexisting sleep problem, sleep deprivation, medications that interrupt or alter sleep architecture, magnesium deficiency, and hormonal factors. There is, in fact, a slight increase in occurrence around puberty.

Somnambulists are typically docile. Some affected individuals begin sleepwalking after an episode of enuresis. Somnambulists may engage in simple behaviors, such as walking into another room and falling back to sleep on the couch, or more complex behaviors, such as getting dressed, taking a walk outside, or preparing and eating food. Sleepwalking episodes that include irrational acts, incoherence, and significant disorientation are called confusional arousals and are considered a variant of sleepwalking. As with all non-REM parasomnias, autonomic arousal is characteristic, as is complete amnesia for the event. Premeditated acts are believed to be impossible, although there have been episodes of life-threatening behavior, murder, and even attempted suicide during these events (Broughton et al., 1994; Guilleminault, Moscovitch, & Leger, 1995; Shatkin, Feinfeld, & Strober, 2002).

The hallmark of a sleep terror is extreme autonomic nervous system activation. A rapid increase in pulse, blood pressure, and heart and respiratory rate, along with profuse sweating, is always observed. Affected children sit bolt upright in bed, scream loudly for a few seconds or minutes, and then promptly fall right back to sleep. They experience complete amnesia for the event and are not harmed in any way.

REM Parasomnias

There are a number of REM parasomnias to which children are sometimes vulnerable as well. The most severe of these, REM sleep behavior disorder, occurs when the body is not adequately paralyzed during REM sleep and is more common among the elderly. Affected individuals commonly act out their dreams, which can result in threatening behavior to themselves and others. Another REM parasomnia, sleep paralysis, occurs when an individual awakens during a REM period while the body is paralyzed. These episodes are highly frightening, as individuals often feel that they are unable to move, breathe, or even open their eyes, yet their brain is actively awake. Finally, nightmares, while frightening, are common and only considered pathological if they occur often (e.g., once or more per week) and the sleep disturbance causes daytime functional impairment. It is important to note that nightmares are common in traumatic stress reactions and are often a by-product of anxiety or depression.

Restless Legs Syndrome

Now most often referred to as Willis-Ekbom Disease, RLS represents a neurological disorder with four characteristics: (1) Symptoms are worse at night and are absent or negligible in the morning; (2) there is a strong and often overwhelming need or urge to move the affected limb(s), often associated with paresthesias or dysesthesias; (3) the symptoms are triggered by rest, relaxation, or sleep; and (4) the symptoms are relieved with movement. The symptoms can be simply uncomfortable at best but painful at worst.

Enuresis

Bed-wetting or enuresis can occur during both REM and non-REM sleep. Most children are dry during the evening by about 4 or 5 years of age, yet some children take longer to train. For a *DSM-5* diagnosis of enuresis, bed-wetting must occur at least twice a week for at least three months, or it must result in significant distress or functional impairment, and the child must be at least 5 years of age (American Psychiatric Association, 2013). Enuresis is sometimes thought of as either "primary," indicating that the child has never been regularly dry, or "secondary," when enuresis occurs in a child who was previously dry for at least six months. In the *DSM*, enuresis is categorized as an elimination disorder, not a sleep disorder.

TREATMENT

Before engaging in treatment, it is important to obtain a complete sleep history. Key components include how many hours the child sleeps each day (including both naps and evening sleep), when he or she goes to sleep, how long it takes him or her to fall asleep, notable awakenings, and any rituals or practices necessary to put him or her to sleep. Special attention should be paid to difficulties falling asleep (early insomnia), staying asleep (middle insomnia), and awakening too early (late insomnia). Parents and children should also be asked directly about sleep pathologies, including enuresis, parasomnias, SDB, family history of sleep problems, and any medications or other methods utilized to promote sleep. A sleep diary is often useful for tracking sleep and helping parents to determine their child's precise vulnerabilities. Sleep diaries generally assess sleep patterns and disruptions, exercise, caffeine use, drugs and alcohol, and stressors that can interfere with sleep. Sample sleep diaries are readily available on the Internet.

A useful tool for pediatric clinicians is the BEARS mnemonic. B stands for bedtime problems; E stands for excessive daytime sleepiness; A stands for awakenings during the night; R stands for regularity of evening sleep time and morning awakenings; and S stands for sleep-related breathing problems or snoring. Using the BEARS mnemonic, clinicians have uncovered twice to four times as many sleep problems in comparison to routine clinical examination (Owens & Dalzell, 2005).

Sudden Infant Death Syndrome

Reducing modifiable risk factors for infants, such as sleeping in a prone position, overbundling, and secondary smoke exposure, has decreased the incidence of SIDS by more than 60% in most parts of the world (Halbower & Marcus, 2003). Other strategies, such as having infants sleep in a supine position, not allowing infants to sleep on their sides, and using a pacifier, may ultimately reduce the incidence still further (Alm, Lagercrantz, & Wennergren, 2006).

Narcolepsy

As narcolepsy is a lifelong disorder, extensive education of the affected child and his or her family is of great importance. Methods to increase daytime alertness and enhance psychomotor functioning are also key. Maintaining a regular sleep–wake schedule; avoiding alcohol and drugs; taking one or two brief, planned naps each day; and engaging in regular exercise are helpful strategies. Avoiding driving and other high-risk activities is also advised. Stimulants, such as modafinil (Provigil) and methylphenidate (Ritalin), are often employed to help with wakefulness, and anticholinergic drugs, such as protriptyline (Vivactil) and clomipramine (Anafranil), are often effective for cataplexy (Kotagal, 2008).

Insomnia

The treatment of insomnia, adult or pediatric, should begin with an adequate history and understanding of the environment within which the child sleeps and lives. Certainly, all other potential psychiatric disorders and psychosocial disturbances should be considered in the history, along with any medical illnesses and medications that can interfere with sleep. Proper sleep hygiene, which is often curative for insomnia, should be reviewed with the family and emphasized as a first intervention (see Table 18.1).

The techniques of sleep hygiene, when employed appropriately, are commonly helpful in settling children and adults back to sleep without further need for treatment. The importance of a sleep–wake schedule, particularly for children, cannot be overemphasized. The folk saying "sleep begets sleep" appears to be the experience of most parents. Consequently, if we wish for our children to sleep well, we should be making sure that they receive plenty of opportunity. Establishing a standard bedtime and routine, which for a child may include bathing, reading a book, or engaging in a quiet and comforting family ritual, is often helpful. Allowing the child to fall asleep in the parents' bed or, conversely, parents falling asleep with their children in the child's bed, while commonly enjoyable and comforting for both parents and children, often leaves the child without the confidence necessary to put himself back to sleep when he awakens naturally throughout the night. Consequently, when overused, these methods of putting children to sleep almost invariably result in the child's calling for the parent each time he awakens throughout the night, resulting in unsatisfactory sleep for both.

For those parents who have fallen asleep with their children every night and now find themselves in a maladaptive pattern with which they are frustrated, behavioral methods are very helpful and typically resolve the problem rapidly. One useful methodology involves leaving the child alone in her room for one additional minute each night until the child

Table 18.1 Sleep Hygiene

- Set a routine sleep-wake schedule.
- Encourage regular exercise and physical activity, but not at night.
- Avoid caffeine within six hours of bedtime.
- Invent a relaxing bedtime ritual, such as bathing and reading together.
- Avoid large meals and large amounts of fluid prior to bedtime.
- Adjust the room temperature as desired.
- Keep noise levels low and the bedroom dark. Use a nightlight if necessary.

is able to fall asleep on her own. For example, on Night 1, the parent explains the plan, noting that she is going to help the child to learn to fall asleep on her own. The parent then bids the child good night and leaves the room for 1 minute. The parent then comes back to the room, rejoins the child, and lies with her until she falls asleep, as on any other night. On Night 2, the parent steps out for 2 minutes before lying with the child, and on Night 3, the parent steps out for 3 minutes, and so forth. This method is often effective within a matter of days, as long as the parent is consistent. Because young children are not generally oriented to time, by the fourth or fifth evening, many parents can stay out of the room for 10 minutes or more, and the child by this time will have fallen asleep on her own.

In the event that a child experiences a new onset of insomnia, the parent may find it helpful to soothe the child by sitting with her for a brief period of time, perhaps reading for a few moments or telling a story, before leaving the room once again so that the child can fall asleep. Adults with insomnia are advised not to read in bed but rather to get up and read on the couch or in another room under dim light for 10 to 15 minutes before once again going back to the bed to try to fall asleep. This method is not necessary for children who can be read to in their beds.

Medications are rarely used for pediatric insomnia, and the Food and Drug Administration (FDA) has not approved any such treatments for children suffering from insomnia. Sedatives are rarely necessary, as behavioral methods most always work well. For those children with psychiatric or medical comorbidities that are causing the insomnia, short-half-life medications (e.g., those rapidly metabolized by the body) are sometimes utilized. The medications typically useful in adults with insomnia are rarely employed with children and younger adolescents. Benzodiazepines, such as lorazepam (Ativan), diazepam (Valium), clonazepam (Klonopin), flurazepam (Dalmane), and temazepam (Restoril), are commonly effective for adults with insomnia, as are related agents, such as zaleplon (Sonata), zolpidem (Ambien), and eszopiclone (Lunesta). Barbiturates are almost never given any longer because of their narrow therapeutic index, abuse and addictive potential, and significant side effects. While tolerance to the somnolent effects of benzodiazepines develops in about four weeks, the anxiolytic effects persist. In the long run, then, these medications are often more useful for anxiety than they are for sleep. In children, the GABA receptors, the primary site of action for these medications, are not fully mature until somewhere between the ages of 15 and 18 years, depending on the child. As a result, a significant minority of children who are given benzodiazepines and similar medications respond paradoxically in a belligerent, agitated, and almost "drunken" manner.

When medications are necessary for the treatment of pediatric insomnia, antihistamines, alpha-2 agonists, and sedating antidepressants are sometimes employed. The antihistamines diphenhydramine (Benadryl), hydroxyzine (Vistaril), and cyproheptadine (Periactin) are all sedating but not without side effects, which can include dry mouth and eyes, tachycardia, urinary retention, paradoxical agitation, confusion, and residual sedation upon awakening, to name just a few. In spite of these side effects, antihistamines are generally well tolerated by children and adolescents. Dosages of both diphenhydramine and hydroxyzine would usually start somewhere between 6.25 and 25 mg, depending on the child; dosages of cyproheptadine would start at between 1 and 2 mg. Perhaps more commonly used, at least among children with ADHD, is the alpha-2 agonist antihypertensive clonidine (Catapres). Clonidine is generally initiated at 0.05 mg at bedtime and can be titrated up to 0.3 mg as needed (see Chapter 3). Sedating antidepressants, such as trazodone (Desyrel) at dosages of 12.5 to 100 mg and mirtazapine (Remeron) at dosages of 7.5 to 15 mg, are also sometimes employed for pediatric insomnia. Increasingly, and perhaps unfortunately, antipsychotics, such as quetiapine (Serzone) and risperidone (Risperdal), are also being used to treat pediatric insomnia, although in the absence of a major psychiatric comorbidity such as bipolar disorder, this type of aggressive treatment is rarely indicated.

Finally, we are beginning to see an influx in the use of herbal medications and dietary supplements, such as melatonin, which has been found effective for treating insomnia in certain groups of children at dosages between 300 mcg and 10 mg. Kava kava, valerian, L-tryptophan, chamomile, passion flower, and lavender are also sometimes marketed and used for pediatric insomnia. With the exception of melatonin, however, which is a reasonable treatment without frequent side effects for most children and adolescents, these medications have not been studied and should be avoided.

Breathing-Related Sleep Disorders

The treatment of OSA and other forms of severe SDB among children typically involves tonsillectomy and adenoidectomy, which almost always resolves the problem. Among adults with OSA, weight loss, sleeping on one's side and stomach (as opposed to the back), and using an air mask that provides continuous positive airway pressure (CPAP) and keeps the airway patent and free of obstruction by the uvula, soft palate, and tongue are often helpful. In more severe cases, septoplasty to repair a deviated nasal septum or tonsillectomy and adenoidectomy for those with residually enlarged tonsils may be necessary.

Parasomnias

The treatment of non-REM parasomnias involves first a series of psychosocial interventions. Educating the family and patient about the pathology itself is of the utmost importance so that they can make any necessary changes to avoid possible recurrences. Violent episodes, as can occur during a confusional arousal, are rarely repeated. However, somnambulism and sleep terrors do commonly recur. Once educated, the family and patient should identify and then avoid possible precipitants, such as sleep disruption and intermittent sleep deprivation. Disruptions will include loud noises while the child is asleep. Limiting evening fluid intake in an effort to decrease the likelihood of awakening to the cues of bladder fullness is also a commonly employed strategy. Locking windows and doors, removing lethal objects (such as knives) from the child's reach, and even placing a movement sensor on the doorpost of a child's room will help to safeguard the house for an active sleepwalker. For those younger children who sleepwalk or experience frequent sleep terrors, enforcing an afternoon nap may be protective, as naps typically decrease the density of Stage 3 sleep in the evening, during which time these parasomnias occur.

Medications may also be employed in the treatment of non-REM parasomnias but are rarely necessary. Although antidepressants tend to decrease REM density, they have been shown to be helpful in non-REM sleep disorders (Mahowald & Schenck, 1996). Their utility may simply rest upon the fact that they disrupt the normal sleep architecture. Benzodiazepines with long half-lives, such as clonazepam and diazepam, are also sometimes helpful. Benzodiazepines tend to decrease non-REM sleep, in contrast to barbiturates, which tend to decrease REM. As indicated previously, however, some children and adolescents will have a paradoxical reaction to benzodiazepines and cannot tolerate their effects. For these children, antidepressants, such as the SSRIs and trazodone, may be useful.

The REM parasomnias, such as sleep paralysis and nightmares, are generally treated simply with psychoeducation. Neither is life threatening, and rarely do they result in significant functional impairment. For those rare cases of REM sleep behavior disorder, a board-certified sleep specialist should be consulted immediately.

Enuresis

The etiology of enuresis is likely to be multifactorial and includes difficulties with bladder muscular stability, central nervous system arousabil-
ity, pontine reflex function, internal sphincter tone, functional bladder
capacity, and nocturnal urine production and a maturational delay in
antidiuretic hormone (ADH) secretion, which inhibits urination. The
final factor is perhaps the most important, as numerous medications
seem to work at this level. Affected individuals probably either do not
produce sufficient ADH or do not respond adequately to the ADH that
they do produce, resulting in enuresis. Secondary enuresis is commonly
caused by urinary tract infections, diabetes mellitus, and in some cases
psychological factors.

The treatment of enuresis, as with all sleep disorders, begins with a
full and complete history. Any prior treatment efforts, behavioral or otherwise, should be ascertained. Education is then provided for the family and patient. Enuresis commonly occurs within families and is more
often seen in males than females. Most children will outgrow enuresis by
10 to 12 years of age, and about 12% to 16% of children become asymptomatic each year, even without treatment. Consequently, education rests
upon supporting the family, helping them to consider behavioral strategies that may be useful, and emphasizing that the family should not
blame, embarrass, or shame the child.

Behavioral treatment efforts begin by discontinuing all caffeine and
alcohol use within six hours of bedtime, as both will inhibit ADH production. Restricting late-night fluid intake to less than 4 ounces of liquid
after dinner is also commonly employed, although we have no data to
support this practice. Some families find it useful to briefly awaken the
child just before the parents go to bed, place him on the toilet, and run
the tap water in order to stimulate the flow of urine. Allowing the child
to void in this manner before placing him back to bed is often helpful in
decreasing early-morning enuresis.

The "bell and pad" or bed-wetting alarm has the highest effective treatment rate and the lowest relapse rate of the behavioral methods (Thiedke, 2003). This practice employs a moisture-sensitive monitor,
often a pad placed atop the mattress or smaller monitors placed on the
child's underwear, which sounds a loud alarm if the child wets. Once the
alarm is triggered, the parents can help the child get to the bathroom to
urinate. This method typically takes about three to four weeks to work.
Some children will naturally relapse after achieving nighttime bladder
control, but if the bell-and-pad method is used subsequently, they can

generally be easily retrained. Other behavioral treatments have not been as consistent in their utility; these include training to increase the functional capacity of the bladder to hold urine; reward systems for children who successfully sleep through the night without urinating in the bed; cognitive and motivational therapies; pelvic floor muscle training; and biofeedback (Abdelghany et al., 2001; Glazener & Evans, 2002; Robson & Leung, 2002; Van Kampen et al., 2002; Yeung, 2003).

The most commonly utilized medication for the treatment of enuresis is desmopressin acetate (DDAVP), a synthetic ADH analog. Dosages typically range between 0.1 and 0.6 mg per evening. Concerns about hyponatremia (low blood sodium) that has resulted in seizures among a small number of children who have received the intranasal form only have recently prompted the FDA to issue a warning advising against treating children with intranasal DDAVP for enuresis.

Other common medications for the treatment of enuresis include the tricyclic antidepressants (TCAs), in particular imipramine (Tofranil). Although most commonly used to treat adult depression, at dosages of 25 to 50 mg, imipramine is often effective for the treatment of enuresis in children and adults. The anticholinergic effects are clearly not the reason for the antienuretic effects, given the fact that other anticholinergic medications are not generally helpful for enuresis. Some suggest that children with enuresis excrete a smaller amount of ADH during sleep and that imipramine restores normal levels of nocturnal ADH secretion (Tomasi, Siracusano, Monni, Mela, & Delitala, 2001). Whenever treating children with TCAs, however, as discussed in Chapter 12, routine electrocardiograms must be performed before and during treatment. Although the dosage of imipramine employed in treating enuresis is much lower than that used to treat depression and is therefore likely to be considerably safer, cardiac parameters must still be followed.

Various antispasmodics are useful for adults who suffer enuresis. These medications include oxybutynin (Ditropan) at a dosage of 2.5 to 5 mg per evening or tolterodine (Detrol) at a dosage of 0.5 to 1 mg per evening. We generally try not to use these medications in children, however, as they can cause excessive sedation and even confusion. In children with particularly difficult-to-treat enuresis, we may sometimes combine treatments, such as desmopressin acetate plus imipramine or oxybutynin. More recently studies have found that atomoxetine (Strattera), an ADHD treatment, is also effective for enuresis. This serendipitous finding was first reported in a case series (Shatkin, 2004) and has now been replicated in a randomized, double-blind, placebo-controlled trial (Sumner, Schuh, Sutton, Lipetz, & Kelsey, 2006).

Treating Sleep Problems Associated With Psychiatric Conditions

As previously noted, many children with ADHD have difficulties with falling asleep or staying asleep. Treatment for these children should begin by reviewing proper sleep hygiene with the parents. Stimulant medications used to treat ADHD also commonly cause sleep impairments. If a stimulant is the cause of the insomnia, the practitioner should consider lowering the dosage of the stimulant or changing to another preparation, perhaps a shorter-acting medication. Paradoxically, for some children with ADHD, adding a low dose of stimulant in the evening may help them to settle to sleep by decreasing their hyperactivity. Changing to a nonstimulant, such as atomoxetine, or using adjunctive agents, particularly clonidine but sometimes sedating antihistamines, antidepressants, or melatonin, is also often useful.

Children with autism spectrum disorders (ASD) often fail to recognize environmental and social cues indicating bedtime. These children may also suffer from poorly developed circadian rhythms because of their social deficits, altered melatonin production, and abnormalities in the hypothalamic-pituitary-adrenal axis (Kulman et al., 2000; Nir et al., 1995; Wiggs & Stores, 1998). Regardless, many of these children require help getting to sleep. As with children diagnosed with ADHD, proper sleep hygiene should be the first intervention. Chronotherapy, or systematically delaying bedtime each night until an age-appropriate bedtime is reached, is sometimes helpful (Piazza, Hagopian, Hughes, & Fisher, 1998). Unstudied medications, but those often utilized for sleep in these children, may include antihistamines, sedating antidepressants, clonidine, benzodiazepines, and antipsychotics. As stated above, melatonin has been studied in small numbers of children affected with developmental disabilities and ASD and has been found effective (Garstang & Wallis, 2006).

Children with depression often exhibit a decreased REM latency, increased total REM, and increased sleep-onset time, all of which tend to dissipate for most children once the depression is treated (Emslie, Rush, Weinberg, Rintelmann, & Roffwarg, 1990). Beyond sleep hygiene and treating all comorbid conditions, no clear data exist on whether or not to treat the symptom of insomnia independent from the mood disorder. For milder cases, a combination of improved sleep hygiene and cognitive behavior therapy (CBT) has been proven effective in managing the insomnia and awakenings associated with depression (Ivanenko et al., 2004). In more severe cases, effective drug therapy may require a combination of an antidepressant with the short-term use of a sedative or hypnotic. Borrowing from adult studies, at the very least practitioners should aggressively treat insomnia associated with bipolar disorder, as a decreased need for sleep is one of the earliest and cardinal symptoms of mania.

The treatment of sleep difficulties in children and adolescents with anxiety disorders involves identifying and treating the primary psychiatric disorder, utilizing sleep hygiene, and then medications as indicated. As with depression, it is not clear how much benefit is gained from treating the symptom of insomnia as a separate entity.

Appendix

Child and Adolescent Psychopharmacology

HISTORY

In 1937, Charles Bradley published "The Behavior of Children Receiving Benzedrine" in the *American Journal of Psychiatry* (Bradley, 1937). Bradley stumbled upon stimulants as a treatment for hyperactive behavior. Amphetamine sulfate (Benzedrine) was marketed in 1928 as an inhaled bronchodilator for children with asthma. Bradley thought that Benzedrine could be useful for the headaches that commonly accompany lumbar punctures. Teachers, however, gave him the feedback that the children who had received Benzedrine were calmer at school and had less disruptive behavior. Bradley observed 30 children aged 5 to 14 years medicated with Benzedrine for one week. He found that the medication calmed and settled hyperactive and impulsive behavior, noting a "spectacular change in behavior . . . remarkably improved school performance" (Bradley, 1937). Bradley's observation marks the beginning of child psychopharmacology. The Emma Pendleton Bradley Hospital in Providence, Rhode Island, is named for his uncle's daughter, Emma Pendleton Bradley, who was stricken with encephalitis at age 7 and became permanently disabled. The Bradley Hospital is the first neuropsychiatric hospital for children in the United States and opened in 1931.

Later that same year, Matthew Molitch published three papers on the use of amphetamine sulfate in children, including two placebo-controlled studies (Molitch & Eccles, 1937; Molitch & Poliakoff, 1937; Molitch & Sullivan, 1937). Two of the studies noted improvements in intelligence testing among those children who had taken medication, and the third report found that 86% of the enuretic boys who were taking the medication stopped bed-wetting but reverted when the medication was discontinued. In 1958, the Conference on Child Research in Psychopharmacology was sponsored by the National Institute of Mental Health. The following year, *Child Research in Psychopharmacology*, the first book devoted to psychopharmacological research in child mental health and based on the proceedings of the 1958 conference, was edited by Seymour Fisher (S. Fisher, 1959). The 1958 conference on child research was important because it was the first time that national scientific attention was focused specifically on the issue of child and adolescent mental health.

Methylphenidate was patented in 1954 but first used to treat "minimal brain dysfunction," or what we now call attention-deficit/hyperactivity disorder (ADHD), in the early 1960s. In 1997 the federal government passed the Food and Drug Administration (FDA) Modernization Act (FDAMA), which encouraged the pharmaceutical industry to voluntarily conduct pediatric drug testing by providing manufacturers with the possibility of an additional six months of patent or marketing exclusivity on their drugs. FDAMA was important because it provided federal support and encouragement for research into the pediatric applications of prescription medications, both psychiatric and general medical.

Only about 20% of the medications available to prescribers in the United States, both psychiatric and general medical, have been FDA approved for use in children and adolescents. Pharmaceutical manufacturers realize that physicians will prescribe medications for children and adolescents regardless of FDA approval because of their need for effective treatments. Once a medication is approved by the FDA for any purpose, a physician may legally prescribe that drug for any indication that he or she sees fit. Consequently, physicians often rely solely on clinical and anecdotal experience and without the benefits of research data when prescribing medications to children and adolescents.

PHARMACOLOGY

There are numerous pharmacological principles that must be understood in order to properly prescribe psychotropic medications. The two most important principles are pharmacokinetics and pharmacodynamics. In simple terms, pharmacokinetics describes how the body processes a medication. The four primary steps include: (a) absorption of the drug, (b) distribution of the drug throughout the body, (c) metabolism of the drug, and (d) excretion or elimination of the drug. Pharmacodynamics describes what the medication does to the body, which results in the therapeutic and unintended side effects of the drug. Stated another way, pharmacokinetics describes the entry of the drug into the body and its elimination from the body, and pharmacodynamics explains the drug's effects on the body.

Absorption and distribution help to determine a drug's speed of onset, whereas metabolism and elimination determine how long a drug will last. Considerable pharmacokinetic variation exists between individuals, and there is a stronger relationship between the concentration of the drug in the plasma and drug effects than the drug dose and drug effects. That is, drug distribution in the body fluids is more important than the dosage taken. There are a number of characteristics that favor absorption of a drug by the body, and generally the opposing characteristics favor excretion. Well-absorbed drugs are usually lipid soluble, nonpolar, and of small molecular size; in contrast to drugs that are not well absorbed and are generally nonlipid soluble, highly polar, and of large molecular size. The body favors nonpolar substances for absorption but typically polarizes them for excretion.

Metabolism is the key to changing drugs into a form that allows their excretion. Covalent bonds occur when atoms share electrons. A polar bond occurs when the electrons are unequally shared. Polar bonds occur when two or more different atoms come together to form a molecule, such as a carbon and an oxygen forming carbon monoxide. Each atom has a different strength of attraction for the electrons circulating around them. The strength of their pull on the electrons is their electronegativity. A greater variation in electronegativity between atoms makes a molecule more polar and favors excretion.

Most cells within the body have a lipid bilayer or a two-layered cell wall that is polar on the outside and nonpolar on the inside. For all practical purposes, the bilayer is impermeable to most water-soluble and polar molecules and ions. Complex proteins and ion channels within the bilayer allow selected molecules and ions to float in and out of the cell. All medications must be able to pass through the lipid bilayer and into the cell if they are to be effective.

Most psychotropic medications are orally administered and absorbed into the circulation through the gastrointestinal tract. Oral administration of drugs, however, is the least reliable and predictable due to the "first-pass effect." Once ingested, contents from the stomach and small intestine are gathered up in the portal venous circulation and passed directly to the liver, the body's detoxification station. After being absorbed by the intestine, most food, drugs, and other gut contents will be metabolized by the liver before entering the body's systemic circulation. The amount of drug making it through the liver on the "first pass" and entering the circulatory system is thereby reduced and accompanied by metabolites of varying pharmacological activity.

The fraction of a drug that reaches the systemic circulation, or that which survives beyond the first-pass effect and is available to exert a biological effect on target tissues, is known as the *bioavailable fraction*. It is only this portion of the drug that actually has a chance of asserting an impact on the body. For many drugs, 80% to 90% is destroyed by the liver during the first pass. The amount of drug that binds to the receptor at the site of action determines the magnitude of the drug effect. Because children have highly metabolically active hepatic enzymes and an increased renal glomerular filtration rate, they metabolize drugs more rapidly than do adults per unit body weight.

Once a drug or its active metabolite arrives at its target, it must bind to its intended receptor. A receptor is a protein on the cell membrane or within the cell cytoplasm or nucleus that binds to a specific molecule known as a *ligand*, such as a neurotransmitter, hormone, or drug, and initiates a cellular response. The ligand, then, induces a change in the behavior of receptor proteins, resulting in physiological changes within the body. Virtually all biological ligand/receptor bonds are reversible.

The distribution of a drug within the body is determined by a number of factors, including the drug's lipid solubility, the rate of drug absorption from the gastrointestinal tract, the pH of the body fluids, differences in regional blood flow, and the *blood–brain barrier*. The blood–brain barrier is a membrane structure that acts to protect the brain from chemicals in the blood while still allowing essential metabolic functions. It is composed of endothelial cells that are packed very tightly in brain capillaries. This high density of endothelial cells restricts passage of substances from the bloodstream. Finally, the amount of albumin or blood protein can also affect drug distribution, particularly for strongly protein bound drugs, such as divalproex sodium (Depakote). Protein binding leaves only the free and unbound portion to act on the body. A significant decrease in albumin, for example, leads to an increase in free drug within the plasma, greater receptor binding, and a risk of drug toxicity. Conversely, a significant increase in albumin can lead to more protein binding and less drug activity.

Most psychotropic drugs are lipid soluble and must undergo extensive metabolism to make them more polar and water-soluble for excretion. Metabolism involves both Phase 1 and Phase 2 reactions. During Phase 1 reactions, oxidation, reduction, or hydrolysis of the parent drug occurs via various enzymes at different tissue sites. Examples include the cytochrome P450 enzymes, which metabolize many drugs; plasma esterases, which metabolize stimulants; microsomal epoxide hydrolases, which metabolize carbamazepine (Tegretol); and flavin-containing monooxygenases, which degrade clozapine (Clozaril) and olanzapine (Zyprexa). Polar metabolites sometimes have pharmacological activity as well, which can be of greater, lesser, or equal potency to that of the parent drug. Norfluoxetine, for example, a metabolite of fluoxetine (Prozac), has a longer half-life and may be up to five times more potent than the parent drug (Pinna, Costa, & Guidotti, 2006).

The cytochrome P450 (CYP) proteins are a large family of iron- or heme-containing enzymes. The CYP 3A family is the most significant CYP 450 enzyme group, found primarily in the liver and small intestine. The CYP 3A family alone metabolizes approximately 30% to 40% of drugs known to be metabolized by human CYP enzymes. Some drugs are not only *substrates* for a CYP enzyme (e.g., metabolized by the enzyme), but also *inducers* or *inhibitors*, which increase or decrease, respectively, the activity of the enzyme or a related enzyme. Carbamazepine is a well-known inducer of CYP 3A4, for example, which when given with oral contraceptives and other drugs metabolized by this enzyme, increases their metabolism and renders them less effective. Conversely, fluoxetine is a well-known inhibitor of CYP 2D6, which when given with other antidepressants and atomoxetine (Strattera), for example, decreases their metabolism and increases their plasma levels.

Phase 2 pharmacokinetic reactions involve conjugation of Phase 1 metabolites or certain parent drugs with endogenous substrates, such as sulfate, acetate, or glucuronic acid, to produce more water-soluble metabolites for excretion. The products of Phase 2 reactions rarely exhibit pharmacological activity.

Most psychotropic drugs follow *first-order elimination kinetics*. In other words, a constant fraction or percentage of the drug is eliminated per unit time. The rate of drug elimination is proportional to the amount of drug in the body, and the rate will increase or decrease with greater or lesser concentrations, respectively, of the drug. First-order elimination kinetics allow for predictions of the impact of dose changes on plasma drug concentrations. The majority of drugs are eliminated in this way. A first-order reaction depends on the concentration of only one reactant, the drug itself. Whereas a constant fraction of a drug is eliminated per unit time when following first-order kinetics, a constant amount of a drug is eliminated per unit time when following zero-order kinetics.

Zero-order elimination kinetics occur for drugs for which there are a very limited number of metabolizing enzymes, leading to quick saturation of enzyme sites even at normal therapeutic drug concentrations. In other words, zero-order elimination kinetics occur when there is a drug without a lot of enzymes to break it down or when the enzymes present have been overwhelmed or supersaturated. Elimination here is constant over time. There is nothing one can do to change the elimination rate. Zero-order elimination kinetics are followed with alcohol, for example, which is why we can metabolize only approximately 8 to 10 grams per hour or one standard drink (e.g., 1 ounce of hard liquor, 4 ounces of wine, or 12 ounces of beer). A zero-order reaction has a rate that is independent of the concentration of the reactants or amount of the drug. Increasing the concentration of the reacting species or the amount of drug will not speed up the rate of the reaction. Though uncommon, the body will resort to zero-order elimination kinetics even for drugs that typically follow first-order elimination kinetics when enzyme saturation occurs at very high concentrations of any drug.

The *steady state* is the point at which an equilibrium is reached between the amount of drug ingested and the amount of drug eliminated, resulting in no net change in plasma concentration over time. Steady state typically occurs after about four and a half half-lives. Likewise, a drug is essentially entirely eliminated from the body, if no more drug is given, after about four and a half half-lives. The *half-life* ($T_{1/2}$) is the time it takes for the plasma concentration to fall by 50% from the initial plasma concentration of the drug. Half-lives are very helpful in determining dosage intervals, and medications are commonly dosed on a schedule equivalent to the half-life of the drug (see Table A.1). Once the drug reaches steady state, it is not generally necessary to keep to a strict schedule of dosing on the half-life, but it is the surest way of maintaining a steady state with minimal fluctuation.

Most clinicians have observed that children and young adolescents often require larger, weight-adjusted dosages and more frequent dosing than adults in order to achieve comparable blood levels and therapeutic effects with most medications. This variation appears to be due to increased rates of metabolism and elimination in children. There are other differences as well in pediatric pharmacokinetics, including chil-

Table A.1 Drug Half-Life

Fraction of drug eliminated and fraction remaining in the body as a function of half-life

Half-lives (n)	Fraction eliminated (%)	Fraction remaining (%)
1	50.0	50.0
2	75.0	25.0
3	87.5	12.5
4	93.8	6.2
5	96.9	3.1

dren's metabolic capacity, renal elimination, tissue differences, and whole-body water. Children and adolescents have greater metabolic capacity than adults and more rapidly eliminate drugs that utilize hepatic pathways, such as tricyclic antidepressants, antipsychotics, and methylphenidate. After the first year of life, the younger the child, the more rapidly the drug will be metabolized in the liver. Children and adolescents are also more efficient in their renal elimination and excrete drugs that rely solely on renal clearance and are not metabolized by the liver, such as lithium, more rapidly than adults. In addition, younger children have a greater glomerular filtration rate and, therefore, more rapidly move plasma through the kidneys.

Children also differ from adults in terms of body tissue. The proportion of body fat is highest in the first year of life, followed by a steady decrease until another increase at puberty. Compared to adults, most children and adolescents have relatively less fatty tissue, which can lead to differences in drug distribution and increased accumulation of lipophilic or fatty agents and their metabolites in their plasma. Although we might predict higher plasma drug levels in children and adolescents because they have fewer fat stores, their increased metabolic rate often more than compensates for the lower fat stores and leads to a lower plasma drug level than in adults.

Finally, as compared to adults, children have a greater volume of extracellular water. For drugs like lithium that are distributed largely throughout the body water, children will generally have a lower plasma concentration than adults because the volume of water distribution is higher in children. Total body water gradually decreases during childhood to adult values of approximately 55% of body weight by 12 years of age. By approximately 15 years of age, adolescent pharmacokinetic parameters resemble those of adults more so than those of children.

Target receptors on the neural substrates that bind drugs may also be different in children. Children are neurobiologically immature when compared to adults. As discussed in Chapter 10, for example, gamma aminobutyric acid (GABA) receptors are not fully mature until later adolescence. Consequently, children who receive benzodiazepine drugs may have a paradoxical reaction to them. Instead of being calmed or relaxed by these medications, children may become agitated, irritable, or belligerent. Additionally, as discussed in Chapter 12, catecholamine receptors in the central nervous system may not be fully developed until adulthood. The fact that children's immature noradrenergic receptors cannot adequately utilize the tricyclic antidepressants may explain the failure of these medications to treat depression in most studies of youth. Likewise, serotonin neural networks continue to develop throughout the third decade of life, which may explain why serotonergic antidepressants appear to be more effective in adults than in children.

EVALUATION AND TREATMENT

Children and adolescents should have a complete psychiatric and medical evaluation prior to starting psychotropic medications in order to determine the potential risks and benefits of treatment. The standard of care for psychiatric disorders requires a careful diagnostic assessment before the introduction of therapy. Because we lack sufficient data in many areas of child psychiatry, we cannot always rely on research to determine the most efficacious treatments and must borrow heavily from our clinical experience. If a practitioner does not have adequate clinical experience and is not confident in his or her ability to diagnose and treat child and adolescent mental illness, consultation with or referral to a specialist is advised. Although our diagnostic nosology and evaluation methods remain imperfect, without an adequate diagnosis an accurate treatment plan cannot be formulated. Appropriate laboratory examinations should also be completed as indicated before the initiation of pharmacotherapy.

Typically, we stipulate that a child must have received a full physical and neurological exam within the past 12 months prior to initiating treatment. The practitioner, if not completing a physical examination himself or herself, should contact the individual who did the last physical examination prior to prescribing medication. In addition to any indicated blood and urine laboratory examinations, routine vital signs, including blood pressure, pulse, height, and weight, should be ascertained in order to follow growth and cardiac parameters. For children and adolescents taking antipsychotics, routine lab work as described in Chapter 15 should be obtained.

Once psychotropic treatment has been agreed upon, the practitioner should provide extensive psychoeducation to the child or adolescent and the family. Successful treatment may also require educating the teacher, coach, and other important collaterals in the child's life. If the grandmother, for example, spends a great deal of time with the child or has particular influence within the family, she should be educated about the need for treatment as well, because without her support the treatment plan is likely to fail.

Parents must be told about all medication options to treat the target symptoms, in addition to the possible benefits and risks of each treatment being considered. Parents should also be educated about the therapeutic dosage range of medication, the medication schedule and dosage titration, the duration of treatment to achieve the desired effect, plans for managing adverse drug reactions or any emergencies that may arise, and the anticipated length of treatment.

Once medication treatment is initiated, a full trial is advised unless the side effects make continued treatment untenable. Practitioners are encouraged to generally start with a low dosage and titrate upward slowly until the desired treatment effect or dosage is achieved. With the exception of stimulants, psychiatric medications commonly take weeks to exert their intended effects. Even with stimulants, it may take weeks or months to achieve the optimal dose and treatment schedule. Consequently, an adequate trial at a therapeutic dosage is required before an individual is considered a nonresponder.

Some parents will prefer that the practitioner not advise their child about medication side effects prior to initiating treatment. As the parent is the legal guardian, their wishes should be respected, but at the same time the prescriber must inform the child in some way that he or she will be taking a new medication that is designed to treat specific symptoms. Providing too much information on side effects to some children and adolescents, particularly those with high anxiety, is sometimes an error, as they will be so fearful of the potential side effects that they will not try the medication or maintain adherence with the treatment plan.

Finally, clinical management of patients being treated with psychotropic medications should include the following: monitoring the target symptoms; evaluating medication efficacy and the need for additional interventions, such as individual or family psychotherapy; providing ongoing support and education to the family and patient about not only the diagnosis, but also the medication and its use; evaluating the need for educational interventions and supports; and evaluating the need for additional case management services.

BLACK-BOX WARNINGS

Subsequent to the passing of the FDAMA of 1997, a number of pharmaceutical companies began studies of their antidepressants in children and adolescents. In the midst of these studies, it was observed that some youth were reporting thoughts of suicide or self-harm after being treated with an antidepressant. Upon recognition that there appeared to be a pattern, the FDA engaged in a review of all studies of antidepressants in children. Nine medications were included in the FDA's review, including fluoxetine (Prozac), sertraline (Zoloft), paroxetine (Paxil), fluvoxamine

(Luvox), citalopram (Celexa), bupropion (Wellbutrin), venlafaxine (Effexor), nefazodone (Serzone), and mirtazapine (Remeron). The FDA analysis included approximately 4,400 patients in 25 placebo-controlled trials, which ranged from 4 to 16 weeks in duration. Sixteen of these studies were for the treatment of major depressive disorder, four were for obsessive-compulsive disorder, two were for generalized anxiety disorder, two were for ADHD, and one was for social anxiety disorder.

Pooled analyses of these studies found an excess of suicidal ideation noted in children and adolescents taking antidepressants. Roughly 4% of those children and adolescents taking medication versus about 2% of those taking placebo reported thoughts of suicide (Hammad, Laughren, & Racoosin, 2006; U.S. Food and Drug Administration, 2004). A subsequent review incorporated additional studies of antidepressants into this analysis and found lower rates of associated suicidality (Bridge et al., 2007). Regardless, no suicides occurred in these trials, but the FDA could not rule out an increased risk of suicide when using these medications. Given these concerns, black-box warnings suggesting that children and adolescents treated with antidepressants "should be observed closely for clinical worsening, suicidality, or unusual changes in behavior" were added to the packaging of all antidepressants. The release of this data and the subsequent FDA response has had both practitioners and parents concerned.

Although we should be cautious when treating with any medication, additional analyses suggest that antidepressants do considerably more good than harm when treating child and adolescent depression. In a 12- to 16-week study of psychotherapy for the treatment of adolescent depression, for example, 12.5% of teens (11 of 88) reported suicidality at some point during treatment, even though no medications were used and they denied suicidality on initial intake interview (Bridge, Barbe, Birmaher, Kolko, & Brent, 2005). The detection of suicidality was improved by specific and systematic assessment, and self-reported suicidality in the week prior to intake predicted the onset of emergent suicidality more accurately than did interviewer-rated concern, treatment assignment, cognitive distortions, and severity of depression. By contrast, among the 25 studies that the FDA analyzed, the assessment instruments varied, as did the methods of assessing for suicidal ideation. Consequently, it is possible that among these 25 studies, some of these youth would have acknowledged suicidal ideation prior to entry into the study were they systematically assessed.

Following the warnings about a possible association between antidepressants and suicidal ideation and behavior in 2003 and 2004, prescriptions for selective serotonin reuptake inhibitors (SSRIs) for the treatment of child and adolescent depression fell by 22% in both the United States and the Netherlands. Between 2003 and 2005, the youth suicide rate increased by 49% in the Netherlands; similarly, the rate increased by 14% in the United States between 2003 and 2004 (Gibbons et al., 2007). These data suggest that for every 20% decline in antidepressant use among patients of all ages in the United States, an additional 3,040 suicides per year would occur. Although not proof of causation, certainly the timing between the antidepressant warnings and subsequent decrease in prescriptions correlates well with the increases in suicide rates. Elevated rates of suicide among youth in the United States persisted between 2004 and 2005, suggesting that the increase seen in the United States between 2003 and 2004 was not an isolated event (Bridge, Greenhouse, Weldon, Campo, & Kelleher, 2008).

Additional data suggest that antidepressant sales of fluoxetine and other SSRIs may be tied to a decrease in overall suicide rate. The U.S. suicide rate held fairly steady for 15 years from 1973 to 1988 at between 12.2 and 13.7 per 100,000. After the introduction of fluoxetine in 1988, the suicide rate gradually declined to 10.4 per 100,000 by the year 2000. This drop was associated with an increase in fluoxetine prescriptions from 2.47 million in 1988 to 33.32 million in 2002. The estimated decrease in suicides during this period totals 33,600. These data suggest that it may have been the increased availability of antidepressants that led to the decrease in suicides (Licinio & Wong, 2005).

Regardless of these studies, we do know that the risk of suicide increases for those with chronic as opposed to acute depression and that the vast majority of teen suicide completers are not taking an antidepressant at the time of the event. About 32,000 Americans commit suicide each year. If antidepressants were responsible for large numbers of suicides, then the reduction in prescriptions should have caused a decrease in the suicide rate. Instead, we saw the opposite. It would appear, then, that the slight increased risk of suicidal thinking as reported by the FDA among children and adolescents is more than balanced out by the protective effect of these medications for the majority of those who take them.

References

AACAP Work Group on Stimulant Medications. (2002). Practice parameter for the use of stimulant medications in the treatment of children, adolescents, and adults. *Journal of the American Academy of Child and Adolescent Psychiatry, 41*(2), 26S–49S.

Abdelghany, S., Hughes, J., Lammers, J., Wellbrock, B., Buffington, P. J., & Shank, R. A. (2001). Biofeedback and electrical stimulation therapy for treating urinary incontinence and voiding dysfunction: One center's experience. *Urologic Nursing, 21*(6), 401–405, 410.

Abelson, J. F., Kwan, K. Y., O'Roak, B. J., Baek, D. Y., Stillman, A. A., Morgan, T. M., . . . State, M. W. (2005). Sequence variants in SLITRK1 are associated with Tourette's syndrome. *Science, 310,* 317–320.

Abikoff, H., Gallagher, R., Wells, K. C., Murray, D. W., Huang, L., Lu, F., & Petkova, E. (2013). Remediating organizational functioning in children with ADHD: Immediate and long-term effects from a randomized controlled trial. *Journal of Consulting and Clinical Psychology, 81*(1): 113–128.

Aboa-Eboulé, C., Brisson, C., Maunsell, E., Mâsse, B., Bourbonnais, R., Vézina, M., . . . Dagenais, G. R. (2007). Job strain and risk of acute recovery coronary heart disease events. *Journal of the American Medical Association, 298*(14), 1652–1660.

Accreditation Council for Graduate Medical Education. (2007). *Child and adolescent psychiatry program requirements.* Retrieved April 5, 2009, from http://www.acgme.org/acWebsite/downloads/RRC_progReq/320pr0101 2006.pdf

Addington, J., Van Mastrigt, S., & Addington, D. (2004). Duration of untreated psychosis: Impact on 2-year outcome. *Psychological Medicine, 34*(2), 277–284.

Adolphs, R., Baron-Cohen, S., & Tranel, D. (2002). Impaired recognition of social emotions following amygdala damage. *Journal of Cognitive Neuroscience, 14(8),* 1264-1274.

Ainsworth, M. D. S., Blehar, M. C., Waters, E., & Wall, S. (1978). *Patterns of attachment: A psychological study of the Strange Situation.* Hillsdale, NJ: Lawrence Erlbaum.

Alam, M. N., McGinty, D., & Szymusiak, R. (1995). Neuronal discharge of pre-optic/anterior hypothalamic thermosensitive neurons: Relation to NREM sleep. *American Journal of Physiology, 269*(5), R1240–R1249.

Alm, B., Lagercrantz, H., & Wennergren, G. (2006). Stop SIDS—sleeping solitary supine, sucking soother, stopping smoking substitutes. *Acta Paediatrica, 95*(3), 260–262.

Aman, M. G., Arnold, L. E., & Armstrong, S. C. (1999). Review of serotonergic agents and perseverative behavior in patients with developmental disabilities. *Mental Retardation and Developmental Disabilities, 5,* 279–289.

Aman, M. G., Collier-Crespin, A., & Lindsay, R. L. (2000). Pharmacotherapy of disorders in mental retardation. *European Child and Adolescent Psychiatry, 1,* 198–207.

Aman, M. G., De Smedt, G., Derivan, A., Lyons, B., & Findling, R. L. (2002). Double-blind, placebo-controlled study of risperidone for the treatment of disruptive behaviors in children with subaverage intelligence. *American Journal of Psychiatry, 159,* 1337–1346.

American Diabetes Association. (2004). Consensus development conference on antipsychotic drugs and obesity (Consensus statement). *Diabetes Care, 27,* 596–601.

American Foundation for Suicide Prevention. (n.d.). *Facts and figures.* Retrieved September 13, 2014, from https://www.afsp.org/understanding-suicide/facts-and-figures

American Medical Association, Physician Masterfile. (2012). Data decoded by the American Academy of Child and Adolescent Psychiatry, March 2013.

American Psychiatric Association. (1952). *Diagnostic and statistical manual of mental disorders.* Washington, DC: Author.

American Psychiatric Association. (1968). *Diagnostic and statistical manual of mental disorders* (2nd ed.). Washington, DC: Author.

American Psychiatric Association. (1980). *Diagnostic and statistical manual of mental disorders* (3rd ed.). Washington, DC: Author.

American Psychiatric Association. (1987). *Diagnostic and statistical manual of mental disorders* (Rev. 3rd ed.). Washington, DC: Author.

American Psychiatric Association. (1994). *Diagnostic and statistical manual of mental disorders* (4th ed.). Washington, DC: Author.

American Psychiatric Association. (2000). *Diagnostic and statistical manual of mental disorders* (4th ed., text revision). Washington, DC: Author.

American Psychiatric Association. (2006). Treatment of patients with eating disorders. *American Journal of Psychiatry, 163*(7), 4–54.

American Psychiatric Association. (2013). *Diagnostic and statistical manual of mental disorders* (5th ed.). Washington, DC: Author.

American Sleep Disorders Association. (2007). *International classification of sleep disorders: Diagnostic and coding manual, ICSD-R.* Westchester, IL: American Academy of Sleep Medicine.

Amiri, S., Farhang, S., Ghoreishizadeh, M. A., Malek, A., & Mohammadzadeh, S. (2012). Double-blind controlled trial of venlafaxine for treatment of adults with attention deficit/hyperactivity disorder. *Human Psychopharmacology: Clinical and Experimental, 27*(1): 76–81.

Amitai, Y., & Frischer, H. (2006). Excess fatality from desipramine in children and adolescents. *Journal of the American Academy of Child and Adolescent Psychiatry, 45*(1), 54–60.

Anderson, J. C., Williams, S., McGee, R., & Silva, P. A. (1987). *DSM-III* disorders in preadolescent children. Prevalence in a large sample from the general population. *Archives of General Psychiatry, 44*(1), 69–76.

Anderson, J. R. (2000). *Cognitive psychology and its implications* (5th ed.). New York, NY: Worth.

Anderson, K. J., Revelle, W., & Lynch, M. J. (1989). Caffeine, impulsivity, and memory scanning: A comparison of two explanations for the Yerkes-Dodson Effect. *Motivation and Emotion, 13,* 1–20.

Anderson, R. N., & Smith, B. L. (2005). Deaths: Leading causes for 2002. *National Vital Statistics Reports, 53*(17), 1–89.

Andreasen, N. C., Rezai, K., Alliger, R., Swayze, V. W., Flaum, M., Kirchner, P., . . . O'Leary, D. S. (1992). Hypofrontality in neuroleptic-naive patients and in patients with chronic schizophrenia. Assessment with xenon 133 single-photon emission computed tomography and the Tower of London. *Archives of General Psychiatry, 49*(12), 943–958.

Angold, A., & Costello, E. J. (1993). Depressive comorbidity in children and adolescents: Empirical, theoretical, and methodological issues. *American Journal of Psychiatry, 150,* 1779–1791.

Angold, A., Costello, E. J., Farmer, E. M., Burns, B. J., & Erkanli, A. (1999). Impaired but undiagnosed. *Journal of the American Academy of Child and Adolescent Psychiatry, 38*(2), 129–137.

Angst, J. (1999). Major depression in 1998: Are we providing optimal therapy? *Journal of Clinical Psychiatry, 60*(6), 5–9.

Angst, J., & Vollrath, M. (1991). The natural history of anxiety disorders. *Acta Psychiatrica Scandinavica, 84*(5), 446–452.

Anthony, J. C., Warner, L. A., & Kessler, R. C. (1994). Comparative epidemiology of dependence on tobacco, alcohol, controlled substances, and inhalants: Basic findings from the National Comorbidity Survey. *Experimental and Clinical Psychopharmacology, 2(3),* 244–268.

Antochi, R., Stavrakaki, C., & Emery, P. C. (2003). Psychopharmacological treatments in persons with dual diagnosis of psychiatric disorders and developmental disabilities. *Postgraduate Medicine Journal, 9,* 139–146.

Apter, A., Pauls, D. L., Bleich, A., Zohar, A. H., Kron, S., Ratzoni, G., . . . Cohen, D. J. (1993). An epidemiologic study of Gilles de la Tourette's syndrome in Israel. *Archives of General Psychiatry, 50*(9), 734–738.

Arias, E., MacDorman, M. F., Strobino, D. M., & Guyer, B. (2003). Annual summary of vital statistics—2002. *Pediatrics, 112*(6), 1215–1230.

Aristotle. *Nicomachean ethics* (Number II. 1109a27; A. I. Bekker, Trans.). http://www.perseus.tufts.edu/hopper/text?doc=Perseus%3Atext%3A1999.01.0054%3Abekker+page%3D1109a

Arnold, L. E. (2000). Methylphenidate vs. amphetamine: Comparative review. *Journal of Attention Disorders, 3*(4), 200–211.

Atkin, C. K. (1995). Survey and experimental research on effects of alcohol advertising. In S. Martin (Ed.), *Mass media and the use and abuse of alcohol* (pp. 39–68). Rockville, MD: National Institute on Alcohol Abuse and Alcoholism.

Avery, K. (2009). The coffee trade and its MDG ramifications. *UN Chronicle, Online Edition*. Retrieved January 28, 2009, from http://www.un.org/Pubs/chronicle/2007/webArticles/111407_coffee_trade.html

Ayers, T. S., Sandler, I. N., West, S. G., & Roosa, M. W. (1996). A dispositional and situational assessment of children's coping: Testing alternative models of coping. *Journal of Personality, 64*(4), 923–958.

Babor, T. F., Hofmann, M., DelBoca, F. K., Hesselbrock, V., Meyer, R. E., Dolinsky, Z. S., & Rounsaville, B. (1992). Types of alcoholics: I. Evidence for an empirically derived typology based on indicators of vulnerability and severity. *Archives of General Psychiatry, 49*(8), 599–608.

Bailey, A., Le Couteur, A., Gottesman, I., Bolton, P., Simonoff, E., Yuzda, E., & Rutter, M. (1995). Autism as a strongly genetic disorder: Evidence from a British twin study. *Psychological Medicine, 25*(1), 63–78.

Baird, G., Pickles, A., Simonoff, E., Charman, T., Sullivan, P., Chandler, S., . . . Brown, D. (2008). Measles vaccination and antibody response in autism spectrum disorders. *Archives of Disease in Childhood, 93*, 832–837.

Bangs, M. E., Jin, L., Zhang, S., Desaiah, D., Allen, A. J., Read, H. A., & Wernicke, J. F. (2008). Hepatic events associated with atomoxetine treatment for attention-deficit hyperactivity disorder. *Drug Safety, 31*(4), 345–354.

Barbaresi, W. J., Katusic, S. K., Colligan, R. C., Weaver, A. L., & Jacobsen, S. J. (2007). Modifiers of long-term school outcomes for children with attention-deficit/hyperactivity disorder: Does treatment with a stimulant medication make a difference? Results from a population-based study. *Journal of Developmental Behavioral Pediatrics, 28*(4): 274–287.

Barbosa, J., Tannock, R., & Manassis, K. (2002). Measuring anxiety: Parent–child reporting differences in clinical samples. *Depression and Anxiety, 15*(2), 61–65.

Barkley, R. A. (1998). *Attention-deficit hyperactivity disorder: A handbook for diagnosis and treatment* (2nd ed.). New York, NY: Guilford Press.

Barkley, R. A., Murphy, K. R., & Kwasnik, D. (1996). Motor vehicle driving competencies and risks in teens and young adults with attention deficit hyperactivity disorder. *Pediatrics, 98*(6), 1089–1095.

Baron-Cohen, S., Allen, J., & Gillberg, C. (1992). Can autism be detected at 18 months? The needle, the haystack, and the CHAT. *British Journal of Psychiatry, 161,* 839–843.

Baron-Cohen, S., Cox, A., Baird, G., Swettenham, J., Nightingale, N., Morgan, K., . . . Charman, T. (1996). Psychological markers in the detection of autism in infancy in a large population. *British Journal of Psychiatry, 168,* 158–163.

Barrett, P. M., Farrell, L., Pina, A. A., Peris, T. S., & Piacentini, J. (2008). Evidence-based psychosocial treatments for child and adolescent obsessive-compulsive disorder. *Journal of Clinical Child and Adolescent Psychology, 37*(1), 131–155.

Barrett, T. B., Hauger, R. L., Kennedy, J. L., Sadovnick, A. D., Remick, R. A., Keck, P. E., . . . Kelson, J. R. (2003). Evidence that a single nucleotide polymorphism in the promoter of the G protein receptor kinase 3 gene is associated with bipolar disorder. *Molecular Psychiatry, 8*(5), 546–557.

Batshaw, M. L. (1993). Mental retardation. *Pediatric Clinics of North America, 40,* 507–521.

Baum, A. E., Akula, N., Cabanero, M., Cardona, I., Corona, W., Klemens, B., . . . McMahon, F. J. (2008). A genome-wide association study implicates diacylglycerol kinase eta (DGKH) and several other genes in the etiology of bipolar disorder. *Molecular Psychiatry, 13*(2), 197–207.

Bawden, H. N., Stokes, A., Camfield, C. S., Camfield, P. R., & Salisbury, S. (1998). Peer relationship problems in children with Tourette's disorder or diabetes mellitus. *Journal of Child Psychology and Psychiatry, 39*(5), 663–668.

Baxter, A. J., & Krenzelok, E. P. (2008). Pediatric fatality secondary to EDTA chelation. *Clinical Toxicology, 23,* 1–2.

Baxter, L. R., Schwartz, J. M., Bergman, K. S., Szuba, M. P., Guze, B. H., Mazziotta, J. C., . . . Phelps, M. E. (1992). Caudate glucose metabolic rate changes with both drug and behavior therapy for obsessive-compulsive disorder. *Archives of General Psychiatry, 49,* 681–689.

Bean, M. K., Stewart, K., & Olbrisch, M. E. (2008). Obesity in America: Implications for clinical and health psychologists. *Journal of Clinical Psychology in Medical Settings, 15*(3), 214–224.

Beardslee, W. R., Versage, E. M., & Gladstone, T. R. (1998). Children of affectively ill parents: A review of the past 10 years. *Journal of the American Academy of Child and Adolescent Psychiatry, 37*(11), 1134–1141.

Beauchamp, G., & Gagnon, A. (2004). Influence of diagnostic classification on gender ratio in schizophrenia: A meta-analysis of youths hospitalized for psychosis. *Social Psychiatry and Psychiatric Epidemiology, 39*(12), 1017–1022.

Beck, A. T., Rush, J. A., Shaw, B. F., & Emery, G. (1979). *Cognitive therapy of depression.* New York, NY: Guilford Press.

Beitchman, J. H., Cantwell, D. P., Forness, S. R., Kavale, K. A., & Kauffman, J. M. (1998). Practice parameters for the assessment and treatment of children and adolescents with language and learning disorders. *Journal of the American Academy of Child and Adolescent Psychiatry, 37*(10), 46S–62S.

Beitchman, J. H., & Youn, A. R. (1997). Learning disorders with a special emphasis on reading disorders: A review of the past 10 years. *Journal of the American Academy of Child and Adolescent Psychiatry, 36*(8), 1020–1032.

Belardinelli, C., Hatch, J. P., Olvera, R. L., Fonseca, M., Caetano, S. C., Nicoletti, M., . . . Soares, J. C. (2008). Family environment patterns in families with bipolar children. *Journal of Affective Disorders, 107*(1–3), 299–305.

Bell-Dolan, D. J., Last, C. G., & Strauss, C. C. (1990). Symptoms of anxiety disorders in normal children. *Journal of the American Academy of Child and Adolescent Psychiatry, 29*(5), 759–765.

Bellini, S., & Peters, J. K. (2008). Social skills training for youth with autism spectrum disorders. *Child and Adolescent Psychiatric Clinics of North America, 17*(4), 857–873.

Ben-Shachar, D., Bonne, O., Chisin, R., Klein, E., Lester, H., Aharon-Peretz, J., . . . Freedman, N. (2007). Cerebral glucose utilization and platelet mitochondrial complex I activity in schizophrenia: A FDG-PET study. *Progress in Neuropsychopharmacology and Biological Psychiatry, 31*(4), 807–813.

Berard, R., Fong, R., Carpenter, D. J., Thomason, C., & Wilkinson, C. (2006). An international, multicenter, placebo-controlled trial of paroxetine in adolescents with major depressive disorder. *Journal of Child and Adolescent Psychopharmacology, 16*(1–2), 59–75.

Berney, T., Kolvin, I., Bhate, S. R., Garside, R. F., Jeans, J., Kay, B., & Scarth, L (1981). School phobia: A therapeutic trial with clomipramine and short-term outcome. *British Journal of Psychiatry, 138*, 110–118.

Bernstein, G. A., Borchardt, C. M., & Perwien, A. R. (1996). Anxiety disorders in children and adolescents: A review of the past 10 years. *Journal of the American Academy of Child and Adolescent Psychiatry, 35*(9), 1110–1119.

Bernstein, G. A., Borchardt, C. M., Perwien, A. R., Crosby, R. D., Kushner, M. G., Thuras, P. D., & Last, C. G. (2000). Imipramine plus cognitive-behavioral therapy in the treatment of school refusal. *Journal of the American Academy of Child and Adolescent Psychiatry, 39*, 276–283.

Bernstein, G. A., Garfinkel, B. D., & Borchardt, C. M. (1990). Comparative studies of pharmacotherapy for school refusal. *Journal of the American Academy of Child and Adolescent Psychiatry, 29*(5), 773–781.

Bernstein, G. A., Hektner, J. M., Borchardt, C. M., & McMillan, M. H. (2001). Treatment of school refusal: One-year follow-up. *Journal of the American Academy of Child and Adolescent Psychiatry, 40*(2), 206–213.

Berry-Kravis, E., Sumis, A., Hervey, C., Nelson, M., Porges, S. W., Weng, N., . . . Greenough, W. T. (2008). Open-label treatment trial of lithium to target the underlying defect in fragile X syndrome. *Journal of Development and Behavioral Pediatrics, 29*(4): 293–302.

Biederman, J., Faraone, S. V., Hirshfeld-Becker, D. R., Friedman, D., Robin, J. A., & Rosenbaum, J. F. (2001). Patterns of psychopathology and dysfunction in high-risk children of parents with panic disorder and major depression. *American Journal of Psychiatry, 158*, 49–57.

Biederman, J., Faraone, S. V., Marrs, A., Moore, P., Garcia, J., Ablon, S., . . .

Kearns, E. (1997). Panic disorder and agoraphobia in consecutively referred children and adolescents. *Journal of the American Academy of Child and Adolescent Psychiatry, 36*(2), 214–223.

Biederman, J., Faraone, S., Milberger, S., Guite, J., Mick, E., Chen, L., & Perrin, J. (1996). A prospective 4-year follow-up study of attention-deficit hyperactivity and related disorders. *Archives of General Psychiatry, 53*(5), 437–446.

Biederman, J., Melmed, R. D., Patel, A., McBurnett, K., Konow, J., Lyne, A., & Scherer, N. (2008). A randomized, double-blind, placebo-controlled study of guanfacine extended release in children and adolescents with attention-deficit/hyperactivity disorder. *Pediatrics, 121*(1), e73–e84.

Biederman, J., Monuteaux, M. C., Spencer, T., Wilens, T. E., & Faraone, S. V. (2009). Do stimulants protect against psychiatric disorders in youth with ADHD? A 10-year follow-up study. *Pediatrics, 124,* 71–78.

Biederman, J., Petty, C. R., Fried, R., Kaiser, R., Dolan, C. R., Schoenfeld, S., . . . Faraone, S. V. (2008). Educational and occupational underattainment in adults with attention-deficit/hyperactivity disorder: A controlled study. *Journal of Clinical Psychiatry, 69*(8), 1217–1222.

Biederman, J., & Pliszka, S. R. (2008). Modafinil improves symptoms of attention deficit/hyperactivity disorder across subtypes in children and adolescents. *Journal of Pediatrics, 152*(3), 394–399.

Biederman, J., Rosenbaum, J. F., Bolduc-Murphy, E. A., Faraone, S. V., Chaloff, J., Hirshfeld, D. R., & Kagan, J. (1993). A 3-year follow-up of children with and without behavioral inhibition. *Journal of the American Academy of Child and Adolescent Psychiatry, 32*(4), 814–821.

Biederman, J., Spencer, T. J., Wilens, T. E., Prince, J. B., & Faraone, S. V. (2006). Treatment of ADHD with stimulant medications: Response to Nissen perspective in *The New England Journal of Medicine*. *Journal of the American Academy of Child and Adolescent Psychiatry, 45*(10), 1147–1150.

Biederman, J., Wilens, T. E., Mick, E., Faraone, S. V., & Spencer, T. (1998). Does attention-deficit hyperactivity disorder impact the developmental course of drug and alcohol abuse and dependence? *Biological Psychiatry, 44*(4), 269–273.

Birmaher, B. (2007). Longitudinal course of pediatric bipolar disorder. *American Journal of Psychiatry, 164*(4), 537–539.

Birmaher, B., Axelson, D., Goldstein, B., Strober, M., Gill, M. K., Hunt, J., . . . Keller, M. (2009). Four-year longitudinal course of children and adolescents with bipolar spectrum disorder. *American Journal of Psychiatry, 166*(7), 795–804.

Birmaher, B., Axelson, D. A., Monk, K., Kalas, C., Clark, D. B., Ehmann, M., . . . Brent, D. A. (2003). Fluoxetine for the treatment of childhood anxiety disorders. *Journal of the American Academy of Child and Adolescent Psychiatry, 42,* 415–423.

Birmaher, B., Axelson, D., Strober, M., Gill, M. K., Valeri, S., Chiappetta, L., . . . Keller, M. (2006). Clinical course of children and adolescents with bipolar spectrum disorders. *Archives of General Psychiatry, 63*(2), 175–183.

Birmaher, B., & Brent, D. (1998). Practice parameters for the assessment and treatment of children and adolescents with depressive disorders. *Journal of the American Academy of Child and Adolescent Psychiatry, 37*(10), 635–835.

Birmaher, B., Brent, D. A., Kolko, D., Baugher, M., Bridge, J., & Holder, D. (2000). Clinical outcome after short-term psychotherapy for adolescents with major depressive disorder. *Archives of General Psychiatry, 57*(1), 29–36.

Birmaher, B., Ryan, N. D., Williamson, D. E., Brent, D. A., & Kaufman, J. (1996). Childhood and adolescent depression: A review of the past 10 years: Part II. *Journal of the American Academy of Child and Adolescent Psychiatry, 35*(12), 1575–1583.

Bissada, H., Tasca, G. A., Barber, A. M., & Bradwejn, J. (2008). Olanzapine in the treatment of low body weight and obsessive thinking in women with anorexia nervosa: A randomized, double-blind, placebo-controlled trial. *American Journal of Psychiatry, 165*(10), 1281–1288.

Bitsko, R. H., Holbrook, J. R., Visser, S. N., Mink, J. W., Zinner, S. H., Ghandour, R. M., & Blumberg, S. J. (2014). A national profile of Tourette syndrome, 2011–2012. *Journal of Developmental and Behavioral Pediatrics, 35*(5), 317–322.

Black, B., & Uhde, T. W. (1992). Case study: Elective mutism as a variant of social phobia. *Journal of the American Academy of Child and Adolescent Psychiatry, 31*(6), 1090–1094.

Black, B., & Uhde, T. W. (1994). Treatment of elective mutism with fluoxetine: A double-blind, placebo-controlled study. *Journal of the American Academy of Child and Adolescent Psychiatry, 33,* 1000–1006.

Blackorby, J., & Wagner, M. (1996). Longitudinal post school outcomes of youth with disabilities: Findings from the National Longitudinal Transition Study. *Exceptional Children, 62*(5), 399–413.

Blader, J. C., & Carlson, G. A. (2007). Increased rates of bipolar disorder diagnoses among U.S. child, adolescent, and adult inpatients, 1996–2004. *Biological Psychiatry, 62*(2), 107–114.

Blader, J. C., Koplewicz, H. S., Abikoff, H., & Foley, C. (1997). Sleep problems of elementary school children: A community survey. *Archives of Pediatrics and Adolescent Medicine, 151*(5), 473–480.

Bleuler, M. (1978). *The schizophrenic disorders: Long-term patient and family studies.* London, UK: Yale University Press.

Bloch, M. H., Landeros-Weisenberger, A., Kelmendi, B., Coric, V., Bracken, M. B., & Leckman, J. F. (2006). A systematic review: Antipsychotic augmentation with treatment refractory obsessive-compulsive disorder. *Molecular Psychiatry, 11*(7), 622–632.

Bloch, M. H., Leckman, J. F., Zhu, H., & Peterson, B. S. (2005). Caudate volumes in childhood predict symptom severity in adults with Tourette syndrome. *Neurology, 65*(8), 1253–1258.

Blunden, S., Lushington, K., Kennedy, D., Martin, J., & Dawson, D. (2000). Behavior and neurocognitive performance in children aged 5–10 years who snore compared to controls. *Journal of Clinical and Experimental Neuropsychology, 5,* 554.

Boachie, A., Goldfield, G. S., & Spettigue, W. (2003). Olanzapine use as an adjunctive treatment for hospitalized children with anorexia nervosa: Case reports. *International Journal of Eating Disorders, 33*(1), 98–103.

Boney-McCoy, S., & Finkelhor, D. (1995). Psychosocial sequelae of violent victimization in a national youth sample. *Journal of Consulting and Clinical Psychology, 63,* 726–736.

Bongers, I. L., Koot, H. M., van der Ende, J., & Verhulst, F. C. (2003). The normative development of child and adolescent problem behaviour. *Journal of Abnormal Psychology, 112,* 179–192.

Bookheimer, S. Y., Ting Wang, A., Scott, A., Sigman, M., & Dapretto, M. (2008). Frontal contributions to face processing differences in autism: Evidence from fMRI of inverted face processing. *Journal of the International Neuropsychological Society, 14,* 922–932.

Borbély, A. A. (1982). A two process model of sleep regulation. *Human Neurobiology, 1*(3), 195–204.

Borchardt, C. M., & Bernstein, G. A. (1995). Comorbid disorders in hospitalized bipolar adolescents compared with unipolar depressed adolescents. *Child Psychiatry and Human Development, 26*(1), 11–18.

Borcherding, B. G., Keysor, C. S., Rapoport, J. L., Elia, J., & Amass, J. (1990). Motor/vocal tics and compulsive behaviors on stimulant drugs: Is there a common vulnerability? *Psychiatry Research, 33,* 83–94.

Borkman, T., Kaskutas, L. A., & Owen, P. (2008). Contrasting and converging philosophies of three models of alcohol/other drugs treatment: Minnesota model, social model, and addiction therapeutic communities. *Alcoholism Treatment Quarterly, 25*(3), 21–38.

Bottlender, R., Sato, T., Jäger, M., Wegener, U., Wittmann, J., Strauss, A., & Möller, H.-J. (2003). The impact of the duration of untreated psychosis prior to first psychiatric admission on the 15-year outcome in schizophrenia. *Schizophrenia Research, 62*(1–2), 37–44.

Bowen, R. C., Offord, D. R., & Boyle, M. H. (1990). The prevalence of overanxious disorder and separation anxiety disorder: Results from the Ontario Child Health Study. *Journal of the American Academy of Child and Adolescent Psychiatry, 29*(5), 753–758.

Bradley, C. (1937). The behavior of children receiving Benzedrine. *American Journal of Psychiatry, 94,* 577–585.

Bradley, S. J., Jadaa, D.-A., Brody, J., Landy, S., Tallett, S. E., Watson, W., . . . Stephens, D. (2003). Brief psychoeducational parenting program: An evaluation and 1-year follow-up. *Journal of the American Academy of Child and Adolescent Psychiatry, 42*(10), 1171–1178.

Brady, J. P. (1991). The pharmacology of stuttering: A critical review. *American Journal of Psychiatry, 148,* 1309–1316.

Brambilla, F., Garcia, C. S., Fassino, S., Daga, G. A., Favaro, A., Santonastaso, P., . . . Monteleone, P. (2007). Olanzapine therapy in anorexia nervosa:

Psychobiological effects. *International Clinical Psychopharmacology, 22*(4), 197–204.

Brawn, T. P., Fenn, K. M., Nusbaum, H. C., & Margoliash, D. (2008). Consolidation of sensorimotor learning during sleep. *Learning and Memory, 15*(11), 815–819.

Bregman, J. D. (1991). Current developments in the understanding of mental retardation: Part II. Psychopathology. *Journal of the American Academy of Child and Adolescent Psychiatry, 30*(6), 861–872.

Brent, D., Emslie, G., Clarke, G., Wagner, K. D., Asarnow, J. R., Keller, M., . . . Zelazny, J. (2008). Switching to another SSRI or to venlafaxine with or without cognitive behavioral therapy for adolescents with SSRI-resistant depression: The TORDIA randomized controlled trial. *Journal of the American Medical Association, 299*(8), 901–913.

Brent, D. A., Holder, D., Kolko, D., Birmaher, B., Baugher, M., Roth, C., . . . Johnson, B. A. (1997). A clinical psychotherapy trial for adolescent depression comparing cognitive, family, and supportive therapy. *Archives of General Psychiatry, 54*(9), 877–885.

Brent, D. A., Kalas, R., Edelbrock, C., Costello, A. J., Dulcan, M. K., & Conover, N. (1986). Psychopathology and its relationship to suicidal ideation in childhood and adolescence. *Journal of the American Academy of Child and Adolescent Psychiatry, 25,* 666–673.

Bridge, J. A., Barbe, R. P., Birmaher, B., Kolko, D. J., & Brent, D. A. (2005). Emergent suicidality in a clinical psychotherapy trial for adolescent depression. *American Journal of Psychiatry, 162*(11), 2173–2175.

Bridge, J. A., Birmaher, B., Iyengar, S., Barbe, R. P., & Brent, D. A. (2008). Placebo response in randomized controlled trials of antidepressants for pediatric major depressive disorder. *American Journal of Psychiatry, 166,* 42–49.

Bridge, J. A., Greenhouse, J. B., Weldon, A. H., Campo, J. V., & Kelleher, K. J. (2008). Suicide trends among youths aged 10 to 19 years in the United States, 1996–2005. *Journal of the American Medical Association, 300*(9), 1025–1026.

Bridge, J. A., Iyengar, S., Salary, C. B., Barbe, R. P., Birmaher, B., Pincus, H. A., . . . Brent, D. A. (2007). Clinical response and risk for reported suicidal ideation and suicide attempts in pediatric antidepressant treatment: A meta-analysis of randomized controlled trials. *Journal of the American Medical Association, 297*(15), 1683–1696.

Brizendine, L. (2006). *The female brain.* New York, NY: Morgan Road Books.

Broadhurst, P. L. (1957). *Emotional Psychology, 54,* 345–352.

Brooks-Gunn, J., & Duncan, C. J. (1997). The effects of poverty on children. *Future of Children, 7*(2), 55–71.

Broughton, R., Billings, R., Cartwright, R., Doucette, D., Edmeads, J., Edwardh, M., . . . Turrell, G. (1994). Homicidal somnambulism: A case report. *Sleep, 17*(3), 253–264.

Brown, A. S., Begg, M. D., Gravenstein, S., Schaefer, C. A., Wyatt, R. J., Bresnahan, M., . . . Susser, E. S. (2004). Serologic evidence of prenatal influenza in the etiology of schizophrenia. *Archives of General Psychiatry, 61,* 774–780.

Brown, A. S., Schaefer, C. A., Wyatt, R. J., Begg, M. D., Goetz, R., Bresnahan, M. A., . . . Susser, E. S. (2002). Paternal age and risk of schizophrenia in adult offspring. *American Journal of Psychiatry, 159*(9), 1528–1533.

Brown, R., Colter, N., Corsellis, J. A., Crow, T. J., Frith, C. D., Jagoe, R., & Johnstone, E. C. (1986). Postmortem evidence of structural brain changes in schizophrenia. Differences in brain weight, temporal horn area, and parahippocampal gyrus compared with affective disorder. *Archives of General Psychiatry, 43*(1), 36–42.

Brownell, K. D., & Napolitano, M. A. (1995). Distorting reality for children: Body size proportions of Barbie and Ken dolls. *International Journal of Eating Disorders, 18*(3), 295–298.

Bruch, H. (1962). Perceptual and conceptual disturbances in anorexia nervosa. *Psychosomatic Medicine, 24,* 187–194.

Brumberg, J. J. (1988). *Fasting girls: The emergence of anorexia nervosa as a modern disease.* Cambridge, MA: Harvard University Press.

Brumberg, J. J. (2000). *Fasting girls: The history of anorexia nervosa.* New York, NY: Vintage Books.

Bryan, T. (1991). Assessment of social cognition: Review of research in learning disabilities. In L. H. Swanson (Ed.), *Handbook on the assessment of learning disabilities: Theory, research and practice* (pp. 285–311). Austin, TX: Pro-Ed.

Buguet, A. (2007). Sleep under extreme environments: Effects of heat and cold exposure, altitude, hyperbaric pressure and microgravity in space. *Journal of the Neurological Sciences, 262*(1–2), 145–152.

Bukstein, O. G., Glancy, L. J., & Kaminer, Y. (1992). Patterns of affective comorbidity in a clinical population of dually diagnosed adolescent substance users. *Journal of the American Academy of Child and Adolescent Psychiatry, 31,* 1041–1045.

Bull, L. (2007). Sunflower therapy for children with specific learning difficulties (dyslexia): A randomised, controlled trial. *Complement Therapies Clinical Practical, 13,* 15–24.

Burke, J. D., Loeber, R., & Birmaher, B. (2002). Oppositional defiant and conduct disorder: A review of the past 10 years: Part II. *Journal of the American Academy of Child and Adolescent Psychiatry, 41*(11), 1275–1293.

Byrd, R. S., Weitzman, M., Lanphear, N. E., & Auinger, P. (1996). Bed-wetting in US children: Epidemiology and related behavior problems. *Pediatrics, 98,* 414–419.

Campbell, M., Cohen, I. L., & Small, A. M. (1982). Drugs in aggressive behavior. *Journal of the American Academy of Child and Adolescent Psychiatry, 21,* 107–117.

Campbell, M., Small, A. M., Green, W. H., Jennings, S. J., Perry, R., Bennett, W. G., . . . Anderson, L. (1985). Behavioral efficacy of haloperidol and lithium carbonate: A comparison in hospitalized aggressive children with conduct disorder. *Archives of General Psychiatry, 41,* 650–656.

Cannon, T. D., Cadenhead, K., Cornblatt, B., Woods, S. W., Addington, J., Walker, E., . . . Heinssen, R. (2008). Prediction of psychosis in youth at high clinical risk: A multisite longitudinal study in North America. *Archives of General Psychiatry, 65*(1), 28–37.

Cantwell, D. (1996). Attention deficit disorder: A review of the past 10 years. *Journal of the American Academy of Child and Adolescent Psychiatry, 35*(8), 978–987.

Carandang, C., Robbins, D., Mullany, E., Yazbek, M., & Minot, S. (2007). Lamotrigine in adolescent mood disorders: A retrospective chart review. *Journal of the Canadian Academy of Child and Adolescent Psychiatry, 16*(1), 1–8.

Cardno, A. G., & Gottesman, I. I. (2000). Twin studies of schizophrenia: From bow-and arrow concordances to star Wars Mx and functional genomics. *American Journal of Medical Genetics, 97*(1), 12–17.

Cardno, A. G., Marshall, E. J., Coid, B., Macdonald, A. M., Ribchester, T. R., Davies, N. J., . . . Murray, R. M. (1999). Heritability estimates for psychotic disorders: The Maudsley twin psychosis series. *Archives of General Psychiatry, 56*(2), 162–168.

Carlson, G. A., Bromet, E. J., & Sievers, S. (2000). Phenomenology and outcome of subjects with early- and adult-onset psychotic mania. *American Journal of Psychiatry, 157*(2), 213–219.

Carlson, G. A., & Cantwell, D. P. (1980). A survey of depressive symptoms, syndrome and disorder in a child psychiatric population. *Journal of Child Psychology and Psychiatry, 21*(1), 19–25.

Carlson, G. A., Loney, J., Salisbury, H., Kramer, J. R., & Arthur, C. (2000). Stimulant treatment in young boys with symptoms suggesting childhood mania: A report from a longitudinal study. *Journal of Child and Adolescent Psychopharmacology, 10*(3), 175–184.

Carlson, G. A., Pine, D. S., Nottelmann, E., & Leibenluft, E. (2004). Defining subtypes of childhood bipolar disorder: Response and commentary. *Journal of the American Academy of Child and Adolescent Psychiatry, 43*(1), 3–4.

Carrasco, M., Volkmar, F. R., & Bloch, M. H. (2012). Pharmacologic treatment of repetitive behaviors in autism spectrum disorders: Evidence of publication bias. *Pediatrics, 129*(5), 1301–1310.

Carter, A. S., O'Donnell, D. A., Schultz, R. T., Scahill, L., Leckman, J. F., & Pauls, D. L. (2000). Social and emotional adjustment in children affected with Gilles de la Tourette's syndrome: Associations with ADHD and family functioning. *Journal of Child Psychology and Psychiatry, 41*(2), 215–223.

Carter, T. D., Mundo, E., Parikh, S. V., & Kennedy, J. L. (2003). Early age at onset as a risk factor for poor outcome of bipolar disorder. *Journal of Psychiatric Research, 37*(4), 297–303.

Case, B. G., Olfson, M., Marcus, S. C., & Siegel, C. (2007). Trends in the inpatient mental health treatment of children and adolescents in US community hospitals between 1990 and 2000. *Archives of General Psychiatry, 64*(1), 89–96.

Casey, B. J., & Jones, R. M. (2010). Neurobiology of the adolescent brain and behavior: Implications for substance use disorders. *Journal of the American Academy of Child and Adolescent Psychiatry, 49*(12), 1189–1201.

Caspi, A., Henry, B., McGee, R. O., Moffitt, T. E., & Silva, P. A. (1995). Temperamental origins of child and adolescent behavior problems: From age three to age fifteen. *Child Development, 66,* 55–68.

Caspi, A., Sugden, K., Moffitt, T. E., Taylor, A., Craig, I. W., Harrington, H., . . . Poulton, R. (2003). Influence of life stress on depression: Moderation by a polymorphism in the 5-HTT gene. *Science, 301*(5631), 386–389.

Cass, H., Gringras, P., March, J., McKendrick, I., O'Hare, A. E., Owen, L., & Pollin, C. (2008). Absence of urinary opioid peptides in children with autism. *Archives of Disease in Children, 93*(9), 745–750.

Castellanos, F. X., Lee, P. P., Sharp, W., Jeffries, N. O., Greenstein, D. K., Clasen, L. S., . . . Rapoport, J. L. (2002). Developmental trajectories of brain volume abnormalities in children and adolescents with attention deficit/hyperactivity disorder. *Journal of the American Medical Association, 288*(14), 1740–1748.

Catalano, R. F., Berglund, M. L, Ryan, J. A. M., Lonczak, H. S., & Hawkins, J. D. (2004). Positive youth development in the United States: Research findings on evaluations of positive youth development programs. *Annals of the American Academy of Political and Social Science, 591,* 98–124.

Centers for Disease Control and Prevention. (2001). *National health interview surveys 1997–2001.* Retrieved from http://www.cdc.gov/nchs/nhis.htm

Centers for Disease Control and Prevention. (2010). *HIV incidence.* Retrieved August 21, 2014, from http://www.cdc.gov/hiv/statistics/surveillance/incidence/

Centers for Disease Control and Prevention. (2013). *Youth violence: National statistics.* Retrieved June 14, 2014, from http://www.cdc.gov/violenceprevention/youthviolence/stats_at-a_glance/lcd_15-19.html

Centers for Disease Control and Prevention. (2014a). *Autism spectrum disorder.* Retrieved July 24, 2014, from http://www.cdc.gov/ncbddd/autism/data.html

Centers for Disease Control and Prevention. (2014b, June 13). Youth Risk Behavior Survey—United States, 2013. *Morbidity and Mortality Weekly Report.* Retrieved August 16, 2014, from http://www.cdc.gov/mmwr/pdf/ss/ss6304.pdf

Centers for Disease Control and Prevention, National Vital Statistics System, National Center for Health Statistics (2010). 10 leading causes of death by age group, United States—2010 [Table]. Retrieved May 28, 2014, from http://www.cdc.gov/injury/wisqars/pdf/10LCID_All_Deaths_By_Age_Group_2010-a.pdf

Chambers, W. J., Puig-Antich, J., Tabrizi, M. A., & Davies, M. (1982). Psychotic symptoms in prepubertal major depressive disorder. *Archives of General Psychiatry, 39*(8), 921–927.

Chang, K. (2007). Adult bipolar disorder is continuous with pediatric bipolar disorder. *Canadian Journal of Psychiatry, 52*(7), 418–425.

Chang, K. D., Blasey, C., Ketter, T. A., & Steiner, H. (2001). Family environment of children and adolescents with bipolar parents. *Bipolar Disorder, 3*(2), 73–78.

Chang, K., Howe, M., Gallelli, K., & Miklowitz, D. (2006). Prevention of pediatric bipolar disorder: Integration of neurobiological and psychosocial processes. *Annals of the New York Academy of Sciences, 1094,* 235–247.

Chang, K. D., Nyilas, M., Aurang, C., van Beck, A., Jin, N., Marcus, R., . . . Findling, R. L. (2007, October). *Efficacy of aripiprazole in children (10–17 years old) with mania.* Poster presented at the annual meeting of the American Academy of Child and Adolescent Psychiatry, Boston, Massachusetts.

Chang, K., Saxena, K., & Howe, M. (2006). An open-label study of lamotrigine adjunct or monotherapy for the treatment of adolescents with bipolar depression. *Journal of the American Academy of Child and Adolescent Psychiatry, 4,* 298–304.

Chang, K. D., Steiner, H., & Ketter, T. A. (2000). Psychiatric phenomenology of child and adolescent bipolar offspring. *Journal of the American Academy of Child and Adolescent Psychiatry, 39*(4), 453–460.

Chang, K., Steiner, H., & Ketter, T. (2003). Studies of offspring of parents with bipolar disorder. *American Journal of Medical Genetics: Part C. Seminars of Medical Genetics, 123C*(1), 26–35.

Charney, D. S. (2004). Psychobiological mechanisms of resilience and vulnerability: Implications for successful adaptation to extreme stress. *American Journal of Psychiatry, 161*(2), 195–216.

Chen, C. Y., Storr, C. L., & Anthony, J. C. (2009). Early-onset drug use and risk for drug dependence problems. *Addictive Behaviors, 34*(3), 319–322.

Chervin, R. D., & Archbold, K. H. (2001). Hyperactivity and polysomnographic findings in children evaluated for sleep-disordered breathing. *Sleep, 24*(3), 313.

Chervin, R. D., Archbold, K. H., Dillon, J. E., Panahi, P., Pituch, K. J., Dahl, R. E., & Guilleminault, C. (2002). Inattention, hyperactivity, and symptoms of sleep-disordered breathing. *Pediatrics, 109*(3), 449.

Children's Defense Fund. (2002). *The state of children in America's union: A 2002 action guide to leave no child behind.* Retrieved from www.childrensdefense .org/pdf/minigreenbook.pdf

Choudhury, M. S., Pimentel, S. S., & Kendall, P. C. (2003). Childhood anxiety disorders: Parent–child (dis)agreement using a structured interview for the DSM-IV. *Journal of the American Academy of Child and Adolescent Psychiatry, 42*(8), 957–964.

Christison, G. W., & Ivany, K. (2006). Elimination diets in autism spectrum disorders: Any wheat amidst the chaff? *Journal of Developmental and Behavioral Pediatrics, 27*(2), 5162–5171.

Cipriani, A., Hawton, K., Stockton, S., & Geddes, J. R. (2013). Lithium in the prevention of suicide in mood disorders: Updated systematic review and meta-analysis. *British Medical Journal.* doi: 10.1136/bmj.f3646

Citrome, L. (2012). A systematic review of meta-analyses of the efficacy of oral atypical antipsychotics for the treatment of adult patients with schizophrenia. *Expert Opinion on Pharmacotherapy, 13*(11), 1545–1573.

Clarke, M. C., Harley, M., & Cannon, M. (2006). The role of obstetric events in schizophrenia. *Schizophrenia Bulletin, 32*, 3.

Cleghorn, J. M., Zipursky, R. B., & List, S. J. (1991). Structural and functional brain imaging in schizophrenia. *Journal of Psychiatry and Neuroscience, 16*(2), 53–74.

Cloitre, M., Scarvalone, P., & Difede, J. A. (1997). Posttraumatic stress disorder, self- and interpersonal dysfunction among sexually retraumatized women. *Journal of Traumatic Stress, 10*(3), 437–452.

Coffey, B. J., Biederman, J., Smoller, J. W., Geller, D. A., Sarin, P., Schwartz, S., & Kim, G. S. (2000). Anxiety disorders and tic severity in juveniles with Tourette's disorder. *Journal of the American Academy of Child and Adolescent Psychiatry, 39*(5), 562–568.

Coffey, B. J., & Park, K. S. (1997). Behavioral and emotional aspects of Tourette syndrome. *Neurologic Clinics, 15*(2), 277–289.

Cohan, S. L., Chavira, D. A., Shipon-Blum, E., Hitchcock, C., Roesch, S. C., & Stein, M. B. (2008). Refining the classification of children with selective mutism: A latent profile analysis. *Journal of Clinical Child and Adolescent Psychology, 37*(4), 770–784.

Cohen, N. J., Davine, M., Horodesky, N., Lipsett, L., & Isaacson, L. (1993). Unsuspected language impairment in psychiatrically disturbed children: Prevalence and language and behavioral characteristics. *Journal of the American Academy of Child and Adolescent Psychiatry, 32*, 595–603.

Cohen, J. A., Mannarino, A. P., & Deblinger, E. (2006). *Treating trauma and traumatic grief in children and adolescents.* New York, NY: Guilford Press.

Conduct Problems Prevention Research Group. (1992). A developmental and clinical model for the prevention of conduct disorder: The FAST track program. *Development and Psychopathology, 4*, 509–527.

Conners, C. K., Casat, C. D., Gualtieri, C. T., Weller, E., Reader, M., Reiss, A., & Ascher, J. (1996). Bupropion hydrochloride in attention deficit disorder with hyperactivity. *Journal of the American Academy of Child and Adolescent Psychiatry, 35*(10), 1314–1321.

Connolly, S. D., & Bernstein, G. A. (2007). Practice parameter for the assessment and treatment of children and adolescents with anxiety disorders. *Journal of the American Academy of Child and Adolescent Psychiatry, 46*(2), 267–283.

Connor, D. F. (2002). *Aggression and antisocial behavior in children and adolescents: Research and treatment.* New York, NY: Guilford Press.

Connor, D. F., Barkley, R. A., & Davis, H. T. (2000). A pilot study of methylphenidate, clonidine, or the combination in ADHD comorbid with aggressive oppositional defiant or conduct disorder. *Clinical Pediatrics, 39*, 15–25.

Connor, D. F., Fletcher, K. E., & Swanson, J. M. (1999). A meta-analysis of clonidine for symptoms of attention-deficit hyperactivity disorder. *Journal of the American Academy of Child and Adolescent Psychiatry, 38*, 12.

Conture, E. G., Schwartz, H. D., & Brewer, D. W. (1984). Laryngeal behavior during stuttering. *Journal of Speech and Hearing Research, 28,* 233–240.

Cooper, W. O., Arbogast, P. G., Ding, H., Hickson, G. B., Fuchs, D. C., & Ray, W. A. (2006). Trends in prescribing of antipsychotic medications for US children. *Ambulatory Pediatrics, 6*(2), 79–83.

Copur, M., Arpaci, B., Demir, T., & Narin, H. (2007). Clinical effectiveness of quetiapine in children and adolescents with Tourette's syndrome: A retrospective case-note survey. *Clinical Drug Investigation, 27*(2), 123–130.

Corkum, P., Moldofsky, H., Hogg-Johnson, S., Humphries, T., & Tannock, R. (1999). Sleep problems in children with attention-deficit/hyperactivity disorder: Impact of subtype, comorbidity, and stimulant medication. *Journal of the American Academy of Child and Adolescent Psychiatry, 38*(10), 1285–1293.

Corkum, P., Tannock, R., & Moldofsky, H. (1998). Sleep disturbances in children with attention-deficit/hyperactivity disorder. *Journal of the American Academy of Child and Adolescent Psychiatry, 37*(6), 637–646.

Correll, C. U., & Kane, J. M. (2007). One-year incidence rates of tardive dyskinesia in children and adolescents treated with second-generation antipsychotics: A systematic review. *Journal of Child and Adolescent Psychopharmacology, 17*(5), 647–656.

Cortese, S., Angriman, M., Lecendreux, M., & Konofal, E. (2012). Iron and attention deficit/hyperactivity disorder: What is the empirical evidence so far? A systematic review of the literature. *Expert Review of Neurotherapeutics, 12*(10), 1227–1240.

Cortiella, C. (2011). *The state of learning disabilities.* New York, NY: National Center for Learning Disabilities.

Costello, E. J., Angold, A., Burns, B. J., Stangl, D. K., Tweed, D. L., Erkanli, A., & Worthman, C. M. (1996). The Great Smokey Mountains Study of Youth: Goals, design, methods, and the prevalence of *DSM-III-R* disorders. *Archives of General Psychiatry, 53*(12), 1129–1136.

Costello, E. J., Egger, H. L., & Angold, A. (2004). Developmental epidemiology of anxiety disorders. In T. H. Ollendick & J. S. March (Eds.), *Phobic and anxiety disorders in children and adolescents* (pp. 61–91). New York, NY: Oxford University Press.

Council on *Communications and Media.* (2010). Children, adolescents, substance abuse, and the media. *Pediatrics, 126*(4), 791–799.

Courchesne, E. (2004). Brain development in autism: Early overgrowth followed by premature arrest of growth. *Mental Retardation and Developmental Disabilities Research Reviews, 10*(2), 106–111.

Couturier, J., & Lock, J. (2007). A review of medication use for children and adolescents with eating disorders. *Journal of the Canadian Academy of Child and Adolescent Psychiatry, 16*(4), 173–176.

Craft, M., Ismail, I. A., Krishnamurti, D., Mathews, J., Regan, A., Seth, R. V., & North, P. M. (1987). Lithium in the treatment of aggression in mentally handicapped patients: A double-blind trial. *British Journal of Psychiatry, 150,* 685–689.

Craney, J., & Geller, B. (2003). Clinical implications of antidepressant and stimulant use on switching from depression to mania in children. *Journal of Child and Adolescent Psychopharmacology, 13*(2), 201–204.

Crisp, A. H. (1980). *Let me be.* London, UK: Academic Press.

Crisp, A. H., & Bhat, A. V. (1982). "Personality" and anorexia nervosa—the phobic avoidance stance: Its origins and its symptomatology. *Psychotherapy and Psychosomatics, 38*(1), 178–200.

Crystal, S., Olfson, M., Huang, C., Pincus, H., & Gerhard, T. (2009). Broadened use of atypical antipsychotics: Safety, effectiveness, and policy challenges. *Health Affairs (Millwood), 28*(5), 770–781.

Csikszentmihalyi, M. (1991). *Flow, the psychology of optimal experience.* New York, NY: Harper & Row.

Curry, J. F. (2001). Specific psychotherapies for childhood and adolescent depression. *Biological Psychiatry, 49*(12), 1091–1100.

Cuthbert, S. C., & Barras, M. (2009). Developmental delay syndromes: Psychometric testing before and after chiropractic treatment of 157 children. *Journal of Manipulative and Physiological Therapeutics, 32*, 660–669.

Daban, C., Vieta, E., Mackin, P., & Young, A. H. (2005). Hypothalamic-pituitary-adrenal axis and bipolar disorder. *Psychiatric Clinics of North America, 28*(2), 469–480.

Dahl, R. E., Kaufman, J., Ryan, N. D., Perel, J., Al-Shabbout, M., Birmaher, B., . . . Puig-Antich, J. (1992). The Dexamethasone Suppression Test in children and adolescents: A review and a controlled study. *Biological Psychiatry, 32*(2), 109–126.

Dalsgaard, S., Kvist, A. P., Leckman, J. F., Nielsen, H. S., & Simonsen, M. (2014). Cardiovascular safety of stimulants in children with attention-deficit/hyperactivity disorder: A nationwide prospective cohort study. *Journal of Child and Adolescent Psychopharmacology.* doi: 10.1089/cap.2014.0020

Dalton, K. M., Nacewicz, B. M., Alexander, A. L., & Davidson, R. J. (2007). Gaze-fixation, brain activation, and amygdala volume in unaffected siblings of individuals with autism. *Biological Psychiatry, 61*(4), 512–520.

Dalton, K. M., Nacewicz, B. M., Johnstone, T., Schaefer, H. S., Gernsbacher, M. A., Goldsmith, H. H., . . . Davidson, R. J. (2005). Gaze fixation and the neural circuitry of face processing in autism. *Nature Neuroscience, 8*(4), 519–526.

Danaei, G., Ding, E. L., Mozaffarian, D., Taylor, B., Rehm, J., Murray, C. J., & Ezzati, M. (2009). The preventable causes of death in the United States: Comparative risk assessment of dietary, lifestyle, and metabolic risk factors. *PLoS Medicine, 6*(4), e1000058.

Davalos, D. B., Compagnon, N., Heinlein, S., & Ross, R. G. (2003). Neuropsychological deficits in children associated with increased familial risk for schizophrenia. *Schizophrenia Research, 67*(2–3), 123–130.

Davanzo, P., Gunderson, B., Belin, T., Mintz, J., Pataki, C., Ott, D., . . . Strober, M. (2003). Mood stabilizers in hospitalized children with bipolar disorder: A retrospective review. *Psychiatry and Clinical Neurosciences, 57*(5), 504–510.

David-Ferdon, C., & Kaslow, N. J. (2008). Evidence-based psychosocial treatments for child and adolescent depression. *Journal of Clinical Child and Adolescent Psychology, 37*(1), 62–104.

Davies, L., Stern, J. S., Agrawal, N., & Robertson, M. M. (2006). A case series of patients with Tourette's syndrome in the United Kingdom treated with aripiprazole. *Human Psychopharmacology, 21*(7), 447–453.

Daviss, W. B., Bentivoglio, P., Racusin, R., Brown, K. M., Bostic, J. Q., & Wiley, L. (2001). Bupropion sustained release in adolescents with comorbid attention deficit/hyperactivity disorder and depression. *Journal of the American Academy of Child and Adolescent Psychiatry, 40*(3), 307–314.

Dawson, G., Webb, S., Schellenberg, G. D., Dager, S., Friedman, S., Aylward, E., & Richards, T. (2002). Defining the broader phenotype of autism: Genetic, brain, and behavioral perspectives. *Development and Psychopathology, 14*(3), 581–611.

Deas, D. (2008). Evidence-based treatments for alcohol use disorders in adolescents. *Pediatrics, 121*(4), S348–S354.

De Bellis, M. D., Zisk, A. (2014). The biological effects of childhood trauma. *Child and Adolescent Psychiatric Clinics of North America, 23*(2), 185–222.

de Groot, C. M., Bornstein, R. A., Spetie, L., & Burriss, B. (1994). The course of tics in Tourette syndrome: A 5-year follow-up study. *Annals of Clinical Psychiatry, 6*(4), 227–233.

DelBello, M. P., Findling, R. L., Earley, W. R., Stankowski, J., & Acevedo, L. D. (2007, October). *Efficacy of quetiapine in children and adolescents with bipolar mania.* Poster presented at the annual meeting of the American Academy of Child and Adolescent Psychiatry, Boston, MA.

DelBello, M. P., Findling, R. L., Wang, P. P., Gundapaneni, B., & Versael, M. (2008, May). *Safety and efficacy of ziprasidone in pediatric bipolar disorder.* Poster presented at the annual meeting of the Society of Biological Psychiatry, Washington, DC.

DelBello, M. P., Hanseman, D., Adler, C. M., Fleck, D. E., & Strakowski, S. M. (2007). Twelve-month outcome of adolescents with bipolar disorder following first hospitalization for a manic or mixed episode. *American Journal of Psychiatry, 164*(4), 582–590.

DelBello, M. P., Kowatch, R. A., Adler, C. M., Stanford, K. E., Welge, J. A., Barzman, D. H., . . . Strakowski, S. M. (2006). A double-blind randomized pilot study comparing quetiapine and divalproex for adolescent mania. *Journal of the American Academy of Child and Adolescent Psychiatry, 45*(3), 305–313.

DeLong, G. R., & Nieman, G. W. (1983). Lithium-induced behavior changes in children with symptoms suggesting manic-depressive illness. *Psychopharmacology Bulletin, 19*(2), 258–265.

DeLong, G. R., Ritch, C. R., & Burch, S. (2002). Fluoxetine response in children with autistic spectrum disorders: Correlation with familial major affective disorder and intellectual achievement. *Developmental Medicine and Child Neurology, 44*(10), 652–659.

DeNavis-Walt, C., Proctor, B. D., & Smith, J. C. (2013). Income, poverty, and health insurance coverage in the United States: 2012. *Current Population Reports*. Retrieved May 27, 2014, from http://www.census.gov/prod/2013pubs/p60-245.pdf

DeVeaugh-Geiss, J., Moroz, G., Biederman, J., Cantwell, D., Fontaine, R., Greist, J. H., . . . Landau, P. (1992). Clomipramine hydrochloride in childhood and adolescent obsessive-compulsive disorder: A multicenter trial. *Journal of the American Academy of Child and Adolescent Psychiatry, 31*(1), 45–49.

Deykin, E. Y., & MacMahon, B. (1979). The incidence of seizures among children with autistic symptoms. *American Journal of Psychiatry, 136*(10), 1310–1312.

Díaz-Caneja, C. M., Moreno, C., Llorente, C., Espliego, A., Arango, C., & Moreno, D. (2014). Practitioner review: Long-term pharmacological treatment of pediatric bipolar disorder. *Journal of Child and Adolescent Psychology and Psychiatry, 55*(9), 959–980.

Díaz-Marsá, M., Carrasco, J. L., Basurte, E., Sáiz, J., López-Ibor, J. J., & Hollander, E. (2008). Enhanced cortisol suppression in eating disorders with impulsive personality features. *Psychiatry Research, 158*(1), 93–97.

Diefenbach, G. J., Reitman, D., & Williamson, D. A. (2000). Trichotillomania: A challenge to research and practice. *Clinical Psychology Review, 20*(3), 289–309.

Diller, L. H. (2002). Lessons from three year olds. *Journal of Developmental and Behavioral Pediatrics, 23*(1), S10–S12.

Dinan, T. G. (1998). Psychoneuroendocrinology of depression: Growth hormone. *Psychiatric Clinics of North America, 21*(2), 325–339.

Dodge, K. A., Pettit, G. S., Bates, J. E., & Valente, E. (1995). Social information processing patterns partially mediate the effect of early physical abuse on later conduct problems. *Journal of Abnormal Psychology, 104,* 632–643.

Domes, G., Heinrichs, M., Michel, A., Berger, C., & Herpertz, S. C. (2006). Oxytocin improves "mind-reading" in humans. *Biological Psychiatry, 61*(6), 731–733.

Donfrancesco, R., & Ferrante, L. (2007). Ginkgo biloba in dyslexia: A pilot study. *Phytomedicine, 14*(6), 367–370.

Donner, J., Pirkola, S., Silander, K., Kananen, L., Terwilliger, J. D., Lönnqvist, J., . . . Hovatta, I. (2008). An association analysis of murine anxiety genes in humans implicates novel candidate genes for anxiety disorders. *Biological Psychiatry, 64*(8), 672–680.

Donovan, S. J., Stewart, J. W., Nunes, E. V., Quitkin, F. M., Parides, M., Daniel, W., . . . Klein, D. F. (2000). Divalproex treatment for youth with explosive temper and mood lability: A double-blind, placebo-controlled crossover design. *American Journal of Psychiatry, 157,* 818–820.

Du, Y. S., Li, H. F., Vance, A., Zhong, Y. Q., Jiao, F. Y., Wang, H. M., . . . Wu, J. B. (2008). Randomized double-blind multicenter placebo-controlled clinical trial of the clonidine adhesive patch for the treatment of tic disorders. *Australian and New Zealand Journal of Psychiatry, 42*(9), 807–813.

Duclos, W. W., Beals, J., Novins, D. K., Martin, C., Jewett, C. S., & Manson, S.

M. (1998). Prevalence of common psychiatric disorders among American Indian adolescent detainees. *Journal of the American Academy of Child and Adolescent Psychiatry, 37*(8), 866–873.

Duffy, A. (2007). Does bipolar disorder exist in children? A selected review. *Canadian Journal of Psychiatry, 52*(7), 409–417.

Duffy, E. (1957). The psychological significance of the concept of "arousal" or "activation." *Psychological Review, 64,* 265–275.

Dufrene, B. A., Doggett, R. A., Henington, C., & Watson, T. S. (2007). Functional assessment and interventions for disruptive classroom behaviors in preschool and Head Start classrooms. *Journal of Behavioral Education, 16,* 368–388.

Dusenbury, L., Khuri, E., & Millman, R. B. (1992). Adolescent substance abuse: A sociodevelopmental perspective. In J. H. Lowinson, P. Ruiz, & R. B. Milman (Eds.), *Substance abuse: A comprehensive textbook* (2nd ed., pp. 832–842). Baltimore, MD: Williams & Wilkins.

Dykens, E. M., Hodapp, R. M., & Finucane, B. M. (2000). *Genetics and mental retardation syndromes: A new look at behavior and interventions.* Baltimore, MD: Paul H. Brookes.

Dyregrov, A., & Yule, W. (2006). A review of PTSD in children. *Child and Adolescent Mental Health, 11*(4), 176–184.

Earley, P. (2006). *Crazy: A father's search through America's mental health madness.* New York, NY: Berkley Books.

Eddy, C. M., Rickards, H. E., & Cavanna, A. E. (2011). Treatment strategies for tics in Tourette syndrome. *Therapeutic Advances in Neurological Disorders, 4*(1), 25–45.

Edwards, M. (1984). Speech disability in children: Some general considerations. *International Rehabilitation Medicine, 6*(3), 114–116.

Egeland, J. A., Hostetter, A. M., Pauls, D. L., & Sussex, J. N. (2000). Prodromal symptoms before onset of manic-depressive disorder suggested by first hospital admission histories. *Journal of the American Academy of Child and Adolescent Psychiatry, 39*(10), 1245–1252.

Eisenberg, D., & Neighbors, K. (2009). Benefits and costs of prevention. In M. E. O'Connell, T. Boat, & K. Warner (Eds.), *Preventing mental, emotional, and behavioral disorders among young people: Progress and possibilities* (pp. 241–262). Washington, D.C. National Academies Press.

Eisenberg, J., Mei-Tal, G., Steinberg, A., Tartakovsky, E., Zohar, A., Gritsenko, I., . . . Ebstein, R. P. (1999). Haplotype relative risk study of catechol-O-methyltransferase (COMT) and attention deficit hyperactivity disorder (ADHD): Association of the high-enzyme activity Val allele with ADHD impulsive-hyperactive phenotype. *American Journal of Medical Genetics, 88,* 497–502.

Eisler, I., Dare, C., Russell, G. F. M., Szmukler, G., Le Grange, D., & Dodge, E. (1997). Family and individual therapy in anorexia nervosa: A 5-year follow-up. *Archives of General Psychiatry, 54,* 1025–1030.

Elder, J. H., Shankar, M., Shuster, J., Theriaque, D., Burns, S., & Sherrill, L.

(2006). The gluten-free, casein-free diet in autism: Results of a preliminary double blind clinical trial. *Journal of Autism and Developmental Disorders, 36*(3), 413–420.

Eley, T. C., & Stevenson, J. (1999). Using genetic analyses to clarify the distinction between depressive and anxious symptoms in children. *Journal of Abnormal Child Psychology, 27*(2), 105–114.

Elia, J., Borcherding, B. G., Rapoport, J. L., & Keysor, C. S. (1991). Methylphenidate and dextroamphetamine treatments of hyperactivity: Are there true non-responders? *Psychiatry Research, 36*(2), 141–155.

Elkins, I. J., Malone, S., Keyes, M., Iacono, W. G., & McGue, M. (2011). The impact of attention-deficit/hyperactivity disorder on preadolescent adjustment may be greater for girls than for boys. *Journal of Clinical Child and Adolescent Psychology, 40*(4), 532–545.

Elliott, G. R., & Smiga, S. (2003). Depression in the child and adolescent. *Pediatric Clinics of North America, 50*(5), 1093–1106.

Emerson, E. (2003). Prevalence of psychiatric disorders in children and adolescents with and without intellectual disability. *Journal of Intellectual Disability Research, 47*, 51–58.

Emslie, G. J., Findling, R. L., Yeung, P. P., Kunz, N. R., & Li, Y. (2007). Venlafaxine ER for the treatment of pediatric subjects with depression: Results of two placebo-controlled trials. *Journal of the American Academy of Child and Adolescent Psychiatry, 46*(4), 479–488.

Emslie, G. J., Heiligenstein, J. H., Wagner, K. D., Hoog, S. L., Ernest, D. E, Brown, E., . . . Jacobson, J. G. (2002). Fluoxetine for acute treatment of depression in children and adolescents: A placebo-controlled, randomized clinical trial. *Journal of the American Academy of Child and Adolescent Psychiatry, 41*(10), 1205–1215.

Emslie, G. J., Rush, A. J., Weinberg, W. A., Kowatch, R. A., Hughes, C. W., Carmody, T., & Rintelmann, J. (1997). A double-blind, randomized, placebo-controlled trial of fluoxetine in children and adolescents with depression. *Archives of General Psychiatry, 54*(11), 1031–1037.

Emslie, G. J., Rush, A. J., Weinberg, W. A., Rintelmann, J. W., & Roffwarg, H. P. (1990). Children with major depression show reduced rapid eye movement latencies. *Archives of General Psychiatry, 47*(2), 119–124.

Emslie, G. J., Ventura, D., Korotzer, A., & Tourkodimitris, S. (2009). Escitalopram in the treatment of adolescent depression: A randomized placebo-controlled multisite trial. *Journal of the American Academy of Child and Adolescent Psychiatry, 48*(7), 721–729.

Emslie, G. J., Wagner, K. D., Kutcher, S., Krulewicz, S., Fong, R., Carpenter, D. J., . . . Wilkinson, C. (2006). Paroxetine treatment in children and adolescents with major depressive disorder: A randomized, multicenter, double-blind, placebo-controlled trial. *Journal of the American Academy of Child and Adolescent Psychiatry, 45*(6), 709–719.

Enderby, P., & Emerson, J. (1996). Speech and language therapy: Does it work? *British Medical Journal, 312*, 1655–1658.

Engleman, H., & Joffe, D. (1999). Neuropsychological function in obstructive sleep apnea. *Sleep Medicine Reviews, 3*(1), 59.

Epstein, J. A., & Spirito, A. (2009). Risk factors for suicidality among a nationally representative sample of high school students. *Suicide and Life-Threatening Behavior, 39*(3), 241–251.

Erenberg, G. (2005). The relationship between Tourette syndrome, attention deficit hyperactivity disorder, and stimulant medication: A critical review. *Seminars in Pediatric Neurology, 12*(4), 217–221.

Erickson, C. A., Stigler, K. A., Posey, D. J., & McDougle, C. J. (2010). Aripiprazole in autism spectrum disorders and fragile X syndrome. *Journal of the American Society for Experimental NeuroTherapeutics, 7*(3), 258–263.

Erikson, E. H., & Erikson, J. M. (1997). *The life cycle completed.* New York, NY: Norton.

Ernst, M., Zametkin, A. J., Matochik, J. A., Pascualvaca, D., Jons, P. H., & Cohen, R. M. (1999). High midbrain [18F] DOPA accumulation in children with attention deficit hyperactivity disorder. *American Journal of Psychiatry, 156,* 1209–1215.

Ersu, R., Arman, A. R., Save, D., Karadag, B., Karakoc, F., Berkem, M., & Dagli, El. (2004). Prevalence of snoring and symptoms of sleep-disordered breathing in primary school children in Istanbul. *Chest Journal, 126,* 1.

Essen, J., & Peckham, C. (1976). Nocturnal enuresis in childhood. *Developmental Medicine and Child Neurology, 18*(5), 577–589.

Estes, A., Shaw, D. W., Sparks, B. F., Friedman, S., Giedd, J. N., Dawson, G., Bryan, M., & Dager, S. R. (2011). Basal ganglia morphology and repetitive behavior in young children with autism spectrum disorder. *Autism Research, 4*(3), 212–220.

European School Survey Project on Alcohol and Other Drugs (2012). *The 2011 ESPAD report.* Retrieved August 16, 2014, from http://www.espad.org/Uploads/ESPAD_reports/2011/The_2011_ESPAD_Report_FULL_2012_10_29.pdf

Evans, G. W. (2003). The built environment and mental health. *Journal of Urban Health, 80*(4), 536–555.

Fairburn, C. G., Marcus, M., & Wilson, G. (1993). Cognitive-behavioral therapy for binge eating and bulimia nervosa: A comprehensive treatment manual. In C. G. Fairburn & G. T. Wilson (Eds.), *Binge eating: Nature, assessment and treatment* (pp. 361–404). New York, NY: Guilford Press.

Fallone, G., Acebo, C., Arnedt, T. A., Seifer, R., & Carskadon, M. A. (2001). Effects of acute sleep restriction on behavior, sustained attention, and response inhibition in children. *Perceptual and Motor Skills, 93*(1), 213.

Falloon, I. R. H., Held, T., Coverdale, J. H., Roncone, R., & Laidlaw, T. M. (1999). Psychosocial interventions for schizophrenia: A review of long term benefits of international studies. *Psychiatric Rehabilitation Skills, 3,* 268–290.

Fan, A. H., & Hassell, J. (2008). Bipolar disorder and comorbid personality psychopathology: A review of the literature. *Journal of Clinical Psychiatry, pii,* ej08r04175.

Fan, Y. T., Decety, J., Yang, C. Y., Liu, J. L., & Cheng, Y. (2010). Unbroken mirror neurons in autism spectrum disorder. *Journal of Child Psychology and Psychiatry, 51*(9), 981–988.

Faraone, S. V. (2000). Genetics of childhood disorders: XX. ADHD, Part 4: Is ADHD genetically heterogeneous? *Journal of the American Academy of Child and Adolescent Psychiatry, 39*(11), 1455–1457.

Faraone, S. V., Biederman, J., Jetton, J. G., & Tsuang, M. T. (1997). Attention deficit disorder and conduct disorder: Longitudinal evidence for a familial subtype. *Psychological Medicine, 27*(2), 291–300.

Faraone, S. V., Biederman, J., Wozniak, J., Mundy, E., Mennin, D., & O'Donnell, D. (1997). Is comorbidity with ADHD a marker for juvenile-onset mania? *Journal of the American Academy of Child and Adolescent Psychiatry, 36*(8), 1046–1055.

Faridi, K., & Suchowersky, O. (2003). Gilles de la Tourette's syndrome. *Canadian Journal of Neurological Sciences, 30*(1), S64–S71.

Feehan, M., McGee, R., Stanton, W., & Silva, P. A. (1990). A 6-year follow-up of childhood enuresis: Prevalence in adolescence and consequences for mental health. *Journal of Paediatrics and Child Health, 26,* 75–79.

Feeny, N. C., Danielson, C. K., Schwartz, L., Youngstrom, E. A., & Findling, R. L. (2006). Cognitive-behavioral therapy for bipolar disorders in adolescents: A pilot study. *Bipolar Disorders, 8*(5), 508–515.

Feingold, B. F. (1975). Hyperkinesis and learning disabilities linked to artificial food flavors and colors. *American Journal of Nursing, 75,* 797–803.

Felitti, V. J., Anda, R. F., Nordenberg, D., Williamson, D. F., Spitz, A. M., . . . Marks, J. S. (1998). Relationship of childhood abuse and household dysfunction to many of the leading causes of death in adults: The Adverse Childhood Experiences (ACE) Study. *American Journal of Preventive Medicine, 14*(4), 245–258.

Fergusson, D. M., & Boden, J. M. (2008). Cannabis use and later life outcomes. *Addiccation, 103,* 969–976.

Fergusson, D. M., & Horwood, L. J. (1994). Nocturnal enuresis and behavioral problems in adolescence: A 15-year longitudinal survey. *Pediatrics, 94,* 662–668.

Fernández, T., Herrera, W., Harmony, T., Díaz-Comas, L., Santiago, E., Sánchez, L., . . . Valdés, R. (2003). EEG and behavioral changes following neurofeedback treatment in learning disabled children. *Clinical Electroencephalography, 34,* 145–152.

Fichter, M. M., Leibl, K., Rief, W., Brunner, E., Schmidt-Auberger, S., & Engel, R. R. (1991). Fluoxetine versus placebo: A double-blind study with bulimic inpatients undergoing intensive psychotherapy. *Pharmacopsychiatry, 24*(1), 1–7.

Filipek, P. A., Accardo, P. J., Ashwal, S., Baranek, G. T., Cook, E. H., Jr., Dawson, G., . . . Volkmar, F. R. (2000). Practice parameter: Screening and diagnosis of autism. *Report of the Quality Standards Subcommittee of the American Academy of Neurology and the Child Neurology Society, 55,* 468–479.

Findling, R. L., Greenhill, L. L., McNamara, N. K., Demeter, C. A., Kotler, L. A., O'Riordan, M. A., ... Reed, M. D. (2007). Venlafaxine in the treatment of children and adolescents with attention-deficit/hyperactivity disorder. *Journal of Child and Adolescent Psychopharmacology, 17*(4), 433–445.

Findling, R. L., Johnson, J. L., McClellan, J., Frazier, J. A., Vitiello, B., Hamer, R. M., . . . Sikich, L. (2010). Double-blind maintenance safety and effectiveness findings from the Treatment of Early-Onset Schizophrenia Spectrum (TEOSS) Study. *Journal of the American Academy of Child and Adolescent Psychiatry, 49*(6), 583–594.

Findling, R. L., Kafantaris, V., Pavuluri, M., McNamara, N. K., Frazier, J. A., Kowatch, R., . . . Taylor-Zapata, P. (2013). Post-acute effectiveness of lithium in pediatric bipolar I disorder. *Journal of Child and Adolescent Psychopharmacology, 23*(2), 80–90.

Findling, R. L., McKenna, K., Earley, W. R., Stankowski, J., & Pathak, S. (2012). Efficacy and safety of quetiapine in adolescents with schizophrenia investigated in a 6-week, double-blind, placebo-controlled trial. *Journal of Child and Adolescent Psychopharmacology, 22*(5), 327–342.

Findling, R. L., McNamara, N. K., Gracious, B. L., Youngstrom, E. A., Stansbrey, R. J., Reed, M. D., . . . Calabrese, J. R. (2003). Combination lithium and divalproex sodium in pediatric bipolarity. *Journal of the American Academy of Child and Adolescent Psychiatry, 42*(8), 895–901.

Findling, R. L., McNamara, N. K., Youngstrom, E. A., Stansbrey, R., Gracious, B. L., Reed, M. D., & Calabrese, J. R. (2005). Double-blind 18-month trial of lithium versus divalproex maintenance treatment in pediatric bipolar disorder. *Journal of the American Academy of Child and Adolescent Psychiatry, 44*(5), 409–417.

Findling, R. L., Preskorn, S. H., Marcus, R. N., Magnus, R. D., D'Amico, F., Marathe, P., & Reed, M. D. (2000). Nefazodone pharmacokinetics in depressed children and adolescents. *Journal of the American Academy of Child and Adolescent Psychiatry, 39*(8), 1008–1016.

Findling, R. L., Reed, M. D., O'Riordan, M. A., Demeter, C. A., Stansbrey, R. J., & McNamara, N. K. (2006). Effectiveness, safety, and pharmacokinetics of quetiapine in aggressive children with conduct disorder. *Journal of the American Academy of Child and Adolescent Psychiatry, 45,* 792–800.

Findling, R. L., Reed, M. D., O'Riordan, M. A., Demeter, C. A., Stansbrey, R. J., & McNamara, N. K. (2007). A 26-week open-label study of quetiapine in children with conduct disorder. *Journal of Child and Adolescent Psychopharmacology, 17,* 1–9.

Fisher, M. (2003). The course and outcome of eating disorders in adults and in adolescents: A review. *Archives of Pediatrics and Adolescent Medicine, 14*(1), 149–158.

Fisher, S. (1959). *Child research in psychopharmacology.* Springfield, IL: Charles C Thomas.

Flament, M. F., Rapoport, J. L., Berg, C. J., Sceery, W., Kilts, C., Mellström, B., & Linnoila, M. (1985). Clomipramine treatment of childhood obsessive-compulsive disorder. A double-blind controlled study. *Archives of General Psychiatry, 42*(10), 977–983.

Flavell, J. H. (1963). *Developmental psychology of Jean Piaget.* Princeton, NJ: D. Van Nostrand.

Fleischhaker, C., Munz, M., Böhme, R., Sixt, B., & Schulz, E. (2006). Dialectical behaviour therapy for adolescents (DBT-A): A pilot study on the therapy of suicidal, parasuicidal, and self-injurious behaviour in female patients with a borderline disorder. *Zeitschrift fur Kinder- und Jugendpsychiatrie und Psychotherapie, 34*(1), 15–25.

Fleming, J. E., & Offord, D. R. (1990). Epidemiology of childhood depressive disorders: A critical review. *Journal of the American Academy of Child and Adolescent Psychiatry, 29*(4), 571–580.

Fluoxetine Bulimia Nervosa Collaborative Study Group. (1992). Fluoxetine in the treatment of bulimia nervosa. A multicenter, placebo-controlled, double-blind trial. *Archives of General Psychiatry, 49*(2), 139–147.

Food and Drug Administration. (2006, February). *Drug Safety and Risk Management Advisory Committee meeting: Table of contents.* Retrieved January 26, 2009, from http://www.fda.gov/ohrms/dockets/ac/06/briefing/2006-4202_00_TOC.htm

Fountoulakis, K. N., & Vieta, E. (2008). Treatment of bipolar disorder: A systematic review of available data and clinical perspectives. *International Journal of Neuropsychopharmacology, 11*(7), 999–1029.

Foxx, R. M. (2008). Applied behavior analysis treatment of autism: The state of the art. *Child and Adolescent Psychiatric Clinics of North America, 17*(4), 821–834.

Frankhauser, M. P., Karumanchi, V. C., German, M. L., Yates, A., & Karumanchi, S. D. (1991). A double-blind, placebo-controlled study of the efficacy of transdermal clonidine in autism. *Journal of Clinical Psychiatry, 53,* 77–82.

Frazier, J. A., Biederman, J., Bellordre, C. A., Garfield, S. B., Geller, D. A., Coffey, B. J., & Faraone, S. V. (2001). Should the diagnosis of attention-deficit/ hyperactivity disorder be considered in children with pervasive developmental disorder? *Journal of Attention Disorders, 4,* 203–211.

Frazier, J. A., Chiu, S., Breeze, J. L., Makris, N., Lange, N., Kennedy, D. N., . . . Biederman, J. (2005). Structural brain magnetic resonance imaging of limbic and thalamic volumes in pediatric bipolar disorder. *American Journal of Psychiatry, 162*(7), 1256–1265.

Freda, L. (2010). Suicide risk assessment and prevention in children and adolescents. *Brown University Child and Adolescent Behavior Letter, 26*(9), 1–3.

Fristad, M. A., Goldberg-Arnold, J. S., & Gavazzi, S. M. (2003). Multi-family psychoeducation groups in the treatment of children with mood disorders. *Journal of Marital and Family Therapy, 29*(4), 491–504.

Fristad, M. A., Verducci, J. S., Walters, K., & Young, M. E. (2009). Impact of multifamily psychoeducational psychotherapy in treating children aged 8 to 12 years with mood disorders. *Archives of General Psychiatry, 66*(9), 1013–1021.

Fruntes, V., & Limosin, F. (2008). Schizophrenia and viral infection during neurodevelopment: A pathogenesis model? *Medical Science Monitor, 14*(6), 71–77.

Gadow, K. D., Sverd, J., Sprafkin, J., Nolan, E. E., & Ezor, S. N. (1995). Efficacy of methylphenidate for attention-deficit hyperactivity disorder in children with tic disorder. *Archives of General Psychiatry, 52*(6), 444–455.

Gagiano, C., Read, S., Thorpe, L., Eerdekens, M., & Van Hove, I. (2005). Short- and long-term efficacy and safety of risperidone in adults with disruptive behavior disorders. *Psychopharmacology, 179,* 629–636.

Galaburda, A. M., Sherman, G. F., Rosen, G. D., Aboitiz, F., & Geschwind, N. (1985). Developmental dyslexia: Four consecutive patients with cortical anomalies. *Annals of Neurology, 18,* 222–233.

Galanter, C. A., Carlson, G. A., Jensen, P. S., Greenhill, L. L., Davies, M., Li, W., . . . Swanson, J. M. (2003). Response to methylphenidate in children with attention deficit hyperactivity disorder and manic symptoms in the multimodal treatment study of children with attention deficit hyperactivity disorder titration trial. *Journal of Child and Adolescent Psychopharmacology, 13*(2), 123–136.

Garber, K. B., Visootsak, J., & Warren, S. T. (2008). Fragile X syndrome. *European Journal of Human Genetics, 16,* 666–672.

Garfield, C. F., Dorsey, E. R., Zhu, S., Huskamp, H. A., Conti, R., Dusetzina, S. B., . . . Alexander, G. C. (2012). Trends in attention deficit hyperactivity disorder ambulatory diagnosis and medical treatment in the united states, 2000–2010. *Academic Pediatrics, 12*(2), 110–116.

Garrison, C. Z., Addy, C. L., Jackson, K. L., McKeown, R. E., & Waller, J. L. (1992). Major depressive disorder and dysthymia in young adolescents. *American Journal of Epidemiology, 135*(7), 792–802.

Garstang, J., & Wallis, M. (2006). Randomized controlled trial of melatonin for children with autistic spectrum disorders and sleep problems. *Child: Care, Health and Development, 32*(5), 585–589.

Gauthier, I., Skudlarski, P., Gore, J. C., & Anderson, A. W. (2000). Expertise for cars and birds recruits brain areas involved in face recognition. *Nature Neuroscience, 3*(2), 191–197.

Geist, R. A. (1985). Therapeutic dilemmas in the treatment of anorexia nervosa: A self psychological perspective. In S. W. Emmett (Ed.), *Theory and treatment of anorexia nervosa and bulimia* (pp. 268–288). New York, NY: Brunner/Mazel.

Gejman, P. V., Sanders, A. R., & Duan, J. (2011). The role of genetics in the etiology of schizophrenia. *Psychiatric Clinics of North America, 33*(1), 35–66.

Geller, B., Cooper, T. B., Sun, K., Zimerman, B., Frazier, J., Williams, M., & Heath, J. (1998). Double-blind and placebo-controlled study of lithium for adolescent bipolar disorders with secondary substance dependency. *Journal of the American Academy of Child and Adolescent Psychiatry, 37*(2), 171–178.

Geller, B., & Luby, J. (1997). Child and adolescent bipolar disorder: A review of the past 10 years. *Journal of the American Academy of Child and Adolescent Psychiatry, 36*(9), 1168–1176.

Geller, B., Tillman, R., & Bolhofner, K. (2007). Proposed definitions of bipolar I disorder episodes and daily rapid cycling phenomena in preschoolers, school-aged children, adolescents, and adults. *Journal of Child and Adolescent Psychopharmacology, 17*(2), 217–222.

Geller, B., Tillman, R., Bolhofner, K., Zimerman, B., Strauss, N. A., & Kaufmann, P. (2006). Controlled, blindly rated, direct-interview family study of a prepubertal and early-adolescent bipolar I disorder phenotype: Morbid risk, age at onset, and comorbidity. *Archives of General Psychiatry, 63*(10), 1130–1138.

Geller, B., Williams, M., Zimerman, B., Frazier, J., Beringer, L., & Warner, K. L. (1998). Prepubertal and early adolescent bipolarity differentiate from ADHD by manic symptoms, grandiose delusions, ultra-rapid or ultradian cycling. *Journal of Affective Disorders, 51*(2), 81–91.

Geller, B., Zimerman, B., Williams, M., Bolhofner, K., Craney, J. L., Delbello, M. P., . . . Soutullo, C. A. (2000). Six-month stability and outcome of a prepubertal and early adolescent bipolar disorder phenotype. *Journal of Child and Adolescent Psychopharmacology, 10*(3), 165–173.

Geller, B., Zimerman, B., Williams, M., DelBello, M. P., Bolhofner, K., Craney, J. L., . . . Nickelsburg, M. J. (2002). DSM-IV mania symptoms in a prepubertal and early adolescent bipolar phenotype compared to attention deficit hyperactive and normal controls. *Journal of Child and Adolescent Psychopharmacology, 12,* 11–25.

Geller, B., Zimerman, B., Williams, M., DelBello, M. P., Frazier, J., & Beringer, L. (2002). Phenomenology of prepubertal and early adolescent bipolar disorder: Examples of elated mood, grandiose behaviors, decreased need for sleep, racing thoughts and hypersexuality. *Journal of Child and Adolescent Psychopharmacology, 12*(1), 3–9.

Geller, D. A., Biederman, J., Stewart, S. E., Mullin, B., Farrell, C., Wagner, K. D., . . . Carpenter, D. (2003). Impact of comorbidity on treatment response to paroxetine in pediatric obsessive-compulsive disorder: Is the use of exclusion criteria empirically supported in randomized clinical trials? *Journal of Child and Adolescent Psychopharmacology, 13,* S19–S29.

Geller, D. A., Hoog, S. L., Heiligenstein, J. H., Ricardi, R. K., Tamura, R., Kluszynski, S., . . . Fluoxetine Pediatric OCD Study Team. (2001). Fluoxetine treatment for obsessive-compulsive disorder in children and adolescents: A placebo-controlled clinical trial. *Journal of the American Academy of Child and Adolescent Psychiatry, 40,* 773–779.

Geller, D. A., Wagner, K. D., Emslie, G., Murphy, T., Carpenter, D. J., Wetherhold, E., . . . Gardiner, C. (2004). Paroxetine treatment in children and adolescents with obsessive-compulsive disorder: A randomized, multicenter, double-blind, placebo-controlled trial. *Journal of the American Academy of Child and Adolescent Psychiatry, 43,* 1387–1396.

Gershon, E. S., Hamovit, J., Guroff, J. J., Dibble, E., Leckman, J. F., Sceery, W.,

... Bunney, W. E., Jr. (1982). A family study of schizoaffective, bipolar I, bipolar II, unipolar, and normal control probands. *Archives of General Psychiatry, 39,* 1157–1167.

Gershon, J. (2002). A meta-analytic review of gender differences in ADHD. *Journal of Attention Disorders, 5*(3), 143–154.

Gfroerer, J. C., Wu, L. T., & Penne, M. A. (2002). *Initiation of marijuana use: Trends, patterns, and implications.* Rockville, MD: Substance Abuse and Mental Health Services Administration, Office of Applied Studies.

Ghaziuddin, N., Kutcher, S. P., Knapp, P., Bernet, W., Arnold, V., Beitchman, J., ... Kroeger Ptakowski, K. (2004). Practice parameter for use of electroconvulsive therapy with adolescents. *Journal of the American Academy of Child and Adolescent Psychiatry, 43*(12), 1521–1539.

Gibbons, R. D., Brown, C. H., Hur, K., Marcus, S. M., Bhaumik, D. K., Erkens, J. A., ... Mann, J. J. (2007). Early evidence on the effects of regulators' suicidality warnings on SSRI prescriptions and suicide in children and adolescents. *American Journal of Psychiatry, 164*(9), 1356–1363.

Gibson, A. P., Bettinger, T. L., Patel, N. C., & Crismon, M. L. (2006). Atomoxetine versus stimulants for treatment of attention deficit/hyperactivity disorder. *Annals of Pharmacotherapy, 40*(6), 1134–1142.

Giddan, J. J. (1991). School children with emotional problems and communication deficits: Implications for speech-language pathologists. *Language, Speech, and Hearing Services in Schools, 22,* 291–295.

Gilbert, D. L., Dure, L., Sethuraman, G., Raab, D., Lane, J., & Sallee, F. R. (2003). Tic reduction with pergolide in a randomized controlled trial in children. *Neurology, 60*(4), 606–611.

Gilbert, D. L., Sethuraman, G., Sine, L., Peters, S., & Sallee, F. R. (2000). Tourette's syndrome improvement with pergolide in a randomized, double-blind, crossover trial. *Neurology, 54*(6), 1310–1315.

Gill, M., Daly, G., Heron, S., Hawi, Z., & Fitzgerald, M. (1997). Confirmation of association between attention deficit hyperactivity disorder and a dopamine transporter polymorphism. *Molecular Psychiatry, 2*(4), 311–313.

Gillberg, C., & Steffenburg, S. (1987). Outcome and prognostic factors in infantile autism and similar conditions: A population-based study of 46 cases followed through puberty. *Journal of Autism and Developmental Disorders, 17*(2), 273–287.

Gittelman-Klein, R., & Klein, D. F. (1973). School phobia: Diagnostic considerations in the light of imipramine effects. *Journal of Nervous and Mental Diseases, 156*(3), 199–215.

Glantz, S. A., Iaccopucci, A., Titus, K., & Polansky, J. R. (2012). Smoking in top-grossing US movies, 2011. *Preventing Chronic Disease, 9,* 120170.

Glazener, C. M., & Evans, J. H. (2002). Simple behavioural and physical interventions for nocturnal enuresis in children. *Cochrane Database of Systematic Reviews, 2,* CD003637.

Glowinski, A. L., Madden, P. A., Bucholz, K. K., Lynskey, M. T., & Heath, A. C. (2003). Genetic epidemiology of self-reported lifetime *DSM-IV* major depressive disorder in a population-based twin sample of female adolescents. *Journal of Child Psychology and Psychiatry, 44*(7), 988–996.

Goetz, R. R., Goetz, D. M., Hanlon, C., Davies, M., Weitzman, E. D., & Puig-Antich, J. (1983). Spindle characteristics in prepubertal major depressives during an episode and after sustained recovery: A controlled study. *Sleep, 6*(4), 369–375.

Goetz, R. R., Puig-Antich, J., Ryan, N., Rabinovich, H., Ambrosini, P. J., & Nelson, B. (1987). Electroencephalographic sleep of adolescents with major depression and normal controls. *Archives of General Psychiatry, 44*(1), 61–68.

Goez, H. R., Scott, O., Nevo, N., Bennnett-Back, O., & Zelnik, N. (2012). Using the test of variables of attention to determine the effectiveness of modafinil in children with attention-deficit hyperactive disorder (ADHD): A prospective methylphenidate-controlled trial. *Journal of Child Neurology, 27*(12): 1547–1552.

Goldberg, J. F., & Ernst, C. L. (2002). Features associated with the delayed initiation of mood stabilizers at illness onset in bipolar disorder. *Journal of Clinical Psychiatry, 63*(11), 985–991.

Goldman, L. S., Genel, M., Bezman, R. J., & Slanetz, P. J. (1998). Diagnosis and treatment of attention-deficit/hyperactivity disorder in children and adolescents. *Journal of the American Medical Association, 279*(14), 1100–1107.

Goldschein, E. (2011). 11 incredible facts about the global coffee industry. *Business Insider.* Retrieved August 15, 2014, from http://www.businessinsider.com/facts-about-the-coffee-industry-2011-11?op=1

Goldstein, B. I., Strober, M. A., Birmaher, B., Axelson, D. A., Esposito-Smythers, C., Goldstein, T. R., . . . Keller, M. B. (2008). Substance use disorders among adolescents with bipolar spectrum disorders. *Bipolar Disorder, 10*(4), 469–478.

Goldstein, D. J., Wilson, M. G., Ascroft, R. C., & al-Banna, M. (1999). Effectiveness of fluoxetine therapy in bulimia nervosa regardless of comorbid depression. *International Journal of Eating Disorders, 25*(1), 19–27.

Goldstein, M. J. (1989). Psychosocial treatment of schizophrenia. In S. C. Schultz & C. A. Tamminga (Eds.), *Schizophrenia: Scientific progress* (pp. 318–324). New York, NY: Oxford University Press.

Goldstein, T. R., Axelson, D. A., Birmaher, B., & Brent, D. A. (2007). Dialectical behavior therapy for adolescents with bipolar disorder: A 1-year open trial. *Journal of the American Academy of Child and Adolescent Psychiatry, 46*(7), 820–830.

Goldstein, T. R., Birmaher, B., Axelson, D., Goldstein, B. I., Gill, M. K., Esposito-Smythers, C., . . . Keller, M. (2008). Psychosocial functioning among bipolar youth. *Journal of Affective Disorders, 91*(2–3), 181–188.

Goldstein, T. R., Birmaher, B., Axelson, D., Ryan, N. D., Strober, M. A., Gill, M. K., . . . Keller, M. (2005). History of suicide attempts in pediatric bipolar disorder: Factors associated with increased risk. *Bipolar Disorder, 7*(6), 525–535.

Goldstein, T. R., Fersch-Podrat, R. K., Rivera, M., Axelson, D. A., Merranko, J., Yu, H., . . . Birmaher, B. (2014, July 10). Dialectical behavior therapy (DBT) for adolescents with bipolar disorder: Results from a pilot randomized trial. *Journal of Child and Adolescent Psychopharmacology, 24* (Epub ahead of print).

Goodman, R. F. (2014). *Children trapped by gaps in treatment of mental illness.* Retrieved August 23, 2014, from http://www.aboutourkids.org/articles/children_trapped_gaps_in_treatment_mental_illness

Goodwin, F. K., & Jamison, K. R. (1990). *Manic-depressive illness.* New York, NY: Oxford University Press.

Goodwin, R., Gould, M. S., Blanco, C., & Olfson, M. (2001). Prescription of psychotropic medications to youths in office-based practice. *Psychiatric Services, 52*(8), 1081–1087.

Gordon, C. T., State, R. C., Nelson, J. E., Hamburger, S. D., & Rapoport, J. L. (1993). A double-blind comparison of clomipramine, desipramine, and placebo in the treatment of autistic disorder. *Archives of General Psychiatry, 50*(6), 441–447.

Gordon, I., Vander Wyk, B. C., Bennett, R. H., Cordeaux, C., Lucas, M. V., Eilbott, J. A., . . . Pelphrey, K. A. (2013). Oxytocin enhances brain function in children with autism. *Proceedings of the National Academy of Sciences, 110*(52), 20953–20958.

Gordon, R. A. (2000). *Eating disorders: Anatomy of a social epidemic* (2nd ed). Malden, MA: Blackwell.

Gorwood, P., Leboyer, M., Jay, M., Payan, C., & Feingold, J. (1995). Gender and age at onset in schizophrenia: Impact of family history. *American Journal of Psychiatry, 152*(2), 208–212.

Gotts, S. J., Simmons, W. K., Milbury, L. A., Wallace, G. L., Cox, R. W., & Martin, A. (2012). Fractionation of social brain circuits in autism spectrum disorders. *Brain, 135*(9), 2711–2725.

Gould, M., Jamieson, P., & Romer, D. (2003). Media contagion and suicide among the young. *American Behavioral Scientist, 46*(9), 1269–1284.

Gozal, D. (1998). Sleep-disordered breathing and school performance in children. *Pediatrics, 102,* 616–620.

Gozal, D., O'Brien, L., & Row, B. W. (2004). Consequences of snoring and sleep disordered breathing in children. *Pediatric Pulmonology Supplement, 26,* 166.

Gracious, B. L., Youngstrom, E. A., Findling, R. L., & Calabrese, J. R. (2002). Discriminative validity of a parent version of the Young Mania Rating Scale. *Journal of the American Academy of Child and Adolescent Psychiatry, 41*(11), 1350–1359.

Greenberg, B. S., Siemicki, M., & Dorfman, S. (1993). Sex content in R-rated films viewed by adolescents. In B. S. Greenberg, J. D. Brown, & N. Buerkel-Rothfuss, (Eds.), *Media, sex and the adolescent.* Cresskill, NJ: Hampton Press.

Greenberg, M. T., Speltz, M. L., Deklyen, M., & Endriga, M. C. (1991). Attachment security in preschoolers with and without externalizing behavior problems: A replication. *Development and Psychopathology, 3,* 413–430.

Greene, R. W., Ablon, J. S., Goring, J. C., Raezer-Blakely, L., Markey, J., Monuteaux, M. C., . . . Rabbitt, S. (2004). Effectiveness of collaborative problem solving in affectively dysregulated children with oppositional-defiant disorder: Initial findings. *Journal of Consulting and Clinical Psychology, 72*(6), 1157–1164.

Greenhill, L., Kollins, S., Abikoff, H., McCracken, J., Riddle, M., Swanson, J., . . . Cooper, T. (2006). Efficacy and safety of immediate-release methylphenidate treatment for preschoolers with ADHD. *Journal of the American Academy of Child and Adolescent Psychiatry, 45*(11), 1284–1293.

Greenhill, L. L., Solomon, M., Pleak, R., & Ambrosini, P. (1985). Molindone hydrochloride treatment of hospitalized children with conduct disorder. *Journal of Clinical Psychiatry, 46*(8), 20–25.

Greenhill, L. L., Swanson, J. M., Vitiello, B., Davies, M., Clevenger, W., Wu, M., . . . Wigal, T. (2001). Impairment and deportment responses to different methylphenidate doses in children with ADHD: The MTA titration trial. *Journal of the American Academy of Child and Adolescent Psychiatry, 40*, 180–187.

Grigorenko, E. L. (2006). Learning disabilities in juvenile offenders. *Child and Adolescent Psychiatric Clinics of North America, 15*, 353–371.

Grilo, C. M., Crosby, R. D., Wilson, G. T., & Masheb, R. M. (2012). 12-month follow-up of fluoxetine and cognitive behavioral therapy for binge eating disorder. *Journal of Consulting and Clinical Psychology, 80*(6), 1108–1113.

Grilo, C. M., Masheb, R. M., & Crosby, R. D. (2012). Predictors and moderators of response to cognitive behavioral therapy and medication for the treatment of binge eating disorder. *Journal of Consulting and Clinical Psychology, 80*(5), 897–906.

Grilo, C. M., Masheb, R. M., & Wilson, G. T. (2005). Efficacy of cognitive behavioral therapy and fluoxetine for the treatment of binge eating disorder: A randomized double-blind placebo-controlled comparison. *Biological Psychiatry, 57*(3), 301–309.

Griswold, K. S., Aronoff, H., Kernan, J. B., & Kahn, L. S. (2008). Adolescent substance use and abuse: Recognition and management. *American Family Physician, 77*(3), 331–336.

Grossman, J. B., & Tierney, J., P. (1998). Does mentoring work? An impact study of the Big Brothers Big Sisters program. *Evaluation Review, 22*(3), 402–425.

Gruber, R., Cassoff, J., Frenette, S., Wiebe, S., & Carrier, J. (2012). Impact of sleep extension and restriction on children's emotional lability and impulsivity. *Pediatrics, 130*(5), 1155–1161.

Guastella, A. J., Einfeld, S. L., Gray, K. M., Rinehart, N. J., Tonge, B. J., Lambert, T. J., & Hickie, I. B. (2010). Intranasal oxytocin improves emotion recognition for youth with autism spectrum disorders. *Biological Psychiatry, 67*(7), 692–694.

Guilleminault, C., Moscovitch, A., & Leger, D. (1995). Forensic sleep medicine: Nocturnal wandering and violence. *Sleep, 18*(9), 740–748.

Guttmacher, L. B., & Cretella, H. (1988). Electroconvulsive therapy in one child and three adolescents. *Journal of Clinical Psychiatry, 49*(1), 20–23.

Haapasalo-Pesu, K. M., Vuola, T., Lahelma, L., & Marttunen, M. (2004). Mirtazapine in the treatment of adolescents with major depression: An open-label, multicenter pilot study. *Journal of Child and Adolescent Psychopharmacology, 14*(2), 175–184.

Hagerman, R. J., Berry-Kravis, E., Kaufmann, W. E., Ono, M. Y., Tartaglia, N., Lachiewicz, A., . . . Tranfaglia, M. (2009). Advances in the treatment of fragile X syndrome. *Pediatrics, 123*(1), 378–390.

Halbower, A. C., & Marcus, C. L. (2003). Sleep disorders in children. *Current Opinion in Pulmonary Medicine, 9*(6), 471–476.

Hammad, T. A., Laughren, T., & Racoosin, J. (2006). Suicidality in pediatric patients treated with antidepressant drugs. *Archives of General Psychiatry, 63*(3), 332–339.

Handen, B. L., & Gilchrist, R. (2006). Practitioner review: Psychopharmacology in children and adolescents with mental retardation. *Journal of Child Psychology and Psychiatry, 47*(9), 871–882.

Handen, B. L., & Hardan, A. Y. (2006). Open-label, prospective trial of olanzapine in adolescents with subaverage intelligence and disruptive behavioral disorders. *Journal of the American Academy of Child and Adolescent Psychiatry, 45*, 928–935.

Handen, B. L., Sahl, R., & Hardan, A. Y. (2008). Guanfacine in children with autism and/or intellectual disabilities. *Journal of Developmental and Behavioral Pediatrics, 29*(4), 303–308.

Hannesdottir, D. K., & Ollendick, T. H. (2007). The role of emotion regulation in the treatment of child anxiety disorders. *Clinical Child and Family Psychology Review, 10*(3), 275–293.

Hardan, A., Birmaher, B., Williamson, D. E., Dahl, R. E., Ambrosini, P., Rabinovich, H., & Ryan, N. D. (1999). Secretion in depressed children. *Biological Psychiatry, 46*(4), 506–511.

Harley, R., Sprich, S., Safren, S., Jacobo, M., & Fava, M. (2008). Adaptation of dialectical behavior therapy skills training group for treatment-resistant depression. *Journal of Nervous and Mental Disease, 196*(2), 136–143.

Harrington, R., Rutter, M., Weissman, M., Fudge, H., Groothues, C., Bredenkamp, D., . . . Wickramaratne, P. (1997). Psychiatric disorders in the relatives of depressed probands: I. Comparison of prepubertal, adolescent and early adult onset cases. *Journal of Affect Disorders, 42*(1), 9–22.

Harrington, R., Whittaker, J., & Shoebridge, P. (1998). Psychological treatment of depression in children and adolescents. A review of treatment research. *British Journal of Psychiatry, 173*, 291–298.

Hauser, P., Zametkin, A. J., Martinez, P., Vitiello, B., Matochik, J. A., Mixson, A. J., & Weintraub, B. D. (1993). Attention deficit-hyperactivity disorder in people with generalized resistance to thyroid hormone. *New England Journal of Medicine, 328*(14), 997–1001.

Hawi, Z., Foley, D., Kirley, A., McCarron, M., Fitzgerald, M., & Gill, M. (2001). Dopa decarboxylase gene polymorphisms and attention deficit hyperactivity disorder (ADHD): No evidence for association in the Irish population. *Molecular Psychiatry, 6*, 420–424.

Hawkins, C., & Williams, T. I. (1992). Nightmares, life events and behaviour problems in preschool children. *Child: Care, Health and Development, 18*(2), 117–128.

Hawton, K., & Harriss, L. (2007). Deliberate self-harm in young people: Characteristics and subsequent mortality in a 20-year cohort of patients presenting to hospital. *Journal of Clinical Psychiatry, 68*(10), 1574–1583.

Hazan, A. R., Lipton, H. L., & Glantz, S. A. (1994). Popular films do not reflect current tobacco use. *American Journal of Public Health, 84,* 998–1000.

Hazell, P., O'Connell, D., Heathcote, D., Robertson, J., & Henry, D. (1995). Efficacy of tricyclic drugs in treating child and adolescent depression: A meta-analysis. *British Medical Journal, 310*(6984), 897–901.

Hazell, P. L., & Stuart, J. E. (2003). A randomized controlled trial of clonidine added to psychostimulant medication for hyperactive and aggressive children. *Journal of the American Academy of Child and Adolescent Psychiatry, 42*(8), 886–894.

Hecker, E. (1871). Die hebephrenie. *Archiv Pathologie Anatomie Physiologie Klinik Medizi, 52,* 394.

Hedley, A. A., Ogden, C. L., Johnson, C. L., Carroll, M. D., Curtin, L. R., & Flegal, K. M. (2004). Prevalence of overweight and obesity among US children, adolescents, and adults, 1999–2002. *Journal of the American Medical Association, 291,* 2847–2850.

Heiervang, E., Hugdahl, K., Steinmetz, H., Smievoll, A. I., Stevenson, J., Lund, A., . . . Lundervold, A. (2000). Planum temporale, planum parietale and dichotic listening in dyslexia. *Neuropsychologia, 38*(13), 1704–1713.

Heinicke, C. M., & Ramsey-Klee, D. M. (1986). Outcome of child psychotherapy as a function of frequency of session. *Journal of the American Academy of Child and Adolescent Psychiatry, 25*(2), 247–253.

Hellings, J. A., Kelley, L. A., Gabrielli, W. F., Kilgore, E., & Shah, P. (1996). Sertraline response in adults with mental retardation and autistic disorder. *Journal of Clinical Psychiatry, 57,* 333–336.

Hellström, A. L., Hanson, E., Hansson, S., Hjalmas, K., & Jodal, U. (1990). Micturition habits and incontinence in 7-year-old Swedish school entrants. *European Journal of Pediatrics, 149,* 434–437.

Hemminki, K., & Mutanen, P. (2001). Genetic epidemiology of multistage carcinogenesis. *Mutation Research, 473*(1), 11–21.

Henggeler, S. W., & Lee, T. (2003). Multisystemic treatment of serious clinical problems. In A. E. Kazdin & J. R. Weisz (Eds.), *Evidence-based psychotherapies for children and adolescents* (pp. 301–322). New York, NY: Guilford Press.

Hepworth, J. (1999). *The social construction of anorexia nervosa.* Thousand Oaks, CA: SAGE.

Herpertz-Dahlmann, B. (2009). Adolescent eating disorders: Definitions, symptomatology, epidemiology and comorbidity. *Child and Adolescent Psychiatry Clinics of North America, 18*(1), 31–47.

Herpertz-Dahlmann, B., & Salbach-Andrae, H. (2009). Overview of treatment modalities in adolescent anorexia nervosa. *Child and Adolescent Psychiatry Clinics of North America, 18*(1), 131–145.

Herschell, A., Calzada, E., Eyberg, S. M., & McNeil, C. B. (2002). Parent–child interaction therapy: New directions in research. *Cognitive and Behavioral Practice, 9,* 9–16.

Hettema, J. M., Neale, M. C., & Kendler, K. S. (2001). A review and meta-analysis of the genetic epidemiology of anxiety disorders. *American Journal of Psychiatry, 158,* 1568–1578.

Heywood, L. (1996). *Dedicated to hunger: The anorexic aesthetic in modern culture.* Berkeley: University of California Press.

Hiastala, S. A., Kotler, J. S., McClellan, J. M., & McCauley, E. A. (2010). Interpersonal and social rhythm therapy for adolescents with bipolar disorder: Treatment development and results from an open trial. *Depression and Anxiety, 27*(5), 457–464.

Hilbert, A., Bishop, M. E., Stein, R. I., Tanofsky-Kraff, M., Swenson, A. K., Welch, R. R., & Wilfley, D. E. (2012). Long-term efficacy of psychological treatments for binge eating disorder. *British Journal of Psychiatry, 200*(3), 232–237.

Hirshfeld, D. R., Rosenbaum, J. F., Biederman, J., Bolduc, E. A., Faraone, S. V., Snidman, N., . . . Kagan, J. (1992). Stable behavioral inhibition and its association with anxiety disorder. *Journal of the American Academy of Child and Adolescent Psychiatry, 31*(1), 103–111.

Ho, B., & Andreasen, N. C. (2001). Long delays in seeking treatment for schizophrenia. *Lancet, 357*(9260), 898–900.

Hollander, E., Anagnostou, W., Chaplin, K., Esposito, M., Haznedar, E., Licalzi, S., . . . Buchsbaum, M. (2005). Striatal volume on magnetic resonance imaging and repetitive behaviors in autism. *Biological Psychiatry, 58*(3), 226–232.

Hollander, E., Bartz, J., Chaplin, W., Phillips, W., Sumner, J., Soorya, L., . . . Wasserman, S. (2006). Oxytocin increases retention of social cognition in autism. *Biological Psychiatry, 61*(4), 498–503.

Hollander, E., Phillips, A., Chaplin, W., Zagursky, K., Novotny, S., Wasserman, S., & Iyengar, R. (2005). A placebo controlled crossover trail of liquid fluoxetine on repetitive behaviors in childhood and adolescent autism. *Neuropsychopharmacology, 30,* 582–589.

Holma, K. M., Melartin, T. K., Holma, I. A., & Isometsä, E. T. (2008). Predictors for switch from unipolar major depressive disorder to bipolar disorder type I or II: A 5-year prospective study. *Journal of Clinical Psychiatry, 69*(8), 1267–1275.

Honda, H., Shimizu, Y., & Rutter, M. (2005). No effect of MMR withdrawal on the incidence of autism: A total population study. *Journal of Child Psychology and Psychiatry, 46*(6), 572–579.

Hoover, D. W., & Milich, R. (1994). Effects of sugar ingestion expectancies on mother–child interactions. *Journal of Abnormal Child Psychology, 22*(4), 501–515.

Howlin, P., Goode, S., Hutton, J., & Rutter, M. (2004). Adult outcome for children with autism. *Journal of Child Psychology and Psychiatry, 45,* 212–229.

Howlin, P., Gordon, R. K., Pasco, G., Wade, A., & Charman, T. (2007). Picture exchange communication system (PECS). *Journal of Child Psychology and Psychiatry, 48*(5), 473–481.

Hoyert, D. L., Mathews, T. J., Menacker, F., Strobino, D. M., & Guyer, B. (2006). Annual summary of vital statistics: 2004. *Pediatrics, 117*(1), 168–183.

Humphreys, K. L., Eng, T., & Lee, S. S. (2013). Stimulant medication and substance use outcomes: A meta-analysis. *JAMA Psychiatry, 70*(7), 740–749.

Hunter, L. C., O'Hare, A., Herron, W. J., Fisher, L. A., & Jones, G. E. (2003). Opioid peptides and dipeptidyl peptidase in autism. *Developmental Medicine and Child Neurology, 45,* 121–128.

Hwang, G. C., Tillberg, C. S., & Scahill, L. (2012). Habit reversal training for children with Tourette syndrome: Update and review. *Journal of Child and Adolescent Psychiatric Nursing, 25*(4), 178–183.

Iacoboni, M., Molnar-Szakacs, I., Gallese, V., Buccino, G., Mazziotta, J. C., & Rizzolatti, G. (2005). Grasping the intentions of others with one's own mirror neuron system. *PLoS Biology, 3*(3), e79. doi: 10.1371/journal.pbio.0030079

Ialongo, N., Edelsohn, G., Werthamer-Larsson, L., Crockett, L., & Kellam, S. (1995). The significance of self-reported anxious symptoms in first grade children: Prediction to anxious symptoms and adaptive functioning in fifth grade. *Journal of Child Psychology and Psychiatry, 36*(3), 427–437.

Indig, D., Copeland, J., & Conigrave, K. M. (2008). Young people who attend specialist alcohol treatment: Who are they and do they need special treatment? *Australian and New Zealand Journal of Public Health, 32*(4), 336–340.

Insel, T. (2013). *Director's blog: Transforming diagnosis.* National Institute of Mental Health. Retrieved June 10, 2014, from http://www.nimh.nih.gov/about/director/2013/transforming-diagnosis.shtml

Institute of Medicine. Board on Health Promotion and Disease Prevention, Immunization Safety Review Committee. (2004). *Immunization safety review: Vaccines and autism.* Washington, DC: National Academies Press.

Ipser, J. C., Stein, D. J., Hawkridge, S., & Hoppe, L. (2009). Pharmacotherapy for anxiety disorders in children and adolescents. *Cochrane Database of Systematic Reviews* (Issue 3). doi: 10.1002/14651858.CD005170.pub2

Itard, J. (1825). Mémoire sur quelques fonctions involontaires des appareils de la locomotion, de la préhension et de la voix. *Archives Générales de Médecine, 8,* 405.

Ivanenko, A., Barnes, M. E., Crabtree, V. M., & Gozal, D. (2005). Psychiatric symptoms in children with insomnia referred to a pediatric sleep medicine center. *Sleep Medicine, 5*(3), 253.

Ivanenko, A., Crabtree, V. M., & Gozal, D. (2004). Sleep in children with psychiatric disorders. *Pediatric Clinics of North America, 51*(1), 51.

Ivanenko, A., Crabtree, V. M., & Gozal, D. (2005). Sleep and depression in children and adolescents. *Sleep Medicine Reviews, 9*(2), 115–129.

Jacobsen, L. K., Hamburger, S. D., Van Horn, J. D., Vaituzis, A. C., McKenna,

K., Frazier, J. A., . . . Zametkin, A. J. (1997). Cerebral glucose metabolism in childhood onset schizophrenia. *Psychiatry Research, 75*(3), 131–144.

Jafarinia, M., Mohammadi, M. R., Modabbernia, A., Ashrafi, M., Khajavi, D., Tabrizi, M., ... Akhondzadeh, S. (2012). Bupropion versus methylphenidate in the treatment of children with attention-deficit/hyperactivity disorder: Randomized double-blind study. *Human Psychopharmacology: Clinical and Experimental, 27,* 411–418.

Jaffe, E., Trémeau, F., Sharif, Z., & Reider, R. (1995). Clozapine in tardive Tourette syndrome. *Biological Psychiatry, 38*(3), 196–197.

James, A., Soler, A., & Weatherall, R. (2005). Cognitive behavioural therapy for anxiety disorders in children and adolescents. *Cochrane Database Systematic Reviews, 19*(4), CD004690.

James, A. C., Taylor, A., Winmill, L., & Alfoadari, K. (2008). A preliminary community study of dialectical behaviour therapy (DBT) with adolescent females demonstrating persistent, deliberate self-harm (DSH). *Child and Adolescent Mental Health, 13*(2), 148–152.

Janowsky, D. S., Kraus, J. E., Barnhill, J., Elamir, B., & Davis, J. M. (2003). Effects of topiramate on aggressive, self-injurious, and disruptive/destructive behaviors in the intellectually disabled: An open-label retrospective study. *Journal of Clinical Psychopharmacology, 23,* 500–504.

Janowsky, D. S., Shetty, M., Barnhill, J., Elamir, B., & Davis, J. M. (2005). Serotonergic antidepressant effects on aggressive, self-injurious and destructive/disruptive behaviors in intellectually disabled adults: A retrospective open naturalistic trial. *International Journal of Neuropsychopharmacology, 8,* 37–48.

Jiang, S., Xin, R., Lin, S., Qian, Y., Tang, G., Wang, D., & Wu, X. (2003). Linkage studies between attention-deficit hyperactivity disorder and the monoamine oxidase genes. *American Journal of Medical Genetics, 105,* 783–788.

Johnson, K. P., & Malow, B. A. (2008). Sleep in children with autism spectrum disorders. *Current Treatment Options in Neurology, 10*(5), 350–359.

Johnston, L. D., O'Malley, P. M., Miech, R. A., Bachman, J. G., & Schulenberg, J. E. (2013). *Monitoring the Future national survey results on drug use 1975–2013.* Retrieved from www.monitoringthefuture.org

Jolin, E. M., Weller, E. B., & Weller, R. A. (2008). Anxiety symptoms and syndromes in bipolar children and adolescents. *Current Psychiatry Reports, 10*(2), 123–129.

Jones, E. A. (2009). Establishing response and stimulus classes for initiating joint attention in children with autism. *Research in Autism Spectrum Disorders, 3*(2), 375–389.

Jones, K. L. (1997). *Smith's recognizable patterns of human malformation* (5th ed.). Philadelphia, PA: W. B. Saunders.

Kadesjö, B., & Gillberg, C. (2000). Tourette's disorder: Epidemiology and comorbidity in primary school children. *Journal of the American Academy of Child and Adolescent Psychiatry, 39*(5), 548–555.

Kafantaris, V., Coletti, D. J., Dicker, R., Padula, G., Pleak, R. R., & Alvir, J. M. (2004). Lithium treatment of acute mania in adolescents: A placebo-controlled discontinuation study. *Journal of the American Academy of Child and Adolescent Psychiatry, 43*(8), 984–993.

Kagan, J., Reznick, J. S., & Snidman, N. (1988). Biological bases of childhood shyness. *Science, 240*(4849), 167–171.

Kagan, J., & Snidman, N. (1999). Early childhood predictors of adult anxiety disorders. *Biological Psychiatry, 46*(11), 1536–1541.

Kairaluoma, L., Narhi, V., Ahonen, T., Westerholm, J., & Aro, M. (2009). Do fatty acides help in overcoming reading difficulties? A double-blind, placebo-controlled study of the effects of eicosapentaenoic acid and carnosine supplementation on children with dyslexia. *Child: Care, Health and Development, 35*, 112–119.

Kalanithi, P. S., Zheng, W., Kataoka, Y., DiFiglia, M., Grantz, H., Saper, C. B., & Vaccarino, F. M. (2005). Altered parvalbumin-positive neuron distribution in basal ganglia of individuals with Tourette syndrome. *Proceedings of the National Academy of Sciences (US), 102*(37), 13307–13312.

Kaminski, J. W., & Fang, X. (2008). Victimization by peers and adolescent suicide in three US samples. *Journal of Pediatrics, 155*(5), 683–688.

Kane, J. M. (2006). Tardive dyskinesia circa 2006. *American Journal of Psychiatry, 163*, 1316–1318.

Kane, J., Honigfeld, G., Singer, J., & Meltzer, H. (1988). Clozapine for the treatment-resistant schizophrenic: A double-blind comparison with chlorpromazine. *Archives of General Psychiatry, 45*(9), 789–796.

Kanner, L. (1965). Infantile autism and the schizophrenias. *Behavioral Science, 10*(4), 412–420.

Kaplan, H. I., & Sadock, B. J. (2007). *Kaplan and Sadock's synopsis of psychiatry: Behavioral sciences, clinical psychiatry* (10th ed.). New York, NY: Lippincott Williams & Wilkins.

Kaplan, H. I., Sadock, B. J., & Greb, J. A. (1994). *Kaplan and Sadock's synopsis of psychiatry* (7th ed., pp. 689–698). New York, NY: Williams & Wilkins.

Kashani, J. H., Barbero, G. J., & Bolander, F. D. (1981). Depression in hospitalized pediatric patients. *Journal of the American Academy of Child Psychiatry, 20*(1), 123–134.

Kashani, J. H., & Carlson, G. A. (1987). Seriously depressed preschoolers. *American Journal of Psychiatry, 144*(3), 348–350.

Kashani, J. H., Carlson, G. A., Beck, N. C., Hoeper, E. W., Corcoran, C. M., McAllister, J. A., . . . Reid, J. C. (1987). Depression, depressive symptoms, and depressed mood among a community sample of adolescents. *American Journal of Psychiatry, 144*(7), 931–934.

Kashani, J. H., Sherman, D. D., Parker, J. R., & Reid, J. C. (1990). Utility of the Beck Depression Inventory with clinic-referred adolescents. *Journal of the American Academy of Child and Adolescent Psychiatry, 29*(2), 278–282.

Kauffman, J. M. (1997). *Characteristics of emotional and behavioral disorders of children and youth* (6th ed.). Englewood Cliffs, NJ: Prentice Hall.

Kavale, K. A., & Forness, S. R. (1995). *The nature of learning disabilities: Critical elements of diagnosis and classification.* Mahwah, NJ: Lawrence Erlbaum.

Kaye, W. H., Klump, L., Frank, G. K. W., & Strober, M. (2000). Anorexia and bulimia nervosa. *Annual Review of Medicine, 51,* 299–313.

Kaye, W. H., Nagata, T., Weltzin, T. E., Hsu, L. K. G., Sokol, M. S., McConaha, C., . . . Deep, D. (2001). Double-blind placebo-controlled administration of fluoxetine in restricting- and restricting-purging-type anorexia nervosa. *Biological Psychiatry, 49*(7), 644–652.

Kazdin, A. E. (1997). Parent management training: Evidence, outcomes, and issues. *Journal of the American Academy of Child and Adolescent Psychiatry, 36*(10), 1349–1356.

Kazdin, A. E. (2003). Problem-solving skills training and parent management training for conduct disorder. In A. E. Kazdin & J. R. Weisz (Eds.), *Evidence-based psychotherapies for children and adolescents* (pp. 241–262). New York, NY: Guilford Press.

Kazdin, A. E. (2005). *Parent management training.* New York, NY: Oxford University Press.

Keenan, K., & Shaw, D. S. (2003). Starting at the beginning: Exploring the etiology of antisocial behavior in the first years of life. In B. Lahey, T. E. Moffitt, & A. Caspi (Eds.), *Conduct disorders in childhood and adolescence* (pp. 153–181). Cambridge, UK: Cambridge University Press.

Keller, M. B., Ryan, N. D., Strober, M., Klein, R. G., Kutcher, S. P., Birmaher, B., . . . McCafferty, J. P. (2001). Efficacy of paroxetine in the treatment of adolescent major depression: A randomized, controlled trial. *Journal of the American Academy of Child and Adolescent Psychiatry, 40*(7), 762–772.

Kemner, C., Willemsen-Swinkels, S. N., deJonge, M., Tuynman-Qua, H., & van Engeland, H. (2002). Open-label study of olanzapine in children with pervasive developmental disorder. *Journal of Clinical Psychopharmacology, 22,* 455–460.

Kendall, P. C., Safford, S., Flannery-Schroeder, E., & Webb, A. (2004). Child anxiety treatment: Outcomes in adolescence and impact on substance use and depression at 7.4-year follow-up. *Journal of Consulting and Clinical Psychology, 72*(2), 276–287.

Kendler, K. S. (2001). Twin studies of psychiatric illness: An update. *Archives of General Psychiatry, 58,* 1005–1014.

Kenny, M. C., & Faust, J. (1997). Mother–child agreement on self-report of anxiety in abused children. *Journal of Anxiety Disorders, 11*(5), 463–472.

Kent, J. L. (2013). Adderall: America's favorite amphetamine. *High Times.* Retrieved June 17, 2014, from http://www.hightimes.com/read/adderall-americas-favorite-amphetamine

Kerr, P. L., Muehlenkamp, J. J., & Turner, J. M. (2010). Nonsuicidal self-injury: A review of current research for family medicine and primary care physicians. *Journal of the American Board of Family Medicine, 23*(2), 240–259.

Kerr, S., & Jowett, S. (1994). Sleep problems in pre-school children: A review of the literature. *Child: Care, Health and Development, 20*(6), 379–391.

Kessler, R. C., Berglund, P., Demler, O., Jin, R., Merikangas, K. R., & Walters, E. E. (2005). Lifetime prevalence and age-of-onset distributions of *DSM-IV* disorders in the National Comorbidity Survey Replication. *Archives of General Psychiatry, 62*(6), 593–602.

Kessler, R. C., Nelson, C., McGonagle, K., Edlund, M., Frank, R., & Leaf, P. (1996). The epidemiology of co-occurring addictive and mental disorders: Implications for prevention and service utilization. *American Journal of Orthopsychiatry, 66,* 17–31.

Kessler, R. C., & Walters, E. E. (1998). Epidemiology of *DSM-III-R* major depression and minor depression among adolescents and young adults in the National Comorbidity Survey. *Depression and Anxiety, 7*(1), 3–14.

Kessler, R. J. (2004). Electroconvulsive therapy for affective disorders in persons with mental retardation. *Psychiatric Quarterly, 75*(1), 99–104.

Keverne, E. B. (2004). Understanding well-being in the evolutionary context of brain development. *Philosophical Transactions of the Royal Society of London, 359*(1449), 1349–1358.

Kieseppä, T., Partonen, T., Haukka, J., Kaprio, J., & Lönnqvist, J. (2004). High concordance of bipolar I disorder in a nationwide sample of twins. *American Journal of Psychiatry, 161*(10), 1814–1821.

Kim, W. J. (2003). Child and adolescent psychiatry workforce: A critical shortage and national challenge; the American Academy of Child and Adolescent Psychiatry Task Force on Workforce Needs. *Academic Psychiatry, 27*(4), 277–282.

Kim, Y. S., Leventhal, B., Koh, Y. J., Fombonne, E., Laska, E., Lim, E. C., . . . Grinker, R. R. (2011). Prevalence of autism spectrum disorders in a total population sample. *American Journal of Psychiatry, 168*(9), 904–912.

King, B. H., Hollander, E., Sikich, L., McCracken, J. T., Scahill, L., Bregman, J. D., . . . STAART Psychopharmacology Network. (2009). Lack of efficacy of citalopram in children with autism spectrum disorders and high levels of repetitive behavior: Citalopram ineffective in children with autism. *Archives of General Psychiatry, 66*(6), 583–590.

King, B. H., State, M. W., Shah, B., Davanzo, P., & Dykens, E. (1997). Mental retardation: A review of the past 10 years: Part I. *Journal of the American Academy of Child and Adolescent Psychiatry, 36*(12), 1656–1663.

King, R. A., Scahill, L., Findley, D., & Cohen, D. J. (1999). Psychosocial and behavioral treatments. In J. F. Leckman & D. J. Cohen (Eds.), *Tourette syndrome—tics, obsessions, compulsions: Developmental psychopathology and clinical care* (pp. 338–359). New York, NY: Wiley.

Kirchner, J. C., Hatri, A., Heekeren, H. R., & Dziobek, I. (2011). Autistic symptomatology, face processing abilities, and eye fixation patterns. *Journal of Autism and Developmental Disorders, 41*(2), 158–167.

Klackenberg, G. (1981). Nocturnal enuresis in a longitudinal perspective. *Acta Paediatrica, 70,* 453–457.

Klein, N. J. (2001). Management of primary nocturnal enuresis. *Urologic Nursing, 21*(2), 71–76.

Klein, R. G., Koplewicz, H. S., & Kanner, A. (1992). Imipramine treatment of children with separation anxiety disorder. *Journal of the American Academy of Child and Adolescent Psychiatry, 31*(1), 21–28.

Klin, A., Jones, W., Schultz, R., Volkmar, F., & Cohen, D. (2002). Defining and quantifying the social phenotype in autism. *American Journal of Psychiatry, 159*(6), 895–908.

Klin, A., Volkmar, F. R., & Sparrow, S. S. (2000). *Asperger sydrome.* New York, NY: Guilford Press.

Klonsky, E. D., & Muehlenkamp, J. J. (2007). Self-injury: a research review for the practitioner. *Journal of Clinical Psychology, 63*(11), 1045–1056.

Knable, M. B., Kleinman, J. E., & Weinberger, D. R. (1998). Neurobiology of schizophrenia. In A. F. Schatzberg & C. B. Nemeroff (Eds.), *Textbook of psychopharmacology* (2nd ed., pp. 589–607). Washington, DC: American Psychiatric Press.

Knutson, J. F., & Sullivan, P. M. (1993). Communication disorders as a risk factor in abuse. *Topics in Language Disorders, 13*(4), 1–14.

Kodish, I., Rockhill, C., & Varley, C. (2011). Pharmacotherapy for anxiety disorders in children and adolescents. *Dialogues in Clinical Neuroscience, 13*(4), 439–452.

Kopelowicz, A., Liberman, R. P., & Wallace, C. J. (2003). Psychiatric rehabilitation for schizophrenia. *International Journal of Psychology and Psychological Therapy, 3*(2), 283–298.

Kotagal, S. (2008). Narcolepsy and idiopathic hypersomnia in childhood. In A. Ivanenko (Ed.), *Sleep and psychiatric disorders in children and adolescents* (pp. 163–171). London, UK: Informa Health Care.

Kotler, L. A., Devlin, M. J., Davies, M., & Walsh, B. T. (2003). An open trial of fluoxetine for adolescents with bulimia nervosa. *Journal of Child and Adolescent Psychopharmacology, 13*(3), 329–335.

Kovacs, M. (1985). The Children's Depression Inventory (CDI). *Psychopharmacology Bulletin, 21*(4), 995–998.

Kovacs, M., Devlin, B., Pollock, M., Richards, C., & Mukerji, P. (1997). A controlled family history study of childhood-onset depressive disorder. *Archives of General Psychiatry, 54*(7), 613–623.

Kovacs, M., & Pollock, M. (1995). Bipolar disorder and comorbid conduct disorder in childhood and adolescence. *Journal of the American Academy of Child and Adolescent Psychiatry, 34*(6), 715–723.

Kowatch, R. A., Findling, R. L., Scheffer, R. E., & Stanford, K. E. (2007, October). *Placebo-controlled trial of divalproex versus lithium for bipolar disorder.* Poster presented at the annual meeting of the American Academy of Child and Adolescent Psychiatry, Boston, MA.

Kowatch, R. A., Fristad, M., Birmaher, B., Wagner, K. D., Findling, R. L., & Hellander, M. (2005). Treatment guidelines for children and adolescents with bipolar disorder. *Journal of the American Academy of Child and Adolescent Psychiatry, 44,* 213–235.

Kowatch, R. A., Suppes, T., Carmody, T. J., Bucci, J. P., Hume, J. H., Kromelis,

M., . . . Rush, A. J. (2000). Effect size of lithium, divalproex sodium, and carbamazepine in children and adolescents with bipolar disorder. *Journal of the American Academy of Child and Adolescent Psychiatry, 39*(6), 713–720.

Kraepelin, E., Barclay, R., & Robertson, G. M. (1919). *Dementia praecox and paraphrenia.* Edinburgh, UK: E&S Livingstone.

Krous, H. F., Beckwith, J. B., Byard, R. W., Rognum, T. O., Bajanowski, T., Corey, T., . . . Mitchell, E. A. (2004). Sudden infant death syndrome and unclassified sudden infant deaths: A definitional and diagnostic approach. *Pediatrics, 114*(1), 234–238.

Kryzhanovskaya, L., Schulz, S. C., McDougle, C., Frazier, J., Dittmann, R., Robertson-Plouch, C., . . . Tohen, M. (2009). Olanzapine versus placebo in adolescents with schizophrenia: A 6-week, randomized, double-blind, placebo-controlled trial. *Journal of the American Academy of Child and Adolescent Psychiatry, 48*(1), 60–70.

Kulig, J. W. (2005). Tobacco, alcohol, and other drugs: The role of the pediatrician in prevention, identification, and management of substance abuse. *Pediatrics, 115*(3), 816–821.

Kulman, G., Lissoni, P., Rovelli, F., Roselli, M. G., Brivio, F., & Sequeri, P. (2000). Evidence of pineal endocrine hypofunction in autistic children. *Neuroendocrinology Letters, 21*(1), 31–34.

Kurlan, R. (2003). Tourette's syndrome: Are stimulants safe? *Current Neurology and Neuroscience Reports, 3*(4), 285–288.

Kurlan, R. (2014). Treatment of Tourette syndrome. *Neurotherapeutics, 11*(1), 161–165.

Kurlan, R., Crespi, G., Coffey, B., Mueller-Vahl, K., Koval, S., & Wunderlich, G. (2012). Pramipexole for TS trial investigators. *Movement Disorders, 27*(6), 775–778.

Kushner, H. I. (1995). Medical fictions: The case of the cursing marquise and the (re)construction of Gilles de la Tourette's syndrome. *Bulletin of the History of Medicine, 69*(2), 224.

Kutcher, S., & Robertson, H. A. (1995). Electroconvulsive therapy in treatment-resistant bipolar youth. *Journal of Child and Adolescent Psychopharmacology, 5*, 167–175.

Lagnato, L. (2013, April 11). U.S. probes use of antipsychotic drugs on children. *Wall Street Journal.* Retrieved July 12, 2014, from http://online.wsj.com/news/articles/SB10001424127887323477604578654130865747470

Lahey, B. B., Loeber, R., Hart, E. L., Applegate, B., Zhang, Q., Green, S. M., & Russo, M. F. (1995). Four-year longitudinal study of conduct disorder in boys: Patterns and predictors of persistence. *Journal of Abnormal Psychology, 104*, 83–93.

La Malfa, G., Bertelli, M., & Conte, M. (2001). Fluvoxamine and aggression in mental retardation. *Psychiatric Services, 52*, 1105.

Landon, T. M., & Barlow, D. H. (2004). Cognitive-behavioral treatment for panic disorder: Current status. *Journal of Psychiatric Practice, 10*(4), 211–226.

Langberg, J. M., Epstein, J. N., & Graham, A. J. (2008). Organizational-skills interventions in the treatment of ADHD. *Expert Reviews of Neurotherapeutics, 8*(10), 1549–1561.

Larson, J. C., Mostofsky, S. H., Goldberg, M. C., Cutting, L. E., Denckla, M. B., & Mahone, E. M. (2007). Effects of gender and age on motor exam in typically developing children. *Developmental Neuropsychology, 32*(1), 543–562.

Larson, M. K., Walker, E. F., & Compton, M. T. (2010). Early signs, diagnosis and therapeutics of the prodromal state of schizophrenia and related psychotic disorders. *Expert Review of Neurotherapeutics, 10*(8), 1347–1359.

Last, C. G., Hersen, M., Kazdin, A. E., Finkelstein, R., & Strauss, C. C. (1993). Comparison of *DSM-III* separation anxiety and overanxious disorders: Demographic characteristics and patterns of comorbidity. *Harvard Review of Psychiatry, 1*(1), 2–16.

Last, C. G., Perrin, S., Hersen, M., & Kazdin, A. E. (1996). A prospective study of childhood anxiety disorders. *Journal of the American Academy of Child and Adolescent Psychiatry, 35*(11), 1502–1510.

Laugeson, E. A., Frankel, F., Mogil, C., & Dillon, A. R. (2008). Parent-assisted social skills training to improve friendships in teens with autism spectrum disorders. *Journal of Autism and Developmental Disorders, 18.*

Law, J., Boyle, J., Harris, F., Harkness, A., & Nye, C. (2000). Prevalence and natural history of primary speech and language delay: Findings from a systematic review of the literature. *International Journal of Language and Communication Disorders, 35*(2), 165–188.

Lawson, D. C., Turic, D., Langley, K., Pay, H. M., Govan, C. F., Norton, N., . . . Thapar, A. (2003). Association analysis of monoamine oxidase A and attention deficit hyperactivity disorder. *American Journal of Medical Genetics, 116B,* 84–89.

Leach, C. E., Blair, P. S., Fleming, P. J., Smith, I. J., Platt, M. W., Berry, P. J., & Golding, J. (1999). Epidemiology of SIDS and explained sudden infant deaths. CESDI SUDI Research Group. *Pediatrics, 104*(4), e43.

Lebowitz, E. R., Motlagh, M. G., Katsovich, L., King, R. A., Lombroso, P. J., Grantz, H., . . . Leckman, J. F. (2012). Tourette syndrome in youth with and without obsessive compulsive disorder and attention deficit hyperactivity disorder. *European Child and Adolescent Psychiatry, 21*(8), 451–457.

Leckman, J. F. (2003). Phenomenology of tics and natural history of tic disorders. *Brain and Development, 25*(1), S24–S28.

Leckman, J. F., & Cohen, D. J. (1996). Tic disorders. In M. Lewis (Ed.), *Child and adolescent psychiatry: A comprehensive textbook* (2nd ed.). Baltimore, MD: Williams & Wilkins.

Leckman, J. F., Goodman, W. K., North, W. G., Chappell, P. B., Price, L. H., Pauls, D. L., . . . Cohen, D. J. (1994). Elevated cerebrospinal fluid levels of oxytocin in obsessive-compulsive disorder. Comparison with Tourette's syndrome and healthy controls. *Archives of General Psychiatry, 51*(10), 782–792.

Leckman, J. F., Walker, D. E., & Cohen, D. J. (1993). Premonitory urges in Tourette's syndrome. *American Journal of Psychiatry, 150*(1), 98–102.

Leckman, J. F., Zhang, H., Vitale, A., Lahnin, F., Lynch, K., Bondi, C., . . . Peterson, B. S. (1998). Course of tic severity in Tourette syndrome: The first two decades. *Pediatrics, 102*(1), 14–19.

Lecomte, T., Leclerc, C., Corbière, M., Wykes, T., Wallace, C. J., & Spidel, A. (2008). Group cognitive behavior therapy or social skills training for individuals with a recent onset of psychosis? Results of a randomized controlled trial. *Journal of Nervous and Mental Disease, 196*(12), 866–875.

le Grange, D., Crosby, R. D., Rathouz, P. J., & Leventhal, B. L. (2007). A randomized controlled comparison of family-based treatment and supportive psychotherapy for adolescent bulimia nervosa. *Archives of General Psychiatry, 64*(9), 1049–1056.

le Grange, D., & Eisler, I. (2009). Family interventions in adolescent anorexia nervosa. *Child and Adolescent Psychiatry Clinics of North America, 18*(1), 159–173.

Leibenluft, E. (2011). Severe mood dysregulation, irritability, and the diagnostic boundaries of bipolar disorder in youth. *American Journal of Psychiatry, 168*(2), 129–142.

Lieberman, J. A., Stroup, T. S., McEvoy, J. P., Swartz, M. S., Rosenheck, R. A., Perkins, D. O., . . . Hsiao, J. K. (2005). Effectiveness of antipsychotic drugs in patients with chronic schizophrenia. *New England Journal of Medicine, 353*(12), 1209–1223.

Leibson, C. L., Katusic, S. K., Barbaresi, W. J., Ransom, J., & O'Brien, P. C. (2001). Use and costs of medical care for children and adolescents with and without attention deficit/hyperactivity disorder. *Journal of the American Medical Association, 285*(1), 60–66.

Leonard, H. L., Swedo, S. E., Rapoport, J. L., Koby, E. V., Lenane, M. C., Cheslow, D. L., & Hamburger, S. D. (1989). Treatment of obsessive-compulsive disorder with clomipramine and desipramine in children and adolescents: A double-blind crossover comparison. *Archives of General Psychiatry, 46*, 1088–1092.

Leonard, H. L., Topol, D., Bukstein, O., Hindmarsh, D., Allen, A. J., & Swedo, S. (1994). Case study: Clonazepam as an augmenting agent in the treatment of childhood-onset obsessive-compulsive disorder. *Journal of the American Academy of Child and Adolescent Psychiatry, 33*, 792–794.

Levin, H. S., & Hanten, G. (2005). Executive functions after traumatic brain injury in children. *Pediatric Neurology, 33*(2), 79–93.

Lewinsohn, P. M., Clarke, G. N., Seeley, J. R., & Rohde, P. (1994). Major depression in community adolescents: Age at onset, episode duration, and time to recurrence. *Journal of the American Academy of Child and Adolescent Psychiatry, 33*(6), 809–818.

Lewinsohn, P. M., Hops, H., Roberts, R. E., Seeley, J. R., & Andrews, J. A. (1993). Adolescent psychopathology: Prevalence and incidence of depression and other *DSM-III-R* disorders in high school students. *Journal of Abnormal Psychology, 102*(1), 133–144.

Lewinsohn, P. M., Klein, D. N., & Seeley, J. R. (1995). Bipolar disorders in a community sample of older adolescents: Prevalence, phenomenology, comorbidity, and course. *Journal of the American Academy of Child and Adolescent Psychiatry, 34*(4), 454–463.

Lewis, M. H., Bodfish, J. W., Powell, S. B., & Golden, R. N. (1995). Clomipramine treatment for stereotype and related repetitive movement disorders associated with mental retardation. *American Journal of Mental Retardation, 100,* 299–312.

Lewis, M. H., Bodfish, J. W., Powell, S. B., Parker, D. E., & Golden, R. N. (1996). Clomipramine treatment for self-injurious behavior of individuals with mental retardation: A double-blind comparison with placebo. *American Journal of Mental Retardation, 100*(6), 654–665.

Libby, A. M., Brent, D. A., Morrato, E. H., Orton, H. D., Allen, R., & Valuck, R. J. (2007). Decline in treatment of pediatric depression after FDA advisory on risk of suicidality with SSRIs. *American Journal of Psychiatry, 164,* 884–891.

Licinio, J., & Wong, M. L. (2005). Depression, antidepressants and suicidality: A critical appraisal. *Nature Reviews Drug Discovery, 4*(2), 165–171.

Liddle, H. A., Rowe, C. L., Dakof, G. A., Henderson, C. E., & Greenbaum, P. E. (2009). Multidimensional family therapy for young adolescent substance abuse: Twelve-month outcomes of a randomized controlled trial. *Journal of Consulting and Clinical Psychology, 77*(1), 12–25.

Lieberman, J. A., Stroup, T. S., McEvoy, J. P., Swartz, M. S., Rosenheck, R. A., Perkins, D. O., . . . Hsiao, J. K. (2005). Effectiveness of antipsychotic drugs in patients with chronic schizophrenia. *New England Journal of Medicine, 353*(12), 1209–1223.

Liebowitz, M. R., Turner, S. M., Piacentini, J., Beidel, D. C., Clarvit, S. R., Davies, S. O., . . . Simpson, H. B. (2002). Fluoxetine in children and adolescents with OCD: A placebo-controlled trial. *Journal of the American Academy of Child and Adolescent Psychiatry, 41,* 1431–1438.

Lindenmayer, L. P., & Kotsaftis, A. (2000). Use of sodium valproate in violent and aggressive behaviors: A critical review. *Journal of Clinical Psychiatry, 61,* 123–128.

Linehan, M. M. (1993). *Cognitive-behavioral treatment of borderline personality disorder.* New York, NY: Guilford Press.

Ling, W., Oftedal, G., & Weinberg, W. (1970). Depressive illness in childhood presenting as severe headache. *American Journal of Diseases of Children, 120*(2), 122–124.

Lish, J. D., Dime-Meenan, S., Whybrow, P. C., Price, R. A., & Hirschfeld, R. M. (1994). The National Depressive and Manic-Depressive Association (DMDA) survey of bipolar members. *Journal of Affective Disorders, 31*(4), 281–294.

Liu, X., Buysse, D. J., Gentzler, A. L., Kiss, E., Mayer, L., Kapornai, K., . . . Kovacs, M. (2007). Insomnia and hypersomnia associated with depressive phenomenology and comorbidity in childhood depression. *Sleep, 30*(1), 83–90.

Loeber, R., Burke, J. D., Lahey, B. B., Winters, A., & Zera, M. (2000). Oppositional defiant and conduct disorder: A review of the past 10 years: Part I. *Journal of the American Academy of Child and Adolescent Psychiatry, 39*(12), 1468–1484.

Loeber, R., & Kennan, K. (1994). Interaction between conduct disorder and its comorbid conditions: Effects of age and gender. *Clinical Psychology Review, 14,* 497–523.

Lohr, W. D., & Honaker, J. (2013). Atypical antipsychotics for the treatment of disruptive behavior. *Pediatric Annals, 42*(2), 72–77.

Loy, J. H., Merry, S. N., Hetrick, S. E., & Stasiak, K. (2012). Atypical antipsychotics for disruptive behaviour disorders in children and youths (review). *Cochrane Database Systematic Review, 9.*

Luby, J., Mrakotsky, C., Meade Stalets, M., Belden, A., Heffelfinger, A., Williams, M., & Spitznagel, E. (2006). Risperidone in preschool children with autistic spectrum disorders: An investigation of safety and efficacy. *Journal of Child and Adolescent Psychopharmacology, 16*(5), 575–587.

Luiselli, J. K., Blew, P., & Thibadeau, S. (2001). Therapeutic effects and long-term efficacy of antidepressant medication for persons with developmental disabilities: Behavioral assessment in two cases of treatment-resistant aggression and self-injury. *Behavior Modification, 25,* 62–78.

Määttä, T., Tervo-Määttä, T., Taanila, A., Kaski, M., & Iivanainen, M. (2006). Mental health, behavior and intellectual abilities of people with Down syndrome. *Down Syndrome Research and Practice, 11*(1), 37–43.

Madsen, K. M., Hviid, A., Vestergaard, M., Schendel, D., Wohlfahrt, J., Thorsen, P., & Melbye, M. (2002). A population-based study of measles, mumps, and rubella vaccination and autism. *New England Journal of Medicine, 347*(19), 1477–1482.

Mahowald, M. W., & Rosen, G. M. (1990). Parasomnias in children. *Pediatrician, 17*(1), 21–31.

Mahowald, M. W., & Schenck, C. H. (1996). NREM sleep parasomnias. *Neurologic Clinics, 14*(4), 675–696.

Makris, N., Biederman, J., Valera, E. M., Bush, G., Kaiser, J., Kennedy, D. N., . . . Siedman, L. J. (2007). Cortical thinning of the attention and executive function networks in adults with attention-deficit/hyperactivity disorder. *Cerebral Cortex, 17*(6), 1364–1375.

Manassis, K., & Monga, S. (2001). A therapeutic approach to children and adolescents with anxiety disorders and associated comorbid conditions. *Journal of the American Academy of Child and Adolescent Psychiatry, 40*(1), 115–117.

Mandoki, M. W., Tapia, M. R., Tapia, M. A., Sumner, G. S., & Parker, J. L. (1997). Venlafaxine in the treatment of children and adolescents with major depression. *Psychopharmacology Bulletin, 33*(1), 149–154.

Mann, J. J., Oquendo, M., Underwood, M. D., & Arango, V. (1999). The neurobiology of suicide risk: A review for the clinician. *Journal of Clinical Psychiatry, 60*(2), 7–11, 18–20, 113–116.

Mannarino, A. P., & Cohen, J. A. (1996). Family related variable and psychological symptom formation in sexually abused girls. *Journal of Child Sexual Abuse, 5*(1), 105–119.

Manni, R., Ratti, M. F., Marchioni, E., Castelnovo, G., Murelli, R., Sartori, I., . . . Tartara, A. (1997). Poor sleep in adolescents: A study of 869 17-year-old Italian secondary school students. *Journal of Sleep Research, 6,* 44–49.

Mano, M. J., Tom-Revzon, C., Bukstein, O. G., & Crismon, M. L. (2007). Changes and challenges: Managing ADHD in a fast-paced world. *Journal of Managed Care Pharmacy Supplement, 9*(13), S-b.

Marazziti, D., Corsi, M., Baroni, S., Consoli, G., & Catena-Dellosso, M. (2012). Latest advancements in the pharmacological treatment of binge eating disorder. *European Review for Medical and Pharmacological Sciences, 16*(15), 2102–2107.

March, J. S., Biederman, J., Wolkow, R., Safferman, A., Mardekian, J., Cook, E. H., . . . Wagner, K. D. (1998). Sertraline in children and adolescents with obsessive-compulsive disorder: A multicenter randomized controlled trial. *Journal of the American Medical Association, 280,* 1752–1756.

March, J. S., Entusah, A. R., Rynn, M., Albano, A. M., & Tourian, K. A. (2007). A randomized controlled trial of venlafaxine ER versus placebo in pediatric social anxiety disorder. *Biological Psychiatry, 62*(10), 1149–1154.

March, J., Silva, S., Petrycki, S., Curry, J., Wells, K., Fairbank, J., . . . Treatment for Adolescents With Depression Study (TADS) Team (2004). Fluoxetine, cognitive behavioral therapy, and their combination for adolescents with depression: Treatment for Adolescents with Depression Study (TADS) randomized controlled trial. *Journal of the American Medical Association, 292*(7), 807–820.

March, J. S., Silva, S., Petrycki, S., Curry, J., Wells, K., Fairbank, J., . . . Ronchon, J. J. (2007). The Treatment for Adolescents with Depression Study (TADS): Long-term effectiveness and safety outcomes. *Archives of General Psychiatry, 64*(10), 1132–1143.

Marcus, R. N., Owen, R., Kamen, L., Manos, G., McQuade, R. D., Carson, W. H., & Aman, M. G. (2009). A placebo-controlled, fixed-dose study of aripiprazole in children and adolescents with irritability associated with autistic disorder. *Journal of the American Academy of Child and Adolescent Psychiatry, 48*(11), 1110–1119.

Marder, S. R. (1998). Antipsychotic medications. In A. F. Schatzberg & C. B. Nemeroff (Eds.), *Textbook of psychopharmacology* (2nd ed., pp. 309–321). Washington, DC: American Psychiatric Press.

Marshall, M., Lewis, S., Lockwood, A., Drake, R., Jones, P., & Croudace, T. (2005). Association between duration of untreated psychosis and outcome in cohorts of first-episode patients: A systematic review. *Archives of General Psychiatry, 62*(9), 975–983.

Martin, A., Koenig, K., Anderson, G., & Scahill, L. (2003). Low-dose fluvoxamine treatment of children and adolescents with pervasive developmental dis-orders: A prospective, open-label study. *Journal of Autism and Developmental Disorders, 33*(1), 77–85.

Mash, E. S., & Wolfe, D. A. (2005). *Abnormal child psychology.* Belmont, CA: Thomson Wadsworth.

Masi, G., Marcheschi, M., & Pfanner, P. (1997). Paroxetine in depressed adolescents with intellectual disability: An open label study. *Journal of Intellectual Disability Research, 41,* 268–272.

Masi, G., Milone, A., Canepa, G., Millepiedi, S., Mucci, M., & Muratori, F. (2006). Olanzapine treatment in adolescents with severe conduct disorder. *European Psychiatry, 21,* 51–57.

Masi, G., Perugi, G., Toni, C., Millepiedi, S., Mucci, M., Bertini, N., & Akiskal, H. S. (2004). Predictors of treatment nonresponse in bipolar children and adolescents with manic or mixed episodes. *Journal of Child and Adolescent Psychopharmacology, 14*(3), 395–404.

Masserman, J. H. (1941). Psychodynamics in anorexia nervosa and neurotic vomiting. *Psychoanalytic Quarterly, 10,* 211–242.

Mayo, N. E., Fellows, L. K., Scott, S. C., Cameron, J., & Wood-Dauphinee, S. (2009). A longitudinal view of apathy and its impact after stroke. *Stroke, 40*(10), 3299–3307.

Mazza, M., Di Nicola, M., Della Marca, G., Janiri, L., Bria, P., & Mazza, S. (2007). Bipolar disorder and epilepsy: A bidirectional relation? Neurobiological underpinnings, current hypotheses, and future research directions. *Neuroscientist, 13*(4), 392–404.

Mazziotta, J. C., Phelps, M. E., & Pahl, J. J. (1988). Cerebral glucose metabolic rates in nondepressed patients with obsessive-compulsive disorder. *American Journal of Psychiatry, 145,* 1560–1563.

McCabe, K. M., Lansing, A. E., Garland, A., & Hough, R. (2002). Gender differences in psychopathology, functional impairment, and familial risk factors among adjudicated delinquents. *Journal of the American Academy of Child and Adolescent Psychiatry, 41*(7), 860–867.

McClellan, J., Kowatch, R., & Findling, R. L. (2007). Practice parameter for the assessment and treatment of children and adolescents with bipolar disorder. *Journal of the American Academy of Child and Adolescent Psychiatry, 46*(1), 107–125.

McClellan, J., & Stock, S. (2013). Practice parameter for the assessment and treatment of children and adolescents with schizophrenia. *Journal of the American Academy of Child and Adolescent Psychiatry, 52*(9), 976–990.

McClellan, J., & Werry, J. (1997). Practice parameters for the assessment and treatment of children and adolescents with schizophrenia. *Journal of the American Academy of Child and Adolescent Psychiatry, 36*(10), 177S–193S.

McCracken, J. T., McGough, J., Shah, B., Cronin, P., Hong, D., Aman, M. G., . . . McMahon, D. (2002). Risperidone in children with autism and serious behavioral problems. *New England Journal of Medicine, 347*(5), 314–321.

McCracken, J. T., Suddath, R., Chang, S., Thakur, S., & Piacentini, J. (2008). Effectiveness and tolerability of open label olanzapine in children and adolescents with Tourette syndrome. *Journal of Child and Adolescent Psychopharmacology, 18*(5), 501–508.

McDonald, C., Marshall, N., Sham, P. C., Bullmore, E. T., Schulze, K., Chapple, B., ... Murray, R. M. (2006). Regional brain morphometry in patients with schizophrenia or bipolar disorder and their unaffected relatives. *American Journal of Psychiatry, 163*(3), 478–487.

McDougle, C. J., Kresch, L. E., & Posey, D. J. (2000). Repetitive thoughts and behavior in pervasive developmental disorders: Treatment with serotonin reuptake inhibitors. *Journal of Autism and Developmental Disorders, 30*(5), 427–435.

McDougle, C. J., Naylor, S. T., Cohen, D. J., Volkmar, F. R., Heninger, G. R., & Price, L. H. (1996). A double-blind, placebo-controlled study of fluvoxamine in adults with autistic disorder. *Archives of General Psychiatry, 53,* 1001–1008.

McGlashan, T. H. (2006). Is active psychosis neurotoxic? *Schizophrenia Bulletin, 32*(4), 609–613.

McIntosh, W. D., Bazzini, D. G., Smith, S. M., & Wayne, S. M. (1998). Who smokes in Hollywood? Characteristics of smokers in popular films from 1940 to 1989. *Addictive Behaviors, 23,* 395–398.

McLaren, J., & Bryson, S. E. (1987). Review of recent epidemiological studies of mental retardation: Prevalence, associated disorders, and etiology. *American Journal of Mental Retardation, 92,* 243–254.

McLoyd, V. C. (1998). Socioeconomic disadvantage and child development. *American Psychologist, 53,* 185–204.

Mendenhall, A. N., Fristad, M. A., & Early, T. J. (2009). Factors influencing service utilization and mood symptom severity in children with mood disorders: Effects of multifamily psychoeducation groups (MRPGs). *Journal of Consulting and Clinical Psychology, 77*(3), 463–473.

Mereu, G., Lilliu, V., Vargiu, P., Muntoni, A. L., Diana, M., & Gessa, G. L. (1995). Depolarization inactivation of dopamine neurons: An artifact? *Journal of Neuroscience, 15,* 1144–1149.

Merikangas, K. R., He, J. P., Brody, D., Fisher, P. W., Bourdon, K., & Koretz, D. S. (2010). Prevalence and treatment of mental disorders among US children in the 2001–2004 NHANES. *Pediatrics, 125*(1), 75–81.

Merikangas, K. R., He, J. P., Burstein, M., Swanson, S. A., Avenevoli, S., Cui, L., ... Swendsen, J. (2010). Lifetime prevalence of mental disorders in US adolescents: Results from the National Comorbidity Survey Replication–Adolescent Supplement (NCS-A). *Journal of the American Academy of Child and Adolescent Psychiatry, 49,* 980–989.

Messenger, D., & Fogel, A. (2007). The interactive development of social smiling. *Advances in Child Development and Behaviour, 35,* 327–366.

Messias, E., & Kirkpatrick, B. (2001). Summer birth and deficit schizophrenia in the epidemiological catchment area study. *Journal of Nervous and Mental Disease, 189,* 608–612.

Meyer, S. E., Carlson, G. A., Youngstrom, E., Ronsaville, D. S., Martinez, P. E., Gold, P. W., ... Radke-Yarrow, M. (2009). Long-term outcomes of youth who manifested the CBCL-pediatric bipolar disorder phenotype during childhood and/or adolescence. *Journal of Affective Disorders, 113*(3), 227–235.

Meyer, V. (1966). Modification of expectations in cases with obsessional rituals. *Behaviour Research and Therapy, 4,* 273–280.

Mikami, A. Y., Hinshaw, S. P., Patterson, K. A., & Lee, J. C. (2008). Eating pathology among adolescent girls with attention-deficit/hyperactivity disorder. *Journal of Abnormal Psychology, 117,* 225–235.

Miklowitz, D. J., Axelson, D. A., Birmaher, B., George, E. L., Taylor, D. O., Schneck, C. D., . . . Brent, D. A. (2008). Family-focused treatment for adolescents with bipolar disorder: Results of a 2-year randomized trial. *Archives of General Psychiatry, 65*(9), 1053–1061.

Miklowitz, D. J., George, E. L., Axelson, D. A., Kim, E. Y., Birmaher, B., Schneck, C., . . . Brent, D. A. (2004). Family-focused treatment for adolescents with bipolar disorder. *Journal of Affective Disorders, 82*(1), S113–S128.

Miklowitz, D. J., Schneck, C. D., Singh, M. K., Taylor, D. O., George, E. L., Cosgrove, V. E., . . . Chang, K. D. (2013). Early intervention for symptomatic youth at risk for bipolar disorder: A randomized trial of family-focused therapy. *Journal of the American Academy of Child and Adolescent Psychiatry, 52*(2), 121–131.

Milberger, S., Biederman, J., Faraone, S. V., Murphy, J., & Tsuang, M. T. (1995). Attention deficit hyperactivity disorder and comorbid disorders: Issues of overlapping symptoms. *American Journal of Psychiatry, 152*(12), 1793–1799.

Miller, A. L., Rathus, J. H., & Linehan, M. M. (2006). *Dialectical behavior therapy with suicidal adolescents.* New York, NY: Guilford Press.

Miller, L., Gur, M., Shanok, A., & Weissman, M. (2008). Interpersonal psychotherapy with pregnant adolescents: Two pilot studies. *Journal of Child Psychology and Psychiatry, 49*(7), 733–742.

Millichap, J. G., & Yee, M. M. (2012). The diet factor in attention-deficit/hyperactivity disorder. *Pediatrics, 129*(2), 330–337.

Millward, C., Ferriter, M., Calver, S., & Connell-Jones, G. (2008). Gluten- and casein-free diets for autistic spectrum disorder. *Cochrane Database of Systematic Reviews, 16*(2), CD003498.

Ming, X., Gordon, E., Kang, N., & Wagner, G. C. (2008). Use of clonidine in children with autism spectrum disorders. *Brain and Development, 30*(7), 454-460.

Minuchin, S., Rosman, B. L., & Baker, L. (1978). *Psychosomatic families: Anorexia nervosa in context.* Cambridge, MA: Harvard University Press.

Mitchell, J., McCauley, E., Burke, P. M., & Moss, S. J. (1988). Phenomenology of depression in children and adolescents. *Journal of the American Academy of Child and Adolescent Psychiatry, 27*(1), 12–20.

Moehler, E., Kagan, J., Oelkers-Ax, R., Brunner, R., Poustka, L., Haffner, J., & Resch, F. (2008). Infant predictors of behavioural inhibition. *British Journal of Developmental Psychology, 26*(1), 145–150.

Molitch, M., & Eccles, A. K. (1937). The effect of benzedrine sulphate on the intelligence scores of children. *American Journal of Psychiatry, 94,* 587, 590.

Molitch, M., & Poliakoff, S. (1937). The effect of benzedrine sulfate on enuresis. *Archives of Pediatrics and Adolescent Medicine, 54,* 499–501.

Molitch, M., & Sullivan, J. P. (1937). The effect of benzedrine sulphate on children taking the new Stanford Achievement Tests. *American Journal of Orthopsychiatry, 7,* 519–522.

Mondraty, N., Birmingham, C. L., Touyz, S., Sundakov, V., Chapman, L., & Beumont, P. (2005). Randomized controlled trial of olanzapine in the treatment of cognitions in anorexia nervosa. *Australas Psychiatry, 13*(1), 72–75.

Monteleone, P., Castaldo, E., & Maj, M. (2008). Neuroendocrine dysregulation of food intake in eating disorders. *Regulatory Peptides, 149*(1–3), 39–50.

Montgomery, P., Bjornstad, G., & Dennis, J. (2006). Media-based behavioural treatments for behavioural problems in children. *Cochrane Database of Systematic Reviews, 1,* CD002206.

Moreno, C., Laje, G., Blanco, C., Jiang, H., Schmidt, A. B., & Olfson, M. (2007). National trends in the outpatient diagnosis and treatment of bipolar disorder in youth. *Archives of General Psychiatry, 64*(9), 1032–1039.

Morgan, D., Grant, K. A., Gage, H. D., Mach, R. H., Kaplan, J. R., Prioleau, O., . . . Nader, M. A. (2005). Social dominance in monkeys: Dopamine D2 receptors and cocaine self-administration. *Nature Neuroscience, 5*(2), 169–174.

Morral, A. R., McCaffrey, D. F., & Ridgeway, G. (2004). Effectiveness of community-based treatment for substance-abusing adolescents: 12-month outcomes of youths entering Phoenix Academy or alternative probation dispositions. *Psychology of Addictive Behaviors, 18*(3), 257–268.

Mossakowski, K. N. (2008). Dissecting the influence of race, ethnicity, and socioeconomic status on mental health in young adulthood. *Research on Aging, 30*(6), 649–671.

MTA Cooperative Group. (1999). A 14-month randomized clinical trial of treatment strategies for attention-deficit/hyperactivity disorder. *Archives of General Psychiatry, 56,* 1073–1086.

Mufson, L., Weissman, M. M., Moreau, D., & Garfinkel, R. (1999). Efficacy of interpersonal psychotherapy for depressed adolescents. *Archives of General Psychiatry, 56*(6), 573–579.

Muhle, R., Trentacoste, S. V., Rapin, I. (2004). The genetics of autism. *Pediatrics, 113*(5), e472–e486.

Mukaddes, N. M., & Abali, O. (2003). Quetiapine treatment of children and adolescents with Tourette's disorder. *Journal of Child and Adolescent Psychopharmacology, 13*(3), 295–299.

Müller, T. D., Föcker, M., Holtkamp, K., Herpertz-Dahlmann, B., & Hebebrand, J. (2009). Leptin-mediated neuroendocrine alterations in anorexia nervosa: Somatic and behavioral implications. *Child and Adolescent Psychiatry Clinics of North America, 18*(1), 117–129.

Muñoz-Solomando, A., Kendall, T., & Whittington, C. J. (2008). Cognitive behavioural therapy for children and adolescents. *Current Opinion in Psychiatry, 21*(4), 332–337.

Munson, J., Dawson, G., Abbott, R., Faja, S., Webb, S. J., Friedman, S. D., . . .

Dager, S. R. (2006). Amygdalar volume and behavioral development in autism. *Archives of General Psychiatry, 63*(6), 686–693.

Murialdo, G., Barreca, A., Nobili, F., Rollero, A., Timossi, G., Gianelli, M. V., . . . Polleri, A. (2000). Dexamethasone effects on cortisol secretion in Alzheimer's disease: Some clinical and hormonal features in suppressor and non-suppressor patients. *Journal of Endocrinology Investment, 23*(3), 178–186.

Muris, P., Merckelbach, H., Gadet, B., & Moulaert, V. (2000). Fears, worries, and scary dreams in 4- to 12-year-old children: Their content, developmental pattern, and origins. *Journal of Clinical Child Psychology, 29*(1), 43.

Murray, C. J. L., & Lopez, A. D. (1996). *The global burden of disease.* (Published on behalf of the World Health Organization and the World Bank.) Cambridge, MA: Harvard School of Public Health.

Myers, L. L., & Wiman, A. M. (2014). Binge eating disorder: A review of a new DSM diagnosis. *Research on Social Work Practice, 24*(1), 86–95.

Nacewicz, B. M., Dalton, K. M., Johnstone, T., Long, M. T., McAuliff, E. M., Oakes, T. R., . . . Davidson, R. J. (2006). Amygdala volume and nonverbal social impairment in adolescent and adult males with autism. *Archives of General Psychiatry, 63*(12), 1417–1428.

Nagaraj, R., Singhi, P., & Malhi, P. (2006). Risperidone in children with autism: Randomized, placebo-controlled, double-blind study. *Journal of Child Neurology, 21*(6), 450–455.

Narrow, W. E., Clarke, D. E., Kuramoto, S. J., Kraemer, H. C., Kupfer, D. J., Greiner L, & Regier, D. A. (2013). *DSM-5* field trials in the United States and Canada: Part III. Development and reliability testing of a cross-cutting symptom assessment for *DSM-5*. *American Journal of Psychiatry, 170*(1), 71–82.

Nasrallah, H. A. (2006). Focus on lower risk of tardive dyskinesia with atypical antipsychotics. *Annals of Clinical Psychiatry, 18*(1), 57–62.

Miglio A. (2013). For quarterbacks, the NFL is no country for old men. Retrieved December 14, 2014, from http://bleacherreport.com/articles/1702238-for-quarterbacks-the-nfl-is-no-country-for-old-men

National Highway Traffic Safety Administration, Department of Transportation. (2013). *Traffic safety facts 2011: Young drivers.* Retrieved August 21, 2014, from http://www-nrd.nhtsa.dot.gov/Pubs/811744.pdf

National Institute for Clinical Excellence. (2004). *Eating disorders: Core interventions in the treatment and management of anorexia nervosa, bulimia nervosa and related eating disorders.* London, UK: Author.

National Institute of Mental Health, Research Roundtable on Prepubertal Bipolar Disorder. (2001). *Journal of the American Academy of Child & Adolescent Psychiatry, 40*(8), 871–878.

National Institute on Drug Abuse. (2008). *Preventing drug abuse among children and adolescents.* Retrieved January 30, 2009, from http://www.nida.nih.gov/Prevention/risk.html

National Institutes of Health. (2014). *How are overweight and obesity diagnosed?* Retrieved August 16, 2014, from http://www.nhlbi.nih.gov/health/health-topics/topics/obe/diagnosis.html

Nelson, J. C. (2007). Augmentation strategies in the treatment of major depressive disorder: Recent findings and current status of augmentation strategies. *CNS Spectrums, 12*(22), 6–9.

Newcorn, J. H., Kratochvil, C. J., Allen, A. J., Casat, C. D., Ruff, D. D., Michelson, D., & Atomoxetine/Methylphenidate Comparative Study Group. (2008). Atomoxetine and osmotically released methylphenidate for the treatment of attention deficit hyperactivity disorder: Acute comparison and differential response. *American Journal of Psychiatry, 165*(6), 721–730.

Newman-Toker, J. (2000). Risperidone in anorexia nervosa. *Journal of the American Academy of Child and Adolescent Psychiatry, 39*(8), 941–942.

Newschaffer, C. J., Croen, L. A., Daniels, J., Giarelli, E., Grether, J. K., Levy, S. E., . . . Windham, G. C. (2007). The epidemiology of autism spectrum disorders. *Annual Review of Public Health, 28*, 235–258.

Newschaffer, C. J., Falb, M. D., & Gurney, J. G. (2005). National autism prevalence trends from US special education data. *Pediatrics, 115*, 277–282.

Niendam, T. A., Bearden, C. E., Rosso, I. M., Sanchez, L. E., Hadley, T., Nuechterlein, K. H., & Cannon, T. D. (2003). A prospective study of childhood neurocognitive functioning in schizophrenic patients and their siblings. *American Journal of Psychiatry, 160*(11), 2060–2062.

Nigg, J. T., & Casey, B. J. (2005). An integrative theory of attention-deficit/hyperactivity disorder based on the cognitive and affective neurosciences. *Development and Psychopathology, 17*(3), 785–806.

Nigg, J. T., Lewis, K., Edinger, T., & Falk, M. (2012). Meta-analysis of attention-deficit/hyperactivity disorder or attention-deficit/hyperactivity disorder symptoms, restriction diet, and synthetic food color additives. *Journal of the American Academy of Child and Adolescent Psychiatry, 51*(1), 86–97.e8.

Nigg, J., Nikolas, M., & Burt, S. A. (2010). Measured gene-by-environment interaction in relation to attention-deficit/hyperactivity disorder. *Journal of the American Academy of Child and Adolescent Psychiatry, 49*, 863–873.

Nigg, J. T., Stavro, G., Ettenhofer, M., Hambrick, D. Z., Miller, T., & Henderson, J. M. (2005). Executive functions and ADHD in adults: Evidence for selective effects on ADHD symptom domains. *Journal of Abnormal Psychology, 114*(4), 706–717.

Nikolas, M. A., & Burt, S. A. (2010). Genetic and environmental influences on ADHD symptom dimensions of inattention and hyperactivity: A meta-analysis. *Journal of Abnormal Psychology, 119*, 1–17.

Nir, I., Meir, D., Zilber, N., Knobler, H., Hadjez, J., & Lerner, Y. (1995). Brief report: Circadian melatonin, thyroid-stimulating hormone, prolactin, and cortisol levels in serum of young adults with autism. *Journal of Autism and Developmental Disorders, 25*(6), 641–654.

Nock, M. K. (2010). Self-injury. *Annual Review of Clinical Psychology, 6*(1), 339–363.

Nock, M. K., Borges, G., Bromet, E. J., Cha, C. B., Kessler, R. C., & Lee, S. (2008). Suicide and suicidal behavior. *Epidemiologic Reviews, 30*(1), 133–154.

Nock, M. K., & Prinstein, M. J. (2004). A functional approach to the assessment of self-mutilative behavior. *Journal of Consulting and Clinical Psychology, 72*(5), 885–890.

Norton, K. I. (1996). Ken and Barbie at life size. *Sex Roles, 34*(3–4), 287–294.

Novak Sarotar, B., Pesek, M. B., Agius, M., & Kocmur, M. (2008). Duration of untreated psychosis and its effect on the symptomatic recovery in schizophrenia: Preliminary results. *Neuroendocrinology Letters, 29*(6).

Nuño-Gutiérrez, B. L., Rodriguez-Cerda, O., & Alvarez-Nemegyei, J. (2006). Why do adolescents use drugs? A common sense explanatory model from the social actor's perspective. *Adolescence, 41*(164), 649–665.

Nybäck, H., Wiesel, F. A., Berggren, B. M., & Hindmarsh, T. (1982). Computed tomography of the brain in patients with acute psychosis and in healthy volunteers. *Acta Psychiatrica Scandinavica, 65*(6), 403–414.

Oberman, L. M., Hubbard, E. M., McCleery, J. P., Altschuler, E. L., Ramachandran, V. S., & Pineda, J. A. (2005). EEG evidence for mirror neuron dysfunction in autism spectrum disorders. *Cognitive Brain Research, 24,* 190–198.

O'Brien, L. M., & Gozal, D. (2004). Neurocognitive dysfunction and sleep in children: From human to rodent. *Pediatric Clinics of North America, 51*(1), 187.

Offord, D. R., Boyle, M. H., Racine, Y. A., Fleming, J. E., Cadman, D. R., Blum, H. M., . . . Woodward, C. A. (1992). Outcome, prognosis, and risk in a longitudinal follow-up study. *Journal of the American Academy of Child and Adolescent Psychiatry, 31,* 916–922.

Ogden, C. L., Carroll, M. D., Curtin, L. R., McDowell, M. A., Tabak, C. J., & Flegal, K. M. (2006). The prevalence of overweight and obesity in the United States, 1999–2004. *Journal of the American Medical Association, 295,* 1549–1555.

Ogden, C. L., Carroll, M. D., Kit, B. K., & Flegal, K. M. (2014). Prevalence of childhood and adult obesity in the United States, 2011–2012. *Journal of the American Medical Association, 311*(8), 806–814.

Okie, S. (2006). ADHD in adults. *New England Journal of Medicine, 354*(25), 2637–2641.

Olfson, M., Blanco, C., Liu, L., Moreno, C., & Laje, G. (2006). National trends in the outpatient treatment of children and adolescents with antipsychotic drugs. *Archives of General Psychiatry, 63*(6), 679–685.

Olfson, M., Blanco, C., Liu, S-M., Wang, S., & Correll, C. U. (2012). National trends in the office-based treatment of children, adolescents, and adults with antipsychotics. *JAMA Psychiatry, 69*(12), 1247-1256.

Ollendick, T. H. (1998). Panic disorder in children and adolescents: New developments, new directions. *Journal of Clinical Child Psychology, 27*(3), 234–245.

Olsson, I., Steffenburg, S., & Gillberg, C. (1988). Epilepsy in autism and autistic like conditions: A population-based study. *Archives of Neurology, 45*(6), 666–668.

O'Malley, P. M., & Johnston, L. D. (2013). Driving after drug or alcohol use by

U.S. high school seniors, 2001–2011. *American Journal of Public Health, 103*(11), 2027–2034.

O'Rourke, J. A., Scharf, J. M., Yu, D., & Pauls, D. L. (2009). The genetics of Tourette syndrome: A review. *Journal of Psychosomatic Research, 67*(6), 533–545.

Oslejskova, H., Kontrová, I., Foralová, R., Dusek, L., & Némethová, D. (2007). The course of diagnosis in autistic patients: The delay between recognition of the first symptoms by parents and correct diagnosis. *Neuroendocrinology Letters, 28*(6), 895–900.

Ospina, M. B., Krebs Seida, J., Clark, B., Karkhaneh, M., Hartling, L., Tjosvold, L., . . . Smith, V. (2008). Behavioural and developmental interventions for autism spectrum disorder: A clinical systematic review. *PLoS ONE, 3*(11), e3755.

Othmer, E., Desouza, C. M., Penick, E. C., Nickel, E. J., Hunter, E. E., Othmer, S. C., . . . Hall, S. B. (2007). Indicators of mania in depressed outpatients: A retrospective analysis of data from the Kansas 1500 study. *Journal of Clinical Psychiatry, 68*(1), 47–51.

Owen, R., Sikich, L., Marcus, R. N., Corey-Lisle, P., Manos, G., McQuade, R. D., . . . Findling, R. L. (2009). Aripiprazole in the treatment of irritability in children and adolescents with autistic disorder. *Pediatrics, 124*(6), 1533–1540.

Owens, J. A., Adolescent Sleep Working Group and Committee on Adolescence, & Council on School Health. (2014). School start times for adolescents. *Pediatrics, 134*(3), 642–649.

Owens, J. A., & Dalzell, V. (2005). Use of the "BEARS" sleep screening tool in a pediatric residents' continuity clinic: A pilot study. *Sleep Medicine, 6*(1), 63–69.

Owens, J. A., & Witmans, M. (2004). Sleep problems. *Current Problems Pediatric and Adolescent Health Care, 34*(4), 154–179.

Padhy, R., Saxena, K., Remsing, L., Huemer, J., Plattner, B., & Steiner, H. (2011). Symptomatic response to divalproex in subtypes of conduct disorder. *Child Psychiatry and Human Development, 42*(5), 584–593.

Palmer, L. J., Knuiman, M. W., Divitini, M. L., Burton, P. R., James, A. L., Bartholomew, H. C., . . . Musk, A. W. (2001). Familial aggregation and heritability of adult lung function: Results from the Busselton Health Study. *European Respiratory Journal, 17*(4), 696–702.

Pandina, G. J., Aman, M. G., & Findling, R. L. (2006). Risperidone in the management of disruptive behavior disorders. *Journal of Child and Adolescent Psychopharmacology, 16*(4), 379–392.

Pandina, G. J., DelBello, M. P., Kushner, S., Van Hove, I., Kusumakar, V., Haas, M., & Augustyns, I. (2007, October). *Risperidone for the treatment of acute mania in bipolar youth.* Poster presented at the annual meeting of the American Academy of Child and Adolescent Psychiatry, Boston, MA.

Papatheodorou, G., Kutcher, S. P., Katic, M., & Szalai, J. P. (1995). The efficacy and safety of divalproex sodium in the treatment of acute mania in adolescents and young adults: An open clinical trial. *Journal of Clinical Psychopharmacology, 15*(2), 110–116.

Papolos, D., Hennen, J., & Cockerham, M. S. (2005). Factors associated with parent reported suicide threats by children and adolescents with community-diagnosed bipolar disorder. *Journal of Affective Disorders, 86*(2–3), 267–275.

Pappadopulos, E., Macintyre, J. C., II, Crismon, M. L., Findling, R. L., Malone, R. P., Derivan, A., . . . Jensen, P. S. (2003). Treatment recommendations for the use of antipsychotics for aggressive youth (TRAAY): Part II. *Journal of the American Academy of Child and Adolescent Psychiatry, 42*(2), 132–144.

Parmeggiani, A., Posar, A., Antolini, C., Scaduto, M. C., Santucci, M., & Giovanardi-Rossi, P. (2007). Epilepsy in patients with pervasive developmental disorder not otherwise specified. *Journal of Child Neurology, 22*(10), 1198–1203.

Parry, P. I. (2012). Paediatric bipolar disorder: Are attachment and trauma factors considered? In J. Barnhill (Ed.), *Bipolar disorder: Portrait of a complex mood disorder* (pp. 165–190). Rijeka: In Tech.

Pasalich, D. S., Dadds, M. R., Hawes, D. J., & Brennan, J. (2012). Attachment and callous-unemotional traits in children with early-onset conduct problems. *Journal of Child Psychology and Psychiatry, 53*(8), 838–845.

Patel, N. C., DelBello, M. P., Cecil, K. M., Adler, C. M., Bryan, H. S., Stanford, K. E., & Strakowski, S. M. (2006). Lithium treatment effects on Myo-inositol in adolescents with bipolar depression. *Biological Psychiatry, 60*(9), 998–1004.

Pathak, P., West, D., Martin, B. C., Helm, M. E., & Henderson, C. (2010). Evidence-based use of second-generation antipsychotics in a state Medicaid pediatric population, 2001–2005. *Psychiatric Services, 61*(2), 123–129.

Patten, C. A., Choi, W. S., Gillin, J. C., & Pierce, J. P. (2000). Depressive symptoms and cigarette smoking predict development and persistence of sleep problems in US adolescents. *Pediatrics, 106*(2), E23.

Patzold, L. M., Richdale, A. L., & Tonge, B. J. (1998). An investigation into sleep characteristics of children with autism and Asperger's disorder. *Journal of Paediatrics and Child Health, 34*(6), 528–533.

Paul, R. (2008). Interventions to improve communication in autism. *Child and Adolescent Psychiatric Clinics of North America, 17*(4), 832–856.

Pavuluri, M. N., Graczyk, P. A., Henry, D. B., Carbray, J. A., Heidenreich, J., & Miklowitz, D. J. (2004). Child- and family-focused cognitive-behavioral therapy for pediatric bipolar disorder: Development and preliminary results. *Journal of the American Academy of Child and Adolescent Psychiatry, 43*(5), 528–537.

Pavuluri, M. N., Henry, D. B., Carbray, J. A., Sampson, G., Naylor, M. W., & Janicak, P. G. (2004). Open-label prospective trial of risperidone in combination with lithium or divalproex sodium in pediatric mania. *Journal of Affective Disorders, 82*(1), S103–S111.

Pavuluri, M. N., Henry, D. B., Carbray, J. A., Sampson, G. A., Naylor, M. W., &

Janicak, P. G. (2006). A one-year open-label trial of risperidone augmentation in lithium nonresponder youth with preschool-onset bipolar disorder.
Journal of Child and Adolescent Psychopharmacology, 16(3), 336–350.

Pavuluri, M. N., Henry, D. B., Devineni, B., Carbray, J. A., & Birmaher, B. (2006).
Child mania rating scale: Development, reliability, and validity. *Journal of
the American Academy of Child and Adolescent Psychiatry, 45*(5), 550–560.

Pavuluri, M. N., Henry, D. B., Findling, R. L., Parnes, S., Carbray, J. A., Moham-
med, T., . . . Sweeney, J. A. (2010). Double-blind randomized trial of risperidone versus divalproex in pediatric bipolar disorder. *Bipolar Disorder,
12*(6), 593–605.

Payton, A., Holmes, J., Barrett, J. H., Hever, T., Fitzpatrick, H., Trumper, A. L.,
. . . Thapar, A. (2001). Examining for association between candidate gene
polymorphisms in the dopamine pathway and attention-deficit hyperactivity disorder: A family-based study. *American Journal of Medical Genetics,
105,* 464–470.

Pediatric OCD Treatment Study Team. (2004). Cognitive behavior therapy, sertraline, and their combination for children and adolescents with obsessive
compulsive disorder: The Pediatric OCD Treatment Study (POTS) randomized controlled trial. *Journal of the American Medical Association, 292,*
1969–1976.

Perepletchilova, F., Axelrod, S. R., Kaufman, J., Rounsaville, B. J., Doublas-
Palumberi, H., & Miller, A. L. (2011). Adapting dialectical behaviour therapy for children: Towards a new research agenda for paediatric suicidal
andnon-suicidal self-injurious behaviours. *Child and Adolescent Mental
Health, 16*(2), 116–121.

Perrin, J. M., Friedman, R. A., Knilans, T. K., American Academy of Pediatrics
Black Box Working Group, & American Academy of Pediatrics Section on
Cardiology and Cardiac Surgery. (2008). Cardiovascular monitoring and
stimulant drugs for attention-deficit/hyperactivity disorder. *Pediatrics,
122*(2), 451–453.

Perry, B. D. (1998). Anxiety disorders. In C. E. Coffey & R. A. Brumback (Eds.),
Textbook of pediatric neuropsychiatry (pp. 579–595). Washington, DC:
American Psychiatric Press.

Peters-Scheffer, N., Didden, R., Korzilius, H., & Sturmey, P. (2010). A meta-analytic study on the effectiveness of comprehensive ABA-based early intervention programs for children with autism spectrum disorders. *Research in
Autism Spectrum Disorders, 5*(1), 60–69.

Peterson, B. S., Pine, D. S., Cohen, P., & Brook, J. S. (2001). Prospective, longitudinal study of tic, obsessive-compulsive, and attention deficit/hyperactivity
disorders in an epidemiological sample. *Journal of the American Academy
of Child and Adolescent Psychiatry, 40*(6), 685–695.

Peterson, B. S., Thomas, P., Kane, M. J., Scahill, L., Zhang, H., Bronen, R., . . .
Staib, L. (2003). Basal ganglia volumes in patients with Gilles de la Tourette
syndrome. *Archives of General Psychiatry, 60*(4), 215–224.

Peterson, C. (2004). Positive youth development: Realizing the potential of youth: Preface. *Annals of the American Academy of Political and Social Science, 591,* 6–12.

Petraitis, J., Flay, B. R., Miller, T. Q., Torpy, E. J., & Greiner, B. (1998). Illicit substance use among adolescents: A matrix of prospective predictors. *Substance Use and Misuse, 33*(13), 2561–2604.

Petropoulos, H., Friedman, S. D., Shaw, D. W. W., Artru, A. A., Dawson, G., & Dager, S. R. (2006). Gray matter abnormalities in autism spectrum disorder revealed by T2 relaxation. *Neurology, 67,* 632–636.

Petti, T. A. (1978). Depression in hospitalized child psychiatry patients. Approaches to measuring depression. *Journal of the American Academy of Child Psychiatry, 17*(1), 49–59.

Pezawas, L., Meyer-Lindenberg, A., Drabant, E. M., Verchinski, B. A., Munoz, K., E., Kolachana, B. S., . . . Weinberger, D. R. (2005). 5-HTTLPR polymorphism impacts human cingulate-amygdala interactions: A genetic susceptibility mechanism for depression. *Nature Neuroscience, 8*(6), 828–834.

Philip, N. S., Carpenter, L. L., Tyrka, A. R., & Price, L. H. (2008). Augmentation of antidepressants with atypical antipsychotics: A review of the current literature. *Journal of Psychiatric Practice, 14*(1), 34–44.

Piacentini, J. C., & Chang, S. W. (2006). Behavioral treatments for tic suppression: Habit reversal training. *Advances in Neurology, 99,* 227–233.

Piazza, C. C., Hagopian, L. P., Hughes, C. R., & Fisher, W. W. (1998). Using chronotherapy to treat severe sleep problems: A case study. *American Journal of Mental Retardation, 102*(4), 358–366.

Pierce, J. P., Choi, W. S., Gilpin, E. A., Farkas, A. J., & Berry, C. (1998). Industry promotion of cigarettes and adolescent smoking. *Journal of the American Medical Association, 279*(9), 511–515.

Pierce, K., Conant, D., Hazin, R., Stoner, R., & Desmond, J. (2011). Preference for geometric patterns early in life as a risk factor for autism. *Archives of General Psychiatry, 68*(1), 101–109.

Pierre, J. M. (2011). Cannabis, synthetic cannabinoids, and psychosis risk: What the evidence says. *Current Psychiatry, 10*(9), 49–58.

Pilkington, H. (2007). Beyond "peer pressure": Rethinking drug use and "youth culture." *International Journal of Drug Policy, 18*(3), 213–224.

Pine, D. S., Cohen, P., Gurley, D., Brook, J., & Ma, Y. (1998). The risk for early adulthood anxiety and depressive disorders in adolescents with anxiety and depressive disorders. *Archives of General Psychiatry, 55*(1), 56–64.

Pinna, G., Costa, E., & Guidotti, A. (2006). Fluoxetine and norfluoxetine stereospecifically and selectively increase brain neurosteroid content at doses that are inactive on 5-HT reuptake. *Psychopharmacology, 186*(3), 362–372.

Pirke, K. M. (1996). Central and peripheral noradrenalin regulation in eating disorders. *Psychiatry Research, 62*(1), 43–49.

Platt, J. E., Campbell, M., Green, W. H., Perry, R., & Cohen, I. L. (1981). Effects of lithium carbonate and haloperidol on cognition in aggressive hospitalized school-age children. *Journal of Clinical Psychopharmacology, 1,* 8–13.

Pliszka, S. R., McCracken, J. T., & Maas, J. W. (1996). Catecholamines in attention deficit hyperactivity disorder: Current perspectives. *Journal of the American Academy of Child and Adolescent Psychiatry, 35*(3), 264–272.

Posey, D. J., Erickson, C. A., Stigler, K. A., & McDougle, C. J. (2006). The use of selective serotonin reuptake inhibitors in autism and related disorders. *Journal of Child and Adolescent Psychopharmacology, 16*(1–2), 181–186.

Posey, D. J., Puntney, J. I., Sasher, T. M., Kem, D. L., & McDougle, C. J. (2004). Guanfacine treatment of hyperactivity and inattention in pervasive developmental disorders: A retrospective analysis of 80 cases. *Journal of Child and Adolescent Psychopharmacology, 14*(2), 233–241.

Posey, D. J., Stigler, K. A., Erickson, C. A., & McDougle, C. J. (2008). Antipsychotics in the treatment of autism. *Journal of Clinical Investigation, 118*(1), 6–14.

Post, R. M. (2007). Kindling and sensitization as models for affective episode recurrence, cyclicity, and tolerance phenomena. *Neuroscience and Biobehavioral Reviews, 31*(6), 858–873.

Preskorn, S. H., Weller, E. B., Hughes, C. W., Weller, R. A., & Bolte, K. (1987). Depression in prepubertal children: Dexamethasone nonsuppression predicts differential response to imipramine vs. placebo. *Psychopharmacology Bulletin, 23*(1), 128–133.

Preti, A., Cardascia, L., Zen, T., Marchetti, M., Favaretto, G., & Miotto, P. (2000). Risk for obstetric complications and schizophrenia. *Psychiatry Research, 96*, 127.

Preti, A., Melis, M., Siddi, S., Vellante, M., Doneddu, G., & Fadda, R. (2014). Oxytocin and autism: A systematic review of randomized controlled trials. *Journal of Child and Adolescent Psychopharmacology, 24*(2), 54–68.

Price, R. A., Kidd, K. K., Cohen, D. J., Pauls, D. L., & Leckman, J. F. (1985). A twin study of Tourette syndrome. *Archives of General Psychiatry, 42*(8), 815–820.

Primack, B. A., Dalton, M. A., Carroll, M. V., Agarwal, A. A., & Fine, M. J. (2008). Content analysis of tobacco, alcohol, and other drugs in popular music. *Archives of Pediatrics and Adolescent Medicine, 162*(2), 169–175.

Pringsheim, T., Davenport, W. J., & Lang, A. (2003). Tics. *Current Opinion in Neurology, 16*(4), 523–527.

Pringsheim, T., & Gorman, D. (2012). Second-generation antipsychotics for the treatment of disruptive behaviour disorders in children: A systemic review. *La Revue Canadienne de Psychiatrie, 57*(12), 722–727.

Prizant, B. M., & Meyer, E. C. (1993). Socioemotional aspects of language and social-communication disorders in young children and their families. *American Journal of Speech-Language Pathology, 2*, 56–71.

Puig-Antich, J., Goetz, R., Hanlon, C., Davies, M., Thompson, J., Chambers, W. J., . . . Weitzman, E. D. (1982). Sleep architecture and REM sleep measures in prepubertal children with major depression: A controlled study. *Archives of General Psychiatry, 39*(8), 932–939.

Pull, C. B. (2004). Binge eating disorder. *Current opinion in psychiatry, 17*(1), 43-48.

Qiu, A., Adler, M., Crocetti, D., Miller, M. I., & Mostofsky, S. H. (2010). Basal ganglia shapes predict social, communication, and motor dysfunctions in boys with autism spectrum disorders. *Journal of the Academy of Child and Adolescent Psychiatry, 49*(6), 539–551.

Rahim, S. I., & Cederblad, M. (1986). Epidemiology of nocturnal enuresis in a part of Khartoum, Sudan: The extensive study. *Acta Paediatrica, 75,* 1017–1020.

Rai, P. R., & Kerr, M. (2010). Antidepressant use in adults with intellectual disability. *Psychiatric Bulletin, 34,* 123–126.

Rana, R., Gormez, A., & Varghese, S. (2013). Pharmacological interventions for self-injurious behaviour in adults with intellectual disabilities. *Cochrane Database of Systematic Reviews* (Issue 4). doi: 10.1002/14651858.CD009084.pub2

Randazzo, A. C., Muehlbach, M. J., Schweitzer, P. K., & Walsh, J. K. (1998). Cognitive function following acute sleep restriction in children ages 10–14. *Sleep, 21*(8), 861.

Rapin, I., & Katzman, R. (1998). Neurobiology of autism. *Annals of Neurology, 43*(1), 7–14.

Rapport, M. D., & Denney, M. A. (1997). Titrating methylphenidate in children with attention-deficit/hyperactivity disorder: Is body mass predictive of clinical response? *Journal of the American Academy of Child and Adolescent Psychiatry, 36,* 523–530.

Rasmussen, S. A. (1984). Lithium and tryptophan augmentation in clomipramine resistant obsessive-compulsive disorder. *American Journal of Psychiatry, 141,* 1283–1285.

Rasmussen, S. A., & Tsuang, M. T. (1986). Clinical characteristics and family history in DSM-III obsessive-compulsive disorder. *American Journal of Psychiatry, 143,* 317–322.

Raznahan, A., Wallace, G. L., Antezana, L., Greenstein, D., Lenroot, R., Thurm, A., . . . Giedd, J. N. (2013). Compared to what? Early brain overgrowth in autism and the perils of population norms. *Biological Psychiatry, 74,* 563–575.

Reber, A. S. (1985). *The Penguin dictionary of psychology.* New York, NY: Penguin Books.

Reddy, L. A., & Pfeiffer, S. I. (1997). Effectiveness of treatment foster care with children and adolescents: A review of outcome studies. *Journal of the American Academy of Child and Adolescent Psychiatry, 36,* 581–588.

Reeves, H., Batra, S., May, R. S., Zhang, R., Dahl, D. C., & Li, X. (2008). Efficacy of risperidone augmentation to antidepressants in the management of suicidality in major depressive disorder: A randomized, double-blind, placebo-controlled pilot study. *Journal of Clinical Psychiatry, 69*(8), 1228–1236.

Regier, D. A., Farmer, M. E., Rae, D. S., Locke, B. Z., Keith, S. J., Judd, L. L., & Goodwin, F. K. (1990). Comorbidity of mental disorders with alcohol and other drug abuse: Results from the Epidemiologic Catchment Area (ECA) Study. *Journal of the American Medical Association, 264,* 2511–2518.

Register, D., Darrow, A. A., Standley, J., & Swedberg, O. (2007). The use of music to enhance reading skills of second grade students and students with reading disabilities. *Journal of Music Therapy, 44,* 23–37.

Remington, G., Sloman, L., Konstantareas, M., Parker, K., & Gow, R. (2001). Clomipramine versus haloperidol in the treatment of autistic disorder: A double-blind, placebo-controlled, crossover study. *Journal of Clinical Psychopharmacology, 21*(4), 440–444.

Research Units for Pediatric Psychopharmacology (RUPP) Anxiety Study Group. (2001). Fluvoxamine for the treatment of anxiety disorders in children and adolescents. *New England Journal of Medicine, 344,* 1279–1285.

Reveley, A. M., Reveley, M. A., Clifford, C. A., & Murray, R. M. (1982). Cerebral ventricular size in twins discordant for schizophrenia. *Lancet, 1*(8271), 540–541.

Rey, J. M., & Walter, G. (1997). Half a century of ECT use in young people. *American Journal of Psychiatry, 154,* 595–602.

Richardson, A. J., & Puri, B. K. (2002). A randomized double-blind, placebo-controlled study of the effects of supplementation with highly unsaturated fatty acids on ADHD-related symptoms in children with specific learning disabilities. *Progress in Neuro-Psychopharmacology and Biological Psychiatry, 26,* 233–239.

Richdale, A. L., & Prior, M. R. (1995). The sleep/wake rhythm in children with autism. *European Child and Adolescent Psychiatry, 4*(3), 175–186.

Riddle, M. A., Bernstein, G. A., Cook, E. H., Leonard, H. L., March, J. S., & Swanson, J. M. (1999). Anxiolytics, adrenergic agents, and naltrexone. *Journal of the American Academy of Child and Adolescent Psychiatry, 38*(5), 546–556.

Riddle, M. A., Reeve, E. A., Yaryura-Tobias, J. A., Yang, H. M., Claghorn, J. L., Gaffney, G., . . . Walkup, J. T. (2001). Fluvoxamine for children and adolescents with obsessive–compulsive disorder: A randomized, controlled, multicenter trial. *Journal of the American Academy of Child and Adolescent Psychiatry, 40,* 222–229.

Riddle, M. A., Scahill, L., King, R. A., Hardin, M. T., Anderson, G. M., Ort, S. I., . . . Cohen, D. J. (1992). Double-blind, crossover trial of fluoxetine and placebo in children and adolescents with obsessive-compulsive disorder. *Journal of the American Academy of Child and Adolescent Psychiatry, 31,* 1062–1069.

Ritvo, E. R., Freeman, B. J., Mason-Brothers, A., Mo, A., & Ritvo, A. M. (1985). Concordance for the syndrome of autism in 40 pairs of afflicted twins. *American Journal of Psychiatry, 142,* 74–77.

Rizzo, C. J., Esposito-Smythers, C., Swenson, L., Birmaher, B., Ryan, N., Strober, M., . . . Keller, M. (2007). Factors associated with mental health service utilization among bipolar youth. *Bipolar Disorders, 9*(8), 839–850.

Rizzolatti, G., & Fabbri-Destro, M. (2010). Mirror neurons: From discovery to autism. *Experimental Brain Research, 200,* 223–237.

Roane, B. M., & Taylor, D. J. (2008). Adolescent insomnia as a risk factor for early adult depression and substance abuse. *Sleep, 31*(10), 1351–1356.

Robbins, D. R., Alessi, N. E., Cook, S. C., Poznanski, E. O., & Yanchyshyn, G. W. (1982). The use of the Research Diagnostic Criteria (RDC) for depression in adolescent psychiatric inpatients. *Journal of the American Academy of Child Psychiatry, 21*(3), 251–255.

Roberts, D. F., Henriksen, L., & Christenson, P. G. (1999). *Substance use in popular movies and music.* Washington, DC: Office of National Drug Control Policy and the Department of Health and Human Services.

Robins, D., Fein, D., Barton, M., & Green, J. (2001). The Modified-Checklist for Autism in Toddlers (M-CHAT): An initial investigation in the early detection of autism and pervasive developmental disorders. *Journal of Autism and Developmental Disorders, 31*(2), 131–144.

Robson, L. M., & Leung, A. K. (2002). Urotherapy recommendations for bedwetting. *Journal of the National Medical Association, 94*(7), 577–580.

Rodenburg, R., Benjamin, A., de Roos, C., Meijer, A. M., & Stams, G. J. (2009). Efficacy of EMDR in children: A meta-analysis. *Clinical Psychology Review, 29*(7), 599–606.

Rogers, S. J. (1996). Brief report: Early intervention in autism. *Journal of Autism and Developmental Disorders, 26*(2), 243–246.

Romero, S., Birmaher, B., Axelson, D., Goldstein, T., Goldstein, B. I., Gill, M. K., . . . Keller, M. (2009). Prevalence and correlates of physical and sexual abuse in children and adolescents with bipolar disorder. *Journal of Affective Disorders, 112*(1–3), 144–150.

Ronan, K. R., & Kendall, P. C. (1990). Non-self-controlled adolescents: Applications of cognitive-behavioral therapy. *Adolescent Psychiatry, 17,* 479–505.

Ropers, H. H., & Hamel, B. C. J. (2005). X-linked mental retardation. *Nature Reviews, Genetics, 6,* 46–57.

Rosenbaum, J. F., Biederman, J., Bolduc-Murphy, E. A., Faraone, S. V., Chaloff, J., Hirshfeld, D. R., . . . Kagan, J. (1993). Behavioral inhibition in childhood: A risk factor for anxiety disorders. *Harvard Review of Psychiatry, 1*(1), 2–16.

Ross, D. P., Shillington, E. R., & Lockhead, C. (1994). *The Canadian fact book on poverty—1994.* Ottawa, ON, Canada: Canadian Council on Social Development.

Rosselló, J., & Bernal, G. (1999). The efficacy of cognitive-behavioral and interpersonal treatments for depression in Puerto Rican adolescents. *Journal of Consulting and Clinical Psychology, 67*(5), 734–745.

Rosselló, J., Bernal, G., & Rivera-Medina, C. (2008). Individual and group CBT and IPT for Puerto Rican adolescents with depressive symptoms. *Cultural Diversity and Ethnic Minority Psychology, 14*(3), 234–245.

Rowe, C., Liddle, H., Caruso, J., & Dakof, G. (2004). Clinical variations of adolescent substance abuse: An empirically based typology. *Journal of Child and Adolescent Substance Abuse, 14*(2), 19–40.

Rowles, B. M., & Findling, R. L. (2010). Review of pharmacotherapy options for the treatment of attention-deficit/hyperactivity disorder (ADHD) and ADHD-like symptoms in children and adolescents with developmental disorders. *Developmental Disabilities Research Reviews, 16,* 273–282.

Rudd, M. D., Mandrusiak, M., & Joiner, T. E., Jr. (2006). The case against no-suicide contracts: The commitment to treatment statement as a practice alternative. *Journal of Clinical Psychology, 62*(2), 243–251.

Ruedrich, S., Swales, T. P., Fossaceca, C., Toliver, J., & Rutkowski, A. (1999). Effect of divalproex sodium on aggression and self-injurious behaviour in adults with intellectual disability: A retrospective review. *Journal of Intellectual Disability Research, 43,* 109–113.

Rumpold, G., Klingseis, M., Dornauer, K., Kopp, M., Doering, S., Höfer, S., . . . Schussler, G. (2006). Psychotropic substance abuse among adolescents: A structural equation model on risk and protective factors. *Substance Use and Misuse, 41*(8), 1155–1169.

Russell, A. T., & Tanguay, P. E. (1996). Mental retardation. In M. Lewis (Ed.), *Child and adolescent psychiatry: A comprehensive textbook* (2nd ed., pp. 502-510). Baltimore, MD: Williams & Wilkins.

Russell, G. (1979). Bulimia nervosa: An ominous variant of anorexia nervosa. *Psychological Medicine, 9,* 429–448.

Rutter, M. (2000). Genetic studies of autism: From the 1970s into the millennium. *Journal of Abnormal Child Psychology, 28*(1), 3–14.

Ryan, N. D., Meyer, V., Dachille, S., Mazzie, D., & Puig-Antich, J. (1988). Lithium antidepressant augmentation in TCA-refractory depression in adolescents. *Journal of the American Academy of Child and Adolescent Psychiatry, 27*(3), 371–376.

Ryan, N. D., Puig-Antich, J., Ambrosini, P., Rabinovich, H., Robinson, D., Nelson, B., . . . Twomey, J. (1987). The clinical picture of major depression in children and adolescents. *Archives of General Psychiatry, 44*(10), 854–861.

Rynn, M. A., Riddle, M. A., Yeung, P. P., & Kunz, N. R. (2007). Efficacy and safety of extended-release venlafaxine in the treatment of generalized anxiety disorder in children and adolescents: Two placebo-controlled trials. *American Journal of Psychiatry, 164*(2), 290–300.

Rynn, M. A., Siqueland, L., & Rickels, K. (2001). Placebo-controlled trial of sertraline in the treatment of children with generalized anxiety disorder. *American Journal of Psychiatry, 158,* 2008–2014.

Saarenpää-Heikkilä, O., Laippala, P., & Koivikko, M. (2001). Subjective daytime sleepiness and its predictors in Finnish adolescents in an interview study. *Acta Paediatrica, 90*(5), 552–557.

Sagud, M., Mihaljevi-Peles, A., Pivac, N., Muck-Seler, D., Simunovi, I., & Jakovljevi, M. (2008). Genetics of schizophrenia in the context of integrative psychiatry. *Psychiatria Danubina, 20*(3), 364–368.

Sallee, F. R., Kurlan, R., Goetz, C. G., Singer, H., Scahill, L., Law, G., . . . Chappell, P. B. (2000). Ziprasidone treatment of children and adolescents with Tourette's syndrome: A pilot study. *Journal of the American Academy of Child and Adolescent Psychiatry, 39*(3), 292–299.

Sallee, F., McGough, J., Wigal, T., Donahue, J., Lyne, A., & Biederman, J. (2008). Guanfacine extended release in children and adolescents with attention deficit/hyperactivity disorder: A placebo-controlled trial. *Journal of the American Academy of Child and Adolescent Psychiatry, 48*(2), 155–165.

Salsman, N. L., & Arthur, R. (2011). Adapting dialectical behavior therapy to help suicidal adolescents. *Current Psychiatry, 10*(3), 18–34.

Sandler, A., Glesne, C., & Geller, G. (2008). Children's and parents' perspectives on open-label use of placebos in the treatment of ADHD. *Child: Care, Health and Development, 34*(1), 111–120.

Sanson, A., & Prior, M. (1999). Temperament and behavioral precursors to oppositional defiant disorder and conduct disorder. In H. C. Quay & A. E. Hogan (Eds.), *Handbook of disruptive behavior disorders* (pp. 397–417). New York, NY: Kluwer Academic/Plenum.

Santisteban, D. A., Suarez-Morales, L., Robbins, M. S., & Szapocznik, J. (2006). Brief strategic family therapy: Lessons learned in efficacy research and challenges to blending research and practice. *Family Process, 45*(2), 259–271.

Sarkar, S., & Grover, S. (2013). Antipsychotics in children and adolescents with schizophrenia: A systematic review and meta-analysis. *Indian Journal of Pharmacology, 45*(5), 439–446.

Saveanu, R. V., & Nemeroff, C. B. (2012). Etiology of depression: genetic and environmental factors. *Psychiatric Clinics of North America, 35*(1), 51–71.

Sawyer Radloff, L. (1991). The use of the Center for Epidemiologic Studies Depression Scale in adolescents and young adults. *Journal of Youth and Adolescence, 20*(2), 149–166.

Saxe, G. N., Ellis, B. H., Fogler, J., Hansen, S., & Sorkin, B. (2005). Comprehensive care for traumatized children. *Psychiatric Annals, 35*(5), 443-448.

Saxe, G. N., Ellis, B. H., & Kaplow, J. B. (2007). *Collaborative treatment of traumatized children and teens: The Trauma Systems Therapy approach.* New York, NY: Guilford Press.

Saxena, K., Howe, M., Simeonova, D., Steiner, H., & Chang, K. (2006). Divalproex sodium reduces overall aggression in youth at high risk for bipolar disorder. *Journal of Child and Adolescent Psychopharmacology, 16*(3), 252–259.

Schaefer, G. B., & Mendelsohn, N. J. (2013). Clinical genetics evaluation in identifying the etiology of autism spectrum disorders: 2013 guideline revisions. *Genetics in Medicine, 15*(5), 399–407.

Schaeffer, J. L., & Ross, R. G. (2002). Childhood-onset schizophrenia: Premorbid and prodromal diagnostic and treatment histories. *Journal of the American Academy of Child and Adolescent Psychiatry, 41*(5), 538–545.

Schapiro, N. A. (2002). "Dude, you don't have Tourette's": Tourette's syndrome, beyond the tics. *Pediatric Nursing, 22*(3), 243–246.

Schechter, R., & Grether, J. K. (2008). Continuing increases in autism reported to California's developmental services system: Mercury in retrograde. *Archives of General Psychiatry, 65*(1), 19–24.

Scheeringa, M. S., & Weems, C. F. (2014). Randomized placebo-controlled D-cycloserine with cognitive behavior therapy for pediatric posttraumatic stress. *Journal of Child and Adolescent Psychopharmacology, 24*(2), 69–77.

Scheffler, R. M., Hinshaw, S. P., Modrek, S., & Levine, P. (2007). The global market for ADHD medications. *Health Affairs, 26*(2), 450–457.

Schmidt, U. (2009). Cognitive behavioral approaches in adolescent anorexia and bulimia nervosa. *Child and Adolescent Psychiatry Clinics of North America, 18*(1), 147–158.

Schneider, C., Corrigall, R., Hayes, D., Kyriakopoulos, M., & Frangou, S. (2014). Systemic review of the efficacy and tolerability of clozapine in the treatment of youth with early onset schizophrenia. *European Psychiatry, 29*(1), 1–10.

Schneider, K. (1959). *Clinical psychopathology.* New York, NY: Grune & Stratton.

Schultz, R. T., Gauthier, I., Klin, A., Fulbright, R. K., Anderson, A. W., Volkmar, F., . . . Gore, J. C. (2000). Abnormal ventral temporal cortical activity during face discrimination among individuals with autism and Asperger syndrome. *Archives of General Psychiatry, 57,* 331–340.

Schulz, H. (2008). Rethinking sleep analysis: Comment on the AASM manual for the scoring of sleep and associated events. *Journal of Clinical Sleep Medicine, 4*(2), 99–103.

Schumann, C. M., Hamstra, J., Goodlin-Jones, B. L., Lotspeich, L. J., Kwon, H., Buonocore, M. H., . . . Amaral, D. G. (2004). The amygdala is enlarged in children but not adolescents with autism; the hippocampus is enlarged at all ages. *Journal of Neuroscience, 24,* 6392–6401.

Schur, S. B., Sikich, L., Findling, R. L., Malone, R. P., Crismon, M. L., Derivan, A., . . . Jensen, P. S. (2003). Treatment recommendations for the use of antipsychotics for aggressive youth (TRAAY): Part I. *Journal of the American Academy of Child and Adolescent Psychiatry, 42*(2), 145–161.

Scull, T. M., Kupersmidt, J. B., & Erausquin, J. T. (2014). The impact of media-related cognitions on children's substance use outcomes in the context of parental and peer substance use. *Journal of Youth and Adolescence, 43*(5), 717–728.

Scully, P. J., Owens, J. M., Kinsella, A., & Waddington, J. L. (2004). Schizophrenia, schizoaffective and bipolar disorder within an epidemiologically complete, homogeneous population in rural Ireland: Small area variation in rate. *Schizophrenia Research, 67*(2–3), 143–155.

Sears, L. L., Vest, C., Mohamed, S., Bailey, J., Ranson, B. J., & Piven, J. (1999). An MRI study of the basal ganglia in autism. *Progress in Neuro-Psychopharmacology and Biological Psychiatry, 23*(4), 613–624.

Sebat, J., Lakshmi, B., Malhotra, D., Troge, J., Lese-Martin, C., Walsh, T., . . . Wigler, M. (2007). Strong association of de novo copy number mutations with autism. *Science, 316*(5823), 445–449.

Seo, W. S., Sung, H. M., Sea, H. S., & Bai, D. S. (2008). Aripiprazole treatment of children and adolescents with Tourette disorder or chronic tic disorder. *Journal of Child and Adolescent Psychopharmacology, 18*(2), 197–205.

Shaffer, D., Fisher, P., Dulcan, M. K., Davies, M., Piacentini, J., Schwab-Stone, M. E., . . . Regier, D. A. (1996). The NIMH Diagnostic Interview Schedule for Children Version 2.3 (DISC-2.3): Description, acceptability, prevalence rates, and performance in the MECA Study. *Journal of the American Academy of Child and Adolescent Psychiatry, 35,* 865–877.

Shaffer, D., Gould, M. S., Fisher, P., Trautman, P., Moreau, D., Kleinman, M., & Flory, M. (1996). Psychiatric diagnosis in child and adolescent suicide. *Archives of General Psychiatry, 53*(4), 339–348.

Shaffer, J. A., Edmondson, D., Wasson, L. T., Falzon, L., Homma, K., Ezeokoli, N., . . . Davidson, K. W. (2014). Vitamin D supplementation for depressive symptoms: A systematic review and meta-analysis of randomized controlled trials. *Psychosomatic Medicine, 76*(3), 190–196.

Shatkin, J. P. (2004). Atomoxetine for the treatment of pediatric nocturnal enuresis. *Journal of Child and Adolescent Psychopharmacology, 14*(3), 443–447.

Shatkin, J. P., Feinfeld, K., & Strober, M. (2002). The misinterpretation of a non-REM sleep parasomnia as suicidal behavior in an adolescent. *Sleep and Breathing, 6*(4), 175–179.

Shatkin, J. P., & Janssen, A. (2012). Atypical psychopharmacologic strategies. In D. R. Rosenberg & S. Gershon (Eds.), *Pharmacotherapy of child and adolescent psychiatric disorders* (3rd ed., pp. 365–398). West Sussex, UK: Wiley.

Shaw, P., Lerch, J., Greenstein, D., Sharp, W., Clasen, L., Evans, A., . . . Rapoport, J. (2006). Longitudinal mapping of cortical thickness and clinical outcome in children and adolescents with attention deficit/hyperactivity disorder. *Archives of General Psychiatry, 63,* 540–549.

Shaywitz, S. E., Shaywitz, B. A., Pugh, K. R., Fulbright, R. K., Constable, R. T., Mencl, W. E., . . . Gore, J. C. (1998). Functional disruption in the organization of the brain for reading in dyslexia. *Neurobiology, 95,* 2636–2641.

Shea, S., Turgay, A., Carroll, A., Schulz, M., Orlik, H., Smith, I., & Dunbar, F. (2004). Risperidone in the treatment of disruptive behavioral symptoms in children with autistic and other pervasive developmental disorders. *Pediatrics, 114*(5), 634–641.

Shelton, R. C., & Weinberger, D. R. (1986). X-ray computerized tomography studies in schizophrenia: A review and synthesis. In H. A. Nasrallah & D. R. Weinberg (Eds.), *Handbook of schizophrenia: Vol. I. The neurology of schizophrenia* (pp. 207–250). Amsterdam, Netherlands: Elsevier.

Sher, L. (1997). Autistic disorder and the endogenous opioid system. *Medical Hypotheses, 48*(5), 413–414.

Sher, L. (2006). Combined dexamethasone suppression-corticotropin-releasing hormone stimulation test in studies of depression, alcoholism, and suicidal behavior. *Scientific World Journal, 6,* 1398–1404.

Sherin, J. E., & Nemeroff, C. B. (2011). Post-traumatic stress disorder: the neurobiological impact of psychological trauma. *Dialogues in Clinical Neuroscience, 13*(3), 263–278.

Shriberg, L. D., & Kwiatkowski J. (1988). A follow-up study of children with phonologic disorders of unknown origin. *Journal of Speech and Hearing Disorders, 53,* 144–155.

Siegel, D. J. (1999). *The developing mind.* New York, NY: Guilford Press.

Sigurdsson, E., Fombonne, E., Sayal, K., & Checkley, S. (1999). Neurodevelopmental antecendents of early-onset bipolar affective disorder. *British Journal of Psychiatry, 174*(2), 121–127.

Sikich, L., Frazier, J. A., McClellan, J., Findling, R. L., Vitiello, B., Ritz, L., . . . Lieberman, J. A. (2008). Double-blind comparison of first- and second-generation antipsychotics in early-onset schizophrenia and schizo affective disorder: Findings from the treatment of early-onset schizophrenia spectrum disorders (TEOSS) Study. *American Journal of Psychiatry, 165*(11), 1420–1431.

Silani, G., Frith, U., Demonet, J.-F., Fazio, F., Perani, D., Price, C., . . . Paulesu, E. (2005). Brain abnormalities underlying altered activation in dyslexia: A voxel based morphometry study. *Brain, 128*(10), 2453–2461.

Simonoff, E., Pickles, A., Charman, T., Chandler, S., Loucas, T., & Baird, G. (2008). Psychiatric disorders in children with autism spectrum disorders: Prevalence, comorbidity, and associated factors in a population-derived sample. *Journal of the American Academy of Child and Adolescent Psychiatry, 47*(8), 921–929.

Singh, N., Ellis, C., & Wechsler, H. (1997). Psychopharmacoepidemiology of mental retardation: 1966 to 1995. *Journal of Child and Adolescent Psychopharmacology, 7*, 255–266.

Skuse, D. H. (2005). X-linked genes and mental functioning. *Human Molecular Genetics, 14*(1), r27–r32.

Smedje, H., Broman, J. E., & Hetta, J. (2001). Short-term prospective study of sleep disturbances in 5–8-year-old children. *Acta Paediatrica, 90*(12), 1456–1463.

Smoller, J. W., Paulus, M. P., Fagerness, J. A., Purcell, S., Yamaki, L. H., Hirshfeld-Becker, D., . . . Stein, J. B. (2008). Influence of RGS2 on anxiety-related temperament, personality, and brain function. *Archives of General Psychiatry, 65*(3), 298–308.

Smoller, J. W., Yamaki, L. H., Fagerness, J. A., Biederman, J., Racette, S., Laird, N. M., . . . Sklar, P. B. (2005). The corticotrophin releasing hormone gene and behavioral inhibition in children at risk for panic disorder. *Biological Psychiatry, 57*(12), 1485–1492.

Snyder, R., Turgay, A., Aman, M., Binder, C., Fisman, S., & Carroll, A. (2002). Effects of risperidone on conduct and disruptive behavior disorders in children with subaverage IQs. *Journal of the American Academy of Child and Adolescent Psychiatry, 41*, 1026–1036.

Sowell, E. R., Levitt, J., Thompson, P. M., Holmes, C. J., Blanton, R. E., Kornsand, D. S., . . . Toga, A. W. (2000). Brain abnormalities in early-onset schizophrenia spectrum disorder observed with statistical parametric mapping of structural magnetic resonance images. *American Journal of Psychiatry, 157*(9), 1475–1484.

Spear, L. P. (2000). The adolescent brain and age-related behavioral manifestations. *Neuroscience and Biobehavioral Reviews, 24*, 417–463.

Spencer, T., Biederman, J., Coffey, B., Geller, D., Crawford, M., Bearman, S. K., . . . Faraone, S. V. (2002). A double-blind comparison of desipramine and placebo in children and adolescents with chronic tic disorder and comorbid attention-deficit/hyperactivity disorder. *Archives of General Psychiatry, 59*(7), 649–656.

Spencer, T. J., Biederman, J., Harding, M., O'Donnell, D., Faraone, S. V., & Wilens, T. E. (1996). Growth deficits in ADHD children revisited: Evidence for disorder associated growth delays? *Journal of the American Academy of Child and Adolescent Psychiatry, 35*(11), 1460–1469.

Spencer, T., Biederman, J., & Wilens, T. (1999). Attention-deficit/hyperactivity disorder and comorbidity. *Pediatric Clinics of North America, 46*(5), 915–927.

Spencer, T., Biederman, J., & Wilens, T. (2000). Pharmacotherapy of attention deficit hyperactivity disorder. *Child and Adolescent Psychiatric Clinics of North America, 9*(1), 77–97.

Spivak, H., & Prothrow-Stith, D. (2001). The need to address bullying: An important component of violence prevention. *Journal of the American Medical Association, 285*, 2131–2132.

Stahl, S. M. (2002). *Essential psychopharmacology of antipsychotics and mood stabilizers.* Cambridge, UK: Cambridge University Press.

Stanley, B., Brodsky, B., Nelson, J. D., & Dulit, R. (2007). Brief dialectical behavior therapy (DBT-B) for suicidal behavior and non-suicidal self injury. *Archives of Suicide Research, 11*(4), 337–341.

State, M. W., King, B. H., & Dykens, E. (1997). Mental retardation: A review of the past 10 years: Part II. *Journal of the American Academy of Child and Adolescent Psychiatry, 36*(12), 1664–1671.

Statista. (2014). *Major League Baseball rosters by average player age in 2014 (in years).* Retrieved August 21, 2014, from http://www.statista.com/statistics/236223/major-league-baseball-clubs-by-average-age-of-players/

Staton, D., Volness, L. J., & Beatty, W. W. (2008). Diagnosis and classification of pediatric bipolar disorder. *Journal of Affective Disorders, 105*(1–3), 205–212.

Steffenburg, S., Gillberg, C., Hellgren, L., Andersson, L., Gillberg, I. C., Jakobsson, G., & Bohman, M. (1989). A twin study of autism in Denmark, Finland, Iceland, Norway and Sweden. *Journal of Child Psychology and Psychiatry, 30*(3), 405–416.

Stehr-Green, P., Tull, P., Stellfeld, M., Mortenson, P. B., & Simpson, D. (2003). Autism and thimerosal-containing vaccines: Lack of consistent evidence for an association. *American Journal of Preventive Medicine, 25*(2), 101–106.

Stein, D., & Laakso, W. (1988). Bulimia: A historical perspective. *International Journal of Eating Disorders, 7*(2), 201–210.

Stein, M. A., Mendelson, J., Obermeyer, W. H., Amronin, J., & Benca, R. (2001). Sleep and behavior problems in school-aged children. *Pediatrics, 107*(4), E60.

Steinberg, A. M., & Beyerlein, B. (2014). UCLA PTSD reaction index: *DSM-5* version. Retrieved September 7, 2014, from http://www.nctsn.org/category/products/mental-healthmedicalchild-welfare-professionals

Steiner, H., Petersen, M. L., Saxena, K., Ford, S., & Matthews, Z. (2003). Divalproex sodium for the treatment of conduct disorder: A randomized controlled clinical trial. *Journal of Clinical Psychiatry, 64,* 1183–1191.

Steiner, H., Remsing, L., & AACAP Work Group on Quality Issues. (2007). Practice parameter for the assessment and treatment of children and adolescents with oppositional defiant disorder. *Journal of the American Academy of Child and Adolescent Psychiatry, 46*(1), 126–141.

Steiner-Adair, C. (1986). The body politic: Normal female adolescent development and the development of eating disorders. *Journal of the American Academy of Psychoanalysis and Dynamic Psychiatry, 14*(1), 95–114.

Steingard, R. J., Zimnitzky, B., DeMaso, D. R., Bauman, M. L., & Bucci, J. P. (1997). Sertraline treatment of transition-associated anxiety and agitation in children with autistic disorder. *Journal of Child and Adolescent Psychopharmacology, 7*(1), 9–15.

Steinhausen, H. C. (2009). Outcome of eating disorders. *Child and Adolescent Psychiatry Clinics of North America, 18*(1), 225–242.

Stephens, C. E. (2008). Spontaneous imitation by children with autism during a repetitive musical play routine. *Autism, 12*(6), 645–671.

Stephens, R. J., Bassel, C., & Sandor, P. (2004). Olanzapine in the treatment of aggression and tics in children with Tourette's syndrome: A pilot study. *Journal of Child and Adolescent Psychopharmacology, 14*(2), 255–266.

Sterling, L., Dawson, G., Webb, S., Murias, M., Munson, J., Panagiotides, H., & Aylward, E. (2008). The role of face familiarity in eye tracking of faces by individuals with autism spectrum disorders. *Journal of Autism and Developmental Disorders, 38*(9), 1666–1675.

Stewart, S. E., Geller, D. A., Jenike, M., Pauls, D., Shaw, D., Mullin, B., & Faraone, S. V. (2004). Long-term outcome of pediatric obsessive-compulsive disorder: A meta-analysis and qualitative review of the literature. *Acta Psychiatrica Scandinavica, 110*(1), 4–13.

Stouthamer-Loeber, M., Loeber, R., Wei, E., Farrington, D. P., & Wikström, P. O. H. (2002). Risk and promotive effects in the explanation of persistent serious delinquency in boys. *Journal of Consulting and Clinical Psychology, 70,* 111–123.

Stowell, R. J. A., & Estroff, T. W. (1992). Psychiatric disorders in substance-abusing adolescent inpatients: A pilot study. *Journal of the American Academy of Child and Adolescent Psychiatry, 31,* 1036–1040.

Stringaris, A., & Goodman, R. (2008). Mood lability and psychopathology in youth. *Psychological Medicine, 11,* 1–9.

Strober, M., Birmaher, B., Ryan, N., Axelson, D., Valeri, S., Leonard, H., . . . Keller, M. (2006). Pediatric bipolar disease: Current and future perspectives for study of its long-term course and treatment. *Bipolar Disorders, 8*(4), 311–321.

Strober, M., Freeman, R., Lampert, C., Diamond, J., & Kaye, W. (2000). Controlled family study of anorexia nervosa and bulimia nervosa: Evidence of shared liability and transmission of partial syndromes. *American Journal of Psychiatry, 157*(3), 393–401.

Strober, M., Freeman, R., Rigali, J., Schmidt, S., & Diamond, R. (1992). The pharmacotherapy of depressive illness in adolescence: Effects of lithium augmentation in nonresponders to imipramine. *Journal of the American Academy of Child and Adolescent Psychiatry, 31*(1), 16–20.

Strober, M., Morrell, W., Lampert, C., & Burroughs, J. (1990). Relapse following discontinuation of lithium maintenance therapy in adolescents with bipolar I illness: A naturalistic study. *American Journal of Psychiatry, 147*(4), 457–461.

Strober, M., Schmidt-Lackner, S., Freeman, R., Bower, S., Lampert, C., & DeAntonio, M. (1995). Recovery and relapse in adolescents with bipolar affective illness: A five-year naturalistic, prospective follow-up. *Journal of the American Academy of Child and Adolescent Psychiatry, 34*(6), 724–731.

Strober, M., & Schneider, M. (2005). *Just a little too thin: How to pull your child back from the brink of an eating disorder.* Cambridge, MA: Da Capo Press.

Stromme, P., & Diseth, T. H. (2000). Prevalence of psychiatric diagnoses in children with mental retardation: Data from a population-based study. *Developmental Medicine and Child Neurology, 42,* 266–270.

Substance Abuse and Mental Health Services Administration. (2001). *The DASIS report—coerced treatment among youths: 1993 to 1998.* Washington, DC: Author.

Substance Abuse and Mental Health Services Administration. (2003). *The National Household Survey on Drug Abuse report.* Rockville, MD: Author.

Substance Abuse and Mental Health Services Administration. (2008a). *The NSDUH report: Misuse of over-the-counter cough and old medications among persons aged 12 to 25.* Retrieved from http://www.oas.samhsa.gov/2k8/cough/cough.cfm

Substance Abuse and Mental Health Services Administration. (2008b). *Results from the 2007 national survey on drug use and health: National findings.* Rockville, MD: Author.

Substance Abuse and Mental Health Services Administration. (2013a). *The NSDUH report.* Retrieved August 16, 2014, from http://www.samhsa.gov/data/2k13/NSDUH098/sr098-UrbanRuralRxMisuse.htm

Substance Abuse and Mental Health Services Administration. (2013b). *Results from the 2012 National Survey on Drug Use and Health: Summary of national findings.* Rockville, MD: Author.

Sumi, S., Taniai, H., Miyachi, T., & Tanemura, M. (2006). Sibling risk of pervasive developmental disorder estimated by means of an epidemiologic survey in Nagoya, Japan. *Journal of Human Genetics, 51*(6), 518–522.

Sumner, C. R., Schuh, K. J., Sutton, V. K., Lipetz, R., & Kelsey, D. K. (2006). Placebo controlled study of the effects of atomoxetine on bladder control in children with nocturnal enuresis. *Journal of Child and Adolescent Psychopharmacology, 16*(6), 699–711.

Sung, V., Hiscock, H., Sciberras, E., & Efron, D. (2008). Sleep problems in children with attention-deficit/hyperactivity disorder: Prevalence and the effect on the child and family. *Archives of Pediatrics and Adolescent Medicine, 162*(4), 336–342.

Susser, E. S., & Lin, S. P. (1992). Schizophrenia after prenatal exposure to the

Dutch hunger winter of 1944–1945. *Archives of General Psychiatry, 49*(12), 983–988.

Swain, J. E., Scahill, L., Lombroso, P. J., King, R. A., & Leckman, J. F. (2007). Tourette syndrome and tic disorders: A decade of progress. *Journal of the American Academy of Child and Adolescent Psychiatry, 46*(8), 947–968.

Swanson, J., Gupta, S., Lam, A., Shoulson, I., Lerner, M., Modi, N., & Wigal, S. (2003). Development of a new once-a-day formulation of methylphenidate for the treatment of attention-deficit/hyperactivity disorder: Proof-of-concept and proof-of-product studies. *Archives of General Psychiatry, 60*(2), 204–211.

Swanson, J. M., Lerner, M., & Williams, L. (1995). More frequent diagnosis of attention deficit-hyperactivity disorder. *New England Journal of Medicine, 333*(14), 944.

Swanson, J. M., Sunohara, G. A., Kennedy, J. L., Regino, R., Fineberg, E., Wigal, T., . . . Wigal, S. (1998). Association of the dopamine receptor D4 (DRD4) gene with a refined phenotype of attention deficit hyperactivity disorder (ADHD): A family-based approach. *Molecular Psychiatry, 3*(1), 38–41.

Swedo, S. E., Garvey, M., Snider, L., Hamilton, C., & Leonard, H. L. (2001). The PANDAS subgroup: Recognition and treatment. *CNS Spectrums, 6*(5), 419–422, 425–426.

Swedo, S. E., Leonard, H. L., Garvey, M., Mittleman, B., Allen, A. J., Perlmutter, S., . . . Lougee, L. (1998). Pediatric autoimmune neuropsychiatric disorders associated with streptococcal infections: Clinical description of the first 50 cases. *American Journal of Psychiatry, 155*(2), 264–271.

Szatmari, P., Brysin, S. E., Streiner, D. L., Wilson, F., Archer, L., & Ryerse, C. (2000). Two-year outcome of preschool children with autism or Asperger's syndrome. *American Journal of Psychiatry, 157*(12), 1980–1987.

Tani, P., Lindberg, N., Nieminen-von Wendt, T., von Wendt, L., Alanko, L., Appelberg, B., & Porkka-Heiskanen, T. (2003). Insomnia is a frequent finding in adults with Asperger syndrome. *BMC Psychiatry, 3*, 12.

Tannock, R., Schachar, R., & Logan, G. (1995). Methylphenidate and cognitive flexibility: Dissociated dose effects in hyperactive children. *Journal of Abnormal Child Psychology, 23*(2), 235–266.

Target, M., & Fonagy, P. (1994). Efficacy of psychoanalysis for children with emotional disorders. *Journal of the American Academy of Child and Adolescent Psychiatry, 33*(3), 361–371.

Tauber, E. S., & Glovinsky, P. B. (1987). New views on the function of REM sleep in the evolution of mammals. *Contemporary Psychoanalysis, 23*, 438–445.

Tcacik, M. (2011). *Why Big Pharma is causing the Adderall shortage*. Retrieved June 17, 2014, from http://www.thefix.com/content/pay-attention-adderall-add-big-pharma7004

Temple, E. (2002). Brain mechanisms in normal and dyslexic readers. *Current Opinion in Neurobiology, 12*(2), 178–183.

Temple, E., Deutsch, G. K., Poldrack, R. A., Miller, S. L., Tallal, P., Merzenich,

. . . Gabrieli, J. D. E. (2003). Neural deficits in children with dyslexia ameliorated by behavioral remediation: Evidence from functional MRI. *Source Proceedings of the National Academy of Sciences of the United States of America, 100*(5), 2860–2865.

Teplin, L. A., Abram, K. M., McClelland, G. M., Dulcan, M. K., & Mericle, A. A. (2002). Psychiatric disorders in youth in juvenile detention. *Archives of General Psychiatry, 59*(12), 1133–1143.

Teri, L. (1982). The use of the beck depression inventory with adolescents. *Journal of Abnormal Child Psychology, 10*(2), 277–284.

Thapar, A., Cooper, M., Eyre, O., & Langley, K. (2013). Practitioner review: What have we learnt about the causes of ADHD? *Journal of Child and Adolescent Psychology and Psychiatry, 54*(1), 3–16.

Thiedke, C. C. (2003). Nocturnal enuresis. *American Family Physician, 67*(7), 1499–1506.

Thomas, A., Chess, S., & Birch, H. G. (1968). *Temperament and behavior disorders in children.* New York, NY: New York University Press.

Thomas, C. R., & Holzer, C. E. (2006). The continuing shortage of child and adolescent psychiatrists. *Journal of the American Academy of Child and Adolescent Psychiatry, 45*(9), 1023–1031.

Thompson, K. M., & Yokota, F. (2001). Depiction of alcohol, tobacco, and other substances in G-rated animated feature films. *Pediatrics, 107*(6), 1369–1374.

Thompson, P. M., Vidal, C., Giedd, J. N., Gochman, P., Blumenthal, J., Nicolson, R., . . . Rapoport, J. L. (2001). Mapping adolescent brain change reveals dynamic wave of accelerated gray matter loss in very early-onset schizophrenia. *Proceedings of the National Academy of Science, 98*(20), 11650–11655.

Thompson, J. W., & Blaine, J. D. (1987). Use of ECT in the United States in 1975 and 1980. *American Journal of Psychiatry, 144*(5), 557–562.

Thunström, M. (2002). Severe sleep problems in infancy associated with subsequent development of attention-deficit/hyperactivity disorder at 5.5 years of age. *Acta Paediatrica, 91*(5), 584–592.

Tiegerman, E., & Primavera, L. (1981). Object manipulation: An interactional strategy with autistic children. *Journal of Autism and Developmental Disorders, 11*(4), 427–438.

Tohen, M., Kryzhanovskaya, L., Carlson, G., Delbello, M., Wozniak, J., Kowatch, R., . . . Biederman, J. (2007). Olanzapine versus placebo in the treatment of adolescents with bipolar mania. *American Journal of Psychiatry, 164*(10), 1547–1556.

Tolstoy, L. (2004). *Anna Karenina.* London, UK: Penguin Classics. (Original work published 1873–1877)

Tomasi, P. A., Siracusano, S., Monni, A. M., Mela, G., & Delitala, G. (2001). Decreased nocturnal urinary antidiuretic hormone excretion in enuresis is increased by imipramine. *British Journal of Urology, 88*(9), 932–937.

Tottenham, N., Hertzig, M. E., Gillespie-Lynch, K., Gilhooly, T., Millner, A. J., & Casey, B. J. (2014). Elevated amygdala response to faces and gaze aversion in autism spectrum disorder. *Social Cognitive and Affective Neuroscience,* 9(1), 106–117.

Tourette's Syndrome Study Group. (2002). Treatment of ADHD in children with tics: A randomized controlled trial. *Neurology, 58*(4), 527–536.

Towbin, K. E., & Riddle, M. A. (1993). Attention deficit hyperactivity disorder. In R. Hurla (Ed.). *Handbook of Tourette's syndrome and related tic and behavioral disorders.* New York, NY: Marcel Dekker.

Towbin, K. E., & Riddle, M. A. (1996). Obsessive-compulsive disorder. In M. Lewis (Ed.), *Child and adolescent psychiatry: A comprehensive textbook* (2nd ed., pp. 684–693). Baltimore, MD: Williams & Wilkins.

Treatment for Adolescents with Depression Study (TADS) Team. (2009). The treatment for adolescents with depression study (TADS): Outcomes over 1 year of naturalistic follow-up. *American Journal of Psychiatry, 166*(10), 1141–1149.

Tremblay, R., Pihl, R. O., Vitaro, F., & Dobkin, P. L. (1994). Predicting early onset of male antisocial behavior from preschool behavior. *Archives of General Psychiatry, 51,* 732–739.

Trimble, M. R. (1996). *Biological psychiatry* (2nd ed.). Hoboken, NJ: Wiley.

Trocmé, N., & Wolfe, D. A. (2001). *Child maltreatment in Canada: Selected results from the Canadian Incidence Study of Reported Child Abuse and Neglect.* Ottawa, ON, Canada: Minister of Public Works and Government Services. Retrieved from www.hc-sc.gc.ca/ppub-dgspsp/publicat/cissr-ecirc/index.html

Tyrer, S. P., Walsh, A., Edwards, D. E., Berney, T. P., & Stephens, D. A. (1984). Factors associated with good response to lithium in aggressive mentally handicapped students. *Progress in Neuro-Psychopharmacology and Biological Psychiatry, 8,* 751–755.

University of Michigan. (2008). *Monitoring the future.* Retrived December 14, 2014, from http://www.monitoringthefuture.org/data/08data.html#2008data-drugs.

University of Michigan. (2013). *Monitoring the future.* Retrieved August 15, 2014, from http://monitoringthefuture.org/data/13data.html#2013data-cigs

U.S. Department of Education, National Center for Education Statistics (2011). *Fast facts.* Retrieved July 13, 2014, from http://nces.ed.gov/fastfacts/display.asp?id=16

U.S. Department of Health and Human Services. (1999). *Mental health: A report of the surgeon general.* Rockville, MD: U.S. Department of Health and Human Services, Substance Abuse and Mental Health Services Administration, Center for Mental Health Services, National Institutes of Health, National Institute of Mental Health.

U.S. Department of Health and Human Services. (2014). *The health consequences of smoking—50 years of progress: A report of the surgeon general.* Retrieved August 23, 2014, from http://www.surgeongeneral.gov/library/reports/50-years-of-progress/

U.S. Department of Health and Human Services, Administration for Children and Families, Administration on Children, Youth and Families, Children's

Bureau. (2013). *Child maltreatment 2012.* Retrieved May 27, 2014, from http://www.acf.hhs.gov/programs/cb/research-data-technology/statistics-research/child-maltreatment

U.S. Drug Enforcement Agency. (2000). Retrieved January 26, 2009, from http://www.usdoj.gov/dea/pubs/cngrtest/ct051600.htm

U.S. Food and Drug Administration. (2004). *Relationship between psychotropic drugs and pediatric suicidality: Review and evaluation of clinical data.* Retrieved February 1, 2009, from http://www.fda.gov/ohrms/dockets/ac/04/briefing/2004-4065b1-10-TAB08-Hammads-Review.pdf

U.S. Surgeon General. (2005). *Surgeon general's advisory on alcohol use in pregnancy.* Retrieved November 17, 2008, from http://www.cdc.gov/ncbddd/fas/documents/ Released%20Advisory.pdf

Uthman, O. A., & Abdulmalik, J. (2010). Comparative efficacy and acceptability of pharmacotherapeutic agents for anxiety disorders in children and adolescents: A mixed treatment comparison meta-analysis. *Current Medical Research and Opinion, 26*(1), 53–59.

Valicenti-McDermott, M. R., & Demb, H. (2006). Clinical effects and adverse reactions of off-label use of aripiprazole in children and adolescents with developmental disabilities. *Journal of Child and Adolescent Psychopharmacology, 16*(5), 549–560.

Van Ameringen, M., Mancini, C., & Oakman, J. M. (1998). The relationship of behavioral inhibition and shyness to anxiety disorder. *Journal of Nervous and Mental Disease, 186*(7), 425–431.

Van den Eynde, F., Naudts, K. H., De Saedeleer, S., van Heeringen, C., & Audenaert, K. (2005). Olanzapine in Gilles de la Tourette syndrome: Beyond tics. *Acta Neurologica Belgica, 105*(4), 206–211.

Van Kampen, M., Bogaert, G., Feys, H., Baert, L., De Raeymaeker, I., & De Weerdt, W. (2002). High initial efficacy of full-spectrum therapy for nocturnal enuresis in children and adolescents. *British Journal of Urology, 90*(1), 84–87.

Van Riper, C. (1973). *The treatment of stuttering.* Englewood Cliffs, NJ: Prentice Hall.

Varanka, T. M., Weller, R. A., Weller, E. B., & Fristad, M. A. (1988). Lithium treatment of manic episodes with psychotic features in prepubertal children. *American Journal of Psychiatry, 145*(12), 1557–1559.

Varley, C. K. (2001). Sudden death related to selected tricyclic antidepressants in children: Epidemiology, mechanisms and clinical implications. *Pediatric Drugs, 3*(8), 613–627.

Verhoeven, W. M. A., & Tuinier, S. (2001). Cyclothymia or unstable mood disorder? A systematic treatment evaluation with valproic acid. *Journal of Applied Research in Intellectual Disabilities, 14,* 147–154.

Verhoeven, W. M. A., Veendrik-Meekes, M. J., Jacobs, G. A., van den Berg, Y. W. M. M., & Tuinier, S. (2001). Citalopram in mentally retarded patients with depression: A long-term clinical investigation. *European Psychiatry, 16,* 104–108.

Vetter, V. L., Elia, J., Erickson, C., Berger, S., Blum, N., Uzark, K., & Webb, C. L.

(2008). Cardiovascular monitoring of children and adolescents with heart disease receiving medications for attention deficit/hyperactivity disorder. *Circulation, 117,* 2407–2423.

Villarejo C., Fernandez-Aranda, F., Jimenez-Murcia, S., Penas-Lledo, E., Granero, R., Penelo, E., . . . Menchon, J. M. (2012). Lifetime obesity in patients with eating disorders: Increasing prevalence, clinical and personality correlates. *European Eating Disorders Review, 20*(3), 250–254.

Virues-Ortega, J., Julio, F. M., & Pastor-Barriuso, R. (2013). The TEACHH program for children and adults with autism: A meta-analysis of intervention studies. *Child Psychology Review, 33*(8), 940–953.

Visser, S. N., Danielson, M. L., Bitsko, R. H., Holbrook, J. R., Kogan, M. D., Ghandour, R. M., . . . Blumberg, S. J. (2014). Trends in the parent-report of health care provider–diagnosed and medicated attention-deficit/hyperactivity disorder: United States, 2003–2011. *Journal of the American Academy of Child and Adolescent Psychiatry, 53*(1), 34–46.

Volkmar, F. R. (1996a). Childhood and adolescent psychosis: A review of the past 10 years. *Journal of the American Academy of Child and Adolescent Psychiatry, 35*(7), 843–851.

Volkmar, F. R. (1996b). Childhood schizophrenia. In M. Lewis (Ed.), *Child and adolescent psychiatry: A comprehensive textbook* (2nd ed., pp. 629–635). Baltimore, MD: Williams & Wilkins.

Volkmar, F. R., & Klin, A. (2000). Diagnostic issues. In A. Klin & F. R. Volkmar (Eds.), *Asperger sydrome.* New York, NY: Guilford Press.

Volkow, N. D. (2004). Imaging the addicted brain: From molecules to behavior. *Journal of Nuclear Medicine, 45*(11), 13N–16N, 19N–20N.

von Knorring, A. L., Olsson, G. I., Thomsen, P. H., Lemming, O. M., & Hultén, A. (2006). A randomized, double-blind, placebo-controlled study of citalopram in adolescents with major depressive disorder. *Journal of Clinical Psychopharmacology, 26*(3), 311–315.

Vriend, J. L., Davidson, F. D., Corkum, P. V., Rusak, B., Chambers, C. T., & McLaughlin, E. N. (2013). Manipulating sleep duration alters emotional functioning and cognitive performance in children. *Journal of Pediatric Psychology, 38*(10), 1058–1069.

Wachsmuth, D., & Dolce, G. (1980). Visual and computerized analysis of EEG during transcendental meditation and sleep. *EEG EMG Zeitschrift fur Elektroenzephalograhie, Elektromyographir und Verwandte Gebiete, 11*(4), 183–188.

Wagner, K. D., Ambrosini, P., Rynn, M., Wohlberg, C., Yang, R., Greenbaum, M. S., . . . Deas, M. D. (2003). Efficacy of sertraline in the treatment of children and adolescents with major depressive disorder: Two randomized controlled trials. *Journal of the American Medical Association, 290*(8), 1033–1041.

Wagner, K. D., Berard, R., Stein, M. B., Wetherhold, E., Carpenter, D. J., Perera, P., . . . Machin, A. (2004). A multicenter, randomized, double-blind, placebo-controlled trial of paroxetine in children and adolescents with social anxiety disorder. *Archives of General Psychiatry, 61,* 1153–1162.

Wagner, K. D., Jonas, J., Findling, R. L., Ventura, D., & Saikali, K. (2006). A double blind, randomized, placebo-controlled trial of escitalopram in the treatment of pediatric depression. *Journal of the American Academy of Child and Adolescent Psychiatry, 45*(3), 280–288.

Wagner, K. D., Kowatch, R. A., Emslie, G. J., Findling, R. L., Wilens, T. E., McCague, K., . . . Linden, D. (2006). A double-blind, randomized, placebo-controlled trial of oxcarbazepine in the treatment of bipolar disorder in children and adolescents. *American Journal of Psychiatry, 163*(7), 1179–1186.

Wagner, K. D., Nyilas, M., & Johnson, B. (2007). *Long-term efficacy of aripiprazole in children (10–17 years old) with mania.* Poster presented at the annual meeting of the American Academy of Child and Adolescent Psychiatry, Boston, MA.

Wagner, K. D., Robb, A. S., Findling, R. L., Jin, J., Gutierrez, M. M., & Heydorn, W. E. (2004). A randomized, placebo-controlled trial of citalopram for the treatment of major depression in children and adolescents. *American Journal of Psychiatry, 161*(6), 1079–1083.

Wagner, K. D., Weller, E. B., Carlson, G. A., Sachs, G., Biederman, J., Frazier, J. A., . . . Bowden, C. (2002). An open-label trial of divalproex in children and adolescents with bipolar disorder. *Journal of the American Academy of Child and Adolescent Psychiatry, 41*(10), 1224–1230.

Wakefield, A. J., Murch, S. H., Anthony, A., Linnell, J., Casson, D. M., Malik, M., . . . Walker-Smith, J. A. (1998). Ileal-lymphoid-nodular hyperplasia, non-specific colitis, and pervasive developmental disorder in children. *Lancet, 351*(9103), 637–641.

Walkup, J. T., Albano, A. M., Piacentini, J., Birmaher, B., Compton, S. N., Sherrill, J. T., . . . Kendall, P. C. (2008). Cognitive behavioral therapy, sertraline, or a combination in childhood anxiety. *New England Journal of Medicine, 359,* 2753–2766.

Wals, M., van Os, J., Reichart, C. G., Hillegers, M. H. J., Ormel, J., Verhulst, F. C., & Nolen, W. A. (2004). Multiple dimensions of familial psychopathology affect risk of mood disorder in children of bipolar parents. *American Journal of Medical Genetics: Part B. Neuropsychiatric Genetics, 127B*(1), 35–41.

Walsh, B. T., Kaplan, A. S., Attia, E., Olmsted, M., Parides, M., Carter, J. C., . . . Woodside, B. (2006). Fluoxetine after weight restoration in anorexia nervosa: A randomized controlled trial. *Journal of the American Medical Association, 295*(22), 2605–2612.

Walter, G., Lyndon, B., & Kubb, R. (1998). Lithium augmentation of venlafaxine in adolescent major depression. *Australian and New Zealand Journal of Psychiatry, 32*(3), 457–459.

Walters, E. E., & Kendler, K. S. (1995). Anorexia nervosa and anorexic-like syndromes in a population-based female twin sample. *American Journal of Psychiatry, 152*(1), 64–71.

Warren Z., Veenstra-VanderWeele, J., Stone, W., Bruzek, J. L., Nahmias, A. S., Foss-Feig, J. H., . . . McPheeters, M. L. (2011). *Therapies for children with autism spectrum disorders: Comparative effectiveness.* Retrieved July 25, 2014, from http://effectivehealthcare.ahrq.gov/index.cfm/search-for-guides-reviews-and-reports/?productid=651&pageaction=displayproduct

Wasserman, G. A., McReynolds, L. S., Lucas, C. P., Fisher, P., & Santos, L. (2002). The voice DISC-IV with incarcerated male youths: Prevalence of disorder. *Journal of the American Academy of Child and Adolescent Psychiatry, 41*(3), 314–321.

Wattendorf, D. J., & Muenke, M. (2005). Fetal alcohol spectrum disorder. *American Family Physician, 15*(72), 279–285.

Webster-Stratton, C., & Reid, M. J. (2003). The incredible years parents, teachers, and children training series: A multifaceted treatment approach for young children with conduct problems. In A. E. Kazdin & J. R. Weisz (Eds.), *Evidence-based psychotherapies for children and adolescents* (pp. 224–249). New York, NY: Guilford Press.

Weinberg, N. Z., Rahdert, E., Colliver, J. D., & Glantz, M. D. (1998). Adolescent substance abuse: A review of the past 10 years. *Journal of the American Academy of Child and Adolescent Psychiatry, 37*(3), 252–261.

Weinstock, H., Berman, S., & Cates, W. (2004). Sexually transmitted diseases among American youth: Incidence and prevalence estimates, 2000. *Perspectives on Sexual and Reproductive Health, 36*(1), 6–10.

Weisbrod, B. (1983). A guide to benefit-cost analysis, as seen through a controlled experiment in treating the mentally ill. *Journal of Health Politics, Policy and Law, 4,* 808–845.

Weiss, M. D., Wasdell, M. B., Bomben, M. M., Rea, K. J., & Freeman, R. D. (2006). Sleep hygiene and melatonin treatment for children and adolescents with ADHD and initial insomnia. *Journal of the American Academy of Child and Adolescent Psychiatry, 45*(5), 512–519.

Weissman, M. M., Pilowsky, D. J., Wickramaratne, P. J., Talati, A., Wisniewski, S. R., Fava, M., . . . Rush, J. (2006). Remissions in maternal depression and child psychopathology: A STAR*D-child report. *Journal of the American Medical Association, 295*(12), 1389–1398.

Weissman, M. M., Warner, V., Wickramaratne, P., Moreau, D., & Olfson, M. (1997). Offspring of depressed parents: 10 years later. *Archives of General Psychiatry, 54*(10), 932–940.

Weissman, M. M., Warner, V., Wickramaratne, P., & Prusoff, B. A. (1988). Early-onset major depression in parents and their children. *Journal of Affective Disorders, 15*(3), 269–277.

Weissman, M. M., Wickramaratne, P., Nomura, Y., Warner, V., Pilowsky, D., & Verdeli, H. (2006). Offspring of depressed parents: 20 years later. *American Journal of Psychiatry, 163*(6), 1001–1008.

Weitzman, M., Rosenthal, D. G., & Liu, Y-H. (2011). Paternal depressive symptoms and child behavioral or emotional problems in the United States. *Pediatrics, 128*(6), 1126–1134.

Wenzel, C., Kleimann, A., Bokemeyer, S., & Muller-Vahl, K. R. (2012). Aripiprazole for the treatment of Tourette syndrome: A case series of 100 patients. *Journal of Clinical Psychopharmacology, 32*(4), 548–550.

Werner, E. E. (1995). Resilience in development. *Current Directions in Psychological Science, 4,* 81–85.

West, A. E., Jacobs, R. H., Westerholm, R., Lee, A., Carbray, J., Heidenreich, J., & Pavuluri, M. N. (2009). Child and family-focused cognitive-behavioral therapy for pediatric bipolar disorder: Pilot study of group treatment format. *Journal of the Canadian Academy of Child and Adolescent Psychiatry, 18*(3), 239–246.

West, S. A., McElroy, S. L., Strakowski, S. M., Keck, P. E., & McConville, B. J. (1995). Attention deficit hyperactivity disorder in adolescent mania. *American Journal of Psychiatry, 152*(2), 271–273.

Westerberg, D. P., & Waitz, M. (2013). Binge-eating disorder. *Osteopathic Family Physician, 5*(6), 230–233.

Whipple, M. O., Lewis, T. T., Sutton-Tyrrell, K., Matthews, K. A., Barinas-Mitchell, E., Powell, L. H., & Everson-Rose, S. A. (2009). Hopelessness, depressive symptoms and carotid atherosclerosis in women: The Study of Women's Health Across the Nation (SWAN) Heart Study. *Stroke 40*(10), 3166–3172.

Whitaker, A., Johnson, J., Shaffer, D., Rapoport, J. L., Kalikow, K., Walsh, B. T., . . . Dolinsky, A. (1990). Uncommon troubles in young people: Prevalence estimates of selected psychiatric disorders in a nonreferred adolescent population. *Archives of General Psychiatry, 47*(5), 487–496.

Wickramaratne, P. J., Greenwald, S., & Weissman, M. M. (2000). Psychiatric disorders in the relatives of probands with prepubertal-onset or adolescent-onset major depression. *Journal of the American Academy of Child and Adolescent Psychiatry, 39*(11), 1396–1405.

Wiggins, L. D., Baio, J., & Rice, C. (2006). Examination of the time between first evaluation and first autism spectrum diagnosis in a population-based sample. *Journal of Developmental and Behavioral Pediatrics, 27*(2), S79–S87.

Wiggs, L., & Stores, G. (1996). Severe sleep disturbance and daytime challenging behaviour in children with severe learning disabilities. *Journal of Intellectual Disability Research, 40*(6), 518–528.

Wiggs, L., & Stores, G. (1998). Behavioural treatment for sleep problems in children with severe learning disabilities and challenging daytime behaviour: Effect on sleep patterns of mother and child. *Journal of Sleep Research, 7*(2), 119–126.

Wilens, T. E., Adamson, J., Monuteaux, M. C., Faraone, S. V., Schillinger, M., Westerberg, D., & Biederman, J. (2008). Effect of prior stimulant treatment for attention-deficit/hyperactivity disorder on subsequent risk for cigarette smoking and alcohol and drug use disorders in adolescents. *Archives of Pediatrics and Adolescent Medicine, 162*(10), 916–921.

Wilens, T. E., Martelson, M., Joshi, G., Bateman, C., Fried, R., Petty, C., & Biederman, J. (2011). Does ADHD predict substance-use disorders? A 10-year follow-up study of young adults with ADHD. *Journal of the American Academy of Child and Adolescent Psychiatry, 50*(6), 543–553.

Wilens, T. E., & Spencer, T. J. (1998). Pharmacology of amphetamines. In R. E. Tarter, R. T. Ammerman, & P. J. Ott (Eds.), *Handbook of substance abuse:*

Neurobehavioral pharmacology (pp. 501–513). New York, NY: Plenum Press.

Wilens, T. E., Spencer, T. J., Biederman, J., & Schleifer, D. (1997). Case study: Nefazodone for juvenile mood disorders. *Journal of the American Academy of Child and Adolescent Psychiatry, 36*(4), 481–485.

Williams, J. B. W. (1985). The multiaxial system of *DSM-III:* Where did it come from and where should it go? *Archives of General Psychiatry, 42*(2), 181–186.

Williams, K., Wray, J. A., & Wheeler, D. M. (2012). Intravenous secretin for autism spectrum disorders (ASD). *Cochrane Database of Systematic Reviews* (Issue 4). doi: 10.1002/14651858.CD003495.pub3

Williams, R. J., & Chang, S. Y. (2000). Comprehensive and comparative review of adolescent substance abuse treatment outcome. *Clinical Psychology: Science and Practice, 7*(2), 138–166.

Wilson, G. T., Wilfley, D. E., Agras, W. S., & Bryson, S. W. (2010). Psychological treatments of binge eating disorder. *Archives of General Psychiatry, 67*(1), 94–101.

Winters, K. C., Stinchfield, R. D., Opland, E., Weller, C., & Latimer, W. W. (2000). The effectiveness of the Minnesota Model approach in the treatment of adolescent drug abusers. *Addiction, 95*(4), 601–612.

Winslow, C. E. A. (1920). The untilled fields of public health. *Science, New Series, 51*(1306), 23–33.

Winterstein, A. G. (2013). Cardiovascular safety of stimulants in children: findings from recent population-based cohort studies. *Current Psychiatry Reports, 15*(8), 379.

Wittchen, H. U., Nelson, C. B., Lachner, G. (1998). Prevalence of mental disorders and psychosocial impairments in adolescents and young adults. *Psychological Medicine, 28*(Suppl. 1), 109–126.

Wolff, J. C., & Ollendick, T. H. (2006). The comorbidity of conduct problems and depression in childhood and adolescence. *Clinical Child and Family Psychology Review, 9*(3/4), 201–219.

Wolraich, M., Milich, R., Stumbo, P., & Schultz, F. (1985). Effects of sucrose ingestion on the behavior of hyperactive boys. *Journal of Pediatrics, 106*(4), 675–682.

Wolraich, M. L., Lindgren, S. D., Stumbo, P. J., Steglink, L. D., Appelbaum, M. I., & Kiritsy, M. C. (1994). Effects of diets high in sucrose or aspartame on the behavior and cognitive performance of children. *New England Journal of Medicine, 330*(5), 301–307.

Wood, J. J., Drahota, A., Sze, K., Har, K., Chiu, A., & Langer, D. A. (2009). Cognitive behavioral therapy for anxiety in children with autism spectrum disorders: A randomized, controlled trial. *Journal of Child Psychology and Psychiatry, 50*(3), 224–234.

World Health Organization. (1993). *The ICD-10 classification of mental and behavioral disorders: Diagnostic criteria for research.* Geneva, Switzerland: Author.

World Health Organization. (2014). *WHO disability assessment schedule 2.0.*

Retrieved June 3, 2014, from http://www.who.int/classifications/icf/whoda-sii/en/

Xie, L., Kang, H., Xu, Q., Chen, M. J., Liao, Y., Thiyagarajan, M., . . . Nedergaard, M. (2013). Sleep drives metabolite clearance from the adult brain. *Science, 342*(6156*)*, 373–377.

Yeganeh, R., Beidel, D. C., Turner, S. M., Pina, A. A., & Silverman, W. K. (2003). Clinical distinctions between selective mutism and social phobia: An investigation of childhood psychopathology. *Journal of the American Academy of Child and Adolescent Psychiatry, 42*(9), 1069–1075.

Yakovlev, P. I., & Lecours, A. R. (1967). The myelogenetic cycles of regional maturation of the brain. In A. Minkowski (Ed.), *Regional development of the brain in early life* (pp. 3–70). Oxford, UK: Blackwell.

Yeh, C., Wu, C., Tsung, H., Chen, C., Shyu, J., & Leckman, J. F. (2006). Antineural antibody in patients with Tourette's syndrome and their family members. *Journal of Biomedical Science, 13,* 101–112.

Yerkes, R. M., & Dodson, J. D. (1908). The relation of strength of stimulus to rapidity of habit-formation. *Journal of Comparative Neurology and Psychology, 18,* 459–482.

Yeung, C. K. (2003). Nocturnal enuresis (bedwetting). *Current Opinion in Urology, 13*(4), 337–343.

Zahn, T. P., Jacobsen, L. K., Gordon, C. T., McKenna, K., Frazier, J. A., & Rapoport, J. L. (1997). Autonomic nervous system markers of psychopathology in childhood onset schizophrenia. *Archives of General Psychiatry, 54*(10), 904–912.

Zarcone, J. R., Hellings, J. A., Crandall, K., Reese, R. M., Marguis, J., Fleming, K., . . . Schroeder, S. R. (2001). Effects of risperidone on aberrant behavior of persons with developmental disabilities: A double-blind crossover study using multiple measures. *American Journal of Mental Retardation, 106,* 525–538.

Zareba, W., & Lin, D. A. (2003). Antipsychotic drugs and QT interval prolongation. *Psychiatric Quarterly, 74*(3), 291–306.

Zemrak, W. R., & Kenna, G. A. (2008). Association of antipsychotic and antidepressant drugs with Q-T interval prolongation. *American Journal of Health-System Pharmacy, 65*(11), 1029–1038.

Zohar, A. H., Apter, A., King, R. A., Pauls, D. L., Leckman, J. F., & Cohen, D. J. (1999). Epidemiological studies. In J. F. Leckman & D. J. Cohen (Eds.), *Tourette's syndrome—tics, obsessions, compulsions: Developmental psychopathology and clinical care* (pp. 177–192). New York, NY: Wiley.

Zucker, R. A. (1996). Longitudinal research on alcohol problems: The flow of risk, problems, and disorder over time. *Alcohol: Clinical and Experimental Research, 20*(8), 93A–95A.

Zuvekas, S. H., & Vitiello, B. (2012). Stimulant medication use in children: A 12-year perspective. *American Journal of Psychiatry, 169,* 160–166.

Index